D1093638

THE
ENCYCLOPEDIA OF
ROBBERIES,
HEISTS, AND CAPERS

THE
ENCYCLOPEDIA OF
ROBBERIES,
HEISTS, AND CAPERS

Michael Newton

☑®

Facts On File, Inc.

The Encyclopedia of Robberies, Heists, and Capers

Copyright © 2002 by Michael Newton

Facts On File, Inc.
132 West 31st Street
New York NY 10001

Library of Congress Cataloging-in-Publication Data

Newton, Michael, 1951–
The encyclopedia of bank robberies, heists, and capers / by Michael Newton.
    p. cm.
Includes bibliographical references and index.
ISBN 0-8160-4488-0
1. Robbery—Encyclopedias. 2. Theft—Encyclopedias. 3. Thieves—Biography.
4. Brigands and robbers—Biography. I. Title.
HV6648 .N49 2002
364.15'52—dc21 2001007057

Facts On File books are available at special discounts when purchased in bulk quantities for businesses, associations, institutions, or sales promotions. Please call our Special Sales Department in New York at (212) 967-8800 or (800) 322-8755.

You can find Facts On File on the World Wide Web at http://www.factsonfile.com

Text and cover design by Cathy Rincon

Printed in the United States of America

VB FOF 10 9 8 7 6 5 4 3 2 1

This book is printed on acid-free paper.

Contents

Introduction

If murder was the first crime, as described in Genesis, then robbery ran a close second. Theft, like homicide, would be a subject of the Ten Commandments, but no criminal penalties were attached to the act of robbery in biblical times. Thieves, if discovered, were required to pay double or triple restitution for stolen property, with failure to do so treated as a case of unresolved debt. Only then, on failure to pay, did a thief risk loss of liberty because he or she could be sold as a slave to make good on the debt.

That lenient attitude toward theft did not last long. Muslim society prescribed mutilation for thieves—typically amputation of the right hand—and execution of thieves was commonplace throughout medieval Europe. Defendants in the western United States were hanged for grand larceny through the early 1850s, at least, with ad hoc lynch mobs or formal "vigilance committees" standing by to do the honors if duly sanctioned courts were soft on frontier crime. No matter how many horse thieves and highwaymen were executed, though, a new crop always waited in the wings to take their place.

It may be argued—and persuasively—that theft, rather than prostitution, is the world's oldest criminal profession. Bandits, burglars, and thieves have been with us always. The first sneak thief was probably a covetous Neanderthal, snatching a brightly colored stone or seashell from some other member of his tribe. Today, that greedy prehistoric's criminal descendants hold up liquor stores and armored cars at gunpoint—or, increasingly, loot banks by means of high-tech software, without setting foot at the crime scene.

Times change, but greed endures.

Thieves have evolved to keep pace with the times and with technology. From robbing travelers on foot—the pilgrim left for dead in Luke's account and succored by a good Samaritan was only one of countless thousands victimized—bandits progressed to horseback raids on caravans and stagecoaches; they raided banks and trains and plundered whole communities. Powered by sail or steam or diesel engines, they have looted ships and ports on every ocean, sea, and major river of Earth. Horses gave way to horsepower around the turn of the last century and outlaws kept pace; 60 years later they were robbing jet airliners at an altitude of 30,000 feet. If we have had no robberies in outer space as yet, it is because the risks thus far outweigh rewards.

The work in hand does not pretend to be a comprehensive view of larceny around the world and throughout time. No book—indeed, no library or cutting-edge search engine—may presume to make that claim. Even with the relatively "narrow" focus on bank and train robberies, piracy, and art and jewel thefts, the text is necessarily incomplete, forever restricted by limitations of economy and space. An overview *is* offered, though, of certain crimes and criminals from ancient times until the present day that have inspired particular interest for their daring, ingenuity, or cruelty. Also included are case histories of bandits whose best-laid plans have gone disastrously—sometimes hilariously—wrong. In addition to felons and their deeds, profiles are offered of certain law-enforcement officers and agencies who tracked the villains down—and some, it must be said, who went badly astray in that pursuit.

No work of this scope is completed in perfect solitude. Despite my extensive collection of criminal lore, critical information on various cases was supplied by—and heartfelt thanks are owed to—David Frasier, author and reference librarian at Indiana University in Bloomington; Heather Locken, computer wizard and treasured friend; and Melanie McElhinney, former Top Ten Materials Coordinator for the Federal Bureau of Investigation. Their assistance was invaluable and is deeply appreciated. Any mistakes in the text are my own, and readers with additional information pertinent to the text are invited to contact the author in care of Facts On File.

Entries A-Z

ADAMS, Edward J.

A notorious bandit of the early 1920s, Eddie Adams was born W. J. Wallace in 1887 near Hutchinson, Kansas. He served his youthful criminal apprenticeship under Wichita's premier fence, JOHN CALLAHAN, before striking off on his own to lead a gang that terrorized Kansas, Missouri, and Iowa with a series of daring bank and train robberies. At age 33, as Prohibition dawned, Adams was infamous throughout the Midwest . . . and he was also running out of time.

On September 5, 1920, teamed with outlaw brothers Ray and Walter Majors, Adams tried to rob Harry Trusdell's illegal casino on Grand Avenue in wide-open Kansas City, Missouri. The resultant shootout left gambler Frank Gardner dead; Adams and the Majors brothers were captured by police. Identified as the triggerman in Gardner's death, Adams was convicted of murder in February 1921 and sentenced to life. His companions were charged with a lesser count of simple robbery and sentenced to five years apiece.

Unwilling to finish his life behind bars and gray walls, Adams escaped from a train en route to the Missouri state prison at Jefferson City. Days later, on February 11, 1921, he joined accomplice Julius Finney to rob a bank and store in Cullison, Kansas. Both men were captured by a posse six days later near Garden Plains. On conviction of bank robbery, Adams drew a 10- to 30-year term at the Kansas state prison in Lansing, that sentence to precede the life term waiting for him in Missouri.

On August 13, 1921, Adams sabotaged the prison power plant at Lansing, scaling a wall under cover of darkness to escape with fellow inmates Frank Foster, George Weisberger, and D. C. Brown. Although Brown was soon recaptured, the others eluded manhunters and remained at large to form the nucleus of a new Adams gang, soon joined by up-and-coming outlaw Billy Fintelman.

September 1921 was a busy month for the gang. Adams murdered Patrolman A. L. Young in Wichita and then rolled on with his gang to rob banks in Roes Hill and Haysville, Kansas, of some $10,000. In the Haysville stickup, Adams pistol-whipped an elderly customer, 82-year-old James Krievell, and left him dying with a fractured skull. On October 8 the gang fought its way clear of a police trap near Anoly, Kansas, wounding Deputy Benjamin Fisher in the exchange of gunfire. Eleven days later, after stealing $500 in silver from a bank in Osceola, Iowa, Adams and company shot it out with a posse near Murray, killing one C. W. Jones before escaping in a car stolen from Sheriff E. J. West. Speeding toward Wichita on October 20, stealing and ditching a series of cars, the gang robbed a record 11 stores in Muscotah, Kansas, then abducted and robbed two motorcycle officers near Wichita, afterward setting fire to their bikes.

On November 5, 1921, the Adams gang scored its biggest take ever, stopping a Santa Fe express train near Ottawa, Kansas, and bagging $35,000 in cash. Celebrating in Wichita on November 20, the bandits were joyriding with prostitutes when police pulled them over for a traffic violation. Frank Foster shot and killed Patrolman Robert Fitzpatrick, and the gang fled southeastward into Cowley County where Adams murdered farmer George Oldham while stealing his car. Two days later, back in Wichita, Adams was traced to a local garage and cornered by police. The bandit chose to shoot it out, killing Detective Charles Hoffman before he was cut down by a storm of gunfire.

ALCORN, Gordon: See SANKEY VERNE.

ALVORD-STILES Gang

Born in 1866, the son of a circuit-riding justice of the peace, Burt Alvord grew up in Tombstone, Arizona, and observed the vagaries of western law enforcement at first hand when the Earp brothers (aka "The Fighting Pimps") waged their ruthless feud against the Clanton and McLowery families. At age 20 Alvord became chief deputy to Sheriff John Slaughter in Cochise County, building a reputation as fearless manhunter while simultaneously pursuing a criminal career on the side. In the mid-1890s Alvord briefly retired to steal Mexican cattle full time, was suspected of several murders in the process, but pinned on a badge once more in 1899 as a constable in Wilcox, Arizona.

There, he met and befriended Billie Stiles, several years younger than Alvord, a native of the Arizona Territory, who had killed his own father at age 12. Despite that indiscretion, Stiles went on to pursue a shady law-enforcement career and soon landed a position as Constable Alvord's right-hand man. They turned to TRAIN ROBBERY, recruiting Arizona bandits Bob Brown, Bravo Juan Yaos, Three-Fingered Dunlap, and the Owens brothers, George and Louis. The gang's last holdup was the robbery of a Southern Pacific train near Cochise, Arizona, on September 9, 1899. All seven were soon arrested, with Stiles alone confessing his role in the heist and offering testimony against his confederates. The bargain set him free, but he double-crossed his benefactors, raiding the jail and wounding a deputy while liberating Alvord and the others.

A new cycle of raiding began, interrupted in 1903 when Alvord and Stiles were captured a second time. They soon broke jail again and tried a new ploy to divert pursuit: Faking their own deaths, they shipped caskets bearing decomposed human remains to Tombstone. Arizona Rangers were not deceived, however, and continued tracking the duo, illegally chasing Alvord and Stiles into Mexico in 1904. Stiles eluded the manhunters, but Burt Alvord was cornered and wounded in a shootout at Nigger Head Gap. Returned to Arizona for trial, he served two years in prison for robbery and then vanished into obscurity. Reported sightings throughout the Caribbean and Latin America climaxed with unverified reports that Alvord died while working on the Panama Canal in 1910.

Billie Stiles, meanwhile, had gone back to law enforcement, working as a deputy sheriff in Nevada under the alias "William Larkin." In January 1908 he shot and killed a fugitive from justice, afterward transporting the victim back to his home. There, the dead man's furious 12-year-old son blasted "Larkin" from his saddle with a double-barreled shotgun. Only afterward was the murdered deputy identified as hunted outlaw Billie Stiles.

ANDERSON, George "Dutch"

A child of Danish nobility, born Dahl Von Teller in 1879, America's future "superbandit" reportedly earned degrees from the Universities of Uppsala and Heidelberg where he studied music and literature, becoming fluent in multiple languages. Emigrating to the United States at the turn of the century, "Anderson" attended the University of Wisconsin but did not graduate. Turning to a life of petty crime about 1907, he served prison terms in Illinois, Ohio, and Wisconsin before the outbreak of World War I.

Police in Rochester, New York, arrested Dutch Anderson in 1917, charging him with a 1913 burglary; conviction on that charge sent him to Auburn state prison with a five-year sentence. There, he met career outlaw GERALD CHAPMAN and the two became fast friends. Both were paroled in 1919 and spent the next two years peddling bootleg liquor in Detroit, Toledo, and New York. The money was good but could have been better. By autumn 1921, teamed with Auburn parolee Charles Loeber, Anderson and Chapman were ready to try the big time.

They crashed it with a vengeance on October 21, 1921, stopping a U.S. mail truck at gunpoint on Leonard Street in New York City and extracting $2.4 million in cash, bonds, and jewelry. Betrayed by a tipster eight months later, all three bandits were captured by New York police on July 3, 1922. Anderson and Chapman were each convicted and sentenced to 25 years in the federal prison at Atlanta,

ANDERSON, Richard Paul

Georgia. Chapman escaped on April 5, 1923, and Anderson followed suit six months later on December 30. Both were later suspected of numerous holdups, and although "Gentleman Gerald" was the more notorious of the pair, authorities considered brainy "Dutch" Anderson the strategist and leader.

Chapman was recaptured in January 1925, betrayed by informer Ben Hance of Muncie, Indiana. When Hance and his wife were murdered eight months later on August 11, police assumed that "Dutch" Anderson had settled the score for his incarcerated friend. By that time Chapman was facing the gallows in Connecticut for a policeman's murder, and Anderson himself was running short of time. On October 31, 1925, Anderson was sighted in Muskegon, Michigan, while passing counterfeit money. Detective Charles DeWitt Hammond tried to make the arrest, but Anderson drew a pistol, blasting away at point-blank range. Though mortally wounded, Hammond wrestled "Dutch's" gun away from him and killed the bandit where he stood.

ANDERSON, Nola, and RYAN, Frank

On February 17, 1915, two masked bandits boarded Southern Pacific Railroad passenger train No. 5 as it was passing through Saugus, California. Confronting engineer Walt Whyers and fireman Fred Harvey at gunpoint, the intruders stopped the train two miles outside town and ordered Whyers to uncouple the mail car from the rest of the train. That done, they drove north another few miles and then stopped a second time. Three express guards barricaded themselves inside the mail car and refused to open up, despite a flurry of gunshots fired through the windows by their assailants. The gunmen finally fled empty handed, unaware that one of the passengers they had abandoned down the line was William Sproule, president of the railroad.

Lawmen scoured the neighborhood for suspects and soon arrested two young hobos. Though innocent, they were able to describe another pair of men seen loitering near the Saugus tracks, pitching horseshoes on the day of the abortive holdup. When the tramps in custody had tried to board train No. 5, the other men had brandished guns and ordered them to find a different car, toward the rear of the train. The nameless gunmen matched general descriptions offered by engineer Whyers and fireman Harvey.

One week after the bungled train robbery, on February 24, two men were arrested in Napa, California, for burglarizing the post office at nearby

Rutherford for $70 worth of postage stamps. They identified themselves to police as Edward Collins and Frank Ryan—the latter an Australian immigrant—but authorities soon learned that "Collins's" real name was Nola Anderson. The Saugus hoboes readily identified both men as the strangers who had threatened them with guns on February 15, but crewmen Whyers and Harvey were not prepared to name them as the robbers under oath. Although never charged with the attempted robbery, Anderson and Ryan both pled guilty to the post-office burglary on March 13, 1915. Judge W. T. Van Fleet sentenced both men to three years in prison. When asked what had turned them to a life of crime, both defendants blamed "dime novels and bad companions," with a special fondness for tales of JESSE JAMES. Ryan was paroled on May 29, 1916, and deported to Australia; Anderson was released from San Quentin on July 4, 1917.

ANDERSON, Richard Paul

Richard Anderson logged the first of his 18 arrests in Buffalo, New York, in 1957 on a charge of robbery. Most of his New York indictments were later dismissed, with the exception of a 1959 conviction for robbery in Elmira, and he moved to St. Louis County, Missouri, in the early 1960s. There, around Mattese, it was the same old story: Charged with theft, burglary and other crimes, Anderson saw most of his cases dismissed for lack of evidence. In March 1963 he was convicted of assault with intent to rob and was sentenced to three years in state prison, but soon he was back on the street and looking for action.

Romance spelled doom for Anderson in 1967. Infatuated with a local girl, Richard broke into her home on July 1 and forced her to join him at a nearby motel, afterward threatening to kill her parents if they pressed rape charges. Denied entry to the family's home two weeks later, he produced a shotgun and killed the girl's parents, Albert and Victoria Fisk, in a fit of rage.

Three days later, with murder charges already pending, Anderson kidnapped a gas-station attendant in Biloxi, Mississippi, robbing his victim and leaving the hostage handcuffed to a tree. FBI agents, hunting Anderson on federal charges of unlawful flight to avoid prosecution, traced him to Long Beach, California, where he was linked to an assault on victim Charles Jordan. Kidnapping charges were filed on July 24, and Anderson's name was added to the FBI's "Ten Most Wanted" list on September 7, 1967.

By mid-November Anderson had settled in Toronto, posing as an American businessman. As it turned out, though, his business was confined to robbery. Anderson looted a Toronto department store of $10,000 on November 24, resurfacing on December 18 to rob a local bank. Despite the ready cash in hand, he grew increasingly unstable, seemingly desperate for pocket money.

On January 16, 1968, Anderson abducted 19-year-old hockey player Sam Kimberly from the Don Mills Plaza, hitching a ride at gunpoint to the Thorncliffe Plaza shopping mall. Arriving at their destination, Anderson ordered Kimberly into the trunk of his car, but the hostage bolted, hurling his skates at Anderson, making good his escape. While Kimberly was flagging down police, Anderson hijacked elderly salesman Alfred Nobel, demanding $100 in cash. Nobel saved himself and secured his liberty with a trip to the bank, withdrawing $50 that apparently satisfied his abductor.

On January 19 Anderson was captured by a team of Toronto detectives who staked out his apartment. Asleep when they entered, he offered no resistance. Various felony counts earned him nine years in Canadian prisons, but the jackpot was waiting in Missouri, where conviction on murder charges brought him a sentence of 60 years. That conviction was overturned on appeal in November 1974, but it did Anderson no good at the time.

Freed on parole in November 1972, awaiting results of his appeal in the United States, Anderson tried to break up a bar fight between rowdy bikers. One of the combatants knocked him down, and Richard came up shooting, wounding two assailants and firing several rounds at a constable who tried to disarm him. Convicted anew on two counts of attempted murder and one count of possessing a dangerous weapon, he was sent back to prison for 12 years.

ARGENTINE Liberation Front: Terrorist robbers

One's freedom fighter is another's TERRORIST, but regardless of the label attached, private guerrilla armies operate outside the law and are thus, at least in theory, cut off from conventional avenues of financial support. Some groups, like the Contras who terrorized El Salvador with the blessing and (illegal) funding from the Ronald Reagan White House, tap monetary sources outside their normal domain. Oth-

ers, already hunted as outlaws, incorporate ransom kidnapping and armed robbery into their tactics, justifying their crimes in the name of revolution and assuming (at least in their own minds) the mantle of modern ROBIN HOODS.

One group that followed this path in South America was the Argentine Liberation Front (FAL), a band of leftist rebels dedicated to overthrowing Argentina's neofascist military junta in the 1970s. FAL gunmen committed their first robbery of record in Buenos Aires, on October 21, 1970, when they invaded and looted the home of Chilean industrialist Jorge Yarur Rey, stealing money, jewelry, and items of personal documentation. Forty days later, on November 30, members of the FAL's Maria Pacheco faction robbed the French Hospital of 8 million pesos (about $23,000). The take on December 18, 1970, was much smaller, FAL gunmen lifting 300,000 pesos from the Spanish embassy in Rosario, setting the building on fire as they fled.

Such tactics by the FAL and other revolutionary groups gave Argentina's military overlords the excuse they needed for tightening the screws of martial law, engaging in a "dirty war" that saw thousands of Argentine citizens imprisoned and tortured and thousands more murdered or missing. The FAL was crushed by repressive tactics, but that did not stop the killing. Military rule endured in Argentina until October 1983 when a civilian president was finally elected.

ART Theft: History

Valuable works of art have drawn attention from thieves throughout recorded history. Unlike cash and precious stones, masterworks of art are highly distinctive and cannot be offered for sale on the open market when stolen. The typical buyer is a wealthy connoisseur-collector who is short on scruples and who will pay handsomely for a specific piece in full knowledge that it can never be publicly displayed. An alternative scenario involves artwork held for ransom by thieves. Although few students of crime give much thought to art theft, it remains a thriving global trade. Estimates of yearly losses in the United States alone range from $50 million to more than $500 million; worldwide, Interpol estimates a yearly market somewhere between $2 billion and $5 billion, making stolen art the world's third-most-popular contraband item (behind narcotics and illegal arms). No single volume can pretend to catalogue all famous art thefts through the ages, but a fair sampling would include the following cases:

1878—England: Burglar Adam Worth stole Gainsborough's painting *The Duchess of Devonshire* from London art dealers Agnew & Agnew. He initially demanded release of an accomplice from prison as his price for returning the portrait but then switched to cash on learning that his friend had already been freed. The painting was finally ransomed for an undisclosed amount in 1901.

1911—France: House painter Vincent Perrugia stole Leonardo da Vinci's *Mona Lisa* from the Louvre in Paris, holding it for two years before he was arrested while trying to sell it in Florence, Italy.

1940–1945—The NAZI LOOTING OF EUROPE saw wholesale removal of art masterpieces from occupied nations and from the possession of families exterminated during Adolf Hitler's "final solution of the Jewish question." More than 50 years later, controversy continues regarding ownership and disposition of some treasures stolen by the Nazis.

1945—Germany: American soldier Joe Meador, a former art teacher, stole 12 medieval artifacts from a cave near Quedlinburg, where they had been hidden by members of the clergy to protect them from Nazi looters in 1943. Meador later returned the artifacts to the United States and died in 1980 without trying to sell them. Two of his elderly siblings were arrested in 1996 when they offered two of the items (a ninth-century manuscript and a 16th-century prayer book) for sale, but charges were dismissed on grounds that the statute of limitations had expired.

1946—New York: Three paintings by Georgia O'Keeffe were stolen from a gallery owned by her husband, Alfred Stieglitz. The Princeton [New Jersey] Gallery of Fine Arts purchased the works for $35,000 in 1975, but O'Keeffe discovered them a year later and sued for their return. Despite a six-year statute of limitations on art theft, a state appellate court ruled for O'Keeffe on July 27, 1979.

1967—Michigan: Sketches by Spanish artist Pablo Picasso and British sculptor Henry Moore, valued at more than $200,000, were stolen from a traveling art exhibit organized by the University of Michigan. FBI agents recovered the pieces from a California auction house on January 24, 1969, but no arrests were made.

1969—Turkey: Various art objects valued at $5 million were stolen from Istanbul's Izmir archaeological museum where a night watchman was killed by the burglars on July 24. Police arrested a German national on August 1 after 128 stolen relics were found in his car.

1969—New York: Seven paintings valued in excess of $500,000 were stolen from a Madison Avenue gallery on the night of November 19, while owner Stephen Hahn discussed the problem of art theft with other dealers. The works taken included paintings by Cassatt, Monet, Pissarro and Rouault.

1970—Maryland: Chagall's painting *Le Petit Concert* was stolen from a private home in Baltimore by unknown thieves. New York art dealer Barry Turpin purchased the painting from reputed ORGANIZED CRIME members in 1979 at a cost of $100,000 and was arrested in 1990 when he offered it for black-market sale at a price of $300,000. On August 25, 1995, a federal jury in New York convicted Turpin of possessing and selling a stolen painting.

1970—California: Two works by Renoir—a miniature oil painting and a sculpture valued at $33,500—were stolen from the Maxwell Gallery in San Francisco on September 7 and were returned by the nervous thieves 12 hours later.

1973—Italy: Eighteen Tuscan and Umbrian paintings from the 14th and 15th centuries, valued at more than $600,000, were stolen from Ravenna's Fine Arts Academy on February 23. Local police recovered the items three days later.

1973—Italy: On March 13 customs officials reported the seizure of 63 Etruscan art works that were stolen from a grave site near Cerveteri, and they publicized the theft of a Tiepolo painting valued at $1.5 million from a church in Rovetta. One day later, customs officers announced the arrest of a French national who was caught smuggling eight stolen paintings out of Italy.

1973—New Jersey: Spokespersons for the Newark Museum acknowledged on April 2 that a fourth-century Roman mosaic purchased for $6,000 from a New York dealer had been stolen from an archaeological site in Syria. Museum administrators declared themselves "absolutely horrified" and promised to return the work.

1973—California: Art collector Norman Simon insisted on May 11 that he owned "clear title" to a 44-inch bronze sculpture of a Hindu god, which had been reported stolen (with other items) from a temple at Sivapuram in southern India. Simon paid $1 million for the statue, part of $16 million spent on Asian art over a two-year period. He freely acknowledged that "most of it was smuggled. I don't know if it was stolen."

1973—Connecticut: Two defrocked priests were indicted on March 16 for stealing hundreds of rare books from the Yale University library over a period of several years. FBI agents recovered hundreds of books and manuscripts from Yale and eight other university libraries when they raided a New York monastery occupied by the thieves. Both pled guilty to conspiracy in October 1973; more-serious charges were dropped in return for their cooperation in recovering the stolen items.

1973—Italy: A rash of stolen-vase reports occupied headlines in spring and early summer. On March 26 police in Modena confiscated a 2,500-year-old Etruscan vase from four men, but no charges were filed, the suspects claiming they had purchased the vase at a flea market. Three months later, on June 25, authorities issued an arrest warrant for Robert Hecht Jr., charged with illegally exporting an ancient Euphronios vase that he sold to New York's Metropolitan Museum for $1 million. Hecht, describing himself as a middleman in the transaction, refused to leave Switzerland for trial in Italy.

1974—Ireland: Members of the Provisional Irish Republican Army invaded the mansion of Sir Arthur Beit outside Dublin, on April 26, 1974, stealing $20 million worth of paintings by Goya, Rubens, and Vermeer. A note to one of Dublin's art galleries threatened destruction of the paintings if four imprisoned PIRA guerrillas were not released, together with a ransom of $1.2 million. Bridget Rose Dugdale, leader of the raid, was arrested, and the works were recovered from her hideout before any ransom was paid. Two days later, another IRA ransom demand for the same prisoners led police to Vermeer's painting *The Guitar Player,* valued at $4.8 million.

1975—New York: Long Island authorities arrested a 50-year-old schoolteacher on December 21, charged with second-degree burglary in connection with a series of art thefts in the Hamptons. Police found more than $1.5 million worth of stolen artwork and antiques at the suspect's Sag Harbor home.

1978—Germany: Burglars entered Hamburg's Künsthalle gallery on July 30, while its alarm system was deactivated for repair, and stole 22 paintings valued at $750,000. Two of the most valuable pieces were Degas's *In Front of a Mirror* and Renoir's *Portrait of Madame Leriaux.*

1978—France: *The Conjurer,* a painting by Hieronymous Bosch, insured for $675,000, was stolen by two gunmen on December 13 from a museum in a Parisian suburb.

1978—Illinois: Three paintings by Cézanne, valued between $2.5 million and $3 million, were discovered missing from the Art Institute of Chicago on December 27. No signs of forced entry were found.

1979—Italy: Thieves invaded a Catholic convent in Rome on June 3, stealing eight Flemish paintings valued at $1.2 million. One painting of Moses, by Rubens, was valued at $600,000.

1981—New York: A graduate student at Columbia University was arrested on October 2 after accepting $11,000 in payment for four rare books, stolen in September from the University College of London. The books were part of a stolen 267-volume collection valued at $2 million. The suspect, a Greek national, faced 20 years in prison for transporting stolen goods via interstate and foreign commerce.

1982—Virginia: Art importer, David Bernstein, pled guilty in Alexandria's federal court to misdemeanor charges of filing false customs declarations on a shipment of pre-Columbian relics from Peru, valued at $288,000. FBI agents also seized 160 art objects valued at $1.4 million from Bernstein's home in New York City. As part of his plea bargain, Bernstein promised to return any art objects that he could not prove to have been purchased outside Peru.

1982—New York: Thieves stole 25 "irreplaceable" Mayan artifacts, valued at $478,000, from the Museum of Natural History over the weekend of September 4–5. Authorities believe that more than one burglar was involved in the theft.

1985—France: Armed bandits staged a daylight raid on the Marmotan Museum, in Paris, on October 27. Nine Impressionist paintings valued at 100 million francs ($12.5 million) were removed in the five-minute holdup. The paintings stolen included Renoir's *Bathers* and five works by Monet, among them his *Impression, Sunrise* (valued at $4.75 million).

1987—Washington, D.C.: A 59-year-old art historian was arrested by FBI agents August 13 for the largest known theft of U.S. historical documents. Items recovered from his home included a 1904 letter signed by novelist Henry James, reported stolen from the Library of Congress. The suspect was arrested while attempting to sell letters from Abraham Lincoln, Winston Churchill, and other historical figures, stolen from the National Archives.

1988—Pennsylvania: A lone gunman entered Philadelphia's Rodin Museum on November 23, overpowered three security guards, and handcuffed them together before stealing a 12-inch bronze statuette, *Man with a Broken Nose,* valued at $75,000.

1990—Massachusetts: Two thieves dressed as police officers invaded Boston's Isabella Stewart Gardner Museum on March 18, tied up museum security guards, and escaped with artwork valued in excess of $300 million. The robbery—still unsolved today—was the greatest of its kind in history; the loot included paintings by Degas, Manet, Rembrandt, and Vermeer, plus other high-priced items. The Massachusetts statute of limitations expired in May 1995 and the bandits remain unidentified. None of the stolen works have been recovered. A $5 million reward offered for return of the paintings has produced many leads but no useful information.

1991—Iowa: On January 31 a federal jury in Des Moines convicted 42-year-old Stephen Blumberg of stealing more than $20 million in rare books from libraries and museums across the United States and Canada. Jurors rejected Blumberg's plea of not guilty by reason of insanity in the series of thefts that involved 21,000 volumes. In August 1991 Blumberg was sentenced to five years in prison and a $200,000 fine.

1991—New York: Wall Street financier Michael Steinhardt paid $1.2 million for the "Phiale of Achytis," a solid-gold bowl for the ritual serving of wine, that was illegally excavated and exported from Sicily in the mid-1980s. U.S. Customs agents confiscated the 2,500-year-old bowl from Steinhardt's home in 1995 and returned it to Italian authorities in February 2000.

1991—New York: A gold-and-jewel-encrusted icon of St. Irene of Chrysovalantou, valued in excess of $800,000, was stolen from a Greek Orthodox church in Queens on December 23. The statue became famous in 1990 after worshipers claimed to see it "weeping" on the eve of the Persian Gulf war. Persons unknown returned the statue by mail on December 28.

1992—Belgium: Brussels businessman Dirck Van Wylinkck lost a $3.1 million Rubens painting, *Unidentified Man Wearing a Ruff,* when he gave it to a pair of men in June as collateral for a business project in Prague, Czechoslovakia. The thieves disappeared, and Van Wylinkck's painting was missing until December 20, 1999, when FBI agents recovered it from a New Jersey collector. No arrests were made.

1993—New York: A six-year court battle climaxed with an order that the Metropolitan Museum

The Pablo Picasso painting entitled *Tête de Femme,* worth more than $1 million, was stolen from the Lefevre Art Gallery in London by an unmasked gunman who walked out of the gallery and sped away in a taxi, leaving his video image and fingerprints behind. It is thought that the theft was commissioned by someone who wanted to enjoy the painting privately. (AP/Wide World Photos)

of Art must return the "Lydian Treasure"—a trove of gold, silver, and glass dating from the time of Croesus—to Turkish authorities. The art objects were stolen from an illegal excavation in the early 1960s, smuggled out of Turkey, and hidden in the museum's basement for nearly two decades.

1994—Illinois: On January 3 a burglar stole Picasso's painting *Tête,* valued at $500,000, from Chicago's Richard Gray Gallery.

1994—Kentucky: Lexington's Headley-Whitney Museum was burglarized on the night of July 17, thieves removing various art objects insured for nearly $1.6 million. Three Ohio men—two of them already imprisoned for other crimes—were charged with the theft in September 1999. Authorities refused to comment on whether the missing items were recovered.

1994—Massachusetts: Mather Brown's 1786 portrait of Thomas Jefferson was stolen by burglars from a Boston warehouse on July 28. Its owner, a descendant of U.S. President John Adams, had stored the painting in preparation for production of a copy.

1999—California: Los Angeles ophthalmologist Steven Cooperman was convicted of fraud in July for arranging the theft of two paintings—a Picasso and a Monet—from his own home in a $17.5 million insurance scam.

1999—New York: Federal prosecutors filed charges on November 9 against a Long Island resident who tried to sell a 16th-century portrait of Jesus stolen by American soldiers from a museum in Weimar, Germany, during World War II. The painting's value was estimated between $150,000 and $400,000. The suspect was arrested after he tried to negotiate a finder's fee for returning the work to its original home at the Kunstsammlungen zu Weimar.

2000—England: Oxford University's Ashmolean Museum was burglarized on New Year's Day, thieves making off with Cézanne's painting *Auvers-Sur-Oise*, valued at $4.8 million. Museum spokesmen termed the theft "not just a criminal act but . . . a very selfish act."

2000—California: A pair of 200-pound bronze monkeys were cut from their granite pedestals at a Folsom subdivision in January and removed by unknown thieves.

See also: JEWEL THEFT.

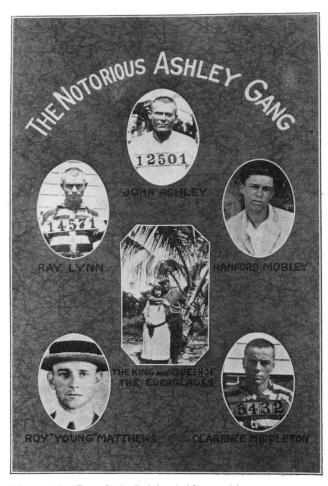

"King of the Everglades" John Ashley and his notorious Florida gang (Florida State Archives)

ASHLEY, John

Born in 1895, self-styled "King of the Everglades" John Ashley fit the mold of the classic SOCIAL BANDIT and is still regarded as a folk hero today by certain residents of southern Florida. Suspected of killing a Seminole Indian at age 16, Ashley evaded capture in that case and went on to lead a notorious gang of bank robbers, bootleggers, pirates, and hijackers that operated from an Everglades hideout between 1915 and 1924. In its heyday the gang robbed 40 banks and made off with close to $1 million in loot while simultaneously hijacking numerous loads of illicit whiskey en route to Florida from the Bahamas. One spokesman for the Sunshine State dubbed Ashley the greatest threat to Florida since the Seminole Wars of the 19th century; newspapers compared him frequently to JESSE JAMES.

The Everglades was Ashley's sanctuary, one story relating his battle with a 12-man posse in the swamp, two of the manhunters wounded before they fled in panic. To the state's impoverished "crackers," Ashley was a symbol of resistance to the bankers, law enforcers, wealthy landowners—even big-city rum-runners whose foreign shipments undermined the local moonshine trade. Indeed, the Ashley gang was more effective than the Prohibition Bureau and the coast guard combined, intercepting so many rum boats that the illicit traffic virtually ceased between Bimini and Florida's Gold Coast.

On land, the gang was known for its haphazard operations: Ashley's bandits were so lazy that they rarely "cased" a bank beyond determining its business hours, to make sure the doors were open. Known (with Henry Starr) as one of the decade's first "motorized bandits," Ashley was still so negligent that he once turned out to rob a bank in Stuart, Florida, without first procuring a getaway car. (He assumed that one of the bank's employees or patrons would have a car parked nearby, and his instinct was true.) Retreating from a holdup, it was not unusual

8

to see the gangsters waving liquor bottles from the window of their Model T, saluting residents who lined the street to watch their boozy getaway.

Such carelessness had a price, however. During one escape, Ashley was shot in the face by a gang member, firing at pursuers. Police found him wandering, dazed with pain, at the edge of the swamp and took him into custody. Fitted out with a glass eye, Ashley was not charged with bank robbery but rather with killing a Seminole subchief and was held in Dade County for trial on charges now widely regarded as false. Brother Bob Ashley invaded the jail and killed a guard while trying to liberate John, but he was forced to flee empty handed and was cornered and killed by deputies a short time later. Surviving members of the gang immediately mailed an ultimatum to the Dade County sheriff and the city of Miami at large.

Dear Sir,

We were in your city at the time one of gang Bob Ashley was brutely shot to death by your officers and now your town can expect to feel the results of it any hor. and if John Ashley is not fairly dealt with and given a fair trial and turned loose simply for the life of a God-damn Seminole Indian we expect to shoot up the hole God-damn town regardless as to what the results might be. we expect to make our apearance at a early date.

The Ashley Gang

Whether mindful of the threat or some other factor, prosecutors dismissed the murder charge and convicted Ashley of bank robbery instead, imposing a 17-year prison term. It hardly mattered, as he soon escaped from custody and returned to the Everglades, resuming command of his gang.

In 1924 Ashley tried his hand at PIRACY, leading his gangsters on an amphibious raid against West End in the Bahamas. His goal was to rob the rum-runners in residence, and although the raiders bagged $8,000 it was still a disappointing take; mere hours before the strike, an express boat had removed a quarter-million dollars from West End to Nassau. At that, the foray was a criminal milestone of sorts, marking the first time in more than a century that American pirates had raided a British Crown colony.

Discouraged by his last maritime venture, Ashley returned to the familiar trade of bank robbery. Police had given up on tracking him by wits alone and now

had an informer in the gang. Though never finally identified, the stool pigeon was later thought to be narcotics addict Clarence Middleton. In February 1924, after Ashley's father skipped bail on a moonshining charge, authorities were told that John and other members of the gang would visit him at home. A trap was sprung and a firefight ensued, Old Man Ashley killed on the spot, and several others wounded while the King of the Everglades slipped through the net unscathed.

The law got lucky nine months later with a tip that Ashley and some members of his gang were on their way to visit Jacksonville. A trap was set at Sebastian, in Indian River County, with a chain and lanterns strung across the road to resemble a construction project. It was dark when Ashley approached with gang members Ray Lynn, Hanford Mobley, and alleged traitor Clarence Middleton. All four stepped from the car to inspect the roadblock, instantly surrounded by a score of deputies with leveled guns. What happened next remains a mystery, but the result was not: Ashley and his companions were riddled with bullets from 20 guns, killed instantly. Officially, it was reported that the gangsters reached for weapons in defiance of a warning to surrender. Among the poor folk who revered him, it was said that Ashley and the rest were handcuffed first and then coldly executed, the marks of manacles still visible on lifeless wrists when they were dropped off at the morgue.

AUSTIN, Earl Edwin
A native of Tacoma Park, Maryland, Austin spent much of his adult life in prison on convictions for grand larceny, forgery, aggravated assault, bank robbery, escape, and threatening the president of the United States. The latter charge resulted from a letter Austin sent to Lyndon Johnson from a penitentiary in Idaho that cost him five more years in custody. A jailbreak artist with a history of firing on police when he was cornered, Austin won parole in February 1979 from Kansas City and immediately headed south to launch another crime spree.

On February 25 Austin robbed a bank in Houston, Texas, of $60,000, making a clean getaway. By mid-July he was linked to at least five other bank jobs in southern states, ranging from Kentucky to Florida. Already sought by federal agents on charges of bank robbery and unlawful flight to avoid prosecution, Austin was added to the FBI's "Ten Most Wanted" list on October 12, 1979.

Five months of investigation paid off for FBI agents on March 1, 1980, when they traced Austin to his rented apartment in Tucson, Arizona. Surrendering without a struggle, the fugitive carried a loaded pistol and more than $10,000 at the time of his arrest; a portion of the loot was marked and thus directly traceable to the Houston bank job in February. Charged in three of his known holdups, Austin was held in lieu of $35,000 bond, subsequently convicted, and returned to prison.

B

BAADER-MEINHOF Gang: See RED ARMY FACTION.

BAILEY, Harvey John

America's best-known bank robber of the 1920s was born at Jane Lew, West Virginia on August 23, 1887. He was not a scofflaw in his early years and was employed as a railroad fireman from 1905 until the U.S. Army drafted him in 1918. After the World War armistice, he went back to his railroad job but found it stale. Prohibition offered exciting new opportunities, and Bailey tried his hand at bootlegging and then switched to safecracking, burglarizing a dozen small-town banks in Iowa and North Dakota after hours. On September 28, 1922, he joined Nicholas "Chaw Jimmy" Trainor and two other gunmen for the daylight robbery of bank in Walnut Hills, Ohio, bagging $265,000 in cash and bonds.

It was the end for Bailey . . . at least for a while. He was suspected of participation in the $200,000 DENVER MINT ROBBERY of December 1922, but in fact he had "gone straight" for the moment, moving his wife and two children to Chicago and investing in a pair of service stations. Bailey kept his nose clean for the next four years, until November 12, 1926, when he helped Charley Fitzgerald, Al Johnston, and one "Slim Jones" loot a bank in LaPorte, Indiana, of $140,000. Three weeks later the gang turned up in Rochester, Minnesota, hitting another bank for $30,000.

A long series of impressive holdups followed. Bailey's gang took a bank in Vinton, Iowa, for $70,000 in cash and Liberty Bonds on August 19, 1927. They did even better at Washington Court House, Ohio, on February 6, 1928, walking off with $225,000 in bonds and currency. On October 25, 1928, they took $55,000 from a bank in Atlantic, Iowa, followed by $80,000 from a heist at Sturgis, Minnesota, on December 18. Six days after that holdup, a bank in Clinton, Indiana, yielded $52,000 in cash and Liberty Bonds. The take from Estherville, Iowa, on August 29, 1929 was disappointing by comparison, a mere $5,320.

The new decade found Bailey working with new allies, including THOMAS HOLDEN and GEORGE "MACHINE GUN" KELLY, among others. At least five gunmen were involved in the chaotic holdup of a bank at Willmar, Minnesota, on July 15, 1930. The bandits got away with $70,000, but three of them—Mike Rusick, Frank "Weinie" Coleman, and "Jew Sammy" Stein—were later found shot to death, their bodies discarded near White Bear Lake. (Reports differ on whether the outlaws were killed by police gunfire during their escape or executed by their comrades for reasons unknown.) On September 9, 1930, Bailey teamed with Holden, Fred Barker and VERNON MILLER to lift $40,000 from a bank in Ottumwa, Iowa. Bailey is commonly named as a member of the gang that took $2,870,000 from a Lincoln, Nebraska, bank on September 17, 1930, but if true, the huge score did not satisfy him. He rebounded on April 8, 1931, to loot a bank in Sherman, Texas, of $40,000, operating with George Kelly, Verne Miller, FRANK NASH, and unknown others.

By early 1932 Bailey and most of his usual cohorts had drifted into the orbit of the large and relatively fluid BARKER GANG. On July 7 of that year Bailey was golfing with fellow gang members Tom Holden and FRANCIS KEATING in Kansas City when they were surrounded by FBI agents and taken into custody. Holden and Keating, escapees from the federal pen at Leavenworth, were taken back to finish out their time; Bailey was searched, and in his pocket G-men found a Liberty Bond stolen from a bank in Fort Scott, Kansas, three weeks earlier. Swiftly convicted of that crime, Bailey entered the Kansas state prison at Lansing on August 17, sentenced to a term of 10 to 50 years for robbery. (A fourth gang member, ex-policeman Bernard Phillips, escaped the FBI trap in Kansas City and was later suspected of squealing to the feds. His later disappearance is regarded as an act of gangland retribution.)

The Kansas conviction was Bailey's first in 12 years of defying the law, and he had no intention of serving one year, much less 50. On May 30, 1933, he was among 11 convicts who escaped from the Lansing penitentiary, using smuggled guns and taking Warden Kirk Prather hostage along with two of his guards. The hard core of the bust-out group also included WILBUR UNDERHILL, JIM CLARK, ROBERT "BIG BOB" BRADY, ED DAVIS, and FRANK SAWYER. Together, they raced southward to find shelter in the historic outlaw sanctuary of Oklahoma's COOKSON HILLS.

The new gang made its first score on July 3, 1933, taking $11,000 from a bank at Clinton, Oklahoma. Underhill went off on his own two days later, robbing a bank in Canton, Kansas, but he was back with the crew on August 9 to crack another Oklahoma bank, at Kingfisher. Bailey carried George Kelly's trademark submachine gun on that raid, afterward driving to Paradise, Texas, where Kelly's father-in-law Robert Shannon ran a pay-as-you-go hideout for felons on the lam. Arriving on August 12, Bailey returned the Tommy gun to Shannon (in Kelly's absence) and accepted some cash left by Kelly in payment of an outstanding debt. He had barely settled down to take a nap when federal agents and local police stormed the ranch, arresting the Shannons and surrounding Bailey with a ring of guns.

It was a fluke, perhaps poetic justice working overtime. The raiders had no clue that Bailey would be present when they hit the farm. Instead, they wanted Kelly and the Shannons for kidnapping Oklahoma City oil man Charles Urschel in July, holding him for $200,000 ransom. Some of the kidnap money, its serial numbers carefully recorded, was neatly folded up in Bailey's pocket when the G-men frisked him, and the prince of bank robbers found himself wrongfully accused of kidnapping under the new Lindbergh law. Tried with the Shannons in September 1933, Bailey was convicted and sentenced to life imprisonment on October 7.

There would be no bustout this time for the legendary outlaw. Bailey served his time and was paroled from federal prison on July 4, 1961—a bleak Independence Day—only to find Kansas authorities waiting for him at the gate. They transported him to Lansing to complete his sentence from three decades earlier. He caught a break on March 31, 1965, was finally paroled, and lived another 14 years in welcome obscurity before he died at Joplin, Missouri, on March 1, 1979.

BANGHART, Basil "The Owl"

A professional stickup artist in the early 1930s, Basil Banghart is ironically remembered today primarily for a crime he did not commit but which nonetheless sent him to prison for life.

The caper was supposed to be a no-sweat proposition under the protection of the powerful Chicago syndicate. Mobster John "Jake the Barber" Factor, facing extradition to England and a possible 24-year prison sentence on a $7 million stock swindle, had contrived his own fake kidnapping in July 1933 to jam the wheels of justice. Icing on the cake was the decision that a stubborn rival bootlegger, Roger Touhy, should be framed for the mythical abduction and thus removed from circulation without a costly shooting war. Unfortunately for the plotters, members of the British consulate saw through the ruse and won a judgment from the U.S. Supreme Court that Factor should be extradited to stand trial in England.

Enter "The Owl" and crime partner Charles "Ice Wagon" Connors, as Jake Factor fell back on Plan B. Factor had told police that he was abducted on the night of June 30–July 1 and was released on July 12, following payment of $70,000 ransom to his abductors. Still, if that story would not fly, perhaps another ransom demand would convince pesky skeptics. Granted, Factor was at liberty and in no danger, but he still contrived another $50,000 extortion bid.

All Banghart and Connors had to do was pick the money up, make it "look real," and they were welcome to the 50 grand.

The drop was scheduled for August 15 on Mannheim Road outside Chicago. It was an obvious double-cross: Three hundred police and FBI agents were waiting at the scene, and a mere $500 was placed in the ransom packet, but Banghart and Connors surprised all concerned: They scooped up the meager reward and shot their way clear of the trap, escaping in a swirl of gunsmoke while the ambushers milled around in hopeless confusion. There was little that Basil and his friend could do but shrug the setup off—there was no question of declaring war on the Chicago mob—and they were soon engaged in more familiar business, joining colleagues Ike Costner and Ludwig "Dutch" Schmidt to take $105,000 from a U.S. mail truck in Charlotte, North Carolina, on November 15, 1933.

The first trial on Factor's kidnapping forged ahead in Chicago, meanwhile, resulting in a hung jury on November 28. Banghart and Costner were in custody by the time the second trial convened on February 13, 1934, the threat of long prison terms for the Charlotte mail robbery giving prosecutors extra leverage in persuading them to testify. There were problems with the deal, of course: Costner had played no part in the August 1933 "ransom" fiasco, and Charles Connors was still at large (found murdered near Chicago by persons unknown on March 14, 1934). It made no difference to the prosecution, though: Costner was more than willing to take his old friend's place and falsely swear that he had joined with Banghart and the Touhy gang to kidnap Jake Factor. Banghart stood firm in denial, describing Factor's machinations on the witness stand, but jurors chose to ignore him, convicting "The Owl," Roger Touhy, and two other defendants of kidnapping. The four drew matching 99-year sentences and were packed off to serve their time at Joliet.

Appeals were fruitless, and Banghart had seen enough of the Big House by 1942. On October 9 he escaped from Joliet with Touhy and five other inmates, including Edward Derlak, Martlick Nelson, William Stewart, St. Clair McInerney, and James O'Connor. FBI agents joined the manhunt at once, using the novel excuse that the escapees had changed addresses without notifying Selective Service, thus violating the federal draft law. Banghart and Touhy were suspected (but never charged) in a $20,000 robbery at Melrose Park, Illinois, on December 18, but if they pulled the job, the money brought no peace.

Escapees McInerney and O'Connor were killed by federal agents in Chicago 10 days later. On December 29, Banghart, Touhy, and Derlak were captured at a nearby address, J. EDGAR HOOVER observing the raid in what would be his last "personal arrest." Conviction on escape charges earned the fugitives another century inside, and Banghart would not survive to see belated justice served in 1954 when a federal judge declared the Factor kidnapping a fraud and frame-up perpetrated by the syndicate and corrupt Chicago officials.

BANK Robbery: history

Famed stickup artist WILLIE "THE ACTOR" SUTTON was once quoted as saying that he robbed banks because "that's where the money was." Sutton insisted to his dying day that no such words had ever passed his lips, but the author of the statement—whoever he was—clearly captured the essence of bank robbery and the motive that drives its practitioners. Banks house money along with other valuables in safe deposit boxes, and as long as they exist, there will undoubtedly be felons seeking to withdraw cash that is owned by others. Whether they do so by stealth or brute force depends on temperament and circumstance. The end result of a successful robbery remains the same.

America's first bank robber was, in fact, a burglar, Englishman EDWARD SMITH, who invaded New York's City Bank of Wall Street with duplicate keys on the night of March 19, 1831, extracting $245,000. He managed to spend $60,000 before his arrest, drawing a five-year prison sentence for his trouble from a court that found his crime unique. America's first bank heist resulting in homicide occurred in 1855 when teller George Gordon was beaten to death by a nocturnal thief who escaped with $130,000. Agents of the PINKERTON detective agency were hired to solve the crime and secured a confession from killer Alexander Drysdale via the unusual technique of persuading him that his victim's ghost had come back to haunt him.

The pattern of nocturnal burglary remained the norm for East Coast bandits in the 19th century, operations reaching their pinnacle with the Bliss Bank Ring in New York City. This three-man gang—including George Miles Bliss, George Leonidas Leslie, and Mark Shinburn—laid out extensive bribes to keep New York police from interfering with their heists. A total of $132,000 was paid out to myopic law enforcers for a single job in 1869, permitting the

Bliss gang to steal $1.75 million from the Ocean Bank.

Out west, by that time, a more direct and dangerous method of looting banks had been devised by outlaw brothers FRANK and JESSE JAMES, operating with their cousins from the YOUNGER clan. As graduates of WILLIAM QUANTRILL's Civil War guerrilla band, accustomed to gun-blazing raids on enemy towns, the James-Younger gang "invented" daylight bank robbery with their first raid at Liberty, Missouri, on February 14, 1866, escaping with $15,000 in gold coins and $45,000 in bonds. Imitators of the James-Younger gang were soon active from California to the Midwest, risking their lives in pursuit of easy money. The inventors of hit-and-run bank jobs met their Waterloo at Northfield, Minnesota, in 1876, but the bloody fiasco and others like it failed to discourage a new generation of bandits. The DALTON BROTHERS, cousins of the Youngers, enjoyed a brief run before they overstepped themselves at Coffeyville, Kansas, in 1892 and were slaughtered while trying to hold up two banks simultaneously.

Every year since 1866 has witnessed multiple bank robberies in the United States, their frequency mounting over time, but the last great era of headline-grabbing SOCIAL BANDITS passed with the Depression years of the 1930s. Between 1930 and 1936 Americans were captivated by the exploits of such bandits as JOHN DILLINGER, CLYDE BARROW and BONNIE PARKER, GEORGE "BABY FACE" NELSON, CHARLES "PRETTY BOY" FLOYD, HARVEY BAILEY, ALVIN KARPIS, and the BARKER GANG, raiding at will from Texas to Wisconsin, New Jersey to California. The Barker-Karpis gang and GEORGE "MACHINE GUN" KELLY dabbled in ransom kidnapping for a change of pace, dodging pursuit by the simple expedient of crossing state lines. Few Americans sympathized with bankers in those days of foreclosures and lost savings, but the mounting death toll of law enforcers and civilian bystanders finally provoked congressional action. Robbery of federally insured banks became a federal crime in May 1934, with FBI agents empowered to hunt down the new generation of "public enemies."

The demise of Dillinger and company demoted American bank robbers from their status as off-color folk heroes, but bandits continued to perfect their craft during and after World War II. Bankers in New York and New Jersey fell prey to a band of "phantom" burglars STANLEY PATREK and JOSEPH STEPKA between October 1944 and May 1945, employing

oxyacetylene torches to crack vaults and safes in place of the traditional dynamite or nitroglycerine. Their scores, while never huge, dazzled detectives at the time and were eventually solved more by dumb luck than any great detective work. The January 1950 robbery of a Brinks vault in Boston set a new record for American bank hauls, with $1,218,211.39 in cash plus $1,557,183.83 in checks and money orders. Perpetrators of the crime were soon added to the FBI's new "Ten Most Wanted" list, the same vehicle that took veteran stickup artist Willie Sutton out of circulation in 1951.

The early 1970s witnessed a rash of incidents wherein bankers and their families were held hostage, compelled under threat of death to furnish their captors with money from various financial institutions. In January 1973 bank president Robert Kitterman, his wife, and his daughter were murdered in their Gallatin, Missouri, home after Kitterman removed $10,000 from his bank. In the wake of that crime, *Newsweek* magazine (February 5, 1973) reported at least 77 similar cases in 1972, with an average ransom of $77,000. Few of the cases resulted in murder, however, and the brutal "fad" seems to have passed in the wake of the Kitterman slaughter while security specialists debated the hopeless task of guarding every banker's home in the United States around the clock.

Although bank robberies are routine in modern America—7,562 were reported in 1996, up 10 percent from 1995's total of 6,915 for an average of one bank heist every 69 minutes—certain cases still make national headlines for the size of the score, the brutality involved, or some peculiar quirk in the robber's technique. A few examples include:

1974—Nevada: Three masked gunmen invaded a Reno bank on September 27, handcuffed nine employees, and escaped with an estimated $1,044,000 in cash.

1974—California: Newspaper heiress Patricia Hearst, kidnapped by the SYMBIONESE LIBERATION ARMY, was apparently converted by her captors and collaborated with the group on various criminal activities, including at least one bank holdup. Despite pleas of "brainwashing," Hearst was later convicted and sentenced to prison.

1977—Illinois: Labor Day weekend witnessed the disappearance of $1 million from the vault of Chicago's First National Bank, unsolved despite the offer of a $100,000 reward. The bank's theft insurance was useless because it contained a $1 million deductible clause.

1978—California: Security Pacific National Bank in Los Angeles was robbed of $10.5 million on October 25, by means of a telephone call transferring funds to another account. The largest bank heist in U.S. history went unnoticed until FBI agents contacted the bank eight days later.

1979—New York: Another slick wire transfer removed $1.1 million from City National Bank on March 25 and shuttled it to an outside account. Banking officials professed themselves "unusually concerned" about the potential for further remote-control heists.

1979—New York: Five armed bandits scored the biggest bank haul in Manhattan history on August 3, stealing $500,000 from a branch of Bankers Trust Company. Their record was shattered on August 21 when two bandits stole more than $2 million from an armored truck outside Chase Manhattan Bank. The latter holdup was one of 13 New York bank heists logged in the hectic two-day period of August 21–22.

1981—New York: America's youngest bank robber on record used a toy pistol to steal $118 from the New York Bank for Savings on February 25. The unnamed nine-year-old, reportedly truant from school since 1979, surrendered to FBI agents on February 27. He was arraigned as a juvenile in family court and released to the custody of his parents.

1986—Florida: Hunted by FBI agents for a series of violent bank holdups, quick-trigger bandits WILLIAM MATIX and MICHAEL PLATT shot it out with G-men in Miami on April 11. Both gunmen were killed in the fierce battle, which also left two federal agents dead and five more wounded.

1993—California: Los Angeles gang member Robert S. Brown drew a 23-year sentence in federal court for training teenage boys to carry out a four-year series of bank holdups. FBI spokesmen linked Brown and accomplice Donzell Thompson (sentenced to 25 years) to a stunning total of 175 bank robberies committed in southern California and Las Vegas, Nevada—the worst spree of serial bank heists in American history.

1997—California: America's first televised bank robbery was broadcast live from Los Angeles on February 28, as bandits EMIL MATASAREANU and LARRY PHILLIPS JR. fought a pitched battle with police under the watchful eyes of circling television-news helicopters. Armed with automatic rifles and shielded by body armor, the gunmen dueled with police for 20-odd minutes before both were fatally wounded.

The United States, of course, has no monopoly on bank holdups. A sampling of foreign endeavors includes the following.

1869—Australia: "BUSHRANGERS" led by Andrew Scott (aka "Captain Moonlite") staged the island continent's first bank robbery in May, stealing more than £1,000 from the London Chartered Bank at Egerton. Scott was captured and served 10 years for that crime; on release, he organized a new gang of raiders in 1879.

1878—Australia: NED KELLY's gang robbed a bank at Euroa, afterward treating 22 hostages to a party at a nearby sheep ranch.

1912—France: A trigger-happy gang of anarchists led by Jules Joseph Bonnot killed three persons and wounded two more during their March robbery of a Parisian bank. Bonnot and an accomplice were killed by police following a six-hour siege in March 1913. Other members of the gang were arrested and convicted of various crimes; two of the gunmen were beheaded on the guillotine.

1935—Greece: A series of bank raids on March 12 netted 70 million drachmas for rebels who later surrendered to Turkish authorities, claiming political asylum.

1937—France: Émile "Crazy Mimile" Buisson pulled the first of his several Parisian bank holdups on December 27. Imprisoned for that caper, he escaped in 1941 and robbed another bank, killing two employees in cold blood. Jailed again, he feigned insanity and was sent to an asylum, from which he escaped in 1947. More crimes followed, until Buisson was finally captured again in 1955 and was guillotined a year later for the murder of a fellow gangster.

1962—France: French "Public Enemy No. 1" Jacques Mesrine received a three-year prison sentence for attempted bank robbery. Released in 1963, he soon returned to crime and committed dozens of holdups before police finally cornered and killed him on November 2, 1979. In one case, Mesrine robbed the same bank twice because a teller angered him by scowling as Mesrine left the place with his first bag of loot.

1969—Uruguay: TUPAMAROS guerrillas robbed the Bank of London and South America on September 10, making off with 5 million pesos ($18,825). On October 8 they invaded the town of Pando and robbed three banks, killing 15 persons in a battle to capture the town's police station.

1970—Uruguay: Tupamaros gunmen raided three banks between June 17 and June 23, netting some 34 million pesos (about $128,000).

1970—Washington, D.C.: Members of the radical Revolutionary Force Seven firebombed local headquarters of the Bank of London and South America, stealing 12 million pesos ($63,000) in the confusion.

1971—England: Taking their cue from a Sherlock Holmes story, "The Red-Headed League" (1890), burglars tunneled under London's Baker Street to penetrate the vault of Lloyd's Bank, stealing cash and other valuables in excess of £1.5 million on September 11.

1973—Lebanon: Five members of the Lebanese Socialist Revolutionary Organization seized 39 hostages at the Beirut Bank of America on October 18, holding them for 24 hours and demanding $10 million to finance Arab attacks on Israel. One hostage was executed before police stormed the bank, igniting a battle that left one policeman and two guerrillas dead, with 17 other persons wounded.

1976—Lebanon: Palestinian guerrillas robbed the British Bank of the Middle East in January. Estimates of total losses varied widely from $20 million to $100 million, including the unrecorded contents of various safe deposit boxes looted by the raiders.

1976—England: Eight gunmen invaded the Mayfair branch of the Bank of America, escaping with $13.6 million in a daring daylight raid. All eight were captured and the loot recovered inside of 48 hours.

1976—France: A gang led by right-wing extremist Albert Spaggiari tunneled beneath the streets of Nice to steal 60 million francs in cash, gems, and bonds from the Société Générale Bank on July 20. The gang left behind a note that read: "Without weapons, without hate, and without violence."

1977—Canada: Burglars equipped with diamond-core drills and a thermal lance tunneled through three feet of steel and cement on January 7 to steal cash, gems, and gold bullion valued at "tens of millions of dollars" from the Vancouver Safety Deposit Vaults Building. Five suspects were in custody by January 11, charged with the crime after a porter at Vancouver International Airport grew suspicious of their unusually heavy luggage.

1977—Switzerland: Four masked gunmen robbed the Swiss Credit Bank at a Geneva shopping mall on December 27, assaulting employees and fleeing with $1.7 million in Christmas receipts from several department stores.

1978—Nicaragua: Three Sandinista rebels stole 120,000 cordobas from a Bank of America branch in Managua on March 17, escaping in a stolen car. A second holdup the same afternoon, this one in Linda Vista, netted the bandits another 150,000 cordobas.

1983—England: Six gunmen took advantage of Easter weekend to overpower a lone guard at London's Security Express Company and stole £7 million. All six were soon captured, ringleaders Terrence Perkins and John Knight each receiving 22-year prison terms.

1983—England: On November 26 a gang of six masked men invaded the Heathrow Airport vaults of Brinks Mat Ltd., dousing a guard with gasoline and threatening to burn him alive if their demands were not met. They escaped with £26 million in gold bullion, £160,000 in platinum, £250,000 in untraceable travelers' checks, and £113,000 worth of uncut diamonds. The theft was significant enough to raise gold prices on the international market to $18 per ounce.

BARKER Gang

The largest bank-robbing gang of the Great Depression era started out as a family affair, growing naturally over time as its original members made friends during sojourns in prison and visits to underworld hangouts across the Midwest. Membership fluctuated over time, with various hangers-on killed or arrested, but throughout its four-year heyday, the loose-knit organization earned a reputation as one of the most successful—and lethal—gangs in a nation that had come to idolize its headline-grabbing outlaws as something akin to folk heroes (or at least as providers of rip-roaring entertainment). In the process, the gang spawned more legends than any other stickup outfit since the old James-Younger gang, and none was more peculiar than the tale of alleged leader Ma Barker.

Born in 1871, a product of Missouri's Ozark Mountains, Arizona Donnie Clark (known as Kate to family and friends) was 11 years old when JESSE JAMES was shot dead near St. Joseph; 10 years later, when the DALTON BROTHERS met their bloody fate at Coffeyville, Kansas, she was married and settled with farmer George Barker. Legend has it that she could not get enough of stories about badmen stealing from the rich to feed their families. Whether true or not, there is no question that Kate Barker grew up in an atmosphere where blood relationships were more important than the rule of law, while institutions such as banks and railroads were regarded in some quarters as the poor man's enemies.

Kate gave her husband four sons in the space of eight years: Herman in 1893, Lloyd in 1898, Arthur (known as Dock) in 1899, and baby Fred in 1901. The Barker farm would not support so many hungry mouths, so George gave up and moved the family to Webb City, near Joplin. Herman and Lloyd were in trouble almost from the moment they hit town, and Kate quickly earned a reputation as a doting mother whose boys could do no wrong in her eyes, ever ready to plead their case while accusing the authorities of harassment and persecution. George, for his part, apparently forbidden to discipline the boys at home, was berated by Kate for any effort to punish their frequent crimes. The date of his departure is uncertain, but he apparently bailed out sometime before the start of World War I in Europe, leaving Kate to raise the boys as she saw fit.

Herman was the first to take a major fall, arrested at Joplin for highway robbery in March 1915. The arrest encouraged Kate to leave the Show-Me State, resettling in Tulsa, Oklahoma, where their over-crowded clapboard bungalow became known as a hangout for delinquents, ex-convicts, and fugitives on the run. Around this time, according to the story later propagated by the FBI's publicity machine, Ma Barker began to direct the criminal activities of her sons and their cohorts, planning holdups down to the last detail, obtaining weapons, medical attention, lawyers—anything and everything, in short, that working outlaws might require. The other version, told by various survivors of the gang, paints Kate as a devoted mother with blind, stubborn faith in her sons, ever ready to defend them but kept in the dark as to ongoing plans of the gang. (Veteran stickup artist HARVEY BAILEY once remarked, "The old lady couldn't plan breakfast.")

Trouble dogged the Barker boys incessantly. Dock was arrested for auto theft in July 1918 and twice escaped from custody. On January 15, 1921, he was arrested in Muskogee with outlaw RAY TERRILL for attempted bank burglary. Dock was discharged on that count by court order, while Terrill went on to serve time. On August 26, 1921, Dock and accomplice VOLNEY DAVIS killed night watchman James Sherrill while burglarizing a Tulsa hospital. Both wound up sentenced to terms of life imprisonment for that crime, though neither would remain in prison. Brother Lloyd, meanwhile, was convicted of a mail robbery at Baxter Springs, Kansas, in January 1922. A 25-year prison term effectively ended his criminal career; by the time he was paroled in 1938,

the other members of his family were either dead or locked away for life.

Fred Barker was next in line for the Big House. After several arrests for vagrancy and "investigation," he was convicted of armed robbery in June 1923 and sentenced to five years in the state reformatory at Granite, Oklahoma. Parole found him unreformed, logging more arrests for bank robbery and burglary. Surviving wounds he suffered in a shootout with Kansas City police, Fred rolled on to Winfield, Kansas, where he was jailed for burglary and larceny on November 8, 1926. Brother Herman escaped capture in that incident; Fred received a sentence of five to 10 years in state prison at Lansing. It was there, while serving out his time, that Fred met Canadian native ALVIN KARPIS, likewise sentenced to 10 years for burglary. The two became fast friends and future crime partners.

Herman Barker may have been lucky in Winfield, but the rest of his luck was all bad. On June 7, 1926, he was caught with accomplice ELMER INMAN in a stolen car at Fort Scott, Kansas. Both were extradited to Oklahoma on outstanding robbery charges, where they made bail and promptly absconded. Herman soon allied himself with the notorious KIMES-TERRILL GANG, participating in the botched burglary of a Jasper, Missouri, bank on January 17, 1927. Surprised by law enforcers, Herman and three associates were trailed to a house in Carterville and were captured there after a shootout that left Herman wounded. Four days later, Herman was transferred to Fayetteville, Arkansas, for trial on charges of robbing a bank at West Fork. He escaped on March 20 with forger Claude Cooper and reached Wyoming in time to kill Deputy Arthur Osborne near Pine Bluff on August 1. Four weeks later, fleeing from a Newton, Kansas, robbery with accomplice Charles Stalcup, Herman killed Patrolman J. E. Marshall in Wichita. Both bandits were hit by police return fire; Stalcup would survive to serve time, but Herman died from a close-range shot to the head. Authorities called it a coward's suicide, but Kate stood firm in the conviction that her eldest son was executed by police.

The only good news coming Ma's way as the Depression set in was Fred's parole from Lansing on March 30, 1931. Alvin Karpis was released on May 10, and they teamed up for a string of petty burglaries that began in Kansas and soon moved on to Oklahoma. Tulsa authorities arrested them with accomplices Sam Coker and Joe Howard one month to the day after Alvin's parole. Coker, an escaped

This is the house in Oklawaha, Florida, in which Ma Barker and her son Fred barricaded themselves on January 16, 1935, before opening fire on federal agents. (AP/Wide World Photos)

convict, was returned to the McAlester state pen to finish a 30-year sentence for bank robbery; Joe Howard made bail and skipped town. Fred Barker was transferred to Claremore, Oklahoma, for trial on an outstanding burglary charge, but he soon escaped and ran home to mother. Karpis pled guilty to a Henryetta, Oklahoma, jewel heist on September 11, 1931, but he returned the loot and saw his four-year sentence suspended on the basis of time served awaiting trial. His next stop was the rented farm near Thayer, Missouri, where Fred and Ma Barker resided with Kate's new paramour, Arthur Dunlop.

The gang was soon back in business, Barker and Karpis determined to shoot their way out of any future confrontations with police. On November 8, 1931, Fred shot and killed Night Marshal Albert Jackson in Pocahontas, Arkansas. (Two local men

were wrongfully convicted and imprisoned for the murder.) When a clothing store in West Plains, Missouri, was burglarized on the night of December 18, Sheriff C. R. Kelly went looking for strangers in town. He found them at a local garage, waiting for repairs on their 1931 DeSoto, and the two men opened fire as Kelly approached, killing him instantly. Four decades later, in his memoirs, Karpis would credit the murder to Fred (though Kelly was struck by bullets from two different guns). In fact, according to the published version, *all* the gang's killing was done by hands other than Alvin's, either in his absence or while he was engaged in some other (nonlethal) action nearby. The aged robber's credibility in that regard is perhaps best judged by recalling that there is no statute of limitations on murder charges in the United States.

Increasing heat soon drove the gang from Tulsa to ST. PAUL, MINNESOTA, where thugs on the run were always welcome for a price. The outfit scored its first big payday on March 29, 1932, when a five-man team including Barker, Karpis, THOMAS HOLDEN, Lawrence DeVol, and Bernard Phillips lifted $266,500 in cash and bonds from the Northwestern National Bank in Minneapolis. A month later, on April 24, a contact at police headquarters telephoned the gang's hideout to report that someone had identified Barker and Karpis as wanted murderers from photos published in a pulp detective magazine. St. Paul authorities were typically generous, stalling their raid for seven hours while the gang packed up and moved on. In the process, Fred and Alvin convinced themselves that the tip had come from Arthur Dunlop. (In fact, the source had been their landlord or his son, depending on which published version is believed.) On April 25, Dunlop's bullet-punctured body was found at Lake Frestead, near Webster, Wisconsin, with a woman's blood-stained glove nearby. Most accounts finger Alvin and Fred as the killers; Karpis, in his memoirs, credits the murder to St. Paul mobster Jack Peifer, carried out as a favor to the Barker-Karpis gang.

From St. Paul the gang moved on to Kansas City, scoring $47,000 from a bank in Fort Scott, Kansas, on June 17, 1932. (Three hapless fugitives arrested in a stolen car that afternoon were wrongly charged, tried, and convicted of the heist.) Eight days later, the take was even better—$250,000 in cash and bonds extracted from a bank in Concordia, Kansas. On July 7, sometime gang members Thomas Holden, FRANCIS KEATING, and HARVEY BAILEY were arrested while playing golf in Kansas City. For Holden and Keating, escapees from Leavenworth, the bust meant a one-way ticket back to prison; Bailey, caught with money from the Fort Scott holdup in his pocket, would be convicted and imprisoned for that crime. A fourth member of the gang, ex-cop Bernard Phillips, evaded arrest on the golf course and was thus suspected of betraying his companions. Phillips later vanished, allegedly killed in New York by outlaws FRANK NASH and VERNON MILLER. Attorney J. Earl Smith, retained by the Barker gang to defend Harvey Bailey at trial, was found murdered in Tulsa on August 18, 1932, reportedly as payback for missing a court date.

September 1932 brought an unexpected gift to Kate Barker when Oklahoma Governor William Murray granted Dock a "banishment parole," with freedom contingent on Dock's permanent departure from the Sooner State. Two weeks later, on September 23, the gang celebrated with a $35,000 bank heist in Redwood Falls, Minnesota. In flight, they sprinkled nails on the road to stall pursuit, escaping even after law enforcers commandeered an airplane to track the getaway car. Once again, fortune smiled on the Barkers: Members of another gang were charged and convicted for the holdup. Nine days before Christmas 1932, seven gang members hit a Minneapolis bank for $22,000 in cash and $92,000 in bonds. A silent alarm brought police to the scene, and two officers were mowed down by Tommy-gun fire outside the bank: Patrolman Ira Evans was hit 20 times, while Leo Gorski stopped five bullets. Both were pronounced dead at the scene. Moments later, switching cars at Como Park in St. Paul, the gang killed 29-year-old Axel Erickson and stole his vehicle.

Banks were still a paying concern for the Barker gang in 1933, as witnessed by the $151,350 stolen from Fairbury, Nebraska's, First National Bank on April 4, gang member Earl Christman killed in the process, but the boys—or Ma, in the official version—were anxious to try something new, a racket with less risk of being gunned down on the street at high noon. They turned to kidnapping for ransom, selecting as their first victim beer magnate William Hamm Jr. Abducted from his St. Paul home on June 15, 1933, Hamm was driven to a hideout in Illinois and released three days later when $100,000 had been handed over on demand.

It was easy money, but old habits die hard. On August 30, 1933 the gang surprised two bank messengers outside the main post office in St. Paul, relieving them of $30,000 in cash before police turned out with guns blazing. Patrolman Leo Pavick was killed in the firefight, with a second officer gravely wounded. A month later, on September 22, the gang was better prepared in Chicago, driving a bulletproofed car equipped with oil slick and smoke-screen devices, when they stopped two Federal Reserve Bank messengers on Chicago's Jackson Boulevard. Patrolman Miles Cunningham was killed when he tried to intervene, and the bandits wrecked their special car while fleeing from the scene. It was all for nothing in the end: The "loot" turned out to be a quantity of worthless checks.

Back in St. Paul for the new year, Karpis and Fred Barker were driving down Portland Avenue when they mistook airline pilot Roy McCord for a policeman and sprayed him with machine-gun fire, leaving him crippled for life. Four days later the nervous gangsters kidnapped local banker Edward Bremer, holding him until February 7 when confused negotiations finally resulted in delivery of a $200,000 ransom. Unknown to the gang, FBI agents had recorded the serial number of each ransom bill, a precaution that would doom political fixers John "Boss" McLaughlin and Harry Sandlovich (aka "Sawyer") when they were caught fencing cash from the kidnapping. Dock Barker, meanwhile, was identified as one of the kidnappers when his fingerprints were lifted from a gasoline can discarded by the gang. Karpis was fingered after G-men traced a flashlight used to signal the ransom drop, and a sales clerk identified Alvin as the purchaser.

Despite those leads, the FBI still had no clue to the existence of the Barker gang per se. The big picture remained obscure until April 1934 when ex-gang member EDDIE GREEN, lately allied with JOHN DILLINGER, was ambushed and fatally wounded in St. Paul. Raving in delirium for eight days prior to death, Green spilled so many details of his criminal career that G-men wore their pencils out and came away with their first glimpse of the cohesive Barker gang. Green's wife, in custody, revealed that Karpis and the Barker boys traveled with an old woman who "posed" as their mother, thus launching speculation on the topic of Ma Barker, gangland mastermind.

Recoiling from the intense heat generated by Edward Bremer's kidnapping, Karpis and Fred Barker took a fling at plastic surgery to help disguise themselves. Their inauspicious choice as surgeon was Chicago's Joseph "Doc" Moran, a one-time physician of dubious ethics and credentials who tended bullet wounds on the sly and offered something less than skillful makeovers to gangsters who were tired of famous fingerprints and faces. The results were painful but unimpressive, Doc Moran adding insult to injury when he began to boast about his criminal associations during alcoholic binges. Moran vanished from Chicago in July 1934, and although no corpse was ever found, the FBI deduced that he was silenced by the Barker gang. Most accounts describe a one-way cruise across Lake Erie with Fred and Alvin; Karpis, for his part, predictably denied participation in the murder but reported that Moran was buried in a Minnesota lime pit.

The gang was scattered once again by early 1935, and it began to unravel in earnest on January 8. That night, FBI agents traced member RUSSELL GIBSON to a Chicago apartment where he tried to shoot it out

and was killed in a fusillade of high-powered rifle fire. Gang member Byron Bolton was captured alive at the scene, and Dock Barker was bagged without resistance in a second raid the same night, commenting to G-men that "This is a hell of a time to be caught without a gun." Back at Gibson's flat, agents found a map of Florida with the Ocala region circled, and Bolton disclosed that Kate and Fred were hiding out near Lake Weir, where Fred sometimes went gunning for a legendary alligator called Old Joe.

Agents tracked their quarry to a cottage rented by the Barkers in November 1934. Surrounded on the morning of January 16, 1935, Fred chose to fight, touching off a battle that raged for nearly five hours, manhunters pouring some 1,500 rounds into the bungalow. Silence fell over the scene at 11:00 A.M., and black handyman Willie Woodbury was drafted to check out the bullet-riddled house. Moments later he called to the agents through a shattered window, "They's all daid!" Inside the house, surrounded by an arsenal of weapons, Fred and Kate Barker lay close together. Fred had stopped 11 bullets, most of them in his left shoulder, apparently from a single burst of machine-gun fire; his mother, meanwhile, was dead from a single shot to the heart, prompting speculation that she may have killed herself or been dispatched by Fred.

At once, the FBI's publicity machine went into overdrive—perhaps, as critics claim, to put the best face possible on the killing of a 63-year-old woman. The campaign included news from Washington that Alvin Karpis had responded to the Lake Weir shootout with one or more letters to J. EDGAR HOOVER, threatening the FBI director's life. (Karpis denied writing to Hoover or anyone else in authority, dismissing the tales as an FBI publicity stunt.) Another 16 months would pass before Karpis was traced to New Orleans and cornered by G-men on May 2, 1936, whereupon Hoover emerged from hiding to "make the arrest" and reap new headlines for himself.

Meanwhile, the sluggish wheels of justice ground away at the surviving remnants of the Barker gang. Seven days after Fred and Kate were killed in Florida, a federal grand jury in St. Paul indicted Dock, Karpis, and 18 others on various charges related to the Bremer kidnapping. The trial opened on April 15 and lasted three weeks; Dock and several codefendants were convicted on May 6 and sentenced to life imprisonment. Shipped off to "The

Rock" of Alcatraz, he served less than three years before staging a *kamikaze* escape attempt with four other inmates on January 13, 1939. Three of the would-be escapees were gunned down by guards, Barker succumbing to his wounds the following day. His last recorded words were accurate, if unremarkable: "I'm all shot to hell."

The rest of the Barker clan was gone by the end of the next decade. Hapless George Barker died at his home in Webb City on February 28, 1941, and was buried at Timberhill Cemetery with Kate, Herman, Dock, and Fred. Brother Lloyd would never share the family plot because there was no one left to bring him home. Returning home late from work on March 22, 1949, Lloyd was shotgunned to death by his wife, who pled self-defense and was later deemed mentally ill. Only Alvin Karpis remained to speak for the gang; sentenced to life for the Hamm kidnapping and then paroled in 1969, he was promptly deported to his native Canada as an undesirable alien.

BARROW, Clyde Chestnut, and PARKER, Bonnie

Though ranked among the more notorious and lethal of the 1930s outlaws, Clyde Barrow and Bonnie Parker were strictly small-timers who never scored more than a few thousand dollars from any given holdup, robbing small shops and gas stations as frequently as they raided banks. Between their petty heists and trigger-happy violence, they earned unsavory reputations not only with law enforcement but among competing bandits who considered themselves professionals. ALVIN KARPIS, for example, once met Clyde and Bonnie in Missouri, recalling that they looked like southern sharecroppers. A gangster friend of Karpis, HERBERT FARMER, dismissed the couple as a pair of "goddamn Texas screwballs."

Born March 24, 1909, Clyde Barrow was in fact the son of a Teleco, Texas, tenant farmer, fifth in a brood that would finally include eight children. He loved guns from childhood, starting with homemade toys and working his way up to the real thing, developing an early reputation as a crack shot. He quit school in the fifth grade, trying his hand at odd jobs before the family abandoned farming and moved to Dallas in 1922, where Clyde's parents ran a gas station. By that time, Clyde and his older brother Ivan (known as "Buck") had agreed that work was for suckers, a necessary evil at the best of time. Theft was so much easier . . . and it was fun.

Bonnie Parker would later write in a famous poem that she "once knew Clyde when he was honest and upright and clean." In fact, Clyde had his first brush with the law in 1926, four years before they met, when he "forgot" to return a rented car. Police came calling and he fled on foot, bullets whistling around his head, but charges were later dropped in deference to his youth. That December, Buck took the blame and the jail time when the brothers were arrested for stealing turkeys, but it was Clyde's second arrest and the beginning of a reputation that would hound him to his grave.

Buck served a week in jail for the turkey caper, and Clyde was waiting when he got out, anxious to pick up where they left off. Accomplice Frank Clause joined them for a long series of burglaries and auto thefts, climaxed by Buck's capture following a Denton, Texas, robbery in October 1929. Clyde escaped on that occasion, but authorities in Waco and Sherman were dogging his tracks, anxious to discuss the presence of his fingerprints on several looted safes and stolen cars. He was a wanted man by the time he rolled into West Dallas and met Bonnie Parker in January 1930.

The queen of America's Depression-era desperadoes was born October 1, 1910, at Rowena, Texas, the second of three children sired by a hardworking bricklayer. She was four years old when her father died, and Bonnie's mother moved the family to Crescent City in search of work. Blond and feisty, something of an exhibitionist in her Sunday school class, Bonnie was recalled as "an adorable child" by her teachers in Crescent City. At age 16 she married Roy Thornton, her high-school sweetheart, and had his name tattooed on her thigh. The relationship was stormy, Thornton walking out on his bride three times between August 1927 and his final exit that December. By 1929 he was serving five years in prison for robbery, and Bonnie was living with her mother in Dallas, working at a diner to make ends meet. The diner folded in November 1929, and Bonnie was visiting a girlfriend in West Dallas, killing time, when dashing Clyde Barrow walked into her life.

By all accounts it was love at first sight for Bonnie and Clyde. At four feet nine inches and 90 pounds, Bonnie was a living doll, one of the few women in Texas who literally looked up to Clyde's runty five feet four inches. Clyde's sister Nell later called Bonnie "the answer to a sister's prayer for a wife for a best-loved brother." They were at her mother's home in Dallas, "mooning on the couch" one night in February 1930, when police arrived with paperwork for Clyde's arrest. Transferred to Waco on March 2, he was convicted on seven counts of burglary and car theft, sentenced to two years in prison with 12 years probation.

The Barrow boys were tired of jails. On March 8, 1930, Buck escaped from the Texas State Prison at Huntsville. Three days later, Bonnie taped a .38 revolver to her thigh and smuggled it into the Waco jail, allowing Clyde to make an unscheduled departure with cellmates William Turner and Emory Abernathy. The trio lasted seven days before a team of railroad bulls arrested them in Middleton, Ohio, and a routine fingerprint check revealed that they were fugitives from justice. Back in Texas, Clyde was stunned to hear his sentence altered by the court, requiring him to serve all 14 years.

Transferred to Huntsville on April 21, Clyde initially corresponded with his "wife" on a near-daily basis. By the summer of 1931, though, Bonnie's letters had begun to taper off, finally stopping altogether. She was dating other men in Dallas, doing her best to forget about Clyde. Brother Buck, meanwhile, had married a preacher's daughter named Blanche on July 1, 1931, and she nagged him into surrendering at Huntsville on December 27 to pay his societal debt.

By that time Clyde had seen enough of prison. His mother was working overtime, pestering the governor with pleas for his release, but Clyde was short on patience. In January 1932, seeking to avoid a prison work detail, Clyde chopped two toes from his right foot with an ax. It was a futile gesture, though: his mother's work paid off in the form of a pardon on February 2, and Clyde came home on crutches. Bonnie dumped her new boyfriend the night Clyde turned up on her doorstep, but their true reunion was delayed until March when Barrow returned from a short-lived job in far-off Massachusetts. The lovers left Dallas together on March 30, 1932, and Bonnie was jailed in Kaufman, Texas, two days later. There had been a stolen car and a high-speed chase, and Clyde had left her in the lurch, escaping on foot while Bonnie was handcuffed and caged. It was in the Kaufman lockup that she penned her first epic poem, "The Ballad of Suicide Sal," recounting the emotions of a woman in prison, abandoned by her gangster boyfriend.

If he had returned to me sometime,
though he hadn't a cent to give,

I'd forget all this hell that he's caused me
And love him as long as I live.

Clyde was busy, meanwhile, raising money the best way he knew how. On March 25 he teamed with hoodlum RAYMOND HAMILTON to rob the Sims Oil Company in Dallas. (Some erroneous accounts place Bonnie at the wheel of the getaway car, although she spent that day and most of the next three months in jail.) A month later, on April 24, Clyde and Frank Clause robbed two gas stations in Magnolia, Texas, netting a total of $35 and two revolvers; they kidnapped both station managers, but released the men unharmed that afternoon. On April 27, 65-year-old John Butcher was shot and killed in the robbery of his gas station at Hillsboro, Texas. Witnesses identified Clyde and Ray Hamilton as the bandits responsible.

The Kaufman grand jury proved sympathetic toward young Bonnie Parker, voting a "no bill" against her on June 17, 1932. She returned to her mother's home in Dallas, lingering there until she left to "visit a friend" in Wichita Falls. In fact, she was reunited with Clyde, her jailhouse bitterness forgotten, more than willing to live and love on the run, supported by ill-gotten gains.

On July 27, 1932, Clyde and Ray Hamilton raided a bank in Willis, Texas, for $3,000. Two days later they held up Grand Prairie's interurban railroad station, rebounding on August 1 to steal several hundred dollars and some diamond rings from the Neuhoff Packing Company in Dallas. On August 5, while Bonnie spent the night with her mother, Clyde and Raymond drove across the border to Stringtown, Oklahoma, for a barn dance. They were sharing an illegal drink in the car when Sheriff C. G. Maxwell and Deputy Eugene Moore strolled over to ask a few questions. Gunfire erupted, killing Moore where he stood, leaving Maxwell gravely wounded. The outlaws wrecked their car in flight but stole a series of others to make their getaway, Clyde calling for Bonnie bright and early on the morning of August 12 at her mother's house.

From Dallas they drove straight through to Carlsbad, New Mexico, where Bonnie had an aunt. They had barely arrived, on August 14, when Sheriff Joe Johns happened by, noticed the out-of-state license plates, and dropped in to pay his respects. It was Bonnie who got the drop on Johns, herding him into the car for a wild ride back to Texas, leaving him unharmed in San Antonio. The gang was spotted stealing another car in Victoria, and shots were exchanged at a roadblock near Wharton on August 30, leaving one officer wounded before the fugitives escaped.

There was too much heat in Texas, so the gang moved north, dropping Ray Hamilton off at his father's place in Michigan for a visit on September 1, Clyde and Bonnie touring Michigan, Missouri, and Kansas over the next month. Reunited with Hamilton in early October, they drifted back to Texas. Conflicting reports blame them for two crimes on October 8: Clyde and Raymond were identified as the bandits who stole $1,401 from a bank in Cedar Hills, while witnesses named Bonnie as the shooter who killed 67-year-old Howard Hall during the holdup of his grocery store in Sherman. (To the bitter end, her family insisted Clyde and Bonnie were in Kansas City when the robberies and homicide occurred.)

Ray Hamilton went off on his own that autumn for a series of holdups with new accomplices, climaxed by his December 5 arrest in Michigan. Extradited to Texas, he was sentenced to 263 years in prison on conviction of murder and multiple robbery counts. Clyde, meanwhile, had stopped in Dallas for a Halloween visit with his family, there recruiting accomplices Hollis Hale and Frank Hardy, rolling on with them to Missouri for a month of small-time heists. The nadir of their sojourn in the Show-Me State came on November 30 when they stole an embarrassing $115 from an Orongo bank, barely escaping in the hail of gunfire from a civilian posse.

The close call and pitiful rewards were too much for Hale and Hardy, two bandits who never lived up to their names. Back in Dallas on December 2, Bonnie and Clyde were joined by William Daniel "Deacon" Jones, a 17-year-old car thief who begged to "go out" with the gang. Clyde agreed, and they blew their first score on Christmas Day, trying to steal a car in Temple, Texas. Owner Doyle Johnson interrupted the thieves and was shot dead on the street. Bonnie blamed Jones for the shooting, while Deacon would later blame Clyde—the first of many controversial incidents in which the truth has been forever lost to passing time. Six days later, Jones was absent when Bonnie and Clyde joined Les Stewart and Odell Chambless to steal $2,800 from a bank at Grapevine, Texas. (Chambless surrendered voluntarily to Dallas authorities on January 18, 1933, and was convicted of robbery.)

Ray Hamilton was chafing at confinement on the Eastham prison farm by January 1933, dispatching pleas for help to Bonnie and Clyde. On January 6,

with W. D. Jones, they dropped by the Dallas home of Raymond's sister, Lillie McBride, to discuss the prospects of a prison break. At that time, Lillie's home was known to cops and cons alike as an underworld safe house where fugitives could grab a home-cooked meal and rest in peace. That night, however, Lillie was in Eastham visiting her brother, and police had occupied the house, expecting fugitive Odell Chambless.

What they got, instead, was the Barrow gang.

The officers waited to spring their trap until Clyde had stepped up on the porch. It was sound strategy but was poorly executed. Deputy Malcolm Davis was killed as Clyde cut loose with a sawed-off shotgun and another officer wounded by flying glass. Jones covered Clyde's retreat with rifle fire, and the outlaws fled into Oklahoma, putting Ray Hamilton's rescue on indefinite hold. On June 26 they kidnapped traffic officer Thomas Purcell in Springfield, Missouri, taking him on an aimless 200-mile drive before they dropped him off again, unharmed. A month later, on February 20, Clyde and Jones teamed with accomplice Monroe Routon to raid a bank in Shiro, Texas, of an undisclosed amount.

Texas had a new governor in early 1933, and Miriam Ferguson celebrated her inauguration with a sweeping series of pardons for state prison inmates. One of those released, on March 22, was "Buck" Barrow. His wife hoped that Buck would go straight, but family came first and he soon met Clyde at Fort Smith, Arkansas, going on to make it a quintet when the gang rented a small house in Joplin, Missouri. It was there, in a town known for its criminal hideouts, that Herb Farmer introduced Alvin Karpis to Bonnie and Clyde. The lovers were trying to sell some Browning automatic rifles, and Farmer privately complained to Karpis, "They're going to be shooting up drugstores and every other damn thing around here. I don't like it."

In fact, he didn't know the half of it.

For security reasons, the gang assumed pseudonyms when they rented the Joplin cottage and paid their utility bills, a practice that aroused police suspicion. Armed with search warrants, a raiding party closed in on April 13, 1933, and a pitched battle broke out at the first glimpse of squad cars. Clyde and Jones were wounded in the shootout, but the whole gang managed to escape. Behind them, Constable Wes Harryman and Detective Harry McGinnis lay dead in the driveway, riddled with bullets; inside the house, police found money from a Springfield bank job, an arsenal of weapons, and Bonnie's ode to

Suicide Sal. They also found numerous snapshots of Bonnie, Clyde, and young Jones posing with weapons and getaway cars. One gag shot of Bonnie holding a revolver and clenching a cigar between her teeth would be published nationwide, advancing her reputation as a hard-bitten "gun moll." (Texas deputy sheriff Ted Hinton, a childhood schoolmate of Clyde's, reports that Bonnie actually held a long-stemmed rose between her teeth in the original photo; some sly reporter penciled in the cigar, Hinton says, to make the photo more dramatic.)

A month after the Joplin shootout, on May 16, Buck Barrow was identified as the gunman who robbed a gas station in Fort Dodge, Iowa. Three days later, the gang scored $2,500 from an Okabena, Minnesota, bank raid, but it was another close shave, running a gauntlet of blazing guns as they raced for the city limits and freedom. On May 20, Bonnie and Clyde became federal fugitives with charges filed in Dallas of violating the Dyer act by driving stolen cars across state lines. Henceforth they would be hunted by the FBI as well as state and local law enforcers.

Near disaster overtook the gang on June 10, 1933, as they drove through the rainy night near Wellington, Texas. A bridge was out, and Clyde lost control of the car in a fiery crash, Bonnie suffering serious burns before she was pulled from the wreckage. Farmer Steve Pritchard stopped to help and found himself a hostage, Clyde and Deacon Jones moving Bonnie into the Pritchard home at gunpoint. A farmhand escaped in the confusion, and police were on the way when someone—either Clyde or Jones, reports vary—fired a panicky shot, drilling Pritchard's sister-in-law through one hand. Outside, the bandits kidnapped two patrolmen and used their car to flee the scene, leaving the hostages tethered to a tree at Erick, Oklahoma.

Bonnie's condition was critical, with second- and third-degree burns over much of her body. On June 19 Clyde went to fetch her sister Billie from Dallas, wanting a relative on hand if Bonnie died. Ted Hinton, on routine patrol, spotted Clyde twice on the highway—coming and going—but a faulty transmission in the squad car allowed Clyde to leave his old friend in the dust. On June 22, two men identified as the Barrow brothers stole $3,600 from a bank in Alma, Arkansas. If true, the next day's events are curious, Buck and Jones setting off to rob a Piggly-Wiggly store in Fayetteville. Returning from that heist, they met Marshal H. D. Humphrey and De-

puty A. M. Sayers on the highway, exchanging shots that left Humphrey mortally wounded.

On July 8 it was a shortage of guns and ammunition that drove the gang to rob a National Guard armory at Enid, Oklahoma, making off with some four dozen .45-caliber Colt automatics. Ten days later they robbed three gas stations in Fort Dodge, Iowa, driving on to the Red Crown Cabin Camp near Platte City, Missouri. Police were on alert for roving bands of strangers in those days, and suspicion brought a full-scale raiding party to the Red Crown Cabins on July 18. Police moved in behind an armored car with tear gas and machine guns, but the gang fought back ferociously, wounding three officers before they escaped in two cars. This time it was a costly victory, Blanche blinded in one eye by a sliver of glass and Buck drilled through the head by a bullet that left him blind, delirious, and weak from loss of blood.

Five days later a civilian posse tracked the fugitives to an abandoned amusement park between Dexter and Redfield, Iowa. Both cars were disabled in the first barrage of gunfire. Buck and Blanche were captured after Buck stopped five more bullets. (He would die, raving incoherently, on July 29; in September at Platte City, Blanche received a 10-year prison sentence for assaulting law enforcers.) Bonnie, Clyde, and Jones were also wounded, but they slipped through hostile lines in the confusion and were able to escape.

It was enough for William Jones. He drifted back to Dallas where police were waiting for him, copies of the Joplin snapshots all they needed to convict him as a member of the "Bloody Barrow" gang. With the electric chair in front of him, Jones did the best he could to save himself, dictating a 28-page confession that described his time with Clyde and Bonnie as a "living hell." According to Jones, he was shackled in chains or "unconscious" during most of the gang's major crimes, occasionally being forced to shoot at police—unwillingly, of course—on pain of death if he refused. To make the story even more bizarre, Jones spoke at length about the sex life of the Barrow gang, describing how both Clyde and Bonnie used him constantly, exhausting Jones with their excessive and perverse desires.

Clyde never held the rambling fairy tale against his one-time friend, expecting Jones to lie if it would save him from the chair. Three generations of reporters, though, have taken Jones's statement as their gospel, overlooking its absurdities and the total

BARROW, Clyde Chestnut, and PARKER, Bonnie

lack of evidence supporting any single charge. Author John Toland swallowed the story whole in 1963, his otherwise exemplary book *The Dillinger Days* accepting "blue-eyed country boy" Jones as the one infallibly honest member of the Barrow gang. Lew Louderback added a new twist in 1968, falsely describing Ray Hamilton as Bonnie's lover before she met Clyde, hinting that Ray's addition to the gang helped satisfy her "insatiable appetite for sex." Crime historian Carl Sifakis continued the trend in 1982, describing the union of Bonnie and Clyde as a collaboration between "a homosexual and a near nymphomaniac." Movies released between 1967 and 1992 have been somewhat kinder to the outlaw couple, painting Clyde as "straight" but impotent until

the last weeks of his life, another claim for which there is no shred of evidence.

While Jones spun his fables in jail, Bonnie and Clyde were back to business as usual. On September 25, 1933, they robbed a McKinney, Texas, grocery and abducted the proprietor, soon releasing him unharmed. On November 15, with an unidentified accomplice, the couple took $2,500 from an oil refinery in Overton Township. One week later, near Sowers, Texas, the couple slipped through another police ambush and vanished.

Clyde finally came to Ray Hamilton's rescue on January 16, 1934. Pistols were stashed along the country road where Hamilton's work crew was chopping weeds, and when the shooting started,

The bullet-riddled automobile in which the bandits Clyde Barrow and Bonnie Parker were trapped, shot, and killed as they sped over a Louisiana road at 85 miles per hour is shown here. (AP/Wide World Photos)

Bonnie and Clyde leaped from cover with accomplice James Mullen, laying down a screen of fire to cover the escape. Two guards were wounded in the melee; one of them, Major Joseph Crowson, died four days later, adding a new murder charge to the list. Among the prisoners who fled with Hamilton, Louisiana native Henry Methvin joined the Barrow gang. It seemed like a good idea at the time.

On February 1 Bonnie and Clyde took a paltry $270 from a bank in Knieram, Iowa. One day later they were suspected (almost certainly in error) of robbing another bank at Coleman, Texas. February 19 found them looting a National Guard armory at Ranger, Texas. Five days later, the gang was suspected of robbing a bank in Galena, Texas; if true, it was the biggest take of their career, the loss reported at $7,100. On February 27 Clyde and Hamilton scored $4,138 from another bank, this one in Lancaster, Texas.

By that time, the Eastham prison break had sparked new demands for the capture of Bonnie and

Clyde. Texas Ranger FRANK HAMER, killer of numerous outlaws in face-to-face showdowns, was assigned on February 10 to track the fugitives across state lines and bring them back dead or alive. His trek would last for 102 days, with Hamer assisted much of the time by Deputy Ted Hinton. In the end, they would employ a combination of detective work and treachery to bag their prey.

Sightings of Bonnie and Clyde continued that spring. They were suspected of robbing a bank in Mesquite, Texas, on March 3, and nine days later Clyde was wrongly identified as the leader of a gang that took $21,000 from another bank in Atchinson, Kansas, wounding Police Chief Willard Linville with machine-gun fire. On April 1 the gang was idling at a rest stop outside Grapevine, Texas, when motorcycle officers E. B. Wheeler and H. D. Murphy rolled up to the scene. When the smoke cleared, both patrolmen were dead, riddled with bullets in the Barrow gang's most controversial shooting. Newspaper reports (and later Henry

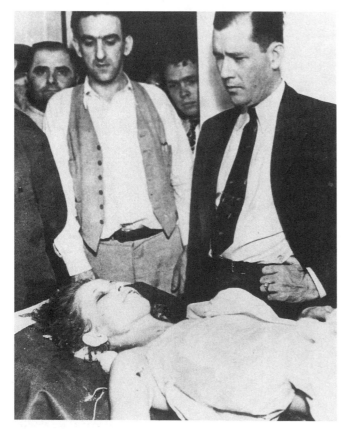

Bonnie Parker in the wake of a fatal police ambush. (From the collection of the Texas/Dallas History and Archives Division, Dallas Public Library)

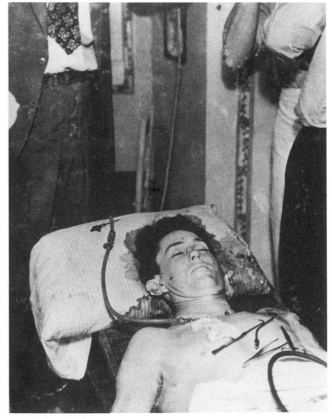

Embalmers prepare Clyde Barrow for his funeral. (From the collection of the Texas/Dallas History and Archives Division, Dallas Public Library)

Methvin) described Bonnie standing over the prostrate victims, pumping bullets into their bodies and kicking them for good measure. Clyde's sister blamed Methvin for killing both officers, claiming he confessed the double murder in her presence. As for Clyde, he later blamed Ray Hamilton, dispatching a letter to law enforcers (complete with his thumbprint in oil) that called Hamilton a "yellow punk," urging detectives to "Ask his girlfriend how they spent Easter." Ray, for his part, claimed that he had left the gang in February on another trip to Michigan.

Five days after the Easter killings, on April 6, Constable Carl Campbell was shot dead in a confrontation with the Barrow gang near Commerce, Oklahoma; Police Chief Perry Boyd was wounded in the gunfight, later testifying that Bonnie, Clyde, and Methvin all fired shots during the brief engagement. It was this incident that encouraged Methvin to leave the gang in mid-April, catching a train back to his father's home in Louisiana, while Clyde rolled on to rob banks at Stuart, Iowa (April 16), in Iredell, Texas (April 20), and at Everly, Iowa (May 3).

Manhunters, meanwhile, had identified the new member of Clyde's gang, tracing his roots to the Pelican State. Father Ivan Methvin lived in a tumbledown shack between Gibsland and Arcadia. He was poor but reasonable, listening attentively as law enforcers spelled out his options. Cooperation meant life for his son; refusal meant a bullet in the head or worse, a date with the electric chair.

The noose was tightening. Ray Hamilton, flying solo once again, was jailed on April 25 after robbing a bank at Lewisville, Texas. On May 18 a federal grand jury in Dallas indicted Clyde, Hamilton, Methvin, and cohort Joe Palmer for stealing government property in their several armory raids. One day later, Bonnie's sister Billie was jailed on suspicion of murder in the Grapevine killings. Barrow gang associate Jack Nichols was arrested on May 20 in Longview, Texas. In Louisiana, manhunters Hamer and Hinton knew Ivan Methvin was expecting a visit from Bonnie and Clyde. He had agreed to bait their trap if son Henry got a pardon from the state of Texas, and the deal was made.

On May 23, 1934, Bonnie and Clyde were approaching Methvin's home when they saw Ivan's truck at the side of the road, one tire apparently flat. They pulled over to help, Clyde munching a sand-

wich and driving in his socks. Across the road, Frank Hamer, Ted Hinton, and four other lawmen sat behind shrubbery, each man armed with a Browning automatic rifle (BAR), surrounded by at least a dozen extra shotguns and pistols.

Like so much else about the story of these outlaw lovers, their final moments remain clouded by gunsmoke and conflicting stories. Were they offered a chance to surrender? Knowing Bonnie and Clyde, does it matter? An estimated 167 bullets ripped through their car in a matter of seconds, dozens piercing each body before they could reach the pistol and shotgun they kept close at hand. A search of the car revealed three BARs, 12 more pistols, several hand grenades, and some 2,000 rounds of ammunition.

Bonnie Parker had anticipated the moment in her second epic poem, "The Story of Bonnie and Clyde."

> *Some day they'll go down together;*
> *they'll bury them side by side;*
> *To few it'll be grief—*
> *To the law a relief—*
> *But it's death for Bonnie and Clyde.*

She was right, except for the funeral arrangements. Both outlaws were returned to Dallas, but they were buried separately—Bonnie in the Parker family plot and Clyde beside his brother "Buck." It hardly mattered to the legend, which had already taken on a life of its own.

The rest was simply mopping up. Ray Hamilton and Joe Palmer were condemned for the murder of Major Crowson at Eastham; Hamilton escaped from death row in July 1934 but was swiftly recaptured and kept his date with the electric chair in May 1935. Bonnie's sister and Floyd Hamilton (Raymond's brother) were acquitted on July 24, 1934, of participating in the Easter Grapevine murders. Henry Methvin got his Texas pardon as promised, but Oklahoma was less forgiving. Convicted of Cal Campbell's murder, Henry was sentenced to die, his penalty later commuted to life imprisonment. Paroled in 1942, he lasted seven more years before the boozy evening when a freight train flattened him, a short walk from his rural home. William Jones, despite his rambling self-exoneration, was sentenced to 15 years for his role in the murder of Deputy Malcolm Davis. Some 20 more defendants were tried on federal charges of harboring Bonnie and Clyde, including the mothers of both outlaws, who were sentenced to 30 days in jail.

BARTER, Richard A. "Rattlesnake Dick"

The son of a British army officer, born 1834 in Quebec, Richard Barter moved to California with an older brother at age 16 working a hard-scrabble gold claim on Rattlesnake Bar on the north fork of the American River. It was a losing proposition, doomed to failure, but Rattlesnake Bar would tag Barter with the nickname that has followed him through history.

When the lure of prospecting paled, Dick Barter turned to crime. In 1853 he was arrested for stealing clothes from a merchant, but jurors acquitted him at trial. On September 12, 1854, he was caught with a stolen mule, convicted of grand larceny, and sentenced to a year in prison despite a claim that his partner had stolen the animal. In later years, Barter cited the alleged injustice as the launching pad for his criminal career. "I left Rattlesnake Bar after my release," he said, "with the intention of leading a better life, but my conviction hounded me at every turn until I could stand it no longer. I have been driven to it, and hereafter my hand is against everybody. I suppose everybody's hand is against me."

Whatever the truth of that case, it is clear that Barter used his prison time to learn tricks of the outlaw trade, befriending veteran holdup artist TOM HODGES and others who would be Barter's future crime partners. In July 1855, with Hodges and others, Barter robbed a messenger of Langton's express near Forest City, California, stealing some $3,000 in gold. On March 12, 1856, with CYRUS SKINNER and BILL GRISTY, he stole 13 mules for use in a $17,000 robbery that targeted a Rhodes and Whitney Express mule train, bearing $17,000 in gold dust from the Yreka Mine to Shasta, California. (Some published accounts contend that Barter failed to get the mules and that the gold was later lost as a result, but such was not the case.)

Five months after the Yreka holdup, Barter rode into the mining camp at Washington, California, for supplies. He was recognized on the street and a band of miners tried to capture him. A flurry of gunfire erupted, leaving one vigilante wounded; Barter escaped with a bullet in his leg. Early October found him jailed in Nevada City with Jim Webster and the Farnsworth brothers, Fred and Jim, for attempted burglary at a local hotel. Using smuggled tools, Barter and Webster tunneled out of their cell, broke open the door to the cell block, and knocked out a guard before escaping into the night.

In the wake of that escapade, Barter's cronies spread the tale that he had fallen down a mine shaft and died. Some law enforcers believed the fable, but "Rattlesnake Dick" was very much alive, recruiting a new gang of his own that included Jim Driscoll, George Taylor, and Aleck Wright. In February 1857 this team cracked the safe in a WELLS FARGO office at Fiddletown, California. On May 3, 1858, they robbed a stagecoach on its run between Nevada City and Auburn. Another stage was taken for $4,500 in gold and coin on November 1, 1858, en route from Rattlesnake Bar to Folsom. Yet another was robbed between Forest Hill and Todd's Hill on January 11, 1859. Altogether, the stage holdups netted Barter's gang a little more than $30,000. Jim Driscoll was the only gang member arrested for those crimes, captured in April 1859 and sentenced to 10 years in prison.

Dick Barter's most persistent enemy was Constable John Boggs of Auburn. So devoted was he to the chase that Boggs was nicknamed "The Nemesis of 'Rattlesnake Dick.'" It chafed at Barter's nerves, prompting him to plot Boggs's death, but a nocturnal stakeout at the lawman's home proved fruitless because the constable was out of town. Disgusted, Barter nailed a peevish letter to his adversary's gatepost: "Have been waiting for you nearly all night."

One near-miss with Constable Boggs occurred on April 28, 1858, when Barter and crony George Taylor were spotted aboard the stage to Folsom. They were wanted at the moment for robbing a nearby ranch, so Boggs stopped the coach in Placer County, ordering the bandits to step out. One disembarked on either side of the coach, both reaching for their guns. Boggs wounded Taylor in one arm, but both gunmen escaped on foot, leaving the constable empty handed and fuming.

Barter was captured several times thereafter and hauled to jail at Auburn, but he always managed to escape from Boggs's lockup, thereby deepening the lawman's hatred. At last, on July 11, 1859, Boggs received a tip that Barter was riding toward Auburn with sidekick Aleck Wright. A posse was dispatched, overtaking the outlaws at 9:00 P.M. In response to their challenge, Barter first called out, "What's up?" and then started to shoot. Wright's gunshots were a second behind him. Deputized tax collector George Martin was killed outright, while Undersheriff George Johnston suffered crippling injury from a wound to his left hand. Still, Johnston was able to return fire, striking Barter in the chest.

Constable Boggs launched an all-night search for the outlaws. Wright was nowhere to be found, but the posse located "Rattlesnake Dick" a mile from the site of his last shootout. He lay dead beside the road, covered with a blanket. In his right hand was a pistol and a note scrawled in pencil. One side read: "Rattlesnake Dick dies but never surrenders, as all true Britons do." On the reverse was written, "If J. Boggs is dead, I am satisfied."

BASS, Sam

A Hoosier native, born July 21, 1851, Sam Bass left Mitchell, Indiana, at 17 to try his hand at gambling. By 1870 he had settled in the Indian Territory (modern Oklahoma), where he raced and rustled horses. The year 1876 found him in Texas where Bass teamed with cronies Jack Davies and Joel Collins to drive 500 cattle north to Kansas. The trio agreed to work on consignment, but in fact they sold the herd as their own and rode on to Deadwood, South Dakota, where they operated a successful brothel. Even with the money pouring in, however, profits always lagged behind expenditures for booze and gambling. Finally, Bass, Collins, and Davies recruited three of their brothel's best patrons—Jim Berry, Bill Heffridge, and Tom Nixon—to form a gang and hit the outlaw trail full time.

They started small, with highway robbery of stagecoaches, but Bass recalled stories of the train-robbing RENO BROTHERS in his native Indiana, deciding to give it a try. On September 19, 1877, the gang invaded a Union Pacific depot at Big Springs, Nebraska, forcing the agent at gunpoint to signal a halt for the eastbound express. The train arrived moments later and duly stopped; Bass and company extracted more than $60,000 in newly minted coins from the baggage car. A passenger was shot while craning out a window to observe the holdup, but he survived to identify Joel Collins as one of the bandits. PINKERTON detectives recognized Collins as a crony of Sam Bass, and so the hunt began—but Bass was nowhere to be found.

He had taken his $10,000 cut from the holdup and decamped to Denton County, Texas, where he soon recruited a new outlaw gang, committing a string of robberies around Dallas–Fort Worth. The first job was disappointing, less than $50 stolen from a stagecoach at Mary's Creek in December 1877. The following month, another stage holdup between Fort Worth and Weatherford netted the gang $400 and two gold watches. Determined to do better, Bass switched back to robbing trains. On February 22, 1878, his gang looted a Texas Central train at Allen Station, west of Dallas. A month later, on March 18, Texas Central was again the loser in a robbery at Hutchins. On April 4 Bass robbed the Texas and Pacific at Eagle Bend, rebounding a week later to hit the same line again, this time at Mesquite.

A classic SOCIAL BANDIT of the era, Bass won friends with his free-spending lifestyle and used a certain primitive charisma to ingratiate himself with otherwise law-abiding Texans. Railroad magnates hated him, of course, but their pleas for a special consignment of Texas Rangers to hunt down the gang were initially rejected. At last, in desperation, the Texas Express Company called on the Pinkerton agency to extend its search for Bass into the Lone Star State.

The manhunters got their first break on May 21, 1878, when a jailed associate of Bass, James W. Murphy, wrote the Texas Rangers, offering to "assist in the capture of the Bass party by joining them and putting them in a position where they could be captured." The price of his cooperation would be freedom. The law enforcers eagerly agreed, arranging for Jim Murphy to "escape" and find his comrades.

Murphy rode with the gang for a month, attempting several times to put Bass on the spot, but each attempt fell through. Finally, he alerted his contacts that Bass planned to rob a bank at Round Rock, 20 miles north of Austin, sometime after July 13. Riflemen were waiting when the gang made its move on July 19, killing outlaw Seaborn Barnes and dropping Sam Bass, wounded, from his saddle. Jim Murphy, forewarned, had found cover by then, but the last of the gang, Frank Jackson, rode back under heavy fire to save Bass and carry him out of Round Rock.

The valiant effort was in vain. A posse found Bass the next day, near death, outside a sharecropper's cabin. Texas Rangers grilled him mercilessly, seeking the identity of his accomplices and the location of alleged buried loot, but Bass refused to squeal. His only comment, as recorded by the frustrated interrogators, was, "Let me go. The world is bobbing around." Bass died on his 27th birthday, and although treasure hunters still seek his legendary fortune, most historians believe Frank Jackson took the secret and the money with him when he disappeared. Although Jackson's fate is unknown, his late comrade was eulogized in "The Ballad of Sam Bass."

Sam Bass was born in Indiana, it was his native home;
At the age of 17 young Sam began to roam.
Sam first came out to Texas, a cowboy for to be—
A kinder-hearted fellow you seldom ever see.

BATES, Albert

A veteran burglar and bank robber of the late 1920s and early 1930s, Bates used a variety of pseudonyms in his effort to avoid arrest, known to some of his associates as George Davis, George Harris, or J. B. King. It did not always work, of course. On March 28, 1916, Bates was convicted of burglary in Nevada, drawing a term of one to 15 years at the state prison in Carson City. He was paroled on November 13, 1917, and lasted 17 months before his next burglary arrest, at Ogden, Utah, on April 22, 1920. Trial on that charge sent him to the Utah state prison on August 3, 1921, and five years passed before he was able to escape, on October 27, 1926.

No matter what he tried, Bates had no luck at staying out of trouble with the law. Convicted of yet another burglary, this time in Colorado, he was dispatched to the state pen at Canyon City on May 10, 1927. Parole released him on July 17, 1930, and Bates predictably set off in search of bad companions.

One of those he found was GEORGE "MACHINE GUN" KELLY, paroled from Leavenworth federal prison a month before Bates won his freedom in Colorado. Bates and Kelly joined forces with unnamed accomplices to rob their first bank at Denton, Texas, on February 6, 1932. On September 21, 1932, the duo teamed with stickup artist EDWARD BENTZ to loot a bank in Colfax, Washington, of $77,000 in cash and bonds. November 30 saw them backed by sidekick Eddie Doll to hit a bank at Tupelo, Mississippi, for another $38,000. (Authorities wrongly blamed CHARLES "PRETTY BOY" FLOYD for that holdup, one of many added to the Oklahoma bandit's rap sheet without justification.)

Bates and Kelly had been lucky so far, but daylight robbery was still a risky trade. It was a rare day during 1932 and 1933 when newspapers did not report another shootout between outlaws and police officers or civilian posses. Bates still wanted to be rich, of course, but what was wrong with finding an easier racket—say, kidnapping, for instance? It was all the rage in early 1933: a gang in ST. PAUL, MINNESOTA, scored $100,000 for brewer William Hamm in June, and the Bates-Kelly team had visions of doubling that payoff.

Their target, Oklahoma City oil man Charles Urschel, was kidnapped at gunpoint from his home on July 22, 1933, and driven to a Texas ranch owned by Kelly's in-laws. After negotiation and a few false starts, the $200,000 ransom was paid on July 30, and Urschel was freed the following day, Bates and Kelly splitting up to go their separate ways while FBI agents took over the case. The Texas ranch was soon identified (either through brilliant detective work or a tip from local authorities; reports vary), and G-men raided the spread on August 12, arresting three of Kelly's in-laws and fugitive bank robber HARVEY BAILEY (who had stopped by to visit and recuperate from his latest stickup). Bates was in Denver by that time, where police coincidentally nabbed him the same day for passing stolen checks.

This time it was the end for Bates and his long-running outlaw career. "Machine Gun" Kelly would remain at large until September 26, but Bates and the other Urschel defendants were already on trial by that time, the lot of them convicted in federal court on September 30. A short week later, on October 7, they were sentenced to life imprisonment and Bates was shipped off to Alcatraz Island, where he died of heart disease on July 4, 1948.

BEACH, Donald, and LINK, Lonnie

On June 1, 1983, two violent thieves invaded the home of a Wenatchee, Washington, gun dealer, beating the man and his wife before making off with 72 firearms, 180 pounds of silver, assorted gems, rare coins, and a quantity of gold. Nearly seven weeks later, on July 17, the gun dealer received a telephone call from one of the thieves-turned-extortionists, offering to sell the stolen items back to him for $19,000 in cash. After hasty consultation with authorities, a meeting was set for 10:30 P.M. the following day at a hotel parking lot in downtown Spokane. Police had the rendezvous site staked out in advance and were prepared to drop a net on anyone who showed up for the payoff.

The suspects were right on time, rolling up in an old-model Lincoln Continental, one man hopping out to approach the gun dealer's car and count the money while his partner remained in the getaway car. Detectives instantly surrounded the scene with guns drawn, but their subjects were not prepared to give up without a fight. A shot fired from the Lincoln fatally wounded Detective Bryan Orchard before the wheelman escaped under heavy fire. Orchard was the first Spokane police officer killed on duty in more than a half-century.

The second thief, meanwhile, ducked through some nearby shrubbery and vanished in the night, but he did not get far. Tracked down by K-9 officers within an hour of the shooting, he was identified in custody as 34-year-old Donald Beach, proud owner of a felony conviction record spanning 15 years. Beach kept his mouth shut in jail, but Spokane police had no need of his help. A witness had seen their second suspect switching cars on his way out of town and had recorded the license number of his backup ride. A trace on the plate identified the car's registered owner as 24-year-old Lonnie Link, well known to police in Washington and Montana for various criminal escapades and paroled in March 1983 from a Montana burglary conviction.

With the shooter identified, running him down was simply a matter of time. Link made it as far as Portland, Oregon, before he was spotted and nabbed by local police, held on a Spokane warrant charging him with first-degree aggravated murder. Returned to Spokane in early August, Link joined Beach in pleading innocent on murder charges. He hedged on the earlier theft, claiming he and Beach were simply go-betweens for unnamed "big men" who had hired them to unload the stolen property. When pressed for names he merely shrugged and said he was afraid to identify his employers in case they might retaliate with a murder contract.

At trial in September 1984, Link claimed that he was unaware that the people who surrounded his car on the night of the shooting were law enforcers. He feared a double-cross or hijacking, Link said, and simply fired in self-defense. Various prosecution witnesses testified that the officers had clearly identified themselves, prompting Link to explain that he was playing the Lincoln's radio and could not hear the many voices shouting, "Freeze! Police!" Jurors dismissed the tale, convicting Link of first-degree murder and fixing his penalty at life imprisonment without parole. Two months later, in November 1984, Donald Beach cut a deal with prosecutors and pled guilty to second-degree felony murder, receiving a life sentence that would leave him eligible for parole in 13 years and five months.

BELL, Tom: See HODGES, THOMAS J.

BENDER Family

Nothing is known of the Bender family's origins beyond the fact that all four members spoke with varying degrees of a Germanic accent. Whether they were actually European immigrants is now impossible to learn, another aspect of the killer brood that shall, like so much else about their lives, remain forever wrapped in mystery.

The family enters recorded history in 1872 as new arrivals in the small community of Cherryvale, Kansas. William Bender was the patriarch, a bearded hulk whose age was estimated in the neighborhood of 60 years. No given name has been recorded for his wife, Ma Bender, some 10 years her husband's junior. Their elder child was John, a brawny moron given to odd fits of giggling. The baby and star of the family was daughter Kate, an attractive blond in her early 20s who quickly emerged as the Bender family spokesperson . . . and, some said, the brains behind their infamous career in crime.

Soon after their appearance on the scene, the Benders built a one-room cabin, 16 feet by 20, on the road between Cherryvale and Thayer. A sheet of canvas cut the room in half, with living quarters on one side, a public room on the other. Travelers could buy a home-cooked meal or rent a cot, but some paid for the rest stop with their lives as the Benders developed a new twist on highway robbery.

In practice, groups of travelers and hard-luck drifters had no problem with the Bender clan; a solitary sojourner with cash or valuables in hand was something else again. The chosen mark was seated at a table, with the canvas curtain at his back. Kate Bender served his meal, distracting him with conversation and a bit of cleavage while her brother or the old man crept up on the victim's blind side and dispatched him with a crushing hammer blow. That done, the corpse was lowered through a trapdoor to the cellar, stripped and looted, and finally buried on the grounds outside. Ma Bender did her part by planting flowers to conceal the graves.

When travelers were scarce, Kate Bender did her part to keep the family business going. On her own, she toured southwestern Kansas, billing herself as "Professor Kate Bender," a medium with contacts in the spirit world. Her public séances earned money for the family, and young male members of the audience were often more impressed with Kate's appearance than her psychic powers. A number of these would-be suitors made the trip to Cherryvale and wound up in Ma Bender's flowerbed.

The family's last-known victim was Dr. William York from Fort Scott, Kansas. Passing through Cherryvale in March 1873, York asked about overnight lodging and was pointed toward the Bender spread. He never made it home, and it was May before his brother, Colonel A. M. York, arrived in search of explanations. Questioning the Benders, York received denials. He declined their hospitality and cautioned them that he would soon return if he could not pick up his brother's trail.

Next morning, on the fifth of May, a passing neighbor saw the front door of the Bender cabin standing open, the family's team and wagon missing. Stepping in, he found the place deserted. Fresh dirt in the cellar marked the grave of William York, and 10 more bodies were unearthed around the cabin, all with shattered skulls. By then the Benders had a two-day lead. Colonel York led a posse in pursuit, but they returned at length with word that no trace of their quarry could be found.

And there the matter rested . . . for a while.

In 1884 an old man matching William Bender's description was arrested in Montana for a homicide committed near Salmon, Idaho. The victim's skull had been crushed with a sledgehammer in that case, and a message was wired to Cherryvale, seeking a positive identification. That night the suspect severed his own foot to escape from leg irons, and he was dead from loss of blood when his breakfast was delivered in the morning. By the time a deputy arrived from Kansas, advanced decomposition had destroyed any hope of a confirmed I.D. (Even so, the "Bender skull" was publicly displayed in Salmon's Buckthorn Saloon until 1920 when Prohibition closed the tavern and the relic disappeared.)

Five years after the bizarre events in Idaho, Cherryvale resident Leroy Dick paid a visit to Michigan, where he identified Almira Griffith and her daughter Sarah Davis as Ma and Kate Bender. The suspects were extradited to Kansas, where seven members of a 13-man panel agreed with Dick's opinion. On the eve of trial, however, a Michigan marriage license was found for one of the women, dated 1872, and all charges were dropped.

In 1909 George Downer, dying in Chicago, told his attorney that he had ridden with Colonel York's posse in 1873. Far from coming up empty, he said, they had captured the "Hell Benders" and meted out brutal vigilante justice, saving Kate for last and burning her alive. The bodies were consigned to an abandoned well, and posse members swore among themselves that they would take the secret to their graves. A year later, before Downer's statement was widely aired, a similar deathbed confession emerged from New Mexico. The source, a man named Harker, admitted taking several thousand dollars from the dead Benders before they went into the well. A search for the burial site was fruitless, the well—if it ever existed—long since vanished in a sea of cultivated corn, but the lynching tale resurfaced in 1940, published by the son of an alleged posse member named Stark.

Did vigilante justice overtake the Benders on a lonely stretch of Kansas prairie some 130 years ago? Or did the lethal clan escape, perhaps to build another roadside lair and kill again? How many victims did they claim *before* they moved to Cherryvale? Today, the only answer to those questions is the brooding silence of the grave.

BENTZ, Edward Wilheim

Despite his notoriety in later life, details are vague about the early years of premier stickup artist Eddie Bentz. The most complete reports suggest that he was "probably" born at Pipestone, South Dakota, sometime in 1895. His father was killed by a runaway horse (date uncertain), whereupon the family moved to Tacoma, Washington. Bentz served teenage time in a reformatory there for burglary before graduating to safecracking and armed robbery in his 20s. Crime historian William Helmer asserts that Bentz participated in 150 robberies or more across the country without being named or indicted, but that account provides no verifiable specifics. Bentz apparently did well enough at robbery to support a lifestyle of understated elegance, collecting a fair number of rare books and coins. Known for his thorough planning and meticulous charting of escape routes, Bentz was a suspect (along with HARVEY BAILEY) in the Lincoln, Nebraska, bank heist that netted $2,870,000 on September 17, 1930, but no charges were filed in that case.

Whether Bentz shared in that record-breaking score or not, he was back in the game by mid-1932, teamed with ALBERT BATES and GEORGE "MACHINE GUN" KELLY to rob a bank at Ponder, Texas, on July 31. (The job was wrongly credited to the Texas-based CLYDE BARROW gang.) On September 21 the same trio knocked over a bank in Colfax, Washington, escaping with $77,000 in cash and bonds. Eight days later, Bentz and unidentified accomplices took down another bank in Holland, Michigan.

Bentz was semiretired and living at Long Beach, Indiana, in 1933, when he was drawn back into active robbery by GEORGE "BABY FACE" NELSON. The target was a bank in Grand Haven, Michigan, and the heist was a fiasco. The gang's getaway driver fled at the sight of a passing patrol car, leaving Bentz, Nelson, and their cohorts stranded. Gang member Eddie Doyle was captured nearby; the others made it to a second waiting car and managed to escape with $30,000 for their trouble. Rumors named JOHN DILLINGER as a participant, but he was probably too busy robbing Indiana and Ohio banks around that time to lend a hand. Nelson reportedly caught up with the offending wheelman later and executed him for bailing out on comrades in a pinch.

The rules changed for bandits on May 18, 1934, when President Franklin Roosevelt signed a package of six anticrime bills, including a statute that placed most bank robberies under federal jurisdiction. Undeterred by the threat of FBI pursuit, Eddie Bentz and unidentified cohorts robbed a bank in Danville, Vermont, on June 4, but the $8,500 take was a major disappointment. Whether Bentz retired after the Danville job or not remains unclear, but he was never positively linked to any other holdups. Still, one was enough to put the G-men on his trail, and they traced him to a Brooklyn, New York, address on March 13, 1936, scouring the house before they found their quarry hiding in a dumbwaiter. In custody, Bentz kept his mouth shut and refused to name his colleagues on the Danville job. Convicted at his trial and sentenced to a prison term of 20 years, he asked to serve his time at Alcatraz, remarking to the judge that "All my friends are there."

BERGL, Joe: Underworld mechanic

The proprietor of Bergl Auto Sales, located on 22nd Street in Chicago, Joe Bergl made his reputation and his fortune by supplying "special" vehicles to clients on the wrong side of the law. A silent partner in the enterprise was Capone gangster Gus Winkler, and Bergl's shop was conveniently situated next door to Ralph Capone's personal speakeasy, the Cotton Club. Bergl specialized in armor-plated vehicles with bulletproof windows, favored by mobsters with more enemies than friends, but he also armed robbers outside the ranks of ORGANIZED CRIME. For them, he tailored getaway cars complete with oil-slick devices and smokescreens to assist in shaking squad cars off their tail.

Bergl's bank-robbing customers included GEORGE "MACHINE GUN" KELLY and members of the wide-ranging BARKER GANG. The latter outfit used one of customized rides in Chicago on September 22, 1933, stopping a team of Federal Reserve Bank messengers on Jackson Boulevard. A patrolman was killed as they fled with a load of worthless canceled checks, and the bandits wrecked their car in flight and left it for police to trace. Gus Winkler was arrested for the robbery two days later, Chicago police naming him as a member of a national stickup syndicate that also supposedly included bandits VERNON MILLER and "Machine Gun" Kelly. Apparently fearful that the threat of heavy prison time might make Gus squeal, persons unknown moved to silence him in gangland style on October 9. Joe Bergl was allowed to live, but his usefulness to the underworld ended with his exposure, and gangsters with a need for special vehicles would henceforth have to deal with his competitor CLARENCE LIEDER.

BIGGS, Everett Leroy

A hard-luck bandit, Everett Biggs was readily identified when he raided a bank in Springfield, Illinois, for $17,600 on September 13, 1966. The next day, federal warrants were issued, charging him with unlawful flight to avoid prosecution, and his name was added to the FBI's "Most Wanted" list on September 21.

Undaunted by his sudden notoriety, Biggs came back strong a month later in Tulsa, Oklahoma. On October 21 he robbed a local bank with accomplices John Frank Larson and Willard McClanahan.

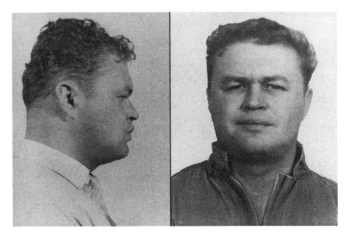

Bank robber Everett Biggs was posted to the FBI's "Ten Most Wanted" list in 1966. (FBI)

The bandits netted $77,606, but the holdup was not without problems. Witnesses described Biggs as "careless and apologetic" after his pistol discharged in a scuffle with a bank cashier.

On December 1, 1966, FBI agents traced John Larson to a rented house in Denver, Colorado. Unarmed at his arrest that afternoon, Larson offered no resistance and was given no opportunity to reach the five guns hidden in adjoining rooms. Three hours later, G-men captured Everett Biggs at a second rented home. Surrounded, Biggs did not attempt to use his .38 revolver. Six other guns and a large amount of cash were recovered by agents in a search of his hideout, the evidence and eyewitness descriptions sufficient to guarantee Biggs a stiff prison sentence.

BIRDWELL, George

A product of the Indian Nation, born in 1894, George Birdwell presented a blend of Irish, Cherokee, and Choctaw stock that was not unusual in those days before the region became modern-day Oklahoma. Published sources disagree on details of his background. Public records indicate that he was shot and wounded by a jealous farmer in 1913, and that the shooter soon divorced his wife as a result of the affair. Author Myron Quimby maintains that Birdwell committed 10 murders and "countless" bank robberies in the 1920s but presents no supporting evidence or details; Birdwell's surviving children, meanwhile, insist that he was a law-abiding farmer until 1930, when he met CHARLES "PRETTY BOY" FLOYD and teamed with the legendary Sooner outlaw to begin to raid banks. In either case, it is remembered locally that Birdwell liked to pass out $20 bills among his neighbors after every job, no petty gesture in the heart of Dust Bowl Oklahoma and the Great Depression.

Birdwell's first known robbery with Floyd occurred on March 9, 1931, when they teamed with WILLIAM MILLER to lift $3,000 from a bank in Earlsboro, Oklahoma. Five months later, George and Floyd hit Shamrock's bank alone, escaping with a paltry $400. Their luck was better on September 8, a raid in Morris, Oklahoma, netting them $1,743, and was better yet three weeks later when they scored $3,850 from a bank in Maud. They returned to Earlsboro on October 14, 1931, and hit the same bank they robbed in March for another $2,498; then they moved on to Conowa and stole $2,500 from another bank on November 5. A bank in Castle,

Oklahoma, gave up $2,500 to the dashing duo on January 14, 1932, and Birdwell (though unrecognized) was probably Floyd's accomplice for the disappointing $800 bank job in Dover, Oklahoma, eight days later.

Large or small, the frequent raids had Oklahoma bankers up in arms and howling at the governor for help. When Floyd rented a house in Tulsa to accommodate his wife and child, it was inevitable that there would be contact with police. Officers spotted Floyd and Birdwell driving through the city on February 7, 1932, but the bandits escaped after wounding one patrolman in a running gunfight. The scene was repeated in a different part of town three days later, and authorities besieged the rented house on February 11, but their quarry escaped out the back while tear-gas shells were being fired inside.

Undaunted by the close shaves in Tulsa, Birdwell and Floyd kept raiding. On March 23, 1932, they tapped a bank in Meeker, Oklahoma, for $500. Birdwell's father died a month later, sheriff's deputies staking out the funeral home in Earlsboro, but the bandits surprised them on April 20, Floyd holding the officers at gunpoint while Birdwell paid his last respects. One day later they looted a bank at Stonewall, making off with $600 from the cash drawers. Another police trap failed to snare the outlaws near Ada on June 7, frustrated sharpshooters speculating that Floyd and Birdwell must have worn full-body armor to survive the fusillade. Their biggest score in months was bagged at Sallisaw on November 1, 1932, when they joined AUSSIE ELLIOTT to steal $2,530, but Floyd and Birdwell were wrongly blamed for the $11,252 robbery of a bank at Henryetta six days later.

It was around this time that Birdwell hatched a plot to rob the Farmers and Merchants Bank in all-black Boley, Oklahoma. Floyd opposed the move, warning that whites were too conspicuous in Boley and the residents unlikely to permit a robbery without resistance. Birdwell forged ahead, recruiting gunmen Charles Glass and C. C. Patterson for backup. He neglected to note that their target date—November 23—was the first day of bird-hunting season in Boley, when sportsmen thronged downtown hardware stores to stock up on shotguns and ammunition.

The holdup went ahead on schedule, Birdwell twirling his .45 automatic like a Wild West outlaw while Glass and Patterson looted the tellers' cages. One drawer was fitted with an automatic alarm, triggered when the last bills were removed, and the commotion alerted bookkeeper H. C. McCormick, over-looked by the bandits in a back room of the bank. Seizing a rifle, McCormick drilled Birdwell through the heart, the dying outlaw finding strength enough to kill bank president D. J. Turner before he collapsed. Roused by the alarm and gunshots, hunters lined the street and let fly as the two surviving bandits fled. Glass was killed outright; Patterson was critically wounded before Boley's sheriff arrived to save him from a second volley. Birdwell lived long enough to reach the hospital in Henryetta, but doctors were unable to save him. C. C. Patterson survived his wounds to serve time in the state prison at McAlester. H. C. McCormick, meanwhile, was rewarded $1,000 and appointed honorary major in the state militia for his sterling marksmanship.

BLANCO, Miguel

A cousin of California outlaw PÍO LINARES, born in 1838, Miguel Blanco was charged in Los Angeles at age 19 with robbing and stabbing a merchant named William Twist. His alleged victim was also the former sheriff of Santa Barbara County, and Blanco confessed the crime, but his confession was discarded by the court as a product of police coercion, and he was acquitted of the charge in April 1857.

Whether or not that first charge was true, Blanco soon emerged as a bandit in his own right, riding with the Linares gang on a series of raids. On May 12, 1858, with Linares and six others, he invaded Rancho San Juan Capistrano, a spread owned by two Frenchmen near present-day Shandon, California. Blanco personally killed one of the ranchers, M. José Borel, while the other—Bartolo Baratrie—was bound and executed by the gang. Linares ordered the death of Baratrie's wife and two ranchhands, but squeamish gang members spared them and thereby sealed their own fate. While fleeing from the looted ranch, the gang met and murdered an Anglo hunter, Jack Gilkey, who lived in a cabin nearby.

Santos Penalta was the first gang member captured, at San Luis Obispo, but he hanged himself in jail without naming his accomplices. It hardly mattered by that time because the survivors of the latest raid were talking to police. On May 22 a posse raided the Linares ranch and flushed four outlaws from cover. Miguel Blanco was among them, but the bandits escaped on foot in thick brush after abandoning their horses. An eight-day, two-county search proved fruitless, law enforcers retiring to wait for the fugitives to surface.

On June 8 Blanco, Linares, and two others visited a ranch 10 miles west of San Luis Obispo. Manhunters were alerted and descended on the ranch on June 10, fighting a skirmish that left Pío Linares wounded. Two days later, a reinforced posse overtook the bandits once more, this time killing Linares while one of their own died and two were wounded. Miguel Blanco and Desidirio Grijalva surrendered after their leader was slain, and both reportedly confessed their role in the lethal raid at Rancho San Juan Capistrano. Vigilantes lynched the pair at San Luis Obispo on June 16, 1858.

BONNY, Anne

Born in 1700, Anne Brennan was the illegitimate daughter of a successful Irish attorney, William Cormac, and his housemaid Peg Brennan. Initially, Cormac sought to avoid scandal by dressing the child as a boy, describing "him" as the child of friends left in Cormac's care, but the charade placed unbearable strain on his home life. Deserting his wife in due course, Cormac fled with his mistress and their child to Charleston, South Carolina, where he abandoned the practice of law and prospered as a merchant. The profits were invested in a great plantation, young Anne taking over household duties when her mother died.

By age 14 neighbors had noted Anne's "robust" body, along with her "fierce, courageous temper." Rumors spread that she had knifed a servant girl to death, but no investigation was pursued. One documented case involved a young man who attempted to molest her on the street: Anne broke his jaw and beat him so severely that he was hospitalized for three months.

At age 16 Anne married penniless seaman James Bonny. Neighbors suspected the groom was after her money, a risk William Cormac laid to rest by driving the newlyweds off his plantation. They drifted to the Bahamas, settling in New Providence, where Governor Woodes Rogers had lately declared open season on pirates. James Bonny signed on as an informer, paid to hang around taverns and brothels, but Anne found more in common with the pirates. Local buccaneers, for their part, liked her style—more so after Anne produced a gun and shot a man who tried to grab her on the street one afternoon.

A general amnesty for pirates ruined the informer business, and Anne soon abandoned her husband in favor of Chidley Bayard, alias "Albert Blackhouse," a fugitive from British justice acting as a fence for pirate loot. Bayard had a live-in mistress at the time, but Anne dispatched her with a well-placed rapier thrust and took the other woman's place before her corpse was cold.

In Bayard's company Anne met such famous privateers as Henry Jennings, Benjamin Hornigold, and the inimitable "Blackbeard," Edward Teach. Before long, she grew tired of Bayard and shifted her affections to John "Calico Jack" Rackham, quartermaster for pirate captain Pierre Bousquet. Overcoming brief resistance, she put to sea with Rackham as part of Bousquet's crew, already scheming to replace the captain with her lover.

In July 1718 Anne persuaded the crew to depose Bousquet and install "Calico Jack." Six months later she gave birth to Rackham's daughter, but the child died in infancy. Stopping off in New Providence, Anne faced an adultery suit filed by James Bonny, but the governor let her off with a warning. Always one to get even, she torched Bonny's new home and shipyard before she set sail on a new voyage of plunder.

At sea Anne Bonny joined in looting scores of ships, proving herself as skilled as any man with a cutlass or pistol. One witness would later testify that she "cursed and swore with the best of males, and never cringed from murder." She dressed in shirt and trousers like a man, but the disguise could not conceal her "breasts the size and strength of melons."

In October 1720 Governor Rogers commissioned an armed sloop under one Captain Burnet, assigned to the sole task of caging Rackham's crew. Burnet overtook his prey while Rackham, Bonny, and the rest were celebrating the capture of a merchant ship, debating the fate of a female hostage. The man-hunters launched their assault, with Bonny, female pirate MARY READ, and one male crewman providing the only resistance. "Calico Jack" was locked in his cabin with a bottle of rum throughout the uneven battle, so infuriating Anne that she afterward spat in his face.

Six members of the crew were sentenced to hang, Bonny and Read postponing their dates with the hangman on grounds that both were pregnant. On the day of Rackham's execution, Bonny dropped by his cell to scold him for cowardice. "If you had fought like a man," she advised, "you need not have been hanged like a dog."

As for Anne, she would never stretch rope. Soon after the birth of her child she vanished from the New Providence lockup, and rumor takes over from there. William Cormac was widely suspected of

paving the way for his daughter's escape, while others blamed a new lover, Michael Radcliffe. Opinions are divided as to whether Anne settled in Charleston under an assumed name or married Radcliffe and migrated west.

See also: PIRATES AND PIRACY.

BOWERMAN, Fred William

A veteran holdup man whose record spanned three decades, Fred Bowerman was pushing 60 years old when he became number 46 on the FBI's "Ten Most Wanted" list. Within two months of his ascension to the limelight, Bowerman's luck—and his life—ran out in a flurry of violence that characterized his long career in crime.

Bowerman was one more in the old tradition of hard-core stickup artists, men such as THOMAS HOLDEN and ALVIN KARPIS who could never turn their backs on an easy woman or an easy bank. Arrested for armed robbery by Illinois authorities in 1932, Bowerman served five years for his first major offense, winning parole in 1937. A year later he was back inside, but not before committing numerous robberies in the Chicago area. Adhering to the bandit's maxim that "You don't live where you pull your jobs," Bowerman resided in Michigan, commuting to Chicago in stolen cars for a series of heists (36 in all) which he committed between June and October 1938. Conviction in the epic string of heists brought more time in Joliet, but Fred was back on the street by 1946, looking for action.

Bowerman was able to avoid detection for a while, but in September 1952 he was identified as one of those who took a South Bend, Indiana, bank for $53,000 in a violent daylight raid. A bank employee was shot and wounded when he raised his hands too slowly for the bandit's taste, and Bowerman was added to the FBI's "Most Wanted" list when a vacancy became available on March 3, 1953.

The heist that finished Bowerman was a chaotic, bloody fracas in the worst Wild West tradition. Fred and three accomplices descended on the Southwest Bank in north St. Louis on the afternoon of April 24. The robbery went well at first, the raiders plucking some $140,000 from the tellers' cages and stuffing it inside a nylon satchel. But a bank employee had been quick enough to trigger a silent alarm, and as Bowerman's gang prepared to evacuate, a strike force of nearly 100 police officers converged on the bank, preparing for a siege. In seconds, as employees

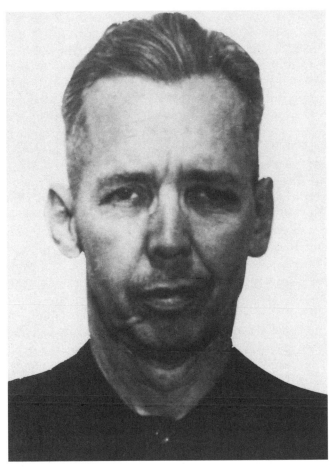

Veteran stickup artist Fred Bowerman died in a 1953 shootout with police. (FBI)

scrambled for the safety of the vault, a full-scale fire-fight was in progress, bandits firing through the windows, gagging on the tear gas that was pumped into the bank. Outside, a police sergeant stopped two bullets, one each in the head and in the neck, before the tide of battle turned.

Attempting to escape, Fred Bowerman was toppled by a bullet in the chest, which pierced a lung and lodged against his spine. Accomplice William Scholl, armed with a shotgun and pushing a female hostage ahead of him, made it as far as the sidewalk. Surrounded, he shoved his captive to the pavement, breaking both her wrists, before a bullet knocked him sprawling. He was digging in his pocket for a backup weapon when police rushed forward to disarm him, dragging him away in handcuffs.

Trapped inside the bank, Bowerman's remaining confederates panicked. One, Frank Vito, put a pistol to his head and killed himself. The lone survivor, one-time college football star Glenn Chesnick, man-

aged to escape on foot (without a dime of loot), but he was captured three days later by alert detectives. At the hospital, Fred Bowerman identified himself as "John W. Frederick," a ruse that fell apart once G-men had a chance to scrutinize his fingerprints. He died on May 1, 1953, of injuries sustained in his last battle with police.

BRADLEY, George Martin, Jr.

A felon whose record dated from 1946, including convictions for counterfeiting, fraudulent checks, armed robbery, and confidence games, George Bradley showed a fondness for deception during his holdups. In 1950 he used a toy pistol to rob the box office of a Cincinnati theater, but plastic weapons did not help his case in court. Sentenced to a term of one to 25 years in prison, Bradley was paroled in March of 1952.

There was nothing fake about the shotgun Bradley carried when he robbed a bank in Stuart, Florida, on January 16, 1961. His two accomplices were captured swiftly, but elusive George was added to the FBI's "Most Wanted" list on April 17. His capture two weeks later could be traced directly to another bluff that blew up in his face.

On May 2, 1961, Bradley entered the First Federal Savings and Loan Association in Davenport, Iowa, carrying a simulated bomb inside a paper bag. Giving employees a glimpse of his "weapon," Bradley demanded $60,000 cash. Instead of paying up, loan officer Paul Josinger snatched the bag from Bradley's grasp, risking death as he hurled the "bomb" across the room. Unarmed, the would-be bandit fled on foot with customers and bank employees in pursuit.

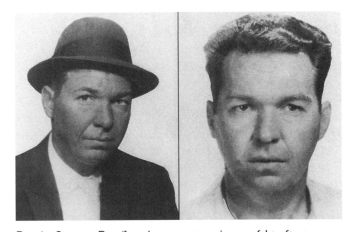

Bandit George Bradley Jr. committed one of his first armed robberies with a toy pistol. (FBI)

Attracted by the chase, Patrolman Ray Musselman cornered Bradley in a nearby alley and held him at gunpoint. Once in jail, George was identified and soon delivered to the hands of federal agents for trial and conviction on outstanding charges.

BRADSHAW, Ford

An Oklahoma outlaw of the late 1920s and early 1930s, Bradshaw was a contemporary of the more notorious Sooner bandit CHARLES FLOYD, whose take from small-town bank jobs frequently exceeded any scores attributed to "Pretty Boy." On November 7, 1933, for instance, Bradshaw joined colleagues Newton Clayton and Jim Benge to loot a bank in Henryetta, Oklahoma, of $11,238. (The heist, ironically, was credited to Floyd, GEORGE BIRDWELL, and AUSSIE ELLIOTT.) A year later, the payoff was even better, when Bradshaw, WILBUR UNDERHILL, and others took $13,000 from a bank in Okmulgee.

Bradshaw was such good friends with Underhill, in fact, that he took it personally when authorities disrupted Wilbur's honeymoon on December 30, 1933, surrounding his rented cottage at Shawnee, Oklahoma, and pouring in a storm of gunfire that left Underhill mortally wounded. The next day, Bradshaw and a carload of his comrades roared through Vian, a hundred miles due east, in a symbolic protest of the shooting, peppering a restaurant, a hardware store, and the town jail with bullets. Such stunts were not inclined to garner public sympathy, and law enforcers took no chances when Bradshaw was finally cornered at Ardmore on March 3, 1934. Reaching for his weapon, Bradshaw was killed where he stood by sheriff's deputy William Harper.

BRADY, Jim, and BROWNING, Sam

This two-man train-robbing team made its first score in October 1894 near Mikon, California (west of Sacramento). Southern Pacific trackwalker John Kelly was on his way home, around 8:00 P.M. on a foggy night when he met a pair of masked strangers armed with rifles. They handed him a lantern and forced Kelly to flag down the eastbound Overland Express a short time later. Taking the engineer and fireman hostage, the bandits persuaded the train's express messenger to open his locked car, wherein they scooped up $50,000 worth of gold and silver coins in four large sacks. The railroad and WELLS FARGO offered $10,000 for capture of the thieves and recovery of the loot, but their only clue so far was the shorter gunman's thick Irish brogue.

Six weeks later, in December 1894, the robbers leaped aboard a moving Southern Pacific passenger train, eastbound from Sacramento. Wearing hoods and brandishing pistols, they surprised the locomotive crew and brought it to a halt. Unable to open the express car's safe, they ordered crewmen to detach the car, but a faulty mechanism foiled their plan and they fled empty handed.

Another holdup went sour for the still-anonymous pair a week later when they boarded Train No. 5 on its slow passage across a bridge spanning the Calaveras River. With drawn guns they ordered the train stopped at Castle, a small railroad station midway between Lodi and Stockton. At gunpoint, the engineer ordered his express guard to open the mail car, but the guard had other plans. Easing the door slightly open, he fired two shots at the bandits—missing both times—then slammed and locked the heavy door again. Threats of dynamite finally forced the guard out, but his captors found the safe impregnable. They settled for stealing the guard's fancy pistol and fled, firing wild shots to frighten the train's passengers.

On March 30, 1895, the Oregon Express was northbound for Portland, rolling through the Sacramento Valley, leaving Wheatland around 2:00 A.M., when two masked gunmen invaded the baggage car. They stopped the train at Reed's Crossing, 10 miles south of Marysville, but once again the heavy safe resisted their best efforts. Frustrated, one of the bandits took the train's fireman hostage, prodding him at gunpoint through the Pullman cars from back to front, relieving startled passengers of $1,000 in cash and 15 gold watches. In the forward Pullman car, they met Tehama County Sheriff John Bogard crouched behind a seat with his revolver drawn. Bogard shot the hooded gunman once, inflicting a mortal chest wound and then shot the fireman twice in a case of mistaken identity. (He would survive.) The second bandit, meanwhile, had circled around behind Bogart and surprised him with a shot in the back, killing the sheriff instantly. Grabbing the bag of loot and leaving his partner to die, the surviving outlaw hopped aboard a waiting bicycle and fled to Marysville, where he evaded searchers and escaped.

The dead bandit was identified as Sam "Big Jim" Browning, aka "Oscar Brown" and "S. McGuire." He had a record of arrests for larceny but lately had gone straight—at least, to all appearances—as a farmhand in the upper Sacramento Valley. The description of his partner in the holdups matched a known associate of Browning's, ex-convict Jim Brady (aka "Henry Williams"). The pistol found beside Browning's corpse was the sidearm stolen from the express guard on Train No. 5 in December.

Fugitive Brady eluded manhunters until July 26, 1895, when he was found dressed as a hobo, lurking under a bridge in Sacramento. Returned to Marysville on a charge of first-degree murder, he pled not guilty at a preliminary hearing on September 2. His trial began on November 4, defense attorneys W. A. Carlin and E. A. Forbes dismissing the state's case as a "chain of rope and sand." Jurors disagreed on November 19, convicting Brady of murder with a recommendation of life imprisonment. At sentencing, he requested confinement at San Quentin, deeming it "healthier than Folsom," but Judge E. A. Davis opted for security and denied Brady's request. The outlaw served 19 years and was paroled on December 2, 1913. He worked a ranch near Galt, California, for several years before his death from natural causes.

An odd footnote to the Brady-Browning holdups was the case of hobo John Harmans, aka "Karl the Tramp." Harmans had been sleeping rough near Mikon on the night of the October 1894 train robbery and had observed the bandits burying their loot. After they fled, Harmans unearthed the stash, pocketed $10,000 of the money, and planted the rest in a new hiding place. He launched an epic spending spree in San Francisco, renting an apartment on fashionable Nob Hill and blowing the rest of his ill-gotten gains on liquor and women. Suspicious detectives pulled him in for questioning, but they had no evidence of any particular crime. By the time they decided to arrest him on general principles Harmans had blown his 10 grand and gone back to a life on the rails. Captured in 1896, he confessed and led authorities to the missing $40,000. Harmans was convicted of grand larceny with a recommendation of leniency and pulled three years at Folsom. On release, he resumed his hobo life style and vanished into obscurity.

BRADY, Robert "Big Bob"

An Oklahoma native born in 1904, Brady was incarcerated for the first time—on a larceny charge—in Kansas at age 15. The state reformatory at Hutchinson failed to reform him, and theft became a way of life for "Big Bob." He was imprisoned on an Okla-

homa forgery charge in 1922 and again three years later for an armed robbery in Nowata County. Free again in 1931, he joined outlaw Clarence "Buck" Adams to loot a Texahoma, Oklahoma, bank of $5,300 on September 15. The outlaws were captured on September 26 at Carlsbad Caverns in New Mexico and were transferred immediately to the Amarillo, Texas, lockup. Brady staged an escape and was shot through the head, but the bullet somehow missed his brain, and he recovered in time for the warden at the McAlester, Oklahoma, state prison to receive him in October.

It seemed no jail could hold "Big Bob," however: Barely 10 months after his incarceration, on July 23, 1932, Brady escaped from McAlester and hit the road. Stopping briefly in Ada, Oklahoma (where his brother ran a legitimate real estate brokerage), Brady robbed for the second time a bank that he had raided prior to his September 1931 arrest. Another bank job in El Dorado Springs, Missouri, followed quickly. On October 1 he stole a new car from a dealer in Liberal, Kansas, and then rebounded the following day to rob a bank at Springer, New Mexico, with Oklahoma native Frank Philpot. Five days before Christmas 1932, Brady was sighted and captured in Des Moines, Iowa; at the time of his arrest, he carried a .38-caliber revolver and a stolen Oklahoma deputy sheriff's badge. By that time, he was wanted in at least four states for different holdups, but Kansas won the honors and sentenced him to life imprisonment at Lansing penitentiary as an habitual criminal.

This time, Brady's sojourn behind bars was even shorter than usual. On May 30, 1933, he joined a mass escape from Lansing that included veteran outlaws HARVEY BAILEY, WILBUR UNDERHILL, JIM CLARK, and seven others. Federal authorities suspected (but could never prove) that pistols used in the breakout were smuggled inside by fugitive bank robber FRANK NASH. To no one's great surprise, the fugitives resumed their criminal careers, robbing a Black Rock, Arkansas, bank on June 16; taking $11,000 from a Clinton, Oklahoma, bank on July 3; and looting a bank in Kingfisher, Oklahoma, on August 9. Two days after the Kingfisher job, gang members met near Shawnee, Oklahoma, to plot the holdup of a bank in Brainerd, Minnesota, but Bailey was coincidentally arrested on August 12 and the plan fell apart.

Brady and Jim Clark thereupon decided that a change of scene might be in order, decamping with their women for an extended vacation in sunny Arizona. On October 6, 1933, they were back in Oklahoma, looting a bank at Frederick of $5,000, carelessly missing another $80,000 in the vault and tellers' cages. Again they fled westward, but they were captured the same day, near Tucumcari, New Mexico. Oklahoma prosecutors waived their charges, and the fugitives were shipped back to Kansas for completion of their interrupted sentences. Briefly held in solitary after their return to Lansing, Brady and Clark were back in the general prison population by January 19, 1934, when they and five other inmates escaped while working on a kitchen detail.

This time, Clark and Brady split up, and "Big Bob" lasted a short three days on his own. On January 22, he was cornered by Undersheriff Harve Lininger and Deputy Ed Schlotman on a farm near Paola, Kansas. Brady chose to shoot it out, but his shotgun misfired and the lawmen killed him where he stood. It was reported that some 2,500 curious citizens lined up to view his body at the local mortuary, before it was shipped back to Oklahoma for burial.

BRADY Gang

The last notorious holdup gang of the 1930s "public enemy" era, this four-man outfit drew its name and inspiration from Alfred James Brady, an Indiana native born at Kentland on October 10, 1910. Enthralled by the bank-robbing exploits of a notorious fellow Hoosier, Brady declared his intention to "make JOHN DILLINGER look like a piker" where crime was concerned. To that end he recruited three accomplices—Charles Geiseking, Rhuel James Dalhover, and Clarence Lee Shaffer Jr.—for a Midwest crime spree that began in October 1935.

Grandiose ambition aside, the gang's first haul was a pitiful $18 taken from a Crothersville, Indiana, movie theater on October 12. During the next two months, the gang struck an estimated 150 drugstores, gas stations, and grocery stores, ranging widely across Indiana and Ohio. It was a grocery stickup that drew their first blood, leaving two policemen wounded at Crawfordsville, Indiana, on November 30, 1935.

In early 1936 the Brady gang switched to jewel heists and scored its first significant success. On March 4 the raiders took $8,000 worth of gems

from a jewelry store in Greenville, Ohio, followed two weeks later by another haul worth $6,800 from a shop in Lima. Their score in Dayton, on April 9, was the gang's all-time best: $27,000 worth of gems, give or take, with a clean getaway. It was all the more perplexing, then, when Brady and company held up a grocery in Piqua, Ohio, killing clerk Edward Linsey on April 22. Five days later they were back in Lima, holding up the same jewelry store a second time.

Their luck went sour on April 29, 1936, when Al Brady was arrested in Chicago. Clarence Shaffer was nabbed at his home near Indianapolis on May 11. Four days later, the handcuffs closed on Rhuel Dalhover, in Chicago. Geiseking remained at large until September 12, 1936, when he was run to earth and captured at Henderson, Kentucky. Jailing the Brady gang was one thing, though; holding its members for a murder trial was something else again. On October 11, in Greenfield, Indiana, Brady, Dalhover, and Shaffer overpowered one of their keepers, escaping from the Hancock County jail. A federal complaint was filed against the fugitives in Cleveland two days later, charging them with interstate transportation of stolen property, and FBI agents were detailed to join in the manhunt.

While Charles Geiseking languished in jail awaiting trial and conviction on robbery charges, his three cohorts took their first fling at bank robbery in the Dillinger tradition. On November 23, 1936, they looted a bank at North Madison, Indiana, of $1,630. On December 16 the target was a bank in Carthage, Indiana, their take $2,158. A four-month hiatus was broken at Farmland, Indiana, on April 27, 1937, when the gang stole $1,427 from a local bank. A month later, on May 25, they bagged $2,528 from another bank in Goodland, Indiana. Fifteen miles down the road, they met a police car and opened fire on sight, killing state policeman Paul Minneman and wounding a deputy sheriff, Elmer Craig.

The gang fled eastward to escape the heat, but they were famous now, as Brady had desired. In Baltimore on August 7, 1937, they were cornered by police but shot their way out of the trap, leaving behind an arsenal of guns and ammunition as they fled. On August 23 the trio hit a bank in Thorp, Wisconsin, escaping with $7,000 in cash. On September 28 they were suspected (perhaps incorrectly) of killing a highway patrolman, George Conn, outside Freeport, Ohio.

It was time to hide again. This time, Al Brady led his cohorts all the way to Maine, but he could not resist the trappings of an era that had passed him by. In Bangor, he went shopping for Tommy guns at a local sporting goods store, perhaps unaware that automatic weapons had been placed under federal regulation by the National Firearms Act of 1934. The dealer had none in stock, but he agreed to take Brady's order—and promptly telephoned police, who flashed a warning to the FBI. It was arranged for the proprietor to summon Brady to collect his nonexistent guns while G-men and police staked out the shop. On October 12, 1937, Brady, Dalhover, and Shaffer walked into the trap. All three drew pistols and went down before a withering barrage of fire; Brady and Shaffer died on the spot; Dalhover survived his wounds to face trial on murder charges and was executed at the Indiana state prison in Michigan City on November 18, 1938. Sixty years later the gang's final shootout was memorialized (albeit with altered names and events) in Stephen King's horror novel *It,* set in the ghost-haunted fictional town of Derry, Maine.

BRANCATO, Anthony

Anthony Brancato was a hard case, living on the fringes of the underworld and serving mobsters bigger than himself when there was work available, content to rape and rob and sell narcotics when times were lean. A Kansas City native, he had gravitated to Los Angeles and there compiled a record of arrests for gambling, dealing drugs and bootleg liquor, plus suspicion in a string of gangland murders. When a sniper murdered Bugsy Siegel in June 1947, homicide detectives hustled Tony in for questioning. They called him back in 1948 when Hooky Rothman, one of Mickey Cohen's goons, was murdered in Los Angeles, and in July 1949 he was interrogated after an attack on Cohen. Further north, in Fresno, he was suspected in the drug-related death of Abe Davidian.

Brancato's bosom pal, another Kansas City boy gone bad, was Anthony Trombino. They had been hauled in together on occasion, and between them they could boast of 46 arrests, including rape and robbery, assault, and other major crimes. They were considered renegades within a world of outlaws, and they had devoted years to making enemies.

On May 28, 1951, four bandits robbed the sports book at the Fabulous Flamingo in Las Vegas,

Mobster and bandit Anthony Brancato was suspected in the 1947 assassination of mob leader Benjamin "Bugsy" Siegel. (FBI)

Nevada, making off with $3,500 in cash. The heist was ill conceived at best, considering the hidden ownership of the casino, doubly so in light of the fact that Tony Brancato neglected to wear a mask. Considering his long and violent record, he was posted to the FBI's "Ten Most Wanted" list on June 27. Two days later, with a lawyer at his side, he surrendered to federal agents in San Francisco, posting a $10,000 bond. Before he had a chance to leave the building, Anthony was rearrested on Nevada's warrant naming him a fugitive from justice. This time he was out of cash and could not post the necessary bail.

Brancato's case became a minor cause célèbre for students of the U.S. Constitution, who accused the state and federal governments of violating Tony's civil rights. Released without bond on a writ of habeas corpus, Brancato fled south to Los Angeles, there teaming up with his sidekick Trombino. They both needed cash for their various lawyers, and neither could stomach the thought of an honest day's work. Their last days are described by author Ovid Demaris in *The Last Mafioso,* a biography of syndicate killer Jimmy "The Weasel" Fratianno.

According to Fratianno, "the Two Tonys" swindled gambler Sam Lazes out of $3,000 he owed to a syndicate bookie. Posing as collection agents for the mob, Brancato and Trombino pocketed the cash and later tried to pressure Lazes for another payment. Added to Brancato's sheer audacity in robbing the Flamingo, it was more than local mobsters were prepared to tolerate.

On orders from the syndicate, Fratianno approached Brancato and Trombino, offering to help them execute a robbery in Hollywood. On August 6 The Weasel kept his date, with gunman Charles Battaglia in tow. Brancato and Trombino occupied the front seat of a car parked on Hollywood Boulevard, Fratianno and Battaglia seated behind them, when the shooting started. Both Brancato and Trombino were killed instantly by multiple shots to the head, their murder "unsolved" until Fratianno entered the federal witness protection program 20 years later.

BRINKS Robbery: Boston, Mass. (1950)

The great Brinks robbery of January 1950 was a year in the making. For 12 months prior to the event, 11 middle-aged Bostonians, including seven men with records of arrests for other crimes, planned every detail of a raid against the Brinks North Terminal garage. They slipped past guards to enter the garage by night in stocking feet and "cased" the floor plan, measured distances, determined which doors swung open in an effort to avoid confusion at a crucial moment. Members of the team broke into a burglar alarm company, making off with samples of the model used by Brinks to study its mechanism in detail. A full-scale dress rehearsal in December 1949 convinced the bandits they were ready for the score.

On January 17 the raiders entered the garage in broad daylight, decked out in simulated Brinks uniforms and rubber Halloween masks. Making their way to the counting room, they held startled employees at gunpoint and looted the vault of $1,218,211 in cash, plus another $1,557,183 in checks and securities. The total haul, much more than $2.7 million, was a record for its time. In less than 15 minutes, it was done.

The conspirators had planned to keep low profiles, sitting on their loot for six years and waiting for the statute of limitations to expire, but one of the team—James "Specs" O'Keefe—began to grumble that his share had not been large enough. Demanding another $63,000, he was angrily rejected by his comrades. "Specs" began to brood about injustice while the gang faced problems on another front.

On May 14, 1952, convict Alfred Gagnon fingered Carlton O'Brien, of West Warwick, Rhode Island, as a planner on the Brinks job. Three days later O'Brien was murdered by persons unknown, but his death, while plugging one leak, also opened another. On December 1, Specs O'Keefe was called before a special grand jury, investigating the holdup. Two weeks later five uncooperative witnesses, named by O'Keefe as participants in the robbery, were cited for contempt when they refused to testify.

It was apparent that O'Keefe would have to go. On June 10, 1964, the contract was assigned to Elmer "Trigger" Burke, the leading freelance hit man of the 1950s. Burke caught up with Specs on June 16, spraying him with machine-gun fire in a wild nocturnal chase through the streets of Boston's Dorchester district. Wounded in the arm and the chest, O'Keefe feigned death and Burke was satisfied, escaping from the scene as squad cars closed with sirens wailing.

(Arrested on June 24, Burke escaped from jail the next day. A year passed before his arrest by FBI agents in South Carolina. Hoping for extradition to Massachusetts for trial on charges of possessing a machine gun, Burke was instead sent to New York on a pending murder charge. Convicted on December 2, 1955, he was sentenced to death two weeks later. Burke died in Sing Sing's electric chair on January 9, 1958.)

The FBI had invested $25 million in its Brinks investigation by the time James O'Keefe started to talk in earnest. Arrested on weapons charges in Leicester, Massachusetts, on August 1, 1954, Specs was sentenced to 27 months in jail. Determined not to take the fall alone, he confessed his role in the heist and named his co-conspirators in late 1955. By that time one of them (Joe Barfield) was deceased. Another, Stanley Gusciora, was incarcerated in Pennsylvania, serving five to 20 years for pulling off a robbery in Pittsburgh. Still at large were Vincent Costa, Michael Geagan, Joseph McGinnis, Adolph Maffie, Thomas Richardson, and James Faherty.

A grand jury hit the surviving suspects with 46 indictments, including 148 separate counts of armed robbery, entering with felonious intent, conspiracy to steal, and putting a person in fear with felonious intent. On January 12, 1956, the FBI tried for a clean sweep of eight outstanding fugitives around the Boston area, but agents came up two men short. James Faherty had evaded authorities beforehand; his longtime partner Thomas Richardson enjoyed a narrower escape. When federal agents cornered Michael Geagan in a bank where Richardson was presently employed, their second suspect managed to slip out unseen in the confusion. Faherty was posted to the "Ten Most Wanted" list on March 19; Richardson was added to the roster April 12.

In spite of massive heat, the fugitives would not desert their Boston stamping grounds. They had been hanging out together since their first arrest in 1934, and togetherness had become a habit. On May 16 a squad of 25 heavily armed FBI agents surprised the pair at an apartment in Dorchester, seizing three guns and $5,009 in cash. The lion's share of loot was never found, but there were indications that it might be working for the robbers. Ex-con William

Cameron had sheltered Faherty for pay, and it was rumored that he may have tipped authorities when he did not receive his rent on time. By June 10 Cameron was dead, shot down by unknown gunmen near his Boston home.

Eight members of the holdup gang, excluding Gusciora and O'Keefe (who turned state's evidence against his friends) were brought to trial in late September 1956. Convicted, they were sentenced to life terms on October 9, serving an average 14 years each before winning parole. When an $18 million movie on the case began production in 1980, Richardson and Adolph Maffie were invited to the set, amused to see their heist presented as a tongue-in-cheek affair. "I'm glad they made something light out of it," Richardson quipped. "People need a few laughs these days."

BRINKS Robbery: Nyack, N.Y. (1981) See MAY 19TH COMMUNIST ORGANIZATION.

BRINKS Robbery: Syracuse, N.Y. (1965) See SINGER, JOEL.

BROWN, Joseph C., and DUNBAR, Charles B.

A pair of unremarkable train robbers and burglars, Joseph Brown and Charles Dunbar provide a case study of police investigative techniques carried out to a successful conclusion in early 20th-century America. The fact that Brown ultimately escaped punishment is a testament to his determination, rather than a failure of the system per se.

On April 16, 1910, two hooded bandits armed with semiautomatic pistols boarded Southern Pacific train No. 10 as it passed through Benicia, California. Engineer Jack Marsh complied with orders to stop his train five miles east of Benicia, one mile west of Goodyear. Express agents in the mail car surrendered their cargo after the bandits threatened them with dynamite; the mail bags were loaded aboard the locomotive, which the bandits then uncoupled and used to make their getaway. Driving the engine to the Goodyear bridge, they stopped again and loaded their haul aboard a waiting boat, paddling off to parts unknown.

Word of the holdup spread rapidly through Alameda, Solano, and Contra Costa counties, and railroad detectives joining forces with police and sheriff's deputies in the manhunt. One bandit had

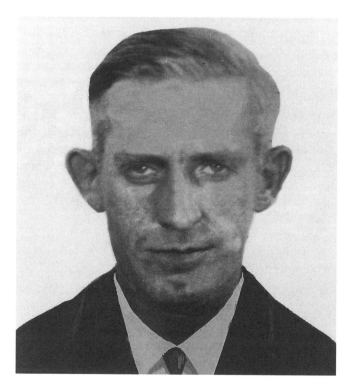

Brinks bandit Thomas Richardson was added to the FBI's "Ten Most Wanted" list six years after the crime, in April 1956. (FBI)

left his overcoat in the locomotive's cab; scattered along the railroad line were empty mailbags, 41 sticks of dynamite, a sawed-off shotgun, and a bandoleer of ammunition. Canvassing the district, investigators learned that two young men had rented a cabin on the outskirts of Martinez—across the Carquinez Straits from the robbery site—on April 1. They kept to themselves and were only seen in public when they rowed their skiff across the strait each day. A farmer found the skiff near Bullshead Point shortly after the holdup; with it detectives recovered a .38-caliber Colt automatic, binoculars, a pair of rubber boots like those worn by one robber, and two pieces of mail from the looted express car.

As the investigation continued, officers learned that a horse and buggy had been stolen from a local farmer on the night of the holdup. A description of the rig was broadcast while law enforcers continued their digging. Two men matching the outlaws' general descriptions had inquired about purchasing dynamite in Martinez one day before a case of explosives was stolen from a local warehouse. One of the shoppers had left a stolen watch to be repaired at a Martinez jewelry store. The discarded shotgun was traced to a shop in Riverside, where it had been stolen (along with four revolvers) in a recent burglary.

The net was tightening, local vigilance increased by Southern Pacific's offer of a $5,000 reward for arrest of the bandits. Three months after the holdup, on July 15, Constable Michael Judge stopped two suspicious characters in Sacramento, determining that their horse and buggy were stolen. A search of their buggy turned up the revolvers stolen from Riverside. Joe Brown and Charles Dunbar were booked on suspicion of burglary and train robbery. They initially denied everything, but Brown cracked on July 19 under grilling by the Solano County sheriff and district attorney. He confessed the train holdup, the Riverside burglary, and the June nocturnal looting of a post office at Armada in Riverside County, where he and Dunbar had stolen cash, another shotgun, and the binoculars discarded in their skiff. Dunbar held out for another three days, but both men admitted their crimes before Justice of the Peace W. W. Reeves at a preliminary hearing on July 22. Tried at Fairfield on August 22, both pled guilty and were sentenced to 45 years in prison. Brown, consigned to Folsom, escaped from a prison road camp on May 11, 1917, and was never recaptured. Dunbar was paroled from San Quentin on Christmas Eve 1919 after serving barely one-fifth of his sentence.

BROWNING, Sam: See BRADY, JIM.

BROWN'S Hole: Western outlaw refuge

A natural sanctuary for all comers, Brown's Hole could scarcely have been more convenient for 19th-century outlaws if prehistoric badmen had sculpted the landscape themselves. It lies where three states meet, a 30-mile-long valley stretching from Wyoming's Sweetwater County across dual borders into Moffat County, Colorado, and Dagget County, Utah. In the days before federal bank-robbing laws, it was a simple matter for hunted men to evade their pursuers without ever leaving Brown's Hole.

The "hole"—pioneer jargon for any place of refuge in the wilderness, large or small—was first inhabited by fur trappers in the early 1820s. One of them—Baptiste Brown, a French employee of the Hudson Bay Company—was prominent enough to give the place his name, although he never had it to himself. Near extinction of local beaver by 1840 drove the trappers out and made way for other settlers, including some ranchers who stole more livestock than they bought or bred.

The Hole's first-known outlaw inhabitants, arriving in 1869, were a true odd couple. Ex-slave Ned Huddleston (aka "Isom ['Quick Shot'] Dart") had run away from his Louisiana masters to fight in America's Civil War, but he strangely chose the Confederacy that enslaved him and drifted into Mexico after General Lee surrendered at Appomattox. In Mexico he killed a priest and had to run again, making his way across the vast Southwest. Somewhere along the way, he met Chang Lee, a Chinese gambler known to win more hands by cheating than by luck. Together, they founded a ranch in Brown's Hole that became an unofficial headquarters for rustlers who operated far and wide across three states.

Rustling was the primary enterprise of bandits operating from Brown's Hole until early 1896, when BUTCH CASSIDY emerged from Wyoming's state prison and began to recruit "long riders" for the bank- and train-robbing gang that soon became notorious as the "WILD BUNCH." Ranging fluidly across a wide area, Cassidy's raiders rode not only from Brown's

Hole, but also Wyoming's "HOLE-IN-THE-WALL" and Utah's ROBBERS' ROOST. All three sanctuaries were periodically raided, searched, and besieged by law enforcers or vigilantes to little effect. The hideouts gradually fell out of use in the early 1900s after Cassidy fled to South America and the men he left behind were killed or captured.

BRUNETTE, Harry

A small-time bank robber of no great reputation in the 1930s, Harry Brunette is remembered today primarily because he was selected by the FBI as an exemplary "public enemy," for propaganda purposes. Without that special (unwelcome) attention, he would almost certainly have been arrested by local police, routinely convicted, and long since forgotten.

As luck would have it, though, the FBI was under fire from various critics in early 1936. Despite its gang-busting reputation and high-profile slaying of various outlaws across the Midwest, the bureau had been widely condemned for its tendency to shoot unarmed suspects and innocent bystanders. More critical, at least to FBI headquarters, were personal attacks on director J. EDGAR HOOVER, pointing out that he had no actual police experience and had never made an arrest in his life. Hoover solved that problem in May 1936 with the staged capture of fugitive ALVIN KARPIS, but what could be done about similar criticism of his second-in-command (and reputed gay lover), Clyde Tolson?

The Karpis capture had taken America's last major bandit out of circulation, and the homicidal BRADY GANG remained too elusive for Hoover's purposes. The answer lay in what Hoover did best: creating a "menace" with strategic leaks to friendly journalists and then rushing in to "save" America and claim the adulation of the press. Harry Brunette became the target, traced to an apartment on New York City's West 102nd Street on December 14, 1936.

Whereas the Karpis arrest had been carefully managed, pulled off without firing a shot, the Brunette raid was a study in chaos, more akin to the 1934 Little Bohemia shootout between G-men and JOHN DILLINGER's gang. New York police initially located Brunette, sought with accomplice Merle Vandenbush for several holdups and the kidnapping of a New Jersey state trooper. After NYPD notified the FBI of Brunette's location as a professional courtesy, Hoover and company descended on West 102nd Street, demanding control of the scene. It was agreed

to raid Brunette's apartment at 2:00 P.M., when he was normally asleep, but G-men broke their word and launched the attack at midnight, 14 hours ahead of schedule, while detectives on stakeout watched in shock. The *New York Times* reported that when officers on site asked Hoover what he was doing, the director "merely shrugged his shoulders."

Things went from bad to worse from there. An FBI agent tried unsuccessfully to shoot the lock off Brunette's door, whereupon Brunette returned fire. Gas grenades were lobbed into the apartment, setting it afire. When firefighters arrived, the situation degenerated even further. As a *Newsweek* reporter observed: "Amid the hubbub, a flustered G-man poked a submachine gun at a husky fireman. 'Dammit, can't you read?' growled the fireman, pointing at his helmet. 'If you don't take that gun out of my stomach I'll bash your head in.'" Brunette finally surrendered, and Tolson was duly photographed leading the bandit away from his bullet-riddled hideout, but the raiders missed Merle Vandenbush entirely.

Next morning, New York Police Commissioner Lewis Valentine and his New Jersey counterpart voiced outrage at what they termed an FBI double-cross that had risked lives needlessly while permitting Vandenbush to escape. J. Edgar Hoover, safely back in Washington, airily dismissed the "unjustified and petty criticism" of his presumed inferior. Two months later, local authorities captured Merle Vandenbush without firing a shot. The fugitive reported that he had been on his way to meet Brunette when the FBI's three-ring circus warned him off. At one point, Vandenbush said, he had been close enough to tap J. Edgar Hoover on the shoulder.

BURKE, Fred "Killer"

An underworld hit man who also freelanced in armed robbery, Fred Burke was born at Mapleton, Kansas, in 1885. Some accounts list his birth name as Thomas Camp, but this—like so much else about his life—remains unclear. It is known that as a youth he ran with Egan's Rats, the notorious St. Louis street gang that spawned so many Prohibition-era mobsters, and the latter 1920s found Burke employed as a "special assignment" gunman for the Al Capone syndicate in Chicago. He was known for impersonating police officers on "contract" murders and for his early use of Thompson submachine guns during bank heists.

By the time of his eventual imprisonment, Burke was wanted for questioning in 20-odd murders across the United States. Detroit police considered him a suspect in the March 1927 Miraflores Apartments massacre of three gangsters, killed on orders from the notorious Purple Gang. He was strongly suspected of killing New York mobster Frankie Yale on orders from Capone in July 1928 and thus committing the Big Apple's first Tommy-gun drive-by assassination. Burke was also the only "confirmed" participant in Chicago's 1929 St. Valentine's Day massacre after one of the submachine guns used to kill seven Capone rivals was seized in a raid on his Missouri home. Ironically, bank robber HARVEY BAILEY maintained that he was drinking with Burke at the time of the slaughter, and while law enforcers dismissed Bailey's testimony on behalf of his friend and sometime accomplice, Burke was never prosecuted for any of those high-profile slayings.

Burke's first significant foray into armed robbery may have occurred as early as April 2, 1923, when some of Egan's Rats held up a U.S. mail truck in St. Louis, escaping with $2.4 million in negotiable bonds. Later that same year, still in St. Louis, Burke was tried and acquitted of participating in the $38,306 robbery of the United Railways Company. With Chicago mobster Gus Winkler, Burke was suspected of stealing $93,000 from a Peru, Indiana, bank on October 18, 1929. Eleven months later, on September 13, 1930, witnesses identified the same pair as two of the three men who looted a South Paterson, New Jersey, bank of $18,000. The final tally of Burke's holdups—like his murder contracts—remains unknown, but Harvey Bailey complained that Burke's "false" identification as a St. Valentine's Day massacre suspect had scuttled a lucrative bank-robbing career for the duo.

It was finally, fittingly, a murder that took Killer Burke off the streets. Living as "Fred Dane" in St. Joseph, Missouri, Burke lost control after a minor auto accident and fatally shot Patrolman Charles Skelly at the scene. Burke escaped, briefly, but the subsequent raid on his home revealed an arsenal including two Tommy guns—one linked by ballistics tests to Chicago's recent massacre, the other to Frankie Yale's death in New York. Burke remained at large and was sporadically active until March 26, 1931, when he was captured near Green City, Missouri, on a farm rented from relatives of Harvey Bai-

ley. Extradited to Michigan and sentenced to life for the Skelly slaying, he bribed guards at Marquette's state prison and thus lived in relative luxury for the better part of a decade. Burke developed diabetes in the late 1930s, and the disease claimed his life on July 10, 1940.

BURROWS, Rube

A late bloomer in the realm of crime, Rube Burrows (or "Burrow," in some accounts) was an Alabama farm boy, born in 1854. At 18 he moved to Texas and worked on his uncle's ranch, apparently content to earn his daily bread through honest labor. By age 32 he had enough cash saved to buy a spread of his own, marry, and start a family.

To this day, no one knows exactly what went wrong.

In December 1886, returning with three male companions from a visit to Indian Territory (now Oklahoma), Burrows was overcome with an irresistible urge to rob the Fort Worth & Denver Express. The four men—now a gang—loitered around the Bellevue, Texas, depot until the train arrived and then flashed guns at the crew in full view of the passengers—who hid most of their valuables before the fledgling outlaws passed among them, collecting a paltry $300 for their effort. In one car the bandits met three armed soldiers—a sergeant and two privates—who were escorting a pair of deserters in shackles, but frightened civilians persuaded the troops not to fire. The sergeant in command was later censured for cowardice by his superiors, while Rube Burrows schemed at ways to minimize the risk of such encounters in his next holdup.

Six months later, in June 1887, the gang struck again, boarding the eastbound Texas & Pacific Express as it left Ben Brooks, Texas. Holding the engineer at gunpoint, Burrows forced him to stop the train on a trestle outside town so that any passengers inclined toward heroism must brave the heights and the meager footing before they could challenge his gang. The take was not recorded on that job, but Burrows was satisfied enough to repeat the procedure at the same spot on September 20, 1887. Press reports of that holdup disagreed on the final score, listing it anywhere from $12,000 to $30,000.

Less than two months later, on December 9, Burrows and accomplice Jim Brock stopped the St. Louis, Arkansas & Texas Railroad's express train at

Genoa, Arkansas, relieving Southern Express Company guards of a Louisiana lottery payoff. Southern Express was a client of the PINKERTON National Detective Agency, placing Burrows on the most-wanted list of law enforcers and private manhunters alike. By December 16 detectives had located a sheriff's deputy who scuffled with three suspicious characters near Genoa on the day of the holdup. All three had escaped, but one lost his raincoat, which was traced by its label to a store in Dublin, Texas, where the sales clerk remembered Jim Brock. In custody, Brock confessed his role in the heist and named Rube Burrows as the mastermind.

The name meant nothing to authorities because Burrows had no record and Brock claimed ignorance of his crony's whereabouts. Pinkerton agents got their break a short time later when Burrows wrote to Brock, still unaware of his arrest. The letter bore a return address in Lamar County, Alabama, and manhunters surrounded the homestead on January 8, 1888. Burrows was already gone, but his brother Jim saw the posse coming and escaped. Two weeks later, a sharp-eyed conductor spied the brothers on a Louisville & Nashville train in southern Alabama. Police surrounded the train on arrival in Montgomery, capturing Jim Burrows after a brief gunfight, but Rube shot his way clear of the trap and vanished.

Instead of making Burrows more cautious, the string of near-misses fueled a dangerous attitude of personal invincibility. Soon after the Montgomery skirmish, Rube shot and killed a Lamar County postmaster who demanded his signature for delivery of a package. The cold-blooded murder made him a pariah in the neighborhood and sent him to the piney woods, a hunted fugitive. Still he raided trains, robbing the Mobile & Ohio near Buckatunna, Alabama, in September, rebounding two months later to hit the Northwestern Railroad in Louisiana. A Pinkerton posse gave chase after that holdup, tracking Burrows for two days through the Raccoon Mountains of Blount County, Alabama, before his expert marksmanship left two trackers dead and three more gravely wounded.

Burrows remained at large for two more years, dodging posses in Alabama's thickly forested hill country. Finally, near the end of 1890, he rode into Linden for supplies and was recognized by a storekeeper named Carter. With two friends, Carter got the drop on Burrows and marched him to the local jail, but Rube escaped from the rickety lockup in less than two hours. Instead of fleeing town, he stole a gun and went looking for Carter, trailing him to the local feed store. Shots were exchanged, Burrows was hit in the stomach, and Carter took a bullet in the arm. More angry than hurt, Carter followed his wounded assailant outside, blazing away until Rube Burrows collapsed in the street, dying from multiple wounds.

BUSHRANGERS: Australian outlaws

The first white settlers of Australia, shipped out of Britain beginning in 1788, were mostly convicts sentenced to "transportation" for a period of years equivalent to prison terms in their native land. Many of the exiles who survived their terms of penal servitude stayed on as colonists, and although the vast majority of those led fruitful, law-abiding lives, a rowdy minority pursued banditry after the fashion of America's Wild West outlaws. These were dubbed "bushrangers" because most lived rough in "the bush" and ranged freely over wide territories in search of homesteads, travelers, and small-town banks to rob. Author Stephan Williams lists more than 1,200 Australian badmen in his *Book of Bushrangers* (1993), and although most are forgotten today, a few—like NED KELLY and DANIEL MORGAN—have been elevated to SOCIAL BANDIT status as Australian folk heroes. As in America, most of Australia's frontier outlaws were imprisoned or exterminated by the early 1900s.

BUSSMEYER, Donald Richard

Heavily tattooed, a known narcotics user, Donald Bussmeyer boasted a record of convictions for auto theft, attempted burglary, assault with intent to kill,

Drug addict and bank robber Donald Bussmeyer was posted to the FBI's "Ten Most Wanted" list in 1967. (FBI)

and robbery with a deadly weapon. On March 2, 1967, with accomplices James Alaway and Russell Jones, he robbed a Los Angeles bank of $75,000, instantly becoming a federal fugitive. Arrested on March 9, Alaway was sentenced to 17 years for his part in the holdup; wheelman Jones, picked up the next day, received a sentence of 10 years. Bussmeyer was indicted on federal bank robbery charges in April 1967 and his name was added to the FBI's "Ten Most Wanted" list on June 28.

Publicity and Bussmeyer's penchant for tattoos led federal agents to his Upland, California, hideout two months later. Closing the net on August 24, raiders captured Bussmeyer, his wife Hallie, and a companion named Gene Harrington. Two pistols were found in the house, but Don Bussmeyer—clad only in shorts—was in no position to resist. A tattoo on his chest, "Don Bussmeyer Loves Joyce," removed any doubt of the fugitive's identity. Bussmeyer was held under $200,000 bond, pending trial and ultimate conviction for the Los Angeles robbery. Harrington and Hallie Bussmeyer, an addict like her husband, were held in custody on charges of harboring a federal fugitive.

C

CALLAHAN, John

Born in 1866, John Callahan got his start in disorganized crime as a bank robber in the days when such raids were still conducted on horseback. Later, while trafficking in bootleg liquor and narcotics from his home base in Wichita, Kansas, Callahan doubled as one of the Midwest's premier "fences," moving stolen bonds and other merchandise, laundering bank loot from other outlaws for pennies on the dollar. His corrupt "treaty" with Wichita's police department made the city a haven for fugitives in the Roaring Twenties, on a par with ST. PAUL, MINNESOTA, in the 1930s. At the same time, Callahan reportedly served as a Faginlike crime coach, teaching his skills to a new generation of up-and-coming outlaws whose number included EDWARD ADAMS and CHARLES "PRETTY BOY" FLOYD. (Some reports claim that Floyd got his start in crime hauling illegal liquor for Callahan during Prohibition before switching to armed robbery as a career.) Convicted of smuggling narcotics in the late 1920s, Callahan served seven years of a 25-year sentence and died peacefully at home in Wichita, on June 8, 1936.

CARLISLE, Will

On February 4, 1916, a lone gunman boarded the Union Pacific Railroad's eastbound Portland Rose near Green River, Wyoming, prodding a Pullman porter through the passenger coaches, chatting amiably from behind his white mask as he relieved male travelers of their cash and pocket watches. Women aboard the train described him as "gentlemanly" because he left their valuables alone.

The performance was repeated on April 14, this time aboard a Union Pacific express in the foothills near Laramie. Press accounts of the second holdup harked back to the days of BUTCH CASSIDY and his "WILD BUNCH," and the nameless robber obviously gloried in his growing reputation. He penned an anonymous letter to the *Denver Post,* promising "to hold up the next Union Pacific train west of Laramie" and enclosed a watch stolen on April 14 to verify his credentials. The letter backfired, though, when the *Post* ran it as a first-page item next morning. A rancher near Cheyenne recognized the handwriting as that of a former employee, Will Carlisle, and the manhunt began.

Identifying Carlisle was one thing; finding him, however, was entirely something else. The courteous bandit struck within a week of his letter's publication, this time on an eastbound train near Walcott, Wyoming. For a change of pace, he bought a ticket and boarded with the other passengers, waiting until the train was underway before he donned his trademark white mask and robbed his fellow travelers. Leaping from the train at Walcott, he twisted his ankle in falling and was captured the following day when members of a sheriff's posse noted his conspicuous limp.

Carlisle was swiftly tried, convicted, and sent to Wyoming's state prison. He spent three years behind stone walls; then he contrived to escape by shipping himself out of prison in a packing crate. Union Pacific trains still lured him, and he soon robbed an eastbound train at Rock River, taking $400 from male passengers before he disembarked. A few days later, the Union Pacific division office in Cheyenne received a telegram that read: "Thanks for the haul on your limited. Some detective force. Carlisle." Another telegram, weeks later, asked investigators, "How's the case going?" More taunts followed, spanning several months, until Carlisle was finally recaptured at his lonely mountain cabin and returned to prison. Tiring of the game, he turned into the classic model prisoner and was paroled in 1936.

CARROLL, Tommy

Described in one published account as "a happy-go-lucky ex-boxer," Midwestern bandit Tommy Carroll decided early that stealing money was more pleasant (and less painful) than having his face pounded in prize fights. His first jail term of record was a 60-day jolt in the Douglas County jail, following a January 24, 1920, arrest "for investigation." On October 24, 1921, Carroll was arrested for larceny in Council Bluffs, Iowa. Convicted of that charge on February 3, 1922, he was sentenced to five years at the Anamosa state reformatory and was paroled in March 1923.

Carroll apparently learned nothing from the experience, either in terms of going straight or evading capture. He did have better luck in dodging felony convictions, though. On November 21, 1924, he was arrested for robbery in Kansas City, but the charge was later dismissed. The St. Louis charge was suspicion of robbery, on August 11, 1925, but again the case was dropped. A year later, on August 18, 1926, Carroll was jailed for auto theft in St. Joseph, Missouri, and then released without trial. On September 15 of that year, Tulsa police arrested him for carrying a concealed weapon but soon dropped the charge. Drifting back to St. Joseph, he was jailed for bank robbery on September 29, 1926, but a jury acquitted him on January 11, 1927.

Carroll's lucky streak ran out on April 1, 1927, when he was convicted of another Missouri holdup and sentenced to five years in state prison at Jefferson City. Parole put him back on the street in time to face federal charges of violating the Dyer Act (transporting stolen vehicles across state lines). Conviction on that count earned him 21 months in Leavenworth, from which he was paroled in October 1931.

Tommy managed to stay out of jail for a year and a half, his movements unknown before he was jailed in ST. PAUL, MINNESOTA, on May 17, 1933, for possession of burglar's tools. That charge was dropped with some assistance from St. Paul's corrupt establishment, and Carroll emerged from jail with a determination to tackle his future crimes in more organized fashion, with plenty of backup.

On October 23, 1933, he teamed with GEORGE "BABY FACE" NELSON, HOMER VAN METER, JOHN PAUL CHASE, and Charles Fisher to loot a bank in Brainerd, Minnesota, making off with $32,000. Two Minneapolis detectives recognized Carroll on November 11, but he shook them off and escaped before they could make an arrest. Feeling the heat, Tommy was glad to run an errand for Nelson, driving south to buy some customized weapons from underworld gunsmith HYMAN LEHMAN in San Antonio, Texas. The trip went sour when Carroll was accosted by police and opened fire on them, killing Detective H. C. Perrow before he escaped.

In February 1934, Homer Van Meter sent Carroll to Crown Point, Indiana, bearing cash to help facilitate the jailbreak of Van Meter's friend, JOHN DILLINGER. As a face unknown to law enforcers who were tracking Dillinger's compatriots, he passed unnoticed through enemy lines. Dillinger escaped from Crown Point on March 3 and was back in action three days later, joining Carroll, Van Meter, Nelson, JOHN "RED" HAMILTON, and EDDIE GREEN to steal $49,500 from a bank at Sioux Falls, South Dakota. Carroll, assigned to watch the street, captured two carloads of patrolmen without firing a shot, but motorcycle officer Hale Keith was wounded by Nelson before the gang fled and drove back to St. Paul.

A week later, on March 13, Carroll was the wheelman when the same crew hit another bank in Mason City, Iowa. The take was slightly larger this time—$52,344—but Dillinger and Hamilton both suffered bullet wounds as they were exiting the bank. Again, the gang fled to St. Paul, but there was too much heat around them now to trust their normal sanctuaries.

It was time for a vacation. The gang retired to Emil Wanatka's Little Bohemia Lodge, near Rhinelander, Wisconsin, in the third week of April 1934. Chicago G-man MELVIN PURVIS learned of the gathering and led a strike force to the lodge, attacking on the night of April 22. The raid left two men dead (including an FBI agent) and four wounded, but all of the gangsters escaped. Carroll fled through the woods to a nearby crossroads community, where he stole a car, and then bogged down on a dead-end logging road 12 miles north of the lodge. He finally escaped on foot while federal agents arrested the gang's several women as a consolation prize. Carroll's wife, Jean Delaney Carroll (aka "Crompton," a sister-in-law of bandit ALVIN KARPIS) was among those briefly detained for harboring fugitives and then released on one year's probation by a sympathetic judge.

Early May 1934 found Tommy Carroll hiding out with Dillinger and Homer Van Meter in a forest shack, outside East Chicago, Indiana. On May 19, the three—along with Nelson and John Hamilton—were indicted by a federal grand jury in Madison, Wisconsin, on charges of harboring fugitives, namely each other. It was the least of Carroll's problems at the moment, but his tension was relieved in late May by a reunion with his wife, violating her probation to hit the road with Tommy one last time.

On June 6, 1934, the Carrolls registered at a tourist camp in Cedar Rapids, Iowa. Next morning, they drove into Waterloo, where a gas station attendant noticed spare license plates in Carroll's new Hudson and alerted police. Tommy and Jean had left the station by that time, ironically parking their car across the street from Waterloo's police garage. Detectives Emil Steffen and P. E. Walker approached the Hudson, spooking Tommy into reaching for his gun. He dropped it underneath the car, then picked it up, and sprinted for a nearby alley. Four shots brought him down, and Carroll died hours later at a local hospital. On June 9 his wife was sentenced to a year and a day in prison for violating her probation.

CASSIDY, Butch

Born Robert LeRoy Parker in 1867, America's most famous bandit of the 1890s was the product of a hard-working Mormon family, raised at Beaver, Utah. His first arrest, at age 13, occurred when Parker helped himself to a pair of trousers from a local store and left an IOU in place of cash. The shopkeeper and sheriff ignored his claims that he intended to pay for the pants next time he came to town, and although he served no time, the experience doubtless colored his attitude toward lawmen and "straight" citizens. Before long, he was actively rustling livestock and changing brands to disguise the thefts. When caught at it in 1884, he fled the area and adopted the name of a cowboy acquaintance—

"Butch Cassidy"—in an effort to spare his kinfolk embarrassment.

Accounts vary on the timing and nature of Cassidy's first major crime, and although none of the reports are indisputable, it seems apparent that he joined the infamous McCARTY GANG sometime in the mid-1880s. Old records of the PINKERTON detective agency identify Butch—with Tom McCarty, Matt Warner, and a fourth outlaw—as a participant in the November 3, 1887, robbery of a train at Grand Junction, Colorado. The holdup was a waste of time for all concerned: The express messenger refused to open his safe even with guns aimed at his head, and the bandits fled empty handed.

On June 24, 1889, with Tom McCarty, Warner, and Burt Maddern, Cassidy robbed a bank at Telluride, Colorado, and escaped with $10,500. The gang used relays of fresh horses to speed their escape—a future Cassidy trademark—and although Maddern was later arrested, carrying a letter to his half-brother that included directions to the gang's campsite, law enforcers arrived too late to catch the rest of the band.

After Telluride, Cassidy returned to cow-punching and rustling for a time. Between 1890 and 1892 he worked on various ranches in Utah and Wyoming, a mild-mannered cowboy by day, a voracious rustler by night. Soon it occurred to him that easy money could be made by selling "protection" to ranchers and their herds, after the fashion of gangland extortionists in Chicago and points east. In the fall of 1892 Butch had enough cash on hand to purchase a ranch of his own near Lander, Wyoming, breeding (and rustling) horses with partner Al Haines. Both were arrested for horse theft in June 1893, but a Uintah County jury acquitted them on June 22. A year later, the law tried again. This time, Cassidy resisted arrest, trading shots with deputies before he was pistol-whipped and handcuffed. Al Haines was acquitted once more, but Cassidy was convicted on July 4, 1894, and sentenced to a two-year prison term. Wyoming's governor pardoned Butch on January 19, 1896, contingent on Cassidy's promise that he would leave Wyoming forever and pursue his criminal activities elsewhere.

On release from prison, Cassidy made a bee line for BROWN'S HOLE, an outlaw sanctuary conveniently situated at the point where Utah, Colorado, and Wyoming meet. Because authorities lacked jurisdiction to pursue felons across state lines, the setting was ideal and bandits gravitated there from far and wide. Loosely known as the "WILD BUNCH," this band welcomed Butch as one of their own and began to include him on various raids. Some accounts mention a Utah bank robbery in early 1896, but details are lacking. Cassidy's first confirmed outing with the Wild Bunch was the August 13, 1896, robbery of a bank at Montpelier, Idaho. With sidekicks ELZA LAY and Bob Meeks, Butch stole $6,165 in greenbacks plus another $1,000 in gold and silver, retreating with their loot to Brown's Hole.

A grim warning of things to come was offered in October 1896 when four members of the "Junior Wild Bunch"—teenage hell-raisers George Bain, Joe Rolls, George Harris, and a fourth lad known only as Shirley—decided to rob a bank at Meeker, Colorado. Rolls was left to hold fresh horses outside town, but his confederates proved too excitable in action, firing several shots inside the bank to cow their victims. Emerging from the bank, the outlaws found themselves surrounded by armed townspeople. More than 100 shots were fired in a few moments, killing all three thieves and leaving four vigilantes slightly wounded. Rolls rode back to Brown's Hole to report the fiasco, and although Wild Bunch members mailed a threat to "smoke up" the town as payback, no retaliatory raid was ever launched.

A few days after the Meeker shootout, on October 19, 1896, senior Wild Bunch members had their own disappointment with a payroll shipment ambushed at Rock Springs, Wyoming. They sprang the trap on schedule, surrounding the awaited buckboard and killing its team, scattering the express guards with a flurry of gunshots, but the strongbox was empty. Tipped off to the presence of suspicious strangers in the neighborhood asking untoward questions about the delivery, authorities had shipped the payroll early on a special train with extra guards.

On April 21, 1897, Cassidy joined Elza Lay and Bob Meeks to steal the payroll of the Pleasant Valley Coal Company at Castle Gate, Utah. They escaped with $8,800 in gold and silver, firing several shots at would-be heroes on their way out of town. A posse gave chase but unwisely chose to travel via locomotive, and the manhunters never even glimpsed their hard-riding prey. Meeks was arrested in Idaho two months later, on June 15, and held for trial in the Montpelier case. Convicted on September 3, 1897, and slapped with a 32-year sentence, Meeks forestalled transfer to state prison by feigning illness and then trying to escape from a local hospital. His leap from a second-story window left one leg so badly broken that it was removed—but the loss won

Meeks his freedom, authorities deciding a one-legged bandit was no further threat to society.

By July 1897 Butch Cassidy was the acknowledged leader of a loose-knit syndicate including the Wild Bunch and the Powder Springs outlaws who hid out at Wyoming's "HOLE-IN-THE-WALL." The latter group included HARRY LONGABAUGH (aka "The Sundance Kid"), who would become Cassidy's best friend and staunchest ally. The gang was notorious enough by early 1898 to be hunted in three states. March of that year witnessed a special conference involving the governors of Colorado, Utah, and Wyoming. All agreed that a special detective force should be organized to hunt down and annihilate Cassidy's raiders. Before the strike force could be fielded, though, America plunged headlong into the Spanish-American War and local banditry took a backseat to the clarion call of imperialism. Wild Bunch members allegedly debated mass enlistment for the duration, but common sense won out over patriotic fervor in the end.

On June 2, 1899, the Wild Bunch staged its first successful TRAIN ROBBERY, six bandits stopping a train nine miles north of Rock Creek, Wyoming—between LeRoy and Wilcox. Butch Cassidy was not present, leaving the details to Elza Lay, Harvey Logan, and "Flatnose" George Curry, but one of the passengers aboard was Douglas Preston, well known to lawmen as Cassidy's attorney. Whatever Preston's role in the incident, the raiders did well, published estimates of their score ranging from $30,000 to $50,000. Rewards of $1,000 for each bandit were posted, and although a special team of bloodhounds from Omaha failed to pick up their trail, a running fight with law enforcers following the holdup left a local sheriff dead. Gang member Harvey Ray, who suffered fatal wounds in the same engagement, was secretly buried by his comrades in the wilderness.

Six weeks later, on July 11, Wild Bunch members Harvey Logan, Elza Lay, and Sam Ketchum hit a train near Folsom, New Mexico. They detached the express car and blew the safe with dynamite, only to find it empty. A posse caught the bandits cooking dinner near Turkey Creek on July 16. Lay was wounded twice by sniper fire before a fierce pitched battle erupted. The bandits fought desperately, killing Huerfano County Sheriff Edward Farr and civilian H. N. Love and wounding another posse member in the leg. Lay and Logan escaped from the trap, leaving Ketchum mortally wounded in the camp. He died of blood poisoning at Santa Fe on July 24. Elza Lay was captured by another posse in

Eddy County, New Mexico, on August 22 after wounding Deputy Rufus Thomas and the posse's civilian guide. Tried as "William H. McGinnis" for the slaying of Sheriff Farr, Lay was convicted and sentenced to life imprisonment on October 10, 1899.

The steady drumbeat of bad news drove Butch Cassidy to desperate measures in early 1900, approaching Utah criminal attorney Orlando Powers with pleas to obtain "a pardon or something" that would let Butch retire from the outlaw life and live peacefully in the Beehive State. Powers scuttled that idea with a reminder that Utah's governor could only issue pardons after a defendant was convicted—and a Utah amnesty would not in any case save Butch from prosecution in the other states where he was wanted.

Understandably discouraged, Cassidy joined Harvey Logan, Harry Longabaugh, and a fourth (unknown) bandit to stop a train at Tipton, Wyoming, on August 29, 1900. By coincidence, the express messenger on board was the same who had defied Wild Bunch raiders in the Wilcox holdup 14 months earlier—and he got his second taste of dynamite that afternoon as three charges shattered the car. Press reports claimed that the gang escaped with $55,000, but the railroad's estimate was more conservative, pegging the loot at a total of $50.40.

Three weeks after the Tipton robbery, on September 19, Cassidy led Logan, Longabaugh, and Bill Carver in the holdup of a bank at Winnemucca, Nevada. Escaping with $32,640, the gang retired to Houston, Texas, for a brief vacation, amusing themselves by sitting for a group photograph. The stunt nearly backfired when the photo was seen by WELLS FARGO detective FRED DODGE, former nemesis of the DALTON BROTHERS, but Butch and company had scattered by the time Dodge organized a posse to hunt them down.

Cassidy led the gang's last raid on July 3, 1901, backed by Sundance, Harvey Logan, and Camilla Hanks. They stopped a train at Wagner, Montana, and demolished the express car with dynamite, but three more blasts were needed to open the safe, the bandits escaping with $65,000 in unsigned bank notes. Logan was captured on December 15, 1901, convicted 11 months later and sentenced to 20 years in state prison. He escaped from custody on June 27, 1903, and robbed another train two weeks later at Parachute, Colorado. A posse overtook the gang on July 9 and Logan was wounded in the ensuing shootout, choosing suicide over surrender.

By that time, Cassidy and Harry Longabaugh had settled on a ranch in Argentina, accompanied by Longabaugh's lover Etta Place, having departed from New York by ship on February 20, 1902. Proud owners of a sheep ranch, they apparently led what one reporter called an "idyllic life" until late 1904 or early 1905 when Pinkerton detectives and local authorities surmised their identity. Reports of a February 1905 bank robbery at Rio Gallegos are vague and unsubstantiated, but Butch and Sundance (with a third unnamed American) almost certainly robbed a bank at Mercedes, Argentina, of $20,000 in March 1906, killing a bank employee in the process. Another bank job at Bahia Blanca netted them $20,000 more a few months later, witnesses describing the third member of the holdup gang as a slender young woman.

Cassidy may have returned to the United States in 1907. Several witnesses claimed to have seen him, and a former employer received a letter from Butch with a U.S. postmark, but most accounts agree that he was back in South America before year's end. With Longabaugh and another Yankee (again unidentified), Cassidy robbed a payroll train at Eucalyptus, Bolivia, afterward hiding out at an abandoned Jesuit mission in the Andes. On December 7, 1907, with Sundance and Etta Place, he stole $10,000 from a bank at Rio Gallegos, Argentina, and shot the horses of a posse that pursued them. The year 1908 found Butch and Sundance in Bolivia, working the Concordia mines while they planned a payroll heist, but it never came off. On December 27, 1908, they robbed a store at Arroyo Pescado, killing the manager before they fled with cash and supplies.

The fate of Cassidy and Longabaugh remained a mystery until 1930 when western writer Arthur Chapman published an article in *Elks Magazine*, describing their alleged demise two decades earlier. According to Chapman, Butch, and Sundance stole a mine payroll near Quechisla, Bolivia, in early 1909. A short time later they were spotted in nearby San Vincente, and troops were summoned, resulting in a ferocious battle. After killing numerous soldiers, Chapman wrote, both bandits gravely wounded, Cassidy finished Longabaugh with a shot to the head and then killed himself. Hollywood memorialized the event (minus the mercy shot and suicide) six decades later with Paul Newman and Robert Redford in the title roles of *Butch Cassidy and the Sundance Kid*.

But was the Chapman story true?

In July 1936 word came from Cassidy's old hangout at Lander, Wyoming, that he had been seen in town the previous year—more than a quarter-century after his supposed death in Bolivia. Aging friends of the bandit confirmed his identity, reporting that Butch had told them he was living full-time in Seattle, Washington, under the name "Bill Phillips." Lawmen scoffed at the story, but reporters started to dig. As luck would have it, though, their investigation proceeded at such a leisurely pace that they missed their man. By the time journalists confirmed the existence of a William Phillips in Seattle he was dead, having succumbed to cancer on July 20, 1937. Cassidy's sister later published a book confirming her brother's survival in the United States until 1937, but the outlaw's fate—like that of JESSE JAMES and JOHN DILLINGER—remains a controversial topic among crime historians.

CAVE-IN-ROCK: Early American outlaw refuge

The outlaw lair known as Cave-in-Rock was precisely what its name suggests—a cave situated on the northern bank of the Ohio River in present-day Hardin County, Illinois. Located equidistant from two river towns, 20 miles downstream from Shawneestown and 20 miles upstream from Golconda, the cave commanded a long view of the river and any boats passing by. When occupied by river PIRATES, it provided an ideal launching point for raids against slow-moving flatboats, and refinements were employed to lure victims without the need for a protracted chase.

Cave-in-Rock was first described to Europeans in a French explorer's journal, written in 1729; its first known appearance on a map, courtesy of a French cartographer, occurred 15 years later. Measured at 160 feet deep, with a fairly uniform width of 40 feet, and a 75-foot ceiling at its entrance, Cave-in-Rock provided ample room for those who sought to spend a night or to build more permanent quarters. Various pioneers and trappers used the cave for shelter during the next four decades, before it was occupied by a counterfeiter named Duff (first name unknown) and his partner Philip Alston. Briefly known as "Duff's Fort" around 1790, Cave-in-Rock sheltered its criminal inhabitants for several years until Duff was killed by hostile Indians and his gang dispersed.

A new breed of badman had settled the cave by 1797. Samuel Mason had been an officer of the Continental army in America's recent rebellion against

England, but he was more interested in profit than patriotism. Accompanied by sons John and Thomas, Mason converted Cave-in-Rock into a makeshift "inn" for weary boaters, supplying food and liquid refreshment for all comers. At the same time he recruited a ruthless band of river pirates to rob and kill his unfortunate guests, chief among them the infamous Harpe brothers. Micajah "Big" Harpe and Wiley "Little" Harpe were the scourge of the frontier after 1795 when they left their native North Carolina and began to travel aimlessly through Tennessee, Kentucky, and the Ohio River Valley. Early American serial killers, the Harpes robbed, murdered, and mutilated many of those they met in their travels, leaving a grisly trail of corpses in their wake. Micajah was caught and killed by vigilantes in 1799, first confessing to a minimum of 20 murders (some reports claim 31). Wiley Harpe joined outlaw James May to kill erstwhile partner Samuel Mason in 1803 and was hanged for that crime in February 1804.

Mason's passing did not leave Cave-in-Rock long unoccupied. By 1809 river pirate James Ford (aka "Jim Wilson") had emulated Mason's trick by naming the cavern Wilson's Liquor Vault and House of Entertainment as a cover for his outlaw enterprise. Ford enjoyed a longer run than Mason, remaining in business at Cave-in-Rock until 1833. That summer, a personal feud between Ford and Kentucky slave trader Vincent Simpson left both men dead, with one of Ford's confederates hanged for Simpson's murder. Dispersed by the ensuing heat, Ford's gang vacated Cave-in-Rock, their passing commemorated years later by establishment of a state park for tourists.

CHAPMAN, Gerald

A career criminal who was born in 1888 and fated to win notoriety as America's premiere "Public Enemy Number One," Gerald Chapman logged his first conviction (for grand larceny) in 1907. He served one year of a 10-year sentence and then went back inside for three more years on a 1908 burglary charge. Convicted of armed robbery in 1911, he was sent to New York's Auburn Prison, where he met future crime partner GEORGE "DUTCH" ANDERSON. Both were paroled in 1919, teaming with accomplice Charles Loeber to create a team of "superbandits," pulling heists across a territory ranging from Chicago to New England. Although "Gentleman Gerald" was the most notorious of the trio, law enforcers considered Anderson to be the brains and leader of the gang.

The gang scored its greatest coup on October 24, 1921, hijacking $1,424,129 in cash and securities from a U.S. mail truck on Leonard Street in Manhattan. More holdups followed, mostly banks, before New York police arrested the trio. All three were convicted of robbery and sentenced to 25 years at the federal lockup in Atlanta. Chapman escaped on March 25, 1923, remaining at large for two days before he was shot and recaptured by authorities. Believed near death, with a bullet in his kidney, he confounded his jailers by fleeing *again,* from the prison hospital, on April 5. Dutch Anderson tunneled out of the pen eight months later, on December 30, and soon rejoined Chapman for another high-profile crime spree.

The press could not resist such a flamboyant villain. On April 23, 1923, under the headline SOMETHING ALMOST HEROICAL, the conservative *New York Times* enthused:

It is getting to be rather difficult to keep in mind the fact that Gerald Chapman is a thoroughly bad man, whose right place is in jail. The difficulty arises from the fact that in his battle with the law he shows qualities— courage, persistence, ingenuity and skill—which it is impossible not to admire. The result is that unless one is careful one finds one's self hoping that he isn't caught, and, so great are the odds against him, that the struggle seems somehow unfair. . . . The temptation is strong to lament that such a man should make of his abilities and peculiarities such miserable employment as devoting them to theft. There must be some explanation of that, however, and the probability is that he is defective. But it does seem hard that his punishment for his crimes should be increased because of his attempts to evade it. That he hates imprisonment is only human, and that he takes desperate risks in his efforts to get out is rather to his credit than his discredit—from every standpoint except the safety of society.

On October 12, 1924, teamed with rookie bandit Walter Shean, Chapman and Anderson tried to rob a department store in New Britain, Connecticut. Patrolman James Skelly interrupted them and was killed in an exchange of gunfire. Captured moments later, Shean boasted to authorities that "My partner was Gerald Chapman!" Warrants were issued for Chapman and Anderson, but the fugitives had fled to Indiana, hiding out in Muncie with a friend, Ben Hance. By the time Chapman was captured there, on January 15, 1925, fan clubs were organized from coast to coast. Admirers sent bouquets of flowers to the Connecticut jail where Chapman was held pending trial on murder charges.

Dutch Anderson, meanwhile, was still at large and bent on an obsessive quest for revenge. Convinced that Ben Hance had betrayed Chapman, Anderson murdered Hance and his wife on August 11, 1925. Next, he tried for loose-lipped Walter Shean but found his target under heavy guard. A few days later, on October 31, 1925, Anderson was spotted on a Muskegon, Michigan, sidewalk by Detective Charles DeWitt Hammond. Challenged by Hammond, Anderson drew a pistol and shot the detective, mortally wounding him, but Hammond fought back. Before collapsing, he wrestled the gun away from Anderson and killed Dutch where he stood.

Back in Connecticut, Gerald Chapman was convicted of Patrolman Skelly's murder and sentenced to hang. His attorney questioned the state's right to execute Chapman as Gerald still owed the federal government 24 years on his mail-robbery conviction, but President Calvin Coolidge solved that problem by commuting Chapman's sentence. Mounting the gallows at Wethersfield on April 26, 1926, Chapman remained philosophical. "Death itself isn't dreadful," he proclaimed, "but hanging seems an awkward way of entering the adventure."

CHASE, John Paul

Once branded by J. EDGAR HOOVER of the FBI as "a rat with a patriotic-sounding name," John Paul Chase was a California native, born the day after Christmas in 1901. He quit grade school to work on a ranch, later serving as a machinist's helper in a railroad yard. Dismissed from that job in 1926, Chase turned his back on the "straight" life and found employment as the chauffeur for a Reno gambler. From there, it was a short step to bootlegging, and while Chase made a living for himself, he never stood out from the crowd. He needed a leader, someone to boss him around, and he found the perfect candidate in GEORGE "BABY FACE" NELSON.

There is no record of Chase's first meeting with Nelson, though it almost certainly occurred in Reno. Nelson had gangland connections there and frequently drove west when the heat was on around Chicago and environs. Rumor has it that Chase may have been the wheelman on a contract murder Nelson carried out in Reno, but no details are available. Their first known crime together, on October 23, 1933, was the theft of $32,000 from a bank in Brainerd, Minnesota. Nelson and Chase were joined in that adventure by companions TOMMY CARROLL, HOMER VAN METER, and Charles Fisher.

By March 1934 Nelson had joined forces with fugitive JOHN DILLINGER, but Chase did not participate in the gang's first holdup that month in Sioux Falls, South Dakota. Reports differ on whether he was present one week later, on March 13, or the next job in Mason City, Iowa. For the most part, Chase was relegated to the role of Nelson's "gofer" in Chicago, fetching take-out meals, acquiring guns and ammunition, carrying messages back and forth between Nelson and Dillinger. It may have been humiliating, but anonymity has its benefits. Chase was not invited on the gang's spring vacation to Little Bohemia Lodge near Rhinelander, Wisconsin, so he missed the April 22 FBI raid that left two men dead, including a federal agent gunned down by Nelson.

The gang's luck had turned. On June 30, 1934, Chase joined Nelson, Dillinger, Van Meter, and two other gunmen to rob a bank in South Bend, Indiana. The take was mediocre—$29,890—and a police officer was killed as they fled. Dillinger himself was killed by FBI agents in July 1934 and Homer Van Meter by ST. PAUL police a month later. Chase and the Nelson gang fled westward again, idling around Reno, but Nelson could never stay away from the Windy City for long. On November 26, 1934, Chase and Nelson stole a car in Chicago, rolling on to Wisconsin, but they found G-men staked out at their intended hideaway. The next day, they were sighted while driving near Barrington, Illinois, and a firefight broke out. Nelson was fatally wounded, but he still managed to kill agents SAMUEL COWLEY and Herman Hollis before he collapsed.

Nelson's death left John Chase at loose ends, virtually friendless in Chicago. Anonymity still served him, investigators and journalists suspecting that Nelson's accomplice in the November 17 shootout was either ALVIN KARPIS or JOHN "RED" HAMILTON, but he needed to get out of town. On November 30, using the name "Elmer Rockwood," Chase answered a newspaper ad for a driver to transport a car to Seattle. He was on the road when Helen Nelson gave his name to federal agents, and he became a fugitive for the first time. Police arrested Chase the day after his birthday, at Mt. Shasta, California, working at a state fish hatchery.

Extradited to Chicago on December 31, 1934, Chase would be the first defendant to face trial under a new law making it a federal crime to kill an agent of the U.S. government. His trial began on March 18, with Chase convicted of Sam Cowley's murder seven days later. He drew a life sentence, confined to The Rock of Alcatraz on December 31, 1935.

That should have ended Chase's story, but a postscript was supplied by J. Edgar Hoover's personal efforts to keep him in prison forever. Chase's first bid for parole was denied in 1950 on the basis of Hoover's objection, and the FBI director's wrath extended even to a prison chaplain who supported Chase. "Watch closely," Hoover wrote in a memorandum to his field agents, "and endeavor to thwart the efforts of this priest who should be attending to his own business instead of trying to turn loose on society such mad dogs."

It is unknown what steps G-men may have taken to "thwart" the Alcatraz chaplain, but John Chase was transferred to Leavenworth in September 1954. Hoover once again opposed his parole bid the following year, announcing plans to prosecute Chase for the murder of agent Hollis if he were released from prison. A federal judge vetoed that plan on grounds that a 21-year delay in prosecution clearly violated constitutional provisions for a "speedy trial," but Chase remained inside until October 1966 when he was finally paroled (once again, over Hoover's objection). The aging outlaw worked as a custodian around Palo Alto, California, until he died of cancer on October 5, 1973. Chase had outlived J. Edgar Hoover by a year, five months, and three days.

CHASE, Vivian

One of the Depression era's most notorious WOMEN BANDITS, Vivian Chase—aka "Gracie Chase" and "Gracie Adams"—was a Missouri native, born in 1902. She married bank robber George Chase at age 20 and was arrested with him in Kansas City on a vague charge of "suspicion" two days before Christmas 1923. Nothing came of that arrest, but George was killed in 1924, leaving Vivian to shift for herself. Two years later, she was implicated with bandits Lee Flournoy, Lyman Ford, and Charles Mayer in the robbery of a Cherryvale, Kansas, bank on May 26, 1926. Authorities deemed it an inside job, indicting bankers Clarence Howard and G. C. Robertson for their part in the heist, but Vivian was acquitted by jurors on March 14, 1928.

Her next known round of crimes, with lover Luther Jordan, involved the robbery of several Kansas City gas stations in April and May 1932. The couple set their sights a bit higher in June with a local bank robbery in North Kansas City, but they were captured soon after; Jordan was convicted and sentenced to 25 years in prison. Vivian was still awaiting trial when she escaped from the Clay County jail in October 1932. While a fugitive, she teamed up briefly with the Egan's Rats gang in St. Louis and then gravitated to the mob run by "Irish" O'Malley, reportedly helping to plan the July 1933 ransom kidnapping of 78-year-old August Luer, a retired banker in Alton, Illinois. The snatch was successful, but Luer was released without payment of ransom after the gang became concerned about his failing health. Most were arrested, with O'Malley captured in May 1935 and sentenced to life imprisonment under the federal Lindbergh Law.

Vivian Chase, meanwhile, eluded local police and FBI agents alike. She returned to the Kansas City area in June 1935 and was suspected, with a male accomplice, of seven local robberies spanning the next three months. Her run ended on November 3, 1935, when she was found dead in a car parked outside St. Luke's Hospital, bound with rope and shot execution-style. Authorities speculated, logically enough, that her death was payback for some perceived double-cross of unidentified criminal cohorts.

CHRISMAN, Marshall Frank

Born in Denver, Colorado, on August 22, 1925, Chrisman logged his first arrest at age 11, proceeding from there to compile a record of adult convictions for burglary, larceny, mail robbery, assault, and receiving stolen goods. Sporting a total of 15 tattoos, he ranked as one of the FBI's most "decorated" fugitives, easily distinguished by his artwork, a missing front tooth, and his vicious temper.

On July 10, 1962, Chrisman and two male accomplices raided a bank in Toledo, Ohio, bagging $12,264 at gunpoint before they escaped in a stolen getaway car. Upon arrest, Chrisman's partners pled guilty to the robbery and were consigned to Ohio's state prison, leaving only their leader at large. Federal warrants charging Chrisman with bank robbery were issued on July 11, and his name was added to the "Ten Most Wanted" list on February 7, 1963. Identified by local officers from his FBI wanted fliers, Chrisman was arrested in Los Angeles on May 21, 1963, returned to Ohio for trial, and convicted.

CHRISTIANSEN, Kenneth Malcolm

Twice honorably discharged from the U.S. Navy, the second time in 1948 (at age 17), Kenneth Chris-

Bank bandit Marshall Chrisman was arrested for the first time at age 11. (FBI)

tiansen was arrested that same year on charges of armed robbery and assault, following a series of hotel robberies in Portland, Oregon. Extradited to California on similar charges, he was imprisoned from 1949 to 1951. Two months after being released on parole, he was picked up again, convicted on two counts of first-degree robbery, and returned to prison with two consecutive sentences of five years to life. Paroled again in May 1956, he was seized by Los Angeles police officers 11 months later, on charges of armed robbery and parole violation. A July 1958 conviction for first-degree robbery put him back behind bars, a new five-to-life sentence running concurrently with his previous terms. Described by authorities as a heavy narcotics user, Christiansen typically employed masks, theatrical makeup, or fake mustaches as a disguise in his holdups.

On Christmas Eve 1963 Christiansen and another inmate escaped from the California state prison at Chino. His companion was soon recaptured in Seattle, but Christiansen remained at large, embarking on a series of "lone wolf" robberies, knocking over a jewelry store in Phoenix; a tavern in Glendale, California; and restaurants and markets in San Gabriel, Santa Monica, La Habra, West Covina, Daly City, San Jose, and San Francisco. A federal warrant charging him with unlawful flight to avoid confinement was issued on February 11, 1964, and his name was added to the FBI's "Ten Most Wanted" list on July 27.

On September 8, 1964, Christiansen held up a seafood restaurant in Silver Springs, Maryland, stuffing his satchel with $6,000 in cash. The job went sour when the owner's wife fled the restaurant screaming, with Christiansen in pursuit, giving the chef time to telephone police. Outside, a pair of milkmen started to chase Christiansen, joined shortly by Patrolman Charles Kriss. In flight, the outlaw traded gunshots with police, but no one suffered any injuries. Disoriented, running in the wrong direction, Christiansen was collared a block from the police station as he tried to commandeer a passing car.

The Maryland fiasco carried sentences totaling 107 years, but Christiansen had no intention of doing the time. On May 18, 1967, while returning from a court appearance in a prison vehicle, Christiansen and fellow inmate Harry McClellan pulled a gun on their guards, handcuffing both to a tree before making their getaway. They dumped the stolen car at Dundalk, there abducting motorist Richard Ruger and forcing him to drive them to Baltimore. Nearing their destination, Christiansen shot Ruger in the chest and pushed him from the car, but Ruger survived his wounds to testify against the kidnappers. Soon recaptured, Christiansen had earned himself another block of prison time, ensuring he would never walk the streets again.

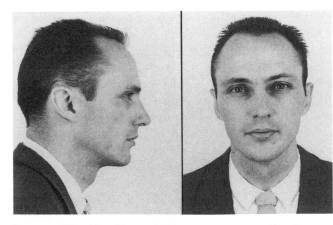

"Lone wolf" robber Kenneth Christiansen specialized in holdups of restaurants and jewelry stores. (FBI)

CLARK, James "Oklahoma Jack"

Not to be confused with equally notorious bandit JIM CLARK (frequent accomplice of outlaws HARVEY BAILEY and ROBERT BRADY), James Clark launched his criminal career as a protégé of master thief HERMANN "BARON" LAMM. Clark was a member of the team Lamm organized and led against a bank at Clinton, Indiana, on December 16, 1930, escaping with $15,567 in cash. A posse gave chase and overtook the gang at Sidell, Illinois, touching off a battle in which Lamm and two other bandits lost their lives. Clark and cohort Walter Dietrich were captured alive and unharmed, convicted of the Clinton robbery, and packed off to Indiana's state prison at Michigan City.

There, they soon made friends with a group of hard-core outlaws including the likes of JOHN DILLINGER, HARRY PIERPONT, CHARLES MAKLEY, and HOMER VAN METER. On September 26, 1933, using pistols smuggled into Michigan City by the recently paroled Dillinger, Clark and Dietrich were among 10 inmates who escaped to launch another round of holdups in the Depression-era Midwest. Unlike his fellow fugitives, however, Clark did not remain long at large. He was recaptured at Hammond, Indiana, two days after the breakout and was promptly returned to prison, where he finished out his days.

CLARK, Jim

Born at Mountainburg, Arkansas, on February 26, 1902, Jim Clark logged his first arrest in Oklahoma at age 21 and earned a stretch in the state reformatory at Granite. On release, he found work in the Texas oil fields but soon tired of manual labor and by 1927 was running illicit liquor across the border from Juarez, Mexico, later serving 30 days in jail for a bungled robbery attempt. The year 1928 found him back in Oklahoma, where he once more tried his hand at robbery without success, drawing a five-year prison sentence on March 31.

In fact, Clark served less than a year of that sentence, but official leniency had no more impact on his lifestyle than had punishment. On March 14, 1932, he was sentenced to two years in prison for stealing a car in Sequoyah County, Oklahoma. Six weeks later, on April 25, he walked away from the prison camp at Colby and became a fugitive from justice. Freedom was short-lived, however. On June 17, members of the BARKER GANG stole $47,000 from a bank in Fort Scott, Kansas. Within hours, police caught Clark riding in a stolen car near Rich Hill, Missouri, with fugitives Frank Sawyer and Ed Davis.

All three were charged and wrongfully convicted of the Fort Scott holdup and packed off the state pen at Lansing.

Imprisonment was bad enough, but the injustice of his sentence left Clark furious, determined not to serve the time. On May 30, 1933, he was among 11 convicts who escaped from Lansing, using pistols smuggled in by friends outside. Authorities suspected bandit FRANK NASH of arranging the break. Besides Clark, the escapees included notorious outlaws HARVEY BAILEY, WILBUR UNDERHILL, and ROBERT "BIG BOB" BRADY. After hiding briefly in the outlaw-friendly COOKSON HILLS of Oklahoma, the fugitives went back to work at the trade they knew best.

On July 3, 1933, the gang robbed a bank at Clinton, Oklahoma, escaping with $11,000. Seven weeks later, on August 9, they looted a bank at Kingfisher, Oklahoma. Bailey's arrest on August 11—like Clark's, for a crime he did not commit—scuttled plans to knock off a bank in Brainerd, Minnesota, but Clark soldiered on, traveling and working with Bob Brady.

Their last job together was a fiasco. On October 6, 1933, Clark and Brady hit a bank in Frederick, Oklahoma, for $5,000. In their haste, they missed another $80,000 in the vault and tellers' cages, but their problems did not end there. Taking three hostages along as they fled, the bandits switched cars at Indiahoma and raced across Texas into New Mexico. Unfortunately, they also left a map in their first getaway car, marked with their escape route, and Oklahoma law enforcers telephoned ahead with descriptions of the fugitives. Stopped by police outside Tucumcari, Clark initially identified himself as "F. N. Atwood," and although authorities briefly mistook him for Wilbur Underhill, fingerprints soon established the true identity of both bandits. Charges were waived in the latest round of holdups, as Clark and Brady returned to serve their time at Lansing.

The escape landed both men in solitary confinement, but restrictions were relaxed enough over the next three months for Clark, Brady, and five other inmates to escape from a kitchen work detail on January 19, 1934. Splitting up outside the prison, Clark left Brady to his own devices, teaming with escapee Frank Delmar to kidnap a schoolteacher, one Lewis Dresser, and steal his car. Dresser was released in Oklahoma, where the fugitives met Clark's girlfriend, Goldie Johnson, waiting with another vehicle. Victim Dresser, for his part, was so rattled by the experience that he wrongly identified Johnson as female bandit BONNIE PARKER.

Clark and Delmar were not long idle. On February 9, 1934, they stole $2,000 from a bank in Goodland, Kansas, but Clark was wounded in both feet as he escaped, shot by a policeman lying underneath a nearby car. Three months later, on May 9, he was well enough to raid a Wetumpka, Oklahoma, bank for $500. On May 31 he returned to rob the same Kingfisher bank he had robbed with Bailey, Underhill, and Brady in August 1933. The target on June 20 was a bank in Crescent, Oklahoma. Soon after, repeating himself once again, Clark stole $13,000 from the same Clinton bank he had helped to rob a year earlier. With Goldie Johnson, he was suspected of raiding a bank at Oxford, Kansas, but both denied the accusation and no charges were ever filed in that case.

By late July 1934, Jim Clark was a certified "public enemy." The governor of Kansas posted a $200 reward for his capture, matched by the state banking association, and the Kansas state police established a special "Clark unit" to track him down. Their efforts paid off on August 1, 1934, when he was found in Tulsa and arrested, held for trial on federal bank robbery charges. Convicted and sentenced to 99 years, he entered Leavenworth prison on January 14, 1935. Clark was transferred to Alcatraz in 1937, but repeated disciplinary infractions sent him back to Leavenworth a decade later. There, he reportedly controlled inmate gambling and loan sharking for the next 10 years until administrators finally noticed and shipped him back to Alcatraz in January 1948. More transfers followed—back to Leavenworth in 1960, on to Seagoville, Texas, nine years later— before Clark was finally paroled on December 9, 1969.

Too old to steal, Clark settled in Oklahoma after his release from prison, married his late brother's widow, and found work as a ranch hand. Later, when that job proved too strenuous, he managed a local bank's commercial parking lot. Clark died on June 9, 1974. At his funeral, three of the ex-bandit's pall bearers were bankers.

CLARK, Russell "Boobie"

A good-natured thief who earned national notoriety as a member of the first JOHN DILLINGER gang, Russell Clark suffered bad luck at the outset of his criminal career, in 1927. Arrested following his first bank robbery, at Fort Wayne, Indiana, Clark was sentenced to a 20-year prison term on December 12, 1927, and packed off to the state penitentiary at Michigan City.

There, he quickly learned that many other holdup men were serving shorter terms for the same offense. Clark's bitterness propelling him into unaccustomed rebellion, insolence, and three failed escape attempts. In 1929, he was ranked among the leaders of an inmate strike that briefly stalled work in the prison's shops.

There was another side to "Boobie" Clark, however; known among his inmate cronies as a joker who was quick to smile and laugh, his friends included Dillinger and a group of hard-core felons such as HARRY PIERPONT, CHARLES MAKLEY, JOHN HAMILTON, and HOMER VAN METER. When Dillinger was paroled in May 1933, he promised to liberate his inmate pals and launched a series of holdups to finance their escape, finally smuggling pistols into Michigan City four months after his release. On September 26, 1933, a group of 10 convicts used the guns to stage a breakout from the penitentiary. Joining Clark in the escape were Pierpont, Makley, Hamilton, JAMES CLARK (no relation to Russell), WALTER DIETRICH, Ed Shouse, Joseph Fox, James Jenkins, and Joseph Burns.

Unfortunately—from the viewpoint of the fugitives—Dillinger had been arrested in Dayton, Ohio, four days before their escape. On October 3, Russell Clark joined Pierpont, Makley, and Hamilton to steal $14,000 from a bank in St. Mary's, Ohio. Nine days later, they liberated Dillinger from his cell in Lima, Ohio, Pierpont murdering Sheriff Jess Sarber in the process. Feeling short of hardware, the gang robbed Indiana police stations in Auburn and Peru on October 14 and 20, making off with various weapons, ammunition, and bulletproof vests.

They were ready for a crime spree that would rock the nation, but Clark reportedly missed the gang's first outing on October 23 when Dillinger and company looted a bank in Green Castle, Indiana, of $18,428 in cash and $56,300 in negotiable bonds. He was back with the team a month later when the team stole $27,789 from a Racine, Wisconsin, bank, taking four hostages along as human shields when they fled. On December 13, the gang chiseled through walls to empty 96 safety deposit boxes of a Chicago bank; the take, while officially listed as $8,700, may in fact have run as high as $50,000 in unreported cash and jewelry.

That score prompted Illinois authorities to publish a list of 21 "public enemies," with Russell Clark ranked fifth behind Dillinger, Pierpont, Hamilton, and Makley. The heat drove them to Florida for the Christmas holidays, but the gang began regrouping in Tucson, Arizona, after New Year's. Clark and girlfriend Opal Long arrived on January 10, with the rest of the mob in place by January 21. Disaster struck a day later when their hotel caught fire and one of the firefighters—an avid fan of pulp detective magazines—recognized two of the guests as Russell Clark and Charles Makley. Authorities were summoned, and the roundup began on January 25, 1934. Clark was the first to be arrested and was pistol-whipped to unconsciousness after he grappled with deputies and tried to draw a gun. Captured later the same day were Dillinger, Makley, and Pierpont. While Dillinger was extradited to Indiana to face murder charges in the death of an East Chicago patrolman, Clark and the others were shipped back to Michigan City and then transferred to Lima, Ohio, for trial in the death of Sheriff Sarber.

The trio was arraigned in Lima on February 15, 1934, encouraged two weeks later by news of Dillinger's escape from custody at Crown Point, Indiana. There would be no hasty exit for Clark and company, however. Pierpont and Makley were convicted of Sarber's murder in March, facing automatic death sentences when their separate juries failed to return with recommendations of mercy. Clark expected the same treatment, yawning and sometimes dozing off during his own trial, but attorney Louis Piquett managed to sway the jury in Clark's case. With triggerman Pierpont already condemned, the panel granted leniency to Clark, and he received a life sentence on March 24.

Still, the three outlaws held out hope that Dillinger would recreate their breakout from Michigan City. Those hopes were dashed on July 22, 1934, with Johnny's violent death in Chicago, and the gangsters shifted to Plan B. On September 22, 1934, using mock pistols carved from soap, Pierpont and Makley surprised their guards, moving on to liberate Clark and six other inmates. They ran out of luck at a set of barred doors, and Clark and the others retreated before a barrage of gunfire from prison guards that left Makley dead and Pierpont gravely wounded. He was carried to the electric chair on a stretcher less than four weeks later.

Russell Clark spent the next 34 years imprisoned at Columbus, Ohio. Diagnosed with terminal cancer, he was finally released on August 14, 1968, and settled in Detroit, where he died on Christmas Eve, after about four months of freedom.

CLIFTON, Daniel "Dynamite Dick"

Although some reports assume that "Dynamite Dick" Clifton earned his nickname blasting safes and railroad express cars, the truth is rather more curious—and less impressive. Early in his outlaw career, this denizen of Indian Territory (modern Oklahoma) apparently decided to increase his deadly reputation as a triggerman by hand-crafting explosive bullets for his six-gun. The process involved hollowed-out bullets and shaved slivers of dynamite, but the precocious experiment was doomed to failure because dynamite—Hollywood special effects notwithstanding—does not explode on impact.

A veteran rustler and whiskey peddler, Clifton joined BILL DOOLIN's outlaw gang in 1892 and participated in most of that outfit's holdups during the next four years. Midway through his tenure with the gang, foolishness almost led "Dynamite Dick" to his doom. While hiding out between robberies, Clifton wrote in his own name to a Tulsa catalog company for a mail-order gun, requesting delivery to Ingalls, Oklahoma. U.S. marshals learned of the order and staked out the Ingalls railroad depot, but they overestimated Clifton's intelligence by relaxing surveillance in broad daylight and thus missed him when he made the pickup one afternoon at 2:00 P.M.

Clifton went his own way when the Doolin gang broke up in 1896, pulling small robberies and reverting to the bootleg trade to make ends meet. As "Dan Wiley," he was arrested for selling whiskey to Indians and sentenced to the usual 30 days in jail. Clifton had nearly completed his sentence when one of the jailers finally saw through his alias and full beard, recognizing the alky peddler as a wanted outlaw. Transported to Guthrie for trial on train-robbery charges, he arrived in time to find cellmate Bill Doolin refining his latest escape plans. They broke out together a few days later, taking a dozen other inmates along for the ride.

Doolin didn't last long: He was gunned down at Lawson on August 25, 1896, and his death propelled Clifton to the apex of Oklahoma's most-wanted list. The day after Doolin's funeral the *Stillwater Gazette* reported that "Marshal Nagle reserved another lot near the grave for the reception of . . . Dynamite Dick." Instead of going on the lam, though, Clifton teamed with Little Dick West to organize a new gang, robbing general stores around Lincoln County while they interviewed prospects. They found a pair of brothers, AL and FRANK JENNINGS, to make it a foursome; a short time later,

brothers Morris and Pat O'Malley brought the team up to strength for a new round of train holdups.

Clifton never really hit it off with Al Jennings, though, and "Dynamite Dick" left his own gang after a few months of sporadic activity. Riding alone on the afternoon of December 4, 1896, 10 miles west of Checotah, he met U.S. deputy marshals George Lawson and W. H. Bussey on the trail. They recognized their man and got the drop on Clifton, but he refused to surrender, lunging for his Winchester rifle. A bullet smashed his arm and knocked him from the saddle, but he ran into the woods and found a cabin, where the lawmen cornered him. Near nightfall, desperate, Clifton burst from the cabin, firing a revolver with his one good hand, and the marshals dropped him in his tracks.

CLOSE, Carl

Born in West Virginia in 1915, Close served with the navy for six months in 1945 before receiving a medical discharge as a psychoneurotic. From those humble beginnings he went on to accumulate felony convictions for embezzlement, bank robbery,

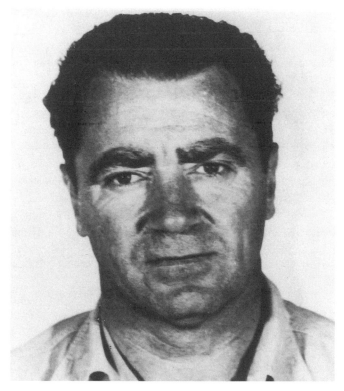

Released from the U.S. Navy on a mental discharge in 1945, Carl Close robbed his first bank four years later. (FBI)

and interstate transportation of stolen funds. On April 21, 1949, Close was arrested in West Virginia with two brothers-in-law, charged with the robbery of two banks in Maryland. A submachine gun and two pistols were confiscated at the time of his arrest.

During their trial on the Maryland charges, Close and his kin escaped from their detention cell but were recaptured moments later. On conviction each received a $15,000 fine, together with a term of 35 years in prison. Close started his time at the federal lockup in Atlanta, where he joined two other inmates in attempting to escape by helicopter from a cellblock roof. Deterred by prison personnel, Close was transferred to Alcatraz, where he remained until September 1954. Shipped out to Leavenworth, he was paroled to Nokomis, Florida, in July 1961. On March 3, 1963, Close skipped town with his brother Harold to launch another crime spree on the eastern seaboard.

On March 8 the brothers raided a Baltimore bank for $21,078, dropping $4,141 en route to their getaway car. Both were charged with bank robbery on a federal complaint issued May 31, and Harold Close was picked up the next day in Roanoke, Virginia, on a charge of vagrancy.

Undeterred by his brother's arrest, Carl hit a bank in Roanoke on June 4, waltzing out with $6,330 in cash. A second federal warrant for bank robbery was issued in his name two days later, and he made the FBI's "Most Wanted" list on September 25.

One day after joining the Top Ten, Close held up a bank in Anderson, South Carolina, stuffing his satchel with $28,262. Unknown to the bandit, a silent alarm had been sounded and local patrolmen were waiting with shotguns as Close left the bank. He surrendered quietly, dropping the loot on command, and officers relieved him of two loaded pistols. Held on $100,000 bond, Close entered a plea of guilty to the Anderson robbery on October 7, 1963, and was sentenced to another 25 years in Leavenworth.

COBLE, William Hutton

Launching his criminal career with a stint in reform school at age 12, Coble went on to serve 19 years of his adult life in various penal institutions. His convictions included robbery, forgery, larceny, housebreaking, and violation of the Dyer Act (transporting stolen cars across state lines), with several jailbreaks

thrown in for good measure. On May 15, 1964, Coble escaped from the city jail in Nashville, Tennessee, where he was confined following conviction for a $34,000 bank robbery at Ardmore. Federal warrants were issued on charges of robbery and prison escape, earning Coble a spot on the FBI's "Ten Most Wanted" list on September 11, 1964.

By that time the fugitive had already settled in Charlotte, North Carolina, arriving in June and renting an apartment under the name of "Marvin Ikard." With a touch of humor, Coble told his landlady he was an FBI agent on secret assignment, swearing her to silence in the interest of national security. In fact, his business was the same as always. On September 30, as the FBI celebrated his posting to the Top Ten list, Coble looted a small bank in Charlotte of $7,226. Five months later, on March 1, 1965, he tried again at the First Citizens Bank, also in Charlotte, but the caper blew up in his face.

Patrolman Jack Bruce, passing the bank on his rounds, witnessed the holdup in progress and summoned assistance. Shots were exchanged as Coble left the bank, carrying a sack filled with $8,869.

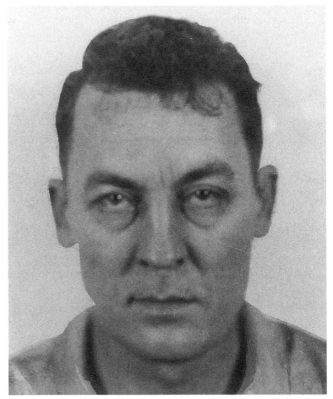

Bank robber William Coble was added to the FBI's "Most Wanted" list in 1964. (FBI)

Fleeing on foot, the bandit approached a station wagon occupied by Mrs. E. B. Vosburgh and her two children. Firing as he approached, wounding the woman in both legs, Coble forced everyone from the car and took off with screeching tires.

Patrolman Bruce arrived seconds too late, flagging down a vehicle driven by Duane Bruch and ordering the startled motorist to "follow that car." Coble led his pursuers on a winding course for 15 blocks before he chose a dead-end street by accident and found himself cut off. He refused to get out of the car until Bruce fired four shots through the windows, at which time the bandit emerged with hands raised in surrender. Local conviction on two counts of bank robbery earned Coble 25 years in the state penitentiary. In the event of his parole, he owed another 15 years to the federal government for violation of national bank robbery statutes.

COLLEARN, Michael, and HAMMONDS, Walker

A pair of Indiana train robbers inspired by the 1866 debut of the RENO BROTHERS, Collearn and Hammonds chose the same town—Seymour, Indiana—as the site of what proved to be their one and only holdup. An eastbound Ohio & Mississippi passenger train was pulling out of Seymour on the night of September 29, 1867, when Collearn and Hammonds boarded the Adams Express car, tied up the messenger, and stole $8,000 from the safe, leaping from the train as it slowed for a trestle outside town.

Unfortunately for the fledgling bandits, Adams Express was a client of ALAN PINKERTON's detective agency, and the famous manhunter himself came west to track the audacious thieves. Pinkerton soon found a witness who had seen the robbers make their leap, noting that one of them was badly injured in the fall, carried away from the scene by his partner. From there, it was an easy job to ask around for any locals who had turned up lame within the past few days. Pinkerton learned that Walker Hammonds had a brand-new limp; more to the point, a neighbor recalled seeing Hammonds the day before the Seymour holdup, modeling a mask identical to one discarded near the crime scene. In custody, Hammonds—a former railroad newspaper vendor who used his knowledge of the trains to plan the crime—confessed his part and named his accomplice. The Adams Express guard identified both bandits, and they were duly convicted of robbery.

CONNER, Terry Lee, and DOUGHERTY, Joseph William

Veteran bank robbers from the 1960s, Conner and Dougherty teamed to perfect the technique of holding bank officers and their families hostage, thereby gaining access to cash hidden in vaults. Conner was suspected of 10 Arizona bank heists in 1972 alone, including two where hostages were held captive overnight. Ten years later, in August 1982, Conner was one of the bandits who held a bank officer and his family prisoner in Bountiful, Utah, before looting the bank vault next morning. Four months later, Conner and Dougherty held an Oklahoma City bank manager and his wife prisoner in their home for eight hours before tapping the victim's bank for $706,000 in cash. Conner earned 25 years in prison for that score, but Dougherty remained at large, raiding banks in Phoenix (January 25, 1984), Salt Lake City (May 3, 1984), and Reno (February 19, 1985) before his ultimate arrest on federal bank-robbery and conspiracy charges. Convicted on those counts, Dougherty soon joined Conner in confinement at the federal penitentiary in El Reno, Oklahoma.

On June 19, 1985, the partners were en route from El Reno to a court date in Oklahoma City, where Dougherty faced trial for the December 1982 holdup. Concealing a razor blade and a handcuff key in his mouth, Conner managed to free himself, holding the blade to a deputy U.S. marshal's throat and demanding a detour. Stripping their captives of guns and official ID, the fugitives dumped their stolen car and left the hostages handcuffed to a tree, commandeering fresh wheels at a nearby truckstop. Using the federal badges to invade a private home, Conner and Dougherty stole fresh clothing before moving on.

New charges filed against the fugitives included escape, theft of government property, and assaulting federal officers, but the runners were not finished yet. On August 12, 1985, they raided a St. Louis bank for $27,000, reverting to form for another strike on September 2. That evening, Dougherty and Conner invaded the home of Richard Woodstock, a bank manager in the Milwaukee suburb of West Allis, Wisconsin. Holding Woodstock's family hostage through the night, they struck the bank next morning, walking out with $574,119 in cash. Some $34,000 was later found in the abandoned getaway car, but the loss did not spoil Dougherty's mood; he had promised that stolen deposit slips would be returned to the bank, and they arrived by mail September 7, safe and sound.

Joe Dougherty was posted to the FBI's "Ten Most Wanted" list on November 6, 1985, while Conner had to wait until August 8, 1986, for another vacancy on the dishonor roll. With cash in pocket, though, the new publicity did not slow the partners down. On June 30, 1986, they barged in on bank manager Raymond Deering in the Vancouver suburb of Hazel Dell, Washington, covering his family through the night with a pistol and a submachine gun. Next morning Conner and Dougherty looted Deering's bank of $225,000 before making good their escape.

By early December 1986 FBI agents had focused their search for Terry Conner on Chicago, where he had family ties. On the morning of December 9 an anonymous phone call led G-men to a motel in suburban Arlington Heights, where Conner was taken without resistance, emerging from his room to seek a cup of coffee. Unarmed at the time of his arrest, he had left his .45-caliber pistol in the motel room. Formally indicted six days later on charges of escape, kidnapping, theft of government property, and assaulting federal officers, he faced a maximum sentence of life imprisonment and a $1.5 million fine.

Friendship would be Joe Dougherty's undoing nine days after Conner's arrest. Federal agents had established surveillance on one Robert Butcher, a crony of Joe's from old prison days, and the trap was sprung on December 18, 1986, when Dougherty met Butcher at a laundromat in Antioch, California. United States marshals were backing the FBI's play because Conner and Dougherty had the distinction of placing on both the bureau's Top Ten and the U.S. Marshal's Top Fifteen lists. Taken into custody without resistance, Dougherty and Butcher (with a third accomplice) faced additional charges of plotting to rob a bank in Antioch.

COOKSON Hills, Oklahoma: Historic outlaw sanctuary

Situated in northeastern Oklahoma where the Sooner State meets Kansas, Missouri, and Arkansas, the Cookson Hills sheltered border-hopping bandits and rustlers for the better part of a century. Including Blue Canyon plus countless ravines and miles of dense forest, the region was populated largely by impoverished Cherokees who had no great, abiding love for Uncle Sam or his deputized agents. Moonshining was a common occupation in the Cooksons,

and fugitives who paid their way in cash were welcome into the mid-1930s.

Belle Starr's gang had a base of operations in the Cookson Hills before the turn of the last century, operating from Blue Canyon; Oscar Poe and his twin cohorts, Bill and George Hart, used the same terrain as a launching pad for raids into southern Kansas. Later, AL JENNINGS found Blue Canyon and the Cooksons most hospitable, as did the notorious KIMES and Jarrett brothers.

By the onset of the Great Depression, the most notorious habitué of the Cookson Hills was CHARLES "PRETTY BOY" FLOYD, Oklahoma's premier "SOCIAL BANDIT," but Floyd was by no means alone. Members of the wide-ranging FLEAGLE GANG enjoyed Cookson hospitality until 1932, when a 15-man posse invaded the hills and captured two gang members, Fred Cody and Frank Lane. That near-unprecedented breach of etiquette persuaded some outlaws to pull up stakes and relocate, shifting their operational headquarters to the Osage Hills outside Wynona, but the Cooksons remained near and dear to the hearts of many hardened fugitives. "Pretty Boy" Floyd—known locally as King of the Bank Robbers—doled out cash to Cookson benefactors through 1933, and when 11 convicts (including HARVEY BAILEY and WILBUR UNDERHILL) escaped from the Kansas state prison in May 1933, they made directly for the Cookson Hills with all due speed.

The end came, more or less, in February 1934 after Oklahoma Governor W. H. Murray received reports that Floyd was hiding in the Cooksons, along with notorious fugitives CLYDE BARROW and BONNIE PARKER. (In fact, Floyd had gone to ground in Buffalo, New York; Bonnie and Clyde, if they were ever in the Cookson Hills at all, had simply passed through on their way to an impending rendezvous with death.) On February 17 and 18, an estimated 350 state and county law enforcers swept through the Cooksons, scouring 100 square miles to purge the district of lawbreakers; 1,000 National Guardsmen were mobilized to guard prisoners, but they were hardly needed for the 19 bush-league offenders who were swept up in the dragnet.

Editorially, the sweep had been a bust, but it was not entirely wasted. During the next eight months, the Barrow gang and Floyd were wiped out by law enforcers in other states; surviving "public enemies" looked elsewhere for a place to hide. If local residents kept on distilling untaxed liquor in the Cookson Hills, that was a matter between them and federal "revenuers," leaving county sheriff's to adopt an attitude of live and let live.

"COOPER, D. B."

On November 24, 1971, Northwest Airlines Flight 305, bearing 42 passengers and crew from Washington, D.C., to Portland, Oregon, and Seattle, Washington, was boarded at Portland by a passenger using the pseudonym "D. B. Cooper." Shortly after takeoff he summoned a flight attendant and showed her a briefcase containing an apparent bomb and then passed her a note for the pilot. The note demanded $200,000 in $20 bills, placed in a knapsack, together with a total of four parachutes. "Cooper" received the cash and parachutes in Seattle, whereupon he released the passengers and two flight attendants; then he ordered the aircraft to take off for Reno, Nevada, and Mexico.

The jet was cruising at 197 miles per hour and an altitude of 10,000 feet when "Cooper" donned two parachutes (one of them used for training, incapable of opening) and leaped from the aircraft with the knapsack full of cash. He was never seen again, alive or dead, but investigators pointed out that he had worn a business suit and street shoes when he jumped into an airstream registered at 69 degrees below zero. Search efforts included employment of 200 troops from Fort Lewis, Washington, scouring a portion of the aircraft's flight path for 18 days in April 1972, and FBI agents reportedly interrogated more than 1,000 suspects without turning up a significant lead. Two men were later arrested for a clumsy attempt to bilk *Newsweek* magazine of $30,000 for a "D. B. Cooper" interview, and although the *Washington Post* reported on September 9, 1975, that Fairfax City resident Harry A. Cooper was under investigation as a suspect lookalike, he was subsequently cleared of all suspicion.

On November 23, 1976, a federal grand jury in Portland indicted "John Doe, also known as Dan Cooper" for aircraft piracy and obstruction of interstate commerce by extortion, describing the elusive subject as "a male Caucasian, age mid-forties, height 5'10" to 6 feet, weight 170–180 pounds, physical build average to well built, complexion olive, medium smooth, hair dark black or brown, parted on left, combed back . . . of greasy appearance, sideburns at low ear level, eyes brown or dark, voice without particular accent, using an intelligent vocabulary, and a heavy smoker of cigarettes." Federal authorities announced that "Cooper's" offense was a capital crime, thereby waiving a five-year statute of limitations.

By that time, "Cooper" had passed into folklore as a near-legendary figure. A song about the hijacking was briefly popular in Washington and Oregon, while T-shirts and bumper stickers commemorating the holdup were on sale within 72 hours of the crime. On November 28, 1976, the residents of Ariel, Washington, celebrated Cooper Caper Sunday with a sky-diving exhibition, a cookout, and sale of souvenir sweatshirts. (A public invitation to "Cooper" was apparently declined.) Four years later, interest in the case was revived by discovery of several thousand dollars in marked ransom bills, found partially buried on the north bank of the Columbia River, near Vancouver, Washington. It remains unclear whether the cash was deliberately buried or washed downstream years earlier and was covered by an accumulation of silt. Most law enforcement officers assume that "Cooper" died in free-fall, but without proof positive he remains a locally cherished figure, one of those who got away.

In August 2000 the *Pensacola News Journal* reported a possible new lead in the "Cooper" case. Jo Weber, a 60-year-old Florida resident, reported that her late husband Duane Weber had confessed to the crime before his death in 1995, at age 70. An ex-convict and Colorado insurance agent, Duane Weber met and wed his spouse in 1977 but kept his secret closely guarded for another 18 years until he entered the terminal stages of kidney disease. Retired FBI agent Ralph Himmelsbach, in charge of the manhunt through 1980, described Mrs. Weber's story as "credible and persuasive," while a forensic artist active on the case described Duane Weber's photos as "about as close a match as possible" to sketches of the phantom skyjacker. Active-duty G-men were more skeptical, reporting that the bureau had investigated Jo Weber's story in 1998 and found the evidence inconclusive. "What we need to bear in mind," a spokesperson told the press, "is that there have been over 1,100 serious suspects and several thousand less serious." Jo Weber, for her part, complains that the FBI ridiculed her and "treated me like scum."

COWLEY, Samuel P.: FBI manhunter

A Utah native, born in 1899, Sam Cowley served as a Mormon missionary before he joined the U.S. Justice Department's Bureau of Investigation (later FBI) in the early 1920s. By the time federal officers were empowered to hunt bank robbers and kidnappers in 1934, he had risen to the rank of inspector. The final, flamboyant phase of Cowley's FBI career began in April 1934 after Chicago G-man MELVIN PURVIS embarrassed the bureau by bungling a raid on an underworld hideout near Rhinelander, Wisconsin. In the process, raiders not only missed the entire JOHN DILLINGER gang but also shot three innocent men (killing one) and lost one of their own, who was gunned down by GEORGE "BABY FACE" NELSON. After that fiasco loosed a storm of media criticism, FBI Director J. EDGAR HOOVER appointed Sam Cowley to lead the Dillinger manhunt, thus superseding Purvis.

Although the hunt for Dillinger remained a cooperative effort, several published sources credit Cowley with negotiating the outlaw's final betrayal by brothel madam Anna Sage, arranged with the cooperation of East Chicago detectives. Cowley and Purvis shared responsibility for the ambush that killed Dillinger outside Chicago's Biograph Theater on July 24, 1934, and although some reports of the event name Cowley as the fatal triggerman, FBI reports are inconsistent and contradictory.

Cowley's moment in the limelight was short-lived. On November 27, 1934, he responded, with 30-year-old Agent Herman Hollis, to reports that "Baby Face" Nelson had been sighted near Barrington, Illinois. Racing to the scene, Cowley and Hollis met Nelson on the highway after Nelson had evaded another FBI team, and battle was joined after Nelson's car veered off the highway.

The odds seemed fairly even: Nelson and accomplice John Paul Chase were armed with a Tommy gun and a Browning automatic rifle, respectively. Cowley also had a submachine gun, while Hollis packed a 12-gauge shotgun. After a preliminary exchange of gunfire, Nelson emerged from cover and stalked toward the FBI car, spraying bullets as he came. Both Cowley and Hollis were fatally wounded, but not before they put 17 holes in Nelson, resulting in his death later that night.

Cowley was treated to a hero's send-off, but he continued to serve J. Edgar Hoover even in death. Four years later, after Melvin Purvis had been hounded from the FBI by his jealous, headline-hungry boss, Hoover published a ghost-written book on the FBI's gang-busting exploits, titled *Persons in Hid-*

ing. The text credits Sam Cowley with solving every major case that had earned Purvis headlines during 1933 and 1934.

CRETZER-KYLE Gang

A notorious Depression-era team of bank robbers, the Cretzer-Kyle gang differed from other headliners by apparently confining their holdups to the West Coast. Known members of the gang included leaders Joseph "Dutch" Cretzer and Arnold Kyle (aka Shorty McKay), with Milton Hartmann (aka James Courey) and John Oscar Hetzer.

The gang's first-known raid occurred on January 31, 1935, when Cretzer, Kyle, and Hartmann robbed a Portland, Oregon, bank of $3,396. Eleven months later, on November 29, the same trio hit a branch bank in the Ambassador Hotel, Los Angeles, for $2,765. On January 23, 1936, they took $6,000 from a bank in Oakland, California, and rebounded the following day to steal $1,475 from another Los Angeles bank. The team liked L.A. so much that they remained there for the next six months, robbing two more banks, one on March 3 ($6,100) and one on July 1 ($1,996). On July 27, 1936, they surfaced in Seattle, taking a local bank for $14,581.

Thus far, the same three bandits had been identified by witnesses on every raid, but variations in technique began on November 27, 1936, when Kyle and Hartmann took $8,000 from another Seattle bank. Milton Hartmann was apparently alone in Los Angeles on January 28, 1937, when he pulled a gun and walked out of a bank with $2,870. Two months later, on March 29, John Hetzer made his first appearance in the lineup, backing Kyle and Hartman on the raid that netted $18,195 from a bank in Portland.

It had been a good run, but the outfit's luck was wearing thin. Eight days after his first-known outing, Hetzer was cornered and arrested by FBI agents in a Los Angeles garage. One day later, G-men laid siege to Hartmann's room at the Stuart Hotel in Los Angeles, but Milton shot himself to death as they closed in. Edna Cretzer was arrested on January 25, 1938, for operating a brothel in Pittsburgh, California, but she quickly posted bond and husband Joe remained at large.

The gang's last gasp came when its surviving members sought a change of scene, transplanting themselves to the midwestern region where holdup gangs had thrived a few years earlier. Arnold Kyle was arrested for drunk driving in Minneapolis on May 18, 1939; he gave his name to officers as "Raymond Palmer," but fingerprints soon confirmed his identity, and he was delivered to the FBI. A guilty plea to federal bank-robbery charges on June 7, 1939, brought Kyle a 25-year sentence at McNeil Island, Washington, near the scene of several holdups. Joe Cretzer held out until August 27, 1939, when FBI agents arrested him in Chicago. Edna pled guilty to charges of harboring her husband on November 6, and Cretzer confessed to one of the Los Angeles robberies on January 24, 1940, joining Kyle at McNeil Island with a matching 25-year sentence.

Unhappy in custody, Cretzer and Kyle assaulted U.S. Marshal A. J. Chitty during one of their court appearances in Washington and tried unsuccessfully to flee the courthouse. The escape attempt cost them five more years apiece, but the worst was yet to come: Chitty suffered a heart attack from the assault, and when he died, both assailants were sentenced to life for his murder. That stunt got them transferred to Alcatraz, where they bided their time before joining in another mass escape attempt on May 24, 1946. Guards summoned a detachment of U.S. Marines to quell the rioting, and when the smoke cleared, Kyle and Cretzer were among the five convicts reported killed in the fighting.

CROWLEY, Francis "Two Gun"

A 20th-century outlaw cast in the mold of a Wild West gunfighter, Francis Crowley was born October 13, 1912, in New York City, the second son of an unwed mother. Rumor named his absentee father as a city policeman, which may help to explain Crowley's lifelong hatred of lawmen. That hatred only deepened in 1925 when his brother John was killed by police, allegedly while resisting arrest for a misdemeanor, disorderly conduct. By age 19, Francis was ready to dish out some payback to society at large and New York's Finest in particular.

On February 21, 1931, Crowley and two other youths crashed an American Legion dance in the Bronx. When several legionnaires tried to eject them, Francis drew a gun and wounded two of his adversaries before he fled the scene. On March 13, sought on charges of attempted murder, he dodged police in an office building on Lexington Avenue, wounding Detective Ferdinand Schaedel in the process. Two days later, Crowley and four accomplices held up a bank in New Rochelle.

On April 15, 1931, Crowley and two sidekicks invaded the basement flat of real-estate broker Rudolph Adler, on West 90th Street. Adler resisted the intruders, whereupon Francis whipped out his trademark pistols and shot the man five times. It was Adler's dog, Trixie, who drove the bandits out empty handed, saving her owner's life.

Twelve days after the Adler shooting, Crowley went joyriding in New York with crime partner Rudolph "Fats" Duringer (aka "Tough Red") and dance-hall hostess Virginia Brannen. Brannen resisted Duringer's sexual advances, prompting him to shoot her dead in Crowley's car. Together, Duringer and Crowley dumped her corpse outside St. Joseph's Seminary in Yonkers.

New York was getting hot for "Two Gun" Crowley, but he stubbornly refused to leave. On April 29 he was spotted driving a green Chrysler sedan along 138th Street in the Bronx, near the Morris Avenue Bridge. Police rolled out in pursuit, but Crowley escaped in a running gun battle. Bullets extracted from a patrol car matched those fired in the Virginia Brannen murder and other recent shootings. Crowley's getaway car was found abandoned nearby the following day, pocked with bullet holes, with bloodstains inside.

On May 6, Patrolmen Frederick Hirsch and Peter Yodice found Crowley parked with 16-year-old girlfriend Helen Walsh on Morris Lane in North Merrick, Long Island. Crowley opened fire as they approached his car, killing Hirsch and driving Yodice back while Francis sped away.

The teenage gunman's time was running out.

On May 7, police traced him to a rooming house on West 90th Street, two blocks from the scene of the Adler shooting in April, where Crowley was holed up in a fifth-floor apartment with Helen Walsh and Fats Duringer. A small army of 150 police officers surrounded the house, armed with rifles, submachine guns, and tear gas, while some 15,000 civilian gawkers gathered to watch the fun. During the next two hours, police fired an estimated 700 rounds into the building while Crowley returned fire from within, dodging from window to window, leaving Helen and Fats to reload his overheated pistols. Several times, Crowley snatched up tear-gas grenades and hurled them back at police. Wounded four times and bleeding profusely, Crowley finally surrendered, but even in his weakened state he remained a dangerous customer. Arresting officers found two pistols strapped to his legs when they patted him down.

Crowley was tried for the murder of Patrolman Hirsch in something close to record time and was convicted on May 29. Fats Duringer, meanwhile, was found guilty of killing Virginia Brannen. Both defendants were sentenced to death on June 1.

Confined to death row at Sing Sing, Crowley maintained his reputation as a violent rebel, stuffing his prison-issue clothing down the toilet, assaulting guards, and fashioning homemade weapons from any available object. As his date with the electric chair grew near, however, he appeared to undergo a change of heart, adopting and feeding a starling that flew into his cell each day. On the last day of his life, January 21, 1932, Crowley resumed his customary swagger. Fats Duringer was the first to go, and when his own turn came, Crowley asked the warden for a rag. "I want to wipe off the chair," he told Warden Lewis Lawes, "after this rat sat in it."

CUNNIFFE, James "Killer"

A New York gang leader, Cunniffe led the seven-man team armed with submachine guns that stopped a U.S. mail truck in Elizabeth, New Jersey, on October 14, 1926. In a blaze of gunfire, the outlaws killed the truck's driver, wounding his assistant and a city policeman before escaping with $161,000 in cash.

The robbery was sensational enough to rate attention in Washington, D.C., where President Calvin Coolidge discussed it with his cabinet on October 16. A day later, 2,500 marines were assigned by the president to guard mail shipments throughout the eastern United States, and it was announced on October 27 that the marine corps would acquire 250 Thompson submachine guns for that task, thus becoming the first U.S. military branch to purchase the "choppers" already famous as gangland's weapon of choice.

"Killer" Cunniffe would never stand trial for his role in the New Jersey mail robbery. On October 31, 1926, a falling-out with gang member William "Ice Wagon" Crowley turned deadly at the Highland Court Apartments in Detroit. Crowley shot and killed Cunniffe, along with Cunniffe's girlfriend, and he was still at the scene when police arrived moments later. A pitched battle ensued, leaving Crowley and Patrolman Ernest Jones dead when the smoke cleared.

CURRENT, Fleet Robert

When Fleet Current robbed a San Francisco restaurant of $1,500 in January 1953, he was running true to form. His record dated back to 1942, with a conviction for burglary in Oakland that had earned him nine months in the county jail. Upon release he would be linked to holdups on the West Coast and around the area of Minneapolis-ST. PAUL.

In August 1948 Current won a grudging compliment from Minneapolis police, for what they called "the smoothest stickup in a generation." Smooth it may have been, but Current's robbery of a local loan company earned him five years in prison. Paroled in May 1951, he traveled west again and picked up with the only trade he knew. A San Francisco robbery cinched Current's nomination to the FBI's "Ten Most Wanted" list, and he was added to the roster on May 18, 1953.

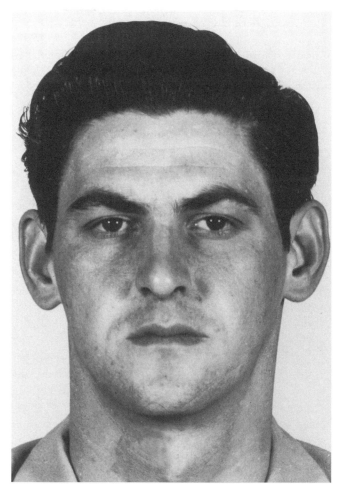

Minneapolis police credited Fleet Current with "the smoothest stickup in a generation." (FBI)

Fleet Current was the kind of thief who stood out in a crowd. A victim of severe tuberculosis, he was so emaciated that his prison comrades dubbed him "The Apple" after his prominent larynx. Witnesses remembered Current easily and linked him to a string of holdups in 1952 and 1953. In late November 1952 he robbed a Minneapolis tavern of $2,500. The San Francisco holdup placed him back in California during January, but The Apple traveled widely. On March 1, 1953, he joined accomplices in robbing a St. Paul dairy to the tune of $22,000. Unsatisfied, he popped up two weeks later for a puny score in Minneapolis, robbing a hotel of $275. Addition to the Top Ten list did not slow Current down: On June 25 he joined two Oakland, California, gunmen to relieve the American Trust Company of $5,148.

Weary from his illness, harried by the need for constant motion, Current sought sanctuary in the great Midwest. He settled on Nebraska, packing up his teenage bride and moving east to Omaha, where he believed that he would not be recognized. It was a fatal error. Agents of the FBI received a tip that put them on The Apple's track, and on July 12 he was taken, with his wife, by G-men acting in coordination with the local sheriff. Caught without a weapon, Current offered no resistance as the agents took him into custody. He was returned to California, there to spend his final days in prison.

D

DALTON Brothers

It may be argued that the Dalton brothers of Missouri were predestined to a life of crime, related by blood as they were to the hard-riding YOUNGER clan, but history suggests a series of deliberate choices leading them along the outlaw trail. Perhaps it was the atmosphere in post–Civil War Missouri, that "MOTHER OF OUTLAWS" where the Youngers were idolized by many (with their cohort cousins FRANK and JESSE JAMES) as heroes of the great Lost Cause. Blood feuds ran deep in that embattled soil, where hard-bitten settlers refused to forget and forgive.

Whatever the cause, we know that only a few of the Daltons went bad. Cass County farmer Louis Dalton married Adeline Younger in 1851, and their union produced a total of 13 children—nine sons and four daughters—of whom 11 lived to adulthood. The sons who would earn notoriety were Grattan (called Grat, born in 1865), William (or Bill, born 1866), Robert (or Bob, born 1868), and Emmett (born in 1871). The family moved from Missouri to Indian Territory (later Oklahoma) in 1882, where brothers Frank and Grat found work as Indian police, driving white squatters off tribal land. Frank soon became a U.S. Deputy Marshal, but it was a bad career move; he was killed in 1884 by horse thieves—replaced by Grat, with brother Bob hired to assist him. Bob killed his first man—one Charles Montgomery, an ex-convict—in 1887; Bob called Montgomery a horse thief, although acquaintances of both men hinted at a possible romantic triangle.

Grat was wounded by outlaws in 1888 but it failed to deter him: He soon took the job of police chief in Osage, with Bob as his chief deputy.

Louis Dalton died in 1890, and his passing seems to have removed the last vestige of restraint from sons Grat, Bob, and Emmett. Bob, though not the oldest, was the brains and spark plug of the fledgling Dalton gang as the brothers doffed their badges and turned to stealing livestock. By June 1890 they were established rustlers, running Cherokee ponies into Kansas for sale. Grat was arrested that winter and briefly jailed at Fort Smith, but former friends in law enforcement dropped the charges, and he struck off for California, where brother Bill had married, settled down, and launched a promising political career. Bob and Emmett, sought on rustling warrants of their own, likewise fled Oklahoma with companions Bill McElhanie, George "Bitter Creek" Newcomb, and "Blackface" Charley Bryant (so called for a powder burn on one cheek, the result of a close-range gunshot). The five briefly ran a faro parlor in New Mexico, but a shootout with unhappy losers left Emmett wounded; he retreated to the Oklahoma hill country with Newcomb while Bob and McElhanie rode on to Bill Dalton's ranch near Paso Robles, California.

A California state assemblyman well settled with his wife and child in San Luis Obispo County, Bill Dalton welcomed his brothers despite their recent troubles with the law. Elected on a platform openly antagonistic to the powerful Southern Pacific Railroad, Bill was already under surveillance by Southern Pacific chief of detectives Will Smith, and the arrival of his outlaw siblings only made Smith more suspicious. On February 6, 1891, a train was robbed at Alila, California (now Earlimart), with fireman George Radliff killed by bandits who left empty handed after the express messenger fled with keys to the safe. Will Smith swore out warrants against Grat and Emmett Dalton—the latter clearly a mistake because Emmett was in Oklahoma—and Grat was captured in Tulare County soon after the holdup. Convicted of robbery and sentenced to 20 years, Grat escaped from careless guards on the train to Folsom Prison, leaping out a window of his carriage as the train crossed a bridge spanning the San Joaquin River. Rewards of $6,000 each were immediately posted on Grat and the still-missing Emmett.

We may never know whether the Dalton's were involved in the Alila robbery, but there is no doubt about the robbery of another train at Wharton, Oklahoma (now Perry), on May 9, 1891. Brother Bob led the team, with Grat and Emmett in tow; they were joined for the outing by Charley Bryant, Dick Broadwell, and Bill Powers. The holdup was flawless, though reports of the take varied widely: Emmett later claimed $14,000, but media estimates ranged from $500 to $1,750. Escaping via Beaver Creek, the bandits stole nine or 10 horses from a local farmer on a whim, and only then was a posse organized to run them down. The vigilantes overtook their quarry but soon had cause to regret it as a blast of gunfire from the gang killed pursuer W. T. Starmer and left another posse member wounded.

Soon after the Wharton holdup the gang struck another train, this one a Leliaetta, Kansas, and again escaped without casualties. A quarrel erupted, though, over division of the spoils, prompting Bob Dalton to dissolve the outfit in a huff. Grat prevailed on his brother to reconsider, and the band—reinforced with fledgling gunman BILL DOOLIN—was back in action on June 1, 1892, stopping a train at Red Rock station on the Otoe Indian Reservation. Grat and Doolin caught the express messenger and his guard playing checkers, defenseless as the outlaws bagged some $1,600. Inside the station, Charley Bryant grew nervous and killed a young telegraph operator, afterward identified by witnesses from the powder burn on his face. A 100-man posse chased the gang for two days, losing them when the raiders split up. The Santa Fe railroad offered a $1,000 reward for Bryant, dead or alive, as he fled to the home of his sister (Bob Dalton's mistress).

Blackface Charley was later captured in Hennessy, Oklahoma, while seeking treatment for syphilis from a local physician. Placed aboard a train to the federal jail in Wichita, Bryant disarmed one of his guards at a stop in Waukomis, dying in a flurry of gunfire that also left Deputy Ed Short fatally wounded.

Shortly before 9:00 P.M. on July 14, 1892, the Dalton gang invaded tiny Adair, Oklahoma, and commandeered the railroad depot, waiting for an inbound train believed to carry major loot. Unknown to the raiders, it also bore 11 armed guards under Captain J. J. Kinney. A firefight erupted as bandits boarded the train; Captain Kinney and three of his men were wounded in an exchange of more than 200 gunshots. Also shot in the crossfire were two local physicians, one of whom—Doctor W.L. Goff—was mortally wounded. The robbers fled unharmed, Emmett Dalton later claiming a take of $17,000 from the raid. Public outrage prompted WELLS FARGO detective FRED DODGE to organize a special "Dalton posse," financed by four railroads and three national express companies, with the specific purpose of tracking and annihilating the gang.

As luck would have it, though, Dodge and his riders never got the chance to do their job.

Bob Dalton had conceived a new plan in his life-long effort "to beat Jesse James": He would rob two banks simultaneously, thereby dazzling both law enforcers and townsfolk and enshrining himself and his brothers as figures of outlaw legend. The town selected was Coffeyville, Kansas. Participants in the raid would include Bob, Grat, and Emmett Dalton, Bill Doolin, Dick Broadwell, and Bill Powers. Doolin dropped out at the last minute—either because his horse went lame en route to Coffeyville or he quarreled with Bob over division of loot from the Adair holdup—and Dalton decided to proceed with five raiders instead of six.

The gang entered Coffeyville sometime after 9:00 A.M. on October 5, 1892, clad in matching linen dusters, armed with six-guns and Winchester repeating rifles. Leaving their horses tied in an alley, the raiders split up: Grat Dalton, Broadwell, and Powers entered the C. M. Condon Bank while Bob and Emmett crossed Coffeyville's main street to the First National Bank. Grat had barely raised his Winchester to cover the Condon Bank's employees when a passer-by glanced through the window, saw the holdup in progress, and sprinted through town raising the alarm. Inside the Condon Bank, meanwhile, Grat's raiders bagged $1,000 in greenbacks and

$3,000 in silver from the tellers' cages and then decided to wait three minutes for a time lock on the bank's main vault to open. When it clicked, they dumped the heavy silver and stuffed their bags with another $19,000 in paper currency. Across the street, with no time lock to slow them down, Bob and Emmett had already jammed their feed sack with $11,000 in greenbacks and gold.

But they were out of time.

Along the street, citizens roused by the early warning cries had armed themselves and had lined up in windows and doorways, on rooftops and in alleys to surround the bandits. Some, too eager to wait, began to fire through the windows of the Condon Bank before they had a clear view of their targets, wounding Dick Broadwell in one arm. Bob and Emmett heard the shots and fled through the First National's back door, confronted first by young Lucius Baldwin, armed with a pistol. Bob shot Baldwin in the chest, mortally wounding him, and the brothers moved on toward the street. Two more vigilantes, Charles Brown and George Cubine, opened fire on Bob and Emmett, but the bandits were better shots, killing both men where they stood. Thomas Ayers, a cashier from First National, ran to the hardware store next door and seized a weapon, stepping out to confront the robbers, but Bob Dalton dropped him with a nonfatal shot to the head. Mat Reynolds, a clerk at the hardware store, followed Ayres outside but missed his assailants as they ducked out of sight; instead, Reynolds saw three bandits emerging from the Condon Bank and nailed Bill Powers with a shot to the chest. Powers returned fire, smashing the clerk's foot, and staggered off toward the alley where his horse was tied.

That alley, fronted by a livery stable, a lumberyard, and Coffeyville's jail, would soon become a slaughter pen. Pursued by a gaggle of amateur gunmen, Broadwell, Powers, and Grat Dalton moved toward their horses. Broadwell was shot again, this time in the back; he crawled into the lumberyard and met employee Charley Gump, drilling Gump's wrist with a bullet that made him drop his pistol. Outside, marksman John Kloehr drilled Grat Dalton with a fatal bullet, but Grat had strength enough to reach a nearby shed, triggering a rifle shot that killed City Marshal Charles Connelly. Bill Powers reached his horse but was shot again, killed before he could mount. Dick Broadwell, meanwhile, emerged from the lumberyard and dragged himself into the saddle, galloping into the combined fire of John Kloehr's rifle and Carey Seaman's double-barreled shotgun.

Dying, Broadwell still managed to travel a mile outside town before he collapsed.

Bob and Emmett Dalton were still unscathed as they reached the alley and their horses. Approaching his mount, Bob took a bullet through the torso from John Kloehr, reeling toward the shed where Grat and Marshal Connelly had died. He triggered two wild rounds before Kloehr dropped him with a chest shot, leaving Emmett Dalton alone on the field. The next barrage wounded Emmett in the arm and pelvis, killing horses on both sides of him as he scrambled aboard. Trotting toward his brother, Emmett was leaning down from the saddle, one hand outstretched toward Bob, when Carey Seaman hit him with a double blast of buckshot and spilled him from the saddle.

Twelve minutes of carnage in Coffeyville left eight men dead or dying; of the four wounded, Emmett Dalton was expected to die, but he surprised his keepers by surviving to stand trial. Of $31,000 stolen from two banks in the abortive raid, all was recovered except for a single $20 bill; its disappearance was never explained. Emmett was sentenced to life imprisonment but was favored with a gubernatorial pardon after he had served 14 years and six months. He later published a memoir—*When the Daltons Rode*—that was produced as a motion picture. Emmett died in Los Angeles on July 13, 1937 at age 65.

Bill Dalton, last of the brothers to go bad, was a belated convert to banditry. News of the Coffeyville massacre scuttled his political career in California, and Bill soon returned to Oklahoma with his wife and child, settling near Kingfisher. He joined forces with Bill Doolin and was present at the battle of Ingalls on September 1, 1893, when a dozen law enforcers tried to corral the gang and lost three of their own in the process. A year later Dalton's wife was arrested at Ardmore for possession of whiskey that her husband had ordered (forbidden as contraband in the territory), and a posse visited the Dalton homestead on September 25, 1894. Bill saw them coming and scrambled out a window but was too late. Deputy Loss Hart drilled him with a single rifle shot, thus writing finis to the career of another infamous Missouri brood.

DANIEL, Francisco "Pancho"

A native of Sonora, Mexico, "Pancho" Daniel traveled north to California with his brother Bernardo in time for the gold rush of 1849. The brothers soon fell in with bad companions, Pancho claiming to have ridden with the outlaw gangs of CLAUDIO FELIZ and JOAQUIN MURRIETA before he and Bernardo decided to lead an outfit of their own. A quick hand with a six-shooter, Daniel boasted of killing 40 men during his decade as a bandit in the Golden State.

Bernardo Daniel met death at the end of a vigilante rope in 1853, but brother Pancho rode on to greater infamy, proficient both at HIGHWAY ROBBERY and raids on California's scattered mission settlements. By 1856 he had teamed with escaped convict JUAN FLORES, late of San Quentin prison, to launch a new series of holdups that put them both near the top of California's "Most Wanted" list. Their final adventure began on January 21, 1857, when the gang, 15 strong, looted two stores at San Juan Capistrano and murdered immigrant shopkeeper George Pflugardt. Sheriff James Barton, of Los Angeles County, led a five-man posse in pursuit of the gang on January 22, overtaking his quarry a day later, near the San Joaquin Hills. A pitched battle ensued, with Daniel killing Sheriff Barton in the first exchange of fire. When the smoke cleared, two other posse members were dead, and Daniel and three of his followers were wounded. The surviving lawmen fled when they ran out of bullets and were pursued to the outskirts of a nearby settlement.

News of the murders galvanized Anglo California. The governor offered a $1,000 reward for information leading to Daniel's arrest, but Juan Flores was captured first on February 3 and lynched by Los Angeles vigilantes 11 days later. It was late March before Sheriff John Murphy found Pancho Daniel hiding in a Santa Clara County haystack, caught with the late Sheriff Barton's distinctive silver-mounted gunbelt.

Daniel was indicted on three counts of murder, and while Angelenos expected swift justice, Pancho surprised them by employing lawyer Kimball Dimmick, an expert at legal delaying tactics. First, Dimmick challenged the Los Angeles jury pool on grounds of prejudice, disqualifying 288 veniremen. Sheriff Jim Thompson was disallowed from choosing more prospective jurors on grounds of his own hatred for Daniel, and Judge Benjamin Hayes finally ordered a change of venue to Santa Barbara County in November 1858. White residents of Los Angeles were outraged, citing lax security at the Santa Barbara County jail and the likelihood of numerous Hispanic jurors at the relocated trial. Unwilling to risk an acquittal, 200 vigilantes stormed the L.A. jail on November 30, removing Pancho Daniel from his cell and hanging him from the crossbeam of the jail-yard gate.

DAUGHERTY, Roy "Arkansaw Tom"

An Arkansas native who habitually misspelled the word when writing his self-chosen nickname, Roy Daugherty was born in 1874 and met outlaw WILLIAM DOOLIN in 1891 when they briefly worked together on a ranch in the northwestern corner of the Razorback State. Daugherty developed an almost childlike admiration for Doolin, verging on hero worship, and he was eager to join Doolin's gang in November 1892 after the demise of the hard-riding DALTON BROTHERS left Doolin without a clique to call his own.

It is uncertain which of Doolin's early raids included Daugherty, but "Arkansaw Tom" was definitely present at Ingalls, Oklahoma, when a posse of lawmen invaded that outlaw sanctuary after midnight on September 1, 1893. Cavorting in the town's brothel when the shooting started, Daugherty grabbed his Winchester rifle and opened up on the posse, ducking scores of bullets as his adversaries riddled the whorehouse. Doolin and comrade George "Bitter Creek" Newcomb were wounded at Ingalls, but they escaped with other members of the gang. Only Roy Daugherty was trapped and left behind, surrendering when he ran out of ammunition and lawmen threatened to burn the house.

Daugherty was charged with killing Deputy Tom Houston—one of three lawmen slain in the battle—and while no proof existed that he fired the fatal shots, jurors convicted him on the basis of his known affiliation with the Doolin gang. Daugherty's youth spared him from the gallows; he was sentenced to 50 years at Leavenworth and served 14 and was pardoned in 1907 after his brother (a clergyman) repeatedly appealed for clemency. Roy went straight for a while, then robbed a bank at Neosho, Missouri, and was shipped back to prison. On release from that term he hit another bank—at Asbury, Missouri—but there would be no more jail cells for "Arkansaw Tom." Cornered by police in Joplin, he drew a pistol and was killed on August 16, 1924.

DAVIS, A. J. "Gentleman Jack"

An enigmatic figure in the annals of early American crime, A. J. Davis was the product of an affluent home and was educated at a small eastern university before he settled in Nevada in the 1860s. A genial, even charismatic man of affluence and social stature, Davis ran the San Francisco Mine at Virginia City before stepping down to lease a mill and start a ranch, raising flowers as a hobby in his leisure time. None of his friends suspected that he led a dual life, scheming after hours as a criminal conspirator and leader of a gang dubbed the "Seven Knights of the Road." Only later, with 20–20 hindsight, would Virginia City locals suggest that Davis's mill—which oddly received no ore shipments—had been leased specifically to remold and market gold bullion that had been stolen in the first TRAIN ROBBERY west of the Rockies.

Second in command of the Davis gang and a treasured spy in Reno's religious community was Sunday School superintendent J. E. Chapman. The other five "knights" were fugitives from justice, wanted on a list of charges that ranged from petty theft to rustling and armed robbery: Tilton Cockerill, James Gilchrist, R. A. Jones, E. B. Parsons, and John Squires. Overlooked by busy law enforcers in the whirl of Reno's red-light district, they killed time with liquor, women, and cards while Davis and Chapman laid plans for a score that would make them all rich.

The plan unfolded with near-military precision. Chapman was sent to Oakland, California, there to ingratiate himself with officers of the Central Pacific Railroad and to discover when their next gold train was headed eastward. No special rules of secrecy were imposed because the railroad employed specially trained, heavily armed WELLS FARGO agents to protect its trains. Chapman discovered that Train No. 1 was scheduled to leave Oakland on November 5, 1870, carrying $41,800 in gold coins, $8,800 in silver bars, plus various bank and commercial drafts for customers in Nevada and Utah. He telegraphed the information to Davis, and the gang swung into action.

The Seven Knights had already colonized a deserted mine tunnel in the Peavine Mountains, overlooking the Central Pacific tracks near Verdi, a logging town 11 miles west of Reno. They sheltered there while the train rolled eastward and then rode on to Verdi and their rendezvous with Train No. 1. R. A. Jones, the appointed wrangler, took their horses from town to Lawton Springs, an old stone quarry seven miles outside of town, and waited for his comrades there.

Nature seemed to conspire with the gang as Train No. 1 rolled into Verdi, visibility obscured by alternating rain and snow flurries. Five bandits boarded the train, unseen by townspeople, quickly getting the

drop on engineer Hank Small, his fireman, and conductor D. G. Marshall. They left town on schedule and stopped the train at Lawton Springs, Small driven at gunpoint to open the express car. Ignoring the silver and bank drafts, Davis's raiders unloaded more than $41,000 in gold and thanked the train's crewmen for cooperating. They divided the loot at once, scattering in different, prearranged directions, unaware that they had missed another $15,000 in gold bars that were hidden under firewood beside the express car's stove. Engineer Small tried to telegraph for help, but the lines had been cut in several places to forestall pursuit.

Wells Fargo offered a $10,000 reward for capture of the outlaws, topped by $15,000 each from the Central Pacific and the state of Nevada. It was the largest reward in the West to date, but manhunters were not about to wait for informants to surface. Wells Fargo detective F. T. Burke was on the case within 24 hours, tracking three of the bandits to a tavern in Sardine Valley, California. James Gilchrist was still there when the posse arrived to collect him; he was frightened by lynch talk into naming his confederates. Washoe County Sheriff Calvin Pegg wired Virginia City authorities to arrest Jack Davis and J. E. Chapman, while pursuit of the others continued.

Despite their preparation for the robbery, escape seemed to be a haphazard affair for Davis's Knights of the Road. E. B. Parsons was literally caught napping, snoring in a hotel bed at Loyalton, California, and was jailed with Squires in Truckee pending extradition to Nevada. Cockerill and Jones were captured at a brothel in Long Valley and driven back to Virginia City, where Davis awaited them in jail. Chapman was the last arrested, lawmen waiting for him at the railroad depot when he returned from his sojourn to Oakland. All seven bandits were under lock and key within four days of the holdup, $39,700 of their loot safely recovered. (Another $3,000, apparently hidden, would never be found.)

James Gilchrist turned state's evidence against his former friends, bargaining for freedom while the rest were held in lieu of $20,000 bond. All six defendants were convicted of robbery on December 23, 1870, Judge C. N. Harris doling out 21-year prison terms to Chapman, Cockerill, Jones, Parsons, and Squires. Davis, although the leader and mastermind of the gang, was sentenced to 10 years without explanation from the bench, prompting speculation that his friends in high places had pulled strings to get him a break. Pardoned after serving less than half of his sentence, Davis squandered his second chance on an ill-conceived one-man holdup of a stagecoach between Tybo and Eureka in White Pine County, Nevada. Express guard Eugene Blair was faster on the draw and killed him with a well-aimed shotgun blast.

DAVIS, Ed

A native of Waurika, Oklahoma, born July 30, 1900, Ed Davis joined the army at age 17 but was prematurely discharged for reasons unknown on January 2, 1918. He drifted aimlessly for a year and then returned to his hometown, pulling a series of small-time robberies with cohorts Oscar Steelman and Earl Berry. Arrested for one heist and sentenced to a two-year term in the state reformatory, he was released in the summer of 1920. Hopping a freight to Kansas, Davis was next arrested in Hutchinson for "train riding" and packing a concealed weapon. Charges were dropped on condition that he leave town the same way he arrived, via boxcar, sans ticket.

Davis apparently kept his nose clean—or, at least, avoided capture—until January 23, 1923, when he teamed with accomplice Bill Sheppard to invade the Rush Springs, Oklahoma, home of oil man Joe McDonald. The loot was unimpressive, amounting to some $50 in cash and $2,425 in jewelry. Davis and Sheppard blew their getaway by hiking five miles northward through fresh snow to their Agawam hideout. Police followed their trail and arrested the embarrassed thieves, both of whom pled guilty and received 10-year sentences at the McAlester state prison.

Davis was paroled in 1928 and managed to avoid further trouble for two years before he served a short jail term in Little Rock, Arkansas. Moving on from there to Texas, he was arrested four times on robbery charges in Crosby, Eastland, and Midland Counties. Skipping bond, he fled to Nebraska and finished 1930 with a jail term for attempted robbery in Columbus.

By the time of his release from custody, Davis had become, if not more competent, at least a more dangerous outlaw. The pain of a persistent ear infection soured his humor, while his long string of arrests encouraged him to violently resist police in future confrontations. Because Davis was still allergic to honest work, the stage was set for tragedy.

Night police chief Ike Veach and Officer J. R. Hill were on routine parole in Marlow, Oklahoma, at 2:00 A.M. on April 20, 1931, when they spotted a suspicious car with three male occupants. Inside the vehicle, armed and ready for trouble, were Davis, Jack Allred, and John Schrimsher. As the officers approached, a shotgun blast blew out the windshield, killing Hill instantly and peppering Chief Veach with buckshot. Despite his wounds, Veach returned fire as the gunmen fled, disabling their car and wounding Allred.

The manhunt was a brief one. Allred was quickly arrested and lodged in a hospital at Duncan, Oklahoma, pending trial on murder charges. Schrimsher was captured near Henderson, Texas, on October 24, surrendering without resistance. Davis lasted one day longer, traced to Joinersville, where he had rented a house (with his wife) under the pseudonym "Paul Martin." All three defendants were convicted at trial, receiving identical life prison terms on August 3, 1931.

Davis was disinclined to end his days in prison, though. On May 26, 1932, with fellow inmates Robert Smith and Edmond Hardin, he escaped from the state pen at McAlester. Hardin chose to flee on foot and was soon recaptured, while Davis and Smith eluded their pursuers in a stolen car. Determined to make it big as an outlaw, Davis soon teamed with veteran stickup artists JIM CLARK and FRANK SAWYER, but their career as a holdup gang was stillborn on June 17 when police caught them riding in a stolen car near Black Rock, Arkansas. Adding insult to injury, the trio was wrongly accused of a bank robbery committed that same afternoon in Fort Scott, Kansas. All three were convicted and sentenced to long prison terms, while the actual robbers—ALVIN KARPIS and the BARKER brothers—got clean away with the loot.

It was too much for Davis to bear. On May 30, 1933, he joined Clark, HARVEY BAILEY, ROBERT BRADY, WILBUR UNDERHILL, and seven other convicts in a mass escape from the Kansas state prison at Lansing. On June 17, Davis drove the getaway car when Brady, Clark, and two other gunmen looted a bank in Black Rock, Arkansas. On August 9 he teamed with Clark and Bailey to hit another bank, this one in Kingfisher, Oklahoma, where all three fugitives were soon identified from prison mug shots. Bailey was arrested three days later in Texas and wrongly identified (and later convicted) as a kidnapping suspect, while Davis launched a series of one-man bank jobs around central Texas and pulling down small scores with such sufficient regularity that law enforcers started to call him "The Fox." By late September 1933 he had enough cash to consider retirement, striking out for California with his wife, debating surgical removal of his various prison tattoos.

Kansas Governor Alf Landon, meanwhile, ordered his state police to spare no effort in tracking down the Lansing fugitives. By November 1933 only Davis and Underhill remained at large, the list pared down to one after Wilbur was cornered and fatally wounded by Oklahoma lawmen on December 30, 1933. Running short of money in Los Angeles, Davis robbed a store and kidnapped owner J. J. Ball, but he was captured and convicted on a list of charges that included three counts of first-degree burglary, six counts of robbery, and two counts of kidnapping and was sentenced to life imprisonment on June 22, 1934. Kansas authorities put a hold on Ed to finish out his Lansing time in case he was ever paroled from the Golden State.

Consigned to Folsom Prison, Davis—dubbed "Old Deafy" by his fellow inmates—was no more acquiescent to confinement than he had been in Kansas. On September 19, 1937, he was one of seven convicts who took the warden and two guards hostage at knifepoint in a bid to escape. Other guards opened fire, leaving one officer and two inmates dead by the time Davis and his four surviving companions surrendered. All five were convicted of murder and sentenced to die. Davis arrived on San Quentin's death row on December 8, 1937, and was executed in the gas chamber eight days later. He left behind a note that read: "No regrets for Old Ed. All considered, my conscience is now resting easy."

At the time of his death, "Old Ed" was 38 years old.

DAVIS, Volney "Curley"
An early member of Tulsa, Oklahoma's "Central Park Gang" in the 1920s, Volney Davis met the BARKER brothers there and teamed up with them to commit various high-profile felonies in later years. His first serious offense occurred in the company of Arthur "Dock" Barker, when they tried to burglarize St. John's Hospital in Tulsa. Night watchman John Sherrill was killed in the process, and while Barker was swiftly arrested, Davis eluded capture for nearly a year before he was reeled in and sentenced to life

imprisonment. He escaped from the state pen at McAlester in January 1925 but remained at large for only 13 days.

Incredibly, despite that record, Davis applied for and was granted a 20-month "leave of absence" from prison on November 3, 1932. (Such leniency was not unusual in Oklahoma, at the time, and ALVIN KARPIS later claimed that the state's decision was assisted by a $1,500 bribe.) Davis was due back at McAlester on July 1, 1934, but there was no doubt that he would not return. In December 1932 he was reunited with girlfriend EDNA MURRAY, aka "The Kissing Bandit," after her third prison break, and both were attached to the Barker-Karpis bank-robbing gang during its period of peak activity. Davis and Murray were both implicated in the January 1934 kidnapping of ST. PAUL, MINNESOTA, banker Edward Bremer, which earned the gang a $200,000 ransom payment.

Interaction between outlaw gangs was common in the early 1930s, and Davis reportedly did a favor for JOHN DILLINGER in April 1934, hiding wounded bandit JOHN HAMILTON at his home in Aurora, Illinois, and afterward helping Dillinger bury his friend when Hamilton died from wounds suffered in a skirmish with police.

Though never charged with any of the holdups he committed as a member of the Barker-Karpis gang, Davis was indicted (with Murray) on January 22, 1935, for participating in the Bremer snatch. He remained at large for two more weeks and then was captured by FBI agents in St. Louis on February 6, but he escaped from federal custody the following day. Davis and his escorts were en route to St. Paul for his trial when their airplane was forced to land at Yorkville, Illinois. Davis promptly slugged a guard and fled in a stolen car, eluding pursuit until he was traced to Chicago and arrested on June 1 by G-man MELVIN PURVIS.

Back in St. Paul, Davis was convicted of participation in the Bremer kidnapping and was sentenced once again to life imprisonment. This time it would stick, as he was shipped off to Alcatraz. "Dock" Barker subsequently died in an attempt to flee The Rock, but Davis did not join his old friend in the break. Stories persist that he also quarreled with Alvin Karpis and once beat his former comrade in a stand-up fistfight. By the time he was finally released, ailing and forgotten, all the fight had gone out of the aged outlaw. Davis died in Oregon in 1978 after a long illness.

DeAUTREMONT Brothers

Oregon's most lethal train robbers struck only once and kept their game in the family. The gang consisted of twin brothers Ray and Roy DeAutremont, born in 1897, and younger sibling Hugh DeAutremont, born in 1905. Ray involved himself with the Industrial Workers of the World and spent most of 1919 at the Monroe, Washington, reformatory on a "syndicalism" conviction arising from his work with the notorious "Wobblies." Hugh graduated from a New Mexico high school in June 1923 and promptly joined his brothers at a logging camp near Silverton, Oregon. Their aging father ran a barber shop in Eugene, but Paul DeAutremont's efforts to instill a solid work ethic in his three sons were wasted. By October 1923 the boys were hungry for adventure and some easy cash.

In retrospect, their one and only crime was said by some to have been doomed by pure bad luck. The target—Southern Pacific Railroad Train No. 13—was chugging southward through Oregon's Siskiyou Mountains at 9:45 A.M. on October 11 when it entered Tunnel No. 13, a few miles out from the Siskiyou Station. Armed with sawed-off shotguns, the three brothers waited for the locomotive and first three cars to emerge, then leaped aboard, and forced engineer Arnold Bates to stop with most of his train still inside the 3,000-feet-long tunnel. With an estimated $40,000 inside the mail coach, the DeAutremont's looked forward to the score of a lifetime.

Roy covered engineer Bates with his shotgun, while Ray and Hugh approached the mail car. Postal clerk Elvyn Dougherty saw them coming and slammed the door as Hugh unleashed two wasted shotgun blasts. Ray then attached a dynamite charge to the mail car's door and the brothers retreated. Years later, in his sworn confession, Roy DeAutremont described what happened next.

Ray gave the detonator a push and the mouth of the tunnel was rocked by a tremendous explosion. It was far stronger than we had planned. In fact, the blast was so severe that the mail clerk was blown to bits. I then took the fireman and started back down the track to uncouple the mail car. But the gassy and smoky air was too thick so I called for the fireman. The fireman and engineer were then marched toward the car. In a few seconds I saw someone coming with a red light from the passenger cars still in the tunnel. I shot at the man, who was a conductor, with my shotgun and at the same time Hugh shot him with his .45 Colt. The man stag-

gered and I could see he was dying. Hugh walked over to him and shot him again, in cold blood. The engineer was put back up into the cab and Hugh told him to pull the main car ahead. He attempted to do this a number of times, but the engine wheels merely spun and the cars failed to move. Hugh then put the engineer back on the ground side next to the fireman while Ray and I looked the thing over to see what could be done about uncoupling the mail car and engine. But there was nothing we could do. So we walked back to the mail car and entered through the blown out front end. Our flashlights would not cut the steam and smoke so we left the mail car. Hugh in the meantime had ordered the engineer back into the cab. The fireman was standing alongside the engine with his arms in the air. Ray and I held a brief consultation as to what to do. We decided to kill the fireman. Ray shot him twice with the Colt. Hugh had the engineer covered and I shouted at him to bump him off and then we would clear out. We didn't want any witnesses. Hugh quickly shot the man in the head with his shotgun. We then fled to our cache which was between two and three miles northwest of the south entrance of the tunnel.

The brothers escaped empty handed, while a second conductor ran to a nearby emergency phone and summoned police from Ashland. Investigators at the scene found a detonator and discarded .45-caliber pistol, along with three empty packs and gunny sacks soaked in creosote that had been dragged along the ground to frustrate bloodhounds. Fanning out from Tunnel 13, other searchers soon turned up a black traveling bag with a railroad shipping tag attached and a pair of greasy denim overalls.

Dozens of suspects were jailed and interrogated after the Siskiyou massacre, but the case was broken by investigative methods worthy of a real-life Sherlock Holmes. Dr. Edward Heinrich, a chemistry professor at the University of California in Berkeley, examined the overalls and reported back to lawmen that their suspect was a left-handed lumberjack, approximately 25 years old, with brown hair and a fair complexion, five feet eight and 165 pounds, and a man of fastidious habits. Lawmen were incredulous until Dr. Heinrich explained the basis for his theory: Strands of hair had been recovered from the overalls, along with Douglas fir needles and fresh pitch from pine trees; furthermore, the garment was worn along its right side only, as where a southpaw might lean against trees while swinging his axe left-handed. If this were not enough, a slip of paper found inside one pocket proved to be a receipt for a registered letter. Further investigation identified the sender as Roy DeAutremont, mailing $50 to brother Hugh in Lakewood, New Mexico, on September 14, 1923.

Authorities traced Paul DeAutremont to Eugene, and he confirmed that his three sons were all lumberjacks, Roy being the lefthanded one. A trace on the discarded .45 Colt, meanwhile, identified its purchaser as one "William Elliott"—whose handwriting matched that of Roy DeAutremont. Express tags on the empty suitcase revealed that Roy had sent it from Eugene, addressed to himself in Portland, on January 21, 1923.

Thus were the Siskiyou suspects identified—but running them to ground was still no easy matter. Federal authorities offered a $6,000 reward; Southern Pacific executives kicked in $7,500, and the Railway Express Company added $900. Sightings were reported from all over the United States, and although each lead was pursued, none proved legitimate. At last, in near desperation, 2,265,000 WANTED fliers were printed in English and five foreign languages and were distributed internationally as the manhunt went global.

Authorities had nearly given up hope by June 1923 when U.S. Army Corporal Thomas Reynolds, stationed on Alcatraz Island in San Francisco Bay, noticed a yellowed poster on the wall and approached his superiors. Reynolds, recently home from a posting in the Philippines, recognized Hugh DeAutremont as one "James Price," an acquaintance from Manila. Jailed within six hours, Hugh admitted his identity but stalled extradition until March 1927 when he was finally returned to the States for trial on first-degree murder charges.

Hugh denied any knowledge of his brothers' whereabouts, but the arrest prompted U.S. postal inspectors to issue a new batch of WANTED fliers. The tactic paid off in early June with a report that the DeAutremont twins had been sighted recently in Portsmouth, Ohio, posing as "Clarence and Elmer Goodwin." FBI agents moved on the lead, tracing the twins to Steubenville, where they were arrested without incident on June 8, 1927. In custody, the brothers admitted fleeing to Detroit after the Siskiyou holdup. Ray had married there and then moved on to Hanging Rock, Roy following a few months later. The twins had stayed together after that, through moves to Portsmouth and Steubenville, Ray's bleached hair failing to disguise him when the new batch of posters was issued.

Speedy extradition landed the twins in Jackson, Oregon, in time for Hugh's murder trial, but news of

their arrival was withheld from the defendant. Jurors convicted Hugh of murder but recommended mercy, whereupon his brothers both filed guilty pleas; all three were sentenced to life terms at the Salem state prison. Hugh was paroled on November 24, 1958, described by his keepers as "a testament to reformation," but he died of cancer in February 1959. Roy DeAutremont was declared insane in 1960 and was transferred to the Oregon State Hospital where he finished his days among madmen. Brother Ray was paroled on October 11, 1961—the 38th anniversary of the Siskiyou slayings—but he had no ready answer for reporters who asked him how it felt to be free after 34 years in a cage. "I'm trying to think of something to say," Ray replied. "Well, you can imagine how it feels, can't you? But one thing is for sure: For the rest of my life I will struggle with the question of whatever possessed us to do such a thing."

DEMBIN, Meyer

A native of New York City's Lower East Side, Meyer Dembin grew up on the streets, running with gangs of local toughs. By the early 1930s he had racked up six arrests for larceny, assault, and robbery, plus one in 1934 on suspicion of murder. All the charges were dismissed for lack of evidence, but Dembin's luck ran out in early 1935. On February 8, with three accomplices, he robbed a bank in Sparkill, New York, of $19,799. Two of the bandits were traced through the license plates of their abandoned getaway car and arrested days later, each receiving terms of 25 years in prison. A third participant was arrested in 1946 and sentenced to 15 years, but Dembin was still at large when his name was added to the FBI's "Most Wanted" list on September 5, 1950.

Fourteen months later, on November 26, 1951, the fugitive surrendered voluntarily to federal agents in New York. Dembin told his captors that he had "gone straight" a decade earlier, about the time he married, but he refused to say where he had been since 1935. He carried no wallet or identification at the time of his surrender, and the labels had been carefully removed from all his clothing.

Picked up once for investigation in El Paso while living on the run, Dembin had been released before officers realized his true identity. Otherwise, he told the FBI, he had been earning $75 to $100 a week, installing hooked rugs. Agents doubted his story, linking his name to unsolved bank robberies in Detroit, Los Angeles, El Paso, and elsewhere, but nothing could be proved in those cases. Pleading guilty to outstanding federal charges on the day he surrendered, Dembin faced a maximum term of 47 years in prison for the Sparkill robbery.

DENVER Mint Robbery

Despite its common designation in the press, this robbery, committed on December 18, 1922, actually involved a Federal Reserve Bank delivery truck *outside* the U.S. Mint in Denver, Colorado. On that Monday afternoon, five gunmen stole $200,000 from the truck and fled after killing a guard, Charles Linton.

The only member of the hit team ever positively identified was Nicholas "Chaw Jimmie" Trainor (aka "J. S. Sloane"), a stickup artist born in 1887. Mortally wounded in the exchange of gunfire with Mint security guards, Trainor was left behind by his accomplices, his corpse found in their bullet-riddled getaway car in a garage on Denver's Gilpin Street on January 14, 1923. Because Trainor was a sometime associate of bank robber HARVEY BAILEY, authorities assumed Bailey must be involved in the caper, but evidence remained elusive.

A month after Trainor's body was found, on February 17, 1923, police in Minnesota raided an abandoned hideout, seizing $80,000 in cash from the Mint holdup and $73,000 in bonds stolen on September 28, 1922, from a bank in the Cincinnati suburb of Walnut Hills, Ohio. Trainor and Bailey were prime suspects in that robbery, as well, but "Old Harve" remained elusive at the moment. The case was finally "solved" 12 years after the fact by executive fiat. On December 1, 1934, Denver Police Chief A. T. Clark announced that the Mint robbery had been carried out by five men and two women. Five unnamed members of the team were dead, Clark claimed. The two survivors named by Chief Clark, Harvey Bailey and JAMES "OKLAHOMA JACK" CLARK—no relation to the chief—were both serving life terms in prison for unrelated crimes. No one was ever charged or brought to trial in the Denver Mint case.

DEVLIN, Edmund James

Ed Devlin's criminal record dated from 1950, listing charges of theft and breaking and entering in his native Connecticut. Later he served prison terms for attempted robbery with violence, armed robbery, assault, and parole violation. FBI files described him as "a reputed Connecticut organized crime gang

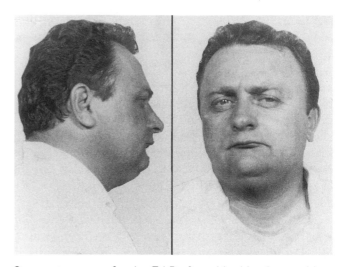

Connecticut gang leader Ed Devlin robbed banks in addition to his duties as an organized-crime racketeer. (FBI)

leader" and a participant in gang warfare against underworld rivals. The bureau also recognized Devlin as the brains of an efficient bank-robbing gang suspected of numerous raids.

On January 9, 1969, three gunmen entered a branch office of the Fairfield County Trust Company in Norwalk, Connecticut, through a back door, brandishing weapons. Their take, an estimated $108,816, set a new record for Connecticut bank robberies. The abandoned getaway car, recovered on January 10, was traced to New York City, where it had been stolen four days earlier. Devlin's two accomplices, Edward Reed and Ralph Masselli, were soon arrested. Masselli made a deal with prosecutors, testifying for the state, and Reed drew 25 years in Leavenworth on conviction of bank robbery, with five years tacked on for transporting a firearm across state lines. Devlin's name was added to the "Ten Most Wanted" list on March 30, 1970, with Masselli remaining in custody pending Devlin's arrest and trial.

On August 15, 1970, FBI agents surrounded the fugitive on a streetcorner in downtown Manchester, New Hampshire. Unarmed, Devlin surrendered without resistance and was returned to Connecticut for trial. In addition to bank robbery, he also faced charges of interstate transportation of stolen property (relating to the cashing of stolen money orders) and failure to appear at a hearing in September 1969 after his indictment on robbery charges. Altogether, it was enough to end his criminal career once and for all.

DE VOL, Lawrence

An Ohio native, born in 1905, Lawrence De Vol moved to Oklahoma at an early age. He soon fell in with bad companions and became a member of Tulsa's notorious "Central Park" gang, logging his first arrest (for larceny) at age 13. By age 22 he had found his calling in life, extracting other people's money from bank vaults at gunpoint.

De Vol's first-known bank job occurred on August 19, 1927, when he joined HARVEY BAILEY, Eddie Fitzgerald, and Harry Morris to lift $70,000 from a jug in Vinton, Iowa. On February 6, 1928, the same gang, joined by one Al Johnston, stole $225,000 in cash and bonds from a bank at Washington Court House, Ohio.

It was not all smooth sailing for Larry, however. Arrested and convicted of a Kansas heist in 1928, he was dispatched to the state reformatory at Hutchinson. There, he met ALVIN KARPIS, and the two of them escaped on March 9, 1929, making their way to Pueblo, Colorado, where they stole a car and headed south. In Woodward, Oklahoma, they burglarized a store, but De Vol was soon recaptured and shipped back to Hutchinson. Despite his recent lapse in discipline, he was paroled before year's end and soon hooked up with Karpis for a string of robberies across Oklahoma and Kansas.

On March 23, 1930, De Vol and Karpis were jailed in Kansas City. Larry posted $1,000 bond on April 1 and promptly skipped town, leaving Karpis to face the music alone.

His status as a fugitive hardened De Vol and made him more violent. In April 1930, with accomplice Jimmie Creighton, he was suspected of robbing and killing two businessmen, brothers, at the Hotel Severs in Muskogee, Oklahoma. On June 25, 1930, he shot and killed two lawmen, Sheriff William Sweet and Officer Aaron Bailey, in Washington, Iowa.

De Vol was reunited with Harvey Bailey on September 9, 1930, stealing $40,000 from an Ottumwa, Iowa, bank as part of a gang that also included THOMAS HOLDEN, FRANCIS KEATING, VERNON MILLER, and GEORGE "MACHINE GUN" KELLY. Two months later, on November 17, he was alone in the robbery of a Hannibal, Missouri, theater, killing Patrolman John Rose in his flight from the scene of the crime.

Little is known of De Vol's movements in 1931 until he turned up in ST. PAUL, MINNESOTA, around Christmas, enlisting as a member of the BARKER GANG. His first outing with the mob occurred on March 29, 1932, when he teamed with Fred Barker, Alvin Karpis, Tom Holden, and Bernard Phillips to loot a Minneapolis bank of $266,500 in cash and securities. On June 17, 1932, Larry joined Barker, Karpis, Holden, Harvey Bailey, George Kelly, Vern Miller, and Francis Keating to steal $47,000 from a bank in Fort Scott, Kansas. The score in Concordia, Kansas, was better on July 25: $250,000 in cash and bonds lifted by De Vol, Barker, Karpis, Jess Doyle, and Earl Christman. The September 30 raid in Wahpeton, North Dakota, was disappointing, by comparison: De Vol, joined by Karpis, Doyle, Fred Barker and his brother Arthur, bagged a mere $6,900. On December 16, 1932, the gang returned to Minneapolis, a seven-man team (including De Vol, Karpis, Doyle, Vern Miller, Bill Weaver, and the Barker brothers) hitting another bank for $22,000 cash and $92,000 in bonds. It was a bloody raid: De Vol killed Patrolmen Ira Evans and Leo Gorski outside the bank, wounding a third officer; Fred Barker later shot and killed a civilian passer-by in St. Paul while the thieves were switching getaway cars.

Arrested by St. Paul police on December 18 (or December 21; accounts vary), De Vol was later convicted of murder and sentenced to life in the state prison at Stillwater, Minnesota. His erratic behavior soon earned him a transfer to St. Peter Hospital for the Criminally Insane, from which he fled with 15 other inmates on June 6, 1936. A month later, on July 8, De Vol joined accomplice Don Reeder to rob a bank in Turon, Kansas. Fleeing into Oklahoma, he was cornered by police at the German Village Tavern in Enid. A shootout erupted, De Vol killing Officer Cal Palmer and wounding a second patrolman before he was riddled with bullets.

DICKERSON, Thomas Everett

Allergic to discipline in any form, Thomas Dickerson had been expelled from Virginia military school in 1939. Thereafter, as a juvenile delinquent and an adult felon, he compiled a record of arrests that testified to his devotion to the "high life." As it turned out, though, his efforts to become a big-time thief were sadly limited by lack of talent. Jailed for 10 to 25 years on an Ohio bank-robbery conviction, Dickerson was finally paroled in January 1953. He lasted barely seven months before he tried another robbery and failed again.

On July 14, 1953, Dickerson held up a loan company in Bethesda, Maryland, fleeing in a car driven by a female accomplice. Arrested the next day in

Arlington, Virginia, he first attempted suicide and then launched a hunger strike designed to dramatize his "cause." Requesting medical attention for the pains of self-imposed starvation, he was transferred to the Spring Grove State Hospital at Cantonsville on September 28. With a companion, also lately transferred, he escaped the next day, severely beating a guard in the process. A federal warrant for unlawful flight was issued on October 2, and Dickerson's name was added to the FBI's "Ten Most Wanted" list on October 10.

Reliance on his family for shelter finally betrayed Tom Dickerson. In mid-December federal agents warned a second cousin in Verdunsville, West Virginia, that they thought the fugitive might try to get in touch. When Dickerson arrived December 21 in company with an uncle, state police and G-men sprang their trap. Dickerson and his uncle (later charged with harboring a fugitive) were taken into custody without a fight. The hard-luck bandit was returned his Maryland sentence, with new time added for the jailbreak.

DICKSON, Bennie and Stella

A short-lived but flamboyant husband-wife holdup team, Bennie and "Sure Shot" Stella Dickson robbed their first bank on Stella's 16th birthday, August 25, 1938. The take from that job, in Elkton, South Dakota, was only $2,174, but they would improve with practice. Two months later, on October 31, they stole $47,233 in cash and bonds from another bank in Brookings, South Dakota.

Police trailed the couple to a Topeka, Kansas, tourist camp, but the Dicksons shot their way out of the trap and escaped separately on November 24, 1938. Bennie drove to South Clinton, Iowa, and stole a fresh car, doubling back to rendezvous with Stella in Topeka on November 25. During the next few days, they battled with police in Michigan, and Stella earned her nickname by shooting out the tires on a patrol car. Taking three men hostage, they stole getaway cars in Michigan and Indiana, eluding their pursuers on narrow back roads.

FBI agents caught up with Bennie Dickson on April 6, 1939, at a St. Louis hamburger stand and killed him when went for his gun. Stella was arrested one day later, in Kansas City and was returned to South Dakota for trial. Convicted of bank robbery, she was sentenced to 10 years in prison.

DILLINGER, John Herbert

America's most famous outlaw since JESSE JAMES was born June 22, 1903, in Indianapolis, the son of German immigrants, his father a successful merchant and landlord. Dillinger's mother died in 1906, and he bitterly resented the woman his father married six years later, thereupon transporting the family to a 60-acre farm near Mooresville, Indiana. Minor run-ins with the law were symptomatic of young Dillinger's unhappiness, but he seemed to make a fresh start in 1923 when he joined the U.S. Navy and shipped out to see the world. It might have been a grand adventure, but Dillinger soon tired of military discipline, deserting that December and returning to Mooresville, where he fooled his family with stories of an early "hardship" discharge. In April 1924 he felt secure enough to woo a local girl and to start to look for work.

Still, honest labor never held much appeal for John Dillinger. By that summer he was hanging out with 31-year-old Edward Singleton, spinning fantasies of easy money. Both men were drunk when they pulled their first job on September 6, 1924, Dillinger trying to rob an elderly grocer at gunpoint while Singleton waited in the getaway car. Unexpectedly, the old man grappled with Dillinger, and a wild shot was fired, prompting Singleton to bolt and leave Dillinger behind to flee on foot. Arrested two days later, he pled guilty on advice of counsel, but the judge disliked his cocky attitude and decided to make an example of Dillinger, slapping him with a sentence of two to 20 years in state prison. He wound up serving eight years and eight months among hardened felons, thus charting the course for the rest of his life. (Singleton took his chances with a jury, and although convicted of conspiracy to rob, he was back on the street within two years.)

At Indiana's Pendleton Reformatory and later at the state prison in Michigan City, Dillinger made friends with a *Who's Who* of Midwestern bank robbers: HARRY PIERPONT, CHARLES MAKLEY, HOMER VAN METER, JOHN "RED" HAMILTON, and others. By the time he was released on May 22, 1933, Dillinger had agreed to help his cronies escape, but to make that happen, he needed cash and plenty of it. Thankfully, Van Meter had provided a list of banks described as easy scores, ready and ripe for the taking.

Times had changed, though, while Dillinger was locked away. The stock market crash of 1929 and ensuing Great Depression had altered the face of

This is a June 1934 FBI "Wanted" poster of John Herbert Dillinger, who was considered "Public Enemy No. 1."
(AP/Wide World Photos)

America, putting millions out of work and closing many banks. Those remaining open were decidedly at risk from roving bands of stickup men, with 631 bank robberies recorded in 1932 alone. Some of the outlaws, including CHARLES "PRETTY BOY" FLOYD and CLYDE BARROW, were already infamous from coast to coast, their bloody front-page exploits providing cheap entertainment for citizens who viewed bankers and their foreclosure notices with utmost contempt. The last great era of the SOCIAL BANDITS had arrived, but it would not last long.

Once on the street, Dillinger quickly joined an Indianapolis gang dubbed the "White Caps," after the foolishly distinctive headgear worn during stickups. On June 9, 1933, he joined gang members William Shaw and Noble Claycomb to steal $100 from an Indianapolis supermarket. The following day he scored a double-header: First, he joined Shaw and Paul "Lefty" Parker to loot a bank in New Carlisle, Ohio, of $10,600; heading homeward, the trio also robbed a pharmacy and a supermarket in Indianapolis. On June 24 Dillinger and Shaw wounded the manager of a Monticello, Indiana, thread factory, escaping empty handed; the holdup of an Indianapolis fruit market that afternoon was a poor consolation. Five days later, Dillinger and Shaw knocked over an Indianapolis sandwich shop. With Shaw and Harry Copeland, Dillinger robbed a Muncie speakeasy on July 15; Shaw, Lefty Parker, and Noble Claycomb were jailed the next day, but Dillinger and Copeland managed to escape the trap. They came back strong two days later in Daleville, Indiana, taking one of Van Meter's banks for $3,500.

By now, police knew Dillinger as "Desperate Dan," a nickname derived in equal parts from his swashbuckling approach to robbery and Noble Claycomb's erroneous identification of his fugitive pal as "Dan Dillinger." Suspected of robbing a Rockville, Indiana, bank on July 19, 1933, Dillinger was definitely teamed with Harry Copeland on August 4, lifting $10,110 from another bank in Montpelier. Four days later, Dillinger was named as a suspect in the holdup of a bank at Gravel Switch, Kentucky. On August 14, in Bluffton, Ohio, he joined Copeland and Sam Goldstein to raid the Citizens National Bank for $2,100. (Goldstein was jailed in Gary eight days later.) On September 6 Dillinger turned up in Indianapolis with Copeland and Harry Crouch (or Crough), robbing a local bank of $24,800. Six days later, Dillinger was suspected of taking another $24,000 from a bank in Farrell, Pennsylvania.

Even with such a busy schedule, Dillinger had not forgotten his vow to his pen pals. On September 12, 1933, he tossed several pistols over the wall at Michigan City, but other convicts found the guns and turned them in before his friends could arm themselves. Next, he arranged for handguns to be hidden in a box of thread shipped to the prison sewing shop, but his luck ran out before the plan bore fruit. On September 22, 1933 he was arrested by police in Dayton, Ohio, and jailed at Lima pending trial on the Bluffton bank-robbery charge.

Four days after Dillinger's arrest, on September 26, 10 Michigan City inmates used the smuggled pistols to escape from custody. The breakout team included Pierpont, Makley, Hamilton, RUSSELL CLARK, JAMES CLARK (no relation), Joseph Fox, Ed Shouse, James Jenkins, Joseph Burns, and Walter Dietrich. James Clark was recaptured on September 28, and Jenkins made it as far as Beanblossom, Indiana, before a civilian posse killed him on September 30. The other fugitives made it to a hideout prearranged by Dillinger and moved on from there to Ohio, where they were met by Harry Copeland. On October 3 they celebrated their escape by looting a bank in St. Mary's, Ohio, of $14,000.

The next order of business was liberating Dillinger, to which end Pierpont, Makley, Clark, Copeland, Hamilton, and Shouse invaded the Lima jailhouse on October 12. Initially posing as lawmen, they were stymied for a moment when Sheriff Jesse Sarber asked to see their credentials. Pierpont responded by shooting and pistol-whipping Sarber (who died that night without regaining conscious-

ness). Dillinger seemed genuinely saddened by the sheriff's death, but he was not about to look a gift horse in the mouth.

A roving bandit gang needs guns, and the outfit augmented its arsenal by raiding an Auburn, Indiana, police station on October 14, walking off with submachine guns, various other weapons, and several bulletproof vests. Six days later they repeated the procedure at a police station in Peru, Indiana. Thus fortified, the gang looted a Greencastle bank for $74,782 on October 23 and was suspected (probably in error) of hitting a South Bend bank for $5,000 the following day. The series of daring raids prompted Indiana Governor Paul McNutt to mobilize National Guard units, while the fugitives retreated to Chicago with their cash.

Already notorious, the gang soon got another boost from the media, thanks to Indiana State Police investigator MATT LEACH. It was his brainstorm to blanket the Midwest with publicity about the "Dillinger gang," hoping veteran robbers Pierpont and Makley would feel slighted, take offense, and possibly dissolve the mob. In fact, however, no one in the outfit took the headlines seriously, the gang rolling on from one job to the next with no recognized leader. Still, the publicity had had its effect: Dillinger and girlfriend Evelyn Frechette narrowly escaped a police trap in Chicago on November 15; officers accidentally shot out their own windshield and then reported a wild running battle to the press. Harry Copeland was captured in Chicago two days later, following an altercation with his lover, and was ultimately convicted and sentenced to 25 years for the Greencastle, Indiana, holdup.

On November 20, 1933, the gang took $27,789 from a bank in Racine, Wisconsin, wounding one policeman in the process and briefly taking another hostage for use as a human shield in their getaway. On December 13 Dillinger and company were named as suspects in a Chicago bank heist. The following day, Red Hamilton had a near-miss with Chicago police when he came to retrieve his car from a local garage, but he escaped on foot after killing Sergeant William Shanley. By December 16 Chicago police had organized a 40-man "Dillinger Squad," and eight of the department's 10 identified "public enemies" were members or girlfriends of the Dillinger gang. Ed Shouse was cornered by police in Paris, Illinois, on December 20, trying his best to surrender, but officers were so excited that they opened fire regardless, killing Indiana state policeman Eugene Teague, while Shouse emerged un-scathed. Two days later, three small-time stickup artists unconnected to the gang were killed in a police raid on a suspected Dillinger hideout in Chicago. Dillinger crony Hilton Crouch, arrested in Chicago on December 23, was later sentenced to 20 years for an Indianapolis bank heist.

The heat in Illinois drove Dillinger and his companions to Florida, where they celebrated New Year's Eve by firing Tommy guns into the surf at Daytona Beach. That same night they were wrongly identified as members of the gang that robbed a Chicago nightclub, gunning down two police officers in the process. Dillinger would later claim that they were still in Florida two weeks later, on January 15, 1934, when three gunmen stole $20,376 from a bank in East Chicago, Indiana. Patrolman William O'Mal-

ley was machine-gunned to death in the holdup, several witnesses naming the triggerman as John Dillinger. One of his sidekicks, apparently wounded by police gunfire, was identified by the same witnesses as Red Hamilton.

Denials notwithstanding, Dillinger was indicted for O'Malley's murder, but bringing him to trial was something else again. Authorities were pleasantly surprised on January 25 by news that Dillinger, Makley, Clark, and Pierpont had been captured in Tucson, Arizona, following a fire at their hotel. A bellboy, whom they paid to rescue their gun-heavy luggage, told his story to the local sheriff, afterward picking their photographs out of a pulp detective magazine. In custody, Dillinger was transferred to the Lake County jail in Crown Point, Indiana, pending trial in the O'Malley case, while his companions

Gangster John Dillinger strikes a pose with Prosecutor Robert Estill, left, while awaiting trial for the murder of police officer William O'Malley during a bank robbery. (AP/Wide World Photos)

went back to Ohio, pending charges in the death of Sheriff Sarber.

Dillinger was held without bond at Crown Point, his trial scheduled to open on March 12, but he had other ideas. Nine days before his slated appearance in court, Dillinger staged his famous "wooden-gun" escape along with murder suspect Herbert Young-blood, fleeing in a stolen car. (Some versions of the story claim the phony gun was carved from soap; others state as fact that one or another of Dillinger's cronies smuggled a real pistol into the jail. A compromise version, published for the first time in 1994, states that Dillinger used a wooden gun carved by a friend on the outside and smuggled into jail.) It was his flight across state lines in a stolen car that led to Dillinger's first federal indictment, under the Dyer Act, and thus placed J. EDGAR HOOVER's G-men on his trail.

Immediately after his escape from Crown Point, Dillinger joined what would soon become known as the "second Dillinger gang," this one including Red Hamilton, Homer Van Meter, EDDIE GREEN, TOMMY CARROLL, and GEORGE "BABY FACE" NELSON. The new gang staged its first raid on March 6, looting $49,500 from a bank in Sioux Falls, South Dakota, wounding a patrolman in the process. Four days later, Dillinger was tentatively identified as the triggerman in a shootout with police at Schiller Park, Illinois. On March 13 the gang took $52,344 from a bank in Mason City, Iowa, but Dillinger and Hamilton were both wounded during the getaway.

The net was tightening. On March 31, 1934, FBI agents ambushed Dillinger and Van Meter in ST. PAUL, MINNESOTA, but the outlaws shot their way out of the trap and escaped. (Ironically, a special grand jury chose that day to release a statement dismissing claims that St. Paul was a notorious criminal hang-out.) Dillinger visited his father in Mooresville from April 5 to April 8, and while FBI spotters observed his homecoming, reinforcements gathered too slowly to prevent his escape. On April 9 G-man MELVIN PURVIS nabbed Evelyn Frechette in Chicago but missed his main quarry parked in a car outside the tavern. Four days later, Dillinger and Van Meter robbed the Warsaw, Indiana, police station, but they gained only two revolvers and three bulletproof vests. On April 19 the gang was suspected of hitting a bank in Pana, Illinois, for $27,000.

It was embarrassing for lawmen and particularly for the gangbusting FBI. Flamboyant Melvin Purvis was enraged at his inability to lay hands on Dillinger,

but he got another chance on April 22, 1934, with reports that the whole gang was idling near Rhinelander, Wisconsin, at Emil Wanatka's Little Bohemia Lodge. Purvis led his team north, arriving after nightfall, but his hasty plans soon fell apart. Barking watchdogs and an unexpected barbed-wire fence delayed his agents, already nervous in the dark, on unfamiliar ground. When three innocent patrons emerged from the lodge and prepared to drive away, the G-men opened fire, killing one and wounding the others. A blazing gun battle erupted, Dillinger and company escaping out the back while Purvis and his men shot up the lodge. It was after sunrise when tear gas flushed several "gun molls" from the bullet-riddled resort. Meanwhile, Baby Face Nelson had killed one federal agent and wounded two more lawmen at a nearby general store, while the rest of Dillinger's gang scattered to the winds. The only gang casualty was Red Hamilton, mortally wounded while crashing a police roadblock near South St. Paul. He reportedly died four days later, buried secretly by Dillinger, Van Meter, and members of the BARKER GANG.

The Little Bohemia raid was a public relations disaster for Purvis and the FBI, but it hardly slowed Dillinger down. On May 1 he was identified as the gunman who slugged and disarmed three police officers in Bellwood, Indiana. Three days later, Dillinger and Van Meter were identified as two-thirds of the trio who took $17,000 from a bank in Fostoria, Ohio, killing police chief Frank Culp and wounding others. On May 18 Dillinger, Baby Face Nelson, and an unidentified third man were blamed for the $25,000 robbery of a Flint, Michigan, bank. The next day, a federal grand jury indicted Dillinger, Nelson, Van Meter, and Tommy Carroll on charges of harboring fugitives—namely, each other. In St. Paul on May 23, Evelyn Frechette and Dr. Clayton May were convicted of harboring Dillinger, each defendant fined $10,000 and sentenced to two years in prison.

Violence flared again on May 24 when East Chicago policemen Lloyd Mulvihill and Martin O'Brien were riddled with submachine-gun bullets after stopping a panel truck occupied by Dillinger and Homer Van Meter. Three days later, Dillinger and Van Meter submitted to plastic surgery performed by Doctors WILHELM LOESER and Harold Cassidy, at the home of Chicago mobster James Probasco. The outlaws hoped to change their appearance and thus avoid capture, but by all accounts the experiment was a miserable failure.

On June 22, 1934, John Dillinger was unofficially proclaimed America's first "Public Enemy Number One" in a speech by U.S. Attorney General Homer Cummings. Two days later, 60 lawmen raided a ranch near Branson, Missouri, on a tip that Dillinger and CHARLES "PRETTY BOY" FLOYD were hiding out there to recover from wounds, but no bandits were found. Five days later, one Albert "Pat" Reilly was arrested by G-man in St. Paul on a charge of harboring Dillinger, but he informed his captors that he believed the elusive gangster to be already dead.

Such rumors notwithstanding, Dillinger was fit enough to rob his last bank at South Bend, Indiana, on June 30, accompanied by Nelson, Van Meter, John Paul Chase, Jack Perkins, and a sixth man identified in some accounts as Pretty Boy Floyd. The gang bagged $29,890, but all hell broke loose as they were leaving. Patrolman Harold Wagner was shot and killed outside the bank—probably by Van Meter, who was also slightly wounded. Four civilians also caught bullets as Nelson sprayed the landscape in one of Dillinger's wildest and bloodiest holdups.

On July 6, 1934, Patricia Cherrington (former girlfriend of the late Red Hamilton) was convicted of harboring Dillinger in Madison, Wisconsin, and sentenced to two years in prison. Eight days later, surviving members of the gang met briefly at a rural schoolyard northwest of Chicago, but their confab was interrupted by two policemen, both of whom were shot and wounded on the spot by Baby Face Nelson.

By that time, Melvin Purvis was already ironing out the wrinkles in another plan to capture Dillinger. A tip from corrupt police in East Chicago had informed him that brothel madam Ann Cumpanas (aka "Anna Sage") would be willing to put Dillinger "on the spot" in return for some help with pesky Immigration officials who sought to deport her as an undesirable alien. Purvis agreed to do what he could for Anna—in fact, precisely nothing—and the madam rewarded him with information that Dillinger planned to attend a gangster movie, *Manhattan Melodrama*, at Chicago's Biograph Theater on the night of July 22. G-men were waiting when Dillinger emerged from the movie house, accompanied by the infamous "woman in red," and he was gunned down on the street in a fusillade that also wounded several bystanders. Stories persist that Dillinger's corpse was plundered en route to the morgue, an East Chicago detective stealing several thousand dollars from the outlaw's pockets, while Melvin Purvis himself claimed Dillinger's ruby ring and diamond stickpin.

Years after the fact, author Jay Robert Nash noted certain discrepancies in Dillinger's autopsy report, promoting a theory that Dillinger actually escaped justice, while small-time hoodlum "Jimmy Lawrence" died in his place. Similar theories surround the deaths of JESSE JAMES and BUTCH CASSIDY and are equally devoid of proof, but Nash did uncover evidence that Dillinger may have been unarmed when he was killed. Tracing the serial number of a Colt pistol, displayed for years at FBI headquarters, that was identified as Dillinger's weapon on the night he died, Nash proved conclusively that the gun in question was manufactured months after Dillinger was shot. Crime historian William Helmer reports an alternate story, that Dillinger *was* armed on July 22 but that J. Edgar Hoover claimed the pistol as a personal keepsake, replacing it with a "ringer" in the FBI trophy case.

DODGE, Fred J.: Wells Fargo detective

A California native, born in 1854, Fred Dodge grew up among the Digger Indians in Butte County, acquiring from survivors of the tribe the tracking skills that later served him so well as a manhunter. Employment as a cowboy, freight handler, storekeeper, and occasional gambler preceded his enlistment with WELLS FARGO in 1879 as an undercover detective. Dodge's first assignment was Tombstone, Arizona, where he had a ringside seat for the bloody conflict between the Earp brothers and the Clanton gang. Dodge posed as a gambler, staying on the fringes of the action and staying alert for any threats to his real employer's banking and express interests.

In later years, while still ostensibly a civilian, Dodge participated in most of the major manhunts for outlaws across Arizona Territory, including the pursuit of bandits who robbed two Southern Pacific trains at Pantana in 1887. A year later, he was present at the Stein's Pass holdup and helped capture the outlaws who nearly killed Cochise County Sheriff John Slaughter. In the wake of that adventure, Dodge dropped his undercover role and went to work in Wells Fargo's Southern Division, including Texas and the Oklahoma Indian Territory. There, after a May 1891 train robbery near Wharton, Dodge launched a long-running pursuit of the DALTON GANG that would consume most of his waking hours for the next 17 months. Dodge tried to plant an informer in the gang—mercenary gunman Jim Matthews—but the plan fell through when Bob Dalton decided the gang was already too large for new members. Next, Dodge joined U.S. deputy marshal Heck Thomas in organizing the "Dalton Posse," a joint effort privately funded by five railroads and three express companies to eradicate the outlaw clan. Dodge and Thomas were "close," they felt—but still a crucial step behind when the gang was massacred at Coffeyville, Kansas, in October 1892.

Eradication of the Daltons meant no rest for Fred Dodge, however. Within a year of the Coffeyville shootout, train robberies had reached an epidemic level in Indian Territory. As Dodge later recalled, "They were coming too fast and thick for one man to work them all." Still, he pressed on, doing his best and jailing more than his fair share of thieves. In 1896 Dodge bought a farm near Bourne, Texas, and settled his family there, but he remained active with Wells Fargo until 1918 when he finally retired from the chase. Dodge died at Bourne on December 16, 1938. A respected local character of whom the local paper wrote:

He had no patience with the rising tendency to glorify early day outlaws as picturesque heroes. He knew them for what they were. We cannot mourn his passing. He was very tired and he had earned his rest.

DONALDSON, Harry: See LOFTUS, HENRY.

DOOLIN, William M. (Bill)

The son of Arkansas farmers, born in 1858, Bill Doolin came late to a life of crime, remaining at home with his family until age 23. Finally tiring of the soil, he drifted into Indian Territory (later Oklahoma) and worked as a wrangler at various ranches along the Kansas-Oklahoma border. On one such job in 1890 or 1891, he met the notorious DALTON BROTHERS, who despite their growing reputation also tried their hands at honest work from time to time (or cased new ranches for potential rustling opportunities, as some would say). In 1891 Doolin attended a party in Coffeyville, Kansas, where too much liquor and noise brought law enforcers to the scene. Shooting broke out and two deputies died, by Doolin's or some other hand. Whatever the truth of the matter, Doolin ran for his life, all the way to the open arms of the Dalton gang.

An Oklahoma historian later called Doolin unique among outlaws of the era in that he "had no wrongs to avenge, no persecutions that drove him into crime." On the contrary, Bill had "tasted the fruits of victory in gunfights and known the excitement and glow that came in train robberies." His first-known outing with the Daltons involved the May 1891 holdup of a train at Wharton (now Perry), Oklahoma, where $1,500 was stolen from the express car. Fleeing past Beaver Creek, the gang rustled a small herd of horses on impulse and then shot it out with a posse that overtook them near Twin Mounds, killing vigilante W. T. Starmer. Four months later, Doolin was along for the ride when the gang robbed another train, this one at Leliaetta, Oklahoma.

And the raiding continued. On June 1, 1892, the gang hit a train at Red Rock station, killing one passenger and escaping with several hundred dollars and a small amount of jewelry. Six weeks later on July 14, Doolin was among the six or eight gang members who invaded Adair, Oklahoma, waiting for the express train to pull in at 9:45 P.M. Surprised by a force of 11 armed guards under Captain J. J. Kinney, the bandits found themselves in a pitched battle, but all members of the gang escaped unscathed. Behind them, they left Kinney and three of his deputies wounded; two local physicians had also been injured—one of them, Doctor W. L. Goff, fatally—by stray shots fired into the local pharmacy.

The last great outing of the Dalton gang occurred on October 8, 1892, in Coffeyville, Kansas. The plan sounded simple enough—split up and rob two banks at once—but the results were disastrous. Bill Doolin missed the massacre, either because his horse went lame en route to Coffeyville or because he had quarreled with Bob Dalton over fair division of loot, and left the gang (reports vary). In either case, he was alive and well, prepared to launch his own gang while the Dalton's made their slow way to Boot Hill.

His first plan was a masterstroke: he mailed a letter to Coffeyville's mayor, threatening to punish the town for gunning down his friends. Instant panic ensued; citizens armed themselves for Doomsday while reinforcements were ordered up; a special trainload of railroad detectives was dispatched to wait at the Coffeyville depot. In the midst of confusion, Doolin led his new gang—including George "Bitter Creek" Newcomb, William "Little Bill" Raidler, and Charlie Pierce—into Caney, 18 miles from Coffeyville, and robbed an unprotected train.

A few days later, on October 21, 1892, the gang stole $18,000 from a bank in Spearville, Kansas, retreating as usual into Indian Territory. Most of the raiders escaped, but gang member Crescent Sam

Yountis drew attention to himself by murdering a farmer for a fresh mount, prompting law enforcers to pursue him with special vigor. Tracked to his sister's home near Guthrie, Oklahoma, Yountis was cornered by a posse and was killed when he went for his gun.

On May 28, 1893, the Doolin gang robbed a train at Cimarron, Kansas, and escaped with $13,000 cash. Another holdup on June 11 proved less fortunate: Unable to open the WELLS FARGO safe with $10,000 inside, the raiders stole $1,000 from a smaller safe and fled with a large posse in hot pursuit. They shook the lawmen off at last but not before a rifle bullet shattered Doolin's foot. He retreated to Ingalls, Oklahoma, where he had secretly married a local woman—one Edith Ellsworth—in April. Edith nursed him back to health, and Doolin was well on the road to recovery when Bill Dalton turned up, looking for work. Unknown to both men, his arrival meant new trouble for the Doolin gang.

Wells Fargo detective FRED DODGE had devoted himself to tracking the Daltons full time for more than a year. Disappointed over missing the action at Coffeyville, he remained dedicated to wiping out remnants of the gang in 1893, and word of Bill Dalton's appearance in Ingalls inspired him to action. Shortly after midnight on September 1, 1893, two wagons rumbled into Ingalls, each with seven armed lawmen aboard. Details of the ensuing pitched battle differ from one report to another, but this much is known: When the smoke cleared, Deputies Tom Houston, Lafe Shadley, and Dick Speed were dead in the street; Doolin and George Newcomb were both wounded, Doolin by a shot to the neck that would pain him for the rest of his life; and young gang recruit ROY "ARKANSAW TOM" DAUGHERTY was captured, held for trial and sentenced to a 50-year prison term on conviction.

Doolin and Newcomb recuperated from their wounds at Hot Springs, Arkansas, launching their next raid in the latter part of 1894. The target was a bank in Southwest City, Missouri, where they bagged $15,000. More shooting erupted as they fled, with Doolin suffering a minor wound. Less fortunate was a pedestrian, former Missouri state auditor J. C. Seaborn, killed on the street as the gang swept past, wounding his brother in the same fusillade.

On April 3, 1895, the Doolin gang hit a train near Dover, Oklahoma, 10 miles north of Kingfisher. An hour's drilling failed to crack the Wells Fargo safe with a $50,000 army payroll inside, and the dis-

gusted bandits settled for some $1,500 in cash, watches, and jewelry stolen from passengers. A posse was organized at El Reno, led by U.S. Deputy Marshal Chris Madsen, and the manhunters literally caught their prey napping, near sundown, beside the Cimarron River. More than 200 shots were fired in the ensuing battle; gang member William "Tulsa Jack" Blake was mortally wounded and left for dead when his comrades escaped into the nearby Glass Mountains. Along the way, raider Red Buck Waightman murdered an elderly farmer while stealing a fresh mount, his wanton act resulting in ouster from the gang after Doolin divided the loot, telling Waightman, "You're too low to associate with a high-class gang of train robbers."

The gang was done, in any case. Dover was Doolin's last raid. Less than a month later, George Newcomb and Charlie Pierce were killed by lawmen in Payne County; DANIEL "DYNAMITE DICK" CLIFTON died in a shootout with marshals a short time later; Bill Raidler was wounded, captured in September, and sentenced to 21 years in prison. Bill Dalton's wife was also arrested in September for running liquor into the Indian Territory; Dalton himself was cornered and killed by a posse on September 25. Outcast gang member Red Buck Waightman was traced to Texas and was killed there by a team of manhunters on October 2, 1895.

In December 1895 word reached Marshal Ben Tilghman that Doolin was relaxing at Eureka Springs, Arkansas, seeking relief from the old bullet wound in his neck that produced occasional seizures and symptoms similar to rheumatism. Tilghman surprised his man at one of the local spas on December 5, arresting him after a brief scuffle and returning him to Guthrie, Oklahoma. There, Doolin turned on the charm for locals and hundreds of tourists who dropped by to visit the jail's star attraction. Security was relaxed enough by January 5, 1896, that Doolin was able to lure a jailer into his cell one night, feigning illness; then he overpowered the guard and fled, releasing three dozen fellow inmates in the process.

Most of the fugitives were swiftly recaptured, one loose-lipped fellow informing lawmen that Doolin planned to leave Oklahoma as soon as he collected his wife and family. U.S. Deputy Marshal Heck Thomas placed the Ellsworth home under surveillance, but another six months passed before the first sighting of Doolin in June. Even then, it was August 1896 before Thomas led a posse to trap the outlaw at his father-in-law's home. Doolin appeared on August 25, surrounded as he stepped down from a wagon in the front yard. He triggered one shot from a Winchester, but the rifle was blasted from his hands. Drawing a six-gun, he fired twice more and then crumpled under a barrage of gunfire, dead before he hit the ground. The posse, proud trophy hunters, removed Doolin's coat and shirt to photograph his bullet-riddled torso as a souvenir of the hunt.

DOUGHERTY, Joseph William: See CONNER, TERRY.

DOYLE, Nathaniel, Jr.

A veteran stickup artist, Nathaniel Doyle ran afoul of federal agents in late 1975 and early 1976, earning his place on the FBI's "Ten Most Wanted" list through a series of wild daylight robberies. In October 1975 a federal warrant was issued on Doyle in Columbus, Ohio, charging him with unlawful flight to avoid prosecution for armed robbery. Three months later a second federal warrant charging him

Bank robber Nathaniel Doyle Jr. was added to the FBI's "Ten Most Wanted" list in 1976. (FBI)

with bank robbery was issued in South Bend, Indiana. In March 1976 Doyle robbed a bank in Fresno, California, escaping from California Highway Patrol officers in a high-speed, bullet-punctuated chase. His name was added to the federal Top Ten list on April 29, 1976.

At 10:00 A.M. on July 15, Doyle and female accomplice Beatrice Brinkley held up a bank in Bellevue, Washington, escaping toward Seattle in a gray sedan. An hour later, Brinkley—already on probation for credit card forgery—was arrested while returning their getaway car to a Seattle rental agency. (Narcotics were also found in her possession at the time of her arrest.) Police routinely checked the address on Brinkley's car-rental contract, confronting her teenage son and fugitive Nat Doyle in the small apartment. Gunfire erupted, wounding Officer Owen McKenna, and Doyle was killed in the exchange; his youthful cohort was taken into custody.

DUNBAR, Charles B.: See BROWN, JOSEPH.

DUNN, Frederick Grant

Frederick Dunn logged his first conviction in 1919 at age 14 when he was sent to the Iowa Training School for Boys at Eldora on charges of breaking and entering and larceny. Paroled in 1921, he was finally discharged in 1924 and was next arrested two months later for the burglary of a general store in Gayville, South Dakota. The proprietor had opened fire on Dunn and two accomplices, striking one of them in the eye. Dunn and his wounded companion were convicted of burglary in November 1924 and sentenced to five years in prison, with Dunn securing parole once more in 1927. Arrested for parole violation in Omaha during May 1928, Dunn was returned to South Dakota's state prison, where he remained until August 1929.

A few weeks later he was linked to the robbery of a bank in Salix, Iowa. Three weeks after that, with a masked accomplice, he held up a store in Sioux City, firing his pistol into the ceiling before he walked out with $67 in cash. In early 1930 Dunn and an accomplice robbed a suburban bank near Sioux City. Arrested in Chicago that February, he was returned to Iowa for trial. Ten days after his arrival in Sioux City, Dunn obtained a smuggled handgun in the jail and led another inmate in a bold escape, shooting one jailer in the thigh when his captor resisted. Dunn managed to elude pursuit but briefly; later in the day,

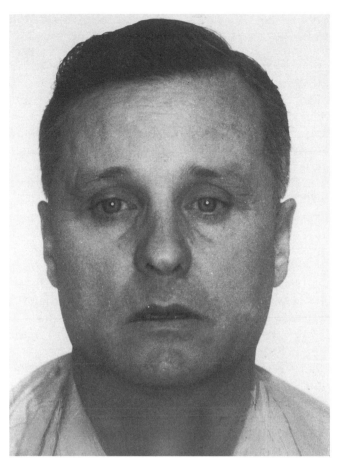

Frederick Dunn's criminal career spanned five decades, from 1919 to 1959. (FBI)

he was surprised by sheriff's deputies in a nearby alley and surrendered after an exchange of gunfire. Sentenced to 40 years for bank robbery and another 30 for assault with intent to kill, Dunn entered the state prison at Fort Madison in March 1930. He was paroled yet again in June 1940.

By that time Dunn had begun to regard himself as a latter-day JOHN DILLINGER, boasting of his prowess at blowing safes with nitroglycerin. On July 2, 1942, he joined two accomplices in looting a Portis, Kansas, bank of $2,861. Although locked inside the vault, a teller freed himself and grabbed a rifle, wounding one of Dunn's companions as they sped away. Outside of town the bandits' vehicle swerved out of control, rolling over several times, but a second getaway car was waiting in the wings and the outlaws eluded pursuers.

On July 21 Dunn and his companions were arrested by the FBI in Denver, Colorado, ultimately sentenced to 15 years on federal charges. (Two women involved in the case as accessories each drew sentences of six years.) Prior to sentencing, hacksaw blades were recovered from Dunn's cell, and he confessed to planning a jailbreak. After consignment to Leavenworth, he was paroled in November 1952, but arrest warrants charging parole violation were issued seven months later. Traced to Kansas City in January 1954, he was found to be in possession of firearms and ammunition and was returned to finish his time in Leavenworth. Dunn was discharged from federal custody on August 16, 1957.

Two months later he was accused of burglarizing a store in Westphalia, Iowa. On November 14 he was arrested in Russell, Kansas, suspected of another burglary in nearby Palco; an indictment on that charge was issued six days later. Dunn was subsequently transferred to the county jail at Lincoln, awaiting trial for the burglary of a grocery store at Sylvan Grove, Kansas, but he escaped from custody on January 11, 1958. Federal warrants charging him with unlawful flight to avoid prosecution were issued on January 16, and his name was added to the FBI's "Most Wanted" list on July 29.

As it developed, Dunn apparently had never fled from Kansas after all. His skeletal remains were found near Ellsworth on September 7, 1959, and finally identified via post-mortem examination on September 18. The cause of death was either suicide or homicide, with murder listed as the safer bet, but either way the rampage of the "modern Dillinger" was over.

DURKIN, Martin James

A professional car thief by trade, 25-year-old Martin Durkin entered criminal history as the first man to kill an FBI agent in the line of duty. It was only the BI (for Bureau of Investigation) in those days, and agents were not authorized to carry firearms, a fact which made the murder less impressive than some later shootouts, but it still propelled Durkin into headlines and resulted in a nightmare chase that ultimately placed him in a prison cell for almost 30 years.

J. EDGAR HOOVER had barely a year on the job as full-time FBI director (and the bureau itself was only 17 years old) on October 11, 1925, when he lost his first agent to hostile fire. G-men had been tracking Martin Durkin for violations of the Dyer Act, a federal law banning transportation of stolen cars across state lines, and Edward B. Shanahan was the agent who tracked him to a Chicago garage. Approaching

Durkin's car, the agent was surprised when Durkin drew a gun and shot him in the chest.

The resulting manhunt was intense, a matter of pride and personal security for every federal agent on the job. According to FBI legend, Hoover summoned an aide to his office on hearing the news of Shanahan's death and ordered, "We've got to get Durkin. If one man from the bureau is killed, and the killer is permitted to get away, our agents will never be safe. We can't let him get away with it."

True or not, the story accurately captured Hoover's attitude. The federal net was flung far and wide, turning up the heat on Durkin no matter where he tried to hide. Matters quickly went from bad to worse in Chicago, where Durkin killed one policeman and wounded another, but he still remained at large. FBI agents traced him to California, where he was linked to a San Diego car theft, and then back through Arizona and New Mexico into Texas. In El Paso he was spotted by a sheriff who noticed the pistol resting beside Durkin and his female companion in a stolen Cadillac. Durkin explained that he was a deputy sheriff from California, passing through town on a vacation. The sheriff agreed to let Durkin retrieve his mythical police ID from a nearby hotel, but Durkin and his lady friend took off into the Texas desert, running scared.

G-men descended on El Paso, heartened by the discovery of Durkin's Cadillac, which had been wrecked and abandoned in a stand of mesquite. A rancher in the neighborhood recalled a man and woman who had shown up on his doorstep, looking for a lift into the nearest town. He had driven them to Girvin and recalled a conversation indicating that they might go on to Alpine, Texas, in hopes of catching a train.

Alpine is the seat of Brewster County, some 50 miles from the Mexican border, but the feds reckoned city-boy Durkin would stay in the States, probably booking passage for some large metropolitan area. A railroad ticket agent in Alpine identified Durkin as the man who had purchased tickets to San Antonio, and there agents learned that Durkin had boarded a train to St. Louis on January 20, 1926. He was scheduled to arrive at 11:00 A.M. that same day, and a hurried telephone call was made to bureau operatives in Missouri. With cooperation from St. Louis police, it was arranged for Durkin's train to stop at a small town outside the city where the station was surrounded by open farmland. Boarding the train in a rush, feds and bluecoats collared Durkin in his private compartment, handcuffing him before he had a chance to reach his guns.

In custody Durkin admitted killing Agent Shanahan, but it was not a federal crime to murder G-men in the 1920s, so Illinois tried him for murder, handing down a 35-year sentence on conviction. The best Washington could do was to try Durkin in federal court for Dyer Act violations, and conviction on those counts cost him another 15 years. Durkin was released from Illinois state prison on August 8, 1945, and transferred directly to the federal lockup at Leavenworth, Kansas. He was finally paroled at age 54 on July 28, 1954.

E

ELLIOTT, Aussie

A Depression-era bandit, Oklahoma-born in 1914, Aussie Elliott robbed his first-known bank at age 18. Convicted and sentenced to prison, he chafed at confinement and escaped from the McAlester state penitentiary on August 14, 1932. He hit the big time soon thereafter, teaming up with veteran outlaws GEORGE BIRDWELL and CHARLES "PRETTY BOY" FLOYD. On November 1, 1932, the trio stole $2,530 from a bank at Sallisaw, Oklahoma. Six days later, they were identified by witnesses as the bandits who looted a Henryetta bank of $11,352, but some reports attribute that raid to the FORD BRADSHAW gang.

Elliott was definitely involved in the $3,000 robbery of a bank at Ash Grove, Missouri, on January 12, 1933. He teamed with ADAM RICHETTI and Edgar Dunbar for that outing, afterward fleeing to the home of Richetti's brother in Bolivar, Missouri. Captured in Creek County, Oklahoma, on May 14, 1933, Elliott endured five months of confinement before escaping on October 28. He spent the last months of his life on the lam, refusing to leave Oklahoma despite the incessant heat. On February 3, 1934, he was cornered near Sapulpa, Oklahoma, in company with bandits Raymond Moore and Eldon Wilson. A pitched battle ensued, ending the lives of all three outlaws; also killed in the engagement were Sapulpa Police Chief Tom Brumley and Patrolman Charles Lloyd.

ELLIS, Frank P. "Frank E. Smith"

Frank Ellis got a rocky start in crime. Convicted of a California bank robbery in 1909, he spent the next 10 years confined at San Quentin. A 1922 burglary conviction in Washington next sent him to the state reformatory, where he stayed through most of 1925. He must have honed his skills in prison, though, because his name would not be linked to any other crimes for five long years.

It should not be supposed that Ellis had gone straight, of course. In retrospect, police identified him as the leader of a gang that stole $50,000 worth of liquor from a Fresno, California, winery in March 1928. A short time later, he planned and carried out the $26,000 burglary of a U.S. post office at Tracy, California. It was TRAIN ROBBERY, though, that gave Ellis his true claim to fame—although, ironically, his first score on the rails was wrongly credited to members of a rival gang.

On June 22, 1929, Southern Pacific Railroad Train No. 36 was stopped by bandits at McAvoy, California, in Contra Costa County. Two of the raiders were aboard the train armed with pistols and Thompson submachine guns, while a third man waited on the tracks, crouched behind a tripod-mounted World War I machine gun. Engineer Joe Barnes was shot in the arm, scuffling with a gunman who invaded his locomotive cab, but otherwise no blood was shed, the bandits herding 15 passengers and crewmen off the train into a trackside ditch.

Inside the mail car, clerk Ralph Tyler was initially defiant, but a storm of 200 machine-gun bullets ripped the car's door from its hinges, whereupon Tyler tossed out canvas bags containing $19,000 in cash. The gang fled in a Hudson sedan, later doused with gasoline and blasted with dynamite at an abandoned cement plant, midway between Bay Point and Concord. Witnesses observed the robbers switching to another vehicle—an Overland coupe—with a blond woman at the wheel. The burned-out Hudson was traced to Los Angeles where it had been purchased by one "James Hendrix." Authorities suspected that "Hendrix" was really Doctor C. O. DeMoss, an ex-physician member of the FLEAGLE GANG, but he was never charged, and police wasted months in pursuit of the wrong criminals.

Three months after the McAvoy holdup, on September 26, masked bandits invaded a bank at Rodeo, California, scooping $27,000 into their satchels. Sheriff Arthur McDonald, off duty, walked in on the holdup and drew his pistol, trading shots with the gunmen until he collapsed with multiple wounds. One of the robbers was also hit, dropping his Tommy gun as he lurched from the bank. A Dodge touring car, waiting outside for the gang, was recovered hours later in the hills above Berkeley. Once again, eyewitnesses had glimpsed the auto switch, describing the gang's second getaway car as a brown Hupmobile sedan with a blond woman driving.

Police still thought they were tracking Jake Fleagle's gang, and they refused to drop the theory even after an informer pointed them toward Frank Ellis, recently seen at the wheel of a brown Hupmobile in San Francisco, where he showed unhealthy interest in the payroll deliveries at several factories. The Hupmobile was traced to a dealer's lot where Ellis had traded in an Overland coupe that resembled the McAvoy getaway car. Accordingly, law enforcers adjusted their hypothesis to treat Ellis as a member of the Fleagle gang, placing various friends and associates under surveillance.

While that exercise was under way, Ellis and company took another shot at Southern Pacific Train No. 36. Five bandits were involved this time on November 7, 1930, when the train was hijacked a quarter-mile out of Berkeley and stopped at the deserted Nobel station. Armed with submachine guns, pistols, and dynamite, the bandits persuaded mail clerk John McClintock to open his car, extracting sacks of currency and coins that totaled nearly $50,000. Loading

their haul into a stolen Studebaker sedan, the thieves dropped a sack containing $1,000 in silver dollars but escaped with the rest of the loot. True to form, the Studebaker was abandoned not far from the point where the Dodge touring car was recovered in September 1929.

Jake Fleagle was dead by this time, gunned down on a Missouri train in October 1930, and three members of his gang executed in Colorado the previous July. Belatedly, police recognized that they were dealing with an altogether different gang and rushed to do their homework on Frank Ellis. Investigators learned that back in 1928, when he purchased the Overland coupe used for the McAvoy robbery, Ellis had listed the Alameda, California, address of brother-in-law Ted Lyda. Lyda, in turn, directed police to an Oakland cottage that Ellis shared with his wife. A raiding party was swiftly organized, including railroad detectives, Alameda County sheriff's deputies, Oakland and Berkeley policemen, U.S. Secret Service agents, and U.S. postal inspectors. They caught Ellis with his pants down, literally, sitting on the toilet in his cottage, and seized two rifles, two pistols, two bulletproof vests, handcuffs, a quantity of narcotics and hypodermic needles, $400 in currency, and several rolls of quarters from the latest holdup.

Though embarrassed, Ellis was not without resources. Law enforcers failed to notice a sedan trailing their convoy as they drove him to the Oakland post office for questioning. On arrival, Ellis shrugged off his captors and ran for the car, which swung in to the curb, an unidentified man at the wheel. Before Ellis could reach the car, though, Secret Service Agent Leonard Schmidt dropped him with a pistol shot, and the getaway driver sped off. Ellis died an hour later, at a local hospital, without making a statement to police. Evalyn Ellis was equally tight-lipped in custody, refusing even to acknowledge that Ted Lyda was her brother. It hardly mattered, though, because crewmen from the McAvoy holdup identified Ellis as one of the train robbers, while another witness identified Evalyn as the Rodeo heist getaway driver. Another search of the Oakland cottage turned up keys to a safe-deposit box, rented in the names of "William and Evalyn Sherrod," where $6,000 in hot loot was recovered.

With Ellis gone and his wife in custody, it still remained for lawmen to identify the other members of his gang. They got a start by questioning ex-convict W. T. Mallahan, Evalyn's brother-in-law who resided in Seattle. Mallahan denied any active link to the gang but admitted that his brother James (another ex-con) had traveled to California with Ellis in November 1930, writing chatty letters home about the Nobel robbery and other jobs. One of the gang members identified by Mallahan was Charles Berta, sought by authorities for various felonies in Seattle and San Francisco (including the murder of San Francisco Patrolman John Malcolm during a holdup).

Investigation of Berta linked him to an October 1930 incident at Hilt, California, where he and a male companion were stopped at a highway quarantine station. A search of their Chrysler sedan turned up two Tommy guns, whereupon the men first tried bribery and then drew pistols and fled. The Chrysler had Washington plates, traced to Seattle buyer "T. H. Ward"—who was, in turn, identified from photographs as Berta. The cashier's check he used to buy the car had been purchased by Seattle attorney John Garvin, who admitted that Berta had been funding Evalyn Ellis's legal defense. Engineer Peter Lemery identified Berta as one of the Nobel train robbers, but he remained at large. Reward-hungry tipsters steered law enforcers to an Oakland apartment occupied by Berta through December 1, 1930, and laundry marks were obtained from some of his discarded clothing and circulated quietly in an attempt to track him down.

Other members of the gang had been identified, meanwhile, from notations in a notebook carried by Frank Ellis. Aside from Charles Berta, they included east coast syndicate gunman Edward J. Kenny, James Sargert (aka "California Eddie") and Edward Shannon. An address from the notebook led detectives to a Seattle apartment house where Shannon had lived until December 5, 1930, as "E. R. Sherwood." From there, he was backtracked to a Seattle hotel that had been abandoned in haste on November 8, Shannon forgetting to collect $195.50 in coins from the Nobel robbery. Traced from Seattle to Olympia, Washington, and back again, Shannon was captured at a roadblock outside Seattle, traveling with three innocent companions, $246 in stolen coins, and a large stash of narcotics. He also carried keys to several safe-deposit boxes, each of which yielded more loot from the Nobel heist.

Charles Berta was the next to fall, traced to the Seattle apartment he shared with a girlfriend. He was out when the raiders arrived, but they caught him a short time later, standing at a nearby bus stop,

dressed in a cadet's uniform. Accosted by police, Berta shouted, "Help! It's a stickup!" His cries drew attention from a passing patrolman, the ensuing confusion permitting Berta to draw one of his two pistols and squeeze off two shots before he was wounded and disarmed. Delivered to U.S. marshals on January 31, 1931, Berta was en route to California for trial when hikers found two suitcases he had stashed on the shore of Lake Washington. Inside the bags were clothing with his laundry marks, a Tommy gun, three rifles, two pistols, and a bulletproof vest.

Seattle authorities nearly bagged Edward Kenny as well, circulating descriptions of his car, but Kenny outran a mail driver who spotted him one afternoon, and he fled eastward to his old haunts on the Atlantic seaboard. On June 12, 1931, he was machine-gunned to death by rival mobsters in Camden, New Jersey, for poaching on their prostitution turf.

Ed Shannon and Evalyn Ellis faced trial in San Francisco on April 28, 1931, for train robbery and conspiracy. The prosecution called 56 witnesses, proving (among other things) that Ellis and her late husband had tried to buy dynamite on June 20, 1929, and failing that had stolen explosives from a quarry storehouse. Convicted on May 4, both defendants were sentenced to 25 years in federal prison. Charles Berta was convicted on identical charges and received the same sentence on September 19, 1931.

James Sargert was the last member of the Ellis gang still at large, identified from photographs by a truant teenager who saw the Nobel robbers together after the holdup. Spurred by a $2,000 reward, an informant tipped police in October 1931 that Sargert was living in Portland, Oregon. He was captured at home on November 5 by a mixed posse of Portland police, U.S. postal inspectors, railroad detectives, and Oregon state troopers. Arrested with Sargert were a girlfriend and auto dealer Ivan Quirk, who had supplied the holdup gang with several cars. Sargert waived extradition and was returned to San Francisco for trial on December 1, was convicted at trial four days later, and was sentenced to a 25-year prison term like his confederates.

The story should have ended there, but confinement grated on some members of the shattered Ellis gang. Charles Berta, with six other convicts, seized rifles and the warden of Leavenworth federal prison on December 11, 1931, escaping in a flurry of gunfire. Three escapees were cornered and killed in a house near the prison; Berta was recaptured after a running battle in a nearby farmer's field. The last man still at large, Earl Thayer of the old AL SPENCER gang, made it as far as Leavenworth proper before he was overtaken and disarmed. James Sargert made his own escape attempt in April 1932 from the federal lockup at McNeil Island, Washington, but he never made it off the island; he was found April 18 concealed beneath some building materials. A second attempt to flee from the Tacoma courthouse, during his February 1933 trial on escape charges, left Sargert dazed from a fall, and he was shipped out to join Berta on The Rock of Alcatraz in 1934.

EMBRY, Ollie Gene

Ollie Embry was a self-styled ladies' man and a two-gun bandit who relied on Benzedrine to quicken his reactions in a holdup. Born in Arkansas, he was arrested for the first time as a highway robber at the tender age of 15 years. By early 1951 he had served time in California, Texas, and Colorado, with a stint at the federal reformatory in El Reno, Oklahoma.

On February 6, 1951, four gunmen entered the Monroe National Bank in Columbia, Illinois, 10 minutes after it reopened from lunch. They lined up employees and swept $8,943 from the cages, scattering two-inch roofing nails in the street to halt pursuers as they fled the scene. Their getaway had been meticulously planned, using three different cars, but luck was running hard against the outlaws. Teenage wheelman Frank Daubauch was soon arrested on a tip from neighbors, and he started to drop names. His cronies Jack McAllister and Patrick Kane (reputed planner of the raid) were picked up hours later; some $8,000 of the loot was recovered by arresting officers. In unison, the bandits gave up Ollie Embry as the one who got away.

The robbery itself had been a federal crime under statutes dating from the 1930s; other charges lodged against Embry included interstate transportation of stolen property and violation of the Dyer Act (the driving of a stolen car across state lines). Embry's name was posted to the FBI's "Most Wanted" list on July 25. He had 10 days of freedom left.

On August 5 a plainclothes officer, James Messick, spotted Embry pumping gas in Kansas City. Messick tipped the FBI, and Lee Boardman, special agent in charge, led a raiding party to the service station where Embry was employed. The agents posed as customers, surrounding Ollie as he bent to check beneath their hood. Comparison of fingerprints conducted at the scene confirmed their recognition of

the fugitive, and he was carted back to Illinois for trial.

EVANS, Chris, and SONTAG, John

A Vermont native, born in May 1847, Chris Evans was still a toddler when his family moved to Canada and failed to make a go of farming. In 1896, with a younger brother, Evans tried his hand at prospecting in California and Nevada, but the "mother lode" eluded him. Settling in California's San Joaquin Valley, Evans married and sired the first of seven children, but he soon lost his homestead when the title proved faulty. Moving on to Tulare, he divided his time between farming and clerking at a local bank. He saved enough money to open a livery stable at Modesto, working with the Southern Pacific Railroad, but a fire destroyed the stable and his livestock, uprooting the family once more. His last fling at honest labor brought Evans back to the soil, farming 20 acres owned by his in-laws near Visalia.

It was there he met the Sontag brothers, Minnesota natives born John and George Constant in the early 1860s, better known by the surname of their stepfather. The brothers had come west in 1878, working for the Southern Pacific out of Fresno, but brakeman John had suffered grievous injury when his ankle was crushed between two railroad cars. His treatment at the railroad's private hospital in Sacramento had been less than satisfactory. Ordered back to work before his leg was fully healed, John had requested lighter duty and was fired instead. Chris Evans befriended the Sontag brothers, sharing their contempt for the Southern Pacific that was a common trait of California farmers in the 1890s, but he had reservations about John, once describing the elder Sontag to his wife as "a bad actor, a man who doesn't possess the hardy qualities of his brother, the cheapest kind of bandit who has it in him to turn traitor."

Those harsh views notwithstanding, Evans allowed John to live with him on the family spread and soon joined the Sontags in planning a series of railroad heists. Their first outing occurred on February 22, 1889, when they boarded a Southern Pacific train at Pixley and forced the engineer to stop two miles south of town. WELLS FARGO agent J. R. Kelly refused to open the express car on demand, so they lobbed a bomb inside and blew the doors off. Conductor Jackson Symington recruited brakeman Henry Grabert and off-duty deputy sheriff Ed Bentley to corral the robbers, but the would-be heroes found themselves outgunned. A shotgun blast killed Grabert outright, while Bentley's left arm was nearly severed at the shoulder by a second shot. The unidentified bandits escaped on horseback with $5,000 in gold.

Eleven months later, at 4:00 A.M. on January 24, 1890, they repeated the exercise with a train leaving Goshen. This time, with the Pixley shootout in mind, the express agent yielded on command and tossed out a sack containing $20,000. It should have been a bloodless coup, but a hobo riding the train free of charge mistook its unscheduled stop for arrival at his destination. One of the bandits, surprised as the man scrambled out from his place beneath one of the cars, shot and killed him on sight.

The gang's third holdup involved Southern Pacific Train No. 19, boarded at Modesto and stopped at nearby Ceres on September 3, 1891. This time, the bandits fired off several warning shots to keep the passengers inside their coaches, but the fusillade alerted Wells Fargo express agents to barricade their car. A bomb blew in the door, but still the agents balked at surrender, threatening to kill anyone who entered the car, hostage crewmen included. A second bomb was thrown, but it failed to explode. By that time, two railroad detectives had crept from their berth and opened fire on the bandits, driving them off empty handed.

The failure drove them eastward to escape impending heat. On November 5, 1891, Evans and the Sontags took $4,800 from a train at Western Union Junction near Chicago and escaped without firing a shot. George Sontag liked the easy pickings, plugging for a spree in the Midwest, but Evans missed his family, and the younger Sontag found himself outvoted two-to-one on a return to California. In passing, the trio tried robbing a train near Kasota Junction, Nebraska, but the abortive job yielded nothing. Law enforcers drew no link between their California killers and the two midwestern jobs until George confessed in custody months later and cleared up the mystery.

The gang's last holdup as a unit occurred at 11:15 P.M. on August 3, 1892, when Evans and the Sontags stopped a Southern Pacific train at Collis, California (near Visalia), and opened the Wells Fargo car with a dynamite charge, severely wounding the express agent. Their loot totaled $15,000 in cash, but $2,000 of the haul turned out to be useless Peruvian coins. Before fleeing the scene, the bandits strapped a bomb to the locomotive's left piston rod, to disable the train and forestall a report of the holdup.

A $25,000 reward offer set tongues wagging around Visalia, where hatred of the railroad ran high and suspects were plentiful. Railroad detective William Smith initially discounted reports that Evans and John Sontag had made disparaging remarks about the Southern Pacific line—indeed, who among their neighbors had not?—but his focus narrowed on learning that both men had bitter dealings with the railroad in their past. Calling at the Evans farm with Deputy Sheriff Ed Witty, Smith asked for John Sontag and quarreled with Eva Evans—Chris's eldest daughter—when she said John was away. The argument was heating up—Smith would admit calling the girl "a goddamned liar"—when Sontag appeared with a shotgun and wounded both officers, driving them into a hasty retreat.

Pausing barely long enough to bandage their wounds, Smith and Witty recruited a posse and rode back to the Evans farm that night, staking out the house. Evans and Sontag had already left, but they returned before dawn and another shootout erupted, leaving Deputy Sheriff Oscar Beaver dead before the outlaws fled a second time. Smith jailed George Sontag as a kind of consolation prize and was startled when the prisoner confessed his role in the Collis holdup and five other robberies. Tried at Fresno in October 1892, George was convicted of the Collis holdup and sentenced to a life term at Folsom Prison.

Brother John and Chris Evans, meanwhile, remained elusive. A Wells Fargo search party found four bags of loot buried in the Evans barnyard, including the worthless Peruvian coins. Indictments for murder and train robbery were filed, but they meant little in the absence of defendants. Lured by reward offers, an informer pointed law enforcers toward an old mining claim that Evans maintained at Sampson's Flat, and a posse was organized to seek him there. Unfortunately for the law officers, they rode into an ambush and were blasted from their saddles. Dead at the scene were V. C. Wilson of Tucson, a former Texas Ranger and leader of the posse, and Deputy Sheriff Andy McGinnis from Modesto. Deputy Witty was wounded again, this time by buckshot in the neck, but Will Smith claimed to have wounded Chris Evans before the two gunmen escaped.

It was his last glimpse of the bandits for 10 months; Evans and Sontag went underground in the Sierras, living in a cave above Dry Creek, a few miles southeast of Camp Badger, near the border of present-day Sequoiah National Park. Hunting and fishing for food, sometimes sleeping over with friends who admired their exploits, the fugitives dodged posses and kept a low profile for the most part, spending Christmas and New Year's at the Evans spread near Visalia, with law enforcers none the wiser. Will Smith learned of that holiday visit after the fact, posting guards around the farm, and Evans took it badly. In April 1893 he and Sontag stopped a stagecoach near Camp Badger, believing Smith and several of his "blood hunters" to be aboard. In fact, there were no law officers in the coach; the passengers were left with their belongings intact, advised by Sontag that he and Evans had "never robbed a person of a cent and never robbed a train."

Local sentiment ran heavily in favor of California's last SOCIAL BANDITS, heightened soon after the Camp Badger incident when Evans mailed a letter to the *Fresno Expositor*. Editors published the note, which was addressed to Chris's wife and closed with a plaintive request that she "kiss the babies for papa." George Sontag's confessions had deflated public claims that Evans and the brothers were innocent men; still, hatred of the railroads ran deep enough with California's farmers and small merchants that it hardly seemed to matter.

On May 26, 1893, Evans and Sontag ambushed another posse near Camp Badger, driving the lawmen away from their hideout with one rider shot through the leg. Two days later, while the bandits were out prowling, a 14-man posse returned in their absence and laid a reverse ambush—determined, some would later say, to take no prisoners. Lawmen opened fire without warning at first sight of Evans and Sontag, toppling Chris from his saddle with a shattered left arm. Sontag, also wounded, joined his partner in the meager sanctuary of a small manure pile, trading shots with the manhunters and holding them at bay while afternoon faded into dusk.

Evans saw his opportunity at nightfall, crawling more than six miles through the woods to reach a neighbor's cabin, where he was admitted without question. Sontag, meanwhile, had been shot at least six times—including one round to the face—and was unfit to travel. Rushed and overpowered by his opponents shortly after dawn on May 29, he died on the wagon ride back to Visalia. Evans was tracked by his blood trail, arrested the same afternoon, and held for trial on charges of robbery and murder.

With money for defense lawyers in short supply, Evans's wife and eldest daughter outraged public opinion by joining the cast of a stage play entitled *The Collis Train Robbery*, playing to a crowded house at San Francisco's National Theater. Local ministers condemned the drama's pandering to "a depraved public taste, glorifying crime, bloodshed and defiance of law," but the women earned $1,700 from their star turn and seemed to have no regrets.

Chris Evans went on trial at Fresno on November 20, 1893, and was convicted of first-degree murder on December 13 with a jury recommendation of life imprisonment. Before he saw the inside of a prison cell, however, daughter Eva befriended café waiter Ed Morrell—an admirer of Evans who served the outlaw's nightly meals—and persuaded him to help Evans escape. Morrell smuggled a pistol in to Evans with his dinner one night and waited across the street with a team and wagon for his hero to emerge. Startled by the unexpected appearance of Police Chief J.D. Morgan, Morrell opened fire with his own sidearm, wounding Morgan but spooking his own team in the process. Flabbergasted as the horses took off with his wagon, Morrell recovered in time to steal a new team and beat a retreat with Evans beside him.

Thus began the last ride of the Evans gang. On January 11, 1894, Evans and Morrell robbed several passengers at the Southern Pacific depot in Fowler, California. Back at Camp Badger in early February, they drove several law enforcers away from their hideout with gunfire, stirring memories of last year's bloody shootouts. Rather than confront the gunmen again on a wilderness battleground, Will Smith spread false rumors that Evans's youngest daughter was dying of diphtheria. When Evans and Morrell arrived to visit her, they were surrounded and gave up their guns without a fight. Evans was packed off at once to begin his life sentence at Folsom. Morrell was convicted of horse theft and sentenced to life; his sentence was commuted in March 1908. George Sontag was pardoned the same week as a belated reward for turning state's evidence in 1892. Chris Evans was paroled on May 1, 1911, in broken health and died penniless in a California poorhouse in January 1917.

EVERETT, Gilbert James

Born June 26, 1939, Gilbert Everett worked variously as a car salesman, a mapmaker, and a topographer when not involved in crime, but his first love was bank robbery. Arrested for robbery at Knoxville, Tennessee, in September 1980, Everett escaped from federal custody later that month and fled to Alabama in a stolen car, racking up new charges for violation of the Dyer Act. Further warrants were issued in November after he took down another bank in

Orlando, Florida, and Everett's name was added to the FBI's "Ten Most Wanted" list on May 13, 1981.

Undaunted by his notoriety, Everett robbed yet another bank—this one in Sacramento, California—in January 1983. The money was his traveling stake, and Everett was northbound, shaking off pursuit as

he lost himself in the wilds of Alaska. It took the better part of three more years, but federal agents traced him to his hideaway and took Everett into custody on August 12, 1985. He was subsequently convicted and sentenced to prison.

FARMER, Herbert Allen "Deafy"

A con man and pickpocket with a long arrest record, Herb Farmer also had a violent side as witnessed by his five-year prison term in Oklahoma for assault with intent to kill. It was there in the state pen at McAlester that Farmer met fledgling outlaw Fred Barker and a host of other outlaws who would be his friends (and later customers) for life. In prison, Farmer sometimes adopted the role of a tutor to younger, up-and-coming felons, one FBI report noting that "it is safe to assume that Fred Barker received considerable education in the school of crime from Farmer."

Once he was paroled, Farmer—also variously known as Harry Garner, William Hilary Baker, and sundry other pseudonyms—found a new line of work, settling on a farm seven miles south of Joplin, Missouri. Farmer had no intention of living up to his name, however; instead, with wife Esther, he operated a lucrative "crook motel," providing safe haven for fugitives on the lam, exchanging hot cars and loot, patching wounds, obtaining weapons— any service, in short, that hunted criminals could not obtain through legitimate channels. At one time or another, Farmer's clients included members of the BARKER-KARPIS gang, CLYDE BARROW and BONNIE PARKER, HARVEY BAILEY, FRANK NASH, and WILBUR UNDERHILL among others. There were no complaints from Farmer's fly-by-night tourists, and Missouri law enforcers could usually be paid to look the other way.

That changed on June 17, 1933, after Frank Nash and four lawmen were killed in the infamous KANSAS CITY MASSACRE. A federal agent was among the dead, prompting J. EDGAR HOOVER to demand answers and arrests at any cost. Investigators quickly learned that three telephone calls had been made from Hot Springs, Arkansas (the scene of Frank Nash's arrest on June 16), to Farmer's place in Missouri. A raid turned up no evidence of any criminal activity, but officers staked out the farm, arresting Herb and Esther when they finally returned on July 7. By that time, FBI agents had persuaded Frances Nash to implicate the Farmers as conspirators in an abortive rescue that had claimed her husband's life. Harvey Bailey and Wilbur Underhill were initially suspected as the triggermen, but G-men later shifted their focus to VERNON MILLER, ADAM RICHETTI, and CHARLES "PRETTY BOY" FLOYD. Before that change of heart, on September 13, 1933, a federal grand jury indicted 10 persons for allegedly obstructing justice in the massacre case. The Farmers were charged, along with Bailey, Underhill, Frances Nash, escaped convict ROBERT BRADY, and four others.

Herb and Esther were both convicted, though Esther would serve no prison time. Her husband was packed off for two years on The Rock at Alcatraz and then returned to Missouri after his release. They sold the farm and moved into Joplin proper, where Farmer died on January 12, 1948. Harvey Bailey was paroled in March 1965 and married Esther in

October 1966. Esther Farmer Bailey survived her second outlaw husband by two years, dying peacefully in 1981.

FARRINGTON, Hillary and Levi

Natives of western Tennessee who worked a hard-scrabble farm before 1861, Hillary and Levi Farrington rode with WILLIAM QUANTRILL's guerrillas in the Civil War, learning banditry as a military tactic with the likes of JESSE JAMES and the YOUNGER BROTHERS. Armed robbery was a hard habit to break in the Reconstruction era, when Southern landowners suffered from the ravages of war, and a push for black political equality threatened the very "southern way of life" below the Mason-Dixon Line. Some angry veterans joined the Ku Klux Klan to wage unending war against the "Radical Republicans" in Washington, while others merely sought to fill their pockets with ill-gotten gains.

In October 1871 the Farrington brothers led a gang that robbed the Mobile & Ohio Railroad on its run through Tennessee, looting the train's Southern Express car and shooting a messenger in the chest. Private detective ALAN PINKERTON dispatched his brothers William and Robert to solve the case, their investigation soon leading them to the Farrington farm. Hillary and Levi were away at the time, but a chat with their mother sent the Pinkerton's sniffing after clues in neighboring Kentucky. William was recalled to New York City on business, but Robert pressed on with an ex-policeman from Memphis, Patrick Connell. They overtook four members of the Farrington gang near Lester's Landing, Kentucky, and a shootout ensued. Pinkerton and Connell both were wounded, but still they managed to beat their adversaries unconscious and clap them in irons, after which Pinkerton removed a bullet from Connell's stomach with a corn knife.

Hillary and Levi Farrington missed that dramatic encounter, but William Pinkerton was relentless. He tracked Hillary to Missouri and arrested him there, but the bandit tried to escape on the homeward journey, tumbling to his death from the upper railing of a stern-wheel riverboat. A few months later, Pinkerton trailed Levi Farrington to Illinois and brought him back to Tennessee alive but all in vain. Shortly before his scheduled trial, a mob of vigilantes stormed the Memphis jail where he was held and riddled him with bullets in his cell.

FBI: U.S. Federal Bureau of Investigation

America's first national police force was created by U.S. Attorney General Charles Bonaparte in May 1908 over stern objections from Congress. The action was illegal, but the U.S. House Appropriations Committee grudgingly approved in January 1909, with specific instructions that the Bureau of Investigation (renamed FBI in 1935) be used only to pursue antitrust violations, postal fraud, impersonation of government officials with intent to defraud, destruction of federal property, violation of federal banking laws, and thefts or murders committed on Indian reservations. Those limits were removed in 1910 when Congress approved funds "for such other investigations regarding official matters under the control of the Department of Justice as may be directed by the Attorney General."

Under that vague mandate, the FBI was soon empowered to investigate "white slavery" (the Mann Act, 1910) and interstate theft of automobiles (the Dyer Act, 1919). World War I saw sweeping persecution of conscientious objectors and "slackers," while the postwar Red Scare launched the FBI's crusade against "radical" thought that has continued with slight variations to the present day. Most crimes—including robbery and murder—were still prosecuted in state courts, unless the heists involved theft of federal property of items from the U.S. mail. Mail thefts led FBI agents to investigate various TRAIN ROBBERIES through the early 1920s; BANK ROBBERY was still beyond the scope of federal authority when such Depression-era bandits as JOHN DILLINGER and HARVEY BAILEY began to make national headlines. FBI mythology further maintains that agents were forbidden from making arrests or carrying firearms until June 1934, but even a casual review of bureau history reveals thousands of arrests made before that date by agents who were frequently armed to the teeth.

The watershed event of FBI law-enforcement history was the KANSAS CITY MASSACRE of June 17, 1933. Federal agents and local police were transporting escaped convict FRANK NASH back to Leavenworth prison when they were ambushed by gunmen in the parking lot of Kansas City's Union Station. The FBI agents were armed, but it did them no good: 30 seconds of gunfire left Nash and four of his seven escorts dead, among them FBI Agent Raymond Caffrey. Investigation demonstrated that most of the fatal wounds were inflicted by another federal agent handling an unfamiliar weapon, but FBI Director J.

EDGAR HOOVER buried that evidence, announcing a long list of gangster suspects before he finally settled on VERNON MILLER, ADAM RICHETTI, and CHARLES "PRETTY BOY" FLOYD as the Kansas City assassins. Miller had indeed organized the bungled rescue attempt, but evidence was slim against Floyd and nonexistent against Richetti. Still, the international publicity was a godsend for Hoover's FBI, and he milked it for all it was worth.

The massacre came at an opportune time for Hoover and his agents. Public outrage echoed in Washington, where on July 13, 1933, U.S. Attorney General Homer Cummings called for sweeping new laws to combat "racketeers." On April 26, 1934, the House Judiciary Committee rushed action on a package of six new anticrime bills that (among other things) penalized robbery of federally insured banks and the murder of their employees. President Franklin Roosevelt signed the bills on May 18, 1934. One month later, on June 18, Congress granted FBI agents full arrest powers and the right to carry firearms without first obtaining "special permission."

The irony of that vote was apparently lost on Americans who followed the FBI's "crime war" via florid headlines. The truth about Kansas City was suppressed for six decades, while FBI agents went about their task of "cleaning up" America. Nine months before they were empowered to arrest or carry weapons, in September 1933, agents seized GEORGE "MACHINE GUN" KELLY in Memphis, spreading a false story that he had nicknamed them "G-men." Eleven weeks before the grant of powers, federal agents fatally wounded Dillinger gang member EDDIE GREEN in ST. PAUL, MINNESOTA. Less than three weeks later, on April 22, Chicago G-man MELVIN PURVIS led a raiding party to Wisconsin and shot it out with the Dillinger gang, gunning down three innocent civilians and losing one of his own men in the process, while the gang escaped en masse.

The tide turned three months later, with the execution-style shooting of John Dillinger in Chicago, followed shortly by the violent deaths of Charles Floyd, GEORGE "BABY FACE" NELSON, RUSSELL GIBSON, "Ma" Barker, and her son Fred. J. Edgar Hoover was criticized in Congress during 1935 for his lack of personal experience with felons, but he remedied that deficiency in May 1936 with the arrest of ALVIN KARPIS, which was staged as Hoover's "personal" capture. Six months later he repeated the performance, this time giving credit to his chief assistant (and

alleged gay lover) Clyde Tolson for the arrest of fugitive bank robber HARRY BRUNETTE.

It was all great publicity for the swiftly-growing FBI, and few Americans questioned the Bureau's tactics when unarmed suspects (or innocent bystanders) were gunned down. Despite rampant criminal behavior that included thousands of illegal burglaries and wiretaps, collaboration with violent racist groups, illegal domestic political surveillance, and outright blackmail, the FBI's pristine reputation remained immune to criticism in mainstream America until Hoover's death in 1972. Probing investigations followed that event and the collapse of President Richard Nixon's corrupt administration, leading Congress to impose new restrictions on FBI activity, but federal jurisdiction survives in respect to bank robbery and has expanded into many other areas, keeping pace with the times and the advance of new technology. Numerous bank robbers have graced the FBI's "Ten Most Wanted" list since its creation in 1950, beginning with Depression-era bandit THOMAS HOLDEN and including WILLIE "THE ACTOR" SUTTON. Violators of state robbery laws may also be pursued by G-men if they cross state lines to avoid prosecution or flee confinement following conviction. Development of computer technology has posed new challenges for federal manhunters, as millions of dollars may be transferred internationally with a few keystrokes.

Pursuit of bank robbers typically involved FBI agents with local police, and the results are not always pretty. Locals frequently accuse G-men of claiming undue credit for arrests or otherwise usurping state and municipal authority. In Los Angeles County, California (as reported by author Sanford Ungar in his book *FBI* [1976]), relations between city police and the county sheriff's office were once so strained that the local FBI field office had to maintain *two* bank-robbery investigation teams, one to collaborate with each contentious agency as a means of keeping peace.

When an FBI investigation succeeds, though, it can be a spectacular event. A case in point occurred on August 28, 1981, when G-men in New York City recovered $50 million in stolen federal home-mortgage guarantee bonds. The negotiable bearer bonds had been reported missing on August 20 by a messenger who claimed to have lost them in the Wall Street financial district. FBI agents posed as underworld brokers for the bonds and met with three suspects at a Midtown luxury hotel. There, G-men paid

$65,000 for bonds worth $500,000 and flashed another $1 million in cash as a sign of good faith. A second meeting was arranged to close the deal, and agents sprang their trap, arresting the trio and recovering the balance of the $50 million shipment. Also seized at the arrest were an additional $1 million in stolen bonds, $2,000 in $100 bills, five pistols, two rifles, a bulletproof vest, and a box of ammunition. The suspects were charged and ultimately convicted on federal counts of embezzlement, theft of public money, and conspiracy.

FELIZ, Claudio

A Mexican bandit active in gold-rush-era California, Claudio Feliz was a brother-in-law of JOAQUIN MURRIETA who turned to crime before his notorious relative hit the outlaw trail. Born in 1832, by age 16, Feliz was prospecting near Sonora, but panning for gold was hard work, and Feliz preferred stealing nuggets from his partners. Fleeing with his loot to Stockton, California, he was caught and briefly jailed but soon escaped from custody.

By late 1850 Feliz was recognized as the leader of a ruthless outlaw gang, loosely organized, impulsive, and violent. The outfit's first raid was recorded on December 5 when Flores led a dozen riders to attack the ranch of one John Marsh, located west of Mt. Diablo in Contra Costa County. They shot and lanced one farmhand to death and then ransacked Marsh's house, making off with $300 cash plus some guns and gold watches. Ten days later the band struck Digby Smith's ranch near San Jose. Smith and a friend, E. G. Barker, were bound before the raiders crushed their skulls with axes and beheaded them with swords, stealing $1,500 and burning Smith's home as they fled. Feliz later confessed the murders to a cellmate. (His only identified accomplice, Miguel Luches, died in a San Francisco knife fight on October 9, 1851.)

On February 12, 1851, Flores and 16 riders attacked Anastacio Chabolla's ranch near San Jose, but they were driven off by gunfire. Separating from the gang, Feliz and his brother Reyes returned to the Southern Mines region where they soon robbed and murdered a fellow Sonoran. Claudio had seven riders with him on June 6 when he raided a store at Campo Seco near Sonora and fled with the safe. Gang member David Hill was captured and lynched at Sonora three weeks later, but Feliz and the rest of his band remained at large, teaming with Joaquin

Murrieta later in the year for raids in the Northern Mines district.

On November 10, 1851, the gang ambushed two travelers near Birdwell's Bar on the Feather River, cutting their throats for a pitiful $34 in gold. A day later, near Honcut Creek, they killed teamster George Mather in similar style and pocketed $500. Before the afternoon was out, they murdered two more travelers and took an ounce of gold from each. Five gruesome murders in two days produced a panic in the goldfields. Yuba County Sheriff Robert Buchanan and Constable Ike Bower surprised Feliz, Murrieta, and several others at a camp outside Marysville on November 12, but the lawmen were lucky to escape with their lives after gunfire erupted. Buchanan was shot in the back but survived, while Bower managed to duck and dodge the storm of bullets.

Claudio Feliz was finally captured in December 1851 and jailed at San Jose on murder charges. He spoke freely with cellmate Teodoro Vásquez, a member of the FRANCISCO DANIEL gang who was already sentenced to hang for grand larceny. Vásquez kept his date with the gallows in February 1852 but first cleared his conscience with a marathon confession of his crimes—and those admitted to him by Feliz. It was too late to take advantage of the windfall, though: Before Vásquez began to sing, Feliz had already escaped from San Jose's aging adobe jail.

On April 5, 1852, the Feliz brothers and several companions—perhaps including Murrieta—camped out at Humbug, three miles from Sonora. Reyes Feliz, returning from some errand, was surprised by law enforcers and arrested for possession of two stolen guns. En route to jail, the posse was attacked by Claudio and company, guns blazing. Reyes escaped in the confusion, but Claudio was shot from his horse and captured. Jailed at Sonora pending action from the local grand jury, Feliz recovered from his wound, biding his time. Amazingly, the charges lodged against him at Sonora were dismissed in August, and he was released, his captors unaware of the escape from San Jose and the murder charges waiting for him there.

Joaquin Murrieta was the big news that summer, and law enforcers searching for him flushed the Feliz gang from hiding in the Sierra Nevada foothills on August 30, 1852. Claudio's band rode hard across the San Joaquin Valley and the Coast Range, invading John Kottinger's home near modern-day Pleasanton on September 10. The rancher proved too much for them, repulsing the bandits in a flurry of gunfire, with no casualties on either side. Three days later, Feliz and his men robbed a traveler on the highway between Monterey and Salinas, breaking tradition by allowing him to live. Their victim sounded the alarm, and Claudio, recognized from his description of the outlaw leader, was tagged with a $3,000 reward.

Driven by the dual motivations of outrage and greed, searchers tracked Feliz and three companions to the home of Manuel Espinosa that Monday night, surrounding the house at 9:00 P.M. Claudio Feliz was shot dead while fleeing the hideout, along with 27-year-old Pablo Valdez. Mateo Andrade survived his bullet wounds and was held for trial. The last of the quarter, Esteban Silva, was captured on September 14 and stabbed to death by vigilantes "while trying to escape." Valdez, the sole survivor, was sentenced to 11 years in prison for robbery and grand larceny, but he escaped in 1854 to resume his criminal career. Reports of his subsequent lynching at San Luis Obispo remain unconfirmed.

FICTION and Film Portrayals of Robbery

No single volume can pretend to list, much less evaluate and analyze the fictional portrayals of crime in print and cinema. Robbery and its results have been staples of literary fiction since author first set pen to paper—in films, since one of the earliest motion pictures depicted Wild West badmen pulling off *The Great Train Robbery* (1904). Cinematic treatments of robbery alone range from the slapstick comedy of the Pink Panther series (1964–82) to the ruthless violence of *Reservoir Dogs* (1992), thereby restricting coverage in this volume to fictional portrayals of real-life robbers and outlaws.

The early American river pirates who made their lair at CAVE-IN-ROCK—including Samuel Mason and the bloodthirsty Harpe brothers—were portrayed as early as 1833 by Judge James Hale in his novel *Harpe's Head*. Fifteen years later, Emerson Bennett created a fictional character to rule the robber's roost in *Mike Fink, a Legend of the Ohio* (1848). Author C. A. Stephens used Mason and the Harpes as background for his boy's adventure, *The Ark of 1803* (1904), and Mickey Mouse creator Walt Disney memorialized Bennett's legend of Mike Fink a half-century later, retaining the Harpes as minor villains and bringing a frontier hero to the fore in his cinematic production of *Davy Crockett and the River Pirates* (1956).

America's romance with the western frontier and its badmen dominated publishing and cinema for several decades, with real-life outlaws claiming their share of ink and celluloid. FRANK and JESSE JAMES, predictably, rank among the favorite subjects of western authors and directors with the resultant offerings varied from the fairly authentic to the frankly bizarre. The James boys featured in no end of dime novels, from the 1870s onward, but a more interesting treatment is found in Susan Dodd's *Mamaw: A Novel of an Outlaw Mother* (1988), which views the brothers and their grim life through a parent's eyes. On screen, one or both brothers have appeared in such features as *Jesse James* (1939), *The Return of Frank James* (1940), *The Return of Jesse James* (1950), *Kansas Raiders* (1950), *The Great Missouri Raid* (1950), *Jesse James's Women* (1954), *Jesse James vs. the Daltons* (1954), *The Great Northfield, Minnesota, Raid* (1972), and *The Long Riders* (1980). Jesse was played for laughs by Bob Hope in *Alias Jesse James* (1959) and took a walk on the weird side six year later in *Jesse James Meets Frankenstein's Daughter* (1965). Lethal cousins of the James boys claim center stage in *The Younger Brothers* (1949) while also playing feature roles in several of the films listed above.

BUTCH CASSIDY and his "WILD BUNCH" were arguably the most infamous 19th-century outlaws after Jesse James, and they have likewise merited attention from novelists and screenwriters. Relevant novels include *The Wild Bunch* by Ernest Haycox (1943), Will Henry's *Alias Butch Cassidy* (1967), John Cooke's *South of the Border* (1989), *Kid Curry's Last Ride* by Warwick Downing (1989), and Lee Nelson's *Cassidy* (1992). In film, Cassidy and accomplice HARRY LONGABAUGH are depicted in *Butch Cassidy and the Sundance Kid* (1969), plus a prequel titled *Butch and Sundance: The Early Days* (1979). Director Sam Peckinpah's stylish-but-gruesome effort *The Wild Bunch* (1969) makes no direct allusion to Cassidy, but Butch rates a passing mention in Brian Fox's novelization of Walon Green's screenplay. Harry Longabaugh also returns—transplanted to Oklahoma and impossibly teamed with the Youngers, the DALTON BROTHERS, and Billy the Kid—for *Return of the Badmen* (1948).

Next to frontier outlaws, the Depression-era bank robbers of 1930–36 have also furnished publishers and Hollywood producers with a bounty of more-or-less fictional plots. JOHN DILLINGER has inspired at least three novels, including *Dillinger* by Jack Higgins (writing as "Harry Patterson," 1983), J. S. Roberto's *1933: The Devil Comes to Henry County* (1989) and Jack Kelly's *Mad Dog* (1992). Poet Todd Moore has also dedicated a series of ongoing epic poems to Dillinger in such collections as *Target Practice* (1985) and *Machine Gun* (1994). On screen, the late desperado's credits include *Dillinger* (1945), *Young Dillinger* (1965), *Dillinger* (1973), *The Lady in Red* (1979), and *Dillinger and Capone* (1995).

The 1930s BARKER GANG and its associates are portrayed in two above-average novels: J. M. Ryan's *Mother's Day* (1969) and Steve Thayer's *Saint Mudd* (1988). Films depicting or inspired by the gang include *Ma Barker's Killer Brood* (1960), *Bloody Mama* (1970), *Big Bad Mama* (1974), *Alvin Karpis: Public Enemy* (1974), *Big Bad Mama II* (1987), and *Public Enemies* (1996). The gang also surfaced briefly in the second episode of *The Untouchables* (October 22, 1959) that outraged FBI Director J. EDGAR HOOVER because Prohibition agent Eliot Ness was depicted erroneously as the slayer of "Ma" Barker and son Fred.

Other 1930s outlaws have also rated attention from Hollywood through the years. CLYDE BARROW and BONNIE PARKER are portrayed in *The Bonnie Parker Story* (1958) and *Bonnie and Clyde* (1967). GEORGE "BABY FACE" NELSON likewise rated two features, the identically titled *Baby Face Nelson* (1957) and *Baby Face Nelson* (1995). Oklahoma bandit CHARLES "PRETTY BOY" FLOYD rated a novel by Larry McMurtry and Diana Oksana, *Pretty Boy Floyd* (1994); he also posthumously starred in four films, including *Pretty Boy Floyd* (1960), *A Bullet for Pretty Boy* (1970), *The Story of Pretty Boy Floyd* (1974, with Martin Sheen appearing as the only actor to portray both Floyd and Dillinger on-screen), and *Kansas City Massacre* (1975). Mild-mannered GEORGE "MACHINE GUN" KELLY appeared larger than life in two films—*Machine Gun Kelly* (1958) and *Melvin Purvis: G-Man* (1974).

Although American film producers have understandably focused on home-grown desperadoes, the legend of Britain's ROBIN HOOD has captivated directors for more than 80 years. Big-screen productions of the tale include *Robin Hood* (1922), *The Story of Robin Hood and his Merrie Men* (1952), *Sword of Sherwood Forest* (1960), *Robin Hood* (1973), *Robin and Marian* (1976), *Robin Hood* (1991), *Robin Hood: Prince of Thieves* (1991) and the comic *Robin Hood: Men in Tights* (1995). Britain aside, Australia has yielded two fine films depicting real-life badmen of the 19th century: *Ned Kelly* (1970) and *Mad Dog Morgan* (1976).

In each of the novels and films cited here, certain liberties have been taken with history in the pursuit of entertainment. Purists may rage at 1973's *Dillinger* for scrambling events, fabricating incidents, and staging one massive firefight to eliminate outlaws actually killed in separate engagements spanning four months and three states, but the purpose of such fictional portrayals has never been transmission of historical data. They are, rather, a form of tribute—albeit profit-motivated tribute in most cases—to the SOCIAL BANDITS who have shaped our common history for good or ill. As such, they are a part of folklore and are thus immune to criticism for their lapses into fantasy.

FINNEY, Julius: See ADAMS, EDWARD.

FLEAGLE Gang: "Wolf Pack of Lamar"

Iowa born in 1890, the youngest of four sons raised by parents of dubious morals, William Harrison Fleagle—known to family and friends alike as Jake—was still a toddler when his family pulled up stakes and moved to Garden City, Kansas. Ostensibly a farming clan, the Fleagles planted crops so rarely and guarded their privacy so zealously that neighbors assumed they were up to no good—bootlegging, perhaps, or some other traffic in contraband. At least where the sons were concerned, it turned out that the neighbors were right.

Active as burglars by the onset of the 1920s, members of the Fleagle gang pulled their first-known bank job at Ottawa, Kansas, stealing $150,000 on November 2, 1923. The next verified hit came three years later on October 16, 1926, when the bandits hit a bank in Marysville, Kansas. The take was a miserable $741, but the Fleagles were clearly busy elsewhere, as verified by regular bank deposits in at least three Kansas towns. Four years later, authorities would document $150,000 in deposits to Garden City banks since 1921, with another $10,000 banked in Dodge City and several thousand dollars more in Scott City. Withdrawals were equally dramatic—up to $60,000 at a time and frequently preceding some dramatic robbery in the Midwest. Throughout the decade-long crime spree, the elder Fleagles somehow managed to survive in style on a 160-acre "horse ranch" that featured neither horses nor crops.

The gang's most notorious holdup occurred in Lamar, Colorado, on May 23, 1928. Four gunmen invaded a local bank at 1:15 P.M. demanding cash, but 70-year-old bank president A. N. Parrish drew a pistol from his desk and shot bandit Howard Royston in the face. Parrish was killed instantly by return fire; his son John—a cashier at the bank—was gunned down while rushing to his father's aid. The robbers bagged $22,500 in cash and $13,700 in Liberty Bonds, taking two bank employees along as human shields when they fled in a late-model Buick sedan. Sheriff L. E. Alderman gave chase, but the gangsters saw him coming and tried to distract him by shoving one hostage from their car 15 miles from Lamar. Alderman kept coming, though, until the outlaws stopped a second time and disabled his car with high-powered rifle fire. Manhunters lost the trail at nightfall, and the gang rolled on. Dr. William Winegar was called from his Dighton, Kansas, home that night to treat Royston; afterward, he was killed with a shotgun blast to the head and left in his car, with a note intended to suggest a revenge-motivated slaying. Bank hostage Everett Kessinger, riddled with bullets and left in a cabin near Liberal, Kansas, was found three weeks later. Fingerprints lifted from Dr. Winegar's car matched those of Jake Fleagle, already wanted by authorities for a 1922 series of boxcar burglaries that targeted the Santa Fe Railroad.

Jake Fleagle had a near-miss in the early spring of 1929 when he, his wife, and his crony Joe Miller were briefly jailed for vagrancy in Stockton, California. Fleagle identified himself to the arresting officers as "W. H. Holden," while his wife passed herself off as "Betty Gramps" (aka Betty Holden or Betty Wright). The charges were a sham; "Holden" and company were suspected of conspiring to rob steel mill payrolls in nearby Pittsburg, but evidence was lacking and the trio were granted bail. Jake gave the cops a handful of Liberty Bonds from the Lamar bank job, and by the time a connection was made, the fugitives had vanished.

On June 22, 1929, three masked bandits armed with Tommy guns and a tripod-mounted machine gun stopped a Southern Pacific mail train near McAvoy, California, riddling a mail car with bullets and escaping with $19,000 in cash. The getaway car was abandoned nearby; police and FBI agents named a friend of Jake Fleagle—physician-turned-gambler Doctor C. O. DeMoss—as the man who purchased it in Los Angeles, using the name "James Hendrix." An FBI background search revealed that Jake Fleagle had served time in Oklahoma for TRAIN ROBBERY, but none of the fingerprints lifted from the train or getaway car were his.

Still, suspicion was enough to power a manhunt, and some rudimentary investigation around Garden City, Kansas, turned up a plethora of bank accounts and safe-deposit boxes maintained by the Fleagle brothers under sundry pseudonyms. Brothers Walter and Fred were jailed in Garden City on "suspicion," their arrests kept quiet to avoid spooking siblings Jake and Ralph. A letter from Ralph soon arrived, postmarked from Kankakee, Illinois, and law enforcers bagged him there, seizing three revolvers, 140 rounds of ammunition, and a set of California license plates from his car. Another safe-deposit box yielded $1,200 in cash and $6,500 in Liberty Bonds, but none were traceable to the Lamar holdup.

The day of Ralph's arrest in Kankakee, a phone call received at his hotel led police to Peoria, where they bagged Doctor DeMoss. He was questioned and then released for "lack of evidence," despite the fact that his Buick sedan was identified as the Lamar getaway vehicle. Searching a Peoria apartment DeMoss had lately shared with Jake Fleagle and his wife, police recovered five rifles, four pistols, a shotgun, and 2,000 rounds of ammunition.

Joe Miller was captured in Reno, Nevada, on July 19, 1929, and held as a suspect in the McAvoy train holdup until a conductor's testimony cleared him of complicity. It did no good, however, as he was extradited to California on unrelated robbery charges and was accused of helping Doctor DeMoss and Jake Fleagle steal $1,400 from a victim named Tom Jenkins several months earlier.

Three weeks later, on August 9, Ralph Fleagle cut a plea with Colorado authorities to escape the death penalty, confessing his role in several bank holdups and naming other members of the gang as brother Jake, Howard Royston, Ernest Rhoda, and George Abshier (aka "Bill Messick"). Ralph admitted calling Doctor Winegar out from his home in May 1928 and writing the note found with Winegar's corpse, but he named Jake as the actual triggerman in that slaying. He directed law officers to San Andreas, California, where Royston was soon arrested; Abshier was captured in Grand Junction, Colorado, where he was known as a resort owner and a bootlegger. In custody on September 18, the gangsters admitted six bank jobs, netting nearly a half-million dollars since 1923, but all steadfastly denied involvement in the McAvoy train heist.

Ralph Fleagle was convicted of the Lamar holdup-murders on October 26, 1929, jurors recommending death despite his bargain with the prosecution. That vote compelled the judge to impose a capital sentence, echoed for Abshier and Royston when they were likewise convicted and condemned. Colorado's supreme court rejected appeals from the three killers on March 13, 1930. Ralph was hanged on July 10, 1930, followed by Abshier and Royston on July 19.

The search for Jake Fleagle continued, meanwhile, federal authorities and railroad police stubbornly refusing to acknowledge his innocence in the McAvoy train heist. (Bank robbery would not become a federal crime for four more years.) As summer 1930 waned, law enforcers learned that Fleagle was corresponding with a professional gambler, soliciting the card sharp's assistance for a robbery in Arkansas. The gambler was persuaded to arrange a meeting with Fleagle, scheduled in their normal manner via personal ads in a midwestern newspaper.

The meeting was set to take place on a passenger train at Yellville, Arkansas, on October 14, 1930. Waiting for Fleagle on the train that afternoon was a posse including two plainclothes officers from Los Angeles, Missouri Pacific Railroad detectives, and U.S. postal inspectors. Fleagle suspected nothing when he boarded the train at Branson, Missouri, 30 miles northwest of Yellville. Confronted with guns, he reached for his own and was dropped in his tracks. He died hours later at a hospital in Springfield without speaking to police. Only later did lawmen acknowledge their error, admitting that the McAvoy train robbery was carried out by the FRANK ELLIS gang.

FLORES, Juan

A native of Mexican California, born at San Jose in 1835, Juan Flores was a teenager when the territory passed into American hands following the Mexican War. Hard on the heels of that change came the gold rush, with ample opportunity for resentful *Californios* to strike back at the Anglo invaders who had stolen their homeland. In such an atmosphere, fraught with racial tension, every holdup smacked of insurrection, while SOCIAL BANDITS like JOAQUIN MURRIETA were elevated to freedom-fighter status in verse and song.

Juan Flores, for his part, starting out small as a bandit, was convicted of stealing horses in Los Angeles and was sentenced to three years imprisonment at San Quentin. He escaped with several other convicts on October 8, 1856, fleeing southward into Santa Clara County, where he soon joined forces with bandit leader FRANCISCO "PANCHO" DANIEL. Other members of the gang included Faustino Garcia, José Jesús Espinosa, Andrés Fontes, Francisco "Guerro" Ardillero, José Santos, Juan Silvas (aka Juan Cataba), Leonardo López, "Piquinini" Galindo, twin brothers Dolores and Lorenzo Ruiz, Antonio María "Chino" Varelas, and Miguel Soto (arrested for robbery with MIGUEL BLANCO in September 1856; acquitted when their confessions were invalidated as products of police third-degree tactics).

By mid-January 1857 the gang was camped outside San Juan Capistrano where Flores had a girl-friend named Chola Martina. The bandits wore out their welcome on January 21 when several gang members raided the settlement, looting two stores and murdering German shopkeeper George Pflugardt. By January 22 a six-man posse was in hot pursuit, led by Los Angeles County Sheriff James Barton; other members of the hunting party included Deputy Sheriff Frank Alexander, Constables William Little and Charles Baker, and civilians Alfred Hardy and Charles Daly.

Barton's posse overtook the Daniel-Flores gang on January 23 near the San Joaquin Hills. A wild shootout erupted; Constables Baker and Little were killed in the first exchange of gunfire. Displaying more courage than common sense, Sheriff Barton then led his three survivors in a head-on charge against the gang, and Barton was shot dead from his saddle by Pancho Daniel. Alexander, Daly, and Hardy fought on, wounding three outlaws before they ran out of bullets; then they turned and fled under fire, pursued by bandits to the outskirts of a nearby settlement. In Los Angeles, City Marshal William Getman deputized 40 men to track the killers but was sickened when he found Barton, Baker, and Little riddled with posthumous gunfire, their corpses looted.

A four-day search around Los Angeles proved fruitless, as the gang rode back to San Juan Capistrano, boasting of the recent shootout. Overnight, the largest manhunt of the gold-rush era was launched, with U.S. troops and vigilante riders watching the border at San Diego. Jim Thompson, new sheriff of Los Angeles County, defied common wisdom by watching the northern escape routes, and his gamble paid off on January 30 when a posse surprised six outlaws at Santiago Canyon. Among the cornered badmen were Juan Flores, Chino Varelas, Jesús Espinosa, Leonardo López, Juan Silvas, and Francisco Ardillero. Varelas quickly surrendered in fear of his life, while Flores, Espinosa and López knotted ropes and clambered down a 200-foot cliff to escape. Flores was wounded by an accidental discharge of his own revolver during the climb, but things went worse for Silvas and Ardillero, who were captured and lynched on the spot.

On January 31, another posse spotted Flores and his fellow fugitives as they ducked into a mountain cave. Heavy gunfire persuaded the outlaws to surrender, and Flores was relieved of Sheriff Barton's gold watch. Held overnight at a nearby ranch, the three bandits escaped when their guards fell asleep on duty. Flores stole horses at Santa Ana and Mission San Fernando, riding alone into Simi Pass on February 3, 1857. Law officers were waiting for him there, and they found the infamous badman unarmed. Flores initially identified himself as Juan Gonzalez Sanchez, but he was quickly identified by one of his captors and transported to jail in Los Angeles. Vigilantes convened in L.A. on February 14 and passed a sentence of death on Flores, removing him from jail with no visible resistance from Marshal Getman. A gallows was erected atop Fort Hill, a quarter-mile away, and Flores was escorted to his death by two Catholic priests before an audience of 3,000 gawkers. From the scaffold, Flores confessed numerous crimes, closing with the remark that he harbored no "ill will against any man, and hoped that no one would bear any ill will against him." For all its pomposity, the hanging was bungled: Flores strangled slowly, after wriggling free of his bonds and trying to pull himself up the taut rope.

Juan Flores was the 12th man executed by Los Angeles vigilantes in their campaign to clean up the town. Despite occasional public references to the "Flores revolution," there was no apparent political motive to any of the crimes committed by the Daniel-Flores gang.

FLOYD, Charles Arthur "Pretty Boy"

The last of America's infamous SOCIAL BANDITS, Charles Floyd was a Georgia native, born February 3, 1904. Seven years later his family moved to Akins, Oklahoma, in the shadow of the COOKSON HILLS, where young Floyd's father opened a small grocery store to augment the meager income from his farm. Reportedly influenced by legends of famous outlaws in his childhood, Floyd—known as "Chock" to his friends—avoided trouble with the law until 1922 when he was arrested for stealing $350 in pennies from the Akins post office. He caught a lucky break when the coins disappeared from police custody and the case was dropped for lack of evidence.

In January 1924 Floyd married Ruby Hargraves, the 16-year-old daughter of a Bixby shopkeeper, and a son (named for boxer Jack Dempsey) was born the following year. The Floyds separated in 1925, Ruby filing for divorce while "Chock" lit out for St. Louis. There, on September 11, he joined accomplices Fred Hilderbrand and Joe Hlavaty to steal $11,934 from a Kroger grocery store. Police apparently confused Floyd with another local hoodlum, one "Pretty Boy" Smith, and the nickname stuck with him even after the mistake was recognized. Arrested with Hilderbrand two days later at Salisaw, Oklahoma, Floyd was returned to St. Louis on September 17. Hilderbrand soon confessed his role in the stickup and implicated his cronies. Floyd pled guilty to first-degree robbery on December 8, 1925, and was given five years, his sentence received at the state prison in Jefferson City 10 days later. Paroled on March 7, 1929, Floyd did not avoid trouble for long.

Two days after his release, police in Kansas City jailed Floyd "for investigation" but quickly released him. Two months later, on May 6, he was arrested for vagrancy and suspicion of highway robbery but was freed the following day. By May 9 Floyd had somehow made his way to Pueblo, Colorado, where he was fined $50 and sentenced to serve 60 days for vagrancy. On September 2, 1929, he was held for investigation in Kansas City under the alias "Joe Scott." Kansas City authorities jailed him again on November 18 for suspicion of robbery but released him next morning.

Bad news from home was waiting for Floyd when he hit the street on November 19. Five days earlier, his father had been shot dead in Akins by shopkeeper Jim Mills in an argument over some shingles. "Chock" Floyd was present in court when a jury acquitted Mills of murder, accepting his plea of self-defense, and when Mills disappeared from Akins soon thereafter, rumors spread that Floyd had killed him in an act of vengeance. The truth, as revealed by Floyd biographer Michael Wallis, was rather different: Fearing retaliation from the Floyd family, Mills had moved west to California, where he died of natural causes years later. "Chock" had reportedly gone looking for his enemy but missed his chance to settle it when Mills left town.

Floyd soon left Oklahoma, heading north again. On February 5, 1930 he teamed with bandits Bob Amos (alias "John King") and James Bradley (alias "Bert Walker") to rob a bank in Sylvania, a suburb of Toledo, Ohio. The take was less than $2,000, and anonymous tips soon alerted Akron police that the bandits might be in their neighborhood. In the predawn hours of March 8, Amos and Bradley were surprised by officers outside an after-hours nightclub. Gunfire erupted, leaving a patrolman dead and Amos in handcuffs while Bradley, wounded, managed to escape. Fourteen hours later, police tracked him to a rented bungalow, bursting in to capture Bradley and Floyd. The raiders seized an arsenal including two sawed-off shotguns, a Tommy gun, a rifle, five pistols, and a quantity of nitroglycerine.

Initially held as material witnesses, Floyd and Amos were indicted for the Sylvania bank robbery on May 20, 1930. Bradley was convicted of murder the following day and sentenced to die; he was executed on November 10. Two weeks later, after a bungled courthouse escape attempt, Floyd pled guilty to robbery on November 24 and received a prison term of 12 to 15 years. By that time, he had warned cellmates that he would "rather be killed than serve a year in prison." "Chock" was as good as his word. On December 10, en route to the Ohio state penitentiary, he leaped from a window of the moving train and escaped, within 10 miles of the prison gates. It was the last time he would ever let himself be taken into custody on any charge.

There was no turning back now for "Pretty Boy" Floyd. On March 9, 1931, he teamed with outlaws GEORGE BIRDWELL and William "Bill the Killer" Miller to lift $3,000 from a bank in Earlsboro, Oklahoma. Two weeks later, Floyd narrowly avoided capture when Kansas City police raided several local nightclubs, including one where he rented a room. Suspecting treachery, he blamed two small-time hoodlums, William and Wallace Ash, for fingering his hideout. On March 27 the Ash brothers were found beside a highway outside Kansas City, each shot execution-style in the back of the head, their burned-out car nearby. The bodies were barely cold before Wallace's widow, Rose Ash, moved in with Floyd, William's widow Beulah providing similar aid and comfort to Miller.

Together, the jolly foursome set off on a bank-robbing spree. On April 6, 1931, Floyd and Miller took $2,262 from the Mount Zion Trust Company in Elliston, Kentucky. Eight days later, they tapped a Whitehouse, Ohio, bank for $1,600 and then settled in at Bowling Green for a few days of rest and relaxation. Police Chief Carl Galliher soon grew suspicious of their free-spending lifestyle and went to visit the strangers with Patrolman Ralph Castner in tow. The officers found Miller and the two women outside a store on Prospect Street. Floyd, across the street, saw the uniforms coming and shouted a warning to Miller before cutting loose with his twin .45 automatics. Patrolman Castner was mortally wounded as he returned fire while Chief Galliher ducked behind a parked car and blasted away at any target visible. Floyd stood his ground long enough to see Miller die, while Beulah Ash suffered a nonfatal head wound. Rose Ash was arrested at the scene, while Floyd escaped on foot, later identified with aid from Kansas City authorities.

Despite the local heat, Floyd went underground in Kansas City, renting meager quarters at a speakeasy, one floor above a mob-owned flower shop on Independence Avenue. Even at the going rate of $100 per night there were still risks involved in sleeping so close to that much bootleg alcohol. Federal agents came calling on the night of July 31, hacking through doors with their axes, barging into Floyd's room. He came up shooting, killing Prohibition agent Curtis Burke where he stood. Floyd escaped in the ensuing chaos but not before he touched off a general firefight. Before it was over, Kansas City officers had killed a hoodlum, one John Calio, while innocent spectator M. P. Wilson was dropped by stray gunfire.

Floyd was too hot to handle after that night's work, even in a mob-controlled town like Kansas City. A federal agent had been killed on syndicate property, and mob boss John Lazia ordered his troops to let the feds have "Pretty Boy," assuming they could find him.

But Floyd was already gone. He surfaced on August 4, 1931, teamed again with George Birdwell to steal $400 from a bank in Shamrock, Oklahoma. The take was better on September 8 when they lifted $1,743 from a bank in Morris. Three weeks later, the First National Bank in Maud, Oklahoma, gave up $3,850. They hit the bank at Earlsboro twice that fall, the second time for $2,498 on October 14. On November 5 it was Conowa's turn: The First National branch was looted of $2,500.

Floyd and Birdwell were moving so rapidly, in fact, that witnesses began to see them in places where they never set foot. One day after the Conowa holdup, "Pretty Boy" was wrongly identified as the lone bandit who took $50,000 from a bank in Strasburg, Ohio. On January 2, 1932, authorities were wrong again, linking him to a shootout that killed six policemen on a farm near Springfield, Missouri. (The actual killers committed suicide three days later.) Floyd and Birdwell, meanwhile, were still in Oklahoma, hiding out in the friendly Cookson Hills, emerging on January 14 to lift $2,600 from a bank in Castle. Eight days later, Floyd and several unidentified confederates scored a paltry $800 from a bank raid in Dover, Oklahoma.

And their luck was wearing thin.

Floyd might be idolized by his impoverished former neighbors, viewed by some as a latter-day ROBIN HOOD, but politicians and bankers took a rather different view, their reward offers mounting. After Oklahoma Lieutenant Governor Robert Burns added $1,000 to the $5,000 bounty already placed on Floyd's head, "Pretty Boy" mailed the first of many letters that he would address to the authorities while living on the lam. It read:

You either withdraw that one thousand at once or suffer the consequences. No kidding. I have robbed no one but moneyed men. Floyd.

Instead of withdrawing the offer, Burns took his message to the radio airwaves. "This is a desperate case," he proclaimed. "Floyd has already terrorized the entire east-central section of Oklahoma with his outlawry. Already six killings and ten bank robberies have been charged to him. He must be stopped." In fact, Floyd had killed no one in Oklahoma, and the only Sooners known to live in fear of "Pretty Boy" were members of the Oklahoma Bankers Association. On the flip side of the coin were tales of Floyd and Birdwell pausing in the middle of bank jobs to burn mortgage papers, handing out cash from their holdups to friends plagued with overdue bills.

In January 1932 Floyd, posing as "Jack Hamilton," rented a house in Tulsa, moving in with ex-wife Ruby and their son, who was enrolled at the neighborhood school. Trouble caught up with him on February 7 when three police officers spotted Floyd's car parked on Admiral Street with two men inside. The officers closed in, but Floyd was faster on the draw, cutting loose with a Tommy gun and wounding Detective Willard Wilson. A running gunfight developed, Floyd and Birdwell stopping only when they turned into a dead-end street by accident and then fled on foot. Patrolman Wade Foor vowed that he had pumped six bullets into Floyd's retreating

back, but if his aim was true, a steel vest must have saved the bandit's life.

Driving was hazardous for "Pretty Boy" in those days. On February 10 he and Birdwell were spotted again, this time at the junction of Fifth Street and Utica Avenue, escaping in another blaze of gunfire. By the next evening, a check on "Jack Hamilton's" license plate led police to Floyd's Tulsa bungalow, and they turned out in force, complete with armored cars, machine guns, and high-powered rifles. Teargas grenades were lobbed through the windows, flushing Ruby Floyd and her son from cover. While officers ran to intercept them, Floyd and Birdwell slipped out the back door and vanished into darkness, so startling police lookouts that they let the bandits go without firing a shot.

The fiasco was humiliating for authorities, the embarrassment compounded when Floyd and Birdwell robbed a bank in Meeker on March 23. Erv Kelley, former sheriff of McIntosh County, came out of retirement in hopes of collecting the bounty on "Pretty Boy" Floyd. Deputized as a special investigator for the occasion, Kelley determined to locate his quarry by watching Floyd's ex-wife. It took time, but the surveillance paid off on April 8 when Ruby and her son left Tulsa to visit the farm of one Cecil Bennett, near Bixby. Convinced that there was a lover's rendezvous in the making, Kelley summoned reinforcements, spotting snipers at strategic locations around the Bennett place. Time dragged while they waited, and four members of the nine-man posse had gone for coffee in Bixby when a car approached and gunfire rang out from Kelley's position at 2:25 A.M., April 9. Deputy William Counts arrived to find Kelley dead, his assailant nowhere in sight. As later reconstructed, he had tried to stop Floyd's car alone, firing off 14 rounds from his Tommy gun before five of Floyd's bullets snuffed out his life. (Unknown to lawmen, Floyd had also suffered three wounds to his legs but would survive.)

Kelley's murder put another $6,000 on Floyd's head, dead or alive, and there was no escaping the heat that spring. George Birdwell's father died in April, and police staked out the Earlsboro funeral parlor, but Floyd caught them napping on April 20 and held them at gunpoint while Birdwell paid his last respects. The next day, Floyd and Birdwell took $600 from a bank in Stonewall, Oklahoma. On June 7 lawmen thought they had the bandits trapped near Ada in Pontotoc County as Floyd's sedan struggled to climb a muddy hill. Sheriff L. E. Franklin later estimated that his men had pumped more than a hundred rounds into the car without visible effect, concluding that Floyd and Birdwell not only wore bulletproof vests but also "steel plates in their sleeves and around the tops of their heads, under their hats."

Or maybe it was just poor shooting.

Rumors constantly surrounded Floyd, mutating into legend. By August 1932 it was supposed that he had teamed up with the ruthless BARKER brothers to loot a bank in Bixby. Claude Chambers of Sapulpa, once a prosecution witness in the 1921 trial of Dock Barker, now claimed that Floyd and the Barkers were sending him death threats 11 years after the fact. H. W. Nave, a former Tulsa cop, declared that Floyd and Birdwell had absconded with his car and clothes, but it was Nave who went to jail for fraud when officers found out that he had sold his mortgaged vehicle to a used-car dealer in Oklahoma City. Floyd was even reported as dead on October 3 after police gunned down two fleeing subjects near Enid, but the ersatz "Pretty Boy" turned out to be a hoodlum named Tom Groggin.

Floyd was very much alive, taking down his last bank with George Birdwell at Sallisaw on November 1. The manager was fond of boasting publicly that "Pretty Boy" could never rob *his* bank, but he was wrong. Some versions of the robbery, perhaps apocryphal, depict Floyd tossing money out the window of his car as he drove out of town, bystanders scrambling for the cash.

About this time, Birdwell conceived a plan to rob the bank in all-black Boley, Oklahoma, but Floyd declined to participate for reasons unknown. Birdwell recruited two accomplices, but only one of them survived the battle of Boley that ensued on November 22, and the survivor was crippled for life. Rumor had it that Floyd attended Birdwell's funeral disguised as a woman, and although he fired off a letter to Boley threatening reprisals, "Chock" had more pressing matters on his mind. Eight days after the Boley fiasco, a score of witnesses named Floyd as the leader of a gang that stole $50,000 from the Citizen's State Bank in Tupelo, Mississippi. Floyd penned a letter to the Memphis *Commercial Appeal* denying any role in the stickup, but his legend had already outgrown the man as sightings multiplied and rumors ran amok.

What Floyd most needed at the moment was another dependable sidekick, and he found one in ADAM "EDDIE" RICHETTI, a fugitive bail-jumper who had walked away from McAlester State Penitentiary in August 1932 determined to serve no more time. The circumstances of their meeting are unknown— some place it in Missouri, others in the friendly Cookson Hills—but they apparently began their partnership by knocking off a dancehall in Wewoka, Oklahoma, in April 1933. Two months later, on June 14, they took $1,628 from a bank in Mexico, Missouri. Less than an hour after the holdup, in neighboring Boone County, Sheriff Roger Wilson and Highway Patrol Sergeant Ben Booth were shot dead at a roadblock established to head off the bandits. Floyd and Richetti were blamed for the murders until 1938, when the actual killer confessed.

Three days after the Boone County shootout, on June 17, Floyd and Richetti were fingered as the gunmen in the most sensational gangland killing since Chicago's St. Valentine's Day massacre of 1929. In fact, the KANSAS CITY MASSACRE was worse because only gangsters and their friends were murdered in Chicago, while the dead at Kansas City's Union Station included four lawmen. Fugitive FRANK NASH had been picked up by G-men in Hot Springs, Arkansas, on June 16, and his captors caught a train to Kansas City where they would be met by escorts for the 30-mile trip to the federal pen at Leavenworth. Instead, they were ambushed by machine gunners in the parking lot; three policemen, an FBI agent, and Nash himself were killed in the blizzard of fire from three weapons.

Or so the classic story goes.

Several witnesses identified one of the shooters, a "fat man," as "Pretty Boy" Floyd, and J. EDGAR HOOVER accepted that judgment as fact, though Floyd denied involvement in the murders to the end of his days. From naming Floyd, it was a short step to assuming that Richetti also must have been on hand, so both men became prime targets for federal agents intent on avenging one of their own. It is worth noting that Floyd and Richetti were definitely seen at Bolívar, Missouri, some 100 miles southeast of Kansas City on the morning of June 16. Richetti's brother worked at a garage in Bolivar, and the bandits stopped by around 7:00 A.M. to have some work done on their car. Sheriff William Killingsworth dropped in a few minutes later, and the outlaws took him hostage, rolling out of town in Joe Richetti's Ford V-8. They abandoned that car near Clinton, Missouri, and commandeered another driven by Walter Griffith, taking Griffith along as an additional hostage. It was 11:00 P.M. when the foursome reached Lee's Summit near Kansas City, and the pris-

Local members of the posse that killed "Pretty Boy" Floyd: (left to right) Officer Curley Montgomery, Chief Huey McDermott, Sgt. Herman Roth, and Capt. Chester A. Smith. (Dawson funeral home)

oners were freed unharmed. Thus, it appears that Floyd and Richetti *were* in town at the time of the Union Station massacre, but their involvement in the crime remains unproven.

Facts hardly mattered at the time, of course, with Floyd and Richetti blamed for seven brutal murders in the space of three days. After Kansas City, the bandits fled to the familiar haven of Oklahoma's Cookson Hills, but even that sanctuary would soon be denied them. Eleven hard-core convicts, including several notorious bank robbers, had escaped from Kansas state penitentiary on Memorial Day 1933, and some of them were thought to be hiding out in the Cookson Hills. To make matters worse, CLYDE BARROW and BONNIE PARKER were seen in the vicinity

in February 1934, after pulling off a lethal prison break in Texas. (About the same time, Floyd was wrongly accused of leading a gang that robbed a bank in Needham, Massachusetts, killing one policeman and wounding two more in the process.) Governor W. H. Murray, disgusted with portrayals of his state as a haven for killers and thieves, ordered an all-out sweep of the Cookson Hills that same month, and 1,000 manhunters began the ugly job on February 17. The 19 men arrested were all small-timers, while Floyd and Richetti fled northward, some reports say as far as Buffalo, New York.

On June 30, 1934, several witnesses identified Floyd as the "fat" member of a gang that robbed a bank in South Bend, Indiana, sparking a shootout that left one policeman dead and two bandits and at least two bystanders wounded. Crime historians argue over Floyd's participation in the holdup to this day, but none attribute Patrolman Harold Wagner's death to "Pretty Boy," variously blaming the crime on HOMER VAN METER or GEORGE "BABY FACE" NELSON. Testimony from two female traveling companions seems to indicate that Floyd was not in Indiana at the time of the holdup but rather hiding out in New York state.

The next reported sighting of Floyd and Richetti occurred on October 11, 1934, when Deputy Will Owens was dispatched to serve some legal papers at a farmhouse near Cresco, Iowa. Owens retreated at sight of the outlaws and then returned with Agent A. G. Haight from the State Bureau of Investigation, but Floyd and Richetti saw the lawmen coming, escaping over dirt roads in a hail of gunfire. (Other reports cast doubt on the sighting, insisting that Floyd and Richetti remained in New York until the early morning of October 19—in which case the Cresco shooters remain unidentified.)

Scattered sightings were reported from Missouri, Minnesota, and Kentucky in the next few days, most (if not all) of them spurious. Floyd and Richetti seemed to be everywhere at once. A bank was robbed of $500 at Tiltonsville, Ohio, on October 19, and two days later Wellsville police chief J. H. Fultz received a report of two men "acting suspicious" on the outskirts of town. Driving out to the scene with a posse, Chief Fultz soon found himself in a blazing gun battle with Floyd and Richetti. The bandits escaped, leaving Fultz and one of his men slightly wounded, but Richetti was captured nearby when he ran out of bullets. Floyd, meanwhile, had flagged down an elderly motorist and stole the old man's car, ditching it to flee on foot when he met another posse combing the district.

"Pretty Boy" ran out of time and luck on October 22 when he was traced to the Cookle farm between Sprucevale and Clarkston, Ohio. He was eating breakfast in the kitchen when an FBI motorcade arrived from East Liverpool, led by none other than Chicago G-man MELVIN PURVIS himself. Despite the eight guns against him, Floyd still tried to run for his life, and the firing squad cut him down at a range of some 200 feet. He lived long enough to confirm his identity and once again deny any part in the Kansas City massacre. Forty-five years later, a member of the raiding party, ex-policeman Chester Smith, claimed that Floyd was finished off execution-style on personal orders from Purvis. FBI spokesmen furiously denied the report, but the fact remains that Smith was the only one of four Ohio policemen present at Floyd's death who was not questioned at the subsequent coroner's inquest; the other three presented contradictory descriptions of exactly where and when Floyd died. Likewise, Smith was the only local officer present whose statement on the shooting has vanished from FBI files.

FOTHERINGHAM, David S., and WITTROCK, Fred

One of America's stranger train holdups occurred on the night of October 25, 1886, 20 minutes after a westbound St. Louis & San Francisco express train left Union Station in St. Louis, Missouri. Messenger David Fotheringham, employed by the Adams Express Company, offered a curious tale of how he came to be bound and gagged in his car, at least $5,000 missing from the safe he was detailed to guard.

As explained by Fotheringham to PINKERTON detectives, a well-dressed stranger calling himself Jim Cummings had entered the express car shortly before departure from St. Louis, presenting the clerk with two letters of introduction. One bore the signature of W. H. Adams, local superintendent of Adams Express; the other was signed by J. B. Barrett, the Adams route agent. Both letters instructed Fotheringham to take Cummings in tow as a trainee and show him the ropes for a typical outing. Fotheringham was pleased to comply, showing his student how to fill out railroad waybills and deal with other paperwork. When they were 10 miles out of town, though, Cummings suddenly jumped his instructor, overpowered Fotheringham, and left him bound on the floor. While cleaning out the safe, he made a point of stating that Jim Cummings was his real name, and that he had once ridden with JESSE JAMES. Apparently content with his confession and the loot he bagged, Cummings retrieved his two letters from Fotheringham, then took his loot, and bailed out as the train approached Pacific Station in Franklin County.

Pinkerton agents openly scoffed at the story, holding Fotheringham under guard in their suite at the Southern Hotel while they checked out the details. Their skepticism increased a week after the heist when the *St. Louis Globe Democrat* published a letter from "Jim Cummings," absolving the clerk of all guilt. The same author wrote to Fotheringham's mother, sending $60, which she used to hire a lawyer and obtain his freedom on a writ of habeas corpus. The Pinkertons, for their part, focused on the postmarks of the letters, mailed from St. Joseph, Missouri, dispatching agents to beat the bushes while a grand jury was convened in St. Louis.

Under close scrutiny, Fotheringham's story began to crumble. Witnesses described him admitting "Jim Cummings" to the express car on October 25 but through a different door than the one specified in his sworn statement. Why the change, detectives asked. A search of the messenger's flat revealed papers on which some unknown forger had rehearsed J. B. Barrett's signature. Confronted with that evidence, Fotheringham finally cracked, admitting complicity in the holdup and identifying his accomplice as Fred Wittrock of Leavenworth, Kansas (30 miles south of St. Joseph, Missouri). Wittrock was the mastermind behind the robbery, Fotheringham insisted. Several other Adams clerks had been approached but rejected the scheme as too risky—though none of them, apparently, saw fit to warn their employer of the impending theft. Lawmen tracked Wittrock to Chicago and arrested him on December 25, 1886, recovering $5,000 from the holdup. Both partners in the crime were duly convicted and sentenced to prison.

FULTS, Ralph

The son of a postal worker, born at Anne, Texas, on January 23, 1911, Ralph Fults was 14 years old when he first ran afoul of the law. Authorities in Aspermont, Texas, caught him with a suitcase full of stolen goods and locked him up, but Fults fashioned a key from a tobacco can and fled a week later, liberating all his fellow inmates in the process while the sheriff visited the county fair. As luck would have it, Fults was the only escapee recaptured. His stunt earned him a trip to the Gatesville reformatory, where he escaped once more on April 16, 1927.

Two years later, in April 1929, Fults was arrested for selling stolen cigarettes to a Greenville, Texas, grocer. The theft earned him a two-year sentence for burglary. He entered Huntsville prison on June 16, 1929, but was later transferred to the notoriously brutal Eastham prison farm. Fults escaped from Eastham on April 8, 1930, with two other inmates and was recaptured five months later while burglarizing a St. Louis hardware store. Missouri gladly sent him back to Texas, where he was paroled on August 16, 1931, despite the 1930 jailbreak.

Fults had been making friends in prison, and he missed them. One of those was stickup artist RAYMOND HAMILTON, who escaped from jail in McKinney, Texas, on January 27, 1932, using hacksaw blades smuggled by Fults. On March 22 Fults joined Hamilton, CLYDE BARROW, and BONNIE PARKER in a failed attempt to burglarize a Kaufman, Texas, hardware store. The store's night watchman sounded an alarm, and the thieves fled in a stolen car. Nervous Clyde steered them into a mud hole, and the car bogged down, Barrow and Hamilton escaping on foot while Fults and Bonnie were captured. Ralph was sentenced to a 10-year prison term on May 11, 1932, and was unaccountably pardoned by the governor on January 10, 1935.

Barely one month later, on February 16, Fults was back on the prowl with Ray Hamilton, stealing eight Thompson submachine guns from a National Guard armory in Beaumont, Texas. On February 24 the partners were in Tulsa, where they stole a car and headed home to Texas. Police nearly bagged them at McKinney, but some fancy driving got them clear and left their pursuers in the dust.

On March 19, 1935, still with Hamilton, Fults met a Houston reporter to discuss the brutality of the Lone Star State's penal system. The interview was a success; Ralph and Raymond celebrated their coup that afternoon with the robbery of a San Antonio grocery store. Three days later, en route to Mississippi, they paused for a nostalgic moment at the Louisiana ambush site where Bonnie and Clyde had been killed by lawmen in May 1934. On March 27, the duo stole a car in Hattiesburg, rebounding the next day with a bank heist at Prentiss, Mississippi. They parted company on March 30, Fults boarding a train to Louisville, Kentucky, while Hamilton returned to Texas and a date with the electric chair.

Arriving in Springfield, Illinois, on April 5, Fults learned of Hamilton's arrest in Fort Worth the same day and booked passage on the first southbound bus out of town. He reached Fort Worth on April 8, perhaps intending to spring Hamilton, but stole a car instead and drove to visit his mother in McKinney. On April 12 Fults stole another car, this one from Renner, Texas. Two days later, joined by an unidentified accomplice, he robbed a Graham, Texas, oil refinery of $900.

It was Ralph's last hurrah. Captured in Denton County, Texas, on April 17, he was shipped back to

115

Huntsville, pending extradition to Mississippi for trial on bank-robbery charges. Conviction on that count in September 1935 earned him a 50-year sentence at Parchman prison farm, one of the South's most infamous penal colonies. In May 1936 Fults led an inmate strike at Parchman and landed in solitary for his trouble. He was graced with a second pardon in January 1944, and this time he went straight. Fults died of cancer in Dallas at age 82 on March 16, 1993.

G

GARCIA, Anastasio

A western lawman turned outlaw, Anastasio Garcia fought for the United States in the war with Mexico (1846–48) and then served as a constable in Salinas, California, during the gold rush. He was part of the posse that killed bandit leader CLAUDIO FELIZ on September 13, 1852, but even while he wore the badge, Garcia tried his hand at crime, working as a hired killer for politician and cattle baron Lewis Belcher, aka the "Big Eagle of Monterey." Garcia reached his point of no return in 1854 when he killed Constable William Hardmount in a dance-hall altercation and was jailed pending trial on murder charges. Garcia's political connections saved him from prison, but his lawless course was set. The confessed slayer of 14 men, Garcia (with his brother Faustino) rode with the gangs of FRANCISCO DANIEL and JUAN FLORES before branching out on his own. One of his protégés, Tiburcio Vásquez, would build on Garcia's teachings to become a feared outlaw in his own right.

On November 10, 1855, Garcia was named as the gunman who killed and robbed attorney Isaac Walt (former speaker of the California state assembly) and ex-constable Thomas Williamson outside Monterey on El Camino Real. An arrest warrant was issued five days later with a $3,000 reward posted for Garcia's capture. Sheriff John Keating led a posse to El Tucho ranch, an outlaw sanctuary 12 miles from Monterey where Garcia was known to reside. Surrounding Garcia's home at 3:00 A.M. on November 16, the law enforcers called for their quarry to surrender. Garcia's first shot struck Undersheriff Joaquin de la Torre in the face, killing him instantly. Using his wife as a human shield, Garcia wounded two more deputies, one of them mortally, before a rifle bullet drilled the woman's chest. Abandoning his wounded spouse—she would survive—Garcia fled with an accomplice believed to be Tiburcio Vásquez. The ex-lawman was spotted by searchers around 1:00 P.M., wounded by a hasty shotgun blast, but he eluded them once more and vanished into the wilderness.

Garcia suspected Lewis Belcher of betraying him, and he took his revenge on June 18, 1856, ambushing the "Big Eagle" and riddling him with buckshot. A fresh pursuit followed that murder, but Garcia remained elusive, wounding a deputy in Santa Barbara County before he vanished again. Finally, four months later, Garcia and two cohorts were surprised by law officers near San Juan Capistrano, surrendering without resistance. Jailed at Monterey on six counts of murder, Garcia never made it to trial. Masked lynchers took him from his cell and hanged him on February 16, 1857.

GARDNER, Roy: "King of the Escape Artists"

While never a tremendously successful outlaw—he was captured and convicted after almost every holdup he committed—Roy Gardner still earned fame within the criminal fraternity as an incorrigible "rabbit," unceasing in his efforts to escape from custody. As such, he was among the first convicts consigned to Alcatraz when that "escape-proof" prison opened during the Great Depression.

A native of Trenton, Missouri, born January 5, 1886, Gardner was eight years old when his family moved to Colorado Springs. He graduated high school there in 1902 and briefly worked the Arizona mines before enlisting for an army hitch that sent him to the Philippines. March 1906 found him in San Francisco, where he deserted from the service a few weeks short of an honorable discharge. Drifting back to the Southwest, he worked as a miner in New Mexico and Arizona until 1908, when an accident at Bisbee left him with a steel plate in his skull. Defense attorneys would surmise, in retrospect, that the head injury somehow set Gardner's feet upon the outlaw trail, but we must bear in mind that his desertion came *before* the accident and that he never lacked for honest work *after* the injury when he was in the mood.

Emerging from the hospital with a more-or-less clean bill of health, Gardner spent five months touring Mexico, apparently making friends with revolutionaries south of the border. On his return to the States, he began to run guns to the rebels but was captured by Mexican authorities with a wagonload of contraband ammunition near Cananea in March 1909. Sentenced to death at Hermosillo, Gardner staged his first jailbreak a few days later, fleeing with three other American prisoners on a long desert trek that brought him back to Arizona. He briefly tried mining again, boxed for prize money in Colorado, and then drifted back to San Francisco in December 1910. Gardner was down to his last dollar when he robbed a Frisco jeweler, but police nabbed him running from the scene. Convicted and sentenced to five years at San Quentin, he saved a guard's life (and suffered serious injury) in a 1912 prison riot. Authorities paroled him six months later in a show of gratitude.

Prison had taught Gardner to use a welding torch, and he found work San Francisco's Mare Island Navy Yard in January 1913, marrying one of his coworkers six months later. Roy left the navy yard to open his own welding shop in London, but an accidental fire sent him back to working for others. His marriage produced a daughter in September 1917, and Gardner became superintendent of welding at a San Francisco shipyard that fall. On the side, he was active in the sale of Liberty Bonds, banking enough money to open another welding shop—this one in

Fresno, California—in February 1919. Luck ran against him once more, and the shop soon folded. Gardner was between jobs in April 1920 when he left his wife and child at home for a quick vacation in Tijuana, Mexico—or so he said.

On April 27, 1920, Gardner robbed a U.S. mail truck en route from San Diego to Los Angeles, escaping with $80,000 in Liberty Bonds and Canadian currency. His follow-through left much to be desired, though: Leaving his hotel room for a nicer suite, Roy left behind several mail bags from the robbery and an old suitcase with his name stenciled on it. Caught within days, he confessed and led authorities to the loot, buried in a field at nearby Del Mar. Gardner pled guilty at trial and was sentenced to 25 years at the federal lockup on McNeil Island, Washington.

Reality set in for Gardner when he boarded a northbound train from Los Angeles to Washington on June 5, 1920. Desperate to escape, he bided his time until the train reached Salem, Oregon. There, with the aid of two Chinese prisoners, Gardner disarmed his guards, held them at gunpoint for several hours (somehow fooling the railroad conductors who passed through the car periodically), and leapt from the train at Portland. From there he walked to Rainier, Washington, and stole a motorboat, cruising downriver to Astoria. His next stop was Bellingham, where he stole a car and drove to Vancouver, British Columbia. Still running, Gardner bought a railroad ticket to Moose Jaw, Saskatchewan, where he found a welding job. A few months later, back in Minneapolis, he demonstrated expertise enough to win employment as a traveling salesman of welding equipment, serving customers throughout the Midwest.

It was a risky endeavor for a federal fugitive, but Gardner made a go of it, banking enough commission money after several months to settle in Davenport, Iowa, as a welding instructor. It was honest work, and the attraction paled before year's end, so he drifted back to California, robbing several railroad mail coaches en route to the Coast. On arrival in Sacramento, Gardner telephoned his wife, now working at a maid in Napa. She arranged to meet him at her home, unaware that law enforcers monitored her phone calls. Gardner eluded manhunters in Napa with uncustomary luck and fell back to the railroad hub at Roseville, California, plotting his next score.

He was immediately suspected on May 19, 1921 when two men stole a pair of mail bags from a train in Sacramento. Skeptics argued that he always worked alone, but the robbery produced a new rash of WANTED posters throughout northern California. It was definitely Gardner who invaded an express car at Roseville on May 20, catching the mail clerk asleep and binding him with leather straps before he rifled the mail bags. Frustrated in his search for major loot, he took a stack of registered mail, stole $11 from the clerk, and bailed out at the Newcastle railroad yard.

More mug shots circulated, prompting a Roseville café owner to finger frequent customer "Neal Gaynor," who enjoyed a chuckle over his perceived resemblance to outlaw Roy Gardner. Lawmen staked out the place and spotted their man on May 23, trailing him from the café to the gambling room of a nearby hotel. Arrested there and held in lieu of $25,000 bond, Gardner pled guilty to mail robbery and received another 25-year sentence, tacked onto his previous term at McNeil Island. Before he was transferred, Gardner offered to return the loot from the May 19 holdup—provided that his wife received the outstanding $5,000 reward—but a trek to the woods on June 9 turned up nothing, federal agents speculating that Gardner planned the jaunt as a means of escape.

The night of his abortive excursion, Gardner was placed aboard a train to Washington, this time wearing double sets of chains and a painful "Denver Boot" clamped to one foot as a hedge against escape. (A Denver boot is a metal clamp that is locked on to practically immobilize the wearer.) In Oregon he asked to use the train's restroom, and permission was granted. Returning from the toilet, he brandished a .32-caliber pistol his captors had somehow overlooked, transferred the chains and the "boot" to his escort, and then relieved them of another gun, some ammunition, and $120 cash before he bailed out near Castle Rock, Washington.

Instead of fleeing this time, Gardner burrowed in, but the effort was in vain. Spotted in Castle Rock on June 14, he ran belatedly but was caught two days later at Centralia. Transported immediately to McNeil Island, he auditioned for the prison baseball team and quickly made the cut. On September 5, 1921, accompanied by two lifers, Gardner fled during a baseball game, cutting his way through a fence, and escaped under fire from the guards. The San Francisco *Call Bulletin* received two letters from Gardner on September 26: One recounted his escape with a bullet in his leg; the other asked President

Warren Harding to commute Gardner's sentence, thus allowing him to "make good" with his wife and daughter. The postmarks were illegible, but postal inspectors confirmed the handwriting as Gardner's.

On November 15, 1921, Gardner tried to rob mail clerk Herman Inderlied at the Phoenix, Arizona, railroad depot. Inderlied overpowered and disarmed the bandit, holding him for police; a search of Gardner's person turned up items stolen from a Maricopa, Arizona, mail pouch the previous week. His trial on the latest mail-robbery charge ended with a hung jury, Gardner's attorney negotiating a plea bargain in return for leniency. The plan fell through, however, when a judge accepted Gardner's guilty plea on December 18 and then promptly slapped him with his third 25-year sentence. This time he was sent to Leavenworth and then transferred to Atlanta in 1925 and to Alcatraz in 1934 when The Rock opened to serve a clientele of incorrigible felons and escape artists.

Ex-wife Dolly Gardner fought for his release on grounds that Roy's head injury had turned him bad against his will, and while U.S. authorities rejected that argument, Gardner still received an unexpected pardon in 1938. He settled in San Francisco where he soon committed suicide by inhaling potassium cyanide in a hotel bathroom. Thoughtful to the last, he left a note warning the hotel's maid of danger from the gas.

GIBSON, Russell "Slim Gray"

A sometime member of the Depression-era bank-robbing gang led by the BARKER brothers and ALVIN KARPIS, Russell Gibson learned thievery as part of Tulsa, Oklahoma's, "Central Park Gang," running with the Barkers, VOLNEY DAVIS, RAY TERRILL, and others of their ilk. He scored his first major holdup on May 24, 1929, joining accomplices Neal Merritt and James "Cowboy" Long to steal $75,000 at gunpoint from a bank messenger in Oklahoma City. Gibson was arrested from that crime but escaped from the county jail prior to trial.

It is unknown how many bank jobs Gibson may have joined in with the Barker-Karpis gang, but his end came with the rest of the outfit in January 1935. FBI agents traced him on January 8 to a Chicago hideout he shared with his wife and other gang associates, but the G-men initially tear gassed the wrong apartment and started a panic in the building. Chicago police officers arrived and nearly opened fire on the feds, believing them to be gangsters. Gibson, meanwhile, armed with a Browning automatic rifle and a .32-caliber pistol, scrambled for the flat's fire escape. Agents were waiting for him there, and his bulletproof vest did no good against the concentrated fire of their high-powered rifles. Gibson was killed instantly; his wife and two companions were arrested on charges of harboring a federal fugitive.

GILBERT, Jesse James

No studies have been made of the relationship between a subject's name and ultimate selection of adult career, but it would seem that any infant christened for America's most famous outlaw has a head start on the road to crime. Such was the case with Jesse James Gilbert, convicted on various charges of burglary, interstate transportation of stolen cars, and parole violation. While confined in a California state prison, Gilbert stabbed a fellow inmate to death and had more time tacked onto his sentence.

On July 20, 1963, Gilbert escaped from San Quentin where he was serving 15 years on a burglary conviction. A federal fugitive warrant was issued on September 24, by which time Gilbert had been linked to California robberies in Los Angeles, Compton, Culver City, Torrance, and Long Beach.

On January 3, 1964, Gilbert and accomplice Edgar Ball Weaver raided an Alhambra savings and loan office for $11,492. Leaving the crime scene, they abducted a female employee for use as a shield, but police gave chase anyway, and shots were exchanged. Sgt. George Davis was struck in the head by a .45-caliber round and killed instantly; Ed Weaver was fatally wounded by return fire from police. In the confusion, Jesse Gilbert managed to escape, and a federal warrant charging him with bank robbery was issued three days later. Gilbert's name was posted to the FBI's "Ten Most Wanted" list on January 27, 1964.

A month later, on February 26, G-men acting on a tip surprised Gilbert in Philadelphia, surrounding him on the street outside the building where he had rented an apartment under the name "Donald Masters." Disguised with a black wig, sunglasses, and an adhesive bandage covering a tattoo on his left arm, Gilbert was armed with a .45 automatic but offered no resistance. A half-hour later, agents dropped by the apartment to arrest Gilbert's traveling companion, one Billie Jo Carder, sought by California authorities for violation of parole on an armed-robbery conviction. Both fugitives were soon returned to prison cells that waited for them in the Golden State.

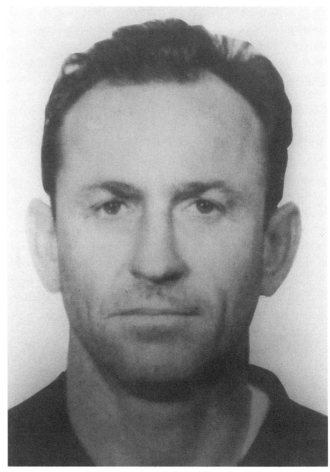

Jesse James Gilbert escaped from San Quentin prison to rob a California bank. (FBI)

GILLIS, Lester M.: See NELSON, GEORGE "BABY FACE."

GIPSON, Andrew Evan

A veteran felon with various jail terms behind him, Gipson was convicted under the Kansas habitual criminal statute for his role in a 1968 bank robbery, during which a state trooper was killed. On conviction Gipson received six concurrent sentences of 40 to 90 years in prison, serving nine years before he escaped from the state penitentiary at Lansing in July 1977. Declared a federal fugitive on charges of unlawful flight to avoid confinement, Gipson was added to the FBI's "Ten Most Wanted" list on March 27, 1978.

On May 24, 1978, two days before his 42nd birthday, Gipson was traced to Albuquerque, New Mexico, where he had spent the past eight months living and working as "Phillip Daigle." Agents collared him without resistance at his job, where he had lately been promoted as the foreman of a construction crew. Gipson's employers were stunned by the arrest, describing the fugitive as "a damn good worker."

GOETZ, Fred "Shotgun" George Ziegler

Fred Goetz was another of those figures, like FRED BURKE and VERNON MILLER, who bridged the gap between organized crime and freelance bank-robbing gangs in the early 1930s. Unlike his peers, however, Goetz spent the first three decades of his life as a respected citizen. Born in 1896, he worked as a landscape engineer before World War I, served as an army pilot in that conflict, and later attended the University of Illinois, where he studied engineering, managed his fraternity house, and excelled in athletics. Goetz graduated in 1922 and his future seemed bright—or, at least, stable—until 1925, when he was arrested for attempting to rape a seven-year-old girl at a Chicago beach (where Goetz worked part time as a lifeguard).

Bond was set at $5,000 on that charge, posted by his parents. Goetz wanted to skip town, but he balked at causing his parents to lose their money. Instead, he planned to raise the cash quickly with another crime. Targeting a local physician who was known to carry large sums of money, Goetz recruited two accomplices for an ill-conceived holdup. They braced their mark outside a Chicago hotel, but the doctor pulled a gun and opened fire, whereupon Goetz shot him dead. He was thus forced to flee empty handed, and his parents lost their money after all.

From attempted rape and bungled robbery, Goetz somehow found his way into Al Capone's bootleg syndicate as a professional killer. Suspicions persist (encouraged by Goetz's own boasting) that he played a role in the St. Valentine's Day massacre of 1929, though proof remains elusive. There is better evidence for his participation, with four gangland accomplices, in the April 16, 1928, robbery of an American Express Company truck in Toledo, Ohio, where the bandits killed a policeman and escaped with $200,000 in cash.

By 1932 or early 1933, Goetz was affiliated with the bank-robbing gang led by ALVIN KARPIS and the BARKER brothers. Well connected with renegade politicians and law enforcers in wide-open ST. PAUL, MINNESOTA, Fred is described in some accounts as the "mastermind" behind that outfit's sudden shift from holdups into kidnapping for ransom. He allegedly planned the abduction of St. Paul brewer William Hamm in June 1933 and eight months later was entrusted to hide half of the $200,000 ransom paid for safe release of another St. Paul resident, banker Edward Bremer. The money was stashed in a garage owned by one of Goetz's in-laws, but the Barker-Karpis mob soon regretted their choice of bagman.

Whether it was alcohol or simple arrogance, something caused Goetz to suffer a falling out with his underworld cronies in the wake of the Bremer kidnapping. Rumors flew that he was often drunk and boasted of his gangland exploits, both with the Barker-Karpis gang and with the Capone syndicate. There was no shortage of suspects on March 21, 1934, when Fred emerged from a Cicero, Illinois, tavern and was torn apart by a volley of shotgun blasts. He died with a $1,000 bill in his pocket, but the Barkers were more interested in their ransom money from the Bremer snatch. Goetz's widow reportedly delivered the cash without complaint, days after her husband was killed.

GOODPASTER, Tanoa

An early contestant for the title of Most Inept Bandit of the New Millennium, 53-year-old Tanoa Goodpaster entered a bank in Indianapolis, Indiana, on February 17, 2000, and handed the teller a note stating that he wished to withdraw $21,000 from his trust-fund account. Being told that his account did not contain sufficient funds, Goodpaster reportedly threatened the teller and was given the cash he desired. Leaving the bank, he crossed the street to a restaurant directly opposite and ordered coffee. Goodpaster was still there, relaxing with his beverage, when police arrived moments later and arrested him on preliminary charges of bank robbery.

GREEN, Eddie

A brainy bank robber of the early 1930s, Eddie Green was known as an expert "jug marker" who not only cased banks in advance but also mapped escape routes and drove them beforehand to ensure a smooth getaway. His alliance with corrupt police and politicians in ST. PAUL, MINNESOTA, also made Green useful for procuring hideouts and making sure his cronies were forewarned of any raids.

A veteran of several different gangs, Green pulled his first recorded bank job on January 28, 1933, with accomplices Earl Doyle, Thomas "Buck" Woulfe, and "Dago" Howard Lansdon. The foursome stopped a bank messenger in North Kansas City and relieved him of $14,500, wounding Marshal Edgar Nall in an exchange of gunfire that also left Woulfe injured. After a shootout with civilian posse members, the gang stole a car from one of their pursuers and fled into Iowa. There, they took fresh license plates from two more vehicles and then kidnapped a pair of Knoxville policemen—Burt Conrey and John Neuman—before heading back to Missouri. The hostages were released unharmed at Unionville on January 29. Tom Woulfe, dying from a bullet wound in his groin, was captured four days later at a hospital in Coffeyville, Kansas, and died soon after his transfer to the lockup in Liberty, Missouri.

Green joined a new team for his next holdup on April 4, 1933. His partners in the holdup of a bank at Fairbury, Nebraska, included Arthur and Fred BARKER, ALVIN KARPIS, FRANK NASH, VOLNEY DAVIS, Jess Doyle, and Earl Christman. The gang made off with $151,350 in cash, but Christman was wounded during their getaway. Green drove him to ex-sheriff VERNON MILLER's Kansas City home to convalesce, but the wound was mortal, and they planted Earl in an unmarked grave outside town.

Green dropped from sight for a time after the Fairbury job and then resurfaced in early 1934 as a member of the reorganized JOHN DILLINGER gang. His first outing with the crew occurred on March 6 when he joined Dillinger, TOMMY CARROLL, HOMER VAN METER, and GEORGE "BABY FACE" NELSON to loot $49,500 from a bank in Sioux Falls, South Dakota. A policeman was wounded in the holdup, but the gang's fortunes were reversed a week later in Mason City, Iowa. Green cased that job with Van Meter, but it still fell apart. The gang bagged $52,344 but left nearly four times as much behind; Dillinger and JOHN HAMILTON were both wounded by gunfire as they fled, along with a civilian passer-by.

Back in St. Paul, Green arranged a hideout for Dillinger and Van Meter, but the FBI was breathing down their neck by then, surprising the outlaws on March 31. Both escaped in a chaotic shootout with the feds, Dillinger wounded once again, and while Green arranged for medical treatment in Minneapolis, his own time was swiftly running out. G-men searched Dillinger's abandoned flat and found Green's telephone number, moving on to occupy his hideout and wait for someone—anyone—to turn up.

It was April 3 before Green and his wife returned to the apartment house in St. Paul. Eddie left his car and was approaching the house on foot when agents opened fire with Tommy guns and cut him down. Reports differ on whether he was ambushed in cold blood or tried to run away, the official report alleging that Green "assumed a threatening attitude . . . accompanied by menacing gestures." Menacing he may have seemed, but Green was unarmed, and the bureau took another beating in the press for its tendency to gun down helpless suspects.

Though mortally wounded, Eddie Green survived for nine more days, raving deliriously in a St. Paul hospital bed. Federal agents stood by to record his every word, gaining extensive knowledge of the Midwest underworld from Green's ramblings. Among his unintended revelations were the FBI's first-ever notice that the Barker-Karpis gang existed, a tip that led within 10 months to the outfit's undoing. Bessie Green, in custody for harboring her husband, confirmed that the Barker-Karpis gang had been responsible for kidnapping Edward Bremer in January 1934, thus producing a new rash of federal indictments.

GRISTY, Bill

A holdup man from California's gold-rush era, Bill Gristy was serving time on robbery charges in the San Francisco County jail when he met outlaws TOM HODGES and HENRY TALBOT. The trio escaped, with several other inmates, from a prison work detail on May 12, 1855, Gristy afterward joining the gang Hodges organized and led under his new alias of "Tom Bell." Additional members of the wide-ranging crew included RICHARD "RATTLESNAKE DICK" BARTER and ADOLPH NEWTON, plus bandit brothers GEORGE and CYRUS SKINNER.

As specialists in highway robbery, the gang preyed often on lone travelers and teamsters, Gristy wounding one victim who tried to escape on the north fork of the Feather River in 1855. That July, the band stole $3,000 in gold from an express messenger near Forest City, California, but a second messenger foiled their attempt five months later, on the run from Shasta to Weaverville.

Gristy participated in the gang's greatest holdup on March 12, 1856, lifting $17,000 in gold dust from the Yreka Mine's mule train en route to Shasta through the Trinity Alps. Six weeks later, on April 22, he was hiding out with George Skinner and

Nicanor Rodriguez near Folsom when lawmen burst into their cabin with sawed-off shotguns leveled. Skinner was killed in the first exchange of fire, and Rodriguez was wounded and captured, but Gristy seized two pistols and shot his way out the front door, escaping into darkness.

On August 11, 1856, with Tom Hodges and four other bandits, Gristy ambushed a stagecoach carrying $100,000 in gold dust near Dry Creek. The express guard and several armed passengers opened fire on the gang, sparking a fierce shootout. A female passenger was killed, and two others and the shotgun rider were wounded, while the gang fled empty handed. Bill Gristy and Juan "Spanish John" Fernandez were prowling the northern California mines by September 9, robbing one man of $14 and stealing two horses from another victim. Spotted by a posse on September 18, both outlaws surrendered and freely confessed to a long list of crimes. Talking saved Gristy's life, and he was returned to San Quentin to finish his time on the interrupted robbery sentence.

HAMER, Francis Augustus: Texas Ranger

A legendary lawman in the Wild West tradition, Frank Hamer was born in March 1884 when Indian raids and stagecoach robberies were still a daily fact of life on the Texas frontier. He grew up with a love of camping and hunting, was familiar with guns almost before he could walk, and built a powerful physique while working in his father's blacksmith shop. By age 22, when he joined the Texas Rangers, Hamer could throw a knife with deadly accuracy and was widely regarded as one of the best shots in Texas. It was a skill that served him well in confrontations with various badmen, and reports credit Hamer with killing at least 53 felons (some reports say 65) during the next quarter-century, though specific names and dates remain obscure.

By the early 1920s, the Texas Rangers had acquired an unsavory reputation in some quarters, known for their political cronyism, outspoken racism, and a history of shootings that sometimes amounted to summary execution of suspects without trial (particularly when those suspects where Hispanic, black, or Native American). The Porvenir massacre of January 1918, in which 15 unarmed Mexican Americans were tortured and shot by a rogue Ranger detachment, brought widespread condemnation but no prosecution of the murderers. Investigation of that incident exposed numerous other cases of flogging, torture, extortion, and murder committed under color of law. Governor Miriam "Ma" Ferguson discharged the entire Ranger Service upon her inauguration in 1925 and then appointed 2,300 "special" Rangers (some of whom, ironically, were convicted felons).

Most accounts stress that Hamer was a "good Ranger," untainted by the many problems dogging the agency, and in fact he did not serve constantly with the Rangers throughout his law-enforcement career. In 1908 he resigned to become town marshal of lawless Navasota, cleaning up that town before he moved on in to serve as a Harris County "special officer" in 1911. March 1915 saw him back with the Rangers, and three years later (two months after the Porvenir slaughter) he was accused of threatening Hispanic state legislator José Canales. No charges were filed in that case, and Hamer was promoted to the rank of senior captain in 1921. Although one published account claims Hamer resigned in protest after the election of 1924, refusing to serve a female governor, he apparently survived the Ferguson shakeup with his rank and reputation intact.

In 1928 Captain Hamer was credited with exposing a curious "reward ring" that operated in response to a standing offer of $5,000, posted by the Texas Bankers' Association, for any dead bank robber. Hamer charged that victims had been framed and murdered by greedy civilians, while other civilians made a practice of tracking down small-time hoodlums, killing them, and presenting them as deceased stickup artists. Coupled with a splash of bad publicity north of the Mason-Dixon Line, Hamer's exposé prompted Texas bankers to insert

Frank Hamer (front row, right) poses with lawmen who helped him slay Clyde Barrow and Bonnie Parker in 1934.
(From the collection of the Texas/Dallas History and Archives Division, Dallas Public Library)

the words "OR ALIVE" on posters that had previously marked bank robbers WANTED DEAD.

Hamer had been officially retired for two years by February 10, 1934, when a special request from Lee Simmons, then head of the Texas state prison system, launched Hamer on the most famous manhunt of his career—the pursuit of bandits CLYDE BARROW and BONNIE PARKER. It took Hamer 102 days to complete his assignment. Trailing Bonnie and Clyde with a bloodhound's tenacity, working in conjunction with Deputy Sheriff Ted Hinton (once a grade-school classmate of Clyde), Hamer learned that Louisiana native HENRY METHVYN was a late addition to the Barrow gang. He was also wanted for multiple murders, a circumstance that permitted Hamer to negotiate from strength when he confronted Methvyn's father at home, arranging a Louisiana ambush for the Lone Star State's most-wanted fugitives. On May

23, 1934, when Clyde and Bonnie were scheduled to visit his home, Ivan Methvyn parked his truck on the highway between Gibsland and Sailes, Louisiana, removing one wheel as if changing a flat tire. Hamer, Hinton, and four other lawmen crouched in nearby bushes, armed with Browning automatic rifles and assorted backup weapons. They were ready and waiting when the outlaws finally appeared.

Some authors have charitably described what happened next as a "shootout," though in fact Clyde and Bonnie received no warning or call to surrender before the posse opened fire, pumping at least 167 bullets through their vehicle and bodies. By that time, Clyde and company had killed so many law officers and civilians that no chance of yet another hair's-breadth escape could be tolerated. Speaking from the center ring of a full-blown media circus, Hamer grudgingly acknowledged that it pained him to shoot a woman, "especially while she's sitting down."

Congress awarded Frank Hamer a special citation for killing Bonnie and Clyde, after which he spent the remainder of the 1930s as a "private agent"—that is, a strikebreaker—for various Texas oil companies. Governor Coke Stevenson recalled him to active duty as a Ranger in 1948, briefly investigating charges of election fraud in two counties where corruption surpassed the accepted norm, but Hamer retired from police work for the last time in 1949. Wounded numerous times in his battles with badmen, Hamer died with his boots off on July 10, 1955, at home in Austin, passing peacefully in his sleep.

HAMILTON, Floyd Garland

A 1930s Texas outlaw whose more famous younger brother, Raymond, ran with the CLYDE BARROW gang on occasion, Floyd Hamilton launched his criminal career as a kind of family affair. On March 16, 1934, with brother Ray, he stole $1,500 from a bank in Grand Prairie, Texas, and eluded the subsequent manhunt. Floyd was less fortunate on April 1, after Raymond and/or Barrow murdered two highway patrolmen near Grapevine. The killings earned Clyde a new tag as Texas "Public Enemy No. 1," but law enforcers couldn't find him, so they jailed Floyd Hamilton instead. The case was admittedly flimsy, and jurors acquitted Floyd of murder charges on July 24, 1934.

Floyd was back with brother Raymond in the new year, looting $1,000 from a Carthage, Texas, bank on February 4, 1935, dodging a posse that raided their Dallas apartment later the same day. Clyde Barrow and girlfriend BONNIE PARKER were long dead by that time, their demise turning up the heat on surviving gang members, and while Raymond soon found himself en route to death row at Huntsville, condemned for the Grapevine double murder, Floyd dropped out of sight for three years, either keeping his nose clean or showing unaccustomed discretion in his criminal exploits.

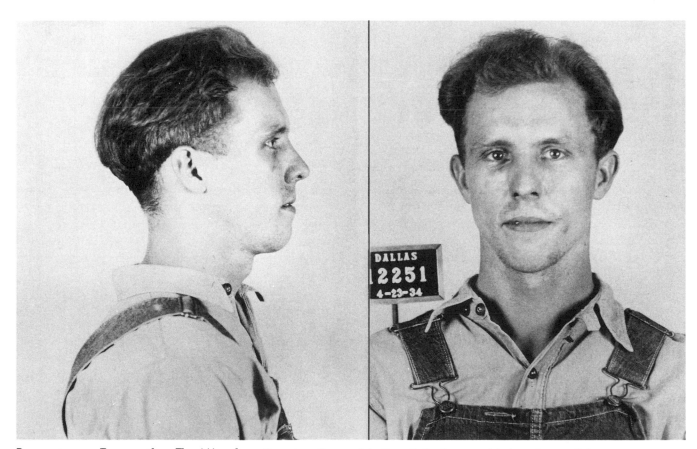

Depression-era Texas outlaw Floyd Hamilton (From the collection of the Texas/Dallas History and Archives Division, Dallas Public Library)

He surfaced again on June 7, 1938, joining accomplice Ted Walters to steal a paltry $685 from a bank in Bradley, Arkansas. On July 21 three gunmen shot their way through a highway-patrol roadblock near Willis Point, Texas, and the rattled officers identified one of the briefly glimpsed shooters as Floyd Hamilton. Ten days later, Missouri officers pursued and lost three "suspicious" characters, afterward naming two as Hamilton and Ted Walters. On August 5, closer to home, Hamilton and Walters blasted their way out of a police trap near Fort Worth. (The missing third gunman was never identified.)

Their luck ran out on August 21, 1938, when both bandits were arrested in Dallas. Convicted in federal court of the Bradley, Arkansas, holdup, both were packed off for long terms on The Rock of Alcatraz. Hamilton was eventually paroled and retired to Grand Prairie, Texas, where he had robbed his first known bank in 1934. He died there of natural causes on July 24, 1984.

HAMILTON, John "Red"

A Canadian native, nicknamed for his dark red hair, John Hamilton earned his living as a carpenter before he turned his hand to crime. On March 16, 1927, he was convicted of "auto banditry"—robbing a gasoline station in St. Joseph County, Indiana—and was sentenced to 25 years in the state penitentiary at Michigan City. There, he met and was befriended by outlaws JOHN DILLINGER, HARRY PIERPONT, CHARLES MAKLEY, HOMER VAN METER, and RUSSELL CLARK, among others. After six and a half years of confinement, Hamilton had seen enough of prison. He gladly went along with Pierpont, Makley, Clark, and six others when they escaped from Michigan City on September 26, 1933, using pistols smuggled in by the lately paroled Dillinger.

The new gang needed money, which they got a week later, stealing $14,000 from a bank at St. Mary's, Ohio. They also needed to repay a favor because Dillinger had been jailed in Lima, Ohio, four days before their escape. Hamilton was along for the ride on October 12 when they raided the Lima jail and liberated Dillinger, Pierpont murdering Sheriff Jess Sarber in the process. Two months later, on December 13, Hamilton was part of the team that invaded a Chicago bank vault to rifle the contents of 96 safe-deposit boxes. Officially, losses totaled $8,700, but other reports place the unreported score closer to $50,000 in cash and other valuables.

One day after the vault raid, Hamilton dropped a car off to get its dented fender repaired at a Chicago body shop. The mechanic pegged it accurately as a "gangster car" and summoned police. Sergeant William Shanley arrived with two patrolmen to stake out the vehicle, bracing Hamilton when he returned. "Red" came up shooting, killing Shanley on the spot and fleeing unscathed, while the patrolmen fumbled with their weapons. Hamilton's girlfriend of the moment, briefly detained, won her freedom by convincing authorities that she did not know that "Red" was an outlaw prior to the shooting.

On January 15, 1935, Hamilton joined Dillinger and a third man to steal $20,376 from a bank in East Chicago, Indiana. Patrolman William O'Malley was killed in the holdup, by a burst of submachine-gun fire, and although Dillinger was charged with the murder, several witnesses claimed that Hamilton—himself wounded in the exchange of gunfire—was the actual triggerman. On December 28, when Illinois issued its first list of "public enemies," Hamilton ranked third on the roster, behind Dillinger and Pierpont.

The gang left Hamilton with an underworld doctor, JOSEPH MORAN, to convalesce in Chicago while the rest of them took off for a vacation in Tucson, Arizona. It was a lucky break for "Red" because Dillinger, Pierpont, Makley, and Clark were arrested in Tucson. Dillinger was packed off to Indiana for trial in the O'Malley murder; his cohorts went back to face charges of killing Sheriff Sarber in Ohio. Pierpont, Makley, and Clark were finished, but Dillinger escaped from custody again on March 3, rallying a new gang that included Hamilton, Van Meter, TOMMY CARROLL, EDDIE GREEN, and GEORGE "BABY FACE" NELSON. (Rumor has it that Hamilton had planned to dynamite the jail where Dillinger was held before Johnny outfoxed his guards with a hand-carved wooden pistol.)

Published sources differ as to whether Hamilton participated in the gang's first holdup at Sioux Falls, South Dakota, three days after Dillinger's jailbreak. The gunmen bagged $49,500, wounding a policemen as they fled the scene in a flurry of gunfire. Hamilton was definitely with the team a week later, however, when they lifted $52,344 from another bank in Mason City, Iowa. It was a chaotic operation: Hamilton and Dillinger were both wounded, despite their bulletproof vests, as they fled the bank in a swirling cloud of tear gas.

The heat was definitely on, newspapers stumbling over each other to report progress in the manhunt. Forewarned by press reports of a police trap in Kentucky, Dillinger and Hamilton stopped to visit "Red's" sister on April 17, in Saul Sainte Marie, Michigan, and then moved on to meet the rest of the gang at Emil Wanatka's Little Bohemia Lodge near Rhinelander, Wisconsin. It was supposed to be vacation time, but FBI agent MELVIN PURVIS had been tipped to the gathering. On the night of April 22 he raided the lodge, shooting three civilians (one fatally) and losing one of his own men in the process before the gang members escaped into darkness.

"Red" Hamilton's luck ran out one day later. While riding with Dillinger and Homer Van Meter, he engaged in another shootout with authorities near south ST. PAUL, MINNESOTA, critically wounded by a bullet as the outlaws made their getaway. Once again, he was delivered to Doctor Moran in Chicago, but this time Moran refused treatment, passing Hamilton off to bank robber VOLNEY DAVIS in Aurora, Illinois. Despite the care of Davis and his outlaw girlfriend, EDNA MURRAY, Hamilton reportedly died on April 30, 1934, and was secretly buried, Dillinger pouring lye over his face and hands in the grave to prevent later identification.

Authorities had no idea that Hamilton was dead, so they indicted him on May 19, with other Dillinger cronies, on charges of harboring his fellow bandits. "Red's" sister was later convicted on an identical charge and briefly sent to prison, her grief compounded with discovery of Hamilton's grave on August 28, 1935. The skeleton was identified from prison dental records, but Hamilton had the last laugh as rumors of his survival continued to circulate. FBI headquarters received several letters claiming that Hamilton was still at large, and years later, one of "Red's" nephews spun a tale of visiting his infamous uncle in Canada. If so, the disappearing act was perfect: No living trace of Hamilton has ever been discovered from mid-April 1934 to the present day.

HAMILTON, Raymond

Born near Schulter, Oklahoma, on May 21, 1913, Ray Hamilton was a lifelong career criminal and escape artist who earned his greatest notoriety in Texas through association with bandits CLYDE BARROW and BONNIE PARKER. That said, he was also aggressive and violent enough to operate on his own—or with other accomplices, including brother FLOYD HAMILTON—and he would outlive his more infamous colleagues, if only by 352 days.

The first of Ray Hamilton's several jailbreaks occurred on January 27, 1932, when he sawed through the bars of his cell in McKinney, Texas, while awaiting trial for auto theft. There is no public record of his first meeting with Clyde Barrow, but the gunmen teamed up three months later to rob a Hillsboro jewelry store and kill proprietor John Bucher on April 30. The pair stole 400 blank money orders from the Port Sullivan post office on June 24 and then resurfaced at Palestine, Texas, on July 16, kidnapping bookkeeper Roy Evans from the Palestine Ice Company and beating and robbing him of $989. Evans identified his attackers from their respective mug shots, and the manhunt was on.

Eleven days after the Palestine kidnapping, Raymond and Clyde robbed a bank in Willis, Texas, making off with $3,000. On August 1 they hit the Neuhoff Packing Company in Dallas, stealing several hundred dollars and a handful of diamond rings. The night of August 5 found them relaxing at a barn dance in Stringtown, Oklahoma, when Sheriff C. G. Maxwell and Deputy Eugene Moore approached their car. Pistols blazed, leaving Moore dead and Maxwell wounded, while the shooters sped away.

Nine days later, while hiding out with Bonnie and Clyde at a relative's home near Carlsbad, New Mexico, Hamilton helped kidnap Sheriff Joe Johns, later dropping him off unharmed in San Antonio. On August 30 the trio fought their way clear of a police ambush near Wharton, Texas, wounding one officer in the exchange of fire.

Hamilton disappeared from view for a time, after that shootout. It was October 8, 1932, before he resurfaced, looting a bank at Cedar Hills, Texas, of $1,401. Police believed his male accomplice in the holdup was Clyde Barrow, but it may have been wishful thinking. On November 9, with sidekick Gene O'Dare, Hamilton tapped a bank in LaGrange for $1,400. O'Dare and gunman Les Stewart helped out on November 25 when Ray returned to Cedar Hills and took another bank for $1,800.

With that as traveling money, Hamilton and O'Dare headed north to Michigan where Raymond spent time with his father. He also spent time with the ladies, drinking in speakeasies and boasting so loudly of his criminal exploits that someone finally tipped police. Arrested with O'Dare on December 5, 1932, Hamilton was swiftly extradited to Texas where conviction on murder and robbery charges earned him a 263-year prison sentence. O'Dare's prison sentence—a mere 50 years—was positively lenient, by comparison.

It was one thing to cage Ray Hamilton, however; holding him was something else, entirely. On January 16, 1934, Bonnie and Clyde ambushed a road crew at the Eastham prison farm, liberating Hamilton and four other convicts. Two guards were wounded in the blaze of gunfire, one of them fatally. Two months later, on March 19, Raymond teamed with brother Floyd and accomplice John Badsden to raid a Grand Prairie, Texas, bank of $1,500. March 31 saw Hamilton rob a bank in West, Texas, Mary O'Dare wheeling the getaway car after Raymond scooped $1,862 from the teller's cages at gunpoint.

The next day, April 1, was Easter Sunday. Hamilton was relaxing with Bonnie and Clyde on a country lane near Grapevine, Texas, when two highway patrol officers pulled up on their motorcycles. Stories differ on what happened next: Clyde's relatives insist to this day that he meant to kidnap the patrolmen for a harmless joy ride, playfully remarking, "Let's take them," before Hamilton cut loose at point-blank range and gunned them down. Conversely, an alleged eyewitness to the crime (albeit a remote one, well beyond gunshot range) later described Bonnie Parker standing over the prostrate forms of Patrolmen E.B. Wheeler and H. D. Murphy, pumping slugs into their bodies. Whoever pulled the trigger, Clyde was promptly designated "Public Enemy No. 1" in Texas, though he denied the murders to the end of his days, once penning a letter that advised detectives to ask Hamilton's girlfriend "how they spend Easter."

In fact, law enforcers could ask Raymond himself because Hamilton and accomplice Ted Brooks had been jailed on April 25, 1934, arrested near Howe, Texas, shortly after stealing $2,300 from a bank in Lewisville. Uncle Sam weighed in on May 18, indicting Ray with Clyde Barrow and two others for the July 1933 theft of weapons from a National Guard armory in Oklahoma. Convicted of the Lewisville heist on May 25, Hamilton saw another 99 years added on to his existing 263-year sentence, but the worst was yet to come. On June 11, Raymond went to trial with co-defendant Joe Palmer for the murder of Major E. M. Crowson, shot in the January 1934 escape from Eastham Farm. Both men were swiftly convicted and sentenced to die.

There would be no rescue from Bonnie and Clyde this time, Hamilton's former benefactors having been riddled by a posse in Louisiana two days before Raymond's Lewisville conviction. Still, he was not without resources. On July 22, 1934, Hamilton, Palmer, and Irwin "Blackie" Thompson—lumped together in press reports as "embryonic DILLINGERS"—used smuggled weapons to shoot their way out of the Huntsville death house and escape. Palmer was recaptured at Paducah, Kentucky, on August 11, promptly confessing the July 26 holdup of a bank in Henderson, Kentucky ($34,237), but Hamilton eluded his pursuers and remained at large.

On February 4, 1935, with brother Floyd, Ray stole $1,000 from a Carthage, Texas, bank; law officers raided their Dallas apartment the same night but came up empty. On February 17, with hoodlum Ralph Fults, Hamilton stole eight Browning automatic rifles from a National Guard armory in Beaumont, Texas. He may have been pleased, five days later, when his sister—Lillie McBride—was acquitted on harboring charges, but 22 other defendants, including relatives of Hamilton, Bonnie, and Clyde, were found guilty as charged and sentenced to various jail terms and fines.

On March 19, 1935, Hamilton allegedly kidnapped Houston journalist Harry McCormick to dictate his exclusive story for publication. Only years later, after Raymond and the statute of limitations had both expired, would McCormick acknowledge the ruse, designed to insulate himself from charges of harboring a public enemy. The story made a splash, but Raymond's last foray into robbery was less impressive, joining Ralph Fults to lift $933 from a bank in Prentiss, Mississippi, afterward capturing 15 members of a civilian posse whom they released unharmed.

On April 6, 1935, Hamilton was sighted and arrested by sheriff's deputies near Grapevine, Texas, scene of his last known murders the previous year. There would be no escape this time, though Hamilton remained cocky and smiling to the bitter end. He was executed with Joe Palmer at Huntsville, in the electric chair on May 10, 1935.

HAMMONDS, Walker: See COLLEARN, MICHAEL.

HARRELSON, Thomas George

A firearms and explosives expert linked to the Aryan Nations movement, Harrelson was another of those home-grown Nazis who seek to "defend the white race" by robbing banks. Between October 1985 and February 1987 he raided at least nine banks in six states, assisted by his fiancée and fellow hard-core fascists. By the autumn of 1986 Harrelson's gang had bagged close to $90,000 for the cause, and his efforts won him a posting to the FBI's "Ten Most Wanted" list on November 26 of that year.

Addition to the list made Harrelson nervous, prompting him to cancel his scheduled wedding. Pregnant and disappointed, fiancée Cynthia Ehrlich still understood her man's commitment to the struggle. Her own father, Klansman Robert Miles, had served prison time in Michigan for bombing school buses as a protest against integration, and he would soon be indicted with other "Aryan" leaders around the country for sedition against the U.S. government.

On January 13, 1987, Harrison's raiders robbed a bank in Little Rock, Arkansas, making off with $11,018 in cash. Four weeks later, on February 9, he robbed a small bank in Warren, Minnesota. Backed up by Cynthia Ehrlich and neo-Nazi Stuart Skarda, he was pursued from the scene by bank employees in private cars, losing his own vehicle when it bogged down in mud on a rural road. Commandeering a grain truck with four hostages, the bandits rolled on toward Argyle, where a police roadblock stopped them cold. Veering into a ditch after a brisk exchange of gunfire, the fugitives surrendered when they found themselves surrounded.

In custody, Harrelson struck a bargain with federal prosecutors, seeking reduced prison time in return for a marathon guilty plea. Aside from the holdups in Warren and Little Rock, he confessed to bank robberies in Fowlersville, Michigan ($7,825); Leslie, Michigan ($13,000); Springport, Michigan ($2,733); Delta, Ohio ($9,800); Rossville, Illinois ($43,911); Drayton, North Dakota ($2,807); and a previous stickup in Warren ($9,800). His reward for the guilty plea was a sentenced of 34 years in the federal penitentiary at Leavenworth, where he presumably remains committed to the Nazi cause, revered as an "Aryan martyr" by comrades still at large.

HEROUX, George Arthur, and PUFF, Gerhard Arthur

A pair of veteran stickup artists who specialized in bank robberies, Heroux and Puff teamed up to loot a bank in Kansas City, Missouri, on October 10, 1951. Six weeks later, on November 23, they cracked another bank in Prairie Village, Kansas, walking out with $62,650. By the time FBI agents began to track them as a federal fugitives, Heroux was also suspected of murdering Massachusetts State Trooper Alje Savela, slain at Barre on August 31, 1951. Heroux's name was added to the "Ten Most Wanted" list on December 19, 1951, with Puff joining him on January 28, 1952.

Evidence recovered from an abandoned getaway car led G-men to scour the state of New Hampshire on July 19, 1952, but the trail was already cold. Six days later, in the Miami suburb of El Portal, Florida, Police Chief Barron Shields and Patrolman Robert Dubray responded to reports of a disturbance at a local residence. Arriving at the scene, they were confronted by Heroux with gun in hand. He forced the officers to take him on a drive that soon became a high-speed running gun battle, as other squad cars joined the lineup. Chief Shields finally brought the pursuit to a close by swerving his car into a tree, stunning Heroux long enough for the fugitive to be disarmed and handcuffed.

Gerhard Puff killed an FBI agent before his capture in 1952. (FBI)

In custody, Heroux refused to offer any information, but an inadvertent comment led the FBI to New York City, where the two fugitives had registered with their wives at the Congress Hotel on July 20, using the names "John Hanson" (for Heroux) and "J. Burns" (for Puff). Heroux had driven on from there to Florida and capture, while Puff and the two women remained in New York.

On the morning of July 26, five federal agents hid themselves in a small waiting room off the lobby of the Congress Hotel, maintaining radio contact with a sixth agent outside. They observed "Mrs. Burns" and "Mrs. Hanson" leaving the hotel with heavy luggage, later found to be packed full of guns and ammunition. Gerhard Puff returned to the hotel a short time later, riding upstairs in the elevator, and the agents took their places to arrest him when he reappeared. Four men were stationed in the lobby, while a fifth—Special Agent Joseph Brock—crouched behind a frosted glass door separating the lobby from a hallway in the rear.

Bank robber George Heroux, half of a deadly 1950s holdup team (FBI)

Puff managed to surprise the agents by descending on the stairs and ambushed Agent Brock, shooting him five times with fatal results. Believing himself in the clear, Puff bolted through the lobby and was halted by a bullet in his leg. A murder charge was added to the other pending counts against him; the women captured in his company were charged with aiding and abetting federal fugitives. Heroux and Puff were convicted at trial and sentenced to long prison terms.

HIGHWAYMEN and Hijacking: History

Robbery of travelers and theft of goods in transit has been a staple practice of career criminals throughout recorded history. The Bible presents one such incident in the parable of the good Samaritan (Luke 10:30–35), and innumerable real-life examples are found in criminal archives. Practitioners of highway robbery—appropriately dubbed "highwaymen"—were routinely condemned in Europe from Medieval times through the early 19th century—whether or not their victims were physically harmed. Similar justice awaited Australian "BUSHRANGERS" and American outlaws who fell into the hands of noose-happy vigilance committees, while those arrested by duly authorized law enforcers might escape with a stiff prison term.

Still, despite the risks involved, variations of highway robbery—dubbed "hijacking" in modern times—have persisted to the present day, keeping pace with technical advances in transportation. From waylaying travelers on foot or horseback, highwaymen soon graduated to stagecoach holdups and TRAIN ROBBERY, moving on from there to aircraft piracy (or "skyjacking") in the 20th century. Armored-car robbery losses reimbursed by insurance between 1973 and 1977 were publicized in 1979 as $8.8 million. In August 1999 FBI spokesmen estimated that losses to cargo theft in the United States alone averaged somewhere between $3.5 billion and $6 billion per year. Such pervasive criminal activity defies easy summarization, but a sampling of notorious incidents may provide an overview of the problem.

1250–1852—India: The Thugee cult, worshipers of Cali, robbed and murdered untold numbers of travelers throughout the subcontinent. No final statistics are available, but British authorities estimated that the cult killed 40,000 victims in the year 1812 alone; one Thug, named Buhram, confessed to 931 murders at his arrest in 1840. At least 4,500 cultists were convicted of various crimes between 1830 and 1848, with 110 condemned for murder. The sect was declared officially extinct in 1852, but occasional reports of cult activity were logged as late as 1867.

1410–1435—Scotland: Sawney Beane's inbred cave-dwelling family robbed, murdered, and cannibalized an estimated 1,000 travelers in County Galway. Captured after a bungled ambush in 1435, the clan was executed en masse without trial, 27 males drawn and quartered, while 21 females were burned alive.

1735—England: Notorious highwayman Dick Turpin joined the Essex Gang, specialists in violent home invasions that included torture of homeowners and rape of any women on the premises, along with general looting. Though romanticized in literature for his exploits with Bonnie Black Bess (his mare), Turpin was in fact a brutal felon who was ultimately hanged at Tyburn for his crimes on April 17, 1739.

1782—England: Irish-born highwayman Michael Martin (aka "Captain Lightfoot") launched his criminal career in concert with another bandit known to history only as "Captain Thunderbolt." Martin emigrated to Massachusetts in June 1818 and tried his hand at honest work, soon failing both as a farmer and a brewer. Back in business as an outlaw by early 1819, he was arrested in October 1821 and hanged on December 22, 1822.

1818—South Carolina: John and Lavinia Fisher lead a gang of early American highwaymen, operating from their home near Charleston. Arrested in the fall of 1818 and convicted of various felonies, the Fishers were hanged together in February 1819.

1853—California: The state's first recorded stagecoach robbery was committed near Sonora, with outlaws such as TOM HODGES and RICHARD BARTER basing their careers on stage holdups during the next six years. Barter's gang alone stole $30,000 from California stagecoaches between November 1858 and January 1859.

1854–1865—Australia: Bushranger DANIEL MORGAN, plying his trade in Victoria and New South Wales, was finally hunted down and killed by authorities who mutilated his corpse, one officer preserving Morgan's scrotum as a tobacco pouch.

1862—Australia: A gang of bushrangers ambushed a payroll shipment at Eugowra Rocks in June, escaping with some £12,000 in gold and currency.

1866—Indiana: The outlaw RENO BROTHERS "invented" train robbery with a holdup at Seymour on October 6, thereby earning the full wrath of the PINKERTON Detective Agency. During the next quarter-century, successful emulators of the Reno gang included FRANK and JESSE JAMES, the YOUNGER BROTHERS, the DALTON BROTHERS, and BILL DOOLIN.

1872—Kansas: The homicidal BENDER FAMILY operated a wayside inn near Cherryvale, robbing and murdering at least a dozen travelers before mounting suspicion forced them to flee the area. Unofficial reports differ on whether the killers escaped or were captured and lynched by vigilantes at some unknown location.

1874–1883—California: Outlaw poet Charles E. Bolton (aka "Black Bart") robbed 27 stagecoaches, gracing his victims in each case with a sample of handwritten verse. Captured November 3, 1883, following a $4,800 holdup, Bolton received a 10-year prison term and was paroled in January 1888. When asked by a reporter if he would continue writing poetry, Bolton replied, "Young man, didn't you just hear me say I will commit no more crimes?"

1920—United States: The advent of Prohibition creates an immediate windfall for hijackers of liquor shipments nationwide. The federal Volstead Act, banning sale and possession of alcoholic beverages, took effect at midnight on January 16; the first liquor hijacking was recorded in Chicago less than 10 minutes later. Hundreds (probably thousands) of booze shipments were hijacked by members of ORGANIZED CRIME during the next 14 years before Prohibition's repeal on December 5, 1933.

1920—New York: A *New York Times* report on February 5 noted the continuation of highway robbery by "motorized bandits" who used automobiles to escape from police. *Armed robbery* soon replaced more familiar terms to describe such events. American police spent the 1920s acquiring cars, motorcycles, and newer weapons to combat roving criminal gangs, but they constantly lagged a step behind their adversaries in adopting new technology.

1931—Peru: The first known hijacking of an aircraft occurred on February 21, followed by a second identical incident two days later. Ironically, the pilot of the first plane—Byron Rickards—would be hijacked again 30 years later, on August 3, 1961. By the late 1960s airline hijacking—popularly dubbed "skyjacking"—had become a popular tactic for political extremists around the world; hundreds of passengers were held for ransom or were taken hostage to force release of imprisoned TERRORISTS. Some skyjackings were also committed for purely mercenary reasons.

1962—Massachusetts: America's largest highway robbery to date occurred on August 14 when bandits stopped a U.S. mail truck outside Plymouth, stealing $1,551,277 in used currency en route from Cape Cod to the Federal Reserve Bank in Boston. Three suspects—two men and a woman—were indicted for the robbery on July 31, 1967.

1967—England: A gang of robbers armed with blackjacks and ammonia overpowered three guards and looted their armored truck in the Islington district of Northeast London on May 1, escaping with 1.9 tons of gold bullion valued at $2 million.

1969—New York: Three men armed with pistols robbed a WELLS FARGO armored truck returning to New York City from Aqueduct Race Track, stealing an estimated $1.4 million.

1971—Washington, D.C.: Convicted mail thief Robert Cudak told a U.S. Senate subcommittee on June 16 that his team of thieves had stolen $100 million worth of goods from 17 American airports between September 1966 and his arrest in September 1970. The hearings were still in progress on June 23 when $20,000 was stolen from a mail pouch at New York's Kennedy International Airport.

1971—Oregon: Unidentified skyjacker "D. B. COOPER" commandeered a commercial airliner out of Portland on November 24, demanding $200,000 in cash and multiple parachutes. He bailed out with his loot over rural Washington state and was never seen again, though some of the ransom money was later recovered from a wilderness area near the drop site. Various proposed solutions to the case have failed to resolve the enduring mystery.

1974—Illinois: Chicago burglars set a new U.S. record on October 20 with the theft of $4.3 million in cash from a vault of the Armored Express Company. Police arrested six suspects in November and recovered $1.5 million of the loot, suggesting that the remainder had been stashed in secret Caribbean bank accounts beyond reach of American authorities.

1977—United States: Bank robber Thomas Hannan hijacked Frontier Airlines Flight 101 over Colorado on October 20, demanding $3 million, two machine guns, two pistols, two parachutes, and a reunion with accomplice George David Stewart (jailed with Hannan after their September robbery of a bank in Atlanta). Hannan forced the pilots to land in Kansas City and there released his hostages, committing suicide aboard the plane after his demands were rejected.

1978—New York: Five or six gunmen surprised the crew of a Wells Fargo armored truck while they were having lunch on Staten Island on December 19. The bandits escaped with cash variously estimated from "in excess of $1 million" to "a shade more than $3 million."

1978—New York: Members of organized crime stole $5.8 million in cash and jewelry from the LUFTHANSA cargo terminal at Kennedy International Airport on December 11. FBI agents arrested two suspects on February 17, 1979, announcing that a third was "missing permanently" and presumed murdered by mob associates. Holdup participant Henry Hill, safe within the federal witness protection program, later offered details of the robbery in his book *Goodfellas,* released as a popular motion picture (with fictional names) in 1990.

1979—Connecticut: Three security guards were killed when gunmen fired through garage windows at the Purolator Security armored car depot in Waterbury on April 16. The thieves escaped with $1.28 million in cash, checks, and jewelry but were captured on April 17 and charged with multiple counts of murder and robbery. Two male defendants were convicted in January 1984 and received 75-year prison terms; their wives pled guilty and received life terms with a minimum of 13 years before parole eligibility.

1980—California: Federal agents blamed a 25-year-old security guard for the August 15 theft of a Brinks armored truck containing $1.85 million from San Francisco International Airport. The fugitive was captured in San Francisco on November 22, 1981, FBI agents reporting that he acted "totally alone" in the theft.

1982—New York: On December 12 burglars stole an estimated $11 million from the Bronx headquarters of Sentry Armored Courier Corporation. Three defendants were convicted of the robbery in 1983, and one turned state's evidence against two other suspects; the last two thieves were convicted in March 1985. Investigation of that massive theft, meanwhile, uncovered financial irregularities at Sentry, and four indictments unrelated to the robbery were issued on February 18, 1983. Sentry's president was charged with stealing $346,000 from company accounts; a vice president was charged with stealing $343,000; Sentry's chairman was charged with stealing $100,000, and a local banker was indicted for assisting the thefts.

1990—New York: Gunmen in suburban Rochester stopped an armored car that was used to transport cash to the Buffalo Federal Reserve office on June 26, stealing $10.8 million in America's second-largest armored car holdup.

1992—Washington, D.C.: On September 15 the FBI announced creation of a special unit to suppress "carjacking"—armed theft of automobiles from their owners—in the nation's capital and environs. Washington and Maryland had logged more than 300 such incidents since January 1992, with thousands more nationwide. Federal legislation was enacted by November, imposing a life prison term for any carjacking resulting in death, but it seemed to have no impact on the new crime wave. An FBI report published on March 6, 1999, declared that 49,000 carjackings had occurred each year from 1992 through 1996, with an average death rate of 27 victims per year.

1993—New York: Gunmen stole $7.4 million from a Brinks armored car depot in Rochester. FBI agents arrested three suspects on November 12, including an ex-policeman employed as a Brinks guard on the night of the holdup, a Melkite Catholic priest, and an illegal immigrant from Ireland. Authorities initially claimed that the robbery was committed to finance the Provisional Irish Republican Army in Northern Ireland but later admitted that no evidence existed to prove any link with the PIRA.

1994—Florida: Bandits attacked and pistol-whipped the crew of a Wells Fargo armored car outside a Fort Lauderdale nightclub on April 11, escaping with $500,000 in cash.

1996—Florida: State authorities arrested a hijacker with $100,000 worth of stolen meat in June. Sentenced to probation, the same thief was jailed again in August 1997, this time with $250,000 in stolen computers. The resultant five-month jail term was not expected to end his criminal career.

HODGES, Thomas J. "Tom Bell"

A native of Rome, Tennessee, born in 1826, Tom Hodges was the product of a respectable family who provided a good education, including some medical training. He served as a military hospital orderly in the Mexican War (1846–48) and settled in California for the postwar gold rush, turning to banditry after he failed as a prospector and a gambler. Convicted of grand larceny in 1851, Hodges was sentenced to five years in state prison—which, in those days, meant a converted ship anchored at Angel Island, in San Francisco Bay. Ailing from hard labor in the Angel Island rock quarry, Hodges was sent to the San Francisco County Jail for medical treatment, where he escaped two days after arriving. Recaptured in 1852, he was lodged more securely in the new state prison at San Quentin.

At "Q," Hodges befriended a clique of professional outlaws, including BILL GRISTY, HENRY TALBOT, and the SKINNER brothers. An imposing figure at six feet two, sporting a full beard and conspicuously broken nose, Hodges combined physical presence with quick wits and genial humor to become a natural leader of the pack in San Quentin. On May 12, 1855, he was assigned with Gristy, Talbot, and Jim Smith to a work detail under Lt. John Gray, a guard whose heavy drinking made him negligent. The four convicts escaped to form the nucleus of what became the Golden State's most notorious holdup gang since the days of JOAQUIN MURRIETA. In honor of the fresh start—or perhaps simply to protect himself—Hodges began to use the name "Tom Bell" and so was known for the remainder of his life.

Bell/Hodges led a gang so large that some active members never worked together or even met each other. A veritable United Nations of crime, the outfit included desperadoes from Australia, Canada, Chile, England, Germany, Mexico, and Sweden in addition to home-grown thieves and killers. Passwords and secret hand signs were employed to let the bandits recognize each other when they met. Aside from the gang's founding fathers, notorious members included Ned Conway, RICHARD "RATTLESNAKE DICK" BARTER, JIM WEBSTER, "English Bob" Carr, Montague "Monte Jack" Lyon, ADOLPH NEWTON, Nicanor Rodriguez, and Juan "Spanish John" Fernandez. Blamed for some of the earliest stagecoach holdups of the gold-rush era, the gang maintained three major hideouts: Mountaineer House, eight miles from Auburn on the Folsom highway, was a stagecoach stop; California House was a hotel-saloon midway between Marysville and Camptonville; the Osage Ranch was a brothel on the road between Sacramento and Nevada City, run by Elizabeth Hood, mother of "Bell's" teenage mistress.

The "Bell" gang's first-known raid involved the July 1855 theft of $3,000 in gold from a Langton's Express messenger near Forest City. Numerous travelers were robbed of gold or pocket change, watches, and firearms; at least one of them survived his encounter with the gang thanks to "Bell's" medical expertise, patching a bullet wound inflicted by quick-trigger Bill Gristy. There were failures, as well—like the bungled holdup of an express coach between Shasta and Weaverville in December 1855—but the gang's reputation was solid enough that "Bell" and company soon were blamed for every unsolved holdup in the Northern Mines district of California.

Their best score ever was executed on March 12, 1856, when the gang took $17,000 in gold dust from a mule train in the Trinity Alps that was traveling from the Yreka Mines to Shasta. "Bell's" riders offloaded the loot onto 13 stolen mules and made their getaway, but retribution was swift for one of the era's greatest holdups. Gang member William Carter was soon arrested and named three accomplices: George Skinner, Dolph Newton, and Nicanor Rodriguez. Newton and cohort Tom Brown were captured a short time later, Brown winning leniency for himself by betraying his comrades. He led lawmen to a hideout on the American River, near Folsom, where George Skinner was killed and Nicanor Rodriguez was captured; Bill Gristy shot his way clear of the trap and escaped. Defendant Carter led authorities to the spot where $14,000 of the missing loot was hidden, but it did him no good. At trial, he was convicted with Newton and Rodriguez, all three sentenced to 10 years in prison.

"Tom Bell," meanwhile, was also on the run. He had a near-miss in March 1856, shooting his way out of an ambush at Newtown, where he stopped to dally with a girlfriend. Four months later, on July 25, he teamed with Ned Conway to rob a peddler, Dick Lash, near Mountaineer House. The bandits tied Lash to a tree and sold his goods, but robbery of lone travelers was losing its appeal, potential risks outweighing the rewards.

It was time, "Bell" thought, to try another stage.

The target was perfect: a coach carrying $100,000 in gold. On August 11, 1856, "Bell" made his move, accompanied by Conway, Gristy, Carr, Jim Smith, and Spanish John. They stopped the stage along Dry Creek, five miles from California House, but the express guard opened fire, quickly joined by several armed passengers. A fierce battle ensued, leaving Spanish John, the express guard and two male passengers wounded; a female passenger was struck in the head by a bullet and killed. The shaken outlaws fled empty handed.

"Bell's" next plan was to start a ranch in the San Joaquin Valley, six miles from Firebaugh's Ferry. Far from going straight, "Bell" planned to use the ranch for cover—a hideout and way station for stolen livestock, doubling as a launching pad for bigger, bolder robberies. The ranch was barely up and running, though, before disaster struck the gang. Bill Gristy and Spanish John were caught near Knight's Ferry on the Stanislaus River and soon named various accomplices. Ten days later, Jack Phillips—the proprietor of Mountaineer House—was arrested and confessed his role as a fence for the gang. "Bell's" downfall, though, was engineered by a different traitor, already in custody.

Charley Hamilton, an African-American member of the "Bell" gang, had been captured near Auburn in August 1856. To save himself from prison or lynching, he bargained with his jailers, agreeing to betray "Tom Bell" in return for freedom and some spending money. Freed on a short leash to rejoin the gang, Hamilton wired Sheriff John Boggs at Auburn on September 30, reporting that "Bell" and two cronies were en route from Folsom to Mountaineer House. A six-man posse met them on the road, confronting "Bell," Ned Conway, and an outlaw known only as Texas Jack. Guns were drawn and Conway died with a bullet in his heart; "Bell" and Texas Jack retreated in a hail of lead, ditching their horses and escaping on foot in the darkness.

"Bell" stole another horse that night, riding hard toward his San Joaquin ranch, unaware that Bill Gristy and Spanish John had revealed the spread's location. Law enforcers got there ahead of him, nabbing brothers Fred and Jim Farnsworth with a herd of stolen livestock. Tired of staking out the ranch after five days, posse men were leaving on October 4 when they met "Tom Bell" on the highway, dressed as a Spanish vaquero. George Belt, commander of the raiding party, told "Bell," "I believe you are the man we have been looking for." "Bell" smiled, replied, "Very probable," and surrendered his weapons without a fight. Transported to nearby Firebaugh's Ferry, "Bell" was told to prepare for immediate execution. At "Bell's" request, his captors permitted him to write two letters. The first was addressed to Elizabeth Hood.

Mrs. Hood—My dear and only friend now in this country:

As I am not allowed the liberty of seeing you, I have been allowed the privilege to write you a few lines, as I have but a few moments to live. I am at a great loss for something to say. I have been most foully betrayed. Bill and John have told things that have never took place. I am accused of every robbery that has been committed for the past twelve months, which is entirely false. I never have committed but three highway robberies in my life—but still I am to blame, and my fate is sealed. I am to die like a dog; and there is not but one thing that grieves me, and that is the condition of you and your family. Probably I have been the instrument of your misfortunes. In my last moments I will think of the many favors you have done me, and if I had fifty kingdoms to present, you should have them all. But alas! I am poor, and my fate is sealed. I would like to give you some advice, but I fear you may think me presumptuous. What I would say, is this: That you had better send the girls to San Francisco to the Sisters of Charity. There, they will be educated and taken care of. Tell all the girls farewell! Tell them to be good girls, and to be very particular to whom they pledge themselves for life. All the money I have is ten dollars, which I have given to Mr. Chism for Sarah. If you ever see Edward S., tell him my fate. I must come to a close for the hounds are thirsting for my blood. Good Bye, forever.

Thos. J. Bell

Bell's second note was addressed to his mother in Tennessee.

Dear Mother:

As I am about to make my exit to another country, I take this opportunity to write you a few lines. Probably you may never hear from me again. If not, I hope we may meet where parting is no more.

In my prodigal career in this country, I have always recollected your fond admonitions, and if I had lived up to them probably I would not have been in my present condition; but dear Mother, though my fate has been a cruel one, yet I have no one to blame but myself. Give my respects to all my old and youthful friends. Tell them to beware of bad associations, and never to enter into any gambling saloons, for that has been my ruin.

If my old Grandmother is living, remember me to her. With these remarks, I bid you farewell forever.

Your only boy,
Tom

At 4:00 P.M., his correspondence finished, "Bell" was taken by his captors to the riverside and hanged from a giant sycamore tree.

HOLDEN-KEATING Gang

Two of America's most notorious stickup artists in the 1920s and early 1930s, Thomas James Holden and Francis Keating began with payroll robberies and then branched out to robbing trains and banks. Holden was the older of the pair, born in 1896, while Keating was three years his junior. Their best score ever was the 1926 theft of $135,000 from a U.S. mail train at Evergreen Park, Illinois. It took federal agents another two years to bag their men, but Holden and Keating were finally convicted and sentenced to matching 25-year prison terms on May 5, 1928.

Packed off to Leavenworth, the crime partners wasted no time in plotting an escape, which they accomplished on February 28, 1930, using trusty passes forged by fellow inmate GEORGE "MACHINE GUN" KELLY. Holden and Keating fled to Chicago and on from there to the underworld haven of ST. PAUL, MINNESOTA, where they promptly organized another holdup gang. Notorious professionals including Kelly, FRANK NASH, and HARVEY BAILEY joined the team for a series of daring robberies in 1930 and 1931, but second-string accomplices had a disturbing mortality rate.

The new gang's first recorded raid occurred on July 15, 1930, when Holden, Keating, Bailey, Kelly, VERNON MILLER, and at least four other gunmen lifted $70,000 from a bank in Willmar, Minnesota. Three of the raiders—Mike Rusick, Frank "Weinie" Coleman, and "Jew Sammy" Stein (aka Silverman)—were later found shot to death at White Bear Lake, reportedly following a dispute with trigger-happy Verne Miller. From Willmar, the gang rolled on to steal $40,000 from a bank in Ottumwa, Iowa, on September 9, 1930, outlaw LAWRENCE DEVOL filling out the depleted ranks. Eight days later, in Lincoln, Nebraska, veteran robber EDDIE BENTZ joined the team to score $24,000 in cash and a whopping $2.6 million in securities from another bank job.

It should have been enough to retire on, but outlaws always want more. On October 2, 1931, Holden and Keating stopped a pair of bank messengers in Duluth, Minnesota, relieving them of $58,000. On October 20, in Menomonie, Wisconsin, Holden and Keating joined accomplices Charlie

Harmon and Frank Weber to steal $130,000 from a local bank. Cashier James Kraft, son of the bank's president, was taken hostage as a human shield for the gang's getaway and then shot to death outside of town. Police later found Harmon and Weber, gunned down and discarded by their confederates, while word spread that the pair had been executed for their wanton murder of Kraft. (An innocent suspect, one Bob Newborne, was later convicted and sentenced to life in prison for the Menomonie holdup.)

The Wisconsin killings may have soured Holden and Keating on leading a gang of their own, but clearly they were not prepared to look for honest work. Instead of going straight, they next attached themselves to a larger and more lethal outfit, run by the BARKER brothers and cohort ALVIN KARPIS. On June 17, 1932, Holden and Keating joined Fred Barker, Karpis, George Kelly, Harvey Bailey, Lawrence DeVol, and Verne Miller to steal $47,000 from a bank in Fort Scott, Kansas. Again, luck was with them, as law enforcers arrested and wrongly convicted three other fugitives from justice, including FRANK SAWYER, JIM CLARK, and ED DAVIS.

Life with the Barker-Karpis gang was not all work, of course. The boys also had time to play, and one of their favorite games was golf. On July 7, 1932, FBI agents surprised Holden, Keating, and Harvey Bailey on a Kansas City golf course, arresting all three, while the final member of their foursome—gang member Bernard Phillips—slipped away in the confusion. (Suspected of squealing to the feds, Phillips was later murdered in New York, reportedly

by Frank Nash and Verne Miller.) Holden and Keating were returned to Leavenworth.

Holden spent the next 15 years inside and then was paroled on November 28, 1947. On June 6, 1949, in Chicago, he fatally shot his wife and her two brothers during a drunken family argument. Described by FBI spokesmen as "a menace to every man, woman, and child in America," Holden was the first fugitive named to the bureau's "Ten Most Wanted" list when that roster was created in March 1950. Fifteen months later, on June 23, 1951, an alert citizen spotted him in Beaverton, Oregon, where he had lived for some time as "John McCullough," employed as a plasterer. Arrested at his job site the same day, Holden was extradited to Chicago, convicted of murder, and died in 1953 while serving a life sentence.

Francis Keating, meanwhile, lived a more peaceful life in retirement than his one-time partner. Upon parole from Leavenworth, he returned to St. Paul, the scene of so many Depression-era holdups, shootouts, and underworld confabs with crooked policemen. Keating died there of heart failure on July 25, 1978.

"HOLE-IN-THE-WALL": Wyoming outlaw refuge

Located in Johnson County, Wyoming—20 miles southwest of Kaycee—this 19th-century bandit sanctuary was first used as a hideout by Chief Sitting Bull, following the Little Big Horn engagement of 1876. Unlike the equally notorious BROWN'S HOLE, this refuge actually *was* a "hole"—or, more precisely, a series of interlocking canyons that made manhunting a high-risk occupation for soldiers or law enforcers tracking fugitives in the region.

Outlaws and their enemies reached Hole-in-the-Wall by following the Powder River, then turning northwestward and passing through a canyon of black rock, and then turning abruptly into yet another canyon etched from brilliant red sandstone past the abandoned settlement of Barnum. The canyon's entrance was so narrow that a pair of lookouts armed with Winchester repeaters could hold a small army at bay. Inside the hideout proper lay Outlaw Ranch, a cluster of one-room log cabins utilized for a quarter-century by some of the frontiers most infamous badmen.

Missouri outlaws FRANK and JESSE JAMES reportedly hid out at Hole-in-the-Wall on one of their flights from the Show-Me State in 1877, followed in

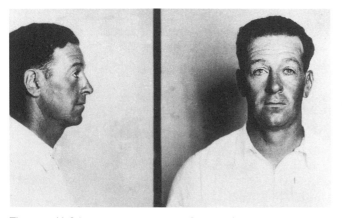

Thomas Holden, a career criminal from the 1920s, became the first fugitive posted to the FBI's "Ten Most Wanted" list in 1950. (FBI)

turn by equally infamous bandits. By the late 1880s, Nate Champion's "Red Sash Gang" dominated rustling over a tri-county range from Hole-in-the-Wall, prompting cattlemen to hire a private army of regulators and draw up a "black list" of 70 rustlers marked for summary extermination. Major Frank Walcott was chosen to lead the drive, backed by 55 seasoned gunmen. Walcott launched his campaign—memorialized as The Invasion—from Denver on April 5, 1892, but unseasonable blizzards slowed the strike force's advance. On arrival at Hole-in-the-Wall the vigilantes met stiff resistance, retreating when their ammo and supplies ran low at the end of a four-day pitched battle. It was a bitter pill for Major Walcott, who had killed only two of the targets on his list.

After Nate Champion's death, "Flatnose" George Curry took command of the outlaws operating from Hole-in-the-Wall, ably assisted by the four Logan brothers from Missouri. Two more offensives were launched by cattlemen and regulators in July 1897, and while the raiders recovered more than 1,000 head of stolen cattle for their rightful owners, the rustlers were unscathed. By year's end Curry and the Logans cast their lot with BUTCH CASSIDY and his "WILD BUNCH," graduating from livestock theft to more adventurous careers in bank and TRAIN ROBBERY. Hole-in-the-Wall remained an active bandit sanctuary through the early 1900s, when Cassidy decamped to South America and the members of his syndicate were jailed, hanged, or gunned down by authorities. Today the canyon is preserved as a point of historical interest for tourists.

HOLTAN, Richard Dean

A South Dakota native, born in February 1935, Holtan put his dismal view of life on display for all to see with identical tattoos on his left wrist and forearm, both reading "Born to Lose." When dead-end jobs as an upholsterer and shipping clerk fell short of meeting Holtan's expectations for the future, he decided that violent crime was worth a try.

On November 19, 1973, he held up a bank in Seattle, walking away with $1,000 in cash. Soon arrested for the robbery, Holtan was placed in a "resident release" program for a one-year trial period in lieu of being sent to prison. Disappearing from the program, he surfaced in Omaha on November 1, 1974, to rob a local tavern. In the course of the holdup, Holtan fired his pistol repeatedly and without provocation at three unarmed victims, killing the bartender and wounding one of his customers.

Federal warrants soon charged Holtan with bank robbery, plus unlawful flight to avoid prosecution for robbery and murder in Omaha. Added to the FBI's "Most Wanted" list on April 18, 1975, he voluntarily surrendered three months later, on July 12, to local police in Kauai, Hawaii. FBI agents took charge of the prisoner, and he was returned to Nebraska for trial and ultimate conviction on charges of murder and robbery.

HOOVER, John Edgar: FBI director and "gangbuster"

A lifelong resident of Washington, D.C., J. Edgar Hoover was the son of a civil servant, born January 1, 1895. Bypassing a traditional college education, he moved directly from high school to night classes at George Washington Law School while working days at the Library of Congress. Shortly after graduation in July 1917, he joined the Department of Justice as a clerk assigned to the alien-registration division. The job's primary fringe benefit was an automatic draft deferment, which kept Hoover safely at home during World War I, pursuing "Bolsheviks" suspected of violating the Alien Enemy Act. In 1921 he was appointed to serve as assistant director of the Bureau of Investigation—renamed the FBI in 1935—under Director William Burns. Mired in scandal for his role in the corrupt regime of President Warren Harding, Burns was fired in 1924, with Hoover named acting director in his place. Six months later, on December 10, 1924, Hoover became permanent director, the post he held until his death on May 2, 1972.

Throughout his career in law enforcement, Hoover's twin obsessions were suppression of the "communist conspiracy" and fervent opposition to black civil rights—the latter position especially ironic in light of recent disclosures that 19th-century census records list his great-grandparents as "B" (for black) and "M" (for mulatto). (A clumsy latter-day amendment to the records lists Hoover, alone of all his siblings, as "m-w," presumably standing for "male white.") Whatever his ethnic roots, Hoover remained a relative unknown in Washington through the 1920s, avoiding the taint of major Prohibition scandals that tarred other federal law-enforcement agencies, content to pursue alleged communists and stage occasional vice raids mandated by federal law.

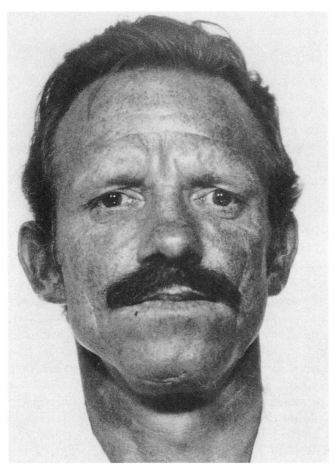

Bank bandit Richard Holtan tattooed both arms with the legend "Born to Lose." (FBI)

In the process, Hoover began to craft his public image, rewriting history to distance himself from the scandalous "Red Raids" of 1920 (which he personally coordinated), while building a myth that he "broke" the 1920s Ku Klux Klan. (In fact, only one Klan member was indicted on federal charges during the secret society's heyday—and that was on a morals charge, for driving his mistress across state lines to enjoy an adulterous liaison in violation of the Mann Act.)

Hoover's first shot at serious headlines arrived with the Great Depression, as a wave of robberies and ransom kidnappings shocked the nation. FBI agents were among the lawmen gunned down on June 17, 1933, in the KANSAS CITY MASSACRE, and Hoover rushed to cash in on the headlines. (First, though, he had to hide the truth—that most of those killed in the firefight were shot accidentally by a clumsy bureau agent armed with an unfamiliar weapon.)

Incensed by the massacre and a spate of high-profile abductions, President Franklin Roosevelt declared America's first "war on crime," assisted by Congress with a package of crime-fighting bills that (a) made interstate kidnapping and robbery of most banks a federal offense, (b) restricted possession of machine guns and other "gangster" weapons, and (c) allowed FBI agents to carry firearms while making arrests. (In fact, of course, the feds had been packing heat and collaring suspects since 1908—but after 1934 it would be *legal*.)

Hoover welcomed his new responsibilities and the newsprint they ensured him. He now had carte blanche to pursue such famous desperadoes as JOHN DILLINGER, GEORGE "BABY FACE" NELSON and CHARLES "PRETTY BOY" FLOYD (accused, most likely in error, of participating in the Kansas City massacre). By September 1933, Hoover's agents also had a new moniker, allegedly labeled "G-men" by kidnapper and bank robber GEORGE "MACHINE GUN" KELLY. It made no difference that the nickname—supposedly common gangland parlance for "government man"—had been concocted from thin air at FBI headquarters in Washington. It looked good in headlines and on theater marquees, boosting Hoover's public stock with a near-daily series of shootouts, arrests, and near-misses.

In April 1936, with the best years of the "crime war" already behind him, Hoover's personal publicity campaign hit a snag in Congress. Tennessee Senator Kenneth McKellar, chairman of the Senate Subcommittee on Appropriations, challenged Hoover's bid for an additional $1,025,000 with some stinging criticism of the bureau's methods—and the fact that Hoover himself had never made an arrest. The latter fact was particularly galling for America's top "gangbuster," and Hoover set about repairing his tarnished image. Orders were issued to all FBI field offices that fugitive bank robber ALVIN KARPIS, the nation's current "Public Enemy No. 1," would be "the director's man," earmarked for personal arrest by Hoover. In fact, Hoover had no intention of risking his life on the street, but he flew to New Orleans after Karpis was spotted there on May 1, 1936, emerging from cover to "arrest" Karpis after the unarmed bandit was surrounded by agents. Six months later, on December 14, Hoover staged a similar sideshow on behalf of his second-in-command (and probably gay lover) Clyde Tolson, with the New York arrest of bank robber HARRY BRUNETTE.

Despite such tawdry theatrics—interspersed with the violent deaths of unarmed suspects and innocent bystanders, deliberate framing of innocent defendants, and a media feud with flamboyant subordinate MELVIN PURVIS—Hoover retained his reputation as a crime fighter par excellence until his death in 1972. Only then, with the director gone and his scandal-laden private files mysteriously vanished, did his public image start to crumble. Rapid-fire exposures revealed a life of racial bigotry and personal corruption, including dozens of gambling vacations subsidized by syndicate mobsters in a period when Hoover denied the existence of organized crime in America. On balance, when Hoover's career of illegal domestic surveillance and blackmail is considered—including thousands of burglaries, illicit wiretaps and buggings, manufacture or suppression of evidence, and subornation of perjury—it is apparent that the FBI's director was a more successful (and more dangerous) criminal than the high-profile bandits he pursued haphazardly in the 1930s.

HUBBARD, Millard Oscar

A habitual criminal whose record spanned 30 years, Hubbard was charged in 1976 with the August 14 robbery of a bank in Tazewell, Tennessee. In short order his name was also linked to bank jobs in Washington and Pennsylvania, as well as in Steubenville and St. Clairsville, Ohio. Sought on federal bank-robbery charges, Hubbard was added to the FBI's "Ten Most Wanted" list on October 19, 1977.

Two days later, federal agents acting on a tip from residents of Lexington, Kentucky, surrounded Hubbard on a visit to the city. Faced with overwhelming odds, Hubbard grabbed a .30-caliber M1 carbine and was wounded twice by G-men, surviving to stand trial in federal court. Conviction on multiple charges—including bank robbery, assault, receipt and possession of a firearm by a convicted felon, and bank robbery with assault—earned him a sentence of 37 years in prison. In July 1979 Hubbard was transferred from the federal penitentiary in Atlanta to a smaller facility at Marion, Illinois. There, on April 29, 1984, he was fatally beaten by another inmate.

HUNT-GANT Gang

Largely ignored by the national press, Alva-Dewey Hunt and Hugh Gant led a Depression-era bank-robbing gang that operated entirely below the Mason-Dixon Line, leaving the Midwest and most of the period's headlines to bandits like JOHN DILLINGER, GEORGE "BABY FACE" NELSON and CHARLES "PRETTY BOY" FLOYD. Aside from geography, the gang's notoriety was also restricted by a tendency to pull small jobs with minimal rewards.

The Hunt-Gant gang's first-known holdup occurred on February 28, 1935, when the raiders stole $4,000 from a bank in Haines City, Florida. A second Florida bank, this one in Mulberry, was looted on August 1, 1935. Seven months later, on March 3, 1936, the robbers scored their all-time record take of $30,459 from a bank in Ybor City, Florida. The Foley, Alabama, robbery of June 2, 1936, was a disappointment by comparison, netting only $7,242. FBI agents were on their trail by then, mopping up the last of the 1930s outlaws, but it took another three and a half years before Hunt and Gant were finally captured by G-men in Houston, Texas. Both were convicted on federal bank-robbery charges and packed off for long terms in prison.

HUSTON, Patrick James

Patrick Huston's record of arrests dated from 1946, with armed robbery dominating the list of felonies. By the early 1970s he had spent a quarter-century behind prison walls, earning himself a reputation as a ruthless gunman. In 1962 Huston and his Queens-based gang shot it out with New York police after a bank robbery in Manhattan. Twelve years later he was still running true to form, joining two accomplices to loot a bank in Queens of $50,000. Captured hours later, each of the bandits was armed with a pistol and a .30-caliber carbine.

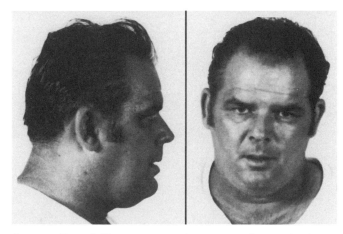

Gunman Patrick Huston pursued a career of armed robbery that lasted from 1946 to 1977. (FBI)

On March 16, 1975, while awaiting trial for the Queens robbery, Huston and his two accomplices escaped from the federal house of detention in New York City. Hiding in a storage room between floors, they sat out a search of the building and then cut through a mesh enclosure, clearing a skylight and descending to the street on a rope made of knotted bedsheets. Charged with bank robbery and unlawful flight to avoid prosecution, Huston was added to the FBI's "Most Wanted" list on March 3, 1976.

Twenty-one months of intensive investigation finally led G-men to Fort Lauderdale, Florida, where Huston had settled. On December 7, 1977, the fugitive left a local tavern, dressed in a blue jogging suit and riding a bicycle. Federal agents were waiting nearby, and Huston was taken into custody without incident, held in lieu of $250,000 bond pending extradition to New York. He was later convicted on all counts and returned to prison.

INMAN, Elmer H.

A Kansas native, born in 1880, Elmer Inman took his first serious fall before World War I, convicted of participation in a jewel robbery at Arkansas City and sentenced to a 10-year minimum in the state prison at Leavenworth. There, he managed to charm Warden J. K. Codding and his family. Inman convinced Warden Codding that he had been "jobbed" (framed) on the charge that sent him to prison, his evident sincerity winning Elmer a job as the warden's chauffeur. Inman was also "wonderfully attentive" to Codding's sickly wife, but his real interest lay with the warden's daughter. Romance blossomed behind bars, and they were married in August 1921, shortly after Inman's parole.

It was a star-crossed union, doomed to fail. While Lavona Inman vainly sought a pardon for her husband in Kansas, Elmer was arrested for stealing a car in Oklahoma and shipped back to Leavenworth as a parole violator. It was soon revealed that Inman had been selling hot jewelry from prison throughout his tenure at Leavenworth, thus adding a new charge of using the mails to defraud. The capper came on November 8, 1921, when his marriage to Lavona was annulled on grounds that Inman—a convicted felon stripped of basic civil rights—was not entitled to marry in Kansas.

Warden Codding must have been relieved, in light of what lay ahead for his near-miss son-in-law. By 1933, Inman held the dubious honor of being named as Oklahoma's "Public Enemy No. 1," climaxing two decades of adventures on the wrong side of the law.

Despite his Kansas problems, Inman was back on the street in 1926, arrested on June 7 while cruising through Fort Scott, Kansas, with Herman BARKER in a stolen car. At the time, Elmer was already wanted on charges of robbing a bank and a post office in Ketchum, Oklahoma. Kansas state authorities were glad to extradite him, but he soon made bail and just as promptly skipped. A few days later, Inman was nabbed again, this time for burglary in Ardmore, Oklahoma, with veteran badman Ray Terrill. On September 27, 1926, Inman and Terrill overpowered a guard in the Carter County jail, making good their escape. Two months later, on November 21, Inman was suspected of joining Terrill and Herman Barker to spring outlaw MATT KIMES from custody in Sallisaw, where Kimes was arguing appeals of his 35-year sentence for robbery and murder.

With that service behind him, Inman was a shoo-in for membership in the Kimes-Terrill gang, but Elmer's bad luck was holding. Arrested two days after Christmas 1926 while burglarizing a store in Oklahoma City, Inman was convicted on February 9, 1927, and sentenced to seven years in prison. En route to McAlester, he escaped from guards near Bolton and vanished once again, rejoining his partners in crime. This time, they tried hiding out in Arkansas, but Hot Springs police jailed Inman and Terrill on November 26, delivering them to Oklahoma authorities. By year's end, Elmer and Terrill were reunited with the

Kimes brothers at McAlester, but none would remain long behind bars. Parole boards were as lax as prison guards in those days, and Inman was once more at large by the early 1930s.

Rumors persist of Elmer's involvement with the BARKER-KARPIS gang in 1932–33, and while his prior association with Herman Barker suggests an affinity for the clan, no evidence exists to support the claim of one author that Inman was "the brains who actually planned each venture" for the gang. By late 1933, in fact, Elmer was teamed with fugitive gunman Wilbur Underhill. They tried in vain to steal a safe from the bank at Harrah, Oklahoma, on December 12, 1933, but weak floorboards doomed the effort as it crashed through to the basement. Next day, when Underhill and two accomplices stole $4,000 from a bank in Coalgate, Inman was mentioned as a probable suspect.

Underhill's luck ran out on December 30 when officers raided his honeymoon cottage at Sallisaw, fatally wounding the "Tri-State Terror" when he tried to escape. Underhill died on January 6, 1934, and law enforcers spotted Inman the following day at a gasoline station in Bowlegs, Oklahoma. Elmer was wounded while resisting arrest; girlfriend Lena Nichols was captured at the same time. Inman would live to see the inside of a prison cell once more. Oklahoma's Public Enemy No. 1 died in custody of natural causes on June 11, 1939.

IRISH Republican Army: Terrorist robbers

Organized in 1916 to support the Irish rebellion against British colonial rule, the Irish Republican Army survived that defeat and the Irish Civil War of 1922, which followed a grant of independence to the Republic of Ireland while maintaining the six counties of Northern Ireland under British authority. Over the next four decades, the IRA waged a sporadic struggle comprised largely of bombing campaigns and assassination of various targets sympathetic to British occupation of Northern Ireland. In 1969 the organization split, with a new Provisional Irish Republican Army (PIRA) maintaining the creed of armed struggle while the Official Irish Republican Army (OIRA) called for a cease-fire. That show of "weakness" caused a further split within the OIRA as more militants defected to form the Irish National Liberation Army.

Financing an illegal war is always challenging without covert support from an established government. PIRA resources in the 1970s and 1980s included limited covert assistance from the Soviet Union and certain Arab nations, more substantial cash and arms donations from Irish Americans in the United States, plus collections and sale of literature in the Republic of Ireland. Still, the war chest was seldom full, prompting a diversion into armed robbery and ransom kidnapping from time to time, as need arose.

One of the first robberies directly linked to the PIRA occurred in England on February 3, 1974, when four gunman stole the equivalent of $80,000 from a bank at Stansted Airport near London. Three months later, on April 26, five PIRA commandos (including one woman, Bridget Rose Dugdale), invaded the Irish home of Sir Alfred Beit, a British millionaire, and stole paintings valued at $19.2 million. A week after the robbery, authorities received a letter demanding $1.2 million for safe return of the artwork, plus immediate transfer of four PIRA prisoners from British jails to a lockup in Ulster. The paintings were recovered by police, undamaged, on May 3, 1974—11 days before the deadline for their threatened destruction. Bridget Dugdale was later arrested and sentenced to nine years in prison for her part in the robbery and extortion attempt.

Armed robbery by PIRA holdup teams became more systematic in the latter 1970s, authorities in the Republic of Ireland estimating that some £2 million had been stolen in bank robberies and payroll heists between January 1978 and August 1979. (No cumulative figures from Northern Ireland were available for the same period.) A major project of the period was a TRAIN ROBBERY near Sallins, County Kildare, which bagged £250,000 for the Provisionals. Several innocent members of the Irish Republican Socialist Party were arrested for that crime, and confessions were extracted via third-degree tactics, resulting in their conviction and imprisonment. PIRA spokesmen approached Irish historian Tim Pat Coogan, requesting that he intercede with the police and explain that the suspects were blameless, but prosecutors refused to listen, preferring defendants in hand to unknown terrorists at large.

Peace talks between British leaders and Republican spokesmen in the late 1990s reduced the level of violence in Northern Ireland, though the habit of killing was difficult to break. Cessation of overt hostilities has likewise eliminated the need for extralegal funding of a covert army, but even if a long-sought peace is finally achieved, it remains to be seen whether veteran robbers will be able to resist the lure of easy money, once political motives are removed.

JACUBANIS, David Stanley

Born at Baku, Russia, in July 1910, David Jacubanis was a rootless drifter, characterized by federal agents as "a man without a country." His 37-year criminal record included convictions for breaking and entering, larceny, auto theft, armed robbery, bank robbery, and carrying a gun without a license. Considered an escape risk at the several prisons where he served his time (including Alcatraz), Jacubanis was rejected for deportation by his native Russia, along with Canada, England, and France.

In March 27, 1962, Jacubanis robbed a bank in Dedham, Massachusetts, of $6,004 at gunpoint. Because the bank was not federally insured, the FBI had no jurisdiction over the robbery proper, but federal warrants were issued charging Jacubanis with unlawful flight to avoid prosecution, along with charges stemming from violation of his federal parole. A second bank robbery in North Smithfield, Rhode Island, on April 5, 1962, added further charges, and Jacubanis was added to the bureau's "Ten Most Wanted" list on November 21, 1962. Eight days later G-men cornered him in Arlington, Vermont, and arrested him without incident, returning him to Massachusetts for trial and conviction on outstanding counts.

A Russian immigrant to the United States, David Jacubanis pursued a criminal career that spanned four decades. (FBI)

JAMES, Alexander Franklin (Frank), and JAMES, Jesse Woodson

Arguably the most famous outlaws in American history, Frank and Jesse James carved themselves an enduring niche as classic SOCIAL BANDITS in the unsettled decades following the Civil War. A medley of excuses was advanced to explain their violent (often cold-blooded) crimes, some apologists still pleading

145

their case more than a century after the fact. In any case, they rank among the 19th century's premier bandits for daring and cruelty, immortalized by their refinement of TRAIN ROBBERY and their "invention" of daylight bank robbery.

The James brothers were born in Clay County, Missouri—Frank in 1844 and Jesse in 1848. Their clergyman father, Rev. Robert James, died in 1851, and their mother remarried to a kindly physician, Dr. Reuben Samuel. All indicators pointed toward a stable, relatively affluent childhood for the two boys—but Fate intervened with the brutal debate over slavery, prompting years of guerrilla warfare in Missouri and "Bleeding Kansas" before all-out civil war began in 1861.

Nothing would ever be the same for Frank and Jesse James.

Missouri was a slave state, though it never left the Union, and Frank James was quick to enlist with the Confederate army in 1861. Captured a short time later, he was paroled in return for his promise to desist from further fighting (a common practice in those days of more genteel warfare). Frank went home and kept his word for a while, but it grated on his nerves to miss so much action, and he soon enlisted with the irregular force led by bandit-turned-guerrilla WILLIAM CLARKE QUANTRILL. It was a violation of parole, but Frank was never much at keeping promises where Yankees were concerned.

Jesse was deemed too young to enlist in 1862, but the war touched him anyway. That June, a troop of Missouri militiamen raided the James farm in Clay County, seeking information on Frank's whereabouts. Jesse was flogged and his stepfather hanged for refusing to talk. Dr. Samuel survived his ordeal but with permanent brain damage. A year later, Jesse's mother and half-sister were arrested and briefly detained by Union forces as Confederate collaborators, further inflaming the hatred of both brothers.

Frank, at least, had an outlet for his rage. Accompanied by cousin COLE YOUNGER, he rode with Quantrill on most of the guerrilla leader's pillaging raids, doing what he could to punish "bluebellies" for their crimes against his family. Frank's description of the experience serves as a blueprint for the postwar creation of his infamous gang.

If you ever want to pick a company to do desperate work or to lead a forlorn hope, select young men from 17 to 21 years old. They will go anywhere in the world you will lead them. When men grow older they grow

more cautious but at that age they are regular daredevils. Take our company and there has never been a more reckless lot of men. Only one or two were over 25. Most of them were under 21. Scarcely a dozen boasted a moustache. Wasn't it Bacon who said when a man had a wife and children he had given hostages to fortune? . . . The truth was we were nothing but great big boys.

But they were deadly, all the same. On May 19, 1863, Frank and others visited Richfield, Kansas, feigning intoxication and boasting of their affiliation with Quantrill. When a squad of Union troops came to arrest them, they were ambushed, three officers killed execution style and two others narrowly escaping under fire. Three months later, on August 20, Frank and Cole Younger were among the guerrillas who sacked Lawrence, Kansas, looting and burning most of the town, inflicting $2 million in damage and killing at least 142 persons, against the loss of one raider slain.

Jesse James missed that slaughter, but the war had months to go and thousands of lives yet to claim. With best friend Archie Clements, Jesse joined Quantrill in 1864 and rode with Quantrill lieutenant William "Bloody Bill" Anderson against the town of Centralia, Missouri, on September 27 of that year. Frank James was also present for the orgy of looting and arson, which included the robbery of an incoming train and summary execution of 24 wounded Union soldiers found aboard. Yankee reinforcements arrived in the midst of the slaughter, but the guerrillas were too much for them, killing another 131 soldiers in pitched combat. Jesse James reportedly killed eight men on his own, including Yankee Major A. V. E. Johnson, who was in charge of the ill-fated relief force.

More than a crack shot and cool head in battle, Jesse was versatile in his service to the Confederacy. Dubbed "Dingus" for his youth and effeminate features, he was used as bait for randy Yanks on at least one occasion, dressing as a girl to lure careless targets within pistol range. It may have been those duties that prompted Jesse to leave Quantrill's service in November 1864, taking Cole Younger with him on the long ride to Arkansas and Indian Territory (later Oklahoma). Frank stayed with Quantrill, meanwhile, as the long war began to wind down.

Many of Quantrill's men ignored the Confederate surrender at Appomattox, as they had ignored the rules of war since 1861. Quantrill himself was fatally wounded on May 10, 1865, by which time Jesse

James had faced his own brush with death. Leading a half-dozen stragglers to surrender at Lexington, Missouri, on April 15, Jesse met a troop of Kansas irregulars and shots were exchanged. Though wounded in a lung, his horse killed beneath him, Jesse still picked off one of enemy and scattered the rest. Found three days later by a local farmer and conveyed to Lexington, he was given a pass by Union officers who assumed that he was dying. Transported to a friend's ranch near Rulo, Nebraska, Jesse recovered and made his way back to Missouri by August 1865. There, he soon fell in love with first cousin Zerelda Mimms (named after his mother), although they did not marry until 1874.

By year's end a new gang was organized around the hard core of the James and Younger brothers, incorporating family friends and survivors of Quantrill's guerrilla band. The gang's first raid was staged on February 14, 1866, in Liberty, Missouri. Ten riders invaded the town at 8:00 A.M., their number including Frank and Jesse James, Cole and Jim Younger, Arch Clements, Bud Pearce, George Shepherd, Payton "Payne" Jones, and Andy McGuire. After looting the bank, they "hurrahed" the town, killing 19-year-old college student George Wynmore in a flurry of gunshots. The take included $15,000 in gold coin and $45,000 in bonds, plus a small amount of silver and greenbacks. The bonds were nonnegotiable, though, and by the time a fence in Texas took his cut for unloading the gold, the raiders cleared $9,000 for their efforts.

Still, it was more profitable than the gang's second bank job, at Lexington, Missouri, on October 30, 1866. That outing bagged a mere $2,000, albeit without any killing. The James and Younger boys were absent when the riders struck again, five bandits raiding a private banking house run by Judge William McLain in Savannah, Missouri, on March 2, 1867. They met their first resistance there when Judge McLain drew a pistol, ignoring a nonlethal chest wound to drive the outlaws empty handed from his home.

Frank and Jesse were back on the job, with the Youngers in tow, on May 23, 1867. That afternoon, 14 riders swept through the streets of Richmond, Missouri, six invading a local bank to steal $4,000 in gold while the rest remained on guard outside. Angry citizens opened fire as the gang prepared to flee, and battle was joined. When the smoke cleared, Richmond's mayor was dead, along with jailer B. G. Griffin and his 15-year-old son. Though witnesses identified the James and Younger brothers as partici-

pants in the holdup, their names were strangely absent from warrants naming suspects Jim and John White, Payne Jones, Dick Burns, Ike Flannery, Andy McGuire, and Allen Parmer (a brother-in-law of the James boys). A posse tracked Jones to a house near Independence, but he shot his way out of the trap, killing manhunter B. H. Wilson and a young girl who had led the lawmen to their target. Dick Burns was caught napping in a farmhouse near Richmond and was lynched on the spot. Andy McGuire received similar treatment a few days later when he was captured outside Warrensburg. Tom Little—not indicted but a suspect all the same—was last to go; arrested in St. Louis and returned to Warrensville, he was removed from jail and lynched before his trial convened.

Apparently satisfied with three lives for three, vigilantes gave up their hunt for the rest of the gang, the James and Younger boys still clear of any public suspicion. On May 20, 1868, Jesse James and Cole Younger entered a bank in Russellville, Kentucky, brandishing pistols after their attempt to change a counterfeit $50 bill was rebuffed. They beat a cashier who refused to open the safe, but he escaped under fire from two more bandits outside, rousing the town with cries for help. Fleeing the bank with $14,000 in gold, silver, and greenbacks, the bandits wounded one man as they swept out of town in a hail of bullets.

The Russellville holdup brought agents of the PINKERTON Detective Agency into play for the first time against the James gang. Investigators traced bandit George Shepherd to the home of his mistress, sparking an all-night battle; Shepherd was wounded and captured as he wriggled through a window shortly after sunrise. Though convicted on minor charges and sentenced to two years in prison, Shepherd was loyal to his cronies, refusing to name other members of the gang.

An 18-month hiatus followed the Russellville holdup, broken on December 7, 1869, when the James brothers and Cole Younger robbed a bank at Gallatin, Missouri. The take was disappointing—a mere $700—and Jesse killed cashier John Sheets in the bargain, escaping in the now-familiar storm of gunfire to elude the posse that gave chase.

The gang's next verified outing occurred on June 3, 1871, when Jesse James and six cohorts looted $45,000 from a bank in Corydon, Iowa. Ex-guerrilla Clell Miller was later arrested on suspicion of participating in the holdup but released for lack of evidence when witnesses could not identify him. On

April 29, 1872, the James brothers and three Youngers stole a paltry $200 from a bank in Columbia, Kentucky, murdering cashier R. A. C. Martin for refusal to open the safe. Five months later, on September 26, three members of the gang struck at the Kansas City fairgrounds, stealing some $10,000 from a runner en route to a nearby bank. One of their horses trampled and injured a 10-year-old girl in the process, prompting false rumors that she had been shot. Another bank was robbed on May 23, 1873, at Sainte Genevieve, Missouri.

The James gang committed its first train robbery on July 21, 1873, near Adair, Iowa. Using an old guerrilla tactic, they uprooted one of the rails, derailing the locomotive in a pile-up that scalded engineer John Rafferty to death and left fireman Dennis Foley with painful burns. Unfazed by the suffering of their victims, Jesse and friends then stole $26,000 from the express car and various passengers, their feat erroneously heralded in press accounts as the "world's first robbery of a moving train." (In fact, that dubious honor belonged to a Hoosier gang, the RENO BROTHERS, who had "invented" train robbery seven years earlier.)

On January 15, 1874, members of the James gang stopped a stagecoach outside Malvern, Arkansas, and robbed the passengers of petty cash. Two weeks later, on January 31, seven bandits commandeered the railroad depot at Gad's Hill, Missouri, to rob an incoming train. Published estimates of the score range from $2,000 to $22,000, but the holdup was notable primarily for Jesse James delivering his own press release on the event. It read:

> The most daring on record—the southbound train on the Iron Mountain Railroad was robbed here this evening by seven heavily armed men, and robbed of —— dollars. The robbers arrived at the station some time before the arrival of the train, and arrested the station agent and put him under guard, then threw the train on the switch. The robbers were all large men, none of them under six feet tall. They were all masked and started in a southerly direction after they had robbed the train. They were all mounted on fine blooded horses. There is a hell of an excitement in this part of the country.

Furious, Missouri's governor posted a $2,000 reward for the capture of each bandit, while the U.S. Postal Department added $5,000 and the governor of Arkansas kicked in another $2,000. Pinkerton agents were spurred to intensify their manhunt, with tragic results. On March 15, 1874, detective John Whicher was stopped near Kearney in Clay County by the James brothers and Clell Miller and carried into Jackson County where he was shot three times and left as a meal for wild hogs. One day later, in the Ozark Mountains to the south, retired lawman E. B. Daniels led Pinkerton officers Louis Lull and James Wright on a search for other members of the gang. They found their prey that afternoon, engaging in a shootout that killed John Younger, while Daniels and Wright also lost their lives. Detective Lull, gravely injured, hung on for six weeks before succumbing to his wounds.

Although Pinkerton executives never admitted seeking vengeance, their next move smacked of cruel retaliation—and wound up producing even greater sympathy for the James boys among their Missouri neighbors. A Pinkerton spy named Jack Ladd had established himself on a neighboring farm, owned by Daniel Askew, to watch the Samuel spread, and he reported on January 5, 1875, that the James boys had come home to visit their mother. A special trainload of detectives was dispatched from Kansas City and the Pinkertons struck that night, lobbing an explosive device—its composition and intent disputed to this day—inside the Samuel home. The resultant blast killed eight-year-old Archie Samuel, severed Zerelda Samuel's right arm at the elbow, and gravely injured the family's black maid.

Frank and Jesse, the bombers soon learned, had not been at home after all.

The outrage was immediate; retaliation took a bit more time. Farmer Askew was shot in his yard on April 12, the James brothers and Clell Miller afterward stopping at another neighbor's house to report, "We just killed Dan Askew. If any of his friends want to know who did it, tell them the detectives did it." Jesse also traveled to Chicago, briefly stalking Allan Pinkerton, but he dropped the planned assassination as too risky.

Mourning ended for the gang on December 13, 1875, when raiders took over the railroad depot at Muncie, Kansas, and looted the incoming train. They bagged some $60,000 from the express safe and various passengers, leaving behind a battered guard and a large shipment of silver bars too heavy to steal. Gang member Bud McDaniels was arrested soon after, drunk and flush with cash in Kansas City. He confessed in custody and drew a two-year prison term, but he soon escaped from state prison, dying in a shootout with the posse that ran him down.

On May 12, 1876, the James gang resorted to highway robbery, stopping a stagecoach between Austin and San Antonio, Texas, to steal an estimated $3,000. Two months later, on July 7, they robbed a train at Rocky Cut, Missouri—near Otterville—of $15,000. Gang member Hobbs Kerry was captured soon after that holdup and spoke freely to law officers, but his accomplices remained elusive—for a while.

Jesse James was already planning a score that would take the gang far from its familiar hunting grounds, all the way to Northfield, Minnesota, for the plunder of a nice, fat bank. Cole Younger opposed the idea but finally joined in against his better judgment, taking brothers Bob and Jim along for the ride. With Frank and Jesse, the eight-man team also included Clell Miller, Bill Chadwell, and Charlie Pitts. On the appointed day—September 7, 1876—Jesse James entered the target bank with Pitts and Bob Younger, leaving his comrades outside to hurrah the startled town. Cashier J. L. Heywood refused to open the safe despite threats and beating, while teller A. E. Bunker escaped from the bank, wounded in a shoulder by Bob Younger as he fled up the street, raising the alarm. Heywood seized the opportunity to reach a pistol in his desk, but Jesse James was quicker, killing the cashier where he stood.

Outside, frightened residents of Northfield grabbed their guns and rushed to join the battle. Nicholas Gustavson, one of those unarmed, was next to die, shot down by the bandits as he crossed the street. By that time, bandits were emerging from the bank into a storm of rifle and shotgun fire. Elias Stacey, firing from a second-story window, blinded Clell Miller with birdshot before Henry Wheeler (a 19-year-old college student) fired a rifle shot and toppled Miller dead from his saddle. Wheeler next shot Cole Younger's hat off, while Stacey stung Bill Chadwell with a shotgun blast. A. E. Manning, proprietor of a nearby hardware store, drilled Cole Younger through the shoulder, while other marksmen killed Bob Younger's horse outside the bank. Bob ran for cover in a nearby alley, but a shot from Wheeler smashed his right elbow. Chadwell, half-blinded by birdshot, was riding out of town when Manning shot him through the heart and left him in the dust. Jim Younger, shot in the face, still managed to gallop out of town. Cole Younger rode back under fire to pluck brother Bob from the street, leaving Miller and Chadwell behind.

Every member of the gang was wounded as they fled Northfield, Frank and Jesse less seriously than their comrades. Multiple posses were organized to pursue them, with hasty rewards of $2,200 made payable for any bandit taken dead or alive. Manhunters found their quarry near tiny Shieldsville on September 11—having traveled less than 15 miles from Northfield over rough ground in four days—and another skirmish ensued, costing the gang another of its horses before the outlaws escaped under fire. The gang split up two days later, Frank and Jesse leaving Charlie Pitts with the Youngers, but the effort was almost too late. That morning they were all surrounded in a forest near Mankato, hemmed in by 400 vigilantes with the roads and bridges covered. At 2:00 A.M. on September 14 the Youngers and Pitts scattered guards at the Blue Earth River bridge and made their escape. Frank and Jesse hid out through the day, breaking through a picket line that night near Lake Crystal. Riding double on one horse, both brothers were wounded in their right legs by a lucky shot from sentry Richard Roberts.

And the hunt went on. Frank and Jesse fought another skirmish with pursuers on September 17, crossing the line into Dakota Territory, but they left one vigilante wounded and escaped to parts unknown. Four days later, the Youngers and Charlie Pitts stopped to buy food at a farm near Madelia, 150 miles southwest of Northfield, and their presence was reported to Sheriff James Gilpin. Surrounded in a nearby stand of timber, Pitts was killed by the posse while the Youngers fought their last battle. All three survived, but it was touch-and-go for Cole and Jim, with 11 wounds each. Convicted at trial, the Younger brothers drew identical 25-year prison terms for the Northfield fiasco.

The James boys, meanwhile, fled all the way to Mexico, later settling in Nashville, Tennessee, as "B.J. Woodson" (Frank) and "J. B. Howard" (Jesse). Frank reportedly joined George "Big Nose" Parrot's gang to rob a train near Medicine Bow, Wyoming, on August 14, 1878, but they came away empty handed after killing two pursuers. The brothers were soon joined by two more survivors of the old days, Bill Ryan (aka "Tom Hill") and Dick Liddil (aka "Charles Underwood"), but they remained inactive until autumn 1879. On October 7 of that year, accompanied by Tucker Basham and Ed Miller (Clell's brother), the gang invaded Glendale, Missouri—22 miles from Kansas City—and robbed an incoming train of $40,000. They left a note with the station agent, signed by all eight members of the team, that read: "We are the boys who are hard to handle, and we will make it hot for the boys who try to take us." Robert Pinkerton had another label for Jesse James, calling him "the worst man, without exception, in America."

Tucker Basham was soon arrested and agreed to turn state's evidence against the rest, a circumstance that prompted arsonists to burn his home. Even so, it was early 1881 before Basham had anyone to accuse. Bill Ryan was arrested and returned to Independence for trial, where a jury surprised observers by convicting him of robbery. The sentence: 25 years.

The raiding continued. In March 1881 the gang robbed a stagecoach at Muscle Shoals, Alabama. On July 10, 1881, they held up a bank in Riverton, Iowa. Five days later, Jesse James and two companions, all wearing false beards, boarded a train at Cameron, Missouri, en route from Kansas City to Davenport, Iowa. Four more bandits came aboard at Gallatin and then stopped the train at Winston, Missouri. They killed a panicky passenger, Frank McMillan, and robbed the express car, though reports of the take vary widely: Newspapers reported a score of $8,000 to $10,000, while Pinkerton spokespeople claimed it was closer to $600. In parting, Jesse executed conductor William Westfall—who had also served on the special Pinkerton train that brought detectives to his mother's home in January 1875.

After the Winston heist and murders, Missouri Governor Thomas Crittenden offered $10,000 each for Frank and Jesse James, with $5,000 outstanding for any other gang member brought to justice. The outfit pulled one more train holdup—at Blue Cut, Missouri, on September 7, 1881—but loyalties were rapidly disintegrating. Jesse killed Ed Miller, fearing he might turn state's evidence to save himself, and Dick Liddil murdered gang member Wood Hite in an argument over a woman (the sister of occasional cronies Charles and Robert Ford). Bob Ford helped hide the corpse, but Liddil afterward feared retribution from Jesse, accepting a lawman's offer of "ample rewards" in return for details on 22 robberies pulled by the gang since 1866.

The Ford brothers, having ingratiated themselves with Jesse James, visited Governor Crittenden to confirm that the outstanding $10,000 reward on Jesse's head would be paid whether he was dead or alive. On April 3, 1882, lately returned from a visit to Belle Starr in Indian Territory, Jesse entertained the brothers at his home in St. Joseph, Missouri, and Bob Ford shot him in the back, killing him instantly. Frank surrendered at the governor's office six months later, on October 5, announcing, "I'm tired of running. Tired of waiting for a ball in the back. Tired of looking into the faces of friends and seeing a Judas." No one was more surprised than Governor Crittenden when a trial jury acquitted Frank of all charges and released him to his family. Frank worked odd jobs thereafter, joining parolee Cole Younger in a Wild West show during 1903, but he left show business a year later and settled on a ranch in Oklahoma. In 1911 he returned to his Missouri home and offered guided tours of the old homestead until his death in 1915 at age 71.

The Ford brothers had little to show for their treachery. Charles was shot to death at home in Richmond, Missouri—an apparent suicide—in 1886. Bob Ford—immortalized in song as "the dirty little coward who shot Mr. Howard"—ran a tent saloon in the mining town of Creede, Colorado, until July 1892 when he was shot and killed by ex-policeman Ed O'Kelley.

As with BUTCH CASSIDY and JOHN DILLINGER, persistent legends insist that Jesse James faked his own death and escaped to Texas, where as "J. Frank Dalton" he allegedly survived until 1951. DNA tests performed on the corpse in Missouri apparently confirmed Jesse's death, but skeptics remained undaunted, exhuming Dalton's corpse at Granbury, Texas, in May 2000. The mystery survived, however, because a misplaced headstone left investigators holding the wrong corpse—in fact, one-armed William Henry Holland, deceased in 1927. At this writing, the search for the "real" Jesse James and his final resting place continues.

JAMES, Jerry Ray

A native of Electra, Texas, Jerry James was sought by the FBI for burglarizing a Mobeetie, Texas, bank on March 16, 1966. Arrested later that year and charged with the robbery of a nightclub in Biloxi, Mississippi, he was held in jail pending delivery to federal agents. Before they arrived, James escaped from jail on December 26 and was named a federal fugitive on charges of unlawful flight to avoid prosecution. On August 16, 1967, his name was added to the bureau's "Ten Most Wanted" list.

The search for Jerry James focused on Tucson, Arizona, in January 1968. On January 23 his wife was arrested at the home she had occupied for 90 days; simultaneously, another raiding party captured a friend of Jerry's, Wayne Padgett, and charged him with harboring a federal fugitive. The rented house was filled with stolen televisions, radios, and other small appliances, along with furs pilfered from stores in Texas, Illinois, and Indiana.

On the afternoon of January 24 G-men in Amarillo, Texas, surprised Jerry James and another Top Ten fugitive, Donald Eugene Sparks, as they sat watching television in another rental house. Unarmed, the men were taken into custody without resistance and James was subsequently convicted on federal bank-robbery charges. Confined to Leavenworth in 1980, he made friends with convicted drug dealer Jamiel "Jimmy" Chagra, reporting conversations in which Chagra allegedly took credit for the 1979 ambush slaying of a federal judge in Texas. Promised his freedom and $250,000 in return for testimony leading to Chagra's conviction, James did his best on the witness stand in 1983, but it was not good enough. Chagra was acquitted on the murder charge, and Jerry James remained in prison.

JARMAN, Eleanor "The Blonde Tigress"

Ranked among the more notorious of the Depression era's WOMEN BANDITS, attractive Eleanor Jarman apparently launched her criminal career in earnest on August 4, 1933. That afternoon, with male accomplices George Dale and Leo Minneci, she robbed James Swock's shoe store on North Avenue, in Chicago. Forty-five minutes later, the same trio held up Gustav Hoeh's haberdashery on West Division Street, but Hoeh was ready with a pistol, wounding Minneci before he was shot and killed. Reporters in the Windy City knew a sensational story when they saw one, and they dubbed Jarman "The Blond Tigress" while police were still trying to learn her real name.

Minneci surrendered to detectives on August 5 outside the Bell Telephone Company's Chicago office and readily confessed his role in the two small-time holdups. He also named his accomplices, fingering George Dale (alias Kennedy) as the triggerman in Gustav Hoeh's murder. It took four more days for police to trace the fugitives, finally arrested at their love nest on South Drexel Avenue. Publication of their photographs brought forward victims who identified the couple as responsible for 37 local robberies; unwilling to be cheated of the "credit" they deserved, Jarman and Dale raised the ante, confessing to 48 holdups. Authorities identified Jarman as

"the brains of the three," calling her "a beautiful but vicious animal" who enjoyed slugging shopkeepers with a blackjack.

On August 30, 1933, all three defendants were convicted of murdering Gustav Hoeh; Dale was sentenced to die, while Jarman and Minneci each drew terms of 199 years in prison. Executed at the Cook County jail on April 19, 1934, Dale allegedly penned one last love letter to Jarman before he took his walk to the electric chair. Eleanor, meanwhile, was dreaming of freedom. On August 8, 1940, she escaped from the women's prison at Dwight, Illinois, and disappeared without a trace. She was never recaptured, entering criminal legend as one of those who got away.

JENKINS, James Francis

Trained as a welder in the army, James Jenkins seldom plied his trade in civilian life, preferring the pursuit of easy money through felonious channels. Inaugurating his criminal career in 1941, he spent a decade running up convictions for burglary, larceny, receiving stolen property, and violation of parole. Convicted in 1948 of pulling off two dozen burglaries in Delaware County, Pennsylvania, Jenkins was paroled in 1950, but other offenses soon put him back behind bars. Conditionally released in 1958, he tried the straight life for a year but found it tedious. An avid bettor on the ponies, Jenkins needed ready cash on hand, and honest labor seemed to offer no immediate reward.

On March 4, 1959, James and sidekick Randall Nuss robbed a bank near Broomall, Pennsylvania, of $17,870. Both men were arrested by FBI agents a week later in Providence, Rhode Island, and returned to Philadelphia for trial, but Jenkins had already seen enough of prison from the inside. Working cautiously for 13 days, he used a smuggled screwdriver to gouge a hole in the wall of his cell, escaping from the Myamensing County jail with two other inmates. Ropes made out of bedsheets were employed as the escapees scrambled to the street from their top-floor cell, a two-hour gap between bed checks granting them a substantial head start on their pursuers.

From the lockup, Jenkins went directly to the home of former cellmate Henry Kiter, free on bail and pending trial on weapons charges. Federal agents traced their man to Kiter's home too late, and Kiter's name was entered on a May 6 warrant charging him with aiding an escape. James Jenkins made the Bureau's "Ten Most Wanted" list on July 21.

Prolific burglar James Jenkins turned to bank robbery in 1959. (FBI)

On August 12 a tip from residents of Buffalo, New York, brought G-men to a small motel where Jenkins and Kiter were registered under assumed names. Jenkins was taking a shower when agents knocked on the door, engaged Kiter in small talk, and then forced their way inside to take the fugitives without a struggle. Neither man was armed, although a sawed-off shotgun was recovered from their car. Returned to Philadelphia where he was eventually tried and convicted, Jenkins heard his new bond set at $50,000. Chuckling ruefully, he asked the bailiff, "Will you take a check?"

JEWEL Theft: History

As with works of art, so precious stones and metals have lured enterprising thieves throughout recorded history. In some respects, stolen gems pose the same disposal problem found in ART THEFT—world-famous stones may be too hot to handle, aside from sale to reclusive collectors—but many such objects offer an escape hatch for wily thieves and fences. Gems can be removed from their settings and sold individually, or they can sometimes be recut to disguise their identity; precious metals, in most cases, may be melted down and recast. An art thief, by contrast, can hardly disguise his loot by penciling a mustache on the *Mona Lisa*.

Jewel thefts through the ages have been so numerous and so diverse that no comprehensive listing is possible. The examples below represent a mere sampling, the proverbial iceberg's tip in a field as diverse and complex as any criminal endeavor known to humankind.

1671—England: Irish rebel Thomas Blood and two companions stole the British Crown jewels from the Tower of London on May 6, shooting a sentry in the process. Captured within the hour, Blood argued for his own acquittal so persuasively that King Charles II pardoned him, restored his lost estates, and granted Blood an annual pension of £500.

1913—France: A pearl necklace valued at £130,000 was stolen from the mail on July 16, after a Parisian broker shipped it to its owner in London. Officers from Scotland Yard recovered the necklace after thieves offered it for sale to a jeweler in Antwerp, Belgium, at a price of 1.5 million francs.

1919—Pennsylvania: A gang of "auto bandits" raided a Philadelphia jewelry store on January 19, escaping with $10,000 in gems.

1920—New York: A series of jewel thefts rocked the state this year. Manhattan jeweler Samuel Schonfeld was robbed of gems worth $100,000 on June 6; a Buffalo jeweler was kidnapped on December 12 and robbed of $70,000 in stones; four days later a jeweler in New York City was murdered by bandits who escaped with gems worth $50,000.

1921—Illinois: Gunmen stole $100,000 worth of uncut diamonds from a Chicago jewelry salesman on November 2.

1922—Illinois: Chicago recorded two more dramatic jewel thefts: On January 17 bandits invaded a local bank, bound the clerks, and stole $25,000 in diamonds from the vault; two months later, on March 20, a jewelry store was raided for stones valued at $100,000.

1923—Illinois: Chicago gunmen surprised a jeweler outside his shop on February 24, stealing $100,000 worth of merchandise.

1924—New York: Armed bandits escaped with gems valued at $100,000 after robbing a delivery truck in downtown Manhattan on June 11.

1924—Illinois: Two gunmen rob a mail train near Rondout on June 12, escaping with $50,000 in jewelry, $450,000 in new currency, and $1.5 million in negotiable bonds.

1924—Michigan: Detroit's Mazer Company was robbed of $125,000 in jewels on July 24.

1924—Illinois: A Chicago jewelry salesman was robbed at gunpoint on October 1, the thieves escaping with gems valued at $200,000.

1925–1926—New York: The brazen gang led by RICHARD WHITTEMORE robbed 10 jewelry stores in New York City and Buffalo between April 5, 1925, and January 11, 1926, escaping with gems worth a total of $506,000. Upon his capture in 1926, Whittemore was convicted and executed for a murder in Maryland.

1930—Illinois: Before adopting bank robbery as his vocation, GEORGE "BABY FACE" NELSON led a five-man gang of home-invading jewel thieves. His first score, on January 6, netted gems worth $25,000 from a Chicago residence. On January 22 the gang stole $5,000 in jewelry from a Lake Forest home.

1932—Texas: Future headline desperadoes CLYDE BARROW and RAYMOND HAMILTON robbed a jewelry store in Hillsboro, killing the proprietor.

1936—Ohio: The BRADY GANG, last noteworthy "public enemies" of the Great Depression, robbed four jewelry stores between March 4 and April 27. The raids—in Greenville, Lima, Dayton, and Piqua—netted an estimated $50,000 in gems.

1950—England: Scottish separatists stole the Stone of Scone from Westminster Abbey on Christmas Day, escaping unseen in the midst of public celebrations and nearly within sight of Scotland Yard. Four suspects returned the stone on April 11, 1951, after receiving promises of amnesty.

1964—New York: Burglars led by Jack "Murph the Surf" Murphy stole 22 gems valued at $380,000 from the American Museum of Natural History on October 29. Their haul included the Star of India (world's largest star sapphire, at 563.35 carats) and the DeLong Star Ruby (103 carats). Murphy and accomplice Allan Kuhn were captured on November 1, but the loot remained elusive, nine of the major stones later surrendered in return for a reduction of charges filed against the thieves.

1972—New York: Well-dressed bandits held employees of Manhattan's Hotel Pierre at gunpoint in the predawn hours of January 2, looting 47 safe deposit boxes of jewelry, cash, and other valuables. Published estimates of the total score ranged from $1 million to $10 million. Five days later, New York police and FBI agents arrested five suspects in the robbery, announcing recovery of stolen property worth $250,000. G-men reported on January 9 that they had found more Pierre loot in Detroit, amounting to some $750,000 in jewelry.

1980—Florida: Miami bandits scored the largest gold heist in American history to date, stealing $8 million worth of the precious metal from a jewelry wholesaler's office.

1982—New York: A burglar removed 25 Mayan artifacts from the American Museum of Natural History on the night of September 4–5. Curators described the items as "priceless," although their total insured value was listed as $478,000.

1983—Florida: Two masked gunmen invaded the office of a Miami jewelry wholesaler, blindfold-

This diamond necklace and bracelet belonging to the duchess of York was stolen and recovered in a locker at New York's Kennedy Airport. The jewels had been a wedding gift to the duchess from Queen Elizabeth. (AP/Wide World Photos)

Two police officers use rubber gloves to handle stolen Oscar statues that were found in a trash bin in Los Angeles. (AP/Wide World Photos)

ing three employees and fleeing with 875 pounds of gold, valued by official estimates somewhere between $6 million and $9 million.

1983—New York: Burglars struck a Manhattan wholesale jewelry firm on April 2, stealing 900 pounds of gold chains valued at $6 million. Police reported that the thieves broke through a wall from an adjoining office, using sledge hammers.

1983—England: Masked gunmen invaded the Brinks-Mat high-security warehouse in Houndslow, West London, on November 26, binding guards before they fled with £113,000 worth of uncut diamonds, £26 million in gold, £160,000 in platinum, and £250,000 in untraceable travelers' checks.

1986—California: Would-be bandit Steven Livaditis invaded Van Cleef & Arpels, a Beverly Hills jewelry store, on June 23, executing two hostages after police surrounded the shop. A third hostage was killed by police gunfire before stun grenades disabled Livaditis. Convicted on three counts of murder, the failed robber was sentenced to death on July 8, 1987.

1995—New York: On December 6 federal authorities charged an airport baggage handler with stealing a diamond necklace and bracelet owned by the Duchess of York, valued at $382,000. The items, received as a wedding gift from Queen Elizabeth II of England, were stolen on December 4 from luggage en route to London.

2000—California: Unknown thieves stole 55 Oscar statuettes from a Los Angeles warehouse shortly before they were scheduled for presentation at the annual Academy Awards ceremony on March 26. Local resident Willie Fulgear found the Oscars in a garbage bin behind a local discount grocery store and summoned authorities, thus earning himself a $50,000 reward and a ticket to the televised ceremony. Two months later, burglars looted Fulgear's home, escaping with $40,000 of the reward money and an unspecified amount of jewelry.

2001—California: Masked gunmen robbed a San Jose jewelry broker in the parking lot behind his store, escaping with $500,000 worth of diamonds on March 22.

JOHNSON, Charles E.

Charles Johnson's record dated back to 1921 with an arrest for burglary when he was still a juvenile. In 1934, his first adult arrest (for a New York robbery) earned him a term of four to eight years in Sing Sing. After shooting a policeman in a failed escape attempt, he was transferred north to Dannemora, the "Siberia" of the New York State penal system. Except for six short months of freedom, Johnson was confined from 1935 to 1952. A year later, New York authorities were seeking him for three-time violation of parole.

On August 28, 1952, Johnson and four other gunmen held up a bank robber, relieving the bandit of loot he had gained from a $50,000 heist in Lakesville, North Carolina, four months earlier. Their victim was in no position to complain, but when arrested for the robbery, he would be quick to point a finger. Federal statutes made Johnson and the others guilty of receiving stolen property, as if the members of his gang had robbed the bank themselves. Johnson's name was added to the FBI's "Ten Most Wanted" list on November 12, 1953.

Bandit Charles Johnson's criminal career spanned the years from 1921 to 1953. (FBI)

Approximately six weeks later, on December 28, a resident of Central Islip, New York, recognized Johnson's photograph in a magazine article covering the Top Ten fugitives. The FBI was notified that afternoon. A dozen G-men backed by local officers converged on a ranch-style home at midnight, bursting in to find their man unarmed in his pajamas and a robe. Johnson did not resist as he was taken into custody, and he was duly convicted at trial.

JOHNSON, Morris Lynn

Kentucky native Morris Johnson was a stickup artist with a laid-back attitude. Boasting adult convictions for bank robbery, escape and rescue, bank robbery with assault, and assault on a federal officer, he balanced his fondness for easy money and automatic weapons with a passion for freedom. Ever restless in confinement, he was a perennial "rabbit," prone to daring escapes from custody.

Breaking parole on his latest robbery conviction in August 1975, Johnson was named in federal warrants charging him with bank robbery and bank burglary, both in Atlanta, Georgia. Briefly recaptured and jailed as a parole violator, he escaped from the federal prison in Atlanta on October 25, 1975.

Named to the FBI's "Ten Most Wanted" list on May 25, 1976, Johnson lasted a month before federal agents acting on a tip captured him in New Orleans on June 26. Held in Selma, Alabama, pending transfer, Johnson confounded his captors by escaping from custody again on November 6. He had promised to send greetings if he ever hit the street again, and Johnson was true to his word. At Christmas the fugitive posted cards to the federal judge and prosecutor responsible for his conviction, along with one of the FBI agents instrumental in his arrest. "I do my thing and you do your thing," the cards read. "If we should ever meet again, it's beautiful." To date, no such meeting has occurred. The fugitive remains at large.

JONES, Phillip Morris

A Florida native with record of convictions for grand theft, Jones was known as an avid gambler with a preference for blackjack and poker. Whenever possible, he liked to use marked cards, but cheating did not always pay, and Jones was constantly in need of cash. In 1968 he turned to robbery and bet the future on his own ability to outwit agents of the FBI.

On February 23, 1968, Jones raided a bank in Bakersfield, California, for $5,637, but luck was running against him, and all but $500 of the loot was recovered from his abandoned getaway car. On April 8, in Winter Haven, Florida, he locked eight bank employees in a vault and escaped to a nearby motel with $79,874. When police arrived, Jones donned swim trunks and posed as a casual poolside lounger; then he stole a car and drove to a local lake. Abandoning the vehicle, he swam 50 yards across the lake, stole a truck, and made good his escape. This time, all but $277 of the bank loot was recovered from Jones's motel room.

The clumsy bandit managed to keep his next score, in the amount of $9,820 stolen on April 30, 1968, from a bank in Weaton, Maryland. Four days later, in Phoenix, he raided a savings and loan association for $2,100, but his time was running out. Identified as the hit-and-run bandit, Jones was indicted on federal bank-robbery charges. His name was added to the FBI's "Ten Most Wanted" list on June 5, 1968.

Three weeks later, tired of running, Jones walked into an FBI office in San Mateo, California, calmly announcing, "You people want me." Special Agent John Breslin accepted a paper sack from Jones, discovering an automatic pistol inside, and the hard-luck fugitive was taken into custody and held for trial. He was subsequent convicted on multiple felony counts.

JONES, William Daniel

A native of Dallas, Texas, born in 1915, W. D. Jones grew up in an era and atmosphere where outlaws were often admired for their defiance of authority and worshiped as heroes in some quarters. He was not, as one author reports, a "former schoolmate" of bank robber CLYDE BARROW, but he was a friend of Clyde's younger brother, and that connection granted him an introduction to Barrow on December 24, 1932. Clyde spoke briefly to Jones and then invited him to join the gang. Jones jumped at the chance to become a real-life badman.

He joined Clyde for their first collaborative felony less than 24 hours later on Christmas Day. Together, they stole a car belonging to Doyle Johnson, in Temple, Texas. Johnson saw the thieves at work and ran outside his house to stop them. Someone fired a pistol shot and dropped him in his tracks; Jones later blamed Clyde, while Barrow's relatives insisted that W. D. himself was the nervous triggerman. It mat-

tered not to Johnson, who was dead before he hit the ground.

Jones witnessed (or participated in) his second murder less than two weeks later. Clyde and girl-friend BONNIE PARKER drove with Jones to visit the West Dallas home of bandit FLOYD HAMILTON's sister, but law enforcers were waiting in ambush. Clyde killed Deputy Malcolm Davis with a close-range shotgun blast, while someone in the car (either Bonnie or Jones) covered his escape with rifle fire. On January 31, 1933, in Oklahoma, Jones helped Clyde kidnap motorcycle officer Thomas Persell on a lark, whisking him off on an aimless 200-mile drive while Jones held the captive at gunpoint. Three weeks later, on February 20, Jones joined Clyde and accomplice Monroe Routon to loot a bank at Shiro, Texas.

The gang's serious holdups resumed after Ivan "Buck" Barrow rejoined brother Clyde. Their first holdup as a team, with Jones participating, was committed near Neosho, Missouri, on April 12, 1933. The next day, police traced the gang to a rented hideout in Joplin, closing in to surround the house, and a pitched battle erupted, leaving two officers dead. (Various snapshots left behind in the Joplin hideout showed W. D. Jones posing with guns and his partners in crime, thus alerting law officers to his identity for the first time.) The comic flip side of such tragic incidents was demonstrated two weeks later in Rushton, Louisiana, when the gang stole a new Chevrolet owned by mortician H. Dillard Dilby. Observing the theft, Dilby and a lady friend gave chase in a second vehicle—only to be taken hostage when the gang doubled back and kidnapped them for sport. Another long ride lay in store (later dramatized in the movie *Bonnie and Clyde*), but the hostages, as usual with Barrow, were released unharmed.

Disaster struck the gang on June 10, 1933. While speeding down rain-slick Texas Highway 203, Clyde swerved their stolen car into a ditch. It burst into flames, and Bonnie was badly burned before she could be extricated from the wreckage. Farmers and policemen who arrived to help were taken hostage at gunpoint, the gang retreating briefly to Jack Pritchard's farmhouse for emergency first-aid. Before they left, one of the gang fired a shotgun blast that wounded Pritchard's wife, crippling one of her hands. Most accounts blame Clyde, but again his surviving relatives name Jones as the jittery gunman responsible. Two policemen were abducted from the scene, cradling Bonnie in their arms as the gang sped on toward Erick, Oklahoma, in a stolen

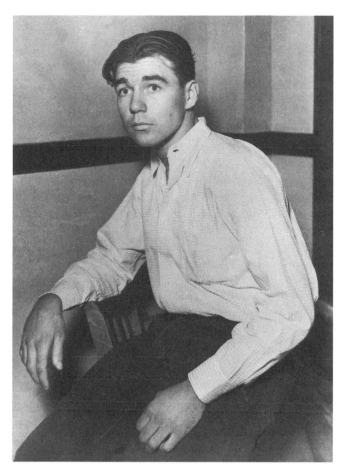

William Daniel Jones, teenage accomplice of Clyde Barrow and Bonnie Parker, spun tales of their aberrant sex life to save himself from the electric chair. (From the collection of the Texas/Dallas History and Archives Division, Dallas Public Library)

car. Clyde left them there, unharmed, with thanks for the consideration they had shown to Bonnie in her suffering.

On June 22, 1933, Jones and Clyde robbed a bank in Alma, Arkansas, of a reported $3,600. The next day, after holding up a Fayetteville grocery store, Buck and Jones were stopped near Alma by Marshal H. D. Humphrey, one of the bandits gunning him down before they escaped. On June 24, Jones and Clyde stole a physician's car from Enid, Oklahoma, as a new addition to their ever-changing motor pool. July 18 saw the gang rob three filling stations at Fort Dodge, Kansas, and they settled next evening at a tourist camp near Platte City, Missouri. Suspicious of the visitors who paid all their bills in small change, local police scanned their WANTED

posters and recognized the tourists as notorious fugitives. Law enforcers closed in on the night of July 19, but the gang shot its way clear once again, leaving two officers wounded despite their steel shields and a "bulletproof" armored car. Five days later, a second posse overtook the gang at Dexfield Park, Iowa, capturing "Buck" (soon to die from his wounds) and his wife Blanche. Jones was wounded by buckshot as he fled on foot with Bonnie and Clyde, but all three escaped to steal another car and clear the area.

Jones's enthusiasm for the outlaw lifestyle had begun to fade. He helped Clyde loot a National Guard armory at Plattsville, Indiana, on August 20, 1933, stealing various weapons and ammunition, but most reports agree that he left the gang by month's end, never to return, after stealing a car from Clarksdale, Mississippi. Authorities traced him to Houston on November 15, 1933, and arrested Jones in a cotton patch, where he was earning honest money for a change. One week later, indicted for Doyle Johnson's murder, the 18-year-old gunman realized that he was on his way to the electric chair.

What to do?

The answer was obvious, but plea bargains were not automatic in the 1930s. Jones had nothing to trade in exchange for his life. He could not give up Bonnie and Clyde because he had no idea where they were. His value as a prosecution witness was likewise nil because no one really expected the outlaw lovers to be captured alive, What he *could* do, however, was enhance the couple's reputation as virtual demons incarnate, ensuring that summary justice, when it came, would enjoy a measure of public approval.

This Jones did, in a 28-page confession rightly described by one author as "a fantastic story of crime and suffering." *Fantastic* was the operative word, as Jones rewrote history from scratch, casting himself in the role of a hapless victim. He had joined Clyde and Bonnie on a whim but instantly regretted it after the Johnson slaying (committed by Clyde, he maintained). When Jones tried to leave the gang, he was taken hostage and forced at gunpoint to participate in robberies and shootouts with police. Not that he ever killed or wounded anyone *himself*, of course: It was always Clyde or "Buck" who did the shooting. Sometimes, Jones averred, he was "unconscious" when the fatal shots rang out. Between raids, he was often chained to furniture or trees. As if this fable were not strange enough, Jones added some salacious frosting to the cake, describing how homosexual Clyde and nymphomaniac Bonnie had taken turns abusing him, keeping him as their personal sex slave for months on end.

It is unclear how many law officers believed the confession, though some historians—including John Toland, author of *The Dillinger Days*—clearly swallowed it whole. Jones won his reprieve from Old Sparky and was sentenced to life imprisonment for the Johnson slaying. Clyde had no hard feelings about W. D.'s outrageous lies; as sister Nell Barrow later wrote, "The stories that W. D. told amused Clyde and never made him mad. He said he hoped the kid put it over and got away with it."

Paroled decades later, Jones lived long enough to see himself portrayed by Hollywood in *Bonnie and Clyde* as dim-witted "C. W. Moss," a composite character combining traits of Jones and Barrow sidekick HENRY METHVIN. Four years later, in 1971, Jones was arrested in Fort Worth for possession of narcotics. His story ended in Houston on August 20, 1974, when he was shot to death in a senseless brawl.

JULIANO, Anthony Michael

A prolific thief, Anthony Juliano was linked with a daring holdup gang responsible for 27 bank robberies in Boston and New York City between 1973 and 1975. On November 11, 1975, a federal warrant was issued in Brooklyn charging him with conspiracy to rob banks; on November 28 a second warrant charged him with violating terms of his release from federal prison on a previous conviction. Juliano's name was added to the FBI's "Most Wanted" list on March 15, 1976.

Seven days later, FBI agents tipped local officers in Mecklenburg County, Virginia, that Juliano was

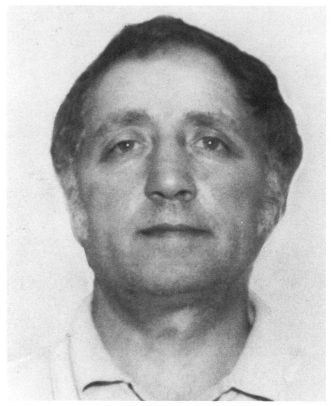

Bandit Anthony Juliano robbed 27 banks between 1973 and 1975. (FBI)

headed their way. At 9:40 that morning, police spotted him at an intersection in South Hill, trailing him onto the open road outside town before pulling him over. Juliano surrendered without resistance and was held in lieu of $1 million bond, pending extradition to New York. His subsequent conviction on multiple felony counts tagged additional time onto his outstanding sentence.

KANSAS City Massacre

In retrospect, FRANK "JELLY" NASH was probably a better jailbreak artist than he was a bank robber. He ran with several holdup gangs in the late 1920s and early 1930s, working at least one bank job with the BARKER-KARPIS outfit, but his major claim to fame (at least, before his gruesome death) was an escape he managed from the federal pen at Leavenworth. Convicted of robbing a mail train in March 1924, Frank spent six and a half years inside, keeping his nose clean and working his way up the ladder to become a trusty before he made his move. Allowed outside the walls from time to time on errands for the staff, Nash failed to return from one jaunt on October 19, 1932, and he was still at large in June 1933 when federal agents tracked him down in Hot Springs, Arkansas.

Hot Springs, in those days, was a notorious hangout for hoods on the lam, where rackets were wide open and protection was acquired by bribing the police. A tip led G-men to the den where Nash spent his idle hours, but they had no power to arrest him, so they brought along Police Chief Otto Reed from McAlester, Oklahoma, to give the bust an aura of legitimacy. On Friday, June 16, Nash was abducted by the makeshift posse from a pool hall run by Hot Springs crime boss Dick Galatas. Twice before they reached Fort Smith and caught a train to Kansas City, they were stopped by bought-and-paid-for lawmen searching for a "kidnap victim," but each time they bluffed the officers and made it through. More

federal men and Kansas City cops were standing by to meet the group at Union Station, prepared to escort Nash the final 30 miles to Leavenworth along back roads.

The train with Nash and company on board arrived at 7:00 A.M. on June 17. The official version of what happened next, embodied in a single paragraph, is found in the 89th and final volume of the FBI's 20,000-page file on the Union Station massacre. It reads:

Frank Nash was escorted by the Head of the FBI's Kansas City Office [Reed Vetterli], together with Special Agent Raymond J. Caffrey, two other representatives of the FBI [Francis J. Lackey and Frank Smith], and Otto Reed, chief of police of the McAlester, Oklahoma, Police Department. Police Officers W.J. Grooms and Frank Hermanson of the Kansas City, Missouri, Police Department, were also given important posts of assignment for this transfer. Frank Nash, upon being removed from the train, was immediately taken to the waiting automobile of Special Agent Caffrey, where he was placed in the left front seat in order that the officers might occupy the rear seat. At this instant two Special Agents [Smith and Lackey] took positions in the rear seat with Chief of Police Otto Reed. Police Officers Grooms and Hermanson, together with the Head of the FBI's Kansas City Office, were standing on the right side of Agent Caffrey's automobile during the time Special Agent Caffrey was walking around the car preparatory to entering the driver's seat. It was when Agent Caffrey approached the left door of this automobile that the three assassins sur-

159

prised the officers from a point in front of and about fif-teen to twenty feet west of the automobile. These men were observed carrying machine guns and other weapons and in approaching the automobile shouted, "Up, up." An instant later the voice of one of the gun-men was heard to say, "Let 'em have it." Immediately a fusillade of gunfire came from the weapons of the attackers. Shots were fired from the front and from all sides of Agent Caffrey's car. Police Officers Grooms and Hermanson were instantly killed in the positions where they stood. Chief of Police Otto Reed was also instantly killed. One agent [Lackey] was severely wounded by bullets which entered his back, and he was confined to bed for several months. Special Agent Caffrey was instantly killed by a bullet which passed directly through his head as he stood beside the car. The prisoner, Frank Nash, was also killed by a misdirected gunshot that entered his skull, thereby defeating the very purpose of the conspiracy to gain his freedom. The other Special Agent [Smith] escaped injury, while the Head of the FBI office [Vetterli] received a wound in the arm. Apparently the assassins started at the front right-hand side of the car and at least two of them proceeded around the auto-mobile, making a complete circle and firing recklessly as they went.

That was and is today the official story, but it had some problems from day one. Patrolman Mike Fan-ning, assigned to patrol Union Station that morning, had fired at one of the shooters—the "fat man"—and saw him drop to the ground. "I don't know whether I hit him or whether he fell to escape," Fan-ning later told the press. "In any event he got up, fired another volley into the car, and ran toward a light Oldsmobile car, which roared west toward Broadway. As the car raced out of the parking lot I saw three men in it, and there may have been more."

The action was not finished yet, however. As the Oldsmobile escaped, Fanning said, "A 1933 Chevro-let car with more gunners swooped past the car [Agent Caffrey's] and riddled it from the rear. I ran into the street, fired two shots into the back of that car, and rushed to the parked Chevrolet. I still didn't know the men in it were officers."

Thus, if Officer Fanning's report was correct, we have *two* cars involved in the shooting, one (the Olds) with three occupants, and the second Chevy containing at least two (and probably more because one was clearly driving and Fanning referred in the plural to "more gunners"). The obvious problem for investigators was identifying those responsible and finding out where they had gone to ground.

Eyewitnesses at the scene were hopelessly con-fused. Survivors Smith and Lackey disagreed on the number of gunmen involved in the ambush, but both initially reported that they had no clear view of the shooters' faces. Agent Vetterli, meanwhile, identified one triggerman from mug shots as ROBERT BRADY, an escaped convict known as an associate of fugitive bank robber HARVEY BAILEY. That I.D. seemed to mesh with testimony from two civilian witnesses, both of whom fingered Bailey as one of the gunners. One of those witnesses also identified the gang's wheelman as WILBUR UNDERHILL, aka the "Tri-State Terror," but problems arose when the witness (Samuel Link) was described in FBI reports as delu-sional, claiming personal friendships with Teddy Roosevelt and various crowned heads of Europe. Another shaky witness, Lottie West from the Travel-ers Aid booth inside Union Station, named the "fat man" among the shooters as CHARLES "PRETTY BOY" FLOYD. Mrs. West told G-men that Floyd had stopped by her booth before the shooting, thus giv-ing her a clear look at his face. That claim was flatly contradicted, though, by several other witnesses who named the "fat man" at the booth as Harry Blan-chard, an employee at Union Station.

Ballistics were another problem for the FBI. Sou-venir hunters looted the crime scene before police managed to secure it, leaving only a handful of .45-caliber cartridge cases behind, and even those were useless without weapons for comparison. There were *other* shells, though, found inside the FBI vehicle where Agent Lackey had fired two rounds from a 16-gauge shotgun, its cartridges specially loaded with distinctive ball bearings instead of the usual buck-shot. Lackey's first shot, whether accidentally or by design, had nearly decapitated Frank Nash, seated directly in front of Lackey in the driver's seat, scatter-ing windshield glass across the Chevrolet's hood. Ball bearings from the shotgun also caused the fatal wounds suffered by Agent Caffrey and Officer Her-manson, although that evidence was swiftly buried by the FBI. Chief Reed, meanwhile, was struck twice in the head, once by a .45-caliber slug and once by a 38-caliber round. Either wound was potentially fatal, but the order of impact was never determined, and although investigators claimed the ambushers all used .45-caliber weapons, none of the five .38s car-ried by lawmen at the scene were ever test-fired for a ballistics comparison with the slug recovered from Reed. The others killed or wounded at Union Sta-tion—Grooms, Lackey, and Vetterli—were all struck by .45-caliber bullets fired from Tommy guns or semiautomatic pistols . . . but who did the shooting?

The first real lead to those responsible for the attack was gained by checking long-distance telephone records, noting several calls made by Frances Nash from Arkansas to various Missouri numbers, following her husband's arrest. One of those numbers belonged to VERNON MILLER, a World War I veteran and ex-sheriff who lost his job in South Dakota for embezzling funds and then went to work as a freelance hit man for various Midwestern gangs. Miller was living with girlfriend Vivian Mathias in Kansas City when he took the call from Frances Nash, and he had called Frances back from a pay phone at Union Station on Saturday morning, shortly before the ambush.

Miller was long gone by the time FBI agents raided his home in Kansas City, but they confirmed his presence in the house through fingerprints. Vern's weren't the only prints retrieved, of course, but none of the others could be identified, even after they were checked against a list of massacre suspects including Bailey, Underhill, Floyd, and Pretty Boy's alcoholic sidekick in various bank holdups, ADAM RICHETTI. More than a year would pass before the feds unaccountably changed their minds, deciding that one of the fingerprints lifted from a beer bottle in Miller's basement really *was* Richetti's after all. That bumped Richetti to the head of J. EDGAR HOOVER's suspect list, and if Richetti was involved in the massacre, who could doubt that Pretty Boy Floyd was along for the ride?

By that time, a full year after the massacre, manhunters had apparently forgotten all about the second carload of gunners, paring their list of suspects down to a trio of Miller, Floyd, and Richetti. Vern Miller was forever beyond their reach, found beaten to death in Detroit in November 1933. Girlfriend Vivian Mathias was subsequently picked up by the feds—abducted, in effect—and illegally held incommunicado until she delivered a statement naming the Union Station triggermen as Miller, Floyd, and Richetti. Floyd had been wounded in the left shoulder during the shootout, Vivian declared, thus accounting for some bloody rags found during the earlier search of Miller's home.

Today we know that Floyd and Richetti hid out with their girlfriends in Buffalo, New York, between September 1933 and early October 1934. Finally tiring of the hermit's life, they left Buffalo in a new Ford V-8 on October 19, traveling as far as eastern Ohio before Floyd lost control of the car on a rain-slick highway and wrecked it near East Liverpool. The girls hiked into town and fetched a tow truck while Floyd and Richetti hid out in the woods nearby. As luck would have it, they were spotted by some passersby who called police. A brief, chaotic shootout ended with Richetti in handcuffs and Floyd having escaped through the woods. Trailed to a local farm on October 22, Pretty Boy was cut down by an eight-man firing squad while trying to flee across an open field. Stories persist that G-man MELVIN PURVIS had him finished off at point-blank range while Floyd lay wounded on the ground.

Pretty Boy's death initially seemed like good news for the FBI, all the more so when one of his .45-caliber pistols was allegedly matched to a shell casing found at Union Station. Unfortunately for the prosecution, though, medical examiners found no evidence of any shoulder wound that would support the story told by Vivian Mathias while she was in federal custody. Intent on touching all the bases, G-men paid another call on Vivian, producing yet another statement. This time she "remembered" that the bloody rags from Miller's home had nothing to do with Floyd after all; they were, she said, the remnants of some first-aid treatment given to a wounded member of the Barker-Karpis gang on another occasion entirely. As for the rest of her affidavit naming the Union Station shooters, Vivian assured the agents that Floyd's shoulder wound "was the only part I wasn't telling the truth about in the first statement."

It was good enough for J. Edgar Hoover, but not for federal prosecutors who declined to file charges on Richetti. Kansas City prosecutor Michael O'Hearn was likewise "inclined to doubt that there is sufficient evidence to convict Richetti," but he was overruled by the masters of K.C.'s political machine, and Richetti was indicted on a single murder count, for allegedly killing Officer Hermanson.

Richetti's trial, commencing on June 13, 1935, was something less than a textbook example of justice in action. The only "evidence" against him was a single fingerprint, allegedly recovered not from the crime scene but from a beer bottle in Vern Miller's home. Ballistically, one cartridge case was said to place "Pretty Boy" Floyd at the massacre site, and prosecutors inferred that Richetti must therefore also have been present. The bulk of the case rested on three survivors of the shootout, and all three apparently perjured themselves on the witness stand. Agent Vetterli had reported to FBI headquarters on the day of the murders that "I am convinced the man who first opened fire from our right, with a machine gun, is Bob Brady"; now, two years later, he told the jury under oath, "I identify the picture of State's Exhibit Number Three of 'Pretty Boy' Floyd as the individual I saw." Agent Smith initially reported seeing one machine-gunner and stated unequivocally that he "was unable to obtain any kind of description of him and was unable to see anyone else who did the shooting"; in June 1935 Smith examined a photo of Vern Miller and told the court, "That was the man who shot at my head." Agent Lackey, two years earlier, had reported to superiors that "there were at least four and possibly more men shooting," although he had only glimpsed two and was "not sure that he could identify either of these men," seen only in a "hurried glance" and "through a none too clean window"; at trial, Lackey not only fingered Richetti as one of the shooters but also denied firing any shots himself, in direct contradiction of physical evidence withheld from the jury.

The verdict was predictable: Richetti was convicted and sentenced to hang. Progress spared him from the gallows, but not from execution. On October 7, 1938, he was the first man to die in Ohio's new gas chamber. Still, there were those who knew the truth, revealed six decades later by journalist Robert Unger. As Unger reports, one G-man on the case confided the real story to federal judge William Becker. "Our agent sitting in the back seat pulled the trigger on Nash, and that started it," he explained. "The machine gunners didn't shoot first. Our guy panicked." With the probable exception of Vern Miller, the identity of those uneasy gunners is unknown today.

KARPIS, Alvin "Old Creepy"

A native of Montreal, Canada, born Francis Albin Karpaviecz on August 10, 1908, America's future "Public Enemy No. 1" moved to Illinois with his parents as a child. He grew up wild and reckless in the same Chicago neighborhood that spawned GEORGE "BABY FACE" NELSON, but the two would only meet years later, as fugitives on the run from police and the FBI. Like other immigrants before him, Karpaviecz soon Anglicized his name and passed into criminal history as Alvin Karpis, dubbed "Old Creepy" for his bug-eyed, slack-jawed stare. An associate of the Depression era's most notorious bandits, Karpis later explained, "I got a kick out of it apart from the money. The action and excitement thrilled

me. I enjoyed the challenge of planning a job and carrying out each step with military precision."

For all that, he got a rocky start in his chosen profession: He was arrested at age 17 for burglarizing a store in Topeka, Kansas, and was sentenced on February 25, 1926, to spend five years in the state reformatory at Hutchinson. Released in the summer of 1929, he returned to Chicago and briefly went straight, working in a local bakery until the October stock-market crash persuaded Alvin's boss to cut back on payroll expenses. By year's end, Karpis was back in the burglary business, teamed with LAWRENCE DEVOL for a series of nocturnal raids in Kansas and Oklahoma. They were arrested together in Kansas City on March 23, 1930. Karpis was packed off to the Kansas state prison at Lansing, where he soon became friends with another young outlaw named Fred BARKER. Fred was paroled a year later in March 1931, and Alvin was close behind him, released from Lansing on May 2. He made a beeline for the Barker home in Tulsa, thus forming the nucleus of what would become the infamous Barker-Karpis gang.

They started small with a series of burglaries around Coffeyville, Kansas, that netted Karpis a pitiful $150 in May and June 1931. On June 10, he was arrested for burglary in Tulsa with Fred Barker, Joe Howard, and escaped convict Sam Coker. Three months later, on September 11, Karpis pled guilty as charged and received a four-year suspended sentence. The Barkers had relocated by then, and Alvin wasted no time in trailing them to their new home, in Thayer, Missouri.

The gang's first bank robbery occurred in Mountain View, Missouri, on October 7, 1931. Karpis joined Fred Barker and two other cohorts, Bill Weaver and Jimmie Wilson, to make off with $14,000 in cash and negotiable securities. On January 5, 1932, the Barker-Karpis gang raided Cambridge, Minnesota, kidnapping the town marshal and stealing $3,000 worth of goods before they fled to ST. PAUL in a stolen car. The score was better in Minneapolis on March 29, 1932, when Alvin, Fred, Lawrence DeVol, THOMAS HOLDEN, and Bernard Phillips looted another bank of $75,000 in cash and $185,000 in bonds.

The last raid was too close to home, and while St. Paul authorities felt compelled to take some action against their resident outlaws, a tipster on the force telephoned ahead, giving Karpis and the Barkers time to vacate their rented house before raiders arrived on April 25, 1932. Authorities had been

Alvin "Creepy" Karpis, shown in a 1936 photo, was one of Kansas's most infamous criminals. (AP/Wide World Photos)

summoned by a neighbor who recognized gang members from their mug shots in a pulp detective magazine, but Fred and Alvin blamed "Ma" Barker's boozy live-in lover, Arthur Dunlop, leaving his bullet-punctured corpse at Lake Frestead, near Webster, Wisconsin, before they moved on to a hideout in Kansas City. The heat followed them, though, with gang members Tom Holden, Francis Keating, and HARVEY BAILEY captured by FBI agents at a local golf course. Uprooted, the gang drifted back toward St. Paul, settling in a bungalow at nearby White Bear Lake.

They began to raid again on June 17, 1932, lifting $47,000 from a bank in Fort Scott, Kansas, and leaving three unlucky fugitives—FRANK SAWYER, ED DAVIS, and JIM CLARK—to take the fall. On July 25 the gang struck in Concordia, Kansas, looting a local bank of some $240,000 in cash and bonds. Still unrecognized, the bandits may have been responsible for another bank holdup, in Beloit, Wisconsin, on August 18, 1932. That same afternoon, attorney J. Earl Smith was found shot to death at the Indian Springs Country Club near Tulsa, Oklahoma. Rumor

had it that Smith had been hired by the Barker-Karpis gang to defend Harvey Bailey after his arrest in Kansas City; Fred and Alvin were understandably disgruntled when Bailey was convicted and sentenced to a prison term of 25 to 50 years.

Arthur "Dock" Barker rejoined the gang in September 1932, paroled from Oklahoma on condition that he leave the state forever, and his return was cause for celebration. On September 23 the Barker-Karpis gang stole $35,000 from a bank in Redwood Falls, Minnesota, rebounding on September 30 to loot another bank, in Wahpeton, North Dakota, of $6,900. Nine days before Christmas, the gang stole $22,000 in cash and $92,000 in bonds from a Minneapolis bank, killing two police officers and wounding a third as they fled; while switching getaway cars in St. Paul, Fred Barker also murdered a civilian passer-by who demonstrated too much interest in the gang's activity.

The outlaws scattered for a time after the Twin Cities holdup-murders, Karpis pausing in Chicago before ranging farther west to Reno, Nevada, where he met and socialized with Baby Face Nelson. Alvin had his tonsils removed by a Reno physician in February 1933, but before month's end he was back in St. Paul, sharing rented quarters with the Barker boys and sidekick Earl Christman. Once again, neighbors grew suspicious, and once again, crooked cops tipped the bandits off in time for them to flee before police raided the flat on March 4, 1933.

Karpis, meanwhile, had cased a fat bank in Fairbury, Nebraska. The gang took it down on April 4, 1933, Karpis accompanied by the Barker brothers, Christman, VOLNEY DAVIS, FRANK NASH, and Jess Doyle. They bagged $151,350 from the vault and tellers' cages, but a wild shootout erupted as they fled, leaving eight persons wounded. One of those was Earl Christman, hurt so badly that he died days later at VERNE MILLER's home and was buried in an unmarked grave outside Kansas City.

It was now, perhaps at the suggestion of gang associate FRED GOETZ, that the Barker-Karpis outfit decided to shift its emphasis from daylight robberies to ransom kidnapping. Their first target, St. Paul brewer William Hamm, was abducted on June 15, 1933, and released four days later after payment of a $100,000 ransom.

It was easy money, but Karpis and the Barkers still craved excitement, along with their ill-gotten gains. On August 30, 1933, they raided a post office in south St. Paul, lifting a $33,000 payroll shipment.

Again there was gunplay—one patrolman was killed on the spot and another gravely wounded. Three weeks later, on September 22, the gang used a special bulletproof car, complete with smokescreen and oil-slick devices, to rob a pair of Federal Reserve Bank messengers on Chicago's Jackson Boulevard. Another policeman was killed in the holdup, and the robbers wrecked their car—traced back to gangland armorer JOE BERGL's garage—but they still managed to escape. It was a wasted effort, after all, as their "loot" from the heist turned out to be a pile of worthless checks.

That disappointment sent Karpis and company back to the drawing board, planning their next foray into the "snatch racket." St. Paul banker Edward Bremer was selected as the target, but four days prior to his kidnapping, on January 13, 1934, Karpis mistook a uniformed airline employee for a policeman, gunning him down on a public street in St. Paul. The victim survived, and Bremer's abduction proceeded on schedule, the February ransom for his safe return exactly double that which the gang had received for Edward Bremer in June 1933.

Thus far, the FBI had no idea that the Barker-Karpis gang even existed. Their kidnappings and several of their robberies had been blamed on other felons, some of whom were ironically tried, convicted, and sentenced to prison for crimes they did not commit. Even so, Karpis felt the need for plastic surgery to change his face and fingerprints. In early March 1934, Alvin and Fred Barker visited underworld surgeon JOSEPH MORAN in Chicago, undergoing painful operations that left them looking battered but otherwise entirely recognizable. (Moran was successful in stripping Alvin's fingerprints, however, a fact that caused Karpis no end of difficulty decades later, when he applied for a passport.) It may have been the shoddy work or Moran's tendency to boast of his gangland connections while drunk (which was most of the time) that resulted in the doctor being taken for a one-way boat ride on Lake Erie, in July 1934.

By that time, the gang's luck had already turned. Sometime associate EDDIE GREEN, lately operating with a gang led by JOHN DILLINGER, was cornered and shot by G-men in St. Paul. He took eight days to die, raving deliriously the whole time, spilling everything he knew about various underworld associates to eager FBI stenographers. By the time Green finally gave up the ghost on April 11, the bureau knew of several wrongful convictions across the Midwest

(though it took no steps to correct them), and G-men had a whole new list of "public enemies" to chase.

May 1934 found Karpis settled in Cleveland, earning his way as hired muscle at a syndicate gambling joint, the Harvard Club. Four months later, he took girlfriend Dolores Delaney to Cuba, where they remained until mid-December 1934. Alvin's next stop was Florida, where Fred and "Ma" Barker had rented a vacation cottage at Lake Weir.

Dock Barker was the first to fall as G-men closed in, captured in Chicago on January 8, 1935. Eight days later, Fred and his mother were killed at Lake Weir, their house surrounded by federal agents in a battle lasting more than four hours. Karpis, Harry Campbell, and their women fled Miami in the wake of those shootings, hiding out at a hotel in Atlantic City, New Jersey. For the sake of appearances, Karpis and Campbell roomed together, using pseudonyms, while the women registered separately and took an adjoining room.

It made no difference, as police came knocking at 5:00 A.M. on January 20. Karpis fired his first shot through the wall of the adjacent room, trying to alert the women, and the bullet struck his pregnant girlfriend in the leg. With that, Karpis and Campbell fled their room, exchanging some 200 shots with police before they reached their car downstairs. Twice they drove around the block, still under fire, hoping the girls would emerge, but finally the bandits fled in a blaze of gunfire, shaking off pursuit while their gun molls were taken into custody. Near Allentown, Pennsylvania, Karpis and Campbell kidnapped Dr. Horace Hunsicker and stole his car. They left Hunsicker bound and gagged in Ohio the following day; his vehicle was later found in Monroe, Michigan.

Two days after the Atlantic City shootout, Karpis and Campbell were among 19 persons indicted for the Bremer kidnapping by a federal grand jury in St. Paul. It was the least of their problems at the moment, though, with G-men on their trail who had a reputation for shooting first and omitting questions altogether. More to the point, the boys needed cash.

On April 24, 1935, the fugitives joined gunman Joe Rich to stop a U.S. mail truck at Warren, Ohio, relieving the drivers of a $72,000 payroll shipment. On November 7, they turned back the calendar with a foray into train robbing, teamed with Freddie Hunter and three other hoodlums to steal $34,000 from Erie Train No. 622 at Garrettsville, Ohio. Karpis and Hunter drove to Port Clinton, Ohio, where they boarded a small airplane recently purchased by Karpis and flew on to Hot Springs, Arkansas. On arrival, Karpis made a gift of the plane to their pilot, parting company with Hunter as Freddie drove on to Texas.

Hot Springs was a criminal haven on a par with St. Paul in those days, and Karpis fit in well with the local denizens. He donated $6,500 to the mayor's reelection campaign and was duly rewarded on March 26, 1936, when police warned him in advance of an impending FBI raid on his local hideout. Frustrated, the feds indicted him on April 22 with seven others for the Hamm kidnapping in St. Paul. A $5,000 reward was posted for his capture, increased five days later when U.S. postal inspectors sweetened the pot with another $2,000.

In Washington, meanwhile, J. EDGAR HOOVER had developed a personal fixation on Karpis. Criticized in Congress for the fact that he had never made an arrest, the FBI's leader determined to silence his critics by personally capturing America's new "Public Enemy No. 1." Stories were spread—and afterward denied by Alvin to his dying day—that Karpis had mailed threats to Hoover in Washington, promising bloody vengeance for the deaths of Fred and Ma Barker. Word went out from Hoover's office to FBI field offices across the nation, informing agents that "Old Creepy" had been marked as "the director's man."

For all the bluster, Hoover was not about to place himself at risk. On May 1, 1936, Karpis was sighted in New Orleans with sidekick Fred Hunter. G-men staked out their lodgings while Hoover caught the next flight south from Washington. Official FBI mythology has Hoover boldly confronting Karpis on the street, grabbing his man as Karpis tried to reach a rifle in the backseat of his car, but the truth was rather different. Karpis and Hunter were unarmed when agents surrounded them that afternoon, in a roadster that had no backseat. Only after they were covered by a dozen guns did Hoover appear from hiding to take charge of the prisoners. Befitting a sideshow, the agents had forgotten to bring handcuffs and were forced to bind the prisoners' wrists with neckties.

Karpis was arraigned in St. Paul six days after his arrest; bond on federal kidnapping charges was fixed at an impossible $500,000. (Harry Campbell and crony Sam Coker were "personally" arrested by J. Edgar Hoover and a small army of G-men the same afternoon in Toledo, Ohio.) Fred Hunter's case moved swiftly. Hunter was sentenced to two years in prison on May 27 for harboring Karpis. On July 14, 1936, Karpis pled guilty to kidnapping William Hamm. He was sentenced to life imprisonment on July 27 and entered Leavenworth Prison two days later. On August 7 the feds reconsidered, shipping Karpis to The Rock of Alcatraz, where he would kill time with Dock Barker.

Unlike Barker, though, Karpis would survive his captivity; he was paroled on January 14, 1969, and immediately deported to his native Canada as an undesirable alien. He published an autobiography, *The Alvin Karpis Story,* in 1971 and moved to Spain two years later. He died at Torremolinos of a sleeping pill overdose on August 26, 1976. (Opinions differ as to whether the OD was accidental or deliberate.) A second memoir, *On the Rock,* was released posthumously in 1980.

KELLY, Edward "Ned"

Australia's premier SOCIAL BANDIT was the son of an Irish ex-convict, transported to Van Dieman's Land (modern Tasmania) in 1841 on conviction of stealing two pigs from his landlord. John "Red" Kelly survived his seven-year sentence on the rugged island and afterward settled in Australia, where he met 18-year-old Ellen Quinn and fell in love. The couple eloped and the first of seven children—Edward, or "Ned"—was born in June 1855. Times were hard in their village of Avenel, 80 miles north of Melbourne, and John Kelly slaughtered a neighbor's heifer for meat in May 1865. The desperate act cost him two months in jail, where he contracted tuberculosis. The disease claimed his life on December 27, 1866, leaving 11-year-old "Ned" as the man of the house.

Influenced by his father's example and that of maternal uncle Jimmy Quinn—another ex-con who ran with rough companions and despised the police—"Ned" Kelly logged his first arrest on October 15, 1869, charged with beating and robbing a Chinese peddler. The charge was dismissed on October 26, but Kelly was marked in the eyes of local law enforcers as a juvenile "BUSHRANGER" (outlaw). In early 1870 he teamed with escaped convict Harry Powers for a fling at highway robbery but was arrested and charged with two counts on May 5, 1870. A magistrate dismissed the charges for lack of evidence, but police nonetheless detained Kelly until June 23 when a second judge threw out the case.

Embittered by his treatment in jail, Kelly clung defiantly to a lawless lifestyle. October 1870 saw him sentenced to six months for assaulting a neighbor. Soon after his release on that charge, "Ned" was jailed again, this time for horse theft, and was sentenced to three years' hard labor at age 16. Released four months shy of his 19th birthday, in February 1874, Kelly was a full-blown desperado with a thick beard and a large chip on his shoulder where law officers were concerned. Four years of honest labor at a sawmill failed to dampen Kelly's hatred of police.

The latter seemed to be a family trait, in fact. Brother Dan, age 15, was charged with stealing a saddle and bridle. Acquitted at trial, Dan remained a suspect in various other crimes, prompting issuance of a warrant for his arrest on charges of rustling livestock. A certain Constable Fitzgerald visited the Kelly homestead on April 15, 1878, seeking to arrest Dan but returned empty handed to headquarters, claiming that the entire family had attacked and attempted to kill him. Ellen Kelly and two friends were arrested on April 16, charged on October 9, 1878, with aiding and abetting an attempt to murder Constable Fitzgerald. All three were convicted at trial, his mother's imprisonment prompting Ned Kelly to declare all-out war on law enforcers in Victoria.

On October 26, 1878, "Ned" Kelly and three accomplices—brother Dan, 21-year-old Joe Byrne, and 18-year-old Steve Hart—confronted a police sergeant and three constables at their camp on Stringybark Creek. When the smoke cleared, three lawmen were dead, the fourth escaping to report the shootout; Dan Kelly, the only outlaw casualty, suffered a minor bullet graze to one arm. A reward of £500 was posted for each of the gunmen, dead or alive, with more than 200 officers drafted to scour the province. Dozens of Kelly friends were jailed on trumped-up charges in the process, but the bandits remained at large, abandoning any pretense of a life within the law.

On December 9, 1878, the gang robbed a bank at Eudora, escaping on horseback with £2,000 in coin and unminted gold. The reward for each bandit was promptly increased to £1,000 but still brought no takers. On February 8, 1879, the gang invaded Jerilderie, New South Wales, and commandeered the local police barracks, jailing local law officers and various townspeople before robbing the bank next morning and fleeing in stolen police uniforms. Rewards on the outlaws were doubled again, the aggregate £8,000 constituting the highest amount ever offered by British authorities for fugitives in a foreign colony.

The Jerilderie raid was followed by a 16-month hiatus for the Kelly gang. Authorities searched the Outback in vain, despite the best efforts of aboriginal trackers, obstructed by a wall of silence from settlers who regarded Kelly and his cohorts as men unjustly persecuted. The fugitives, meanwhile, were busy at their hideout in the swamps near Greta, forging suits of armor that weighed 80 pounds apiece. The bucket-shaped helmet for "Ned" Kelly's outfit weighed another 15 pounds, but he was able to support the costume—barely—on his six-feet frame.

It would be useful when he launched his next campaign.

On June 27, 1880, Dan Kelly and Joe Byrne invaded the home of police informer Aaron Sherritt, shooting him dead despite a guard of four constables around the house. News of the murder brought a special trainload of police from Melbourne to Glenrowan, and while "Ned Kelly" planned to derail the train three-quarters of a mile from the Glenrowan station, his efforts to uproot the track were unsuccessful. Falling back on the town in early morning darkness, the gang commandeered the Glenrowan Hotel while 16 constables laid siege outside. Outnumbered four to one and hampered in their movements by the heavy suits of armor, Kelly and his cohorts waged a fierce battle. Wounded in one arm, Ned escaped through a hotel window and fled on foot into the bush, drawing lawmen after him. Another fierce exchange of gunfire left Kelly stunned, whereupon police disarmed and arrested him. Back at the hotel, with Joe Byrne dead from bullet wounds, Dan Kelly and Steve Hart shot themselves after police set the building on fire.

"Ned" Kelly recovered from his wounds in time to stand trial for murder on October 28, 1880. Convicted on all counts, Kelly told the court, "A day will come, at a bigger court than this, when we shall see which is right and which is wrong. No matter how long a man lives, he has to come to judgment somewhere." After the judge, Sir Redmond Barry, sentenced Kelly to hang, the defendant told Barry, "I'll see you where I'm going." Kelly was hanged on November 11, 1880, his last words from the gallows recorded as "Such is life." Judge Barry, it was noted by the outlaw's friends, fell ill two days before Kelly's execution and died shortly thereafter.

KELLY, George "Machine Gun"

"Some men are born great," George Ade wrote in 1920, "some achieve greatness, and others have it pinned on them." The same could easily be said of notoriety, and no one proves the point better than 1930s desperado George "machine gun" Kelly.

The name was false, for starters. He was born George F. Barnes Jr. in Chicago on July 17, 1900, and used that name for the first half of his life. The well-respected Barnes family moved to Memphis when George was a toddler, and he graduated high school there, enrolling briefly at Mississippi A&M in September 1917. Four months later he dropped out to drive a taxi. In September 1919 Barnes married Geneva Ramsey in Clarksdale, Mississippi, and went to work for her father's construction company. Their first child, a son, was born in November 1920, by which time George had soured on honest work, lured by the quick and easy money to be earned from bootlegging in Prohibition.

His new trade prospered for a while, but George logged his first arrest near Ridgeway, Tennessee, on May 30, 1924. At trial in October, he was sentenced to six months in jail and a $500 fine, but he was pardoned on appeal. His second son was born in January 1925, but the marriage was shaky. George divorced Geneva on New Year's Day of 1926 and launched himself into a full-time life of crime, complete with a new moniker.

As George Kelly, he was arrested and briefly detained for bootlegging in Santa Fe, New Mexico, on March 14, 1927. Police picked him up again in Oklahoma City four months later. The charge in Tulsa on July 24, 1927, was simple vagrancy—a catch-all sometimes used to roust suspicious characters and run them out of town. On January 13, 1928, George was arrested by federal officers for running booze onto an Oklahoma Indian reservation. That charge earned him a three-year passport to Leavenworth prison, where he soon became acquainted with a very different class of criminal.

Among the friends George made at Leavenworth were notorious stickup men THOMAS HOLDEN, Francis Keating, and FRANK "JELLY" NASH. Mild-mannered Kelly served them well from his position as a prison trusty, forging passes that permitted Holden and Keating to escape on February 28, 1930. No one suspected his role in the break at the time, and George was paroled on schedule, four months later, ready to cash in on the gratitude of his fugitive cronies.

On July 15, 1930, Kelly joined Holden, Keating, HARVEY BAILEY, VERNON MILLER, and three other gunmen to steal $70,000 from a bank at Willmar, Min-

nesota. (Gang members Frank Coleman, Mike Rusick, and Sam Silverman [aka Jew Sammy Stein] were later found shot to death at White Bear Lake, following a dispute with quick-trigger Verne Miller.) On September 9, 1930 the same lineup, plus veteran robber LAWRENCE DE VOL, took $40,000 from a bank at Ottumwa, Iowa. Two weeks later, on September 24, Kelly married for the second time, in Minneapolis, to Katherine Thorne.

Legend has it that Katherine changed everything. An ambitious young woman, suspected (but never charged) in the murder of her first husband, she made no attempt to reform George Kelly. Instead, she focused on polishing his image, making him a more notorious and respected outlaw. Katherine may or may not have bought George his first Tommy gun and ordered him to practice with it; he did, gaining such proficiency that he (allegedly) could blast a row of walnuts off a wooden fence. True or not, she definitely capitalized on those practice sessions, retrieving spent cartridge casings and handing them out to friends as souvenirs of their acquaintance with "Machine Gun" Kelly.

It is unknown if Kelly's prison pals knew anything about the rash publicity campaign, but they welcomed George on at least one more bank job. On April 8, 1931, he joined Bailey, Frank Nash, Verne Miller, and others to loot $40,000 from a bank at Sherman, Texas.

Holdups were fine, and made for flashy headlines, but Katherine Kelly had her eye on the snatch racket. On January 27, 1932, George and accomplice Eddie Doll kidnapped Howard Woolverton, a banker's son from South Bend, Indiana, but the Great Depression had already staged a preemptive strike, and Woolverton was released two days later when his family was unable to raise a $50,000 ransom.

George came away from his first kidnapping empty handed and reverted to what he knew best. On February 6, 1932 he joined ex-convict ALBERT BATES and others to rob a bank in Denton, Texas. Four months later, on June 17, he teamed with Tom Holden, Francis Keating, Verne Miller, Harvey Bailey, Larry De Vol, FRED BARKER, and ALVIN KARPIS in Fort Scott, Kansas, lifting $47,000 from another bank. On September 1, 1932, with Bates and EDDIE BENTZ, Kelly stole $77,000 from a bank at Colfax, Washington. Tupelo, Mississippi, was the target on November 30, when Kelly teamed with Bates and Eddie Doll to bag $38,000 in a bank heist wrongly attributed to CHARLES "PRETTY BOY" FLOYD.

It was time to try another kidnapping. On July 22, 1933, Kelly and Bates snatched oil man Charles Urschel from his home in Oklahoma City, collecting a $200,000 ransom before they released him on July 31. The abduction was a family affair, with Urschel held captive at the Paradise, Texas, ranch of Kelly's in-laws, Robert and Ora Shannon. Katherine Kelly's tendency to brag, including careless comments made to "friendly" Texas law officers, blew the hideout's cover on August 12 when a mixed party of sheriff's deputies and FBI agents raided the farm and arrested the Shannons. They also bagged Harvey Bailey, who stopped over to recuperate from minor wounds. In Bailey's pocket was a wad of Urschel ransom money, given to him by George Kelly in repayment of a loan. Al Bates was arrested the same day in Denver and shipped back to Oklahoma for trial.

It was bad luck for Bailey, convicted and sentenced to life for a crime he did not commit, but the Kellys remained at large, hunted by authorities from coast to coast. The end came on September 26, 1933, in Memphis and spawned a myth that endures to the present day. As told by spokesmen for the FBI, "Machine Gun" Kelly cowered before their guns, pleading, "Don't shoot, G-men! Don't shoot, G-men!" In truth, he was arrested by Memphis police, with federal agents cast in a supporting role, and Kelly's only comment was: "I've been expecting you." Still, the legend would endure, FBI agents playing their role as G- (for "government") men to the hilt.

Arraigned in Memphis on September 27, the Kellys pled not guilty to kidnapping charges and were held in lieu of $100,000 bond. Three days later, Al Bates, Harvey Bailey, and the Shannons were convicted at the first Urschel trial. George and Katherine were returned to Oklahoma City on October 1, and their trial began eight days later, resulting in conviction and matching life terms on October 12. George was shipped off to Alcatraz and later transferred back to his old home at Leavenworth, where he died of a heart attack on July 18, 1954. Katherine and her mother were released on bond in June 1959, pending appeal of their convictions. Their attorneys claimed that the women had been framed by overzealous G-men, a contention circumstantially supported by the FBI's strange refusal to produce its documentary files on the case under court order. All charges were dismissed, accordingly, and the women were officially absolved after spending 26 years in prison.

KENDRICK, John Allen

An inveterate felon, Kendrick was first arrested by Baltimore police in May 1923 on charges of larceny and murder. Convicted of larceny and a reduced assault charge, he drew five years in prison, discharging his sentence on December 4, 1928. An arrest on concealed-weapons charges earned him two and a half years in February 1930. Kendrick escaped on September 2, 1931, but his freedom was short lived; indicted in March 1932 for shooting a police officer in Washington, D.C., he was sentenced to 10 years in the federal reformatory at Lorton, Virginia, from which he escaped on July 3, 1933.

In flight Kendrick allied himself with the notorious (and misnamed) "Tri-State Gang," a collection of holdup artists active in Pennsylvania, Maryland, the District of Columbia, Virginia, and North Carolina. On May 4, 1934, he was one of three Tri-State gangsters charged by a federal grand jury at Wilmington, North Carolina, with theft from a shipment in interstate commerce. Arrested at Johnson City, Tennessee, in June 1934, he was briefly returned to Lorton before a transfer to "The Rock" at Alcatraz. Another transfer, in July 1941, landed Kendrick in Leavenworth, where he finished his federal sentence. Instead of being freed, he was returned to New Jersey for completion of his interrupted sentence there on concealed-weapons charges, finally winning parole in June 1943.

Always quick on the trigger, Kendrick was arrested in June 1947 for shooting an underworld associate in the nation's capital. Conviction on December 10 earned him a term of three to 10 years in Leavenworth, from which he was paroled in March 1954. Nine months later, on December 14,

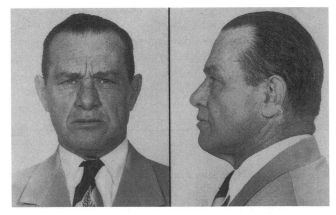

John Kendrick, a member of the notorious "Tri-State Gang" whose holdup career spanned four decades (FBI)

he was identified as the gunman who shot another Washington resident in the throat, leaving his victim critically wounded. Indicted for that incident in August 1955, he was charged a month later with unlawful flight to avoid prosecution, and his name was added to the FBI's "Ten Most Wanted" list on November 2.

It took federal agents a month to trace their man, catching him in Chicago on December 5, 1955, and taking Kendrick into custody without resistance. Returned to Washington for yet another trial, the vicious triggerman received a sentence that would finally remove him from the streets.

KERVAN, Emmett Bernard

A victim of tuberculosis, Emmett Kervan did not let his illness stop him from compiling an impressive record of arrests and felony convictions from coast to coast. At one time or another, charges filed against him ran the gamut from possession of a deadly weapon, burglary, and grand theft to the relatively sophisticated offense of counterfeiting. Kervan never had much luck at crime, but his expensive tastes prevented him from going straight.

On February 5, 1959, a lone bandit entered the Merchants Bank and Trust Company in Norwalk, Connecticut. Drawing a pistol from one coat pocket, he produced a sack from the other and ordered a startled teller to fill it up. An estimated $30,000 went into the sack before he fled, eluding local roadblocks to make his getaway.

That afternoon police received a phone call from a trucker who had nearly been forced off Route 136 south of Norwalk, a few minutes after the holdup. The car that nearly clipped him was a large, black sedan bearing license plates with white numbers displayed on a green background. Federal agents answering the holdup call were cautiously encouraged when they realized that only three states—Washington, New Hampshire, and Michigan—fit the bill. (A fourth state, Florida, also used white-on-green, but only single plates were issued, while the suspect vehicle had license tags on front and back.)

The bandit's car was found abandoned on a street in Buffalo, New York. The plates were stolen, but a registration slip led agents back to Norwalk, where the suspect had allegedly resided. Sketches of the thief were quickly recognized by workers at a Norwalk hospital, where Kervan was employed before he turned his hand to robbery. His name

Emmett Kervan pursued an active criminal career despite suffering from tuberculosis. (FBI)

was added to the FBI's "Most Wanted" list on April 29, 1959.

By that time Kervan had already moved to Texas. Reaching El Paso in February, he had passed a month in various motels before acquiring an apartment. Known locally as a big spender, laying out some $500 per week on living expenses, Kervan impressed his landlady as "a nice gentleman." Another woman who began to date the fugitive knew nothing of his record; she was told that he had come to Texas for his health, beset by chronic asthma.

Agents of the FBI, meanwhile, pursued their man through grim, methodical examination of hotel registers and used-car receipts across the nation, finally homing in on El Paso. Kervan was traced to his apartment and surprised there, in pajamas, on May 13, 1959. He surrendered without resistance, and agents recovered $20,000 of the Norwalk loot when they cleaned out his safety deposit box two days later. Returned to Connecticut for trial, Kervan pled guilty to a robbery charge and was sentenced to prison.

KIMES-TERRILL Gang

Ranked among the most notorious bank robbers of the 1920s, Matthew Kimes and Ray Terrill were as well known for their jailbreaks as for theft of other people's money. So determined were they to avoid confinement, it was said, that every member of their gang swore a blood oath to liberate all captured comrades or to die in the attempt. And die they would, but not before they ran up an impressive score of looted banks.

Ray Terrill got his start with Tulsa's "Central Park Gang," which also spawned the BARKER brothers, VOLNEY DAVIS, and other headline desperadoes of the 1930s. On January 15, 1921, as "G. R. Patton," he was arrested with Arthur "Dock" Barker for attempting to burglarize a bank in Muskogee. Convicted of second-degree burglary and sentenced to three years in prison, Terrill was paroled on March 1, 1923. He promptly joined Al Spencer's gang, in time for the March 26 robbery of a bank at Mannford, Oklahoma, with two men killed in the ensuing chase and shootout. Five months later, on August 20, Terrill joined Spencer, FRANK NASH, and others to commit Oklahoma's last TRAIN ROBBERY, lifting $20,000 in cash and bonds from the Katy Limited near Okesa.

Spencer was cornered and killed by authorities on September 15, 1923, whereupon Ray Terrill organized his own gang, recruiting such stalwarts as Herman Barker, WILBUR UNDERHILL, and ELMER INMAN. They preferred to strike by night, burglarizing banks and stores across the Southwest, staging their raids in a distinctive style: With stolen trucks, the gang extracted safes and drove them back to Barker's Radium Springs Health Resort, near Salina, Oklahoma. Once the safes were cracked and emptied, they were trucked to a nearby bridge after nightfall and dumped into the Grand River. All went well for three years until Terrill and Inman were arrested for burglary in Ardmore, Oklahoma. Convicted and sentenced to 20 years in prison, they escaped together on September 27, 1926, and Terrill went looking for new partners in crime.

He found them in a pair of fellow Oklahoma natives, George and Matthew Kimes.

The Kimes brothers robbed their first bank together at Depew, Oklahoma, on June 30, 1926. One day before the holdup, Matt had staged his first jailbreak, escaping custody in Bristow, Oklahoma, where he had been charged with auto theft. On August 20 the brothers stole $5,000 from a bank in Beggs, Oklahoma. Six days later, they led the gang that simultaneously robbed two banks at Covington. Police overtook them in Sallisaw on August 27 where the brothers killed Deputy Perry Chuculate, kidnapping Sallisaw's police chief and another hostage for their flight into Arkansas. On August 28 they were trapped near Rudy at the home of cousin Ben Pixley; both brothers were wounded before they threw down their guns. George was convicted of bank robbery and sentenced to 25 years at the McAlester state prison; Matt got 35 on conviction of killing Deputy Chuculate.

Ray Terrill rode to the rescue on November 21, 1926, invading the Sallisaw jail where Matt Kimes was lodged prior to transfer. Backed by Herman Barker and Elmer Inman, Terrill liberated Kimes, and so a dynamic new bank-robbing unit was born.

The gang made its first raid on January 10, 1927, Herman Barker joining Kimes and Terrill to steal $42,950 from a bank at Sapulpa, Oklahoma. One week later, the same trio and two accomplices were surprised by law officers while burglarizing a bank after hours, in Jasper, Missouri. The thieves fled in two cars, Matt Kimes and a pair of unknowns escaping into Kansas after a wild chase. Terrill and Barker were trailed to a house in Carterville near Joplin; gunfire erupted, Barker was wounded, and both men were taken into custody.

No trial was needed for Terrill, who already owed the state 20 years for his 1926 conviction. Catching Ray was one thing, though; holding him turned out to be a very different proposition. On January 19, en route to a cell at McAlester, he leaped from the moving police car and made his escape on foot, soon rejoining Matt Kimes for a new round of holdups.

On May 12, 1927, Ray Terrill was named as a prime suspect in the daylight theft of $207,000 from a bank in McCune, Kansas. Six days later, with Kimes and nine other gunmen, he looted two banks at Beggs, Oklahoma, of $18,000; Marshal W. J. McAnally was shot and killed on the street when he tried to intervene.

The double score in Beggs would be the Kimes-Terrill gang's last raid. Matt Kimes and sidekick Raymond Doolin were captured in Arizona near the Grand Canyon on June 24, 1927. Matt was returned to Oklahoma where another murder conviction sent him to prison for life. Terrill and Elmer Inman were arrested in Hot Springs, Arkansas on November 26, 1927, and soon joined the Kimes brothers at McAlester. Ray would end his days there, but Matt Kimes still had friends looking out for his interests. On November 26, 1934, he was granted a six-day leave of absence from prison to go quail hunting with his attorney. Another leave was granted in November 1945, and this time he fled, robbing a bank at Merton, Texas. Warrants were outstanding on that charge when Kimes was run down by a poultry truck in North Little Rock, dying of his injuries on December 1, 1945.

KLING, Thomas

Arrested for the first time at the tender age of 10 in 1916, Kling went on to compile a bulky arrest record, leaning heavily toward counts of robbery and assault. The latter charges stemmed primarily from his employment as a strong-arm goon for corrupt labor unions on the New York waterfront, where he was known as "Mad Dog," an enforcer with a reputation for brutality. Kling served a term of 15 years in New Jersey, finally emerging on September 18, 1947. Two years later he was suspected as the bandit in a New York tavern robbery, but he remained at large, eluding police.

On March 9, 1950, Kling teamed with veteran bandit WILLIE SUTTON and accomplice John De Ventura for the robbery that netted $63,933 from the Manufacturer's Trust Company in Sunnyside, Queens. That holdup earned Sutton a place on the FBI's "Most Wanted" list, and Kling was likewise

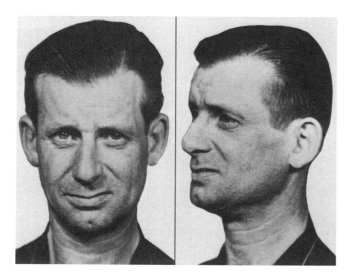

Career criminal Thomas Kling logged his first arrest at age 10. (FBI)

added to the roster on July 17, 1950. His good fortune, while it lasted, seemed caught up with Sutton's. When Willie was arrested by New York police on February 18, 1952, Kling had only two days of freedom remaining. Nabbed with three accomplices on February 20, he was held for trial with Sutton on assorted charges stemming from the Sunnyside holdup. John De Ventura turned state's evidence to save himself and testified against his cronies at their trial. Kling and Sutton each drew 29-year sentences upon conviction, effectively putting both men out of action forever.

KNIGHT, Thomas Otis

When Miami industrialist Sydney Gans arrived at his office on the morning of July 17, 1974, he found one of his employees waiting to greet him. The circumstance was not unusual, but Thomas Knight was no ordinary worker, the M1 carbine in his hands no common greeting. Prodded at gunpoint, Gans returned to his car and drove Knight back to the Gans family home, there parking in the driveway. Under orders from his captor, Gans began to tap the horn of his car, finally attracting his wife's attention and drawing her outside, where she was also taken prisoner.

With two hostages under the gun, Knight directed Gans to the City National Bank in downtown Miami where Gans withdrew $50,000 from his personal account. While the cash was being counted, Gans informed bank president Daniel Gill of his predicament. By the time Gans left the bank, a police helicopter was circling overhead, with squad cars closing on the scene.

Detecting the pursuers, Knight directed Gans to speed away, leading police on a wild chase that ended on a rural expressway 10 miles from Miami. Killing both hostages with single shots to the head, Knight ditched the car and fled on foot. Six hours later, with 200 police and federal agents closing in, he was flushed from the swampy undergrowth by tracking dogs and tear gas, shuttled back to the Dade County jail under guard.

Knight's trial was pending on September 19 when he escaped from jail in company with 11 other inmates. Charged in federal warrants with unlawful flight to avoid prosecution for murder and kidnapping, Knight was added to the FBI's "Ten Most Wanted" list on December 12. He lasted until New Year's Eve when G-men and local officers traced him to an apartment in Smyrna Beach, Florida, bursting in to catch him by surprise. Though heavily armed at the time of his arrest, Knight had no opportunity to resist in the face of overwhelming firepower. He was returned to Miami for trial and ultimate conviction on outstanding charges. Sentenced to death for murder, he remains on death row at this writing.

LaBANTA, Jean

A tight-lipped forger and train robber, Jean LaBanta kept details of his early life to himself, treating friends and lawmen alike to a virtual wall of silence. Born around 1879, he left his first official tracks in April 1911 when he was convicted of grand larceny in San Benito County, California, and sentenced to two years' imprisonment at San Quentin. Paroled in early 1913, he was soon back at work on the wrong side of the law, sought by authorities in several California counties for writing rubber checks. Placer County was the first to issue a warrant, seeking fugitive "Clyde Kaufman" on charges of forging checks worth $65. Arrested at a San Francisco hotel on January 20, 1914, LaBanta seemed almost insulted by the charges filed against him, quietly informing his captors that he was responsible for "much more classier crimes" than mere check-bouncing.

In fact, that proved to be the case. Background investigation soon inflated LaBanta's total of fraudulent checks to a whopping $40,000, but the most surprising news was not revealed for two weeks after his arrest. Finally, after marathon interrogation, LaBanta confessed to three mail robberies committed against the Southern Pacific Railroad.

His first score, on October 14, 1913, was a disappointing $100. In that holdup, a masked LaBanta had invaded the express car of Southern Pacific Train No. 23 during a mail exchange at Burlingame, brandishing a pistol, pulling sacks over the heads of two guards, and forcing them to sit in a corner while the train pulled out and rolled toward San Francisco. The guards did not see him jump off, and the small take for high risk apparently did not discourage LaBanta from trying again.

On November 17, 1913, he boarded Southern Pacific Train No. 77 as it left the San Jose railyard. Again, he held the clerks at gunpoint and hooded them with sacks while he rifled the mail, leaping clear on the approach to Burlingame. His score, while not recorded, was again described as small. Southern Pacific took the holdups seriously, though, and henceforth express guards on the northern California runs would all be armed.

LaBanta heard the news and moved south to Los Angeles. He also recruited a sidekick for the first time, enlisting one Jean Dolley (aka "Jim Barry"), lately paroled after serving 18 months in San Quentin on a forgery conviction. On January 10, 1914, two minutes before the 10:15 P.M. departure of Southern Pacific Train No. 9 from Los Angeles, LaBanta and Dolley invaded the mail car, cowing the clerks with their pistols, stealing an estimated $600, and leaping clear on the approach to Burbank.

The mail clerks identified Dolley from mug shots, and he was quickly arrested and, on February 10, indicted by a federal grand jury. He pled guilty on March 6 and received a five-year sentence at San Quentin. LaBanta's coincidental forgery arrest and subsequent confessions closed the case. Jean was indicted with Dolley on February 10 but saved time by pleading guilty the very next day. His prison time for three train holdups totaled 54 years, reduced to 25 when a judge made the sentences concurrent. LaBanta was paroled on September 24, 1926 and promptly disappeared into obscurity.

LAMM, Hermann K. "Baron"

A pioneer of "scientific" bank heists, Hermann Lamm was born in Prussia around 1890, following national tradition with pursuit of a military career. Shortly before the outbreak of the First World War, he was caught cheating at cards and forced to resign in disgrace from his regiment. The shame of it drove him to emigrate, and Lamm wound up in Utah where he tried his hand at armed robbery without much success. While spending most of 1917 in Utah's state prison, Lamm applied his military training to the field of robbery and thus evolved a style that would be emulated by successful bandits through successive generations.

Lamm believed in planning each holdup as if it were a full-scale military campaign, leaving nothing to chance. His technique, when perfected, included preparation in three phases. First, Lamm would spend several days examining the target, drawing detailed floor plans, learning how the vault or safe was operated and who possessed the combination to its locks. Next, a series of rehearsals were conducted with hand-picked personnel, sometimes using detailed mock-ups of the target bank. Each member of the holdup team had a specific task and a strict deadline, timed to the second, for completing his job. Finally, escape routes were charted and timed; skilled drivers—often with race-track experience—manned the wheels of high-powered, nondescript cars, equipped with maps of the escape route that included block-by-block instructions with suggested driving speeds.

On release from prison, "Baron" Lamm employed his Prussian style of larceny with such finesse that he remained at large and comfortably fixed for nearly 13 years, looting banks across the United States. His demise, when it came, was a product of unforeseen circumstance that made his last outing a bizarre—but fatal—comedy of errors.

Baron Lamm's last target was the Citizens State Bank in Clinton, Indiana, seven miles from the Illinois border. On December 16, 1930, he entered the bank with three mismatched accomplices: 71-year-old G.W. "Dad" Landy; 26-year-old Walter Dietrich; and overalls-clad JAMES "OKLAHOMA JACK" CLARK. Outside, at the wheel of their getaway car, sometime

rum runner W. H. Hunter nervously scanned the main street.

Unknown to Lamm, Clinton's residents had established a kind of vigilante neighborhood watch in that first year of the Great Depression when bank heists had become a near-daily event nationwide. The proprietor of a nearby barbershop, watching through his window, saw a friend enter the bank behind Lamm's raiders. When the friend did not emerge, the barber grabbed a shotgun and proceeded toward the bank, in time to see the bandits rushing out with $15,567 in cash.

W. H. Hunter saw the shotgun and panicked, squealing through a U-turn that bounced one wheel over the curb and blew out the tire. Limping on a dented rim, the bandits reached their stolen switch car, unaware that the owner had installed a governor, an automatic control machine to prevent his elderly father from speeding. Unable to drive more than 35 miles per hour in the second vehicle, Lamm and company still reached the third, only to find that its radiator was nearly dry. The engine was smoking and threatening to stall by the time they entered Illinois and switched cars for the last time—piling into a vehicle with only one gallon of fuel in its tank!

The chase ended near Sidell, Illinois, when the bandits' car ran out of gas. Surrounded by nearly 200 police and vigilantes, the raiders fought for their lives. Lamm and Hunter were killed by the posse, while aging Dad Landy shot himself. Dietrich and Clark survived the battle and were swiftly returned to Clinton for trial, conviction, and sentencing to life imprisonment five days after the holdup.

Baron Lamm was gone, but his philosophy of scientific robbery lived on in his disciples. Dietrich and Clark carried the gospel with them to Indiana's state prison at Michigan City, where they found an apt pupil in young JOHN DILLINGER. Less than three years later, on September 26, 1933, they were among 10 Michigan City convicts who escaped using pistols smuggled in by Dillinger after his parole. Fellow fugitives HARRY PIERPONT, CHARLES MAKLEY, JOHN HAMILTON, and RUSSELL CLARK were pleased to adopt Lamm's methods of planning bank jobs in their crime spree that rocked the Midwest during the next four months.

LEACH, Matthew: 1930s lawman

A Croatian native, born Matthew Lichanin, future lawman Matt Leach followed the example of many other first-generation Americans by Anglicizing his name to get ahead in the land of opportunity. He abandoned life as an Illinois factory worker to serve in World War I and then sought a peacetime career in law enforcement. As captain and commander of the Indiana State Police in 1933, Leach had 42 men under his command (including office clerks) when he set out to capture desperado JOHN DILLINGER and his gang. It was a quest that placed Leach's life in peril and ultimately cost him his career.

A strong advocate of using psychology to capture and prosecute criminals, Leach sometimes employed a childhood stutter while interrogating suspects, several times evoking such sympathy from felons that they "helped" him out by confessing their crimes. Leach was conscious of parolee Dillinger's various holdups between June and September 1933, tracking the outlaw before he rated anything more than local press coverage. He missed his chance on September 22, 1933, when Dillinger was arrested in Ohio, jailed at Lima pending prosecution for a bank holdup at Bluffton. At the time of his arrest, Dillinger carried a sketch that resembled the layout of Indiana's state prison at Michigan City, but Captain Leach dismissed the drawing as insignificant.

He learned of his mistake four days later when 10 convicts escaped from Michigan City, using pistols purchased and smuggled into the prison by Dillinger. The fugitives included HARRY PIERPONT, CHARLES MAKLEY, RUSSELL CLARK, JOHN HAMILTON, and JAMES CLARK. On October 12, 1933, Pierpont and company raided the Lima jailhouse, freeing Dillinger and killing Sheriff Jess Sarber in the process. During the next eight days, they looted two Indiana police stations for weapons and then committed the first of their daylight bank robberies at Greencastle, Indiana, on October 23, 1933.

Indiana Governor Paul McNutt ordered a state investigation of the Michigan City breakout on September 29, 1933, and while the probe confirmed Dillinger's involvement in smuggling the contraband weapons, Harry Pierpont was still considered the brains of the gang. Matt Leach was not encouraging about the short-term future, when he summarized the situation for reporters. "After a lot of people have been killed and banks robbed," he declared, "we'll wind it up and Pierpont will get the works."

To reach that goal, Leach fell back on psychology and took a shot at Pierpont's ego. In future statements to the press, Leach habitually referred to "the Dillinger gang," hoping to thereby infuriate Pierpont and create fatal dissension in the group. Leach had misjudged his man, however, and while Dillinger apparently enjoyed the press reports, Pierpont ignored them, concentrating on the task of robbing banks.

On November 15, 1933, Leach's men joined forces with local police to set a trap for Dillinger outside a Chicago doctor's office. A wild car chase ensued, and while officers in one patrol car shot out their own windshield, Dillinger and girlfriend Evelyn Frechette escaped without injury. Press reports of a dramatic "shootout" prompted Dillinger to make a series of telephone calls to Matt Leach, taunting the lawman at his Indianapolis headquarters.

One month after the Chicago debacle, on December 20, Leach dispatched his men out of state a second time, scrambling in response to claims that Dillinger had been sighted in Paris, Illinois. Instead, they found Michigan City escapee Ed Shouse, lately separated from the gang after a quarrel with Russell Clark, but Leach's troopers were primed for gunplay and they wound up shooting at each other, Officer Eugene Teague killed by a burst of friendly fire.

Reeling from the embarrassment, still focused on Harry Pierpont as the primary target of his psychological warfare, Leach ordered round-the-clock surveillance of Pierpont's family. Overzealous police arrested Harry's mother and younger brother on a visit to Terre Haute, in defiance of Leach's hands-off order, and while Mrs. Pierpont berated detectives in custody, Harry fumed and plotted Leach's murder. He actually drove to Indianapolis, waiting across the street from Leach's office with gun in hand, but scrubbed the plan when a companion emerged with Leach from the building, blocking Pierpont's line of fire.

Authorities in Tucson, Arizona, got the glory for rounding up Dillinger and company, on January 25, 1934, and while Leach requested extradition of all four captured fugitives, Ohio pressed its claim to Pierpont, Makley, and Russell Clark for the slaying of Sheriff Sarber. Dillinger alone was scheduled for trial on Indiana murder charges, for killing Patrolman William O'Malley during a bank heist in East Chicago during January 1934. That trial was averted by Dillinger's escape from custody on March 3, 1934, and while Leach continued to pursue his personal bête noire for the rest of Dillinger's short life, he would never again come close to netting his quarry.

Incensed by FBI domination of the latter-day Dillinger manhunt, Leach found himself increasingly at odds with headline-hungry J. EDGAR HOOVER in Washington, D.C. When Leach insisted that confederates had slipped a pistol to Dillinger, thus facilitating his March escape from jail at Crown Point, G-men belittled Indiana's top cop by hyping the story of a hand-carved wooden gun. After Dillinger was gunned down in Chicago on July 22, 1934, Leach claimed that the fatal shots were actually fired by an Indiana detective rather than by one of Hoover's special agents; furthermore, he said, Dillinger had been unarmed when he was killed, and $7,000 had been stolen from his corpse and delivered to the widow of Patrolman O'Malley.

Leach's feud with the FBI finally went public in 1937, during the wide-ranging hunt for members of the trigger-happy BRADY GANG. Hoover charged that Leach had counseled Indiana citizens to withhold cooperation from federal agents, thus delaying capture of the homicidal fugitives. Donald Stiver, chief of Indiana's Department of Public Safety, requested Leach's resignation on September 4, 1937, giving Leach no choice but to comply. Embittered, Leach spent several years writing a tell-all book that never found a publisher. He was returning from New York, winding up an unsuccessful bid to sell his manuscript, when he died in a car crash on the Pennsylvania Turnpike.

LEHMAN, Hyman S.: 1930s gangland armorer

The son of a respected Texas family and a gunsmith of renown among Depression-era desperadoes, Hyman Lehman specialized in customizing weapons at his shop in San Antonio. He was not averse to selling standard Thompson submachine guns if the price was right, but Lehman's true joy came from converting "civilian" firearms into full-automatic weapons that were tailored for use by bank robbers and contract killers. His specialty was the "baby machine gun"—a Colt .38-caliber semiautomatic pistol converted to full-auto fire, with an oversized ammunition magazine and a foregrip resembling that of a Tommy gun, to help the shooter control his weapon in the heat of battle.

Lehman's list of customers was a virtual *Who's Who* of Midwestern outlaws in the early 1930s: CHARLES "PRETTY BOY" FLOYD was acquainted with Lehman, and bootlegger Roger "The Terrible" Touhy, framed by Chicago FBI agents for a kidnapping that never occurred, had one of Lehman's "baby machine guns" in his car when he was arrested in Wisconsin, with three cohorts, on July 19, 1933; JOHN DILLINGER also favored the full-auto Colts, leaving one behind when he fled a ST. PAUL, MINNESOTA,

hideout on March 31, 1934, losing another three weeks later when he evaded FBI raiders at Little Bohemia Lodge near Rhinelander, Wisconsin.

Lehman's most consistent patron may well have been GEORGE "BABY FACE" NELSON, who purchased his first consignment of modified weapons on a trip to San Antonio in early 1933. That November, Nelson, his wife, and Dillinger crony HOMER VAN METER enjoyed Thanksgiving dinner at Lehman's Texas home. Barely two weeks later, on February 11, 1934, Nelson sent TOMMY CARROLL to pick up more guns from Lehman, but the visit was aborted when Carroll shot and killed San Antonio Detective H. C. Perrow. On April 22, 1934, Nelson used one of Lehman's special automatics to kill FBI agent W. Carter Baum and critically wound two more law officers during the Rhinelander skirmish.

That gun was never found, but the customized pistol seized by G-men at Little Bohemia Lodge was traced via serial number to the Colt factory in Hartford, Connecticut, and on from there to a Fort Worth distributor who had sold it (unmodified) to Hyman Lehman. There was, as yet, no federal law against civilian ownership or manufacture of machine guns—that would come a few weeks later with the National Firearms Act of 1934—and while prosecutors tried to charge Lehman with possession of stolen U.S. government property (a .45-caliber pistol), that count was later dropped. Texas, meanwhile, had restricted possession of machine guns with a state law in October 1933, and Lehman was convicted on that charge and sentenced to a five-year prison term in 1935. He won reversal of that verdict on appeal, and jurors deadlocked at his second trial in 1936, reportedly voting 11–1 for conviction.

Federal prosecutors suspected bribery of the holdout juror in that case, but they could never prove it, and five years of nagging failed to convince the Lone Star State's attorney general that Lehman should face a third trial. "Witness problems" were cited, along with packed court calendars, and the charge was finally dismissed for good in 1941. Lehman, retired from gunsmithing, remained in San Antonio for another four decades, producing custom boots and saddles for the cowboy set.

LIEDER, Clarence: 1930s gangland armorer

Clarence Lieder owned the Oakley Auto Construction Company, located at the corner of Division Street and Oakley on the Near North Side of Depression-era Chicago. In that capacity, he competed with fellow artisan JOE BERGL in building bulletproof cars for syndicate mobsters and bank-robbing members of "disorganized crime." A longtime friend of GEORGE "BABY FACE" NELSON, Lieder also sheltered JOHN DILLINGER and HOMER VAN METER at his garage in early 1934 when they were too hot to find sanctuary at more traditional underworld hideouts around the Windy City. Lieder closed his shop and left Chicago shortly after Dillinger was killed by FBI agents, and Nelson fled westward, in July 1934.

LINARES, Pío

The son of a Mexican bandit who went straight and became a respected rancher after moving to California in 1820, Pío Linares grew up in San Luis Obispo and followed in his father's wayward footsteps after the Mexican War, when the gold rush inaugurated a decade of wild times in the Golden State. Banditry seemed to run in his blood, as Linares was also a cousin of notorious desperado MIGUEL BLANCO.

Linares apparently got his start in crime rustling livestock during 1853 and 1854. By 1855 he was suspected of robbing and killing several travelers along El Camino Real; no definitive body count is available, but his name was linked to numerous homicides during the next three years. A fairly constant resident of San Luis Obispo when not absent from home on raids, Linares was known as a swaggering bully who frequently threatened his neighbors with knives and pistols. Still, the Hispanic community sheltered him because most of his actual victims were Anglos.

A typical crime for the Linares gang was the robbery and murder of two Basque livestock buyers, M. Graciano and Pedro Obiesa, near Mission San Miguel on November 30, 1857. Linares and company were immediate suspects, having been seen in the vicinity at the time of the double slaying, but only one gang member was captured: Nieves Robles, arrested in a San Luis Obispo gambling parlor and acquitted of all charges on March 8, 1858, after the gang provided a defense attorney. The acquittal made Linares even more brazen, prompting him to harass and threaten the town's judge in broad daylight, according to witnesses.

On May 12, 1858, Linares, Miguel Blanco, and six others raided Rancho San Juan Capistrano near modern Shandon, California. Blanco killed the owner of the ranch, a Frenchman named M. José Borel, and the bandits made off with $2,700 in cash, plus jewelry and several gold watches. In flight, they killed a neighboring rancher, Bartolo Baratrie, and a hunter named Jack Gilkey whom they met along the trail. Survivors of the rampage alerted law enforcers in San Luis Obispo, and a manhunt was swiftly organized.

Gang member Santos Peralta foolishly showed up in town after the raid and was jailed by Sheriff Francisco Castro. That night, an interview with attorney Walter Murray and a group of local vigilantes went badly for Peralta. The visitors wanted names of Peralta's fellow outlaws, but Murray recalled the outcome: "He was silent as the grave. We left him hanging from the roof of his cell." If Sheriff Franco had any complaints about the mob's unorthodox tactics, he kept them to himself.

The morning after Peralta's lynching, word came that Linares and his riders had been sighted on the ranch he kept within a mile of town. A 15-man posse rode out to investigate, pursuing Miguel Blanco and three others over two counties for the next eight days. Their quarry proved elusive, but they caught another friend of Linares, Joaquin Valenzuela, when he crossed their path by accident.

On May 22, 1858, a posse returned to Pío's spread, surrounding the house at 3:30 A.M. and calling for him to surrender. Linares was home this time, but he refused to go quietly, sending out his wife, his brother, and a houseguest in his place. Vigilantes fired the roof of his adobe to smoke Linares out and shot a rifle from his hands when he emerged, but still he was too fast for them. Linares vanished on foot in the darkness, briefly pursued by posse member Julian Garcia. Returning from the chase, Garcia was mistaken for Linares by his comrades and shot several times, but he managed to survive his wounds.

At dawn on May 22 a mass meeting was held in San Luis Obispo, with 148 male residents signing the roster of a new vigilance committee pledged to wiping out the Linares gang. As a first step in that direction, they publicly hanged Joaquin Valenzuela and then offered a $3,000 reward for the remaining fugitives. Next caught and lynched was gang member Luciano "El Mesteno" Tapia, followed by Jose Antonio Garcia on June 8.

The night of Garcia's hanging, Linares, Blanco, and two other bandits camped out on a spread 10 miles from San Luis Obispo. Pío's father had once owned the ranch, but its current owner—Captain John Wilson—had little sympathy for Mexicans and none at all for outlaws. On the morning of June 10, bandit Rafael "El Jero" Herrado approached Wilson's shepherd, attempting to buy food, but the shepherd ran instead to Wilson, and a 30-man posse was summoned from town. They found the gang's horses, but Linares and his men fled into thick woods, escaping after an exchange of gunfire that left Linares and vigilante Walter Murray with painful leg wounds. By dusk, more than 100 men had surrounded the woods, engaging the bandits in a 10-minute battle on June 12. One member of the posse was killed and two others wounded before a bullet struck Linares in the head and ended his life. Miguel Blanco and Desederio Grijalva surrendered to the posse and were hanged on June 14. Herrado slipped away unseen, somehow, and was never apprehended.

LINK, Lonnie: See BEACH, DONALD.

LITCHFIELD, Robert Alan

Born in 1948, Robert Litchfield was a truck driver who turned to armed robbery in 1983. During the next two years he raided at least 15 banks in Florida, drawing a 60-year sentence upon his conviction in 1985. Confined to the federal prison at Talladega, Alabama, Litchfield escaped on February 4, 1986, and returned to the trade he knew best. During the next six months he robbed three more banks in Florida and Michigan, resulting in issuance of new federal warrants on August 29, charging Litchfield with bank robbery and escape from a federal institution. His name was added to the FBI's "Ten Most Wanted" list on January 20, 1987.

Four months later, on May 14, Litchfield entered the First Security Bank in Boise, Idaho, brandishing a pistol and threatening employees with a shoebox that allegedly contained a bomb. In fleeing with a briefcase full of cash, he dropped a business card belonging to his one-time federal parole officer, based in West Palm Beach, Florida. Descriptions of the bandit rang a bell, and the parole officer tentatively identified Litchfield, recalling that hoax bombs were employed in several of the fugitive's Florida robberies.

Narrowing their search pattern, G-men were ready to move when they received a telephone tip on May 20, placing Litchfield and his wife near Lake Tahoe on the Nevada-California border. FBI agents and federal marshals descended on the residence in force, capturing Litchfield without a struggle. His wife was also taken into custody on a charge of jumping bail; the fugitives were returned to Alabama pending disposition of their latest felony indictments.

LOESER, Wilhelm: 1930s underworld physician

A native of Prussia, born on November 8, 1876, Loeser immigrated to the United States at age 12 with his mother and five siblings. The family spent a decade in Iowa and then moved on to Kansas. Loeser graduated from medical school in Chicago in 1905 and practiced briefly in Kansas before returning to the Windy City, where he doubled as a physician and a pharmacist. A skilled surgeon, once dubbed "a magician with a knife," Loeser still desired more luxury than his legitimate practice could provide. In 1931 he was convicted of selling narcotics and was sentenced to three years in prison. Lawyer Louis Piquett helped arrange Loeser's parole after 18 months, and the disgraced doctor fled to Mexico. He returned to Chicago in 1934 on learning that a $10,000 bribe could keep him out of prison, but obtaining the money was a problem.

And Louis Piquett had the solution.

Two of Piquett's more notorious clients, bank robbers JOHN DILLINGER and HOMER VAN METER, were in urgent need of a cosmetic overhaul. Both men wanted their faces altered and their fingerprints eliminated—services that Piquett assured them Dr. Loeser could provide for a mere $10,000. The bandits paid up front, Piquett holding the money, and Loeser (assisted by Dr. Harold Cassidy) spent two days with his patients on May 27 and 28 at the home of Chicago mobster James Probasco.

Dillinger wanted several facial moles and scars removed, along with a dimple in his chin and a depression on the bridge of his nose. Loeser did what he could, tightening the outlaw's cheeks with kangaroo tendons, but Dillinger swallowed his tongue under general anesthetic and nearly suffocated. Van Meter, meanwhile, wanted similar facial alterations plus removal of an anchor tattoo from his right arm. A caustic solution was used to burn away fingerprints, but it failed to do the trick. (Two months later, Dillinger's corpse was identified by prints at the Chicago morgue.) Mutilated and in agony, the robbers were dissatisfied, to say the least. Van Meter threatened Loeser with a Tommy gun, clutched in bandaged hands, but he was finally persuaded to spare the doctor's life.

Louis Piquett, meanwhile, saw a way to profit from the fiasco. Citing the surgery's failure, he paid Loeser only $5,000, while keeping the other five grand for himself. (The notion of a refund to Dillinger somehow slipped Piquett's mind.) FBI agents killed Dillinger on July 22, 1934, and Loeser was arrested two days later in Oak Park, Illinois.

Probasco was seized by G-men on July 25, but he "committed suicide" the following day, allegedly leaping from the 19th-story window of an office occupied by federal agent MELVIN PURVIS.

Then again, it may not have been an accident, after all. Various suspects had accused Purvis and his G-men of beating them in custody, sometimes dangling prisoners from the open windows of their high-rise office to extract confessions. Loeser himself would complain of FBI beatings that "smashed his nose all over his face," friends noting "a significant change . . . in Loeser's appearance" after he entered federal custody. Whatever the persuasion, Loeser agreed to testify against Louis Piquett in federal court, but Piquett won a surprise acquittal and Loeser was returned to prison as a parole violator on the old narcotics charge. A clemency petition, filed in April 1935, outlined his devil's bargain with Purvis and FBI Inspector SAM COWLEY, and Loeser was released on September 21. That same day, Dr. Harold Cassidy received one year's probation for his part in the surgery performed on Dillinger and Van Meter.

LOFTUS, Henry, and DONALDSON, Harry

A mismatched pair of would-be desperadoes, described in some accounts as the last of America's classic train robbers, Loftus and Donaldson launched their brief criminal career under the influence of a romantic fantasy and swiftly learned that life rarely imitates art. Their contribution to the railroad-holdup saga was a final act that owed more to slapstick comedy than high drama or adventure.

Henry Loftus was a Wisconsin native who grew up bored in the 1920s. To relieve small-town tedium, he devoured dime novels of the American frontier, developing a "Wild West complex" that his family acknowledged, humoring Henry, confident that he would outgrow it. Loftus was 25 years old and still living at home when he logged his first arrest for burglary, but a sympathetic hometown judge suspended his sentence and released him on probation. A short time later, in 1936, Henry's father moved the family to Chicago, where he opened a shoe store. Henry hung around the Windy City for a few more months and then announced that he was leaving, heading west to seek fame and fortune in the wide open spaces.

His companion on that journey of discovery was Harry Donaldson, a Canadian who shared Henry's fascination with the Wild West in general and its

outlaws in particular. Together, in 1937, they booked passage on the Santa Fe Railroad to El Paso, Texas, apparently expecting the locomotive to double as a time machine. They were disappointed on arrival to discover that the city had paved streets and automobiles, with nary a gunfighter or an Apache warrior in sight. The city boys tried to compensate by purchasing two cowboy outfits, complete with chaps and 10-gallon hats, but the anachronistic garb only made them the butt of rude jokes. At last, near desperation, they bought two sway-backed horses and rode westward, searching for the *real* frontier.

Two weary days on the trail brought them to Deming, New Mexico, and a final confrontation with reality. The West, as portrayed in the novels they loved, no longer existed—if, in fact, it ever had. Where other young men might have been discouraged, though, Loftus and Donaldson decided to make their dreams come true. They sold their horses and used the money to buy a pair of six-guns with hand-tooled holsters, spending the last of their cash on two train tickets back to El Paso. By the time they arrived, they had hatched a plan to revive the era of BUTCH CASSIDY and JESSE JAMES.

Their first target, in November 1937, was the Southern Pacific Railroad's westbound Apache Limited. An hour out of El Paso, Loftus—in full cowboy costume—rose from his seat and confronted conductor W. M. Holloway with a drawn pistol. "I thought he was drunk," Holloway recalled. "I didn't think it was a holdup. I was afraid that gun was going off when the amateur's hands started shaking."

Shaky or not, Loftus covered Holloway while Harry Donaldson moved among the passengers, collecting several men's watches but coming up empty on cash. Frustrated and nervous, Donaldson panicked and shot a male passenger in the hip when the man made an unexpected sudden move. Loftus moved forward to help his partner, but he was tackled and wrestled to the floor by off-duty brakeman W. L. Smith, riding the Apache Limited as a passenger. They grappled on the floor until Henry's gun went off, mortally wounding Smith. At that point, enraged passengers swarmed both bandits, punching and kicking them in a frenzy. One witness later said, "If it hadn't been that we had women passengers on the coach, those robbers would have been beaten to death."

As it was, they faced charges of robbery and murder, with swift convictions and harsh sentences a foregone conclusion. It was a tragicomic end to the era of railroad holdups that began with the outlaw RENO BROTHERS seven decades earlier.

LONGABAUGH, Harry "Sundance Kid"

Born in 1870, Harry Longabaugh kept the details of his childhood to himself, sharing little with friends or the law enforcers who hunted him in later life. He may have come from Pennsylvania, as some stories claim, but he first attracted public notice on the Suffolk ranch in Wyoming, located at the mouth of Lodgepole Creek. He turned up there in 1887, claiming to be a Colorado wrangler, and was put to work. A series of fights with coworkers established his reputation for hot-tempered violence, and Longabaugh was arrested in August 1887, accused of stealing $80 (or a horse; reports vary) from an old man in Lusk, Wyoming. Convicted and sentenced to 18 months, as a juvenile he was spared the rigors of state prison and confined instead to the Crook County jail at Sundance—from which he drew his famous nickname.

Released in February 1889, Longabaugh returned to a life of crime. His name was linked to a pair of Wyoming train robberies—at Big Timber and Malta —during 1892. The latter raid landed Longabaugh in jail with three accomplices, but he soon escaped and fled to the outlaw hideaway dubbed HOLE-IN-THE-WALL, where he met gang leader BUTCH CASSIDY sometime in 1892 or 1893. Accounts differ on whether Longabaugh immediately joined Cassidy's far-ranging "WILD BUNCH" or remained a solo act for several more years, enlisting only after he met Cassidy a second time on a Wyoming ranch.

In either case, Sundance was part of the Cassidy gang by August 1896 when he helped rob a bank at Montpelier, Idaho. A year later he was jailed with three confederates, following another bank heist in Belle Fourche, South Dakota, but the crew broke jail in Deadwood and returned at once to the outlaw trail. On June 5, 1899, he joined Wild Bunch members Harvey Logan and "Flat Nose" George Curry to rob a train at Wilcox Siding, Wyoming. When Sheriff Joe Hazen led a posse in pursuit, the outlaws made a stand and killed him, the fatal shot reportedly fired by Logan.

A new century brought no letup in robberies for the Sundance Kid. On August 29, 1900, he joined Cassidy, Logan, and two unknown accomplices to rob a Union Pacific train at Tipton, Wyoming. Initial reports claimed the bandits had scored $55,000, but the actual take was more modest—a mere $50.40, in fact. Adding insult to injury, the gang learned that a $100,000 military payroll, scheduled for the August 29 run, had been delayed at the last moment.

On September 19, 1900, Longabaugh joined Cassidy and Bill Carver to steal $32,640 from a bank in Winnemucca, Nevada. They retreated to Fort Worth after the holdup, meeting Logan and Ben Kilpatrick. In a whimsical moment, the five robbers posed for a group photograph, but the prank nearly blew up in their faces when a copy of was glimpsed by WELLS FARGO detective FRED DODGE. Sundance and company were gone by the time Dodge organized a posse, but the near-miss was too close for comfort. The gang's last reported job on U.S. soil was a train robbery near Wagner, Montana, on July 3, 1901. Longabaugh joined Cassidy, Logan, and Camilla Hanks for that outing, blasting the express car open with dynamite to steal $65,000 in currency.

The combined attention of regular law enforcers and PINKERTON detectives now combined to break up the Wild Bunch, prompting Butch and Sundance to seek new horizons. Traveling with girlfriend Etta Place, an ex-schoolteacher three years his junior, Longabaugh met Cassidy in New York City on February 1, 1902, and the trio sailed for Buenos Aires on February 20. On arrival, Longabaugh deposited $12,000 in a local bank, applying for a land grant from the Argentine government. It was granted, and the partners settled in as cattle ranchers for a time, although reports persist of their involvement in far-flung criminal activities. Pinkerton detectives had followed their spoor to Argentina, where officials apparently offered to keep an eye out for Butch and Sundance if they tried to leave the country, but the surveillance—if it existed at all—did nothing to restrict their movements.

The first report of trouble came in 1905, when Longabaugh was allegedly caught in flagrante delicto with a neighbor's wife and was forced to wing the jealous husband with a bullet. In March 1906, with a third (unidentified) American, Longabaugh and Cassidy robbed a bank at Mercedes, Argentina, killing the banker before they escaped with $20,000. A few months later, at Bahía Blanca, they took another bank for 20 grand; the third member of the gang was described by witnesses as a slender young woman. A posse gave chase but retired after Butch and Sundance shot their horses.

Longabaugh and Place may have returned to the United States for a visit in 1907. Some accounts place them in New York and Denver, where Place was reportedly hospitalized for appendicitis. Before her release, legend has it, Sundance met some of his old friends in a local saloon and drank to excess, wounding the bartender in a senseless shootout.

Back in South America before year's end, Longabaugh and Place rejoined Cassidy, ranging freely over Argentina and Bolivia. With a third American (again, unidentified), Butch and Sundance robbed a train at Eucalyptus, Bolivia, and stole a sizeable payroll, hiding out afterward at the abandoned Jesuit mission of Cacambaya on the eastern slope of the Andes. On December 7, 1907, Longabaugh, Cassidy, and Etta Place robbed a bank in Río Gallegos, Argentina, of $10,000, shooting the mounts from under posse members who pursued them. Back in Bolivia during 1908, Butch and Sundance briefly worked the Concordia mines, apparently casing a potential payroll robbery, but it appears they never tried to score. Two days after Christmas 1908, they robbed a store at Arroyo Pescado, killing the manager, looting the safe, and forcing employees to load their pack horses with supplies.

Time was running out for the daring *Bandidos Yanquis*. Etta Place permanently dropped from sight after the Arroyo Pescado holdup, her fate a matter of eternal speculation. In early 1909 Butch and Sundance stole a mine payroll near Quechisla in southern Bolivia. Sometime later (reports vary from two days to "several weeks"), they were spotted in the village of San Vincente, and troops were summoned to arrest them. The result was a pitched battle in the heart of town, dramatized by Hollywood 60 years later. An uncertain number of soldiers were killed, and both bandits were gravely wounded before Cassidy finished Sundance with a shot to the head and then took his own life. A popular alternative version has Butch somehow wriggling from the trap and returning to America. A variation on that theme suggests that Longabaugh's companion was not Cassidy at all but the unnamed accomplice who had joined them in at least two previous holdups.

LUFTHANSA Airport Robbery

The largest robbery in history at New York's JFK International Airport began in the predawn hours of December 11, 1978. Kerry Whalen, a security guard for Lufthansa Airlines, was on patrol in the cargo terminal parking lot when met a group of masked men, armed with rifles and pistols, emerging from a dark-colored van. One of the bandits pistol-whipped Whalen and took his wallet, threatening to kill

Whalen, then visit Whalen's home, and kill his family if the guard failed to cooperate. Inside the terminal, the masked bandits quickly rounded up seven more Lufthansa employees, forcing one of them to summon night supervisor Rudy Eirich via intercom. On arrival at the cargo terminal, Eirich was forced to open the company's vault, whereupon the robbers fled with $5 million in cash and some $875,000 in jewelry.

Police and FBI agents were immediately notified, recognizing the signs of a professional heist. Involvement by ORGANIZED CRIME was suspected, and that suspicion was borne out within hours of the holdup as underworld informers offered tips about the gang responsible. One high-ranking member of the Columbo crime family told an FBI contact that the crew responsible was run by James Burke, aka "Jimmy the Gent," a known associate of Brooklyn Mafioso Paul Vario. The same informer named Burke's son Frankie and three other hoodlums— Tommy DeSimone, Angelo Sepe, and Anthony Rodriguez—as members of the holdup team, but the informer was never called to testify. Instead, G-men displayed mug shots of their suspects to Lufthansa employees who had glimpsed the bandits removing their masks as they fled on December 11. Several agreed that the robbers "resembled" Sepe, DeSimone, and Rodriguez, but the tentative ID was insufficient to support indictments. It *did* support court orders for surveillance, including bugs and homing devices planted in several mob vehicles, but the Lufthansa suspects defeated eavesdroppers by playing their car radios at full blast, evading FBI spotter planes and helicopters by driving into JFK Airport's restricted air space.

While the strange surveillance of Jimmy Burke's crew was in progress, authorities pursued a parallel line of investigation, working on a theory that the Lufthansa heist had been an "inside job." One of the airline's cargo supervisors, Louis Werner, boasted of involvement in the crime, and background investigation showed that he owed $20,000 to a syndicate bookie named Marty Krugman. Interrogation of Werner's friends and co-workers revealed his secret life as a habitual gambler who frequently lost. Already suspected of setting up an earlier Lufthansa airport robbery, in which thieves escaped with $22,000 in foreign currency, Werner was now a logical suspect in the latest airport crime. Suspicion turned to certainty when agents learned that Werner had prevented a Brinks truck from picking up the cash and jewels on December 8, falsely reporting that he needed an absent supervisor's signature to release the loot. A friend of Werner's at work, Peter Gruenewald, seemed nervous when questioned by law enforcers. Arrested as a material witness on February 16, 1979, when authorities learned he had scheduled a flight to Japan, Gruenewald quickly agreed to testify against Werner in return for immunity on all charges.

"Jimmy the Gent," meanwhile, was busy cleaning house, disposing of potential witnesses—and members of the holdup team whose share of the Lufthansa proceeds diminished Burke's cut. Suspect Parnell Edwards was the first to go, shot six times in his Queens apartment on December 18, 1978. Marty Krugman, owed $500,000 from the holdup, disappeared forever on January 6, 1979. Tommy DeSimone vanished eight days later, never to be seen again. One of Burke's couriers, Richard Eaton, had just returned from a money-laundering trip to Florida when police found him on January 17, bound with wire in his Brooklyn apartment, neck broken. DeSimone's mistress, 27-year-old Theresa Ferrara, was reported missing on February 10; three months later, on May 18, her dismembered torso washed ashore near Toms River, New Jersey, and was identified via X rays.

Federal prosecutors had only Lou Werner to charge with the Lufthansa heist, at that point. Convicted of conspiracy on May 16, 1979, Werner faced a 25-year prison sentence for his role in the crime.

Authorities hoped he might "roll over" on surviving participants, but that list grew increasingly shorter. On the very day of Werner's conviction, two more Lufthansa suspects—Joseph Manri and Robert McMahon—were found shot to death in a car, parked in Brooklyn. Yet another suspect, Paolo LiCasti, was killed a month later, his corpse left on a smoldering trash heap in Brooklyn. By year's end, the list of dead or missing suspects had expanded to include Anthony Stabile, Angelo Sepe and his teenage girlfriend Joanne Lombardo, and Louis Cafora and his wife Joanna. James Burke, meanwhile, had been arrested for parole violations on April 13, 1979 but remained untouchable in the Lufthansa case.

Prosecutors got lucky, after a fashion, in May 1980. Another Burke associate, Henry Hill, was facing life imprisonment for multiple narcotics violations when he cut a deal to testify against his one-time friends. Unable to link James Burke directly to the Lufthansa robbery, Hill provided testimony proving Burke responsible for the January 1979 murder of Richard Eaton. Convicted of that crime on February 19, 1985, Burke was sentenced life in prison. Hill, meanwhile, vanished into the federal witness protection program; his story—and that of the Lufthansa holdup—was later dramatized in the 1990 film *Goodfellas*. No one else was ever prosecuted for the Lufthansa holdup, and none of the loot was recovered.

MAK, Kwan Fia: See WAH MEE CLUB MASSACRE.

MAKLEY, Charles

A native of St. Mary's, Ohio, born November 24, 1889, eighth-grade dropout Charles Makley turned to crime in his teens, graduating from petty theft to bootlegging and bank robbery in at least three Midwestern states. He cultivated the appearance of a prosperous businessman, with a gift of gab and a talent for bluffing his way out of trouble. Between holdups, he sometimes worked as an insurance agent and claimed to have addressed a civic luncheon after robbing one bank in the 1920s. While the story may have been apocryphal, it fairly captured his engaging personality.

His charm notwithstanding, Makley still had his share of run-ins with the law. In 1921 he was arrested by Detroit police on charges of receiving stolen property. Three years later, in July 1924, he was convicted of a Wichita robbery and sentenced to 15 years in prison. Paroled in June 1928, he was free only a matter of days before he robbed a Hammond, Indiana, bank and was captured again, drawing a sentence of 10 to 20 years at the state prison in Michigan City.

There, Makley soon made friends with a hard core of professional stickup artists, including HARRY PIERPONT, HOMER VAN METER, JOHN "RED" HAMILTON, RUSSELL CLARK, and a young JOHN DILLINGER. Dillinger was paroled in May 1933, committed to

liberating his pals. He was arrested on September 22 for an Ohio bank robbery, but not before he had arranged the prison break. Four days later, using pistols smuggled in by Dillinger's accomplices, Makley, Pierpont, Hamilton, Clark, and four other convicts escaped from Michigan City. Their top priorities were stealing cash and repaying Dillinger for his help.

On October 3, 1933, Makley joined Pierpont, Hamilton, and Clark to steal $14,000 from a bank in Makley's hometown. Nine days later, they liberated Dillinger from jail in Lima, Ohio, killing Sheriff Jesse Sarber in the process. On October 14 the gang stole weapons and bulletproof vests from a police station in Auburn, Indiana; six days later, in Peru, Indiana, they repeated the stunt, adding more hardware to their arsenal. It came in handy on October 23 when they raided a Greencastle bank for $74,782. By year's end, the gang was so notorious that five of its members led Illinois's list of "public enemies": Makley ranked fourth, behind Dillinger, Pierpont, and Hamilton.

Their brief but spectacular run ended on January 25, 1934, when Makley, Dillinger, Pierpont, and Russell Clark were captured by authorities in Tucson, Arizona. Dillinger was shipped to Indiana for trial in the murder of an East Chicago policeman, while his three cohorts faced capital charges in the death of Sheriff Sarber. Before extradition to Ohio, they were briefly returned to Michigan City, their guards reporting that Makley quailed at the sight of those gray prison walls. "Do me a favor," he allegedly requested of his keepers. "Shoot me in the head, so I won't have to go back in there."

No bullet was forthcoming, but if Makley wished to die, Ohio prosecutors were willing to accommodate him. Held under heavy guard at Lima, supervised by Sheriff Don Sarber—the son of their victim—Makley, Clark, and Pierpont were arraigned on February 15, 1934. Each was tried separately in March 1934, with all three convicted. Reunited for sentencing on March 24, Makley and Pierpont heard themselves condemned to die in the electric chair, while Clark received a life prison term. Three days later, they were transferred to the Ohio state prison at Columbus.

Escape was their only hope for survival as the clock ran down. On September 22, 1934, Makley and Pierpont gave it their best shot, brandishing fake guns carved from soap and blackened with shoe polish, slugging a guard and freeing Russell Clark from his nearby cell. The desperate trio cleared two doors and were working on a third when Clark panicked and ran back to his cage. Guards with real guns arrived on the scene moments later, killing Makley and wounding Pierpont. Harry would recover from his wounds in time to keep his date with the electric chair on October 17, 1934.

MATASAREANU, Emil Dechebal, and PHILLIPS, Larry Eugene, Jr.

Los Angeles may be the bank-robbery capital of the world. Police recorded 1,126 bank heists in 1996, including 222 confrontations described by FBI spokesmen as armed "take-over" incidents in the tradition of Depression-era bandits such as JOHN DILLINGER and ALVIN KARPIS. Even so, serious violence is rare, and law enforcers in the City of Angels were woefully unprepared for the havoc unleashed by a pair of determined bandits on the last day of February 1997.

Emil Matasareanu, a Romanian native born in 1966, emigrated to the United States with his parents as a child and grew up in the Los Angeles suburb of Altadena, California. An overweight and introverted youth who suffered teasing from his peers, Matasareanu found solace in his home computer and went on to graduate from the DeVry Institute of Technology, afterward running his own business as a computer technician and software designer. On the side he helped his mother run a private home for the mentally disabled and still found time to revisit Romania

in search of a bride. Married there, he brought his wife back to California and fathered two sons. Somewhere along the way, he met another L.A. resident, Larry Phillips Jr., and they became good friends. The common interests bonding them appeared to be firearms and crime.

On October 23, 1993, Phillips and Matasareanu were stopped by Los Angeles police for a traffic violation and arrested when the officers spotted an arsenal of weapons and other curious items in their vehicle. The items seized that day included two AK-47 assault rifles; four semiautomatic pistols; 1,616 rounds of ammunition; six smoke grenades; two homemade bombs; three drum-type magazines for automatic weapons; two bulletproof vests; one gas mask; six holsters; three different California license plates; two 200-channel police scanners with earpieces; $244 cash in a plastic bag from Sears; a stopwatch; and various items apparently intended for disguises (including three ski masks, several wigs, sunglasses, gloves, miscellaneous clothing, and two cans of gray spray-on hair dye). Phillips later pled guilty to felony false impersonation of a police officer and misdemeanor weapons possession, serving 99 days in jail and receiving three years' probation. Matasareanu pled guilty on two misdemeanor weapons counts and served 71 days, also with three years' probation.

The arrests opened a floodgate of trouble for Emil Matasareanu. Authorities soon shut down the "home" he operated with his mother, and his computer business subsequently failed. Brain surgery was required in July 1996 to repair a blocked artery that had triggered grand mal seizures, and Matasareanu's wife left him around the same time, taking their two children with her. The rash of bad luck might help explain his later violent behavior, were it not for the October 1993 arrest. Whatever drove him to the last chaotic act of his life, Matasareanu's fascination with illegal weapons and paramilitary gear clearly predated the collapse of his private and professional life by at least three years.

At 9:15 A.M. on February 28, 1997, Matasareanu and Phillips entered a Bank of America branch in suburban Van Nuys, intent on transacting some unorthodox business. Both were dressed all in black from ski masks to boots. In preparation for the raid, they had donned bulky "Level III-A" body armor that was capable of stopping military rounds; additionally, they had cut up several Kevlar vests and stitched homespun bulletproof garb from the fragments, shielding their arms and legs from gunfire.

Both carried fully automatic AK-47 rifles with 100-round magazines, backed up by pistols and spare 30-round magazines for the long guns.

The bandits came in shouting, firing automatic bursts into the ceiling as they ordered 10 employees and 32 customers to hit the floor. One bank patron was struck with a rifle butt for failure to silence his wailing child. More gunfire shattered the Plexiglas doors that separated customers from the vault and tellers' cages. Somewhere in the midst of chaos, an alarm was sounded, either from the bank or by some passer-by, and police cars began to descend on the scene. Emerging from the bank with an undisclosed amount of cash, Matasareanu and Phillips found themselves confronted by at least 15 squad cars and the first wave of a massive response that finally included 200-plus law enforcers.

The bandits came out shooting, touching off a wild fight that lasted three-quarters of an hour. Thousands of shots were fired—more than 1,100 from the bandits' two rifles alone as they emptied magazines, reloaded, and resumed the battle. Patrol officers at the scene quickly found themselves outgunned and retreated to a nearby gun shop, B&B Sales, where they commandeered two AR-15 semiautomatic carbines, a shotgun, and several high-powered rifles with telescopic sights. Still the robbers fought on, their body armor deflecting countless bullets, while television helicopters circled overhead and beamed the firefight live to a nationwide audience. Reporters from the *Los Angeles Times* braved gunfire at ground level (and won their newspaper a Pulitzer Prize for front-line coverage of the melee).

Midway through the shootout, Larry Phillips separated from his partner and their getaway car, strolling almost casually along the sidewalk while firing at police officers all around him. When his AK-47 jammed, he dropped the rifle and drew a handgun, fighting on until the weapon was shot from his hand. Stooping to retrieve it, he then apparently committed suicide with a close range shot to the brain—though one confusing media report claimed Phillips "died when he shot himself as a police bullet hit his head."

Emil Matasareanu, meanwhile, climbed into the getaway car and drove slowly away from the bank, firing randomly at officers along the way. Police shot out his tires, whereupon he left the crippled vehicle and tried to commandeer a parked truck, off-loading weapons and equipment from the trunk of his car while officers kept up a withering fire. The truck refused to start, however, and Matasareanu retreated

on foot, discarding his empty AK-47 in favor of an M16 assault rifle from his mobile arsenal. Wounded 29 times, his last weapon empty, Matasareanu finally surrendered, sprawling semiconscious in the street.

What happened next remains a point of controversy mired in litigation. Most accounts agree that the shooting stopped by 10:00 A.M., but no medics reached Matasareanu until 11:10 A.M., when he was pronounced dead from blood loss. Surviving members of his family filed suit against LAPD for wrongful death, charging that officers deliberately let Matasareanu "bleed to death on the ground from a nonfatal wound." Trial on that lawsuit, filed in April 1997, was delayed until February 2000 and continues without a verdict at this writing.

Aside from bandits Matasareanu and Phillips, casualties from the shootout included 11 wounded police officers and at least six injured civilians. One of the wounded was described in early press reports as an accomplice to the holdup, police spokespersons claiming that two or three more bandits had escaped from the scene and were still at large. Those accounts were retracted by March 1, 1997, with Matasareanu and Phillips named as the only gunmen on the scene. Curiously, attorneys for Matasareanu's family in the civil lawsuit still maintain that at least two unknown bandits escaped from the crime scene on February 28—apparently unseen by law officers or media photographers. Police sources speculate that Matasareanu and Phillips may have robbed two more banks in May 1996—one in Canoga Park and the other in Van Nuys—but no evidence has been produced to link them with those crimes.

MATHEWS, Robert Jay: See ORDER, THE.

MATIX, William Russell, and PLATT, Michael Lee
Born at Dayton, Ohio, on May 25, 1951, William Matix graduated from high school at nearby New Madison in 1969. His childhood was uneventful except for a severe stutter that followed him into military service as a young adult. Matix joined the U.S. Marine Corps in October 1969 and was honorably discharged as a sergeant in July 1972 after serving at posts in Hawaii and on Okinawa. Returning home to Ohio, he worked as a factory laborer in Troy for 13 months and then sought relief from tedium in uniform once more. This time Matix joined the U.S. Army, serving from August 1973 to August 1976 when he was honorably discharged (again as a sergeant).

The second military tour changed everything for Matix. He finally beat his stutter under treatment at Walter Reed Army Hospital and met his future wife, Patricia Bukanich, while still in therapy. At his final duty station—assigned as a military policeman to Fort Campbell, Kentucky—Matix met the other most important figure in his life: Sergeant Michael Lee Platt.

The son of a career navy officer, Platt was born at San Diego, California, on February 3, 1954. His father was transferred to Pearl Harbor in 1965 and then to Alameda, California, a year later. By 1970 the Platts were settled in Yuma, Arizona, where Michael—an accomplished athlete—graduated from high school in 1972. He joined the U.S. Army immediately after graduation and served honorably for seven years, rising to the rank of staff sergeant with a specialty in physical activities. In October 1975 he married Regina Lylen, 16 months his senior. Upon meeting William Matix at Fort Campbell, the two men became good friends, but their comradely relationship was interrupted by Matix's discharge in August 1976. Platt went on to serve a tour of duty in Korea from April 1978 until his discharge in May 1979. On leaving the service he settled in Regina's hometown Miami, Florida. By 1983 Platt was the owner, with his brother, of a successful landscaping business.

Things had not gone so well for William Matix in the meantime. Married following his 1976 military discharge, Matix and wife Patricia moved frequently, trying their luck in various locations throughout New York and Ohio before they finally settled in Columbus. A qualified chef who graduated from New York's Culinary Institute of America in December 1978, Matix tried various jobs and seemed satisfied with none. The sole bright spot in those years was a 1983 visit from his old friend Mike Platt—and then disaster struck.

On December 10, 1983, Patricia Matix and a female coworker were stabbed to death by an unknown assailant on the job at a Columbus Hospital. The crime was never solved, although in light of subsequent events, Columbus authorities now suspect Platt of committing the double murder. Matix's father suffered a stroke on the same day Patricia was killed, his health declining steadily until he died of cancer in April 1984. Matix responded to the double loss with a flurry of activity at his church, proclaiming himself a newly "born-again" Christian. Insurance settlements in his wife's case paid him an estimated $180,000, but Matix was bitter, fuming that the hospital and insurance carriers had cheated him. Soon after his father's death, Matix left for Miami, taking a job with Platt's landscaping company.

Platt and Matix picked up where they had left off at Fort Campbell, becoming inseparable. They delighted in out-of-state hunting trips and deep-sea fishing, once returning with a seven-foot trophy marlin on the hook. Platt's marriage began to suffer after Matix came to town, Platt indulging in adulterous affairs that were poorly hidden from his wife. Raging arguments included threats of death against Regina Platt; Michael insisted that she have sex with Matix, and Regina grudgingly complied in an effort "to save the marriage." Secretly, she hired a lawyer and confided her suspicions that Matix and her husband were involved in "something illegal." The lawyer hired a private eye to shadow them, but no conclusive evidence of any criminal activity was found. Regina told her friends that Michael had repeatedly threatened her life. An anonymous female caller allegedly warned Regina in the fall of 1984 that "You'll be gone by Christmas."

On November 13, 1984, Regina Platt attempted suicide with an overdose of antidepressant medication, but doctors pumped her stomach and saved her life. On December 20 she met a friend at a Miami shopping mall and broke down in tears, again insisting that her husband planned to kill her. Next morning she was found dead, nude in bed, nearly decapitated from a shotgun blast to the mouth. Platt claimed that he was sleeping in another room when the gunshot woke him. Authorities measured the weapon, compared it to Regina's diminutive stature, plotted trajectories, and finally ruled the death a suicide—but several Miami detectives remain convinced that Platt in fact murdered his wife.

With Regina gone, Platt and Matix had even more time for each other. Their first joint project was construction of a mysterious earthen mound beside Platt's house. Platt described it to curious neighbors as a cesspool, but it more closely resembled a makeshift bunker of the type favored by hard-core "survivalists" for storage of weapons and paramilitary supplies. Platt's neighbors were relieved—but still mystified—when the mound disappeared overnight in mid-October 1985.

The unorthodox landscaping venture coincided with an ongoing rash of violent crime in Miami and environs. On April 30, 1985, a WELLS FARGO guard was confronted by three armed men wearing ski masks outside a branch bank in Miami Lakes. The gunmen escaped with an estimated $100,000, fleeing in a stolen car.

Five days later, on June 5, two bandits bungled their attempted holdup of a Wells Fargo truck outside a Miami steak house, leaving the scene empty handed. They rebounded on June 21, killing 41-year-old Wells Fargo guard Miguel Porto-Perra and robbing his truck of an estimated $40,000 while it stood outside a Southern Bell in Coral Gables.

Emilio Briel, a 25-year-old Miami resident, vanished without a trace on October 4, 1985, while target shooting at a flooded rock quarry in rural Dade County. Missing with him was a .22-caliber rifle and his car—a 1977 gold-colored Chevrolet Monte Carlo. His skeletal remains were found by hikers near the rock pit five months later, on March 1, 1985.

Six days after Emilio Briel disappeared, on October 10, two armed men wearing ski masks and army fatigues robbed a Loomis armored truck outside a Miami restaurant, escaping with an undetermined amount of cash. At 12:30 P.M. on October 16, 1985, a man armed with a shotgun confronted Wells Fargo guard José Sanchez as he (Sanchez) was unloading a cash delivery for a Winn Dixie store on Southwest 104th Street. After a shouted order to "Freeze!" the gunman fired a blast, wounding Sanchez in the thigh; he then panicked and fled empty handed while his companion/getaway driver peppered the truck with semiautomatic rifle fire. Another Loomis truck was the target on October 17 in suburban Kendall, but the driver held off two would-be robbers with pistol fire.

At noon on November 8, 1985, two masked men invaded a bank on Miami's South Dixie Highway, brandishing a rifle and a shotgun, pistols on their hips. Holding tellers and customers at gunpoint, the bandits helped themselves to $41,469 in cash that had been delivered moments earlier by a Wells Fargo truck. Witnesses described their getaway car as gold Monte Carlo.

Violence continued into the new year, with another robbery at 10:30 A.M. on January 10, 1986. Ernesto Marange's Brinks truck was parked four blocks from the scene of the November 8 bank heist, about to make another bank delivery, when two gunmen sprang from ambush. One shot Marange in the back with a shotgun; the other wounded him twice with a .223-caliber rifle. The bandits then grabbed

$54,000 and fled the scene in Ernesto Briel's Monte Carlo, unaware that a witness to the holdup was trailing them. The witness watched them switch cars, escaping in a white Ford pickup truck, but he failed to get the second vehicle's license number in his rush to alert police.

Miami FBI agents were startled by the string of violent robberies, collaborating with local authorities in an effort to round up the gang. Law enforcers were still seeking viable clues on March 12, 1986, when another target shooter—30-year-old José Collazo—was accosted by two gunmen at the same rock pit where Ernesto Briel vanished in October 1985. Brandishing weapons, the strangers forced Collazo to enter the water and then shot him four times and left him for dead, stealing his black Chevrolet Monte Carlo, a .22-caliber rifle and a .38-caliber revolver.

Collazo's Monte Carlo surfaced one week later, on March 19, when the bandits struck again. In a startling display of audacity, they returned to the same bank where they had robbed the Brinks truck on January 10, this time invading the bank itself to steal $8,338 at gunpoint. Bystanders noted the description and the license number of the bandits' getaway car, authorities quickly tracing it back to the recent Collazo murder attempt.

G-men and local detectives still had no clues to the identity of their roving quarry, but a geographical pattern had emerged from the string of holdups. Miami's FBI field office deployed its C-1 Squad, a "reactive" unit assigned to floating field surveillance, hoping for a swift response next time the bandits tried to score.

As it happened, the agents did not have long to wait.

G-men were covering four separate area banks on the morning of April 11, 1986, when agents Ben Grogan and Jerry Dove spotted José Collazo's stolen Monte Carlo at 9:20 A.M., cruising past a shopping mall in suburban Kendall. The agents followed their suspects southward on Southwest 82nd Avenue for several blocks before turning on their blue light and siren in an effort to stop the Monte Carlo. A high-speed chase ensued, joined by six more G-men in multiple cars. The pursuit ended when fugitives Platt and Matix inadvertently trapped themselves, swerving off the main highway into a cul-de-sac.

They were immediately blocked and sandwiched between FBI vehicles, sirens wailing, their din soon punctuated by rapid-fire gunshots. Michael Platt, riding shotgun in the Monte Carlo, was the first to open fire with a .223-caliber Ruger Mini-14 semiautomatic rifle. Within the space of a minute or less, Platt blazed off 13 shots, wounding agents Gordon McNeil and Ed Mireles in the gun hand and left arm, respectively. Agents Grogan and McNeill returned fire in that first exchange, their pistol shots striking driver Bill Matix in the head, the neck, and the wrist.

Platt, struggling to crawl through the Monte Carlo's passenger-side window (with his door jammed shut against a parked car), was struck next in the arm, the back, the thigh, and the foot by shots from agents Dove and Gil Orrantia, but the torrent of fire failed to slow Platt down. Scrambling across the hood of a resident's car, Platt dropped behind the vehicle and returned fire with one of two .357 Magnum revolvers he carried, striking Agent McNeill a second time and leaving him temporarily paralyzed. An FBI report of the firefight describes the chaos that ensued.

[Agents] Grogan and Dove, from the area of Vehicle D [on the FBI's chart of the battle] began firing on the subjects. Following a period of intense gunfire, subject William R. Matix apparently took [agents] Grogan and Dove under fire with a shotgun. This was evidenced by a pattern of #6 shot down the driver's side of Vehicle D. While Matix exchanged fire with [agents] Grogan and Dove, Michael Lee Platt left cover of his vehicle and proceeded down the passenger side of car D, leaned over the trunk of it, shooting [agent John] Hanlon, who was down, in the groin area, and shooting and killing [agents] Grogan and Dove. During this period of time, [agent Ron] Risner was firing on Platt.

Immediately after shooting the Agents, Platt and Matix approached the Bureau vehicle marked as car D, apparently to effect their escape. Both of them entered the vehicle. At this point, [agent] Mireles, who was apparently semiconscious, and was slightly behind the car, opened fire on the subjects in the FBI car, utilizing his Bureau-issued shotgun. [Agent] Mireles was forced to fire the gun one-handed. He rolled over on his back, put the shotgun between his legs, racked it with his right hand, forced himself up, pointed it over the rear bumper of the car and fired at the subjects. He apparently fired five rounds of 00 buckshot, puncturing the car in the left front fender, driver's window, and through the windshield. Somehow in this round of fire he hit the subject Platt through both feet. [Agent] Mireles then rose to his feet, drew his service revolver, and advanced on car #6 firing and inflicting fatal wounds on both subjects.

Ten minutes of furious action left Platt and Matix dead, along with agents Grogan and Dove. Of the six other G-men involved in the shootout, only Ron Risner emerged without injury. Platt had sustained 12 gunshot wounds and "multiple superficial abrasions of the face"; partner Matix had been shot six times (including five shots to the face and neck).

In the wake of the April 11 firefight, FBI spokespeople speculated publicly that Matix and Platt were members of a larger "loosely organized gang of South Dade armed robbers who specialize in armored car holdups." FBI Director William Webster suggested that the bandits might be linked to some terrorist organization. "We don't have enough information to make a definitive statement," Webster told reporters, "but we are looking at this aspect very, very closely." Another G-man told the media that "many factors"—ranging from costumes and choice of weapons to "cold and calculated" behavior in the last moments of their lives—suggested ties to unnamed extremist organizations.

In the last analysis though, Matix and Platt were positively linked only to the Briel and Collazo shootings, plus the robberies accomplished with their stolen cars. Weapons stolen from Briel and Collazo were found at Platt's home when G-men searched it following the shootout of April 11, 1986. No other suspects in the string of holdups were identified, no organizations branded with involvement in the robberies and murders.

MAY 19th Communist Organization

America's most active left-wing TERRORIST group of the 1970s and 1980s was known by a variety of names. Members were prone to call it "The Family" but also adopted the more formal title of the May 19th Communist Organization, so called after the shared birthday of Ho Chi Minh and Malcolm X. Later, in an effort to divert official scrutiny, the group would issue communiqués under the alternate names of the Revolutionary Fighting Group, the Armed Resistance Unit, and the Red Guerrilla Resistance. The ruse worked for a while, persuading law enforcers that they were dealing with several terrorist factions rather than one.

In hindsight, once the group's 20-odd members had been rounded up for trial, the most amazing thing about the May 19th cadre was not its fanaticism, but rather the way in which it had merged tattered remnants of several earlier groups, emerging as a virtual *Who's Who* of the radical left. Leader Jeral Wayne Williams (aka "Mutulu Shakur") was a defector from the Republic of New Afrika, as were May 19 members Cheri Laverne (aka "Nehanda Obafemi"), Samuel Lee Smith (aka "Mtayari Shabaka Sundiata") and Cecilio "Chui" Ferguson. Drop-ins from the Black Panther Party and the spin-off Black Liberation Army (BLA) included Nathaniel Burns (aka "Sekou Odinga"), Edward Lawrence Joseph (aka "Jamal Baltimore"), Donald Weems (aka "Kuwasi Balagoon"), and Marilyn Jean Buck (known to law enforcement as the only white member of the BLA). Representing white radicalism with ties to the Students for a Democratic Society and its bomb-happy Weatherman Underground faction were the likes of Judith Clark, David Gilbert, Linda Sue Evans, Susan Lisa Rosenberg, Laura Whitchorn, and Kathy Boudin (last seen publicly in 1970 when she fled naked from the rubble of a Weatherman bomb factory in Greenwich Village). Other players on the team included practicing physician Dr. Alan Berkman and Silvia Baraldini, a legal aide to radical defense attorney Susan Tipograph.

The May 19th cadre had its roots in New York City's ghetto, dating back to 1970 when Jeral Williams and several others founded Lincoln Detox, a drug rehabilitation center in the South Bronx. Already active in the Republic of New Afrika, Williams mixed left-wing politics with chemical counseling at Lincoln Detox, but it took him another six years to progress from words to action. On December 6, 1976, Jeral's raiders botched their first attempt to rob an armored truck outside the Mellon Bank in Pittsburgh, Pennsylvania. Shots were fired, but no one was wounded. Williams escaped in the confusion, while Chui Ferguson and accomplice Raymond Q. Oliver were nabbed at the scene.

Something was obviously lacking, but the group became lucky in March 1977 when Sam Smith was paroled after serving six years for the robbery of a Brooklyn grocery store. Two months later, on May 26, Williams led a four-man team that robbed a meat-packing plant in the South Bronx, making off with an undisclosed amount of cash. On June 28 Marilyn Buck, serving 10 years on weapons charges related to her role in the Black Liberation Army, was granted furlough time to visit attorney Tipograph, but she went underground instead, soon lending The Family her expertise on firearms and fake identification.

Things were definitely looking up for the revolution. On October 12, 1978, a four-man raiding party "expropriated" $8,380 from a bank in Lower Manhattan. Two months later, on December 19, Marilyn Buck went along for the ride when Williams and three others stopped a pair of armored-truck guards inside Bamberger's (a mall in Livingston, New Jersey), relieving them of $200,000 in cash. The group bided its time for a while after that, Williams spinning pipe dreams of revolutionary tomorrows, finally purchasing a Harlem brownstone in August 1979 to house a combination "freedom school" and acupuncture clinic. It would take another year to get the project rolling, though; in the meantime, there were places to go and people to rob. On September 11, 1979, Williams and five accomplices hit another Bamberger's—this one in Paramus, New Jersey—surprising two more armored-truck guards and escaping with $105,000.

Armed robbery was fun, but it was only part of the May 19th program. One of the group's primary goals was the liberation of "political prisoners," loosely defined as any nonwhite radicals jailed for acts of terrorism or clashes with police. One such was William Morales, a leader of the Puerto Rican separatist Fuerzas Armadas de Liberación Nacional (FALN). A client of attorney Susan Tipograph, Morales had already lost both hands in a bomb-making mishap, but he still managed to escape from the prison ward of New York's Bellevue Hospital on May 21, 1979, using bolt cutters smuggled into the lockup by "persons unknown." (Tipograph was the one and only contact visitor Morales had before he fled, and girlfriend Dylcia Pagan later told FBI agents that "a female attorney" smuggled the bolt cutters into Bellevue strapped to her leg. Bellevue officials confirm that Tipograph was not searched, nor did she pass through the usual metal detectors on her last visit with Morales.) While the Morales breakout was not a May 19th project per se, the fugitive bomber was sheltered by members of the group, his injuries tended by Dr. Berkman before he fled to Mexico.

Encouraged by the Morales affair and their recent successful holdups, May 19th members planned a full-fledged jailbreak of their own. On November 2, 1979, a 10-member team liberated Joanne Chesimard, billed in media reports as "the queen of the Black Liberation Army," from her New Jersey jail cell, briefly holding two guards hostage, afterward assisting Chesimard with her flight from the United States to Cuba, where she presumably lives to this day.

It was a heady moment, but the movement was in constant need of cash—for weapons and explosives, rent on safe houses, and upkeep on the acupuncture clinic—and the quickest way to get more money was to steal it from "The Man." On February 20, 1980 Williams led an eight-member team to rob an armored car outside a department store in Greenburgh, New York, but they bungled the job and fled empty handed. They were luckier on April 22, scoring their biggest haul yet in the amount of $529,000, looted from another armored car at Inwood, New York.

Still, there seemed to be more failures than successes in those giddy days. Between October 1980 and May 1981 the gang botched at least nine robbery attempts on armored cars: four in Nanuet, New York; three in Danbury, Connecticut; and two in the Bronx. Even the December 1980 parole of Chris Ferguson, after serving four years for the bungled Pittsburgh raid, provided no relief from the long run of misfortune.

The discouraged guerrillas finally got lucky again on June 2, 1981, with their assault on a Brinks truck in the Bronx. One guard was killed and another wounded in the holdup, while the May 19th bandits escaped with $292,000 in cash. The score almost made up for their next two failures, clumsy passes at an armored truck in Nanuet, and it encouraged Williams to pursue his plans for another Brinks holdup, code-named "The Big Dance."

A dozen members of The Family were involved on October 20, 1981, when the cadre jumped a Brinks truck in Nyack, New York, killing a guard, wounding the driver, and then making off with a whopping $1.6 million. Moments later, a suspicious civilian saw them switching getaway cars, piling into a Honda and a U-Haul truck, and called police. Officers overtook the fugitives on the New York State Thruway, and once again the bandits opened fire with automatic weapons. Sergeant Edward O'Grady and Patrolman Waverly Brown were killed in the exchange of fire before their assailants fled in the Honda and an Oldsmobile that had been following the U-Haul truck. More officers took off in hot pursuit, and while the Oldsmobile escaped, the Honda crashed and was surrounded. Handcuffed on the spot were Kathy Boudin, Sam Brown, and David Gilbert. Every penny of the Brinks loot was recovered at the scene.

A trace on the Oldsmobile's license number led authorities to a safe house in East Orange, New Jersey, recently occupied by Marilyn Buck. Buck was not home to greet them when the raiders crashed her pad, but they found clues that pointed them toward other hideouts in New York. Also discovered in the East Orange house were fingerprints identified as those of Donald Weems, an ex-Panther once indicted for conspiracy, who had escaped from a New Jersey prison in May 1978 while serving a 29-year sentence for assault with intent to kill.

On October 23 police in Queens surrounded a Family hangout, summoning the occupants to exit with their hands raised. Instead, the two men in the house started to shoot, and police energetically returned fire. Sam Smith was killed in the exchange, while Nathaniel Burns was wounded and captured alive. New evidence recovered from the bullet-riddled house helped fill in certain gaps for the authorities, identifying other members of the May 19th gang.

Jeral Williams, meanwhile, needed money if he wanted to remain at large. On November 23, 1981, he teamed with Cheri Dalton to rob an armored car in Arlington, Virginia, collecting a paltry $1,900 for his trouble. Also on the lam, Donald Weems and fugitive cop-killer Anthony LaBorde robbed a bank in Metter, Georgia, on December 21, 1981, but their time was swiftly running out. LaBorde was captured in Philadelphia 17 days later, and raiders found Weems on January 20, rousting him from the Bronx apartment he shared with his male transsexual "old lady." Chui Ferguson and Edward Joseph were also caught in New York on March 26, 1982, but Jeral Williams slipped through the net once again, his fancy footwork earning him a place on the FBI's "Ten Most Wanted" list. Silvia Baraldini was captured on November 9, and six days later the long arm of the law reached out to grab fugitive William R. Johnson (aka "Bilal Sunni-Ali") in Belize.

Even with Williams and others still at large, authorities believed the worst was over. They were mistaken, for the May 19th commandos were about to demonstrate their talent as chameleons, switching names and tactics as they carried on their private war against "Amerika." In December 1983 they bombed the Staten Island federal building, a subsequent communiqué claiming credit for the blast in the name of the Revolutionary Fighting Group. Similar statements were issued in the wake of three more bombings: One blast damaged the entrance to the National War College at Fort McNair in Washington, D.C., on April 26, 1983;

Katherine Boudin, who was arrested in connection with the Brinks robbery in Nanuet, New York, in 1981, is escorted into police headquarters. (AP/Wide World Photos)

another rocked the Washington Navy Yard Computing Center on August 18; yet another damaged the U.S. Capitol Building on November 7, 1983. Federal agents sought the bombers in vain, unaware that they were chasing remnants of the May 19th Communist Organization.

Captured members of the clique, meanwhile, were making their way through the courts. On Sep-

tember 3, 1983, following a five-month trial, Nathaniel Burns and Silvia Baraldini were convicted of conspiracy and racketeering; Ed Joseph and Chui Ferguson were convicted as accessories; William Johnson and sometime prostitute Iliana Robinson were acquitted. Twelve days later Judy Clark, Dave Gilbert, and Donald Weems were convicted of robbery and murder in the Nyack case, following a two-month trial in Goshen, New York. Kathy Boudin pled guilty on similar charges in White Plains on April 26, 1984. On June 14 of that year, Samuel Brown was convicted of murder and robbery following a six-week trial in the same White Plains courtroom.

And still the shrunken remnant of the May 19th cadre refused to die. Calling itself the Red Guerrilla Resistance in 1984, the group took credit for bombing the Israeli Aircraft Industries building in New York City on April 5; the Washington Navy Yard officers' club on April 20; and the South African consulate in Manhattan on September 26. The feds finally got lucky on November 29, 1984, arresting Susan Rosenburg and cohort Timothy Adolf Blunk (husband of Silvia Baraldini) as they unloaded weapons and explosives at a rented miniwarehouse in Cherry Hill, New Jersey. Seized in the raid were 100 blasting caps, nearly 200 sticks of dynamite, more than 100 cartridges of gel explosives, and 24 bags of blasting agent.

The radical group's last bombing occurred on February 23, 1985, when an explosion rocked the Patrolmen's Benevolent Association headquarters in New York City. Six weeks later, on May 11, Marilyn Buck and Linda Evans were spotted leaving a safe house in Baltimore and were trailed all the way to New York, where they were arrested outside a diner in Dobbs Ferry. Two weeks after that, Dr. Berkman was arrested in Pennsylvania with traveling companion Elizabeth Duke. (The doctor was held without bond, but Duke made bail and promptly disappeared.) Laura Whitehorn was traced to an apartment she shared with Linda Evans in Baltimore and was arrested there. Jeral Williams remained at large until February 11, 1986, when he was run to ground in California and soon extradited to New York for trial.

And trials there would be. On March 18, 1985, despite the best efforts of attorney Susan Tipograph, defendants Blunk and Rosenberg were convicted in New Jersey on eight of nine counts related to illegal possession of explosives; on May 20 they each received sentences of 58 years. That same month, Linda Evans was indicted by federal grand juries in three separate jurisdictions. At her first trial, in New York, she was convicted on November 21, 1985, of harboring fugitive Marilyn Buck and was sentenced to five years in prison. A second conviction in Louisiana, on nine counts of using false I.D. to purchase firearms, earned Evans another 45 years behind bars. Laura Whitehorn, convicted in New York for making false statements on a passport application, received a two-year prison term in February 1987 and was paroled a year later. Also in 1987, Dr. Berkman was convicted on weapons and explosives charges, plus use of false ID, and was sentenced to 10 years in prison. A year later, Jeral Williams and Marilyn Buck were tried in a New York federal court for the Nyack holdup and the Chesimard prison break, drawing 50-year prison terms on their conviction for murder, armed robbery, and racketeering.

And still, federal prosecutors were saving the best for last. One day after Buck and Williams were convicted in New York, the government announced indictments of seven May 19th defendants on five conspiracy counts related to the bombing spree of 1983–85. All but two of those indicted were already serving time: Elizabeth Duke had vanished underground and never reappeared, while Laura Whitehorn was already free on parole after serving half of her two-year sentence in New York. Of the others, Dr. Berkman was in failing health, recently diagnosed with Hodgkins disease, and the charges against him were later dismissed. Defendants Blunk and Rosenberg appealed their indictments to the U.S. Supreme Court, where the charges were thrown out on grounds of double jeopardy. The remaining trio—Buck, Evans, and Whitehorn—fought the case through numerous legal delays until 1990 when each pled guilty on two of the original five counts. In return for their pleas, Whitehorn drew a 20-year sentence, while Buck was sentenced to 10 years (consecutive to her outstanding 50-year term), and Evans got life (consecutive to her sentences in Louisiana and New York). It was, at long last, the end of the dance for the May 19th guerrillas and their abortive revolution.

MAYS, Lohman Ray, Jr.

Born February 19, 1943, in Dallas, Texas, Mays was a soft-spoken felon with a long record of violent crimes behind him. Variously convicted of murder,

armed robbery, aggravated assault, and concealing stolen property, by early 1969 he was confined as an habitual offender, linked to the February 22 murder of a man in Kannapolis, North Carolina. Mays escaped from prison on July 1, 1984, afterward robbing banks in Spartansburg, South Carolina, (on July 16) and in Orleans, Vermont (on September 14). Named in federal warrants charging him with bank robbery and unlawful flight to avoid confinement, Mays was added to the FBI's "Most Wanted" list on February 15, 1985.

Agents stalked their man with caution, conscious of the fact that he had shot and wounded a policeman in the past. Mays was alleged to travel with an attack dog and a small arsenal of weapons, but he offered no resistance when a flying squad of G-men traced him to Wyoming and arrested him on September 23, 1985. Returned to North Carolina for completion of his life sentence, the fugitive faced additional prison time for the robberies committed after his escape.

McCARTY Gang

There is no obvious reason why two of Dr. William McCarty's seven children should become notorious outlaws, while their siblings led productive, blameless lives. A Confederate army surgeon in the Civil War, Dr. McCarty moved his family from wartorn Tennessee to Montana in the wake of Dixie's defeat. Abandoning medicine for a rancher's life, he soon moved again, this time to the somewhat milder climate of southern Utah. In 1874 brothers Thomas and William McCarty joined others in pursuing and killing a band of Navajo raiders who slaughtered one of their calves. A stint at mining in Nevada failed to satisfy the brothers, and they were back in Utah by the late 1870s, taking over the ranch when their father pulled up stakes and left for Oregon.

Their switch from ranching to banditry was apparently a deliberate, calculated choice. Tom McCarty sold his ranch for $35,000 before he hit the outlaw trail, and brother Bill allegedly served a brief apprenticeship with Missouri gunman Cole YOUNGER, though where he found time before Younger's September 1876 arrest remains a mystery. It is known that Bill McCarty tried his hand at rustling in Minnesota—and wound up in state prison there after killing his accomplice in a quarrel over their loot. Pardoned on his promise to leave the Badger State forever, Bill took another fling at rustling in

Utah with Tom and then rode west to try farming with brother George in Oregon.

In Bill's absence, Tom McCarty found new cronies in the persons of Willard Erastus Christiansen (aka Matt Warner) and Robert LeRoy Parker (aka BUTCH CASSIDY). Joined by Tom's son Lewis, the trio rustled stock from Arizona and New Mexico in 1884, expanding to tap Mexican herds with the addition of gunmen Joe Brooks and Josh Swett. Swett was wounded by *federales* on one border crossing, but the raids were profitable enough to make it worth the risk. Matt Warner listed many holdups from this era in his subsequent autobiography, with himself, Tom McCarty, and Cassidy forming the hard core of the gang, dubbed by friends the "Invincible Three."

The gang attempted its first TRAIN ROBBERY on the night of November 3, 1887, east of Grand Junction, Colorado. They piled boulders on the track and succeeded in stopping a train, but a courageous express messenger refused to open the safe with pistols at his head, and the bandits gained nothing of value. McCarty had better luck in Denver on March 30, 1889, brandishing a vial of clear liquid—said to be nitroglycerine—while he demanded cash from tellers at a local bank. Warner waited outside to cover the street, and the duo escaped with $21,000 in cash. Another bank job followed at Telluride, Colorado, on June 24, 1889, McCarty and Warner teamed with Butch Cassidy to steal $10,500. A posse including the bank's president lost its collective nerve and gave up the pursuit when McCarty left threatening notes on the trail.

Flush with money from their recent holdups, McCarty and Warner bought a log cabin on the outskirts of Afton, Wyoming, where McCarty wooed and wed 14-year-old Rosa Rummel in September 1889. That winter was a hard one, prompting McCarty and Warner to loot Afton's only store, distributing goods to their hungry neighbors and paying the shopkeeper half value—$1,150—for the stolen goods. Both fled the area when spring brought police to their door, moving on to rob a Butte, Montana, gambling joint of $1,800 as a traveling stake.

The farming life had soured for Bill McCarty by that time, and he rejoined brother Tom, forging a new trio in Butch Cassidy's absence. Their first joint operation was the holdup of a store in Sparta, Oregon, for $600. On October 8, 1891, the gang stole $3,450 from a bank at Wallowa, Oregon. One month later, on November 3, they struck another bank at Summerville and fled with $5,000. Walla

Walla, Washington, was next on the list, but that bank job was canceled after post office detectives intercepted Warner's messages to Tom McCarty. Instead, the raiders hit a bank at Enterprise, Oregon, and bagged $9,000 for their trouble. Following a bank heist at Baker, Oregon—a few miles from Bill's failing ranch—the trio hid out for three days in Bill's haystack, besieged by a posse armed with guns and dynamite, finally escaping when Bill's wife let the manhunters ransack their house. Warner joined Butch Cassidy for a rustling foray near Belle Fourche, South Dakota, in April 1892, later describing the war on cattle thieves that was declared as a result.

This move to exterminate cattle rustlers and put an end to cattle rustling seemed to us like the final blow to the Old West. We listened to Butch Cassidy's eloquent call to action, grabbed our Winchesters, and rode out to defend and preserve the Old West. Our peculiar way of defending the Old West was to get a good tough outfit of horses together and plenty of artillery, make a fast dash up into the Belle Fourche or Johnson County country, take a big herd of cattle right from under the noses of the cattle kings, and show 'em they couldn't get away with their game of murdering and exterminating rustlers. . . . "If we let 'em get away with what they've started," said Butch, "this here won't be a free country any longer."

The gang got a preview of grim days ahead on September 24, 1892, when they robbed a bank at Roselyn, Washington. They went in expecting to find $100,000 in cash but finally settled for barely one-fifth that amount. While Warner and Bill McCarty were bagging the loot inside, Tom McCarty shot a passer-by and drew a crowd that had the makings of a lynch mob. Pursued into the wilderness, they managed to escape at last, but not before Matt Warner nearly drowned crossing a river, dragged beneath the surface by his heavy money belt. Reports of the holdup—staunchly denied by Warner and the rest—named George McCarty as a member of the raiding party, while his wife Nellie was described as holding the gang's horses.

Warner and his wife were blessed with the birth of a daughter on December 30, 1892, but the happy event used up all his good luck. A few days later, lawmen posing as cowboys surprised Matt at home and arrested him for the Roselyn job. George McCarty soon joined him in jail, where a slick lawyer promised acquittal in return for a hefty lump sum. Warner drew up a map to the spot where his gold cache was buried, but still the lawyer stalled. Finally, the bandits tunneled out of jail in broad daylight, but they were swiftly recaptured, with McCarty shot and wounded in the process. Their lawyer demanded more money for bribes, and the case—incredibly—was officially dropped for lack of evidence on July 24, 1893. Warner later estimated that his freedom cost him a total of $41,000 in bank loot.

Tom and Bill McCarty staged their last bank job at Delta, Colorado, on September 7, 1893, joined by Bill's son Fred. Cashier A. T. Blatchley raised the alarm before Tom McCarty killed him with a gunshot to the head. Fleeing with a mere $700, the bandits found their exit barred by townsfolk armed and ready to defend their savings. Bill McCarty was the first to drop, spilled from his saddle by a deadly gunshot to the head. Son Fred dismounted to help his father and died where he stood—both McCarty's cut down by keen-eyed W. Ray Simpson, an employee of the local hardware store. Tom's horse was wounded, but it carried him outside of town to the point where fresh mounts stood in wait. Behind him lay the bloody ruins of his family—and all but $100 of their meager loot.

It was the end the McCarty gang. Tom turned to trapping in Wyoming in between abortive plots to kill Ray Simpson and then tried his hand at cattle ranching at the outlaw refuge of BROWN'S HOLE. Some law officers blamed him for a bank job at Montpelier, Idaho, in August 1896, but the real culprits in that heist were Butch Cassidy's "WILD BUNCH." A static fixture around ROBBER'S ROOST through the mid-1890s, McCarty vanished without a trace at decade's end, his fate unknown even to members of the family. Some said he was shot at Green River, Utah, but Matt Warner maintained that McCarty was killed by persons unknown in Montana's wild Bitterroot country.

As for Warner himself, he tried going straight for a while in 1895 but without success. His wife's diagnosis with terminal cancer put him back on the wrong side of the law. Hired with sidekick William Wall to run some miners off their Vernal, Utah, claim in May 1896, Warner wound up killing two instead and narrowly avoided lynching at the hands of outraged prospectors. Butch Cassidy robbed a bank in August to raise Warner's bail, but Warner declined the offer and stood trial with Wall that September. Both were convicted of murder and sentenced to five years

apiece, while the man who hired them for the shooting—affluent businessman E. B. Coleman—was acquitted and allowed to leave the state.

Warner was released from prison on January 21, 1900. Eight months later, Utah Governor Heber Wells paid the former outlaw $175 to approach Butch Cassidy with a tentative amnesty offer. Warner went looking for his old friend, but new holdups by the Wild Bunch prompted Wells to withdraw the offer. Warner went straight—more or less—after prison, first running a saloon at Green River, Utah, and then moving on to Price, where he variously found employment as a policeman, bootlegger, night watchman, and justice of the peace. In 1912 he ran for sheriff of Carbon County under his birth name of Willard Christiansen but failed to make the cut. One local wag later suggested that he would have had a better chance with such voters as Matt Warner, cashing in on his old notoriety.

McCOLLUM, Ben Golden

Born in Macum, Kentucky, Ben McCollum moved to Oklahoma with his family at the age of four. An unremarkable childhood provides no clue to his selection of a criminal career, but the choice was not auspicious. In 1929 he robbed banks in Prague and Checotah, Oklahoma, for a total of $7,000, but the take would scarcely compensate McCollum for the prison term of 40 years he earned upon conviction. Inside, he quarreled habitually with fellow inmates, cutting two of them "to ribbons" with a homemade knife. Both died, and the brutality of the assault brought McCollum a death sentence. Three times he faced the electric chair, and three times stays of execution saved his life. McCollum's sentence was commuted to a life term in 1935, but he did not intend to finish out his days behind gray walls.

It took a while to find an opening, but McCollum finally escaped from Oklahoma's state prison at McAlester on May 1, 1954. His name was added to the FBI's "Most Wanted" list on January 4, 1957, but another 14 months would pass before he was caught.

After escaping from McAlester, the fugitive drifted aimlessly for more than two years, working odd jobs around the country before he finally settled in Indianapolis in September 1956. As "George Napier" he rented a room and found work at Sunnyside Sanatorium, a county hospital serving tuberculosis victims. From all appearances McCollum had gone straight, content to work and lead a normal life.

In fact, it was an effort to improve his situation honestly that ended the charade. On March 7, 1958, McCollum applied for and received a new job at Indiana's state school for the blind. He was scheduled to start work on Monday, March 10, but an employee at the school recalled a published photo lineup of the FBI's Top Ten fugitives and tipped the bureau off to "Napier's" address. McCollum was arrested that same evening; three days later, after waiving extradition, he was transferred back to Oklahoma to complete his prison terms.

METHVIN, Henry

A Louisiana native, born April 8, 1912, Henry Methvin was a footnote figure in the saga of Depression-era bank-robbing gangs, remembered primarily for his role in the deaths of CLYDE BARROW and BONNIE PARKER. At that, his association with the Barrow gang was accidental, stemming from a prison break in which he was initially supposed to have no part.

Methvin was serving 10 years on a Texas robbery conviction at the Eastham prison farm when Clyde and Bonnie came to liberate cohort RAYMOND HAMILTON on January 16, 1934. In the confusion and resultant hail of bullets, leaving one guard dead and another wounded, Methvin and three other inmates joined Hamilton in making a run for freedom. Hamilton first ordered them to go back, but Clyde was more generous, willing to liberate any convict who happened along. While the other three fugitives soon split off on their own, Methvin would remain with the Barrow gang until the bitter end, five months later.

A month after the breakout, on February 19, Henry joined Clyde and Ray Hamilton to burglarize a National Guard armory at Ranger, Texas, making off with arms and ammunition under cover of darkness. Eight days later, with Clyde and Hamilton, he used the new hardware to steal $4,138 from a bank in Lancaster, Texas. Bonnie and Clyde repaid the favor on March 1, driving Methvin to visit his father near Gibsland, Louisiana.

Henry was present on April 1, 1934, at Grapevine, Texas, when motorcycle officers E. B. Wheeler and H. D. Murphy were shot and killed by the Barrow gang. Conflicting reports from kinfolk and alleged eyewitnesses variously identify Clyde, Bonnie Parker, Methvin, or Ray Hamilton as the shooter. Clyde himself was inconsistent in assigning blame: He told relatives that Methvin had opened fire after mis-

Henry Methvin, final accomplice of Clyde Barrow and Bonnie Parker, whose father helped arrange the outlaw couple's death (From the collection of the Texas/Dallas History and Archives Division, Dallas Public Library)

understanding Clyde's suggestion that they "take" the officers, meaning disarm them and abduct them for a joy ride; later, in a note to the authorities, Clyde fingered Hamilton for the double murder.

Whatever the truth of the matter, Methvin was present at another slaying five days later, after Clyde's car bogged down in the mud near Commerce, Oklahoma. Surprised by two lawmen on patrol, the bandits opened fire, killing Constable Cal Campbell and wounding Police Chief Percy Boyd. They took Boyd along as a hostage, later releasing him at Mangle Corner, Kansas, near Fort Scott.

Life had become an endless cycle of pursuit and evasion by then. On April 7, Bonnie, Clyde, and Methvin stopped at a café in Stillwater, Oklahoma, but then left their meal unfinished when a uniformed patrolman wandered past. On April 30, accompanied by Joe Palmer, the gang stole $2,800 from a bank in Kansas. On May 1, the gang was linked to a bank heist in Sac City, Iowa. Two days later, they stole $700 from another bank at Everly, Iowa. By May 6 they were back in Dallas for a family reunion of sorts, driving on from there to revisit Methvin's father in Louisiana. On May 19, in Shreveport, Bonnie and Clyde parked outside a diner and sent Henry in for sandwiches. While he was waiting at the counter, a police car passed by, prompting Clyde to drive off without Methvin. Henry hitchhiked back to Ruston, where his father Ivan lived.

At that point, Bonnie and Clyde had just four days to live.

In the accepted version of the story, Methvin told his father that a rendezvous had been arranged in case the gang was separated. Henry was supposed to meet his cronies on a deserted stretch of highway south of Arcadia, Louisiana. Ivan Methvin, harassed by law officers in pursuit of his son and the rest of the gang, allegedly passed the information on to a Louisiana sheriff, who in turn alerted Texas manhunter FRANK HAMER and his mobile posse to set up an ambush. In return for putting Bonnie and Clyde on the spot, Ivan Methvin was allegedly promised that Henry would be spared execution for the Grapevine murders. Henry himself may not have known about the trap.

On May 23, Ivan Methvin is said to have parked his truck near the appointed rendezvous and removed one of the wheels, as if changing a flat tire. When Bonnie and Clyde cruised by moments later, they stopped to help and were riddled from ambush by six lawmen firing high-powered Browning automatic rifles. An alternate scenario, suppressed for more than 60 years and offered as the "true story" in the late 1990s, contends that Ivan Methvin played no voluntary role in the ambush at all. Instead, the later story goes, he was stopped on the highway at gunpoint and bound to a tree, his truck disabled by law officers as a lure for Bonnie and Clyde.

Either way, the trap was effective, and Henry got his free pass on the Grapevine double murder. Sadly, for his peace of mind, Frank Hamer had no power to negotiate for Oklahoma prosecutors in the case of Constable Campbell. Extradited to the Sooner State for trial on that murder charge, Methvin was convicted and sentenced to death on December 20, 1935. His sentence was commuted to life imprisonment on September 18, 1936, and he was paroled on March 20, 1942.

Once again, however, Methvin showed himself unable to stay out of trouble. In November 1945 Louisiana authorities jailed him for fighting and carrying a shotgun. Eleven months later, he was arrested for attempted robbery and drunk driving, near Shreveport. It was the booze that finished him on April 12, 1948: Methvin was drunk and reeling on a railroad track, unmindful of the train that came along behind him and snuffed out his life. Despite persistent rumors that his death was willful retribution for the ambush of Bonnie and Clyde, no evidence of murder was ever produced.

MILLER, Vernon C.

Born at Kimball, South Dakota, on August 26, 1896, Verne Miller moved to Huron, 35 miles northeast, and went to work as an auto mechanic in 1914. Two years later he joined the U.S. Army and served on bandit-chasing patrols along the Mexican border. America entered World War I in 1917, and Miller was dispatched to France with the 18th Infantry, where he was decorated for valor and rose to the rank of color sergeant. Home again in late 1918, he joined the Huron police force as a patrolman.

Miller's choice of a career in law enforcement was apparently designed to fill his pockets rather than to serve the public. In May 1920 he resigned from the Huron Police Department to run for sheriff of Beadle County, charming enough voters to win the race that November. Tiring of the job in early 1922, Miller withdrew $4,000 in county revenue from the bank and vanished. Investigators tracked him down, and he was convicted of embezzlement on April 4, 1923, and dispatched to the state prison. While confined, he served as the warden's personal chauffeur, winning parole in September 1924.

There was no going back to the straight life for Miller. Prohibition was in full swing across America, and there were profits to be made outside the law. In October 1925 Miller paid a $200 bootlegging fine in Sioux Falls, South Dakota, but received no jail time. He was increasingly unstable, with a hair-trigger temper aggravated by drug abuse and advanced syphilis, making him prone to outbreaks of explosive violence. On February 3, 1928, Miller was indicted for killing one Minneapolis policeman and wounding another, but the charges were ultimately dropped for lack of evidence.

By that time, Miller was recognized in the Midwestern underworld as a gun for hire to bootleg gangs and other racketeers. In 1930, after a friend of Miller's was killed by members of Al Capone's gang in Chicago, the ex-lawman took it upon himself to exact revenge. On June 1 he trailed three suspects to a resort hotel at Fox Lake, Illinois, and killed them with a barrage of submachine-gun fire. Survivors of the Bugs Moran gang were initially suspected in the killings, thus allowing Miller to escape retaliation from Capone.

As the beer wars wound down in Chicago, Miller looked around for other criminal pursuits that fit his personality and settled on bank robbery. His first known holdup, netting $70,000 from a Willmar, Minnesota, bank on July 15, 1930, saw him teamed with HARVEY BAILEY, THOMAS HOLDEN, FRANCIS KEATING, GEORGE "MACHINE GUN" KELLY, and at least three others for a daring daylight raid. A month later, on August 13, Miller quarreled with fellow gang members over some alleged "double-cross" resulting from the heist. In a fit of rage, he killed the three offenders—Frank "Weinie" Coleman, Mike Rusick, and Sammy Silverman (aka Jew Sammy Stein)—and dumped their bodies at White Bear Lake.

The lethal outburst did not seem to trouble Miller's surviving partners in crime. On September 9, 1930, he joined Bailey, Holden, Keating, Kelly, and LAWRENCE DE VOL to lift $40,000 from a bank in Ottumwa, Iowa. Another 40 grand was bagged on April 8, 1931, when Miller struck a Sherman, Texas, bank with Bailey, Kelly, FRANK "JELLY" NASH, and others. After Sherman, Verne apparently retired from bank jobs to resume his career as a contract killer, but he kept in touch with old friends, always willing to help out if there was money to be made.

Miller's most infamous crime was undoubtedly the KANSAS CITY MASSACRE of June 17, 1933. On that date, joined by at least two other gunmen, he attempted to liberate captive Frank Nash from the custody of police and FBI agents transporting him from Arkansas to complete an interrupted prison term at Leavenworth. When the smoke cleared at Union Station, Nash and four lawmen were dead, and two other federal agents were wounded. Every major outlaw in the region was suspected of involvement in the slaughter, but G-men finally identified Verne Miller, ADAM RICHETTI, and CHARLES "PRETTY BOY" FLOYD as the gunmen responsible.

At least in Miller's case, they were correct.

Verne fled to the east coast, hiding out with members of the Abner "Longy" Zwillman mob in New Jersey until his temper got the best of him and

sparked another senseless murder. Miller left Orange, New Jersey, for Chicago on October 24, 1933, posing as a salesman for an optical supply house. By October 31 he was settled into the Windy City apartment of girlfriend Vi Mathis, but FBI agents raided the flat next morning. Miller shot his way clear of the trap, but he was running out of time.

On November 29, 1933, Verne Miller's bullet-riddled body was recovered from a roadside ditch a few miles from Detroit. It was a classic gangland execution, but the motive has remained a subject of debate. Was Miller killed for murdering a member of the Zwillman gang a month earlier? Had Capone's outfit finally nailed him for the Fox Lake massacre of 1930? Was his execution payback for the bungled Kansas City "rescue" of Frank Nash?

It made no difference in the end. Verne Miller had so many enemies that it was difficult to list them all, and no one mourned his passing. He was buried at White Lake, South Dakota, on December 6, 1933.

MILLER, William "Billy the Killer"

A native of Ironton, Ohio, born in 1906, William Miller earned his lethal nickname at age 19 by killing his brother Joseph in a fight over a woman. The slaying occurred on September 18, 1925, in Beaver County, Pennsylvania, but jurors at Miller's murder trial believed he had suffered enough from the loss of his sibling, voting to acquit him on all charges.

The near-miss failed to make an impression on "Billy the Killer." In August 1930 he was arrested in Lakeside, Michigan, and charged with several robberies that spanned the Wolverine State and Ohio. He escaped from jail in Lucas County, Ohio, on September 2, running all the way to Oklahoma and a working partnership with bandits GEORGE BIRDWELL and CHARLES "PRETTY BOY" FLOYD.

The trio stole $3,000 from an Earlsboro, Oklahoma, bank on March 9, 1931, Floyd and Miller striking off for Kansas City while Birdwell remained on more familiar turf. In Kansas City the boys were drawn to a pair of sisters, Rose Ash and Beulah Baird. Unfortunately, Rose was married and Beulah was dating her brother-in-law. Miller and Floyd solved the domestic problem on March 25, executing jealous brothers William and Wallace Ash, leaving their corpses in a car parked on the city's outskirts. Neither of the women seemed to mind; they instantly decamped with Floyd and Miller, hitting the highway with their outlaw paramours.

197

On April 6, 1931, Floyd and Miller stole $2,262 from a bank at Elliston, Kentucky. Eight days later in Whitehouse, Ohio, they cracked another bank for $1,600. Their luck ran out in Bowling Green on April 16 when police recognized Billy Miller on the street and a shootout erupted. Floyd came to Miller's aid, killing Patrolman Ralph Castner in the exchange of fire, but Miller was dead when the smoke cleared. Beulah Baird was also wounded in the crossfire and was arrested with her sister on a charge of harboring fugitives from justice.

MITCHELL, Henry Randolph

A daring gambler who loved to bet the ponies, Henry Mitchell passed a fair amount of time at racetracks, where the regulars knew him as "Little Mitch." Unfortunately, Mitchell rarely backed a winner, and his quest for cash propelled him into crime. In early January 1948 he was released from prison on completion of a 10-year term in Florida, where he had been convicted of grand larceny and burglary. He should have gone straight, but the nags were running at Hialeah, and Little Mitch had never been much good at staying out of trouble.

On January 21, with an accomplice at his side, Mitchell celebrated his release from prison with a visit to the Perkins State Bank in Williston, Florida. Brandishing pistols, the bandits walked out with $10,353, becoming instant fugitives under the federal bank-robbery statutes.

Mitchell's accomplice was captured soon after the crime, but Henry was still at large when the FBI's "Ten Most Wanted" list was created in March 1950. Posted as number four on the original roster, he became the first of the worst to confound federal agents. The fugitive warrant against Mitchell was dismissed on July 18, 1958, after eight years and four months of fruitless searching. "Little Mitch" would have been 63 years old at the time, and an FBI spokesman in his hometown of Louisville, Kentucky, conceded that dismissal of the warrant "might mean he was dead."

MOLINA, Ramon

A 32-year-old resident of Indianapolis, Indiana, Ramon Molina logged his first arrest in February 2000 after a domestic argument turned violent. Police responding to a neighbor's call found Molina's 30-year-old wife unconscious in the couple's apartment and delivered her to a local hospital. There, upon regaining consciousness, Joaquin Molina said that her husband had choked her and forced her to swallow a handful of prescription medicine. Empty pill bottles and bruises on her throat confirmed the story, landing Molina in jail on charges of battery and criminal confinement. He made bail, facing a court date on March 14, 2000, but Molina had spent his last night in custody.

Unknown to Hoosier lawmen at the time of his arrest for wife beating, Molina was a serial bank robber who was responsible for eight Indianapolis holdups since October 1999. His spree had begun on October 2 with the robbery of a Bank One branch on East Washington Street. He next surfaced on October 29, robbing First Indiana Bank on West 86th Street, and he then rebounded to hit a Bank One branch on the same street one day later. Bank One was again the target on December 13, 1999, when Molina looted the branch at Keystone Crossing. On January 5, 2000, he scored a triple play, robbing two branches of National City Bank and a Union Planters Bank on the same day. Another Union Planters branch, this one four blocks away from Molina's first score on West 86th Street, was robbed on January 28.

Police and FBI manhunters had surveillance video footage of Molina in action, but they had so far failed to recognize him thanks to various disguises that included baseball caps, wigs, fake beards, and an occasional sling for one arm. Likewise, while witnesses had described his turquoise compact car, no one had recorded the license-plate number. The phantom bandit never displayed a weapon during any of his holdups, but he was fond of making sinister comments, such as "Death is here. Make it wait."

At 9:15 A.M. on March 10, 2000, Molina entered the CIB Bank on Emerson Way, Indianapolis, and leaped over the cashier's counter. He produced a plastic bag and ordered a teller to fill it with money, but the teller claimed she could not open the cash drawers. Frustrated, the robber grabbed a money bag from one of the bank's customers and fled to his waiting car. An alert was broadcast, and police quickly spotted Molina's turquoise Mitsubishi compact, speeding along 56th Street. Two squad cars followed the bandit home to his apartment house on Emerson Way, where the officers called for his surrender. Instead, Molina drew a snub-nosed revolver and killed himself with a shot to the head.

Investigators found the stolen money bag in Molina's car, compared his likeness to their surveillance pictures from previous robberies, and soon closed the case. Official estimates described Molina's take from eight holdups as "at least $25,000."

MONTONEROS: Terrorist robbers

A TERRORIST group confined to Argentina, organized in 1970, the Montoneros initially supported a return from exile of deposed dictator Juan Perón. Upon Perón's return to power in 1974, however, the group found itself dissatisfied with his performance, escalating its terrorist assaults on the Argentine government and foreign investors. Operating without international links or foreign support, the Montoneros supported themselves with a vigorous campaign of bank robbery and ransom kidnappings. By 1976 terrorist violence in Argentina had reached such a state that authorities responded with a no-holds-barred "dirty war," effectively suspending civil liberties and waging ruthless campaigns that effectively dissolved the movement.

MONTOS, Nick George

Born in Tampa, Florida, in 1916, Montos was first arrested at age 14, receiving brief probation on a charge of possessing stolen property. In 1934 he drew a prison term of 18 months for auto theft, and two years later he escaped from the Miami jail where he had been confined for owning burglar's tools. Recaptured quickly, he was sentenced to a year in Raiford prison. On release he moved to Alabama, swiftly racking up convictions there for burglary and grand larceny. Sentenced to the road gang, Montos made an unsuccessful break for freedom, winding up in Kilby Prison near Montgomery. At Kilby, Montos picked up further training with machinery and tools, while stamping license plates. Unwilling to complete the course, he fled from custody on October 20, 1942, and was recaptured as a federal fugitive in June 1943.

Returned to Kilby, Montos staged another break in February 1944. Four other inmates joined him as he propped a ladder up against the prison wall and scrambled clear. Police arrested him in Illinois, suspecting him in a string of burglaries, and shipped him back to Alabama—where, incredibly, he won parole in 1949. Arrested for a burglary in Anniston, he bargained down to a charge of possessing burglar's tools and escaped with a $500 fine. Moving to Georgia, Montos was indicted for a Coweta County burglary and jumped bond before the case was called for trial. A March 1951 burglary in Hattiesburg,

Mississippi, saw him convicted, but that case was on appeal when Montos earned himself a nomination to the FBI's "Most Wanted" list.

On August 11, 1951, Montos and two cronies entered the home that 74-year-old Render Carter shared with his 65-year-old sister near Alma, Georgia. Both elderly victims were bound and the old man cruelly pistol-whipped before the thieves ransacked their home and stole $1,000. As they fled, the woman managed to untie herself and telephoned police, resulting in a hot pursuit. Near Waycross, Montos and a habitual criminal named Robert Mathus bailed out of the speeding car. Their wheelman subsequently lost control and was captured when he rolled the vehicle.

By summer 1952 the FBI knew Montos and a mistress, traveling as "Mr. and Mrs. James Lewis," had been sighted in Chicago. A raiding party missed the fugitive in June when Nick abandoned his apartment suddenly, without informing neighbors he was leaving. Added to the Top Ten list September 8, he was the subject of reports that placed him anywhere from Texas to the isle of Puerto Rico. None of the reports were accurate. In fact, by early 1953 the fugitive had run back to Chicago.

Nick's old accomplice from the Georgia robbery, Bob Mathus, had been added to the Top Ten list on March 16; he was arrested three days later in Louisiana. In April, Chicago police arrested one William Ellison for participation in a $15,000 bank job; burglar tools found in his car were covered with the fingerprints of Nick George Montos, and the hunt moved back to northern Illinois.

An auto dealer in Chicago told the FBI that he had sold a car to Montos and a woman three days prior to Ellison's arrest. The fugitive had listed an address in Caseyville, five miles from East St. Louis. Federal agents showed Nick's mug shot to the current occupants, and they in turn identified a former tenant, "Jimmy Hastings," who had occupied the house from mid-September 1952 through early April 1953.

On May 6, 1953, the missing vehicle was purchased by a used-car dealer in Reno, Nevada. Airline-ticket records tracked Montos and his lady friend, using pseudonyms, to Denver and then to Oklahoma City. In the meantime, agents in Chicago had connected Montos to a local ring of burglars that ranged far and wide to execute heists. Four members of the gang had been arrested in Kentucky with an arsenal of weapons in their car while they were robbing a bank at Fulton. In February 1954 Montos was identified as one of three men who invaded the home of a wealthy Kenosha, Wisconsin, art dealer, making off with paintings valued at $200,000. One of Nick's accomplices on that score was Chicago mobster Americo De Pietto. When the stolen artwork was recovered by authorities in Melrose Park on February 28, the loot bore fingerprints of both De Pietto and Montos.

In the spring of 1954, a friend of Montos, deportee Arthur Colucci, turned up in Chicago after illegally reentering the United States. The FBI allowed Colucci to remain at liberty, establishing surveillance on his home in the belief that Montos would eventually pay a visit to his chum. The bet paid off on August 23, and Nick surrendered peaceably when he was suddenly surrounded by a ring of weapons. Sentenced to a seven-year term for the Wisconsin art theft, Montos first owed 14 years to state and federal authorities in Mississippi for the Hattiesburg burglary. In case he ever won parole, a Georgia prosecutor put in dibs to try him for the brutal robbery of Render Carter, which had drawn life terms for Nick's accomplices.

On January 10, 1956, Montos escaped from the Mississippi prison farm at Parchman, using a hacksaw to cut through the staple securing a door latch and tossing blankets over a barbed-wire fence to make his getaway with fellow inmate Robert Jones. A federal warrant was issued next day on charges of unlawful flight to avoid confinement, and on March 9, 1956, Montos had the dubious honor of becoming the first felon ever posted twice to the FBI's "Most Wanted" list.

Publicity attendant on his two-time status numbered Nick's days of freedom. On March 29 an alert citizen in Memphis, Tennessee, recognized Montos and Jones as the same "James Harmon and party" who had recently checked into a local motel. G-men established a command post at the motel, closing in at 3:00 A.M. on March 30. Blocking the driveway with cars, 14 agents ringed the suspects' room before a telephone demand was made for their surrender. Thirty seconds later, tear gas shells were blasted through the windows, flushing out both fugitives. Inside their room, the raiders confiscated seven guns, three bottles of narcotics, body armor, and $4,300 in cash. The weapons included a sawed-off shotgun and a small-caliber weapon disguised as a pen, both held in violation of prevailing federal law.

On June 25, 1956, the fugitives appeared in federal court in Memphis. Montos entered a guilty plea to firearms and narcotics charges, drawing an eight-year prison term. Jones earned six years for posses-sion of illegal weapons. One month later, Montos went to trial in Georgia for the brutal 1952 robbery that had put him on the Top Ten list originally. Sentenced to death in that case, he won an appeal on legal technicalities and was retried in May 1957. At his second trial, Montos received a prison term of 10 to 20 years.

MORAN, Joseph P.: Underworld physician

An Illinois native, born in 1905, Dr. Joseph Moran had a fair start in private practice before he began to drink heavily and watch his better patients desert him. To make ends meet and keep his shot glass full, Moran became a "pin artist," performing illegal abortions, but he was convicted and sentenced to prison. His underworld connections served him at the time of his parole when Moran was appointed as the official physician for the Chicago Chauffeurs', Teamsters' and Helpers' Union with an office on the ground floor of the Irving Park Hotel.

By that time, Moran was a physical wreck, still addicted to booze, but shaky hands were better than none at all when a bandit or hit man was wounded in action and needed emergency care on the sly. Dr. Moran was adequate at stitching cuts and extracting bullets, his clients including JOHN "RED" HAMILTON of the DILLINGER gang, but he overreached himself in 1934 when he began to advertise himself as plastic surgeon to the stars of gangland. For a price, Moran suggested, he could permanently rid a fugitive of fingerprints or change a patient's face so radically that he could not be recognized by witnesses or law enforcers.

The beginning of the end for Doc Moran was his association with the BARKER GANG. In March 1934 Moran operated on two leaders of the violent outfit, Fred Barker and ALVIN KARPIS. The result was more akin to butchery than surgery, with little to show for the $1,250 Moran was paid. He did eradicate Karpis's fingerprints, though—so effectively, in fact, that decades later Alvin would have difficulty obtaining a passport in his native Canada.

Sloppy surgery was one thing, but Moran took his underworld ties a step further. After the Barker-Karpis gang kidnapped Minnesota banker Edward Bremer in January 1934, Moran helped move the ransom money through his office in Chicago. It may have seemed like an adventure at the time, but Moran's ego and alcoholism betrayed him six months later. Drinking with gang members at the Casino Club outside Toledo, Ohio, Moran began to throw his nonexistent weight around, telling the Barker crew, "I have you guys in the palm of my hand."

What he held, in fact, was his own death warrant.

Soon after that stormy conversation—some say the same night—Doc Moran disappeared, never to be seen again. Reports vary on the manner of his execution. Alvin Karpis, in a self-serving memoir published 35 years after the fact, claimed that Moran was executed by Arthur and Fred Barker and planted in a Michigan lime pit. The tale more widely told has Fred and Karpis taking Moran on a one-way boat ride across Lake Erie. Associates of the Barker gang recalled Fred telling them, "Doc will do no more operating. The fishes probably have eat him up by now."

MORGAN, Daniel South "Mad Dan"; "Mad Dog"

A notorious Australian "BUSHRANGER," Daniel Morgan operated under so many different pseudonyms in the mid-19th century that his true identity is now obscure. During 11 years of banditry, he variously called himself "John Smith," "Billy the Native" and "Sydney Bill," along with such nicknames as "the Swagman's Friend" and "the Traveler's Friend." Morgan was no great friend of travelers encountered in his rambling, though, robbing enough of them that the law officers who hunted him dubbed their elusive prey "Mad Dan" or "Mad Dog."

Australian sources suggest that *none* of Morgan's many names were accurate. Born at Appin (near Campbelltown, New South Wales) in 1830, he was apparently the illegitimate son of a Sydney laborer named Fuller (or Fulton) and a woman named Owen (aka "The Gipsy"). How Dan Morgan acquired his "official" name is anyone's guess, but he was using it on April 18, 1854, when he robbed a traveling peddler near Castlemaine. Arrested at East Charlton on May 7, Morgan was tried before Judge Redmond Barry—who condemned EDWARD "NED" KELLY 26 years later—and received a 12-year prison term, the first two years to be served in irons aboard the grounded ship *Success*. Paroled on June 23, 1860, Morgan was declared a fugitive after two short months of freedom for failure to report.

Morgan apparently went straight, more or less, for the next 14 months, breaking wild horses—and stealing his favorites—on a ranch in Victoria's Kings River district. Known as "Down-the-River Jack" during this period, "Jack" ran afoul of the law in

August 1861 when two squatters—Edmund Bond and Evan Evans—trailed a stolen horse to his cave and found Morgan asleep. Asking no questions, Evans fired a shotgun blast, wounding Morgan with 27 pellets, but he still escaped to New South Wales. Still trading on his "strange affinity with horses," Morgan spent the best part of two years rustling livestock and breaking wild ponies for sale to legitimate buyers.

Morgan's return to full-time "bushranging" apparently dated from June 17, 1863, when he robbed three travelers at Walla Walla, followed by the holdup of seven more locals near Germantown the next day. On July 29 he stopped at Wallandool station, tying three residents to trees before he looted the store. Enhancing Morgan's reputation as a SOCIAL BANDIT was the claim that the Wallandool station robbery sprang from revenge against merchants who cheated employees or mistreated homeless "swagmen" (drifters). Various accounts claim that "during the remainder of [Morgan's] lifetime, few stations turned any traveler or swagman away" from their doors without an offer of hospitality.

On August 13, 1863, Morgan and companion "German Bill" encountered police magistrate Henry Baylis on the highway between Wagga Wagga and Urana. Baylis recognized the outlaws and eluded the bandits' pursuit to find refuge on a nearby ranch. Rallying a posse, Baylis overtook the pair on August 26, and German Bill was fatally wounded, his body found in the desert two days later. Magistrate Baylis, for his part, was seriously wounded by return fire from Morgan but recovered after a painful convalescence.

On the night of August 27, 1863, a shepherd (and suspected police informer) named Haley was murdered in his hut on Urangelline Creek. Authorities blamed Morgan for the crime, despite a total lack of evidence. Mad Dan's reputation was further enhanced with the November 1863 invasion of Walla Walla station, where he questioned employees about their working conditions and told the proprietor "that it was reported the men on the station were not properly treated. If no amendment took place, he declared his intention of avenging the men."

A short time later, still in the first week of November, Morgan stole expensive horses from Burrumbuttock and Kidston's stations and then stopped at Bulgandry station and forced the owner to write out £30 checks for each of his employees. (A messenger reached the Albury bank in time to stop payment on the checks.) Near the end of November, after Mittagong station proprietor Isaac Vincent voiced his desire to meet Morgan, Mad Dan paid a visit and burned Vincent's woolshed, afterward forcing the station's cook to whip up a feast for the shearers.

In early January 1864 Morgan and two accomplices robbed a Corowa storekeeper. On January 22 Morgan stole a horse from Round Hill station, dropping out of sight until he robbed the Germantown-Tumbarumba mail on April 12, escaping on a horse stolen from Jerilderie. A £500 reward was posted for his capture, but he was still at large on June 19, 1864, when he invaded Round Hill station with two companions. Drunk and showing off with pistols, Morgan accidentally wounded two bystanders in the hand and the knee, respectively. Neighbor John Heriot was sent to fetch a doctor from Walla Walla, but Morgan grew suspicious after Heriot departed and pursued him, overtaking the rider as he turned toward Germanton and the authorities. Morgan shot Heriot and carried him back to the station where he soon died. The reward for Morgan's capture doubled to £1,000.

Six days after the Round Hill station murder, on June 24, Morgan met two police officers on the Tumbarumba road, killing Sergeant David McGinnity in an exchange of pistol fire. Posses combed the countryside for Morgan, but he always stayed one step ahead of his pursuers, fatally ambushing Senior Sergeant Smyth near Doodle Cooma Swamp on September 3, 1864.

WANTED posters issued on Morgan described him in early 1865 as "35 years of age, 5 feet 10 inches high, long black hair, long beard with brown tinge on points, long nose, very sharp and straight down face, sallow complexion with brown spots like freckles, loose jointed, seems to have weak knees, speaks slowly and quietly, lost top of third finger of right hand, the nail growing over it, tumour about the size of a pigeon's egg on back of head." Even that remarkable description failed to pin him down however, and Morgan resurfaced near Kyemba on January 15, 1865, robbing a group of road contractors and their Chinese laborers, afterward burning their tents and shooting one Chinese in the arm. In rapid succession he then robbed two mail shipments near Albury, held up two peddlers at Pulletop, and cut the telegraph lines outside Sydney.

Ten weeks of fruitless searching ensued, capped by reports that Morgan had surfaced in Victoria, publicly threatening to "take the flashness out of the Vic-

torian police." No raids were forthcoming, however, until he stole a horse at Tallangatta, New South Wales, and rode on to rob McKinnon's station at Tarwonga on April 5, 1865. One day later he raided the spread of Evan Evans—who had wounded Morgan back in August 1861—and torched the squatter's haystacks. Riding northwestward, he stopped at Warby's farm near Wangaratta on April 8, forcing the family to cook him breakfast. Evening found him at Peechelba station where he spent the night. A female tenant, Alice Keenan, slipped out to summon police, and the farm was surrounded by morning with "Mad Dan" trapped inside.

Morgan was unaware of lawmen waiting for him as he left the house at 8:00 A.M. on April 9. Despite a standing order not to fire, one of the officers shot him on sight, and he died several hours later. Vengeful police then mutilated Morgan's corpse, one officer flaying the dead outlaw's face (for which he received "a severe reprimand"), while another took Morgan's scrotum for a tobacco pouch. Though buried in an unmarked grave on the outskirts of Wangaratta cemetery, Morgan retained enough admirers in death that his grave was kept tended, and law officers were periodically forced to uproot shrubs and flowers planted in the dead of night. Private parties bought Morgan a headstone in 1911, whereupon local authorities countered the show of respect by erecting a public toilet on his grave.

MORSET, Palmer Julius

Arrested for the first time in Nebraska on a 1922 charge of horse theft, Palmer Morset drew a term of one to two years in state prison. The charge in 1928 in Illinois was robbery; one year to life in Joliet was Morset's sentence. Paroled in 1935, a violation sent him back to jail in 1938. He was released again in May 1940, but the horse-thief-turned-robber showed no signs of going straight.

In early 1950 Morset was connected to a string of holdups in Chicago, victimizing finance companies. With an accomplice, he was captured on March 20 while attempting to escape from their latest job. With officers in close pursuit, the bandits wrecked their car and were arrested as they tried to flee on foot. In March 1951 Morset's bond was forfeited when he failed to appear for trial. Unlawful flight would be the federal charge, and Morset's name was added to the FBI's "Most Wanted" list on February 7, 1955.

By that time, Morset had been hiding out in Indianapolis for nearly four years, and he had another year of freedom left. Living as "Thomas Rooney," joined by his wife, the fugitive found work as a salesman for a local manufacturer of water softeners. From all appearances he had sworn off crime and had settled down to be a model of domestic mediocrity.

It almost worked.

The FBI would not explain precisely how it traced Morset at last. Leonard Blaylock, special agent in charge for Indianapolis, credited "investigative procedures" when Morset was seized at his home on March 2, 1956. For his part, Morset seemed relieved. "I knew it was going to happen," he said. "I am tired of running. I'm glad it's over."

"MOTHER of Outlaws": State of Missouri

The Show-Me State's intimate relationship with "disorganized crime" spans more than a century, beginning in the days of America's sectional strife before the Civil War and continuing into the Great Depression of the 1930s. Along the way, Missouri spawned more than its share of badmen—and badwomen, too—creating what historian Paul Wellman called "a veritable dynasty of outlaws," inextricably linked "not by blood, but by a long and crooked train of unbroken personal connections, and a continuing criminal heritage and tradition handed down from generation to generation."

And, as we shall see, there was a fair number of blood relations, too.

Missouri's history of violent crime rightly begins in 1820 with a congressional debate over slavery that climaxed with the Missouri Compromise. Under terms of that agreement, Missouri was admitted to the Union as a slave state, while human bondage was banned in the new state of Maine and in all future states north of latitude 36°30'. That uneasy truce was broken in 1854, with passage of the Kansas-Nebraska Act, abolishing the 36°30' deadline for slavery while permitting residents of the Kansas and Nebraska territories to decide the issue for themselves. Predictably, Free-Soilers rushed to Kansas from the North, while residents of Missouri and various southern states rode north to cast their votes for slavery. The result was a grim preview of America's Civil War that saw the strife-torn territory nicknamed Bleeding Kansas.

Kansas kept bleeding through secession of the Confederate states and the outbreak of civil war in April 1861, racked by a series of cross-border raids conducted by guerrillas variously known as Missouri ruffians or Kansas Jayhawkers and Red Legs. Chief among the Confederate raiders was WILLIAM CLARKE QUANTRILL, a career criminal and psychopath whose unsanctioned cavalry unit served as a training ground for notorious postwar bandits including the YOUNGER BROTHERS and their first cousins, brothers FRANK and JESSE JAMES. Following Quantrill's August 1863 raid on Lawrence, Kansas, where more than 140 unarmed men and boys were executed in cold blood, Union authorities deepened Missouri's well of hatred by forcibly driving Confederate sympathizers from their homes in the border counties of Jackson, Cass, Bates, and Vernon. Quantrill's men retaliated for the harsh reprisals with new atrocities—including the September 1964 raid on Centralia, Missouri, which witnessed America's first known incident of TRAIN ROBBERY.

Cessation of hostilities in April 1865 meant nothing to Quantrill's Missouri guerrillas. Though Quantrill himself was killed two months later, the James-Younger gang remained active with various other alumni of the border wars. Jesse and Frank "invented" daylight bank robbery with a raid at Liberty, Missouri, on February 14, 1866; other holdup targets in the gang's home territory included the Kansas City fairgrounds (September 1872), a bank in Sainte Genevieve (May 1873), another bank at Gads Hill (January 1874), plus trains robbed at Otterville (July 1876) and Glendale (October 1879). PINKERTON detectives lost three of their own and at least one civilian collaborator while stalking the James-Younger gang in Clay County during 1874–75, but they succeeded only in winning more sympathy for the bandits by bombing the James home in a nocturnal raid. Turncoat Bob Ford finally killed Jesse James at his home in St. Joseph on April 3, 1882, and collected the outstanding reward.

By that time, Missouri's outlaw tradition was too well entrenched to be rooted out by even the most determined manhunters. Some of the state's wayward sons gained notoriety only after they moved west—like the train-robbing MCCARTY brothers, Bill, George, and Tom, who served as mentors for a young BUTCH CASSIDY. Cassidy's "WILD BUNCH," in turn, made room for such Missouri stalwarts as the deadly Logan brothers—Harvey, John, and Lonny. Another infamous Missourian was Nick Ray, gunned down in Wyoming with "King of the Rustlers" Nate Champion.

A unique product of the Missouri border wars, Myra Belle Shirley was raised at Carthage, where her father ran an inn and sometimes sheltered Quantrill's raiders. It may have been here that Myra first met Cole Younger, but their early flirtation was broken off when the Shirley clan left Missouri in 1863, following brother Ed's death in a skirmish with Union soldiers near Sarcoxie. Resettled in Texas, Myra was barely 18 in 1866 when Cole Younger sought her out and reportedly fathered a daughter named Pearl out of wedlock. Nine years later, Myra set up housekeeping with Jim Reed, a cousin of the James brothers and an occasional member of their bank-robbing gang. Myra's tenure as common-law aunt to the James Boys was brief; by 1880 she was found in Oklahoma, living with outlaw "husband" Sam Starr. There, as Belle Starr, she went on to name her settlement Younger's Bend, establishing it as a refuge for bandits and rustlers.

Back in Missouri, meanwhile, hard-working Louis Dalton had married Adeline Younger, an aunt of the lawless brothers, and raised a brood of 13 children. All but four of those were honest like their parents, but the DALTON BROTHERS who went bad—Grat, Bill, Bob, and Emmett—were notorious enough to make the family name synonymous with banditry. As with the James-Younger gang at Northfield, Minnesota, in 1876, the Daltons met disaster when they left their home state, gunned down in an attempt to rob two banks at Coffeyville, Kansas, in October 1892. A survivor of the gang who missed that fatal raid, BILL DOOLIN, organized his own team of "long riders" who ranged across three states, including a $15,000 bank robbery at Southwest City, Missouri, in 1894 (killing former state auditor J. C. Seaborn) and a train heist at Dover in May 1895.

Another son of Missouri who hit the outlaw trail in the late 19th century was Marion Hedgepeth, a Kansas City delinquent and safecracker who pulled a seven-year sentence at the Jefferson City state prison in 1883. On his release in 1890, Hedgepeth put a gang together and tried his hand at TRAIN ROBBERY. His first job, in Omaha, netted only $1,000 on November 4, 1890. The gang did better on November 12, lifting $5,000 from a train near Chicago, but Hedgepeth did best on familiar ground, stealing $25,000 from a train at Glendale, Missouri, on November 30. That stake carried him all the way to California, but he was captured in San Francisco on February 10, 1891 and was returned to Missouri for trial and a 12-year sentence to state prison. Hedgepeth's last appearance in headlines was occasioned by his marginal involvement with swindler and serial killer Herman Mudgett (aka "H. H. Holmes") as part of an insurance scam that turned to murder. After years of being tight-lipped with police, Hedgepeth grew angry after Mudgett stiffed him on his payoff from a swindle and contributed information that would help land Mudgett in jail (where he later confessed close to 30 murders and was hanged).

By the time the Daltons and Bill Doolin met their bloody fates, a new generation of Missouri outlaws was already waiting in the wings. Arizona Donnie Clark was born near Springfield in 1872 and later married in Missouri; as Kate "Ma" BARKER she bore four sons between 1899 and 1903, all of them brutal and addicted to the lure of stolen cash. Joplin, Missouri, was a recognized underworld haven in those days, second only to ST. PAUL, MINNESOTA, as a wide-open hoodlum sanctuary. Herman Barker was arrested there for highway robbery in March 1915. A friend of Herman's, future "Tri-State Terror" WILBUR UNDERHILL, was picked up for a Joplin burglary in February 1919, while Arthur "Dock" Barker was charged with a local jailbreak 12 months later. CHARLES "PRETTY BOY" FLOYD pulled his first known holdup in St. Louis, bagging a modest $55 in August 1925. Sixteen months later, Herman Barker and sidekick Ray Terrill were arrested for burglarizing a bank in Jasper, Missouri.

The Great Depression of the 1930s brought bank-robbing gangs their greatest notoriety since the era of Jesse James—and Missouri remained in the thick of the action. A sampling of noteworthy events from the period includes:

July 20, 1931: A federal Prohibition agent and an unarmed bystander were fatally wounded after liquor raiders surprised "Pretty Boy" Floyd in their raid on a suspected liquor warehouse. Floyd escaped in the confusion.

October 7, 1931: Fred Barker, ALVIN KARPIS, and others robbed a bank at Mountain View, Missouri, fleeing with an estimated $14,000.

June 17, 1932: Bandits JIM CLARK, ED DAVIS, and FRANK SAWYER were arrested at Nevada, Missouri, on suspicion of robbing a bank at Fort Scott, Kansas. In fact, that job was pulled off by the Barker-Karpis gang, while Clark, Davis and Sawyer had abandoned their plan to hold up another bank at Rich Hill, Missouri, the same afternoon. The trio were wrongly convicted of the Fort Scott robbery and sentenced to long prison terms.

July 7, 1932: Lawmen surprised fugitives THOMAS HOLDEN, FRANCIS KEATING, and HARVEY BAILEY at play on Kansas City's Old Mission Golf Course, taking the veteran bandits into custody without resistance.

November 30, 1932: CLYDE BARROW, Hollis Hale, and Frank Hardy stole $80 from a bank at Orongo, Missouri, fleeing after a shootout with guards.

January 12, 1933: Outlaws ADAM RICHETTI, AUSSIE ELLIOTT, and Edgar Dunbar lifted $3,000 from a bank at Ash Grove, Missouri.

January 31, 1933: Clyde Barrow kidnapped Patrolman Tom Persell after a routine traffic stop in Springfield, Missouri. Persell was later released without injury.

April 13, 1933: Two Joplin detectives were killed while attempting to capture the Barrow gang. Snapshots and poetry found in the gang's apartment helped elevate Bonnie and Clyde to the status of national figures.

June 17, 1933: Fugitive FRANK "JELLY" NASH and four lawmen were shot and killed at Kansas City's Union Station. VERNON MILLER was identified as the mastermind of a bungled rescue attempt, while FBI agents later named Adam Richetti and "Pretty Boy" Floyd as Miller's accomplices. Bureau files that were suppressed for six decades demonstrate that several of those killed or wounded at Union Station were accidentally shot by a careless FBI agent.

July 19, 1933: The Barrow gang battled police at the Red Crown Tourist Camp near Platte City, Missouri. Buck Barrow was mortally wounded in the exchange of fire, which also left two officers badly injured.

January 6, 1934: Wilbur Underhill was buried at Joplin after dying in an Oklahoma shootout with police.

The end of the Depression terminated Missouri's apparent love affair with outlaws, but notorious badmen still emerged from the state with some regularity. Between 1950 and 1988, at least eight felons posted to the FBI's "Ten Most Wanted" list were captured in Missouri, while nine others—including serial bank robbers GEORGE HEROUX, GERHARD PUFF, and ROBERT VAN LEWING were sought by G-men for crimes committed in the Show-Me State. The James and Younger boys remain local heroes to many Missourians, still ardently defended on grounds that lawmen "did them wrong" and thereby somehow forced them into lives of crime.

MURRAY, Edna "Rabbits"; "The Kissing Bandit"

A Depression-era female bandit who thrived on the excitement of holdups and hot pursuit, Edna Murray participated as a full partner in the robbery of several banks with her lover, VOLNEY DAVIS. Her media nickname derived from Edna's habit of kissing male robbery victims. Associates in the BARKER GANG more often called her "Rabbits," in honor of her knack for breaking out of jail.

Murray's most notorious bust-out occurred on December 13, 1932, from the women's state prison at Jefferson City, Missouri, where she was confined on a 25-year sentence for highway robbery. Soon reunited with Davis, Murray maintained a family tradition of falling for outlaws. Her sister, Doris O'Connor (aka "Vinita Stanley"), was the live-in lover of another Barker gang member, Jess Doyle.

On April 23, 1934, Murray and Davis opened their Aurora, Illinois, home to JOHN DILLINGER, HOMER VAN METER, and JOHN "RED" HAMILTON, the latter badly wounded by police following an FBI raid on the gang's vacation hideout near Rhinelander, Wisconsin. Hamilton had been rejected by Doctor JOSEPH MORAN in Chicago, and his wounds proved mortal. When he died, a short time later, Davis and Murray joined the covert funeral party, planting Hamilton's corpse in an unmarked grave.

On January 22, 1935, Murray was among the Barker gang associates indicted for conspiracy to kidnap Minnesota banker Edward Bremer for $200,000 in January 1934. Volney Davis was already in jail, but he escaped on February 7, ironically the same day that Edna was captured with Jess Doyle in Wichita, Kansas. Murray's brother, Harry C. Stanley, was convicted on March 12, 1935, of harboring Edna and sentenced to six months in the Sedgewick County jail, with a $1,000 fine. Edna was convicted with various other conspirators in the Bremer snatch on May 6, 1935, and sentenced to federal prison. Three months later, she directed FBI agents to John Hamilton's grave outside Aurora, Illinois.

MURRIETA, Joaquin

America's most famous (or infamous) Hispanic outlaw was born in 1830 at Vayoreca, an adobe village 15 miles south of Alamos, in the southern part of Mexico's Sonora state. He took his notorious surname from a stepfather in early childhood, after his real father—a farmer named Carrillo—died prematurely. In late 1848 Murrieta joined his wife and her three brothers—Claudio, Jesús, and Reyes Feliz—in migrating to California to pan for gold in the Southern Mines district.

Legend has it that Joaquin Murrieta was driven to a life of crime by heartless Anglo racists who flogged him, raped his wife, and lynched his half-brother, driving the family from its gold claim, but no such attack was recorded by California law enforcers in the gold-rush era. Rather, it was brother-in-law CLAUDIO FELIZ who first turned outlaw from simple greed in the spring of 1849. By December 1850 Feliz led California's most violent gang of HIGHWAYMEN, staging murderous raids against ranches and killing travelers for a handful of gold dust.

The violence increased after Murrieta joined the gang full time in the latter part of 1851. On November 10 the raiders waylaid a miner and his black servant near Birdwell's Bar on the Feather River, cutting their throats for two ounces of gold (worth $34). One day later, they lassoed traveler George Mather from his wagon and stabbed him to death, stealing $500. Before the afternoon was out they robbed and killed two more victims, John Gardner and C. Jenkinson, for a grim body count of five slain in two days.

Yuba County Sheriff Robert Buchanan enlisted two deputies and trailed the gang to a point south of Marysville on November 12, 1851, engaging the bandits in a shootout that left Buchanan gravely wounded. He survived to hunt another day, while reinforcements jumped the gang a second time on the east bank of the Yuba River, but again the bandits shot their way clear and escaped.

In December 1851 the gang executed a suspected informer, a Mexican named Trinidad, in San Jose. They also plotted to assassinate Marshal George Whitman but failed to follow through on the scheme. Claudio Feliz was soon arrested and charged with murder, carelessly boasting of his crimes to a cellmate in San Jose, but he managed to escape from jail before the other convict spilled everything he knew in a fruitless effort to save himself from the gallows.

On April 5, 1852, Murrieta was idling with the Feliz brothers and several companions at a mining camp near Sonora when Reyes Feliz was arrested for possession of two distinctive stolen guns. Murrieta's gang ambushed the arresting party en route to Sonora, engaging in a firefight that left one gang member dead and Claudio Feliz wounded in custody; Reyes escaped in the confusion. Against all odds,

Claudio confounded his prosecutors with an acquittal at trial and was released to rendezvous with his comrades in August 1852.

Murrieta was not idle in the meantime. Three weeks after the Sonora shootout, on April 25, he led Reyes Feliz and Pedro Gonzales on a sweep through the San Joaquin Valley. They lassoed farmer Allen Ruddle from his wagon, shot him to death, and robbed his corpse of $400 before stealing 20 horses from a ranch on Orestimba Creek. A posse gave chase, but the bandits were captured by Indian tribesmen instead, relieved of their mounts, and released on foot 100 miles north of Los Angeles. Ruddle's wealthy family offered a $3,000 reward for capture of his killers, prompting bounty hunter Henry Love to take up the pursuit. Love caught Pedro Gonzales on June 16, but his outlaw companions escaped once more and hid out in Los Angeles.

Claudio Feliz came back with a vengeance in late August 1852, leading a series of raids that left at least five victims dead around Sonora and Jamestown. Surrounded by law enforcers at a hideout on the Salinas River, Claudio was killed on September 13, 1852, leaving brother Reyes and Joaquin Murrieta to lead the gang in his stead. Teamed with notorious rustler Salomon Pico, they raided ranches throughout Los Angeles County that autumn. Murrieta was also blamed for the ambush murder of Joshua Bean on November 7 at Mission San Gabriel. (Bean's younger brother, Roy, would later be famous in Texas as a "hanging judge" who dubbed himself "The Law West of the Pecos.") Joaquin evaded a vigilante dragnet on November 8, but Pico and Reyes Feliz were arrested with three other bandits. All denied killing Bean, but Feliz and Benito Lopez confessed three other slayings. Feliz was lynched on November 29; Lopez and sidekick Cipriano Sandoval were hanged without trial six days later.

Joaquin Murrieta returned to his old haunts in the southern California mining district, emerging in January 1853 as the leader of a brand-new gang. Their first raid was logged in Calaveras County, where they stole $310 in gold dust from a group of Chinese miners at San Andreas and stabbed one of their victims to death. On January 21 four more miners were robbed and killed near the scene of the previous crime. Constable Charles Ellis led a posse in pursuit on January 22, shooting it out with the gang before Murrieta and company escaped, killing miner John Carter in the skirmish. That same night—January

WILL BE
EXHIBITED
FOR ONE DAY ONLY!

AT THE STOCKTON HOUSE!
THIS DAY, AUG. 19, FROM 9 A. M. UNTIL 6 P. M.

THE HEAD
Of the renowned Bandit!

JOAQUIN!
AND THE
HAND OF THREE FINGERED JACK!
THE NOTORIOUS ROBBER AND MURDERER.

"JOAQUIN" and "THREE-FINGERED JACK" were captured by the State Rangers, under the command of Capt. Harry Love, at the Arroya Cantina, July 24th. No reasonable doubt can be entertained in regard to the identification of the head now on exhibition, as being that of the notorious robber, Joaquin Murrietta, as it has been recognized by hundreds of persons who have formerly seen him.

Joaquin Murrieta was a major attraction both in life and after his death. (Courtesy of Carl Sifakis)

22—Murrieta's gang raided a quartz mill on O'Neil Creek, killing two watchmen and suffering casualties of their own. On January 23 a party of 300 outraged miners followed blood trails to the hideout of a wounded bandit—a Mexican dubbed "Big Bill" and suspected of several murders—and hanged him on the spot. Two more suspected outlaws were spotted at Cherokee Flat; one was killed while trying to escape the mob, and his comrade was captured and lynched.

His losses failed to slow Murrieta down. Chinese miners remained favorite targets as the gang roved at will, robbing and killing two more near Angel's Camp, looting several other claims before a posse could be organized. Some of the new brutality was initiated by gang member Bernardino Garcia—aka "Three-Fingered Jack"—a psychopath who took personal pleasure in slitting the throats of Chinese victims.

On February 5, 1853, Murrieta and Garcia forced a ferryman to carry them across the Mokelmne River in Amador County. Three days later the gang raided a Chinese camp on the Consumnes River, wounding two miners and stealing some $6,000 in gold for their best score yet. Fleeing toward Jackson with a $1,000 reward on their heads, they looted two more Chinese camps for lesser sums. More raids followed on February 13 near Jackson, where the gang killed two Chinese and an Anglo miner named Joseph Lake. Manhunters overtook Murrieta's band nearby as they counted their take in a ravine. The gang lost it all in a furious shootout, forced to abandon their mounts and stolen gold as they escaped on foot. Two days later the gang was surrounded at Ophir but shot its way clear, leaving straggler Antonio Valencia behind to be lynched.

Exaggerated tales of Joaquin Murrieta's prowess quickly spread throughout the Golden State. He was said to lead a gang of 50 men, perpetually garbed in bulletproof chain mail. Some of the far-flung sightings were occasioned by simple confusion and the bandit's use of pseudonyms. At one point in late February 1853, it was believed that Murrieta's gang included no less than five bandits named Joaquin, their surnames listed on official warrants as Muriati [sic], Ocomorenia, Valenzuela, Botellier, and Carrillo. In fact, though, there were only two Joaquins—Murietta and Valenzuela—with the spare names employed to confuse Anglo law enforcers.

The gang surfaced with another flurry of activity on February 20, 1853, holding 200 Chinese at gunpoint in a camp near Rich Gulch, killing three miners, and fleeing with an estimated $10,000 in gold dust and nuggets. With the law enforcers hot on their trail, the bandits raided several more Chinese camps on February 22, leaving three victims dead and five wounded and stealing another $3,000 in gold. California's governor offered a $1,000 reward for Murrieta on February 23 after the attempted murder of an Anglo traveler at Reynold's Ferry. Finally, with daily sightings reported from Monterey to Los Angeles, the state legislature authorized creation of a ranger force to hunt Joaquin for three months, each deputy being paid $350 per month.

Harry Love led the team, beginning his search on May 17, 1853. It took nearly two months for Love's rangers to nab their first suspect, but the July 10 arrest of Jesús Feliz was worth the wait. Whether through bribery or threats, Love turned Feliz against his former comrades and persuaded him to track the gang. The end came in a flurry of gunfire on July 25 when Love's riders overtook Murrieta's band near Cantua Creek, killing Joaquin, Bernardino Garcia, and one other bandit. Posse members beheaded Murrieta and severed Garcia's famous three-fingered hand, preserving both trophies in spirits for public display. The relics found their way to a San Francisco gun shop, where they were exhibited until the great earthquake and fire of 1906 razed the block and consumed them in flames.

N

NASH, Frank "Jelly"

A determined thief whose career spanned three decades, Frank Nash was born at Birdseye, Indiana, on February 6, 1887. His family moved to Paragould, Arkansas, six years later, and his mother died there of tuberculosis in March 1899. Frank and his father moved again—to Hobart, Oklahoma—in 1902. There, his father built and ran the Nash Hotel, but Frank was driven by an urge to see the world. He joined the army in 1904 and served in the Philippines and was honorably discharged with the rank of sergeant in 1907.

It is unknown exactly when Nash turned to crime, but he logged his first arrest, for burglarizing an Oklahoma store, on May 22, 1911. Six more arrests would follow by year's end—one for each month between June and October—but none of the cases resulted in conviction. Nash managed to stay out of jail until March 6, 1913, when he shot crime partner Nollie Wortman near Elk Creek, Oklahoma. Wortman died on March 29, and Nash was convicted of his murder in August and sentenced to life at the state prison in McAlester. He was pardoned by Oklahoma's governor on July 10, 1918, to rejoin the U.S. Army, and he served with the 90th Division in France during the final months of World War I.

Frank's second tour of duty in uniform did nothing to relieve his yen for easy money. On October 18, 1919, with two accomplices, he raided a bank at Corn, Oklahoma, and blew the safe open with explosives. Arrested the following day near Tuttle,

Nash stalled his trial for nine months but could not escape the inevitable outcome. On August 4, 1920, he was sentenced to 25 years for robbery, but a lenient warden released him on December 22, 1922, granting a 60-day leave of absence for "business reasons."

The business was larceny, as Nash teamed with AL SPENCER's bank- and train-robbing gang. The outfit allegedly robbed 42 banks in 1922 and 1923, with Nash presumably joining in some of the raids. On August 20, 1923, he accompanied Spencer and five others to commit Oklahoma's most recent train robbery, near Okesa, lifting $20,000 in cash and bonds from the Katy Limited. The Katy was a U.S. Mail train, which made the holdup a federal crime. Spencer was killed by an Oklahoma posse on September 15, while Nash fled into Mexico. He returned to the United States two months later, and was arrested by U.S. Marshal Alva McDonald near Sierra Blanca, Texas, on November 9. On March 3, 1924, Nash was sentenced to 25 years at Leavenworth for mail robbery and assaulting a mail custodian.

In his years at Leavenworth, Nash met many of the veteran outlaws who would be his friends and accomplices in the last phase of his criminal career. They included HARVEY BAILEY, THOMAS HOLDEN, Francis Keating, and GEORGE "MACHINE GUN" KELLY. Despite his felonious acquaintances—admittedly difficult to avoid while serving hard time—Nash behaved as a model prisoner and was favored with a trusty's privileges. The folly of that decision was demonstrated on October 19, 1930, when he fled Leavenworth and never looked back.

Tom Holden and Francis Keating had escaped eight months earlier with aid from Nash and George Kelly. Some reports place Nash in their company, pulling various jobs, but Frank's next documented robbery occurred on April 8, 1931. That afternoon, he joined Harvey Bailey, VERNON MILLER, and a character known only as "Dutch Joe" to lift $40,000 from a bank in Sherman, Texas. George Kelly met the gang with a second getaway car at the Louisiana border, and they shook off their pursuers.

Some reports place Nash with the Holden-Keating gang on October 20, 1931, for the chaotic holdup of a bank at Menomonie, Wisconsin. The thieves made off with $10,000 in cash, but the bulk of their loot—some $120,000—proved to be nonnegotiable securities. Gunfire erupted during the holdup, and two bank employees were killed along with gang members Charlie Harmon and Frankie Webber. Two weeks later, on November 2, Nash may have been the third gunman who helped Holden and Keating steal $58,000 from two bank messengers in Duluth, Minnesota, but published sources disagree on his participation in that robbery.

Possible substantiation of the Holden-Keating link is found in ST. PAUL, MINNESOTA, where Nash joined Holden, Keating, Fred Barker, and ALVIN KARPIS for a New Year's Eve party at Harry Sawyer's Green Lantern saloon on December 31, 1931. Six months later, on June 17, 1932, Nash may have participated in the BARKER GANG's theft of $47,000 from a bank in Fort Scott, Kansas. Other reported members of the raiding party were Holden, Keating, Karpis, Fred Barker, LAWRENCE DE VOL, Vernon Miller, Harvey Bailey, and perhaps George Kelly. Three other outlaws—JIM CLARK, ED DAVIS, and FRANK SAWYER—were arrested and wrongfully convicted of the Fort Scott heist, while the Barker gang remained comfortably anonymous.

Guilty or not on the Fort Scott holdup, Frank Nash had exactly one year left to live.

Another "maybe" job for Nash occurred at Concordia, Kansas, on July 26, 1932, when an armed gang stole $240,000 in cash and bonds from a local bank. Known participants in the holdup included Fred Barker, Alvin Karpis, Lawrence De Vol, Jess Doyle, and Earl Christman, with some published accounts calling Frank Nash a member of the team.

His last known bank heist, committed on April 4, 1933, at Fairbury, Nebraska, was another bloody fiasco. Teamed with Fred and Arthur Barker, Alvin Karpis, VOLNEY DAVIS, Jess Doyle, and Earl Christman, Nash helped loot $37,000 from the bank, but another wild shootout erupted, leaving eight persons wounded. One of those was Christman, who died from his injuries several days later. Eight weeks later, on May 30, Nash was named by authorities as the probable source of several firearms smuggled into the Kansas state prison at Lansing, used in a mass escape whose participants included Harvey Bailey, BOB BRADY, WILBUR UNDERHILL, Jim Clark, Ed Davis, Frank Sawyer, and five other inmates.

Nash and his wife, Francis, left St. Paul in early June 1933, headed for wide-open Hot Springs, Arkansas. There, they lived as Mr. and Mrs. Frank Harris, Nash compounding the confusion by occasionally calling himself "Doc" Williams. It did no good because the FBI was now on his trail. On June 16 Nash was arrested in Hot Springs by two G-men and an Oklahoma police chief, Otto Reed. Frank's captors drove him to Fort Smith, where the party boarded a train to Kansas City, en route to Nash's waiting cell at Leavenworth.

Nash never made it.

He was barely out of town before his wife reached out for help from gangland cronies in Chicago. Louis Stacci pulled the strings, making arrangements with Vern Miller to meet Nash's escorts in Kansas City at Union Station and release him from custody. The net result of that attempt, memorialized in headlines as the KANSAS CITY MASSACRE, left Nash and four lawmen dead in a blaze of gunfire. FBI director J. EDGAR HOOVER correctly named Miller as one of the shooters but may have veered off into fantasy with his pursuit of suspects ADAM RICHETTI and CHARLES "PRETTY BOY" FLOYD. Floyd was eventually shot to death and Richetti hanged, but another 60 years would pass before FBI files on the massacre were opened for public scrutiny, revealing that Nash and several of the dead lawmen were actually shot by a nervous FBI agent, seated behind Nash in one of the government cars.

It was an ignominious death for one of the Depression era's leading bandits, but it made no difference in the end. Nash was buried beside his parents at Paragould, Arkansas, on June 21, 1933. Lou Stacci and three others were convicted of obstructing justice in Kansas City, each sentenced to two years in federal prison and a $10,000 fine.

NAZI Looting of Europe

Historians generally agree that Adolf Hitler and his Third Reich cronies rank among the worst mass murderers in human history. Other despots—typically Joseph Stalin and Mao Zedong—are sometimes credited with higher body counts, but no rival candidate for top "honors" can claim so many victims within a relatively short time. Stalin, after all, ruled the Soviet Union for three decades (1923–53), while Mao held sway over China from 1949 to 1976. Hitler's "Thousand Year Reich," by contrast, survived for barely 12 years, from March 1933 to April 1945.

Discussions of the Nazi role in World War II and the Holocaust typically focus on loss of human life, with estimates ranging from 12 million to 26 million victims, but many histories neglect to mention that Hitler's regime also perpetrated the greatest armed robbery of all time, looting a score of nations for a haul that included tons of gold and silver, stocks and currency, precious gems by the crate, artwork and antiques, real property, and raw materials—even the clothing, eyeglasses, and dental fillings of individual victims. More than six decades after the rampage began, authorities still disagree on the final tabulation, and much of the Nazi loot remains missing.

Hitler himself sprang from humble beginnings to cultivate staggering greed. His salary as chancellor of Germany (briefly refused before Der Führer changed his mind) amounted to only DM60,000, but personal expenditures by Hitler of DM305 million are documented between 1933 and 1945, with the true total doubtless much higher. A mediocre artist in his youth, Hitler spent millions of Deutsch marks on artwork—including da Vinci's *Leda and the Swan* and Reubens's *Madonna with Child*—before his troops began in 1938 to steal every painting they could find. In 1933 alone, Hitler earned DM1,232,335 from various unofficial sources, including sales of *Mein Kampf* and his controlling interest in the Ehr Publishing Company, which owned 50 percent of all German newspapers in 1933 (90 percent by 1944). Ehr Publishing alone was worth DM10 billion at the height of Hitler's power—about $20 billion at modern rates.

Hitler would never be content with a legitimate paycheck, though, any more than he was content to rule Germany alone. His first victims, as forecast in the pages of *Mein Kampf*, were the Jews whose combined property holdings in Germany, Austria, and the Sudetenland were valued between DM10 billion and DM12 billion (between $2.5 billion and $3 billion). Between 1933 and 1938, as racist legislation progressively excluded Jews from the various professions, many sold their businesses and homes to "Aryans" at punitive discounts and fled the Reich (after paying an "escape tax" to the Nazi government). Others deposited the bulk of their savings in theoretically neutral Swiss banks, where the accounts would later be frozen and stripped from their owners. By December 1935, an estimated 40 to 50 percent of all Jewish businesses in Germany had been liquidated, an "Aryan" farmer in Franconia gloating after he purchased a synagogue for the paltry sum of DM700. After the *Kristallnacht* pogrom of November 1938 and Hermann Göring's announcement of a program "to exclude the Jews from the economic life of Germany," most were stripped of their remaining property without any pretense of compensation.

At the same time, a Nazi revolution was under way in the German art world. Hitler's regime considered any non-Germanic works "degenerate" and unworthy of respect—but that opinion never stopped high-ranking Nazis from turning a profit on art they despised. In 1935, Berlin art dealer Karl Haberstock sold various French impressionist works purged from German museums to an unnamed "important" French buyer for DM5 million; another purge two years later brought Haberstock another fortune, including sales to Jewish collectors in France who would later be robbed of their purchases by Nazi occupation troops. An auction at Lucerne, Switzerland, on June 30, 1939 featured 126 paintings and sculptures by "degenerate" artists including Braque, van Gogh, Picasso, Klee, Matisse, Kokoschka, and 33 others, purged from nine major German museums. The auction raised SFR500,000, immediately converted into British pounds sterling and banked in London for the benefit of Nazi leaders, while the contributing museums got nothing. Hitler, Göring, and other top Nazis were busy compiling personal art collections, meanwhile, with Göring's plunder so well organized by 1937 that he threatened to outstrip the Führer in extravagance.

Germany's first major conquest, albeit virtually bloodless, was the invasion and annexation of Austria on March 13, 1938. Jewish property with a declared value of RM8 billion ($2 billion) was mostly left behind by owners who escaped—and many were not fortunate enough to get away with what little they could carry. Baron Louis de Rothschild was arrested while trying to flee the country, 919 priceless paintings seized by the SS from his

Vienna collection. Brother Alphonse de Rothschild lost even more, a total of 3,444 paintings and art objects confiscated by the Nazis. Gentile collectors and gallery owners benefited along with the occupying army: Some 10 percent of all acquisitions by Viennese galleries between 1938 and 1950 came from Jewish owners, either sold for a pittance in haste or stolen outright. By the summer of 1939, 18,800 Jewish businesses in Austria had been closed or confiscated, including 606 factories. Owners who were paid anything received RM35 billion less than the fair market value of their property; the rest were simply robbed at gunpoint. Drunken Nazis burglarized Sigmund Freud's Vienna apartment, stealing $12,000 in cash; when he died in September 1939, the Nazis helped themselves to another $375,000 bequeathed for the maintenance of his four sisters. (All four were later murdered in the Holocaust.)

Czechoslovakia was next on Germany's hit list, with the Sudetenland formally annexed on September 30, 1938, and occupied the following day. Widespread plunder was already in progress by the time Hitler dissolved greater Czechoslovakia on March 14, 1939, with looted Jewish property alone valued between $600 million and $1 billion. By 1940, Czech Jews were required to declare any property worth more than 10,000 crowns ($300), with said property seized and stored at 60 repositories scattered around Prague. Jewish bank accounts were frozen and then looted by Nazis, with more than 30 million crowns ($1 million) siphoned off to the Reichsprotektor's account in Prague during one three-week period of 1941 alone. In Slovakia, where Jews owned 44 percent of all real estate, 23 percent of all businesses, and 33 percent of capital investments, the Nazis liquidated 10,025 firms within a year of occupation, selling off 2,223 to "Aryan" buyers.

In the summer of 1939, Hitler ordered Dresden museum curator Hans Posse to "build up the new art museum for Linz Donau" by any means available—in effect creating a vast collection of art works for the Führer's personal enjoyment and profit. An order issued on July 24, 1939, declared that Posse and his scavengers had first claim on any art confiscated or "safeguarded" in occupied lands. On his first flying tour of Vienna, Posse took 182 paintings for Linz and 87 more for other Nazi collections in Germany. By July 1940 Posse had collected 474 priceless paintings, and the end was nowhere in sight.

Hitler's conquests thus far had been unopposed by Britain or France, but his next move—the invasion of Poland on September 1, 1939—would officially spark World War II. Plunder was essential now, second only to the mass murder of Jews in Hitler's mind, because Germany had already expended its $120 million prewar gold reserves and most of Austria's as well. Warsaw Jews owned 40 percent of the city's residential real estate in 1939, with Jewish firms employing 40 percent of Poland's industrial labor force nationwide—all ripe for the taking as Germany's blitzkrieg advanced, dividing the nation with Russian invaders from the east. More than 700,000 Polish homes and farms were seized by Nazis for the benefit of "Aryan" invaders. In the Lødz district, Germans seized control of 70 banks, 3,500 textile shops and factories, and some 8,500 retail shops—all stolen without compensation to their rightful owners. Polish farmers who retained their land were compelled to fork over half of their grain to feed their oppressors. In all, Jewish property valued between $2 billion and $3 billion was stolen by Nazis during their occupation of Poland.

Poland's collapse also prompted leaders of Bulgaria, Hungary, and Romania to ally themselves with the Axis powers, collaborating with German forces in the wholesale theft of Jewish property valued between $1.4 billion and $3.4 billion. In Hungary, all Jewish business were closed, and any assets valued above 3,000 Pengös ($300) were confiscated, along with all vehicles, radios, and telephones. When German occupation troops eventually fled the country, they took with them 24 boxcars of Jewish property, including 88 sacks of precious metals, 630 kilos of "worn" gold objects (including dental fillings taken from murdered Jews), 12 kilos of diamonds larger than three carats each, 65 kilos of smaller diamonds, 2,700 carpets, plus carloads of porcelain, silver, watches, and various art objects.

Art was a primary target of Nazi looters in Poland, as elsewhere. Within a week of the invasion, SS troops seized a repository of classic Veit Stoss sculptures, received in Berlin by the first week of October 1939. Extensive looting of Polish homes and museums proceeded apace with the occupation, spearheaded by a team of German art historians working under Göring confidant Dr. Kajetan Mühlmann. By the winter of 1940 Mühlmann's raiders had stolen the most important artworks in Poland, stashing them in Krakow and publishing an elegant catalog of their booty. Lesser works were held in reserve or handed directly to new Polish governor Hans Frank (Hitler's former defense attorney).

Hitler's next target was Norway, invaded by German shock troops on April 9, 1940. Looting of Jewish property began at once, belatedly legalized by the Quisling puppet government on October 26, 1942. Norwegian police were used by their German conquerors to conduct most of the raids, including 1,381 documented seizures of personal property. Estate files were maintained in 1,053 of those cases, making it impossible for the other 328 victims or their heirs to file postwar claims for recovery. Denmark, invaded the same day as Norway, surrendered to Hitler without resistance, its small gold reserve instantly absorbed by the Reich and shipped back to Berlin, while Jewish property was looted in the now-familiar pattern.

A month and one day after the Norway invasion, on May 10, 1940, Hitler's blitzkrieg was turned against the Low Countries of Belgium, Holland, and Luxembourg. Nazis seized 161 tons of gold in Holland, valued at $1 million per ton, and shipped most of it to banks in neutral countries. Jewish property valued between $300 million and $510 million stood ripe for plunder in Holland alone, where Nazis followed the Norwegian pattern, dragooning native police to rob the homes of 140,000 Jews. In the first year of occupation, 16.9 million cubic feet of personal belongings were stolen from 17,235 apartments, whose Jewish tenants had either fled in advance of the invasion or had been deported eastward to their deaths. On the banking front, Jewish accounts were blocked, each family permitted maximum withdrawals of 250 guilders per month. Even those paltry withdrawals were banned by the end of 1942—although Jews were still permitted to *deposit* cash, if they desired, for the benefit of their persecutors. A reported 25 million guilders ($130 million) was collected at one bank and stolen by Nazis in 1940; by 1942 the sum at that one bank had risen to 213 million guilders ($1 billion). A spring 1942 decree required Dutch Jews to surrender all remaining valuables for "storage" under German care, including coins, bonds, jewelry, stamp collections, artwork, and antiques. Most of the stocks, valued at some 350 million guilders, were quickly sold; 12 million guilders worth remained for shipment to Berlin in September 1944. Nazis also confiscated Jewish-owned buildings valued at some 200 million guilders, selling off the property to finance construction of two Dutch concentration camps and to pay for "maintenance" of the inmates. Between 1940 and 1945, Dutch Jews lost property valued around $3.5

billion at modern rates. Small wonder, then, that Allied investigators later called it the "most ruthless large-scale robbery modern Holland had ever seen."

As usual, priceless art was stolen wherever the Nazi forces set foot. German art expert Edouard Plietzsch joined the Gestapo at the Hague on September 7, 1940, analyzing and looting the city's major art collections. Hitler personally received six pieces from the prestigious Jaffé collection, with nine more earmarked for the Führer's crony Heinrich Hoffmann. Hans Posse's team of thieves were late at the scene of the crime, embarking for Holland on June 13, 1941. Art deemed too "degenerate" for Nazi collection was sold to the highest international bidder, one source reporting that income banked in Holland from the sale of stolen art averaged DM4.5 million *per day* by June 1941.

Belgian leaders had seen the war coming, packing off 1,751 gold ingots valued at $223 million for safekeeping in France, but the transfer was only a delaying tactic for Nazi looters who would seize France itself a month later. By the summer of 1943, Nazi conquerors were shipping Belgian gold—falsely stamped as German in origin—to numbered bank accounts in neutral Switzerland and Sweden. Meanwhile, Jewish property in Belgium valued at $140 million fell into German hands immediately and was liquidated as in other occupied nations. The amount of Jewish property seized in Luxembourg remains uncertain, lumped together in most accounts with an estimated $50 million seized in Denmark, Norway, and Estonia.

France, likewise invaded on May 10, 1940, was the mother lode for Hitler and company. Presumed safe behind its "impregnable" Maginot Line, France not only harbored vast wealth of its own but had also become a repository for gold, art, and other valuables from panicky neighboring countries. Jewish property valued between $400 and $800 million was an early target of the Nazi invaders, as elsewhere in Europe. Jewish bank accounts were frozen, with FFr1.29 billion trapped in one Paris bank. An "Aryanization" law of July 22, 1941, provided for sale of Jewish property to create a "common fund" for sustenance of impoverished Jews—who, of course, never saw the money. A blanket fine of FFr1 billion, levied against Jewish property on December 14, 1941, permitted Germans to steal the money from frozen bank accounts. Another FFr12,039,892 was confiscated from Jewish prisoners corralled at Drancy. Between June 1940 and May 1944, 42,227

Jewish businesses were seized, 9,680 of them sold off to "Aryan" proprietors. Nazis and their collaborators looted 1,708 Jewish apartment buildings, 4,869 shops, and 1,930 artisan establishments—stealing an estimated FFr3 billion by 1943. A report dated August 8, 1944 lists 69,512 Jewish apartments "cleansed" by looting; their contents filled 674 freight trains with 26,984 boxcars. French thieves also used the invasion as a cover for wholesale robbery of Jews: Their loot for April 1941 alone included FFr142 million in cash, 17 gold bars, 502 silver pieces, 450 kilos of clothes, and "thousands of metric cubes of antique furniture and rare carpets." Entire Jewish libraries were stolen—118,000 books and 760 crates of archival material from three Parisian institutions—while the Nazis established special warehouses for storage of looted musical instruments (three for pianos alone). The last shipment of stolen musical instruments to Germany, including 46 pianos, left France as late as July 21, 1944. Records for 1942 document 40,000 tons of antique furniture stolen from Jews in France and shipped out to Germany.

As elsewhere under Nazi occupation, fine art was a primary target of the invading looters. Members of the Rothschild clan residing in France lost artwork valued conservatively at FFr2 billion. The best pieces were predictably shipped back to Germany, while tons of lesser art were stored in Paris. Between October 1940 and July 1944, Nazi records show that 21,093 art pieces were transported to the Fatherland, including 5,281 paintings, 2,437 historic pieces of furniture, and 583 tapestries. The largest single shipment, employing 35 freight wagons, reached Germany on March 15, 1943. Dr. Otto Kümmel, director of the Berlin Museums, followed close behind Hitler's advance troops, identifying the top Jewish art dealers in Paris by mid-July 1940. French police were employed to pillage their galleries, transporting the loot to the German embassy for storage, its removal to Germany authorized by Hitler on December 31, 1940. Hitler himself received 32 pieces from the Rothschild collection in February 1941, including paintings by Vermeer, Hals, Boucher, and Rembrandt. Göring personally claimed another 59 paintings, plus antique furniture including six commodes and two 18th-century desks. Göring's special Luftwaffe loot train carried the bounty back to Berlin, secure under guard.

Altogether, German art analysts worked 16-hour days in Paris, cataloging 218 major collections of art-

work from Arnhold to Zach. Thousands more items were taken from lesser collections: Between April 1941 and July 1944, 138 boxcars carried 4,174 cases (22,000 individual lots) from France to Germany, where the loot was stashed in various castles and monasteries scattered around the country. Two thousand objects were stolen from the Military Museum at the Invalides in April 1941, including 150 large antique cannon. Göring's Luftwaffe cleaned out the French Air Museum, while libraries and collections in Alsace-Lorraine were likewise pillaged. At the Cathedral of Strasbourg, Nazi vandals cleaned out various treasures and dismantled the huge stained glass windows for shipment back to Germany.

Again, those works of art deemed too "degenerate" or Jewish were sold or traded for the benefit of greedy Germans. Hermann Göring profited from the sale of classic works by Vermeer, Rembrandt, Cézanne, van Gogh, Matisse, Renoir, Léger, Picasso, and other masters. In April 1941 he traded 25 stolen impressionist works to a Lucerne gallery for six German paintings. A short time later, he traded 25 more for a Rembrandt and two tapestries. In all, Göring made 18 such trades between March 1941 and November 1943; at least 10 similar transactions were arranged for Hitler, Martin Bormann, and Joachim von Ribbentrop. In March 1943, German thieves sold off 330 collected works by minor Dutch artists of the 17th century. Hitler's Linz collection spent FFr50 million to purchase another 262 paintings in October 1943, while 22 were handed to French middleman P. E. Lefranc for private sale.

Individual families were hard hit by Nazi ART THEFT in France. Paul Rosenberg left 162 major works with a bank at Libourne outside Bourdeaux when he fled to the United States. George Wildenstein banked 329 works in Paris, put 82 in the Louvre, and still left a priceless cache for the Nazis to steal from his Paris gallery and home. The Bernheim-Jeune family sent 28 paintings, including seven by Cézanne, to friends in the Dordogne where the works were later seized. Miriam de Rothschild outfoxed her persecutors by burying much of her collection near Dieppe, but she forgot to mark the sand dune, and the priceless works have never been recovered. Alfred Rosenberg, assigned by Hitler to personally oversee collection of art from "abandoned" Jewish homes and galleries in France, later estimated that objects worth some DM1 billion were stolen during the first six months of German occupation. Countless other items were seized during the next four years, photographs of the major works filling 39 volumes bound in leather and trimmed with gold leaf, which Hitler—dubbed "the greatest art thief of all time" by one historian—spent hours poring over at his leisure.

Other looting in France included the assessment of punitive "occupation costs" at FFr400 million per day—some 60 percent of the French government's total income. Agricultural supplies were highly valued by the Nazis, who stole 3 million tons of wheat, 2 million tons of oats, 700,000 tons of potatoes, 75,000 tons of butter, and 50,000 tons of cheese during the occupation. Thirsty Germans helped themselves to 87 million bottles of champagne and 50 percent of France's national wine production at the same time. In terms of crucial raw materials, the Nazis expropriated 73 percent of all French iron ore, 80 percent of all copper and nickel, 55 percent of all aluminum, 70 percent of all wool, 84 percent of all cotton, and 87 percent of all linen produced. Transportation being vital to the blitzkrieg, Hitler's troops naturally confiscated all of France's petroleum reserves and 80 percent of all new oil produced, 85 percent of new motor vehicles, and 30 percent of all French railroad cars (including 4,000 locomotives). Large machinery confiscated by the Nazis included a massive steel-bending machine from the Althom factory in Belfort, valued at FFr700,000. The wholesale robbery of France finally ended on August 8, 1944, as Allied troops approached Le Mans. (A German train including five boxcars filled with 148 cases of stolen art was captured by French forces at Le Bouget, on August 27, 1944.) By then, Nazis had robbed 71,619 homes and shipped 1,079,373 cubic meters of personal property eastward in 29,436 railroad cars. After ranking Nazis skimmed the cream of the crop, remaining items were distributed as compensation for German victims of Allied bombing raids.

Four months after France was occupied, in October 1940, Hitler teamed with his Italian and Bulgarian allies to capture Greece. Nazis immediately helped themselves to Jewish property valued between $40 million and $60 million, pursuing their usual guidelines for plunder. Another $50 million to $100 million in Jewish property would also be stolen from Italy, but wholesale looting of Hitler's Axis partner was delayed until the Allied invasion of 1943 threatened Benito Mussolini's control in that country. The Nazis had other battles to fight, meanwhile, and their next target lay to the east.

Shortly after midnight on June 22, 1941, German troops invaded western Russia and its neighboring states of Latvia, Estonia, and Lithuania. Most of the three smaller countries had been overwhelmed by July 14 when Nazi troops captured Minsk. Jewish property in the areas overrun was valued between $570 million and $820 million, while Yugoslavia (captured a few weeks earlier) yielded another $100 million to $160 million in Jewish property ready for looting. Kiev fell on September 17, and SS troopers in Novgorod busied themselves with the theft of 11-feet bronze doors from the city's 12th-century cathedral. Art collections everywhere in occupied Russia were seized for "safekeeping," flying squads of Nazi specialists removing the cream of the crop as usual while lesser works were left to the commanders of the occupation force. In Kiev alone, where Nazi looters stripped not only museums and libraries but also churches and scientific institutes, the list of stolen art objects deemed worthy of special notice filled three and a half single-spaced pages. To exploit Russia's natural resources, the Germans established "Eastern Monopoly Companies," variously specializing in oil, chemicals, textiles, tobacco, minerals, hides, and agricultural goods. Within three years the Nazis stole 10 million tons of grain, 3 million tons of potatoes, 600,000 tons of meat, and huge amounts of dairy products. At a local level, individuals were cruelly victimized—as in the case of a Kiev professor's widow who traded her jewelry collection for 16 pounds of millet to survive.

Fascist Italy, although an ally of the Führer, also suffered occupation by his Nazi "supermen." As early as 1940, the former Medici villa of Poggio a Caiano and two other nearby palazzos were requisitioned by Germans and were filled with stolen artwork that included an eight-ton bronze statue of Cosimo I de' Medici on horseback. At Cava, near Salerno, another repository held 37,000 art objects looted from the Royal Palace and various museums or private collections; by 1943, when the Allies invaded Italy, the hoard had grown to include 60,000 items. In August 1943 the Germans hid 187 crates of stolen art at the remote monastery of Monte Cassino, 50 miles north of Naples—just in time to see it flattened by an Allied bombing raid. In retreat from the Allied juggernaut that year, Nazi looters destroyed what they could not remove—50,000 priceless books burned at Naples on September 26 and 80,000 more at Nola four days later. A truck convoy left Florence on July 4, 1943, evacuating

532 stolen paintings and 153 pieces of sculpture to a mountain refuge where the treasure was concealed.

Whether a thief is looting modest homes or whole nations, disposal of property other than cash requires accomplices, the "fences" who buy and sell stolen goods while skimming off a handsome profit for themselves. Neutral Turkey dealt with both sides throughout World War II, its prewar gold reserve of 27 tons inflated by war's end to an impressive 216 tons. Postwar American reports suggest that German banks transferred at least $400,000 worth of gold ingots and assorted coins ($4 million at modern exchange rates) to Turkey in 1945, most of it earmarked for the personal benefit of Joachim von Ribbentrop. In the process, Turkey increased its gold reserves more than 250 percent, from $88 million to $221 million. Fascist Spain increased its gold reserves 248 percent in six years (from $42 million to $104 million) by trading with Nazis. Neighboring Portugal shared Spain's good fortune, receiving an estimated $50 million in Reichsbank transfers, as much as $100 million in looted gold, and Belgian diamonds by the carload. Swedish banks received some $31 million in gold bullion from Germany, much of it stolen by Nazis from Belgium and Holland; the national gold reserve increased nearly three-fold (from $160 million to $456 million) between 1939 and 1945. During the same years, more than $4.1 million was transferred from Berlin to the German embassy in Buenos Aires, Argentina. By 1945, the U.S. State Department estimated, $20 million in German loot had been shipped from Swiss banks to Argentina during the war, including $1.8 million banked by Hermann Göring personally. Argentine dictator Juan Perón was less modest, admitting the receipt of some 680 million pesos ($200 million) from Germany. Even the Vatican cashed in on Hitler's crime spree, accepting 2,500 gold bars from Germany, stamped with false prewar dates.

Those riches notwithstanding, neutral Switzerland surpassed all other nations in its wartime profiteering from the Nazi scourge. Ironically, Swiss banks received deposits both from European Jews and from their Nazi persecutors, using the façade of neutrality to lure customers from both camps as the blitzkrieg enveloped the continent. German Jews were among the first to try hiding their assets in Switzerland, but while their cash was always welcome, they were not. A minimum of 30,000 were expelled by Swiss authorities, delivered to the waiting hands of the Gestapo, while their money remained "safe" in num-bered accounts; some wealthy Jews were favored with asylum after payment of a hefty "Jew tax" mollified the Swiss government. In August 1939 alone, Swiss banks received 17,000 transfers of funds from Poland, most of them from Jews who did not survive the Holocaust to claim their money.

For all the panicked Jews contributed to Switzerland's economy, though, they could never compete with Nazi looters. Despite their posture of neutrality, 200 Swiss financial and political leaders gathered in November 1940 and petitioned their government to show greater sympathy for Nazi investors, turning a blind eye to deposits of gold and other merchandise obviously stolen from occupied nations. A 1942 investigation of the Swiss Bank Corporation, charged with laundering stolen securities for German depositors, was quickly dropped "in the public interest" after strategic applications of political pressure. The same year witnessed initial deposits of gold looted from Holland, finally totaling 14,748 tons ($161 million). Swiss bankers also cheerfully accepted diamonds seized by Nazis from Jewish dealers in Antwerp and Amsterdam, while art dealers in Zurich and Basel grew fat from the trade in stolen paintings, sculpture, and other artifacts. The most sinister trade was that in Jewish jewelry that was seized for "safekeeping" on arrival at various concentration camps —and the gold fillings ripped from victims after death. As a consequence of trade with Hitler's Reich, Switzerland saw its prewar gold reserve more than double in six years, from $503 million to $1.04 billion. Between 1941 and 1945, identifiable German deposits in Swiss banks soared from SF332 million to SF846 million. Swiss auditors valued German accounts in Switzerland at some $250 million by war's end; the U.S. embassy countered with a more realistic estimate exceeding $1 billion.

The neutral Swiss were warned repeatedly about their close relationship to Hitler as the war dragged on. On February 22, 1944, the United States formally cautioned Switzerland and other neutrals against importing, purchasing, or storing Nazi gold. On May 11—less than a month before D-Day— Switzerland received another pointed warning from the United States. In July 1944 Allied nations demanded that the Swiss Bankers Association stop accepting Nazi loot; the association responded with a curious demand that the Allies recognize "legitimate" German ownership of all assets deposited in Switzerland before D-Day. October 1944 witnessed an apparent concession, as Swiss authorities froze certain bank accounts in German-occupied nations—but only after the Nazis had withdrawn, leaving their loot behind. In effect, the Swiss action blocked *victims* of Nazi theft from recovering their property even after the Germans had fled. Meanwhile, truck convoys from Munich and Nuremberg continued transporting "large sums" of gold, cash, and securities to the safety of Swiss banks. In January 1945 Allied spokespersons exposed the funneling of gold and other loot between Swiss banks and Argentina, once again demanding—in vain—that the illicit traffic cease.

Germany's sweeping tide of victory began to ebb in 1943 with armies defeated in North Africa and repulsed in Russia and in Italy. Allied bombing of the Fatherland threatened Hitler's stolen art, much of it transported for storage in salt mines southeast of Salzburg in the Austrian resort district of Salzkammergut. Red Army forces in Estonia captured the town of Vyr in September 1944, discovering a repository of furniture looted from the Catherine Palace. Elsewhere about town, they found more loot hidden in shops and private homes; cooks at a local cafeteria were using two 18th-century Japanese bowls from Pavlovsk to mix dough, while a heap of small sculptures and leather-bound books was found in a roadside ditch outside town. In Riga, Russian soldiers recovered 400 stolen paintings, 8,000 cameos, and various other art objects. In Germany proper, while Hitler braced himself for suicide, Hermann Göring began to evacuate his stash of loot in January 1945, moving it first to a castle outside Nuremberg and then on to Berchtesgaden in April. On April 23, believing the Führer had lost control of himself and his country, Göring cabled an offer to assume command, but Hitler responded by branding him a traitor.

It hardly mattered by that time, as Allied troops uncovered treasure troves throughout the prostrate Fatherland. On Easter Sunday 1945, the U.S. Army breached a network of tunnels near Siegen where civilians and prisoners of war shared space with stolen art. The hoard included 600 paintings from Rhineland museums, 100 sculptures, the manuscript of Beethoven's Sixth Symphony, six cases of gold, and silver shrines containing relics of Charlemagne. Another cache at Ransbach included 3,305 crates or boxes and 140 textile bundles of stolen art objects, filling nine rooms. At Hungen, eight large buildings were crammed with stolen Jewish books and religious artifacts, earmarked for a "racial studies insti-

tute" the Nazis never got around to building in Bavaria. U.S. troops captured a German train, including 24 carriages packed with Reichsbank bullion, when they found the train sidelined near a mine that was filled with looted treasure at Merkers. At Bernterode, on May 1, 1945, American soldiers found a cache labeled with Hitler's name, initially mistaken for his crypt, with contents including 271 stolen paintings, four huge caskets, plus tapestries, and jeweled swords and scepters arranged to resemble "the setting for a pagan ritual." One week later, at the village of Grosscotta (near Dresden), Russian troops found a quarry tunnel filled with unpacked paintings by artists including Rembrandt, Titian, and Raphael.

Hitler's suicide and V-E Day left Allied victors to begin the task of cataloging Nazi loot recovered amidst the ruins of the Thousand-Year Reich. Hermann Göring's private cash at Berchtesgaden filled six separate buildings with more than 1,000 paintings and sculptures, the paintings alone valued at $500 million. (Walter Hofer, a Göring aide, staunchly insisted that the loot was "all legally paid for.") By June 1945 U.S. occupation forces had amassed 4,000 crates containing 15,000 gold and silver bars, plus coins and jewelry stolen from the inmates of various concentration camps. A few months later, the list had grown to include 22,000 gold and silver bars, 3,326 bags of gold coins, and eight bags of gold wedding rings. The stash also included a large quantity of apparent gold dental fillings. In July 1945 an American team began to inventory stolen art concealed by Nazis at Alt Aussee, including portions of the various Rothschild collections and art removed from Belgium, Budapest, and Italy. The final tally included 6,577 paintings, 2,300 drawings and water colors, 954 prints, 137 sculptures, 129 pieces of arms and armor, 122 tapestries, 78 pieces of furniture, 79 baskets of unsorted objects, 1,881 cases of books, 484 cases "thought to be archives," and 283 cases with contents unclassified. Heinrich Himmler's personal escape fund was found in a rural barn, some $2 million worth of foreign currency, plus gold bars, coins, and jewelry. Even then, the Allied catalogs could be misleading: A summary of 340,846 items captured in Munich seemed massive enough, but one "item" was a library of 3 million volumes, while another held 1.2 million.

Such discoveries notwithstanding, vast amounts of wartime loot lay unrecovered by the Allies. British analysts estimated that some $252 million in gold remained hidden in Germany after the initial sweep of loot repositories; American spokespersons placed the total at $293 million. Total wartime thefts of gold alone were said to include $223 million from Belgium, $161 million from Holland, $84 million from Italy, $50 million from Czechoslovakia, $46 million from Austria, $23 million from Russia, $12 million from Poland, $5 million from Luxembourg, and $4 million from Danzig, plus unspecified "large amounts" from the Balkan states and various private parties.

Tracking the Nazi loot that got away became a mystery to challenge Sherlock Holmes. Britain's government estimated art thefts alone at some $144 million; New York's Metropolitan Museum of Art raised the ante to $2.5 billion. Reichsbank records documented transfers of gold worth $400 million to Swiss banks—which in turn transferred at least $138 million to banks in Spain and Portugal. A total of 3,859 gold ingots were shipped from Bern to Lisbon, where "visibly worried" Portuguese bankers fretted over the stolen loot within their vaults, "as if the bank held the *Mona Lisa* itself without even retouching it." Ignoring tiny Liechtenstein and its fat banks, Allies ordered the remaining neutrals on July 31, 1945, to surrender all property held by Axis powers within their borders. The stubborn Swiss were threatened with a global blockade but remained defiant; rather than surrender their ill-gotten gains, Swiss authorities audaciously billed France FFr82 million for the deaths of 63 Swiss nationals executed as collaborators or common criminals. Embarrassed by the crimes of its own Vichy regime, France settled the dubious claim for FFr55 million. In May 1946 the Allies demanded a lump-sum payment of $88 million from Switzerland but finally accepted only $51 million—roughly one-fifth of the estimated loot received from Hitler's Reich. Adding insult to injury four months later, Swiss authorities accepted SF200,000 in bribes to furnish fugitive Nazi war criminals with false travel papers, thus allowing them to flee the continent.

No country suffered more from Nazi art theft than did France, but postwar prosecution of those involved was halfhearted at best. Notorious collaborator P. E. Lefranc was jailed in April 1945; several other profiteers were fined by the courts. Twenty-one more defendants were fined between September 1945 and 1947 when the push ran out of steam. In Holland, several "economic collaborators" were

indicted, but the only one imprisoned was art forger Hans van Meegeren, who died soon after his trial in 1947.

The Nazis left mountains of dead in their wake, and thus created another problem in the form of "heirless" property, whether in bank accounts held by the neutral powers or in caches of recovered loot. Dutch auditors had compiled a list of 70,000 Jewish bank accounts by 1949; 45,000 had no living heirs; applicants filed claims to only 23,000 of the remainder. In January 1947 Swedish authorities sold 74 percent of their wartime Nazi loot and delivered proceeds to the victorious Allies. Swiss bankers remained vague on the total of their heirless assets: in 1946 they reported SF248,000 in "dormant" accounts; three years later they revised the estimate to SF309,000; by 1962 the total topped SF2 million. A Swiss law from 1891 absolved the government from any vestige of fairness in the "ultimate disposal of assets in Switzerland of foreigners who died without heirs," and Swiss negotiators blamed a "Jewish conspiracy" for their ongoing persecution, but world opinion still carried some marginal weight in Bern, especially as journalists revealed the horrors of the Holocaust.

In early 1947 Switzerland agreed to pay Jewish refugee organizations a total of $12.5 million, but the offer was soon withdrawn. A token payment of $2.6 million was released that spring, while Allied auditors continued to insist that Switzerland held Axis assets valued at $1 billion. In May 1948 the Allies denounced Switzerland's "untenable position" and declared that its government had made "no contribution whatsoever to the common effort" of rebuilding war-torn Europe. Swiss authorities flatly rejected a demand for immediate payment of SF20 million to aid refugees. Jewish organizations were outraged in December 1949, when the Swiss announced that the heirless assets of some 2 million Poles held in Switzerland amounted to a paltry SF500,000. Polish officials and the U.S. State Department countered with claims ranging from $5 million to $50 million, whereupon Swiss bankers grudgingly acknowledged a revised total of SF645,000 (barely $150,000). Hungarian authorities joined the fray in March 1950 when Switzerland balked at returning heirless assets to that nation. An abrupt turnaround occurred on April 20, 1951, when the United States, France, and England dropped their quest for heirless assets in Switzerland, accepting the Swiss government's written assurance that such items were "trivial" or nonexistent, worth "at most SF1 million." In November 1952 the Swiss Minister of Justice chaired a meeting "to discuss the fate of money deposited by foreigners in Switzerland who were killed because of Nazi violence and wartime events"; the assembled leaders agreed to expropriate said heirless funds "for social purposes."

Elsewhere, in the French zone of occupied Germany, military authorities permitted Germans to retain all heirless assets and denied all Jewish claims for restitution, declaring that any available funds should be used for the "common good" of Germany and France. In France itself, officials seized most of the FFr12 million stolen from Jewish prisoners at Drancy and in 1951 auctioned off most of their unclaimed jewelry and other personal items for government benefit. A total of 61,257 stolen art objects were recovered in France, some 38,000 still missing from the state's master list. By September 1949, 45,441 pieces had been returned to their rightful owners; the remaining 15,861 pieces were deeded in perpetuity to various French museums. A commission to investigate robbery of Jews by Nazi and Vichy officials was established in January 1997, but its work proceeded with agonizing slowness: in 1999 some 62,460 boxes of Vichy records were still officially sealed, thereby frustrating any effort to identify the heirs to stolen property.

Switzerland was not the only neutral country reluctant to give up its wartime bonanza in Nazi loot. Sweden conducted prolonged negotiations before returning 14 tons of stolen gold to Holland and Belgium, transferring $90 million in Nazi assets to international relief organizations. Even then, another 7.5 tons of "suspect" gold remained in Sweden's treasury. In 1947, Argentina transferred $320 million in Nazi gold to New York City for deposit in the Federal Reserve Bank. Spain and Portugal waited until 1997 to admit receipt of nearly $100 million in currency via Reichsbank transfers; a year later, the two governments acknowledged receipt of looted gold worth $204 million at wartime rates ($2.4 billion today). No accounting has yet been made for 1,230 carats of Belgian diamonds stolen by Germany in 1940 and then shipped to Spain and Portugal, their current price listed at $3.41 billion.

Restitution in occupied nations was as problematic as in neutral countries. Allied forces returned numerous shipments of stolen art to Austria, and while some 10,000 pieces were returned to lawful owners, a 1950 State Department report identified

Austria's largest public auction house as a major "fence" of stolen artwork from the war years. In 1958 a government agency was established to sell "heirless" assets worth $220,000 (or $2.2 million today); artwork withheld from sale included 8,422 pieces stored at a monastery in Mauerbach and later donated to "needy" museums. In 1969 a catalog of the Mauerbach hoard—once dismissed by an Austrian statesman as minor "baubles and kitsch"—listed 657 paintings, 250 drawings, 84 water colors, 365 pieces of silver, 114 rare books, 35 pieces of furniture, and other objects. The paintings included works by da Vinci, Botticelli, Bruegel, Archipenko, and Teniers. On October 30, 1996, the Mauerbach cache was finally sold for charity at a pro bono auction by Christie's, supervised by the World Jewish Congress. One still life by French artist Abraham Mignon sold for $1.35 million.

Matters were equally grim in Czechoslovakia, where a Russian puppet state supplanted Hitler's Reich in 1945. It would be March 1994, after the fall of European communism, before a new government announced the return to prewar owners of 30 communal Jewish properties seized by the Nazis (including the Jewish Museum); at the same time, however, 202 other communal properties were retained by the state, 40 of them privatized and sold under a new Czech law that barred compensation of the original owners. Another 100 of the communal properties were released in May 1995, but the damage was done. Overall, British auditors estimated that Czech banks and institutions had collaborated to rob Holocaust survivors of property worth £1.2 billion.

In the Netherlands, compensation of Jews for stock looted by the Nazis began in 1953; the owners were allowed 90 percent of the stock's original face value—but only if they gave up any claim to ownership. The Dutch thus paid 41 million guilders ($150 million) for stocks valued at 349 million guilders (nearly $1.3 billion) in 1953. More than 20,000 Dutch art objects were recovered from Nazi thieves after World War II, while another 10,000 or more remain missing; of the items recovered, 3,000 of the most expensive remain "under custodianship" today, still in official hands. When Dutch Jews sought return of "heirless" property worth 4.5 million guilders in 1985, the state countered with a nonnegotiable offer of 2.1 million guilders. Four government commissions were established to investigate Jewish claims in 1997, but the fate of many assets stolen by the Reich remains in doubt today. A further insult to survivors of the Holocaust was delivered by various European life insurance companies, which have refused to pay off on policies valued at $250 million in 1940 ($2.5 billion today); some of the firms insist their records were "lost during the war," while others demand nonexistent death certificates from the families of victims killed in concentration camps.

For a half-century after the war, Switzerland set the standard for delay and diversion in return of "heirless" assets. A report from 1964 acknowledged that the government had lied in 1951 about the state of dormant accounts in Swiss banks: Rather than SF1 million, as originally stated, the 1,048 dormant accounts identified in 1964 were valued at SF9,469,882 ($2.5 million)—still far below the amount claimed by Jewish refugee organizations. By 1969, auditors had identified 132 heirs in the United States and Israel who collectively were entitled to SF1.6 million. Three years later, the Swiss acknowledged holding SF10.8 million in wartime deposits, but SF5.4 million was promptly declared "unclaimed" and returned to various banks. In 1975 the Swiss admitted possession of SF463,954 owned by Polish Jews—previously estimated at SF541,000 (in 1949), SF23,300 (1954), and SF17,550 (in 1958)—transferring the "true" amount to Poland's National Bank without explanation of the wild discrepancies. In the 1990s, the World Jewish Organization accused Switzerland of involvement in a "£15 billion Nazi art scandal," further claiming that stolen deposits of Jewish wealth in Swiss banks ranged somewhere between $22.3 billion and $106.4 billion. The Swiss retreat began in January 1997 when Crédit Suisse offered a SF100 million ($72 million) lump-sum payment to Holocaust survivors; a month later President Arnold Koller raised the amount to SF7 billion, payable in yearly installments of SF350 million. A Swiss report of May 1997 acknowledged postwar seizure of Nazi gold worth $580 million in 1945 ($5.6 billion today), while an "accidental" fire the same month destroyed 6,000 cases of archival bank records, rendering further evaluation impossible.

Shamefully, the Allied record of compensating wartime victims is hardly an improvement on neutral states. A military document from 1946 describes Allied gold seizures of 377 tons; after repatriation of the stolen gold, 3 tons curiously remained with the Bank of England, while New York's Federal Reserve Bank kept 2.5 tons. The 5.5 tons of hot gold were finally allocated for a Holocaust reimbursement fund in December 1997, but payments remain problem-

atic. The same is true of stolen art recovered by the Allies. On February 29, 2000, England's National Museum Directors' Conference climaxed months of investigation into Nazi art thefts with publication of a catalog that detailed stolen works retained by British galleries. The list of 350 treasures held by 10 major institutions—100 at London's National Gallery and 80 at the Tate Gallery, also in London—included paintings by Picasso, Monet, and Renoir, valued in the tens of millions of dollars. All admittedly had "gaps or question marks" in their histories since 1933, but ethical questions had not prevented their collection. Survivors of Austrian refugee Elizabeth Glanville were the first to have a stolen painting returned, on March 13, 2000. Experts predict that the quest for Nazi loot will continue well into the 21st century.

NELSON, George "Baby Face"

Chicago native Lester Joseph Gillis was born on December 6, 1908 and grew up in the stockyard district with his widowed mother. Despite (or because of) his short stature and "baby face," he ran with a tough street gang and may have been acquainted with future "Public Enemy No. 1" ALVIN KARPIS. (Author Myron Quimby calls them "fast friends," while Karpis, in his autobiography, recalled meeting Gillis for the first time in Reno, Nevada, years later.) With or without such cohorts, Lester was well on his way to a criminal career by his early teens.

In 1922 Gillis logged his first arrest, for auto theft. It was his attitude in custody that earned him an indefinite sentence to the St. Charles Reform School, but he learned to play the game inside and was paroled for good behavior in April 1924. From there it was in and out of jail: back to St. Charles as a parole violator in September 1924; free again in July 1925; locked up once more that October; paroled yet again on July 11, 1926. By then, at age 18, he was old enough to visit state prison if he crossed the line again.

The next two years are vague because Gillis managed to avoid arrest. Various published accounts suggest that he drifted westward, probably driving stolen cars, and ultimately made his way to California. En route he may have stopped off in Reno, serving as a chauffeur and muscle for an unnamed "small-time gambler." It is furthermore alleged that he tried his hand at bootlegging during Prohibition in San Francisco or Los Angeles (perhaps both). The only certainty is that he traded his "sissy" name for something more impressive. He settled on George Nelson and preferred "Big George," although it scarcely fit his stature. The nickname that stuck, to Lester's chagrin, was "Baby Face," and while few dared use it in his presence, he would enter American criminal history as Baby Face Nelson.

By 1928 Gillis/Nelson was back in Chicago, sporting a bankroll and looking for trouble. Reports of his alleged affiliation with the Al Capone mob are unverified, although rumors of his employment as a "torpedo" for Capone are faithful to Nelson's quick-trigger temperament. There was a gentler side as well, however, and it blossomed after a fashion when he met and married Helen Wawrzyniak, a pretty 16-year-old. Her parents loathed Nelson, so the newly-weds made their way westward, retracing George's earlier flight from Chicago. Again there are uncon-firmed reports of bootlegging, punctuated by two arrests in San Francisco: one for carrying a pistol, the other on suspicion of robbing a gas station. Neither charge was prosecuted, and Nelson must have spent *some* time at home because he fathered two children (son Ronald, born in 1929, and daughter Arlene the following year).

Parenthood never much agreed with Big George Nelson or his wife. Back in Chicago, they left the children with Nelson's mother. Arlene would grow up with Mary Gillis, referring to her mother as "Aunt Helen," while Ronald was later sent to live with a sister of Helen's in Bremerton, Washington. Around that same time Nelson joined a pair of small-time stickup artists—Harry Lewis and Stanton Ran-dall—for a series of robberies in 1930. On January 6 the gang invaded Charles Richter's home on Lake Shore Drive, Chicago, and stole jewelry valued at $25,000. Sixteen days later in Lake Forest, they took another $5,000 worth of gems from the home of lawyer Stanley Templeton. On March 31 the Chicago victims were Count and Countess Von Bülow, relieved of $95 cash and some $50,000 in jewelry.

The gang's performance was less impressive when they switched to robbing banks. On October 3, 1930, they bagged $4,600 from a bank in Itasca, Illi-nois, while the following month they got nothing at all from a November 7 raid in Plainfield, foiled by bulletproof glass on the teller's cages. On November 22 they scored another four grand from a bank in Hillside, Illinois, with Nelson claiming half of the loot for himself. (It was apparently the Hillside heist

that stuck him with his hated nickname, after news-papers described the gang's triggerman as "a young man with a baby face.") Their luck ran out on Janu-ary 13, 1931, when police nabbed Lewis and Ran-dall at their separate Chicago dwellings.

Two days later, Nelson robbed a jewelry store on Chicago's Michigan Avenue and was caught in the act by a police stakeout squad. Booked on a charge of armed robbery, his tough talk and appearance jogged official memories. A lineup was arranged for victims of the Hillside bank job, and Nelson was quickly identified. Convicted on July 15, he received the maximum sentence of one year to life in state prison. An abortive jailbreak in December added more time to his sentence, and things went from bad to worse when he was belatedly identified as one of the Itasca bandits. Transferred to Wheaton, Illinois, for trial in February 1932, Nelson was convicted once again, drawing a new sentence of one to 20 years. It began to look as if he would die in prison if he could not find a shortcut back to liberty.

On February 17, 1932, Nelson boarded the Rock Island Special in leg irons, handcuffed to a guard for the trip back to Joliet State Prison. On arrival in Joliet, the guard hailed a taxi at the station, standard practice in those days for the short ride to the prison. Inside the cab, Nelson produced a gun as if by magic, disarmed his escort, and ordered the cabbie to drive out of town. They found a nice, secluded spot, where Nelson removed his chains and then pistol-whipped both men into unconsciousness before stealing the cab driver's cap, coat, and taxi. (The source of the pistol remains unknown, though both his escort and the cab driver were ultimately cleared of suspicion.)

Determined not to spend another day in jail, Nel-son fled westward again, stopping only when he reached San Francisco and ran out of road. Most sources agree that he found work as "Jimmy Bur-nett" with mobster Joe Parente's San Francisco syn-dicate. Prohibition would last through December 1933, and there was still money to be made from bootleg booze. One of Nelson's new friends in the alky racket was hoodlum JOHN PAUL CHASE, who appeared to regard Big George with a kind of mis-placed hero worship. Before long, Nelson had enough money to send for Helen, and she gladly joined him on the coast.

Life was good for a while until Nelson's mug shots and the tale of his escape were published in *True Detective Story* magazine. Panicked by the thought of exposure and return to prison, Nelson and Helen fled to Reno, where Nelson had criminal ties. It was there, according to Alvin Karpis, that he met Nelson for the first time. Decades after the fact, Karpis claimed he had arranged introductions to a bank-robbing gang in ST. PAUL, MINNESOTA. The last time he saw Nelson, Karpis recalled, Big George was painting his fingertips with acid in an effort to remove his prints.

Whatever "Old Creepy's" role in the move, Nelson and Helen did in fact head east to Minnesota. St. Paul was a notorious criminal hangout, where boss Harry Sawyer ran the show and kept things quiet, more or less, until he took a fall for holding ransom money gathered by the BARKER gang, but that fiasco was still a few years down the road when the Nelsons hit town.

Once again, the details of Nelson's career are vague for the early months of 1933 until he teamed with veteran stickup artist EDDIE BENTZ. On August 18, 1933, with Bentz and others, Nelson took $30,000 from a bank in Grand Haven, Michigan. Accomplice Earl Doyle was captured, but the rest of the gang got away clean. On October 23, with accomplice TOMMY CARROLL and unknown others, Baby Face bagged another $32,000 from a bank in Brainerd, Minnesota.

Nelson had officially hit the big time, and trouble was not far behind. On March 4, 1934, Nelson committed his first verified murder, gunning down 35-year-old Theodore Kidder in St. Paul. The circumstances of the shooting are predictably unclear. Kidder, variously described in published accounts as a paint salesman or an employee of a sporting goods store, was returning from a children's party with his mother-in-law when he was called by name and shot from a car with several men inside. No motive for the shooting was apparent, but witnesses described Nelson and his Ford sedan, complete with California license number 6-H-475. Author Lew Louderback places fugitive outlaw JOHN DILLINGER in Nelson's car that afternoon—a possibility, although Dillinger had escaped from jail in Crown Point, Indiana, just the day before. Dillinger biographer Russell Girardin claims that his subject did not reach St. Paul until March 6, while author Myron Quimby has Nelson and Helen fleeing Minnesota after the murder, driving to Washington state (where Nelson allegedly performed a contract killing for the mob), then catching a train back to Chicago, and rolling on from there to rob a South Dakota bank with Dillinger—all in the span of two days! On balance, crime historian Mel

Heimer may well be correct in his theory that Kidder was slain in the wake of some illegal firearms transaction arranged through the shop where he worked.

Whatever the truth of Kidder's execution and Nelson's immediate reaction, all sources agree that he joined Dillinger, HOMER VAN METER, EDDIE GREEN, JOHN HAMILTON, and Tommy Carroll to steal $49,500 from the Security National Bank in Sioux Falls, South Dakota, on March 6. Bystanders called police and motorcycle officer Hale Keith was hit by submachine gun fire as he approached the bank, suffering wounds to the abdomen, both arms, and one leg. Most reports attribute the shooting to Nelson, though the culprit may well have been Carroll, stationed on the sidewalk out front with a Tommy gun to hold gawkers at bay.

One week later, on March 13, the same gang took the First National Bank of Mason City, Iowa, for $52,344. Again there was shooting: Dillinger and Hamilton both suffered flesh wounds, while bystander R. H. James, secretary of the local school board, was shot in the leg. Modern accounts of the holdup universally name Nelson as the shooter, describing him in near-maniacal terms, but no triggerman was specifically identified at the time.

Gang members scattered after Mason City, ducking the heat, and Nelson may have traveled west once more with Helen in tow. John Paul Chase would later blame Nelson for the March 22 disappearance of Roy Frisch, a prosecution witness in a case of mail fraud filed against Reno gamblers Bill Graham and Jim McKay, but no corpse was recovered and no one was charged in Frisch's presumed death. On April 3 FBI agents shot and mortally wounded Eddie Green in St. Paul; Green survived for eight days, reportedly spilling everything he knew to the feds before he died. Dillinger girlfriend Evelyn Frechette was arrested in Chicago on April 9, but John slipped through the net unseen. Four days later, Dillinger and Van Meter looted a police station in Warsaw, Indiana, making off with weapons and bulletproof vests.

The gang was back together on April 20, 1934, regrouping near Rhinelander, Wisconsin, at Emil Wanatka's Little Bohemia Lodge. Present for the group vacation and strategy session were Nelson and Helen, Dillinger (flying solo since his lover's arrest), Hamilton and Patricia Cherrington, Van Meter and Marie Comforti, Tommy Carroll and wife Jean Crompton, and Crompton's brother-in-law Albert "Pat" Reilly, a small-time hoodlum from St. Paul.

Someone reported the gang's whereabouts to Chicago G-man MELVIN PURVIS on Sunday, April 22, and he mobilized a strike force of FBI agents. By that night the lodge was surrounded, but the federal strategy was poor, to say the least. Some of the agents got entangled in a barbed-wire fence, while others blundered through the woods and set Wanatka's dogs to barking. Finally, in desperation to do something right, they opened fire on three innocent members of the Civilian Conservation Corps who were mistaken for gangsters as they drove away from the lodge.

The fusillade killed one man and wounded the other two, while alerting the outlaws to danger. Dillinger and company fled on foot through the forest, leaving their women behind to face charges of harboring fugitives. Nelson, armed with a .45-caliber pistol modified to full-automatic fire by H. S. LEHMAN, made his way to a nearby crossroads, invading the general store run by Alvin Koerner and his wife. He was on the verge of stealing Koerner's car and taking Alvin along as a hostage when another vehicle approached. Constable Carl Christensen was driving; his passengers, out looking for a telephone to summon reinforcements to the lodge, were FBI agents Jay Newman and W. Carter Baum.

The three lawmen were stepping from their car when Nelson opened fire. Constable Christensen was hit eight times, while Agent Newman took a bullet in the forehead, but both would survive. Agent Baum was not so lucky, choking to death on his own blood after a .45 slug drilled his throat. Nelson, meanwhile, took off in the constable's Ford, driving as far as Squaw Lake before the car died on him. Tramping through the woods, he later met a Chippewa Indian known to history simply as "Catfish" and spent the next few days with his reluctant host in Catfish's shack. In due course Nelson made his way back to Chicago, still keeping a low profile, putting out feelers to surviving members of the holdup gang. Myron Quimby reports a Nelson sighting on April 30, Baby Face supposedly roughing up three policemen, restrained from killing them by companion Homer Van Meter, but no location is given and no other source records the incident.

More definite is Nelson's participation in a June 30 bank heist at South Bend, Indiana. Others present certainly included Dillinger, Van Meter, and John Paul Chase; a fifth bandit was identified by several witnesses as Oklahoma outlaw CHARLES "PRETTY BOY" FLOYD. A sixth member of the holdup team was said to be Jack Perkins, a childhood friend of Nelson,

though jurors later acquitted him of joining in the raid. South Bend was the gang's bloodiest holdup yet, police arriving on the scene with the robbery in progress and both sides cutting loose with everything they had. Van Meter was wounded in the withering crossfire, as were two bystanders and two bank employees. Patrolman Howard Wagner was killed by submachine gun fire, and while Myron Quimby names Nelson as the triggerman, most sources blame the murder on Homer Van Meter.

South Bend, with its disappointing take of $29,890, would be Dillinger's last holdup. Three weeks later he was shot and killed by G-men in Chicago. A month after that, Van Meter was riddled with police bullets in St. Paul. Nelson, meanwhile, shot and wounded two state policemen as they approached his Chicago hideout on July 15, 1934. Afterward, with Helen (free on probation from the Rhinelander arrest), he followed the usual pattern of fleeing westward to the wide open spaces of Nevada, moving on from there to California once again. Promoted to "Public Enemy No. 1" with Dillinger's death, Nelson still would not sever his Midwestern ties, despite the heat that awaited him there. By autumn Nelson and Helen were reported in southeastern Wisconsin, where they were said to have rented a cottage near Lake Geneva. FBI agents had the place staked out on November 27, 1934, when Nelson arrived with his wife and John Chase, but a young G-man showed himself on the porch as the bandits approached and Nelson sped from the scene, leaving the feds to broadcast his license-plate number.

Crossing into Illinois, southbound, the fugitives soon met another car headed in the opposite direction. Federal agents Thomas McDade and William Ryan spotted their license tag and swiftly made a U-turn in the middle of the highway, only to find that Nelson had done the same. The cars passed each other a second time; then Nelson, spoiling for a fight, whipped around in another U-turn and started chasing the feds. Chase, seated in back with a powerful Browning automatic rifle (BAR), opened up on the G-men while Agent Ryan returned fire with his pistol, both cars racing along at top speed.

Moments later, a third car with two more FBI men—Inspector SAMUEL COWLEY and Special Agent Herman Hollis—fell in behind Nelson, joining the parade. Near Barrington, Illinois, a lucky shot from Agent Ryan disabled Nelson's fuel pump and forced the bandit car to a halt, while their frightened quarry escaped. A few miles down the highway, McDade stopped the car and leapt out, taking cover with Ryan in some tall grass at roadside. Together they waited with guns drawn, expecting the gangsters to overtake them at any moment.

Nelson and company, meanwhile, had run out of steam near the entrance to a city park on the northwest edge of town. Helen jumped into a ditch for cover as her husband and Chase scrambled out of the car. Chase still clutched his big BAR, while Nelson carried a Thompson submachine gun; nearby, Agents Cowley and Hollis, likewise armed with a Tommy gun and shotgun, screeched to a halt and crouched behind their vehicle, already under fire. Hollis ran for a nearby telephone pole, seeking a better line of fire, but Nelson caught him on the run and dropped him with a bullet through the head. A group of highway workers planting trees nearby would later describe Nelson advancing on the FBI vehicle with his Tommy gun blazing from the hip, "just like Edward G. Robinson in the movies." Inspector Cowley was chopped down by the incoming fire, mortally wounded, but not before he squeezed off several blasts at Nelson with his shotgun.

Abandoning their useless car and piling into Cowley's Hudson, Nelson told Chase, "You'll have to drive. I'm hit." In fact, a medical examiner would later count 16 buckshot wounds in his legs, but a .45 slug had done the real damage, ripping through Nelson's stomach, liver, and pancreas. Transported to the home of a friend in Niles Center (present-day Skokie), Nelson died a short time later and was found next morning, naked and wrapped in a blanket, near St. Paul's cemetery.

The rest came down to mopping up. Helen Nelson—briefly headlined as the first female "Public Enemy No. 1"—surrendered on November 29 and was returned to Wisconsin as a probation violator. Another charge of harboring her fugitive husband was filed, but Helen saved herself from serious prison time by fingering John Chase (still unidentified at the time) as Nelson's accomplice. Traced to Mount Shasta, California, where he found work at a fish hatchery, Chase was arrested by FBI agents on December 27, 1934. Upon conviction for Inspector Crowley's murder, he was sentenced to life and ultimately died in federal prison. The Niles Center residents who sheltered Nelson in his final hours were never publicly identified or prosecuted, the lapse explained by rumors naming them as FBI informants

whose futile efforts to save Baby Face might have embarrassed the bureau if revealed in open court.

NESBIT, William Raymond

Sought by FBI agents on a charge of unlawful flight to avoid confinement, William Nesbit was a jewel thief with a taste for homicide. In league with two accomplices, he staged a daring robbery in Sioux City, Iowa, that netted the gang $37,000 worth of gems, but then he ran afoul of paranoia and the roof fell in.

Suspecting two associates, a man and woman, as potential squealers, Nesbit and his cronies opted for assassination as a cheap insurance policy. Transported to a rural area in South Dakota, the man was shot and killed, the woman gravely wounded. Nesbit thought her dead, but he would not be satisfied with any less than absolute obliteration of the bodies. Dragging both victims into a shack jammed with 3,500 pounds of dynamite and 7,000 pounds of black powder, Nesbit lit the fuse and made a swift retreat. Incredibly, the wounded woman managed to escape before the blast, which rattled windows in a five-mile radius. She lived to testify against the gunmen, sending them away for terms of life that were reduced by order of the court to 20 years.

Nesbit escaped from the South Dakota state penitentiary on September 4, 1946. Evidence of interstate flight made him a federal fugitive, and he was still at large when the FBI created its "Ten Most Wanted" list in March 1950. Posted to the original list as number three, Nesbit became the program's first arrestee on March 18.

Living off the land since his escape from prison, Nesbit was holed up in a cave beside the Mississippi River, outside ST. PAUL, MINNESOTA, when a pair of teenage boys observed him that Saturday morning. The youth recognized Nesbit from mug shots printed in the local newspaper and immediately summoned police. While Nesbit made his journey back to prison, facing extra time for the escape, the boys were flown to Washington where they received the personal congratulations of FBI Director J. EDGAR HOOVER.

NEWMAN, Eugene Francis

Brooklyn born in 1928, Gene Newman was a wild, ungovernable youth who often stole from members of his family. His first arrest was logged at age 15 for petty larceny, and he was sent to the reformatory at New Hampton, New York, for an indeterminate period. Drafted into the navy as "Daniel Lyons" in April 1943, Newman went AWOL in August 1945. Court-martialed a month later, he was sentenced to one year in a disciplinary barracks, with completion of his term followed by a bad-conduct discharge in 1946. Arrested by New York City police for burglary in April 1947, he was convicted six months later and sentenced to 10 years in the state reformatory. Parole put him back on the street in December 1949, but he was not reformed. Arrested for the theft of a government vehicle on February 27, 1951, he gave his name as "Elvin Hall," pleading guilty to theft of government property and violation of the Dyer Act, prohibiting transport of stolen cars across state lines. On April 2 Newman was sentenced to 18 months in prison, with an additional five years probation. Released in June, he was returned to the authorities in New York state for violating his parole.

A free man once again by summer 1955, Newman spared no time or energy in plotting out another heist. On August 3, with two accomplices, he tried to rob an armored tuck in Buffalo, New York—and the result was a fiasco. The bandits, wearing stocking masks, with Newman brandishing a submachine gun, sprang their trap with the arrival of the truck in the security company's garage. Inside the armored van lay a half-million dollars in American and Canadian currency, lately retrieved from a race track at Fort Erie, Ontario. Bursting into the garage, Newman shot and wounded one of the guards, holding the others at bay while his allies collected the loot.

Unfortunately for the outlaws, Newman's wounded victim was alive and on the move. Unseen by his assailants, the injured officer managed to reach a tower overlooking the garage area, there sounding an alarm that brought employees and patrolmen on the run. The startled bandits dropped their loot and took off empty handed. Newman commandeered a car at gunpoint, but a fault in the ignition left them stranded. Picking up a second car, the gunmen led police on a wild chase, spraying their pursuers with automatic fire before they dumped their latest car in a residential neighborhood. Splitting up, they took refuge in two separate houses and were soon surrounded by police.

A new battle erupted, shattering the normal calm of tree-lined streets, and tear gas was employed to flush a pair of outlaws from their bullet-riddled sanctuary. Newman managed to escape in the confusion, while his two accomplices were being cuffed and bundled into waiting squad cars. Posted to the FBI's

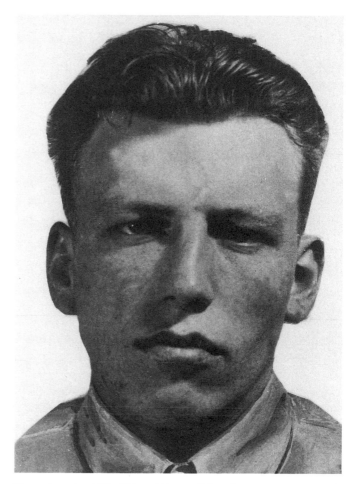

Posted to the FBI's "Most Wanted" list for a 1955 armored truck robbery, Eugene Newman was never apprehended. (FBI)

"Most Wanted" list on May 28, 1956, Eugene and his machine gun had already disappeared without a trace. A few days short of nine years later, federal process was dismissed on May 11, 1965. Gene Newman is another one of those who got away.

NEWTON, Adolph "Big Dolph"

A Swedish immigrant to California, Adolph Newton briefly tried his hand at prospecting for gold, before deciding it was easier to steal loot than to dig it from the earth. Convicted of robbery and imprisoned at San Quentin, he made friends with bandit leader TOM HODGES and later escaped to join his crony's holdup gang, riding with such notorious outlaws as RICHARD "RATTLESNAKE DICK" BARTER, BILL GRISTY, JIM WEBSTER, and the SKINNER brothers, George and Cyrus.

On March 12, 1856, Newton participated in the gang's greatest score of all time, stealing $17,000 in gold dust from a mule train en route from the Yreka Mine to Shasta through the Trinity Alps. Gang member William Carter was quickly arrested, naming Newton, George Skinner, and Nicanor Rodriguez as accomplices in the holdup. Sacramento law enforcers were alerted, jailing Newton and crony Tom Brown in early April. While "Big Dolph" refused to talk, Brown directed manhunters to a hideout near Folsom, where George Skinner was killed and Nicanor Rodriguez arrested after a furious shootout. Newton, for his part, was convicted of robbery once again and sentenced to serve 10 more years at San Quentin.

NG, Benjamin: See WAH MEE CLUB MASSACRE.

NG, Wai-Chiu: See WAH MEE CLUB MASSACRE.

NUSS, Randall: See JENKINS, JAMES.

NUSSBAUM, Albert: See WILCOXSON, BOBBY RANDELL.

O

ORDER, The

Spawned by decades of racist, anti-Semitic propaganda from groups including the Ku Klux Klan, Aryan Nations, National Alliance, and the Christian Identity movement—a cult whose followers believe Jews are the literal spawn of Eve's copulation with Satan in the Garden of Eden, while nonwhite "mud people" are soulless subhumans—The Order was America's first example of a hard-core neo-Nazi TERRORIST group. Its leaders publicly declared war against "ZOG"—the so-called Zionist Occupation Government in Washington, D.C.—and proved themselves willing to kill in that pursuit. Along the way they supported themselves by means of high-profile robberies, distributing much of their loot to like-minded fanatics.

The Order's immediate inspiration came from *The Turner Diaries,* published in 1978 by neo-Nazi activist William Pierce. A one-time physics professor and aerospace research consultant, Pierce quit his job in 1966 to join George Lincoln Rockwell's American Nazi Party. Emerging as a principal leader of the party after Rockwell's 1967 assassination, Pierce organized his own National Alliance three years later and built it over time into America's most active font of fascist propaganda. In *The Turner Diaries,* penned pseudonymously as "Andrew McDonald," Pierce described a futuristic Jewish conquest of America, resisted by militant whites from "The Order" who fight to defend "the true seed of Christ." *The Turner Diaries* provided a handy blueprint for right-wing

terrorism—and, according to federal prosecutors, inspired the 1995 Oklahoma City bombing committed by Timothy McVeigh, claiming 168 lives.

Before McVeigh, though, there was Robert Jay Mathews. Born at Marfa, Texas, in 1953, Mathews at age 21 joined a band of tax resisters called the Sons of Liberty. Legal problems resulting from that crusade drove him to sparsely settled Metaline Falls, Washington, in 1975 and he joined the National Alliance three years later in time to catch *The Turner Diaries* hot off the presses. The fantasy took Mathews by storm, and he plunged full time into the delusional world of neo-Nazi resistance and revolution against "ZOG." In September 1983 he was a keynote speaker at an Arlington, Virginia, meeting of the National Alliance, telling his audience that "the time for war has come."

Within a month he was prepared to launch that war himself.

Mathews founded his real-life version of The Order in mid-October 1983, recruiting allies from sundry factions of the lunatic fringe. Richard Butler's Aryan Nations contributed Bruce Carroll Pierce (no relation to William), Randolph Duey, Gary Lee Yarbrough (an ex-convict and Butler's chief of security at Hayden Lake, Idaho), and Thomas Bentley (principal of Butler's "Aryan Academy"). From James Ellison's Arkansas-based Covenant, Sword, and Arm of the Lord (CSA), came Randall Rader, David Tate, Jackie Lee Norton, and Jean Craig (mother of Mathews's live-in girlfriend Zillah Craig).

Klan members David Eden Lane, Frank Lee Silva, and Thomas Martinez signed on with the team. Richard Harold Kemp and Bill Soderquist pitched in for the National Alliance. Other recruits included RICHARD JOSEPH SCUTARI, Andrew Virgil Barnhill, Ardie McBrearty, Kenneth Loff, and Denver Drew Parmenter. Putting on German airs in the best neo-Nazi style, Mathews and company sometimes referred to The Order as *Bruders Schweigen*—loosely translated as "Silent Brotherhood."

Order members staged their first raid within two weeks of the group's creation, robbing an adult video shop in Seattle. The score was so disappointing—a mere $369—that Mathews abandoned robbery for the time being and tried his hand at counterfeiting. Bogus $50 bills were cranked out on a press at "Pastor" Butler's Aryan Nations compound, but the product was so poor that Bruce Pierce landed in jail on December 3, 1983, following his first attempt to pass the funny money. Released on bond two days before Christmas, Pierce rejoined his comrades for new adventures.

By that time Mathews had already pulled his first bank job, on December 18 in a northern suburb of Seattle. Operating solo, Mathews bagged $25,952, but a red dye pack exploded on the run to his getaway car. Some of the loot was ruined, but he cleaned the rest with paint thinner and funneled it into the cause. Around the same time, Bruce Pierce and Gary Yarbrough stole $10,000 worth of electronics equipment from Spokane-area stores, moving on to rob an Idaho truck stop of several thousand dollars. The gang's next bank job, in Spokane, netted a meager $3,600 on January 30, 1984. Starting a trend, the thieves donated $100 to Butler's Aryan Nations and sent another $200 to Michigan Klan leader Robert Miles.

Holdups were not the purpose of The Order's "racial holy war," but they kept the wheels turning. On March 16, 1984 Mathews led a four-man team that stole $43,345 from a Continental Armored Transport truck in Seattle. With that success behind him, Mathews tried another fling at counterfeiting, recruiting veteran "paper-hangers" Robert Emil Merki and wife Sharon in a fruitless effort to produce $10 bills. Bruce Pierce pled guilty to federal counterfeiting charges on April 3, 1984, expecting probation, but the judge slapped him with a two-year prison sentence. Begging time to put his affairs in order, Pierce was granted three weeks and promptly fled into hiding.

On April 22, 1984—one day before Pierce was scheduled to enter prison—The Order bombed a Seattle porn theater, phoning in more bomb threats on April 23 as a diversion for the holdup of an armored car in suburban Northgate. The seven-man raiding party escaped with $230,379 in greenbacks, $4,432 in Canadian currency, and $301,334 in useless checks. Mathews sent $40,000 of the loot to the Aryan Nations, kept $85,000 to finance The Order's future operations, and divided the rest with his team. By way of celebration, Pierce and Richard Kemp firebombed a Boise, Idaho, synagogue on April 29.

The Order committed its first murder less than one month later. A loose-lipped member of Aryan Nations, one Walter West, had been babbling rumors about The Order around Hayden Lake, his drunken conversations reported back to Mathews and company. On May 27 David Tate and Randolph Duey killed West near the Butler compound, shooting him once in the head and crushing his skull with a sledge-hammer before they planted him in a shallow forest grave. (No one was ever prosecuted for the murder; despite later guidance from a remorseful gang member, law officers never found West's grave.)

Killing a comrade might produce some qualms among "Aryan warriors," but executing a "Jew rabble-rouser" became their next labor of love. The target was Alan Berg, acerbic host of a Denver radio talk show who insulted David Lane and other local racists on the air. Despised by The Order as a mouth-piece for "ZOG," Berg was marked as the first official casualty of the new holy war. Lane drove the car that trailed Berg home from work on June 18, 1984; Bruce Pierce and Richard Scutari sprayed Berg with machine-gun fire, leaving him dead in his driveway.

For their next armed robbery, the Mathews team left nothing to chance. National Alliance member Charles Ostrout was a vault supervisor at the Brinks armored-car company's depot in San Francisco where he brooded daily over the promotion of "unqualified" black employees. Ostrout's boss and roommate, Robert Allen King, shared his friend's Nazi sympathies and collaborated in leaking information on cash shipments to The Order. Their ticket to official membership was a blueprint for the gang's greatest heist, carried off outside Ukiah, California, on July 16, 1984. Mathews led the 11-man team that stopped a Brinks armored truck and stole $3.6 million from the outnumbered guards. In flight, Bruce Pierce dropped a bundle of $10,000, found five months later by hikers in the nearby woods.

More critically, Mathews himself dropped a pistol registered to Andrew Barnhill—and thereby gave FBI agents their first hint that The Order existed.

Despite some grumbling from his followers, Mathews followed his established practice of dispensing loot to ranking bigots nationwide. Recipients of his largesse from the Ukiah heist included the Aryan Nations; Robert Miles in Michigan; Frazier Glenn Miller's North Carolina Knights of the KKK (later the White Patriot Party); Texas Klansman and Aryan Nations "ambassador at large" Louis Beam; Tom Metzger's California-based White Aryan Resistance; and Missouri's Church of Israel, an Identity congregation led by Dan Gayman. Federal agents were busy tracing Barnhill's gun, meanwhile; raiding his last known address on August 4 they found literature from the Aryan Nations, press clippings on the April 1984 Northgate holdup, and printed "Rules of Security" that bore the names of seven Order members. Long-distance telephone records connected the conspirators and put G-men on their trail.

In fact, the feds had scored their big break without knowing it when Order member Tom Martinez was arrested for passing counterfeit money on June 29, 1984. Facing trial and near-certain conviction on October 1, Martinez agreed to roll over and serve as an FBI spy inside The Order. He was reunited with his unsuspecting comrades in time to receive a six-page handout from Mathews headed *Bruders Schweigen* Staff." According to the document, Mathews (code named "Carlos") had divided the United States into six regions and appointed provisional commanders for the revolution: Robert Miles "Fox" would serve the Midwest; Denver Parmenter "Sandals" had authority over the Pacific Northwest; Tom Metzger "Bear" had the west coast; Louis Beam "Lone Star" was assigned the western district; Glenn Miller "Rounder" had the southern and southeastern U.S.; and William Pierce "Eagle" took command of the Northeast.

It was a blueprint for revolution, but members of The Order had more pressing matters on their mind in October 1984—like staying out of jail. Gary Yarbrough was nearly captured by FBI agents near Samuels, Idaho, on October 18, but he shot his way clear of the trap. Tom Martinez, in his role as double agent, arranged a Portland, Oregon, meeting with Mathews for November 24. G-men were waiting when Mathews arrived with Yarbrough in tow, but Mathews escaped after a pistol was shot from his hand. Yarbrough was captured at the scene while

Mathews fled to regroup with the remainder of his dwindling army. Their first order of business was a formal declaration of war against "ZOG."

We, the following, being of sound mind and under no duress, do hereby sign this document of our own free will, stating forthrightly and without fear that we declare ourselves to be in full and unrelenting state of war with those forces seeking and consciously promoting the destruction of our faith and our race.

Therefore, for Blood, Soil, and Honor, for the future of our children, and for our King, Jesus Christ, we commit ourselves to Battle. Amen.

The signatories—whose soundness of mind remained open to question—included Mathews, Bruce Pierce, Richard Scutari, Randolph Duey, Robert and Sharon Merki (using her maiden name, Donohue), and Frank Silva. Other signatures were collected later, from Ian Royal Stewart (son of the Merkis) and two more Klansmen, Mark Franklin Jones (aka "Steve Brant") and Michael Stanley Norris (aka "Paul Anderson").

Instead of launching a new offensive, though, members of The Order fled into hiding. Mathews, Duey, and the Merkis (with their son) hid out at a compound on Whidbey Island in Puget Sound, while the other "Aryan warriors" scattered nationwide. FBI agents besieged Whidbey Island on December 7, 1984, capturing Duey and the Merkis, while Mathews fought them to a standstill from his bunker command post. On the morning of December 8 G-men fired 40-mm flares into the hideout, setting it afire. Flames and exploding ammunition finished Mathews, his charred remains extracted from the rubble as it cooled.

Sweeping arrests rolled up most of The Order's surviving members over the next four months. David Tate and Frank Silva made a run for James Ellison's CSA compound in Arkansas, stopped along the way by two Missouri traffic cops on April 15, 1985. Tate killed one officer and wounded the other, abandoning a van filled with automatic weapons and explosives near the murder scene. Silva was captured the same day at a campground in Benton County, Arkansas; Tate was arrested on April 20, following an FBI siege at the CSA compound near Three Brothers, Arkansas. In the wake of that arrest James Ellison and five other CSA members were named in a 20-count indictment charging conspiracy to manufacture and possess illegal weapons—some of which had been sold to The Order. All six pled guilty in

August 1985: Ellison and Kerry Noble received five-year prison terms, while three other defendants saw their two-year terms suspended. In a separate case, CSA members Bill Brugle and Richard Smalley were convicted of supplying The Order with weapons. Brugle pled guilty and received an 18-month sentence (all but one month suspended) and a $3,000 fine; Smalley went to trial and was convicted, sentenced to one year in prison. Other CSA members were subsequently convicted on bombing charges and for interstate transportation of stolen cars.

Richard Scutari proved to be The Order's most elusive fugitive. Indicted with his compatriots in April 1985 on federal charges that included racketeering, conspiracy, and transporting stolen cash across state lines, Scutari was added to the FBI's "Ten Most Wanted" list on July 11, 1985. He remained at large until March 19, 1986, when G-men captured him in San Antonio, Texas. By that time, it was all over but the jail time for his fellow warriors.

Brinks employee Charles Ostrout was the first to fold, pleading guilty to conspiracy on April 29, 1985, drawing a five-year prison term when he turned state's evidence against his fellow Nazis. Others who pled guilty prior to trial included: Denver Parmenter (20 years); Robert and Sharon Merki (20 years each); Tom Bentley (seven and a half years); Randall Rader (six years suspended); Kenneth Loff (five years); Robert King (five years); Ian Stewart (five years, all but six months suspended); Mark Jones (suspended); Jackie Norton (suspended); George Franklin Zaengle (suspended); and William Anthony Nash (credit for time served pending trial). Charges were waived against Bill Soderquist in return for his turning state's evidence against the remaining defendants.

With Scutari still at large in the summer of 1985 and David Tate facing life without parole for murder in Missouri, 10 members of The Order remained to face trial in Seattle's federal court. All 10 were convicted on December 30, 1985. Bruce Pierce and Randolph Duey each were sentenced to 100 years; Gary Yarbrough and Richard Kemp received 60-year terms; 40-year terms were handed to Andrew Barnhill, Jean Craig, Randall Evans, David Lane, Ardie McBrearty, and Frank Silva; Michael Norris got off easy with a five-year prison term. Richard Scutari filed a guilty plea following his 1986 arrest and was sentenced to 60 years in prison. Defendants Lane and Pierce were convicted at a second federal trial in November 1987 for violating Alan Berg's civil rights

and drew additional terms of 150 years each; in Lane's case, the sentence was made consecutive with his previous 40-year term, for a total of 190 years. (Scutari was acquitted in the 1987 trial.)

Hate is persistent, and the saga of The Order did not end with the sweeping convictions in Seattle. Even before the 10 defendants heard their verdicts read, efforts were in motion to create The Order II—also dubbed the *Bruder Schweigen* Strike Force II. The new group's founders were all members of Aryan Nations, including Eldon "Bud" Cutler (Gary Yarbrough's replacement as chief of security at Hayden Lake); Aryan Nations security officer David Dorr and his wife Deborah (volunteer assistants to the Yarbrough legal defense team); Edward and Olive Hawley (roommates of the Dorrs in Athol, Idaho); Robert Pires and Kenneth Shray.

The new Order was a bumbling imitation of its predecessor. Bud Cutler was arrested in August 1985 for paying an undercover policeman to kill government witness Tom Martinez; his conspiracy trial opened in December 1985, and he received a 12-year prison sentence on March 21, 1986. Two weeks before that sentence was pronounced, on March 6, David Dorr botched an attempt to bomb the home of a Jewish businessman. Five months later, on August 7, the Dorrs bombed a custom auto shop in Kootenai County, Idaho. Two weeks later David Dorr and Robert Pires murdered fellow Aryan Kenneth Shray after deciding (mistakenly) that he was a spy for "ZOG."

The reign of terror was briefly interrupted in September 1986 when the Dorrs and Pires made an appearance on the Oprah Winfrey television show, but they were back in action by September 16, firebombing the home of a Catholic priest in Coeur d'Alene who had criticized the Aryan Nations. Ten days later, biting the fascist hand that fed them, members of The Order II stole computer and video equipment from the Hayden Lake compound for use in their private crusade. On September 26 they tried to emulate The Order's successful tactic from April 1984, planting bombs around Coeur d'Alene as diversions for the robbery of two banks and a National Guard armory, but the plot fizzled out and all five conspirators were soon arrested.

Robert Pires crumbled in custody and agreed to turn state's evidence against his cronies, pleading guilty to Kenneth Shray's murder in February 1987 before he vanished into the federal witness-protection program. All five conspirators were indicted on racketeering charges in February 1988; the Dorrs and Hawleys pled guilty eight months later, David Dorr sentenced to 20 years while his wife and Ed Hawley drew eight-year terms, and Olive Hawley was sentenced to six years (suspended) and five years' probation. Pires pled guilty to racketeering on January 9, 1990 and received a 20-year sentence.

Federal prosecutors, meanwhile, saw an opportunity to strike a death blow at America's festering neo-Nazi movement. CSA's James Ellison was bargaining for a reduced sentence, spinning tales of conspiracy involving his fellow far-right big-wigs on the racist fringe. In April 1987 sedition charges were filed against 17 notorious defendants. Named in the indictments were five imprisoned members of The Order, including Andrew Barnhill, David Lane, Ardie McBrearty, Bruce Pierce, and Richard Scutari. CSA members charged in the case included William Wade and his son Ivan; Lambert Miller; David Michael McGuire (Ellison's son-in-law); and Richard Wayne Snell (already condemned in Arkansas for the 1984 murders of a Jewish pawnbroker and a black policeman). Also indicted, for receiving stolen money from The Order and allegedly conspiring in its crime spree were racist leaders Richard Butler, Robert Miles, Louis Beam, and Glenn Miller.

Miller, already a fugitive on earlier federal charges, was captured in Missouri on April 30, 1987. On January 4, 1988, he pled guilty to possession of grenades and to making terroristic threats, his sentence of five years in prison and five years' probation conditional on turning state's evidence in the sedition case. Louis Beam dodged the FBI dragnet that bagged 11 of his codefendants on April 23, 1987, escaping with his wife and daughter to Mexico. Added to the bureau's "Ten Most Wanted" list on July 14, he was captured by G-men and Mexican police at Guadalajara, on November 6, 1987. Beam surrendered without resistance, but his wife opened fire on the lawmen with a pistol, wounding one Mexican officer before she was disarmed.

Trial commenced before an all-white, all-male jury at Fort Smith, Arkansas, in February 1988. Prosecutors had faith in their case, including testimony from James Ellison that defendants Beam and Butler had joined him for a secret meeting with Bob Mathews in 1983, plotting war against "ZOG" from the Aryan Nations compound in Idaho. Glenn Miller admitted to receiving $200,000 in stolen loot from The Order and furnished names of others who had profited from the crime spree. Tom Martinez repeated his

turn as a star witness, joined on the stand by defectors Zillah Craig, Bill Soderquist, and Denver Parmenter. Despite their testimony, though, jurors returned on April 7, 1988, with a verdict acquitting all 13 defendants on all counts.

Disappointed prosecutors found solace in the fact that 10 of those acquitted would remain in prison for years to come, some of them for life. David Lane, Bruce Pierce, and Richard Scutari plotted to escape from Leavenworth federal prison in January 1989, but their plan was foiled when prison administrators were tipped off in advance. Robert Miles retired from active racist pamphleteering to care for his invalid wife in 1990 and subsequently died of natural causes. Richard Snell was executed in Arkansas on April 19, 1995, hours after a racist bombing in Oklahoma City claimed 168 lives. Richard Butler's Aryan Nations filed bankruptcy and pulled up stakes in September 2000 after losing a multimillion-dollar damage suit resulting from a 1998 assault by Butler's ex-convict "security guards" against two female motorists outside the Hayden Lake compound.

ORGANIZED Crime: Robberies

Widely portrayed in FICTION AND FILM as a mildly sinister purveyor of illicit goods and services, primarily involved with such consensual crimes as gambling, prostitution, and narcotics, U.S. organized crime actually has a long tradition of involvement in robbery and HIJACKING. Early street gangs in cities such as New York and Chicago existed primarily as vehicles for burglary, armed robbery, and extortion, stealing literally anything and everything available. One notorious New York gang, the Hudson Boatmen, maintained a fleet of skiffs from which they looted cargo vessels on the Hudson River.

The advent of Prohibition in January 1920 opened a new age for hijackers of alcohol with the first booze shipment stolen in Chicago 10 minutes after the federal Volstead Act took effect on January 16. During the next 14 years before the "noble experiment" was repealed in December 1933, hundreds of liquor consignments were stolen across the United States with thousands of smugglers and gangsters murdered in battles over bootleg routes and sales territories. The net result of Prohibition was the creation of a nationwide crime syndicate—including but never limited to the Sicilian Mafia—which remembered and maintained its tradition as a subculture founded on strong-arm theft.

The Great Depression saw organized crime shift from bootlegging to widespread gambling and racketeering, but the men (and women) involved still had a taste for good old-fashioned larceny. Freelance bandits such as JOHN DILLINGER, ALVIN KARPIS, and CHARLES "PRETTY BOY" FLOYD were frequent clients of organized crime, renting hideouts between holdups, seeking out underworld sources for weapons, armored getaway cars, and medical treatment when wounded in action. Around the country, various communities—typified by ST. PAUL, MINNESOTA—earned reputations as mob-owned sanctuaries for outlaws on the run. Regional crime families also "taxed" independent thieves, permitting holdups and burglaries in their respective territories in return for a percentage of the loot.

Underworld theft and hijacking increased after World War II with crack teams of burglars and thieves active from coast to coast. Shipments of liquor and cigarettes are often stolen for sale at discount rates (minus state and federal taxes), while various luxury items ranging from furs and jewelry to expensive cars are hijacked in mass quantities. Where such crimes were detected, they rarely brought swift punishment. A 1960s study by the Joint New York State Legislative Committee on Crime found that 99.5 percent of hijacking arrests in New York resulted either in dismissal of charges or punishment with small fines and probation. For one year examined, 6,400 arrests were recorded for criminal possession of stolen property; those arrests resulted in 904 indictments, with only 225 convictions and 30 defendants confined to state prison. Pervasive corruption greases the machine, as in the case of eight New York Mafia figures arrested for hijacking, each found in possession of stolen women's clothing valued above $100,000: all eight received terms of probation and fines of $2,500 each from the same judge, renowned among cops and mobsters alike as being "on the pad" for hefty bribes. While on probation in that case, the same eight men were rearrested a total of 17 times for robbery, burglary, and possession of stolen property—but the same judge rejected all prosecution attempts to revoke their probation and send them to jail.

New York mob associate Henry Hill described the local operation at its peak for journalist Nicholas Pileggi in *Wise Guy* (1985). Working with a crew of hijackers led by Jimmy Burke, Hill—a relative small-timer with the syndicate and never a "made" member of the Mafia—still managed to maintain an affluent lifestyle on the proceeds of theft.

It was overwhelming. None of us had ever seen such opportunities for such money before. The stuff was coming in on a daily basis. Sometimes I'd go to Jimmy's house and it looked like a department store. We had the basement of Robert's [Lounge, a supper club] so loaded down with stuff that there was hardly enough room to play cards. Freight foremen and cargo workers used to bring the stuff to us on a daily basis, but still we felt we had to go out and snatch the trucks ourselves. Waiting for the loads to come to us wasn't cooking on all burners.

The gang's single biggest score was logged on December 11, 1958, when members of Burke's crew stole $5.8 million in cash and jewelry from the LUFTHANSA AIRLINES cargo terminal at Kennedy International Airport. FBI agents arrested two mob suspects on February 17, 1979, declaring that a third robber was "missing permanently," allegedly killed by underworld associates to ensure his silence.

Robbery and burglary remain a way of life for many members of organized crime today, with losses of public and private property ranked in the billions of dollars per year. Las Vegas mobster Anthony "Tony the Ant" Spilotro ran a crew of thieves in the late 1970s and early 1980s, dubbed "The Hole-in-the-Wall Gang" for their favored tactic of smashing through walls with sledgehammers and looting affluent boutiques, restaurants, and private homes. For some mobsters, regardless of their wealth and daily insulation from routine underworld affairs, the thrill of robbery seems almost as alluring as the loot they steal.

OTSUKI, Ted Jeffrey

Only the second Asian fugitive to rate inclusion on the FBI's "Ten Most Wanted" list since its creation in March 1950, Ted Otsuki made the federal dishonor roll nearly four decades later. In 1979 he invaded the Los Fresno, Texas police station, overpowering the officers inside and destroying their communications equipment before crossing the street to rob a bank. Convicted on charges of armed robbery, bank robbery, and as a felon in possession of a firearm, he was sentenced to a long term in the federal prison at Leavenworth, Kansas. Paroled in the 1980s, he continued his career in crime after winning conditional freedom.

Confronted by Boston police officers in 1986, Otsuki killed one and wounded another before fleeing the city. Federal agents tracked him to Dayton, Ohio, and from there to Chicago, filing charges of unlawful flight to avoid prosecution. By the time his name was added to the Top Ten list on January 22, 1987, Otsuki had left tracks in Harlingen, Texas, and in San Francisco, where a rented self-storage locker yielded two suitcases filled with explosives. Outstanding federal warrants included charges of unlawful flight, felon in possession of a firearm, and possession of an unregistered firearm. Otsuki was captured in Harlingen on October 10, 1988, and was returned to Boston for trial. In May 1989 he was convicted of murder and sentenced to life imprisonment.

PARKER, Bonnie: See BARROW, CLYDE.

PHILLIPS, Larry Eugene, Jr.: See MATASAREANU, EMIL.

PIERPONT, Harry "Pete"
A blue-eyed cop-hater known for his unpredictable violence, Hoosier native Harry Pierpont was born at Terre Haute, Indiana, on October 13, 1902. Geneticists would later argue that a birth defect—fused second and third toes on both feet—suggested a genetic bent toward impulsive behavior; others blamed Lena Pierpont for coddling her son and excusing his transgressions. Despite a troubled youth he managed to avoid arrest until March 1922 when a hometown resident spotted Harry in the act of auto theft and tried to intervene. Pierpont drew a pistol and fired four shots, inflicting minor wounds and landing in Pendleton Reformatory on a charge of assault with intent to kill.

Mrs. Pierpont lobbied tirelessly for Harry's release, informing Pendleton's superintendent that her son had been struck on the head with a baseball bat some years earlier, sending him briefly to a mental institution. Whether the tale was true or not, the superintendent had Harry's number, informing Mrs. Pierpont's attorney that "He is in a measure, mustang and must be curbed. I think it can be done with kindness and time better than with force and an early release." When Lena protested, the superintendent wrote to her: "This young fellow has been as wild as a March Hare. . . . I only wish I could write a different letter to you, but this boy has put a 10 rail fence up for me and it is hard to climb."

Hard or not, Pierpont was paroled in early 1924. He wasted no time in plotting his next crime, joining would-be outlaw Earl Kinder—the brother of Pierpont's girlfriend—to rob a bank in Kokomo. The heist was bankrolled by Pearl Elliott, proprietor of a Kokomo brothel, but Harry neglected to mention her name when he was arrested, thereby securing a valuable friendship. On May 6, 1925, Pierpont was shipped back to Pendleton on a 10- to 21-year sentence for armed robbery.

Pierpont's first order of business at Pendleton was making new friends, including veteran outlaws CHARLES MAKLEY, and JOHN "RED" HAMILTON, plus a young JOHN DILLINGER. Harry's second priority seemed to be trouble, ranging from backtalk and spitting at guards to an abortive escape attempt, drilling through the bars of his cell. That caper earned him a transfer to Indiana's state prison at Michigan City, soon followed by Hamilton and Makley. John Dillinger, denied parole in early July 1929, missed his pals enough to seek and receive a transfer to maximum security.

Pierpont maintained his reputation as a troublemaker at Michigan City, absorbing brutal punishment without a whimper and emerging as de facto leader of a gang including older, wiser convicts. By the time Dillinger joined the crew on July 15, 1929, Pierpont had already bungled four escape attempts. His chief competition for dubious honors as Michigan City's most-punished inmate was HOMER VAN METER, another friend of Dillinger whom Pierpont hated on sight. The feeling was mutual and they would never rob a bank together, although both rode with Dillinger in the years to come.

By the time Dillinger was paroled on May 22, 1933, Pierpont had given him a list of outlaw contacts—including Noble Claycomb and his White Cap Gang in Indianapolis—who would help Dillinger collect money and weapons to break his friends out of prison. Whorehouse madam Pearl Elliott and 22-year-old Mary Kinder joined in the conspiracy, climaxed on September 26, 1933, when several handguns were smuggled into the sewing shop at Michigan City. Pierpont led the daring break that afternoon, escaping with Makley, Hamilton, RUSSELL CLARK, JAMES CLARK (no relation), Walter Dietrich, Ed Shouse, Joe Jenkins, and Joseph Fox. (Earl Kinder missed the bust-out, confined to the prison hospital with a terminal case of tuberculosis.) The escapees split up as soon as they hit the street, Pierpont joined by Makley, Hamilton, Shouse, and Russell Clark in stealing a car from a nearby gas station. September 27 found them at the Indianapolis home of Mark Kinder, joined that night by bandit Harry Copeland before rolling on to Chicago.

John Dillinger, ironically, had been arrested for bank robbery four days before his friends broke out of prison; on September 28 he was transferred to the Allen County jail at Lima, Ohio. Never one to forget a favor, Pierpont pledged himself to liberate Dillinger from custody before he faced trial on the Ohio charges—but first the new gang needed operating money. With Hamilton, Makley, and Clark, Pierpont stole $14,993 from a bank at St. Mary's, Ohio, on October 3, 1933. The fugitives stopped at Fred Pierpont's house near Leipsic, Ohio, after the holdup, and Harry gave his brother the getaway car—a new Oldsmobile—as a personal gift.

On October 7, the gang made a dry run past Sheriff Jesse Sarber's jail in Lima, returning that night to the Leipsic farm and stashing their cars in Fred Pierpont's barn. Five days later, with Clark and Makley, Pierpont invaded the Lima jail, the trio posing as detectives who had come to question Dillinger. When Sheriff Sarber asked to see their badges Pierpont shot him and then pistol-whipped the lawman as he lay dying. Dillinger seemed saddened by the

kindly sheriff's death, but he did not hesitate to flee in company with his former cellmates. Sarber's wife readily identified the fugitives from their mug shots, and police raided the Pierpont farm at Leipsic that night, briefly jailing brother Fred for possession of a stolen car.

The new gang needed weapons to pursue its chosen course of holdups. On October 14, 1933, Pierpont, Dillinger, and Walter Dietrich raided the Auburn, Indiana, police station, making off with guns, ammunition, and bulletproof vests. One week later the trio repeated their feat in Peru, Indiana, escaping with another small arsenal. On October 23 eight gunmen—including Pierpont, Makley, Hamilton, Dillinger, Clark, Harry Copeland, and two unidentified accomplices—robbed a bank at Greencastle, Indiana. Newspapers reported the take at $75,000, but Dillinger later claimed the robbers only bagged $32,000, prompting some historians to speculate that the holdup may have been an "inside job" orchestrated to cover bank losses. A month after Greencastle, on November 20, Pierpont led Dillinger, Makley, Clark, Hamilton, and gunman Leslie Homer in stealing another $28,000 from a bank in Racine, Wisconsin. The gang wounded a patrolman and a cashier, taking another policeman, the bank president, and a female teller along as human shields to effect their escape.

Inspired by the gang's rash of sensational exploits, Indiana State Police commander MATT LEACH had a brainstorm in autumn 1933. Because he seemed unable to capture Pierpont's gang, Leach would instead use psychology in an effort to break up the team. As a means to that end, he circulated stories about the fearsome "Dillinger Gang," believing that Pierpont's wounded ego would prompt him to defect—or perhaps even kill his young protégé in a jealous rage. In fact, Pierpont laughed off the stories and did not seem to mind when Dillinger took them more seriously. Within the gang itself, Harry remained the unchallenged leader.

Frustrated, Matt Leach advised local law officers to keep watch on Pierpont's relatives in hopes that Harry would turn up someday for a family reunion. When word came in early December 1933 that Lena Pierpont and son Fred were driving toward Terre Haute in a new Auburn roadster, Leach alerted the Vigo County sheriff but advised against making arrests. Local lawmen ignored the warning and detained both Pierponts, infuriating Harry to the point that he marked Leach for death.

Driving to Indianapolis, Pierpont stood across the street from Leach's office one afternoon, aiming a pistol as the lawmen emerged, but a companion of Leach blocked his aim and Pierpont gave up on the plan.

It was time clearly for a break. On December 20, 1933, the gang arrived in Daytona Beach, Florida. Pierpont was accompanied by Mary Kinder; Dillinger traveled with girlfriend Evelyn Frechette; Russell Clark was paired off with mistress Opal Long; while "old man" Charley Makley traveled solo. Three days after Christmas, Illinois law enforcers released their newest list of "public enemies," ranking Pierpont number two behind Dillinger. If the list caused any qualms, the outlaws hid them well, celebrating New Year's Eve by firing Tommy guns into the surf outside their rented bungalows.

The team was back in action on January 15, 1934, robbing a bank in East Chicago, Indiana. Patrolman William O'Malley was killed in a flurry of machine-gun fire, witnesses identifying Dillinger as the trigger man. The gang fled to Chicago afterward, Pierpont and Mary Kinder moving on from there with Dillinger and Evelyn Frechette. On January 20 the foursome began to drive south to rendezvous with Makley, Russell Clark, and Opal Long in Tucson, Arizona.

The gang should have been safe in Tucson, but a fire broke out at their hotel a few days after they arrived; one of the bellboys was suspicious of the large tip he received for rescuing the gang's gun-heavy luggage. Police were notified, the fugitives swiftly identified from wanted posters, and the gang was rounded up without resistance on January 25. Frechette and Opal Long were released in Tucson five days later, while Dillinger was shipped back to Indiana for trial in the O'Malley murder; Pierpont, Makley, Clark, and Mary Kinder were routed to Chicago and then Michigan City (on February 1); the three men were finally delivered to Lima, Ohio, on February 10 to face trial in the death of Sheriff Sarber. (Mary Kinder, briefly charged with complicity in the September 1933 prison break, was released without trial on February 17, 1934.)

Pierpont's murder trial convened at Lima on March 6—three days after Dillinger escaped from jail at Crown Point, Indiana (using a smuggled pistol or a hand-carved wooden gun; reports vary). Taking the witness stand on March 11, Harry grinned as Prosecutor Ernest Botkin accused him of stealing $300,000 from various Midwestern banks. "Well, at

least if I did," Pierpont replied, "I'm not like some bank robbers—I didn't get myself elected president of the bank first." His trial judge ordered the comment stricken while spectators laughed, but Pierpont was not finished yet.

"That's the kind of man you are, isn't it?" Botkin demanded.

"Yes," Pierpont said. "I'm not the kind of man you are, robbing widows and orphans. You'd probably be like me if you had the nerve."

Spectators may have enjoyed Harry's nerve, but the jury convicted him of first-degree murder that same afternoon, with no recommendation of mercy. Makley and Clark were convicted six days later, but their jury split on the penalty phase: mercy for Clark and none for Makley. On March 24 the three bandits were sentenced; Pierpont and Makley were condemned, while Clark received a term of life imprisonment. They entered the state prison at Columbus together on March 27, 1934.

As veteran breakout artists, Pierpont and Makley were bound to try their hand at cheating the electric chair. Taking their cue from Dillinger (or his legend), they whittled guns from soap on September 22, 1934, blackened them with shoe polish, and used the "weapons" to force their way out of the cell block. Russell Clark briefly joined them, but the adventure ended at a locked steel door. Pierpont and Makley were hammering the door with their fists when armed guards arrived and opened fire. Makley was killed outright, while Pierpont recovered in time to keep his October 17 date with "Old Sparky."

On the eve of his execution, reporters asked Pierpont for details of the Michigan City escape, but they had to settle for his enigmatic smile. "Today," he said, "I am the only man alive who knows the 'who's' and 'how's' and as my end comes very shortly I'll take that little story with me on the last walk."

PINKERTON Detective Agency
Established in 1856, the Pinkerton Detective Agency served as de facto national police force of the United States between 1861 and 1908, when the FBI was established under the U.S. Department of Justice. Though privately employed and officially devoid of any law enforcement status, Pinkerton agents traveled widely throughout the United States and abroad for nearly a half-century, serving both government masters and large corporations while they pursued some of America's most notorious bandits.

Company founder Allan Pinkerton was a native of Glasgow, Scotland, born in 1817. Raised in the Gorbals slum district, he grew up with an intimate knowledge of rowdy lawbreakers, taking that expertise with him when he emigrated to Canada at age 25, in April 1842. Dissatisfied with his prospects north of the border, Pinkerton soon moved to Chicago and joined the sheriff's department in neighboring Kane County. When not chasing criminals, he earned a reputation as an outspoken abolitionist in that era of sectional strife over slavery. In 1850 Pinkerton was hired as a U.S. postal agent, assigned to stop a plague of mail thefts in Chicago. Six years later, with partner Edward Rucker, he founded Pinkerton & Company as the nation's first major private detective firm. Rucker dropped out before year's end and Pinkerton resigned his other jobs to run the company full time, enlisting brothers Robert and William to help him.

The Pinkerton agency obtained its first railroad contracts in January 1861, as the approach of civil war sparked fears of Confederate sabotage along Union rail lines. By spring of that year, with the shelling of Fort Sumter, Pinkerton helped establish a presidential security team that would evolve into the U.S. Secret Service. During the next four years, his agents pursued counterfeiters and Confederate spies with equal zeal, pledged to defend the Union from traitors within and enemies without.

The Pinkerton brothers solved their first TRAIN ROBBERY in January 1866 after an enterprising thief stole $700,000 in cash, bonds, and jewelry from a railroad express car in Connecticut. Nine months later and 400 miles further west, they were thrown into pursuit of the outlaw RENO BROTHERS, desperadoes raiding across three states from their base of operations at Seymour, Indiana. Two years elapsed—and Allan Pinkerton survived two gang-related attempts on his life—before the Renos were brought to heel, jailed in Indiana, and dispatched by lynch mobs before they faced trial for their crimes.

Although Pinkerton agents pursued countless felons across the continent, they were probably best known in the 19th century for their long-running war with a band of Missouri outlaws related by blood, FRANK and JESSE JAMES, together with their cousins the YOUNGER BROTHERS. Pinkerton agents hounded the James-Younger gang from May 1868 until Jesse James was murdered by associate Bob Ford in 1882, but the action was most heated in 1874–75 when blood was spilled on both sides. Three Pinkerton men were killed in the space of two days, March 15–16, 1874, while stalking the James and Younger boys in Missouri's Ozark country; outlaw John Younger also died in one of the shootouts, but the other bandits always managed to escape. Pinkerton agents bombed the home of Frank and Jesse's mother in January 1875, crippling the old woman and killing half-brother Archie Samuel in a move that only increased local sympathy for the fugitives. Pinkerton's men had nothing to do with the battle that broke the original gang in September 1876 at Northfield, Minnesota, but outstanding reward money clearly prompted Bob Ford to gun Jesse down in April 1882.

The Pinkerton agency's next notorious targets about the turn of the century were BUTCH CASSIDY and the members of his hard-riding "WILD BUNCH," linked to numerous bank and train robberies spanning six western states. Various Wild Bunch raiders were imprisoned, were hanged, or died with their boots on battling posses between 1898 and 1903, but Cassidy slipped through the net, escaping to South America with sidekick HARRY LONGABAUGH in February 1902. There, beyond the reach of American manhunters, they survived until early 1909—and Cassidy may have lived much longer, if legends of his escape from Bolivian troops and return to the United States are true.

Allan Pinkerton never witnessed his agency's pursuit of Cassidy and company. Two years after Jesse James was killed, Pinkerton fell on a city street and bit his tongue, developing a gangrene infection that claimed his life in June 1884. Robert Pinkerton led the agency until his death in 1907, followed by brother William, deceased in 1923. Allan Pinkerton II incorporated the agency in 1926 but died four years later, leaving the reins to Robert Pinkerton II. His death in 1967 severed family ties to the company his uncle had founded more than a century earlier, but he left it in good form, with 45 branch offices and 13,000 employees across the United States and Canada. Thirty years later, an expanded Pinkerton Security Services boasted 250 offices and 50,000 employees worldwide.

PIRATES and Piracy

Pirates have been recognized and their exploits recorded for as long as human beings have sailed the seas and oceans of our planet. Some have become infamous for their deeds, while others achieved the near-heroic status of classic SOCIAL BANDITS. Every portion of the globe has witnessed piracy in one form or another, and it continues today in some regions, despite a popular misconception that maritime piracy was wholly eradicated in the late 18th or early 19th century.

The Phoenicians freely raided ships of hostile nations as early as 1100 B.C.E., and the problem of piracy was well known to ancient Greeks and Romans, described by historian Milton Meltzer as "a steady trade" in the Mediterranean Sea from the earliest of times. It ranked as big business—a primitive form of ORGANIZED CRIME—by 150 B.C.E. with captured passengers and seamen sold as slave labor to the owners of large estates. Two major centers of early Mediterranean piracy were Side in Pamphlia and the small island of Delos. Rome's senate gave the illicit traffic a nod in 167 B.C.E. by granting Delos preferential trade status; it was later declared a free port after Roman legions seized territory formerly owned by Rhodes. Thereafter, the docks at Delos were modernized and expanded to the point where historian Strabo reports them able to ship and receive an average 10,000 slaves per day. Delos was finally sacked during one of Rome's numerous wars, in 88 B.C.E., and pirates themselves completed the destruction 19 years later after which the center of slave trading moved to Rome proper.

Piracy became a political issue for Rome when seagoing bandits threatened the empire's ability to replace field troops, as in Rome's war with the Cimbri (or Germanic) tribes. The king of Bithynia was ordered to provide replacement troops for Rome's legions but declined on the ground that most of his able-bodied men had been kidnapped and sold into slavery by pirates. Rome's first military move against Mediterranean pirates was launched in 102 B.C.E. with indifferent results. Contradictory policies of suppression and encouragement vied for primacy during the next 35 years until maritime traffic was brought to a virtual standstill in 69 B.C.E. As reported by Roman historian Appian—

No sea could be navigated in safety, and land remained untilled for want of commercial intercourse. The city of Rome felt this evil most keenly, her subjects being distressed and herself suffering grievously from hunger by reason of populousness. But it appeared to her to be a great and difficult task to destroy such large forces of seafaring men scattered everywhither on land and sea, with no heavy tackle to encumber their flight, sallying out from no particular country or visible places, having no property or anything to call their own, but only what they might chance to light upon. Thus the unex-ampled nature of this war, which was subject to no laws and had nothing tangible or visible about it, caused perplexity and fear. . . . And now the pirates contemptuously assailed the very coasts of Italy, around Brundisium and Etruria, and seized and carried off some women of noble families who were traveling, and also two praetors with their very insignia of office.

Julius Caesar himself was kidnapped and ransomed by Aegean pirates in 78 B.C.E., gathering troops on his release and returning to find his late captors in the midst of a drunken celebration, whereupon he executed 350 men (including 40 who were crucified). In 67 B.C.E. the Roman senate gifted General Pompey with extraordinary powers to rid the Mediterranean of pirates by any means necessary. To that end, Pompey organized a fleet of 270 ships, with 120,000 infantry and 4,000 horsemen to sweep the Mediterranean coastline. Before the end of his ruthless campaign, Pompey captured 377 pirate ships, sacked 120 forts or cities occupied by freebooters, and killed an estimated 10,000 pirates. That bloodbath ended the Mediterranean threat for a time, but piracy continued unabated in the Red and Black Seas, which had been largely neglected by the Roman navy.

Residents of northern Europe and the British Isles, meanwhile, had trouble of their own with pirates as the Roman Empire slipped into decline. One victim, kidnapped by Irish pirates in C.E. 405, spent six years as a slave before he managed to escape; years later, as Saint Patrick, he returned to spread Christianity throughout the Emerald Isle. Scandinavian VIKINGS began three centuries of coastal raiding in June 793 with an amphibious assault on Lindesfarne, on the North Sea coast of present-day Scotland. Viking raids for loot and slaves continued throughout Britain, France, and Germany until 1103 when Norse raiders under Magnus Barelegs were defeated in Ulster, their commander slain in battle by Irish defenders.

Mediterranean piracy resumed with a vengeance in 1492, when Muslim rule in Spain was broken, the defeated Moors driven back to their native North Africa. A new generation of Barbary pirates established strongholds at Tripoli, Algiers, and Sallee (now Salé, Morocco). At the same time, Christopher Columbus discovered a New World for European mariners to explore and colonize, with maritime outlaws following close behind. French pirates were raiding Spanish settlements in the Western Hemisphere by 1506; Dutch traders were active in the

Caribbean by 1542; and English colonists established their first North American outpost in 1607. Colonial rivalry and European warfare prompted the licensing of numerous "privateers"—officially sanctioned pirates financed by governments or private investors who paid their sponsors as much as 50 percent of the loot from each voyage, recruiting seamen on the basis of "no prey, no pay." One such, Sir Francis Drake, bagged £40,000 worth of stolen gold, silver, and pearls on his first privateering voyage in 1573. Half a world away, Mediterranean pirates led by the red-bearded Barbarossa brothers waged ruthless guerrilla war against seagoing Christians and sold them into slavery, a peril that persisted until 1830.

Although piracy remained a global problem through the 17th and 18th centuries, any mention of pirates to an American or European audience commonly evokes visions of Caribbean raiders, complete with eye patches, peg legs, and parrots perched on their shoulders. That image has been heavily influenced by treatments of pirates in FICTION AND FILM, but it is also true that the West Indies were a happy hunting ground for pirates from the early 1500s through the mid-19th century. Most of the pirates freely recognized today were active in that area and age, their exploits told, repeated, and embellished until it is difficult—sometimes impossible—to separate fact from legend.

Among the most notorious (and exalted) of Caribbean pirates was Captain Henry Morgan, a native of Wales who traveled to Barbados at age 20 in 1655. Reports differ on whether Morgan was an indentured servant or an ensign in the Royal Navy, but in either case he soon made his way to Tortuga and there enlisted with the pirate crew of Edward Mansfield, rising through the ranks to assume command with Mansfield's death in 1667. A year later, Morgan sacked Puerto Príncipe (now Camagüey), Cuba. His next target was Portobello, Panama—then the third-richest city in Central America—but it nearly proved to be his last excursion: Morgan's flagship exploded during celebration of the victory, killing some 300 pirates, but Morgan survived with only minor injuries. A taunting postexplosion message from the president of Panama infuriated Morgan, and his revenge was assured by Morgan's June 1670 commission as an admiral and commander-in-chief of Royal Navy forces in the West Indies, assigned to raid Spanish shipping and settlements. In January 1671 Morgan led 1200 men across the isthmus to storm Panama City, defeating a force nearly twice that size in a two-hour battle that left between 400 and 600 persons dead. When the pirates retired from the field, they took with them 200 pack-mules laden with gold, silver, and other booty, estimated by one of Morgan's surgeons at £70,000. Knighted by King Charles III in 1674, Morgan was appointed governor of Jamaica and held office until his removal in 1683 on grounds of habitual drunkenness and alleged improprieties. He died five years later, at age 53.

Another troop of pirates who attempted to duplicate Morgan's sack of Panama in April 1680 found the one-time capital city deserted, most of its dwellings destroyed by fires that had raged for a month after Morgan's attack, but there was no shortage of targets throughout the New World. Capture of prize ships and ransom of hostages remained the pirates' mainstay, with special flags designed to intimidate merchant seamen. A black flag emblazoned with a skull (dubbed "Jolly Roger") identified pirates to their intended victims and warned that any resistance would be met with annihilation. Red flags replaced the black if surrender was not forthcoming, indicating that the offer of mercy was withdrawn. Caribbean-based pirates ranged as far afield as Newfoundland and the west coast of Africa, reaching their peak with an estimated 5,500 active buccaneers (a Spanish word for "pirate") in the decade between 1714 and 1724. Though rebellious by nature and lawless by definition, many pirates nonetheless recognized a basic code of conduct, formalized by certain captains as a list of written rules. One such was posted by Captain Edward "Ned" Low in 1723. It read:

1. The captain shall have two full shares; the master is to have one share and one half; the doctor, mate, gunner and boatswain, one share and one quarter.
2. He that shall be found guilty of taking up any unlawful weapon on board the privateer or any other prize by us taken, so as to strike or abuse another in any regard, shall suffer what punishment the captain and majority of the crew shall see fit.
3. He that shall be found guilty of cowardice in the time of engagements, shall suffer what punishment the captain and majority of the company shall think fit.
4. If any gold, jewels, silver, etc. be found on board of any prize or prices to the value of a piece-of-eight, and the finder do not deliver it to the quartermaster in the space of 24 hours he shall suffer what

punishment the captain and majority of the company shall think fit.

5. He that is found guilty of gaming, or defrauding one another to the value of a real plate, shall suffer what punishment the captain and majority of the company shall think fit.

6. He that shall have the misfortune to loose [*sic*] a limb in time of engagement, shall have the sum of six hundred pieces-of-eight, and remain aboard as long as he shall think fit.

7. Good quarter to be given when craved.

8. He that sees a sail first, shall have the best pistol or small arm aboard of her.

9. He that shall be guilty of drunkenness in time of engagement shall suffer what punishment the captain and majority of the company shall think fit.

10. No snapping of guns in the hold.

Pirate crews generally destroyed their rules of engagement if capture seemed imminent because the lists were signed by all aboard and thus constituted a formal confession. Low's list survived, however, with another posted the same year by Captain John Phillips.

1. Every man shall obey a civil command. The captain shall have one share and a half of all prizes. The master, carpenter, boatswain and gunner shall have one share and [a] quarter.

2. If any man shall offer to run away or keep any secret from the company, he shall be marooned with one bottle of powder, one bottle of water, one small arm and shot.

3. If any man shall steal anything in the company or game to the value of a piece-of-eight, he shall be marooned or shot.

4. If at anytime we should meet another marooner [pirate], that man that shall sign his articles without the consent of our company shall suffer such punishment as the captain and company shall think fit.

5. That man that shall strike another whilst these articles are in force shall receive Moses's Law (that is, forty stripes lacking one) on the bare back.

6. That man that shall snap his arms or smoke tobacco in the hold without a cap on his pipe, or carry a candle lighted without a lantern, shall suffer the same punishment as in the former article.

7. That man that shall not keep his arms clean, fit for an engagement, or neglect his business, shall be cut off from his share and suffer such other punishment as the captain and the company shall think fit.

8. If any man shall lose a joint in time of an engagement, he shall have 400 pieces-of-eight. If a limb, 800.

9. If at any time we with meet a prudent woman, that man that offers to meddle with her without her consent, shall suffer present death.

Pirate captains and crewmen were drawn from all races and nationalities. Dutch pirates, called Sea Beggars, stopped raiding long enough to help William of Orange liberate their homeland in 1571–72. Frenchman Jean Bart captured 80 British ships in the late 17th century before he joined the French navy and was ennobled by King Louis XIV in 1694. Francis L'Olonnais, a French former slave on a Spanish plantation in the West Indies, reserved special hatred for Spaniards, once ripping out a captive's heart and eating parts of it raw; he also severed the tongues of prisoners who refused to give up their valuables until he was himself captured and dismembered alive by Darien tribesmen. Roche Brasiliano, a Dutch buccaneer, roasted Spaniards alive on a spit if they were caught withholding loot. Montbars of Languedoc (aka "The Exterminator") cited cruelty to American Indians as his motive for torturing Spaniards to death. Black Caesar, the lone survivor of a sunken slave ship, washed ashore at Biscayne Bay and later earned a fearsome reputation for his raids along the Florida Keys where a channel on Elliott Key still bears the name Caesar's Creek in his honor. Black Caesar was hanged by British authorities in 1718, but his name resurfaced in the 1820s, assigned to a fugitive slave from the United States who led a pirate crew and once captured a Spanish galleon 800 miles east of Cuba, claiming 26 tons of silver.

Despite such examples, the most notorious Caribbean pirates were either British subjects or first-generation Americans, often privateers commissioned by the king of England or his lord high admiral who tired of sharing their loot and went into business for themselves. In the month of October 1720 alone, British pirates captured 16 French ships around Dominica and Martinique, torturing their captives and hanging the governor of Martinique, who was found aboard one vessel. A favorite stopover for Caribbean pirates was the Bahamas, where British authorities sought to suppress piracy by appointing Woodes Rogers—himself a former privateer—as royal governor. As a first step toward eradicating piracy, Rogers issued a blanket amnesty for any buccaneers who voluntarily retired. The lure of open sea and easy money proved irresistible to some, however, their number including:

Captain William Kidd, a native of Scotland born in 1645, who went to sea as a youth and was commissioned as a privateer in 1689 by King William III. Loot from that occupation established Kidd as a legitimate New York mariner and ship owner in 1690; five years later he received a royal commission to hunt pirates in the Red Sea and Indian Ocean, but he returned to full-time piracy by February 1696, ranging from West Africa to the Caribbean. Captured in the spring of 1701, Kidd was convicted of piracy and murder and was publicly hanged for his crimes on May 23, 1701.

Captain Bartholomew Roberts, a Welshman born in 1682, captured more than 400 prize ships between 1719 and early 1722. One Portuguese galleon contributed 40,000 moidores (about £50,000) to his war chest, and Roberts also looted the port of Trepassy, Newfoundland, in June 1720. Roberts died in combat with the Royal Navy frigate *Swallow* off Cape Lopez (on the Atlantic coast of modern-day Gabon) on February 5, 1722.

Captain Edward Teach (aka "Blackbeard") may have been a Carolina native, though some reports cite his birthplace as Bristol. Teach shipped out of Jamaica with licensed privateers during the War of Spanish Succession (1701–14) and continued with the pirate's trade at war's end in partnership with "Gentleman Pirate" Stede Bonnet. Bonnet tired of the game and accepted the amnesty offered by Governor Rogers, whereupon Teach assumed full control of a fleet including six ships and some 400 pirates. He raided along the Atlantic coast from North Carolina to Philadelphia, earning sufficient notoriety that Teach ranked as a special target of the November 1718 "Act to Encourage the Apprehending and Destroying of Pirates." That law offered £100 for Teach, dead or alive; other pirate captains were worth £40, while £20 was offered for their ranking officers, £15 for each inferior officer, and £10 for each common pirate captured. Three days after the act was passed, on November 17, 1718, Teach was killed in a battle with Royal Navy seamen that left 10 sailors and nine more pirates dead.

Captain Edward Low went to sea as a pirate in 1720 after his wife died and he lost his job in Boston. Known for his extreme cruelty to captives and crew alike, Low lost many crewmen to desertion but still managed to capture 140 prize ships between 1722 and 1724. He harbored special hatred for the Por-

tuguese, commonly beheading or disemboweling any prisoners from Portugal. After one Portuguese captain tossed 11,000 gold coins overboard to keep them from Low, Low's pirates massacred all 32 men aboard the captured ship. Low displayed the same ferocity toward New Englanders after June 1723, when the U.S. Navy captured one of his vessels, executing Captain Charles Harris and 25 of his 48 men. Low disappeared without a trace in the spring of 1725, and his fate remains unknown.

Captain John Rackham, nicknamed "Calico Jack" after his favorite underwear, was perhaps best known for enlisting female pirates ANNE BONNY and MARY READ to sail and fight with his crew of buccaneers. Rackham and company were captured by the Royal Navy in October 1720 after an engagement wherein the two women proved themselves more courageous fighters than their male counterparts. Rackham, Read, and Bonny were among six members of the crew condemned for murder, but the women's lives were spared on discovery that both were pregnant.

Altogether, an estimated 600 Anglo-American pirates from the West Indies were executed in the decade between 1716 and 1726. The New World pirates were suppressed but not eradicated, reports of scattered outbreaks persisting through the early 1840s, while Chile's government licensed privateers to raid Spanish shipping as late as 1865. The Far East remained a hotbed of pirate activity from the west coast of India (where Maratha pirates led by the Angria family plundered ships of the East India Company through the first half of the 18th century) to the Philippines (where Ilanun pirates remained active around Borneo and New Guinea through 1862). Most notorious of Asia's pirates were the Chinese *ladrones,* rebels against the Manchu dynasty who terrorized the coast of Cochin China (now the southern part of Vietnam) through the early 19th century. Ching Yih led the *ladrones* until 1807 when he died in a typhoon, but the pirates thereafter remained loyal to his wife, former prostitute Ching Yih Sao. At the peak of her power, Ching Yih Sao commanded a fleet of 800 large junks and 1,000 smaller boats, with the total strength of her personal army estimated between 70,000 and 80,000 pirates. In time, Ching Yih Sao took a new lover, bisexual opium addict Chang Paou, and placed him in command of her Red Squadron. Ching Yih Saou later retired from piracy to run a casino in Canton, while Chang Paou joined the

Manchu army and rose to the rank of brigade-general before his death at age 36.

Despite a prevailing belief that pirates became extinct sometime in the mid-19th century, sporadic attacks continue to the present day, and some authorities suggest that the problem is getting worse. The early 1960s saw a flurry of ship seizures in the Caribbean, though most were politically motivated, carried out by rebels seeking asylum from oppressive regimes. On January 22, 1961, for example, two crewmen and 24 armed passengers—all members of the Portuguese National Independence Movement—seized a Portuguese cruise ship and killed its third officer, diverting the vessel from its Lisbon-to-Florida course and demanding refuge in Brazil. Asylum was granted to the gunmen after they released their hostages in Recife. Seven months later, on August 8, a Cuban freighter was hijacked by 10 crewmen armed with pistols and diverted to Norfolk, Virginia, where the insurgent anticommunists requested and were granted political asylum.

By 1982 the threat of piracy was significant enough to rate a formal definition by the United Nations Convention on the Law of the Sea (UNCLOS), namely "any illegal acts of violence or detention, or any act of depredation, committed for private ends by the crew or the passengers of a pirate ship or a pirate aircraft" targeting ships or airplanes outside the jurisdiction of any recognized state. Within the jurisdiction of a functional government, the same crimes were identified as "armed robbery against ships." Between 1982 and 1986, an average of 25 pirate attacks were reported each year, particularly along the west coast of Africa; by 1991, the number of attacks had doubled to 50 per year, with a heavy concentration in the Strait of Malacca. Action shifted to the South and East China Seas in the latter 1990s with 98 pirate raids reported from the South China Sea alone in 1998. By 1999, 158 of the year's 285 pirate attacks were reported from Southeast Asia, with 113 of those occurring in Indonesian waters. Worldwide, the International Maritime Organization recorded 2,289 pirate attacks on shipping between July 31, 1995, and April 30, 2001.

Authorities concerned with piracy report that merchant vessels are the primary targets of modern buccaneers, an increasing trend as computer-age technology allows giant tankers and cargo ships to travel with skeleton crews, often fewer than two dozen sailors. New technology also favors pirates in

another way—permitting access to speedboats, automatic weapons, cellular telephones, and global positioning satellite gear. The problem is exacerbated by increasing lawlessness in Southeast Asia, especially Indonesia, since the 1997 Asian currency crisis. Operating on a scale comparable to ORGANIZED CRIME, latter-day pirates frequently infiltrate shipping companies, port authorities, and national customs services, while small crews of six to 10 men assault selected target ships. One large-scale operator, arrested in August 1999, was Singapore native Chew Cheng Kiat, accused of launching 21 hijackings from his "mother ship," a converted tanker named the *MT Pulau Mas*. Captured vessels were transformed into "phantom ships"—repainted, reflagged, and sold with their multimillion-dollar cargoes in Chinese ports of call.

Modern pirates remain as lethal as their forebears in many cases, with 51 victims murdered in 1997 alone. Most of those deadly attacks occurred off the coasts of India, Iran, Pakistan, and Sri Lanka; in one case, pirates slaughtered the 11-man crew of a merchant ship, then rifled the ship's safe, and left the vessel adrift at sea. A year later, in 1998, 23 crewmen were murdered aboard the *MV Cheung Son*. (Thirteen suspects in that case were captured and later executed by Chinese authorities.) In September 1998 the Japanese cargo ship *Tenyu* disappeared en route from Indonesia to Korea with a shipment of aluminum; three months later it turned up in the Chinese port of Zhangjiagang, renamed the *Sanei-1*. Its original crew of 13 Chinese and two Koreans had mysteriously vanished without a trace, replaced by 16 Indonesians.

Pursuit and prosecution of modern pirates remains erratic and largely ineffective, with various factors contributing to the problem. Financial hard times—especially in Asia—had led to dramatic reduction in the size of navies and coast-guard units with a corresponding reduction in service. Some naval units, particularly in the Far East and Africa, have turned to piracy themselves as a means to supplement dwindling income. Geography also plays a part, as in Indonesia where some 60,000 islands offer endless hiding places for small craft and criminal crews. Most frustrating of all are the governments that sometimes seem to encourage maritime piracy. In April 1998 the Malaysian *Petro-Ranger* was seized by pirates, Captain Ken Blyth threatened with death before he ordered his crew to surrender. The ship was later stopped and impounded by Chinese authorities, with the pirates still aboard. Incredibly, the police arrested Captain Blyth and jailed him for 30 days, while the pirates were returned to Indonesia with no charges filed against them.

By the final months of the 20th century, pirate attacks were being recorded worldwide at an average rate of one raid every 48 hours. A sampling of the cases includes—

April 1999: The Cypriot-registered tanker *Valiant Carrier* was hijacked in the Malaccan Strait with a full load of fuel. Pirates hurled Molotov cocktails onto the deck, routing panicked crewmen before they stormed the bridge, stabbing three ship's officers and one seaman's seven-month-old daughter. The ship was left adrift; control was recovered three miles short of collision with an island that would have caused a massive oil spill.

October 1999: Ten pirates boarded the Japanese cargo ship *Alondra Rainbow,* setting 17 crewmen adrift on a raft without food or water for more than a week. The Indian navy later sighted the ship, sailing under a new name and the flag of Belize, and captured it after a two-day chase. In custody, the pirates admitted bartering its cargo of aluminum ingots for weapons, earmarked for separatist guerrillas in Sri Lanka.

February 2000: The cargo ship *MV Hualien* vanished with 21 crewmen off the coast of Taiwan. The ship and crew remain missing today.

February 2000: Pirates armed with automatic weapons boarded the *MT Global Mars,* a Japanese tanker carrying 6,000 metric tons of palm oil, off the Malaysian coast on February 23. Seventeen crewmen were held captive for 13 days and then set adrift in a small boat. The crewmen were rescued on March 10 off the coast of Thailand, but the *MT Global Mars* remains missing.

January 2001: A gang of five to 10 armed pirates raided five fishing boats off the coast of Patharghata, Bangladesh, stealing an estimated $5,000 in cash from the various crews on New Year's Day. The same gang hijacked three more ships off Manderbaria, Bangladesh, on the same afternoon, scoring another $9,000 in cash.

February 2001: A 12-man gang of pirates boarded the fishing boat *Dilruba* off Patharghata, Bangladesh, on February 7, wounding one crewman with gunfire and stealing supplies valued at 8 million Taka ($139,373).

March 2001: Armed robbers attempted to board the cargo ship *Actuaria* on three successive nights

while it was berthed at Chittagong, Bangladesh. In each case the pirates were repelled by crew members with no injuries reported.

March 2001: The Panamanian tanker *Lingfield* was boarded by eight pirates east of Bintan, Indonesia, on March 7. The raiders bound and blindfolded three ship's officers, stealing $11,000 in cash from the *Lingfield*'s safe before they escaped in a speedboat.

March 2001: Armed pirates looted the Panamanian cargo ship *Jasper* off the coast of Kosichang, Thailand, on March 9, escaping with some $87,000 in cash. Members of the Thai Mafia were suspected.

March 2001: Six pirates armed with knives boarded the Indonesian cargo ship *Inabukwa* off the Malaysian coast on March 15, blindfolding crewmen and marooning them on an uninhabited island, making off with the ship and its cargo of pepper and tin ingots, valued at $2,170,000. Philippine authorities recovered the *Inabukwa* 10 days later and arrested the pirates.

April 2001: Pirates armed with high-powered weapons strafed a fishing boat off Zamboanga in the Philippines on April 2. Two crewmen were killed and a third was gravely wounded, but the gunmen fled without boarding the vessel.

May 2001: Four pirates armed with long knives boarded the Panamanian cargo ship *Marine Universal* at anchorage in Lagos harbor, Nigeria. One crewman was taken hostage and thrown overboard before the thieves stole various ship's stores and escaped.

Overall, the International Maritime Organization reported 50 incidents of piracy in the first quarter of 2001. Of those, 18 occurred in the South China Sea, 14 in the Malacca Strait, 13 in the Indian Ocean, four on the coast of West Africa, and one in the Philippines. Twenty-four of the ships were steaming at sea when attacked, while 26 lay at anchor in various ports. Violence was threatened in 22 cases, and physical attacks were reported in another eight; the remainder of cases involved thieves who fled when detected, without display of weapons. Four attacks involved gangs of more than 10 pirates, five to 10 raiders were counted in seven cases, and fewer than five were involved in 10 more. (No estimate of numbers was provided in the other 29 incidents.) No suspects were arrested in the 50 cases, once again suggesting why piracy has become the modern crime of choice for armed robbers in various parts of the world.

PLATT, Michael Lee: See MATIX, WILLIAM RUSSELL.

POEHLKE, Norbert Hans: Bank robber and murderer

On May 31, 1984, a truck driver found the body of 47-year-old Siegfried Pfitzer, shot once in the head with a 9-mm pistol, at a highway rest stop near Marbach, Germany, not far from Stuttgart. Police soon determined that Pfitzer's missing car had been used by the bandit who robbed a bank in Erbstetten, 10 miles from Marbach, on the same day, smashing the teller's glass cage with a sledgehammer to reach the money inside. In the wake of the robbery, Pfitzer's vehicle was abandoned less than a quarter-mile from the scene of the murder.

Seven months later, on December 21, 37-year-old Eugene Wethey was found shot to death at a rest stop near Nuremburg. On December 28, a hammer-wielding bandit used the dead man's car to flee a plundered bank in the village of Cleerbroun, 10 miles from Marbach. Police recognized the pattern, but it put them no closer to a suspect, and they could only wait while the homicidal robber plotted the next move.

On July 22, 1985, Wilfried Schneider, age 26, was found shot to death in a parking lot near his home, in the village of Beilstein-Schmidhausen. The murder weapon was identified as a Walther P5 pistol, routinely carried by many police officers, and authorities were not surprised with Schneider's car turned up at the scene of an attempted bank robbery in Spiegelberg, seven miles to the northwest. On that occasion, though, an armed teller forced the thief to flee without his intended loot.

Two months later, on September 29, antiterrorist officers were searching the Ludwigsburg railroad station for bombs when they found a police uniform in one of the lockers. The garments were traced to Chief Inspector Norbert Poehlke, a 14-year veteran of the Stuttgart constabulary, who claimed the uniform was left in Ludwigsburg for a quick change after a relative's funeral. Investigation revealed no recent deaths in Poehlke's family, but one of his daughters had died of cancer in March 1984 after a long siege that left the inspector with debts of some $400,000. Authorities now had their motive for robbery, and recent deviations in Poehlke's behavior indicated a potential for sudden, unpredictable violence.

The investigation was still in progress when Poehlke requested sick leave on October 14, 1985. A week later, police stopped by his home to ask him some questions, but they found only corpses. Poehlke's wife, Ingeborg, lay slumped in the bathroom, shot twice in the head, while in a bedroom his son Adrian had been shot once. A third child, son Gabriel, was missing from the home.

Three days later, on October 23, Inspector Poehlke and his missing son were found at the beach near Brindisi, in southern Italy. They were together in Poehlke's car, both shot with his Walther service pistol in an obvious murder-suicide. Ballistics tests confirmed that Poehlke's gun had also slain the first three victims in the murder series and the case was closed.

POPE, Duane Earl

A mild-mannered Kansas farm boy, widely admired and respected in his home community, Duane Pope was every parent's dream. Respectful of his elders, regular in church and school, the young man clearly had potential. Captain of the varsity football team during his senior year at MacPherson College, Pope graduated on May 30, 1965, at age 22.

Five days later, his world exploded.

College football star Duane Pope murdered four victims during a Nebraska bank heist. (FBI)

At 11:15 A.M. on June 4, 1965, Pope parked a green rental car outside the Farmers State Bank in Big Springs, Nebraska. He cut a dashing figure as he entered, dressed in suit and tie, the briefcase that he carried making him resemble a young lawyer or executive. Inside the bank Pope spoke with the president, elderly Andreas Kjelgaard, about a farm loan. Informed that the bank did not engage in such transactions, Duane opened his briefcase and withdrew an automatic pistol with a silencer attached. Moving swiftly into the cashier's cage, Pope scooped $1,598 into his bag, but the vault was secured with a time lock, and he could not afford to wait.

Kjelgaard, age 77, was forced to lie down on the floor beside his nephew Frank, cashier Glenn Hendrickson, and bookkeeper Lois Hothan. Moving down the line, Pope shot each hostage twice—once in the nape of the neck, once in the back—before casually leaving the bank. Of the four, only Frank Kjelgaard would survive his wounds, paralyzed from the waist down by a bullet to the spine.

FBI agents were immediately involved in the case, investigating the federal offenses of bank robbery and murder of a bank employee. Pope had rented the getaway car in his own name, and snapshots of the smiling murderer were readily identified by witnesses. His name was added to the Bureau's "Ten Most Wanted" list a week after the massacre on June 11, 1965. That same day, a short time after the announcement was released, Pope telephoned police in Kansas City to surrender. Convicted of triple murder and lesser charges in Nebraska, he was sentenced to die.

POPE, Harry Raymond

A veteran hoodlum from the neighborhood of Dallas, Texas, born in 1920, Harry Pope ran up a record of convictions for burglary, attempted burglary, drunken driving, and narcotics possession by age 30. Dubbed "the walking arsenal" after the shotgun and three pistols he habitually carried, Pope was not averse to violence. An associate of racketeers and contract killers, he possessed the reputation of a fast-gun artist who would shoot it out with officers in lieu of passively submitting to arrest.

On November 23, 1958, police in Phoenix, Arizona, surprised Pope in the act of burglarizing a drug store. Harry shot his way out of the trap but lost his right eye to a bullet in the process and was quickly captured. Free on bail, he disappeared before his trial and fugitive warrants were issued for his arrest. On

Armed robber Harry Pope was known to friends as "the walking arsenal." (FBI)

August 11, 1959, his name was added to the FBI's "Ten Most Wanted" list, citing federal charges of unlawful flight to avoid prosecution.

Two weeks later, on August 25, police in Lubbock, Texas, got a tip that Pope was hiding at a local trailer park. At 4:15 P.M. a team consisting of two federal agents, five patrolmen, and a single Texas Ranger stormed the trailer, catching Pope unarmed and browsing through a newspaper. Arrested with him, on a charge of harboring a federal fugitive, were Los Angeles residents Clifton and Christine Thompson. For all his fearsome reputation, Power opted to surrender in the face of overwhelming odds. "We saw them getting out of the cars," he said, "but I knew I didn't have a chance. There were too many of them, and they were armed too heavily. If there had been just three, that would have been good odds, but eight was too many. I'm not stupid."

POWER, Katherine Ann, and SAXE, Susan Edith

A Denver native, Katherine Power attended Catholic schools before leaving home to complete her education at Brandeis University in Waltham, Massachusetts. There she met lesbian Susan Saxe and they soon became lovers, Saxe introducing Power to feminism, radical politics, and the struggle for "liberation" in America. Saxe graduated from Brandeis in June 1970, devoting herself to the movement full time; Power was starting her senior year when violence and death intervened to cut short her studies.

Together, Saxe and Power were charged with stealing automatic weapons from the Newburyport Arsenal in Massachusetts during the late summer of 1970. They needed the firepower for "political" bank robberies, and Saxe was eventually charged in connection with a Philadelphia bank raid that netted $6,240 on September 1, 1970.

Three weeks later, on September 21, the target was a bank in Boston. Saxe and Power recruited three ex-convicts—Stanley Bond, William Gilday, and Robert Valeri—for muscle on the job, Katherine staying with the "switch" car a mile from the scene. Saxe and her three gunmen were leaving the bank when Patrolman Walter Schroeder pulled up in his squad car, first on the scene in response to a silent alarm. Cut down in a hail of bullets fired by Gilday, Schroeder died at the scene, his murder placing the crime in a whole new perspective.

The three apolitical stickup men were captured in short order: One was nabbed while disembarking from a cab outside his home; another was picked up as he tried to board an airplane in Grand Junction, Colorado; number three was caught in Worcester, Massachusetts, after a wild chase in which he seized two hostages before surrendering. Feeling no loyalty to their radical cohorts, the three outlaws talked freely. Saxe and Power were indicted on charges of murder, bank robbery, and theft of government property, topped off with counts of unlawful flight to avoid prosecution. Their addition to the FBI's "Ten Most Wanted" roster on October 17, 1970, brought the list up to its all-time maximum of 16 fugitives. (Gilday, meanwhile, was sentenced to life imprisonment for Patrolman Schroeder's murder. Valeri and Bond received lesser terms on conviction for manslaughter and robbery; Valeri survived to see parole, while Bond was killed in 1972 when a bomb he was building in prison exploded prematurely.)

Radical bank robber Katherine Ann Power, seen here in a 1996 photo, eluded FBI agents for 23 years after a 1970 holdup. (FBI) (AP/Wide World Photos)

On March 27, 1975, Susan Saxe was arrested by police in Philadelphia. She struck a bargain with prosecutors on June 9, pleading guilty to the arsenal theft and the Philadelphia bank job, on the condition that she would not be compelled to testify about events since 1969. On June 24, 1975, Saxe pled not guilty to charges of murder and robbery in Boston; a jury disagreed, convicting her of armed robbery and manslaughter. Released from prison in 1982, Saxe left through a rear exit to avoid the press and promptly vanished into obscurity.

While Saxe was serving her time, Katherine Power had gone straight in more ways than one. By 1977 she had settled in Corvallis, Oregon, and two years later had a son named Jaime. Power remained on the bureau's Top Ten list until June 15, 1984, when her name was quietly removed. As a former Boston prosecutor told reporters, "Of the five, the weakest case is against her and, well, it's been so long, who'd want to prosecute her now?"

As it turned out, in fact, both state and federal prosecutors would eventually have their chance and neither would decline.

In 1992 Power married longtime companion Ron Duncan and became co-owner of a Corvallis coffee house, but all was not well on the home front. Suffering from clinical depression, she entered therapy that same year. As described by her therapist, Power "started to see her life through the lens of this depression, and when that happened, the fog lifted." Attorneys in Oregon and Massachusetts spent more than a year negotiating with authorities before Power surrendered in Boston on September 15, 1993. The same day, she pled guilty in Suffolk County Superior Court to charges of armed robbery and manslaughter. Nine days later, in federal court, she also pled guilty to theft of government property, concerning the National Guard armory heist in Newburyport. As part of her plea bargain, the feds recommended in that case a five-year sentence to be

served consecutively with her pending time in state prison. On October 6, 1993 Judge Robert Banks imposed a sentence of eight to 12 years plus 20 years probation, with a specific provision that Power not be allowed to profit from sale of her story. Power appealed the latter provision, and the U.S. Supreme Court rejected her appeal on January 8, 1996.

PUFF, Gerhard: See HEROUX, GEORGE ARTHUR.

PURVIS, Melvin Horace, Jr.: 1930s FBI manhunter
The son of an affluent southern planter, Melvin Purvis Jr. was born at Timmonsville, South Carolina, on October 24, 1903. He graduated from the University of South Carolina with a law degree in 1925 and spent the next two years with a law firm in the Palmetto State. Purvis joined the FBI on February 4, 1927, under curious circumstances. Although two years below the minimum age set by Director J. EDGAR HOOVER for prospective G-men, Purvis was admitted to the bureau after Hoover received a personal call from South Carolina's senior U.S. senator and New Deal champion Ed "Cotton" Smith—thus giving the lie to Hoover's frequent claim that FBI recruiting was immune to political patronage.

Purvis enjoyed rapid advancement through the bureau ranks, ensconced by 1932 as special agent in charge of the Chicago field office. His startling rise apparently owed more to personal friendship with Hoover than any outstanding performance on Melvin's part, as indicated by their personal correspondence between 1927 and 1934. Initially in awe of Hoover, Purvis addressed him with all due respect until Hoover penned an order to "stop using MISTER" in written salutations. Henceforth, Purvis cheerfully addressed his boss in Washington as "Dear Chairman" or "Dear Jayee" (from Hoover's initials). Hoover's joke-ridden letters to Purvis included observations on one U.S. attorney's "mental halitosis" and suggestions that Hoover secretary Helen Gandy carried a torch for Purvis. If Melvin turned up for 1932's Halloween Ball, Jayee suggested, Ms. Gandy might be persuaded to greet him in a "cellophane gown."

Purvis might have passed his FBI career as an executive nonentity but for a geographic accident. His Chicago assignment placed him at the heart of bandit country in the Great Depression, and Purvis

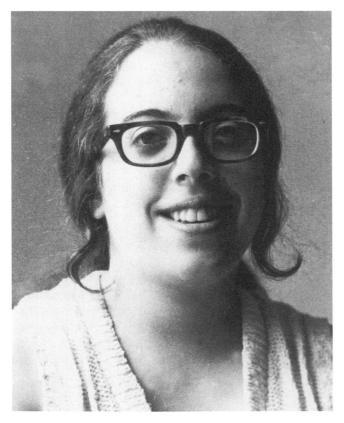

Power's accomplice, Susan Saxe, remained at large for more than four years following the robbery that claimed a Boston policeman's life. (FBI)

Melvin Purvis, left, who directed the capture and slaying of John Dillinger, shakes hands with William Stanley, the acting attorney general, while meeting with J. Edgar Hoover, head of the FBI. (AP/Wide World Photos)

was involved in some of the era's most notorious cases. Unfortunately for the bureau's reputation, he had a tendency to bungle manhunts or veer to the other extreme and "frame" cases with perjured testimony.

An early example of Purvis ineptitude was seen in his hunt for fugitive bank robber FRANK "JELLY" NASH. Purvis enlisted an American Indian ex-convict, one War Eagle, as his prime informant on that case, with humiliating results. War Eagle not only fingered an innocent man in that case but also loaned Purvis a stolen car for use in the abortive raid. It was small consolation to Purvis when other G-men captured Nash in June 1933, then lost their lives in the bloody KANSAS CITY MASSACRE while transporting Jelly back to Leavenworth federal prison.

Purvis saw a chance to redeem himself that same month when brewer William Hamm Jr. was kidnapped from ST. PAUL, MINNESOTA, and ransomed for $100,000. Hamm's abduction was carried out by the wide-ranging BARKER GANG, but Purvis had other suspects in mind—specifically Chicago bootlegger Roger "The Terrible" Touhy and three gangland associates, arrested with automatic weapons on July 19, 1933, following an auto accident near Elkhorn, Wisconsin. There was no clear reason to suspect the Touhy gang of snatching Hamm, but they were wanted in Chicago for the June 30 ransom abduction of career criminal Jerome "Jake the Barber" Factor—later proved to be a hoax.

It was enough for Purvis, pushing for indictments under the new Lindbergh Law that made interstate kidnapping a federal offense. In the absence of anything resembling evidence, Purvis fell back on a combination of third-degree tactics and perjured tes-

249

timony to make his case. As Touhy later described his experience in FBI hands—

I went into the jail in excellent physical shape. When I came out, I was twenty-five pounds lighter, three vertebrae in my upper spine were fractured, and seven of my teeth had been knocked out. Part of the FBI's rehabilitation of prisoners, I supposed. . . .

They questioned me day and night, abused me, beat me up, and demanded that I confess to the Hamm kidnapping. Never was I allowed to rest for more than half an hour. If I was asleep when a team of interrogators arrived at my cell, they would slug me around and bang me against the wall. . . .

I couldn't have confessed if I had wanted to. I didn't know what Hamm looked like, how the ransom was paid, where he was held, or anything else. Neither did [codefendants] McFadden, Stevens, or Sharkey. But it seemingly made no difference.

Touhy's complaint might be dismissed as typical sour grapes from a lifelong felon were it not for Purvis's own description of how the FBI handled its prisoners. "The escaped prisoner was 'invited' to accompany the special agent to the federal building," Purvis gloated, "and sometimes these invitations were engraved on the minds [sic] of the escape[e] in a very definite fashion and they were accepted." Nor were innocent witnesses safe from bureau terrorism. In the Hamm case, prospective defense witness Edward Meany was told by G-men, "If you go to St. Paul to testify for Touhy you'll be sorry—and maybe you won't come back."

It was all in vain, despite public claims from Purvis that "We have an ironclad case." Indicted for Hamm's kidnapping on August 12, 1933, Touhy and his three codefendants were acquitted by a St. Paul jury on November 28. Instead of being freed, however, they were held for delivery to Chicago authorities for trial in the fabricated Factor snatch. It was too much for defendant Willie Sharkey, who hanged himself in jail two days after the Hamm acquittal.

Purvis pulled out all the stops for the next trial in Chicago, pressuring known felons to lie under oath and implicate Touhy in a "kidnapping" staged by Factor to avoid extradition to England on felony charges. Members of the Al Capone syndicate collaborated in the frame-up to rid themselves of a troublesome competitor—and still Touhy nearly wriggled through the net. Jurors in Chicago failed to reach a verdict the first time around, and a mistrial was

declared on February 2, 1934. Prosecutors finally got it right three weeks later; Touhy and his three confederates were convicted of kidnapping and sentenced to 99-year prison terms. J. Edgar Hoover cheered the travesty of justice as "a credit to the entire Bureau," ranking Touhy among the "most vicious and dangerous criminals in the history of American crime."

Another quarter-century would pass before a federal judge exposed the FBI's corrupt activities in Touhy's case. Meanwhile, Melvin Purvis had found a new "public enemy" to pursue through florid headlines. Bank robber JOHN DILLINGER had emerged as one of America's most notorious bandits in the latter part of 1933—twice escaping custody, sought for the murder of an Indiana policeman and numerous robberies, teamed with such quick-trigger outlaws as HOMER VAN METER and GEORGE "BABY FACE" NELSON for a free-wheeling rampage across the Midwest. Chicago was the center of Dillinger's violent universe, and Purvis recognized the stakes involved in stopping him. If there were any doubts, "Jayee" Hoover dispelled them in a letter dated April 3, 1934, closing with the remark: "Well, son, keep a stiff upper lip and get Dillinger for me, and the world is yours."

Purvis got his chance less than three weeks later, with reports that Dillinger's gang could be found at the Little Bohemia Lodge near Rhinelander, Wisconsin. Keeping local law enforcers in the dark, Purvis led a team of G-men north to raid the lodge on April 22, the outcome a grim fiasco by any standards. FBI agents opened the battle by shooting three innocent civilians, killing one of them, while Dillinger and company escaped in a blaze of gunfire, vanishing into the woods. "Baby Face" Nelson ambushed three officers at a nearby store, killing FBI Agent W. Carter Baum and fleeing in a stolen car. Purvis arrested Nelson's wife and two other gang molls, charging them with harboring federal fugitives, but they received suspended sentences in May 1934. Purvis further compounded his embarrassment on May 29 with a premature announcement of Dillinger's death.

Hoover's relationship with Purvis changed dramatically in the wake of Little Bohemia. The director's "Dear Mel" letters were supplanted by terse communiqués addressed to "Dear Mr. Purvis," their tone accusatory. On June 4, 1934, Hoover chastised Purvis for failure to implement some unspecified order, noting that "You have absolutely no right to ignore instructions." Twelve days later, when Purvis went golfing and missed a call from Washington, Hoover cabled that "There is no reason why the Agent in Charge should not leave word where he can be reached at any time." Agent SAMUEL COWLEY was dispatched from bureau headquarters to supervise the Dillinger manhunt, undermining Chicago's star G-man to the point that subordinates soon dubbed him "Nervous Purvis."

Melvin redeemed himself, after a fashion, on July 22, 1934. Alerted by a brothel madam and the corrupt local detectives who accepted her bribes, G-men tracked Dillinger to the Biograph Theater, Purvis and Cowley in joint command of the ambush party. Fearing another black eye, Purvis warned his agents in advance: "Gentlemen, you know the character of John Dillinger. If we locate him and he makes his escape it will be a disgrace to our Bureau." Cut down on the sidewalk in a hail of gunfire, Dillinger had no chance to escape that night, but rumors persist that he was shot without warning, perhaps while unarmed—or that a "ringer" was set up to die while Dillinger himself vanished to parts unknown.

J. Edgar Hoover had forgotten his promise to give Purvis "the world" in exchange for Dillinger's scalp, but he managed a private note to Melvin's father in South Carolina, noting that Purvis "conducted himself with that simple modesty that is so characteristic of his makeup. . . . He has been one of my closest and dearest friends." Close enough, at least, for Hoover to ignore reports that Purvis and his men routinely questioned suspects while dangling them from the 19th-story windows of the FBI's Chicago office. Five days after Dillinger was slain, one such detainee—hoodlum John Probasco, owner of the house in which Dillinger and Homer Van Meter underwent plastic surgery in May 1934—"committed suicide" by tumbling from one of those windows. Allegations persist that G-men dropped Probasco to the street, accidentally or otherwise, when he refused to incriminate others.

Hoover soon regretted his mild praise of Purvis, when Chicago's top G-man bagged another trophy. This time the quarry was CHARLES "PRETTY BOY" FLOYD, named with partner ADAM RICHETTI as a trigger man in the Kansas City massacre of June 1933. Purvis personally led the firing squad that cornered Floyd near East Liverpool, Ohio, on October 22, 1934, wounding Pretty Boy as he tried to flee across an open field. Officially, Floyd died from wounds sustained while resisting arrest. Four decades passed before the last surviving member of the posse told the

media a different story. According to Patrolman Chester Smith, Floyd had been wounded and disarmed when Purvis tried to question him about the Kansas City murders. Floyd responded with a string of curses, whereupon Purvis ordered an FBI subordinate, "Shoot into him." Smith supported his tale with a bloodstained .45-caliber Tommy gun slug, allegedly extracted from Floyd's torso at a local funeral home. (Despite clear rifling marks on the bullet, no specific weapon dating back to 1934 was found for ballistic comparison.)

Floyd's death put Purvis on the media fast track. Eleven weeks later, on January 8, 1935, he personally arrested Arthur "Dock" Barker in Chicago, thereby finally capturing one of the real Hamm kidnappers. Purvis scored another publicity coup on June 1 with the Chicago arrest of Barker gang member VOLNEY DAVIS, wanted on multiple murder and robbery charges. New indictments were filed—against the right suspects, this time—in the Hamm kidnapping and the January 1934 abduction of banker Edward Bremer, also in St. Paul, where FBI investigation soon toppled the corrupt regime of Harry Sawyer. Chicago fixer John "Boss" McLaughlin got the window-dangling treatment from Melvin's G-men, but his complaints were all in vain as he found himself indicted for conspiracy to pass Bremer ransom loot.

It was too much for J. Edgar Hoover. Never one to share the limelight, Hoover sent a "Dear Sir" note to Purvis in March 1935, accusing Purvis of public drunkenness. Purvis denounced the report as an "unmitigated and unadulterated lie," his protest undercut by newspaper accounts of Melvin brandishing his pistol in a Cincinnati store, botching a phone call to Hoover in Washington, and then staggering off to his car. Friends and relatives of Purvis believe Hoover planted the story himself, but the damage was done. Hounded by reports of poor performance, Purvis left the FBI by summer's end. (Contradictory accounts date his resignation from July 10, July 12, and August 5.)

Hoover wasted no time in expunging Purvis from the official FBI record. Once named as Dillinger's slayer, Purvis vanished from bureau accounts of the shooting, variously replaced by Sam Cowley (killed by "Baby Face" Nelson in November 1934), G-man Charles Winstead, or East Chicago detective Martin Zarkovich. No mention of Purvis appeared in Don Whitehead's *The FBI Story,* published with Hoover's full cooperation in 1956, or in the motion picture version released three years later. Officially, at least around FBI headquarters, Melvin Purvis had ceased to exist.

In real life he enjoyed somewhat greater success, moving from Chicago to San Francisco, where he returned to the practice of law. In 1936 Purvis published his autobiography, *American Agent,* while lending his famous face and name to promotion of various products ranging from cars to razor blades. He introduced a radio series, *Top Secrets of the FBI,* and served as chief of the Post Toasties "Junior G-Man Club," thousands of American children mailing box tops in return for badges, cap guns, codes and passwords, microscopes, and "G-man" baseball mitts.

In 1938 Purvis returned to his native South Carolina as a full-time lawyer. Three years later, with America's entry into World War II, he was called for active duty in the U.S. Army Reserve, working with military intelligence through the African and Italian campaigns, later briefly assigned to the War Department's War Crimes Office. Discharged in 1946, Purvis returned to legal practice in Florence, South Carolina, dividing his time between courtrooms and operation of local radio and television stations. Twice summoned to advise congressional investigators in Washington, Purvis was nominated for a federal judgeship in 1952, but negative reports from Hoover scotched the deal.

The Touhy case returned to haunt Purvis in 1954 when U.S. District Judge John P. Barnes declared the Factor case a mockery of justice. Barnes found that "the Department [of Justice] did evince an astounding disregard for Touhy's rights and indulged in practices which . . . cannot be condoned." Furthermore, Barnes ruled that the Illinois state attorney's office and the FBI had "worked and acted in concert to convict Touhy of something, regardless of his guilt or innocence." Briefly liberated on Barnes's order, Touhy was soon hauled back to serve his time for an October 1942 prison break. Finally released on November 24, 1959, Touhy enjoyed three weeks of freedom before old rivals from the bootleg era gunned him down on December 16.

Melvin Purvis outlived his late victim by 75 days. On February 29, 1960, Purvis died at his home in Florence from a self-inflicted gunshot wound. A local coroner described his death as accidental; FBI spokespersons countered with a whispering campaign that it was suicide. In either case, the gun involved was not—as frequently reported—the pistol Purvis carried on the night John Dillinger was killed. Rather, it was a .45-caliber automatic presented to Purvis by Chicago G-men on the occasion of his 1935 retirement.

In death, ironically, Purvis has managed to eclipse J. Edgar Hoover as a symbol of the 1930s gang-busting FBI. Cinematic portrayals of Purvis run the gamut from cold-blooded executioner to swashbuckling action-adventure hero. Ben Johnson's portrayal in *Dillinger* (1973) inflated Purvis's reputation by crediting him with the single-handed capture of GEORGE "MACHINE GUN" KELLY plus the slayings of Theodore "Handsome Jack" Klutas and WILBUR UNDERHILL. Cowboy star Dale Robertson played Purvis twice—in *Melvin Purvis, G-Man* (1974) and *Kansas City Massacre* (1975)—wielding a Tommy gun and corn-pone accent against half the Depression era's notorious bandits. Don Cortese's Purvis in *Public Enemies* (1996) is a self-styled "gunfighter," personally responsible for picking off Ma Barker and her outlaw sons. "Jayee" Hoover, meanwhile, is best remembered as the man who wiretapped Martin Luther King while declaring ORGANIZED CRIME the figment of a journalist's overheated imagination, held in near-universal disdain by post–cold war historians.

Q

QUANTRILL, William Clarke "Charley Hart"

The Confederacy's most controversial field commander (though never a commissioned officer), William Quantrill still inspires heated debate whenever buffs or scholars argue details of the Civil War. Revered by some Confederate apologists as a "hero" or military "genius" of the American Civil War, Quantrill is equally reviled by others as a common thug or worse—a psychopathic serial killer. Whichever side of the debate prevails, one point is clear: Quantrill's guerrilla unit served as a training ground for some of the most infamous and deadly outlaws of the postwar era, his brutal tactics emulated for years after General Robert E. Lee surrendered at Appomattox.

A native of Ohio, Quantrill was born at Canal Dover in 1837. Violence and criminality seemed inbred on his father's side: One paternal uncle was a pirate, another served time for attempting to murder his wife, and a third swindled and abandoned seven brides in swift succession. Quantrill's father, Thomas, was a trustee of the local school board who embezzled funds and viciously assaulted the man who exposed him, beating his accuser with a red-hot poker.

It is therefore no surprise, perhaps, that Quantrill displayed a sadistic streak in early childhood, delighting in the torture and dismemberment of helpless animals. Once, for a "joke," he locked the young caretaker of a local church in the belfry and threw away the key, leaving her trapped for 24 hours without food or water before she was freed. When torturing animals—and later in combat—Quantrill was heard to emit maniacal laughter, "a sort of gay, nervous chuckle" heard most often after he had claimed a life. During the Civil War, his battle-hardened followers "found it rather eerie and even a little frightening"—all the more remarkable in a troop known for collective and individual ferocity.

In 1853 Quantrill was elevated from the rank of student to teach in Canal Dover's school. His father died the following year, leaving the family strapped for cash, and Quantrill fled westward in lieu of helping to support his mother and siblings. February 1856 found him teaching school in Fort Wayne, Indiana; a year later he moved on to "Bleeding Kansas," where a referendum over slavery had sparked a gruesome preview of the civil war that lay ahead. In Kansas Quantrill earned a reputation as a thief and was banished from the settlement of Tuscarora Lake for stealing from his neighbors. Drifting to Fort Leavenworth, he took the name "Charley Hart" and signed on as an army teamster, traveling as far as Salt Lake City. A failure at prospecting in Colorado, Quantrill drifted back to Kansas in the latter part of 1859. March 1860 found him—still as "Charley Hart"—in the hotbed of abolitionism that was Lawrence, Kansas.

It was in Lawrence that Quantrill made the transition from petty thief to outlaw and killer of men. Teamed with notorious bandit Jake Herd, Quantrill pursued fugitive slaves as a bounty hunter and was not above kidnapping free blacks for illegal sale below the Mason-Dixon Line. Devoid of anything resembling scruples, he could argue either side of the Free Soil controversy and sometimes ran livestock with John Stewart, a New Hampshire minister turned militant abolitionist and professional rustler. Lawrence grew too hot for Quantrill after he stole a quantity of explosives and torched an abolitionist's home to settle a personal quarrel.

Fleeing Lawrence, Quantrill stopped at Pardee and there met four young Quaker abolitionists—Charles Ball, Chalkey Lipsey, Edwin Morrison, and Albert Southwick. As "Charley Hart," he offered to serve as their guide on a raid into Missouri, where they hoped to liberate the families of three escaped slaves. Southwick stayed behind in Kansas, but Quantrill led the other three into a trap where they were killed by slave owners, Quantrill personally dropping Lipsey with a shot to the head. Back in Kansas on March 25, 1860, he surrendered to law officers for trial on outstanding charges in Lawrence. Albert Southwick and friends sought revenge for Quantrill's treachery, but a gang of Missouri "border ruffians" rescued him from jail in the nick of time and carried him away to safety.

War broke out on April 12 with the shelling of Fort Sumter in South Carolina, but the outbreak found Quantrill ensconced with a tribe of slave-owning Cherokees in Indian Territory (later Oklahoma). He joined the First Cherokee Regiment, fighting for Dixie, and helped lift Yankee scalps at Wilson's Creek, Missouri, on August 10, 1861. Thereafter, Quantrill enlisted with a Confederate military unit led by General Sterling Price, but he tired of military discipline after a brief skirmish in September and soon left the army, residing with a mistress at Blue Springs, Missouri.

The border war in Kansas and Missouri was conducted chiefly by guerrillas—Kansas "Jayhawkers" or "Red Legs" versus Missouri's pro-Confederate raiders. Quantrill organized his own band of gunmen in December 1861, recruiting "some of the most psychopathic killers in American history," whose goal was "nothing more than robbery, revenge, or nihilistic love of violence." The troop included William "Bloody Bill" Anderson, slayer of 54 men; John Thrailkill (who spent the war stalking and slaying 18 of the 20 bluecoats he blamed for killing his fiancée's father); brothers FRANK and JESSE JAMES; their cousins Cole and Jim YOUNGER; George Todd; Archie Clements; John McCorkle,

and a host of other gunmen sworn to Quantrill's "Black Oath."

In the name of God and Devil, one to punish, the other to reward, and by the powers of light and darkness, good and evil, here under the black arch of heaven's avenging symbol, I pledge and consecrate my heart, my brain, my body, and my limbs, and I swear by all the powers of hell and heaven to devote my life to obedience to my superiors; that no danger or peril shall deter me from executing their orders; that I will exert every possible means in my power for the extermination of Federals, Jayhawkers and their abettors; that in fighting those whose serpent trail has winnowed the fair fields and possessions of our allies and sympathizers, I will show no mercy, but strike with an avenging arm, so long as breath remains.

In the event that a guerrilla failed to keep his pledge, each of Quantrill's riders was sworn to

pray an avenging God and an unmerciful devil to tear out my heart and roast it over flames of sulphur; that my head may be split open and my brains scattered over the earth; that my body be ripped up and my bowels torn out and fed to carrion birds; that each of my limbs be broken with stones and then cut off by inches, that they may be fed to the foulest birds of the air; and lastly, may my soul be given into torment that it may be submerged in melted metal and be stiffened by the fumes of hell, and may this punishment be meted out to me through all eternity, in the name of God and the Devil. Amen.

By early February 1862 Union troops were actively hunting "Quantrill and his gang of robbers" around Blue Springs. A skirmish on February 19 left Quantrill with a dead horse and a minor leg wound, two of his raiders killed before the rest escaped.

The violence escalated from that point. On March 7 Quantrill's band rode into Aubry, Kansas, "screaming and swearing like devils," executing five unarmed civilians before they looted homes and shops, burning one store to the ground. Eleven days later they struck a Union camp at Liberty, Quantrill personally killing one sentry before his men captured and disarmed the rest of the troop. The next day, March 19, Major General Henry Halleck issued a statewide order commanding that guerrillas be executed as common criminals when captured. Quantrill accepted the challenge on March 22, personally murdering an unarmed Yankee sergeant and a bridge toll keeper in Kansas City. "Boys," he shouted to his troops on that occasion, "Halleck issued the order, but we draw the first blood!" One day after the Kansas City murders, Union cavalry tracked Quantrill to a sympathizer's home and fought another skirmish that claimed three lives. The guerrillas lost most of their horses and scattered on foot into the wilderness. More battles followed on March 30 and 31, Quantrill's raiders escaping each time and finally disappearing for the best part of two months.

Quantrill launched a new series of raids in late May 1862, striking outnumbered Union patrols, robbing the U.S. mail repeatedly, and sniping at a ferry on the Little Blue River. On July 8 he fought the first of several running battles with Union cavalry, evading pursuit at last after killing 11 Yanks and wounding 21 more. Quantrill admitted losing five men on the trail; his pursuers claimed 18 guerrilla kills.

At 4:30 A.M. on August 11, 1862, supported for the first time by regular Confederate troops, Quantrill struck Independence, Missouri, and captured a small Union garrison, liberating inmates from the county jail on the dubious theory that everyone incarcerated must be loyal rebels. A month later, on September 9, Quantrill led 140 riders into Olathe, Kansas, seeking vengeance for the recent execution of guerrilla Perry Hoy at Fort Leavenworth. The raiders killed and mutilated 14 unarmed civilians and then fled with Union cavalry in hot pursuit. The chase wound through four counties in the next 10 days, frustrated Yankees seizing the opportunity to liberate 60 slaves and burn the homes of several outspoken Confederate sympathizers.

Retreating southward on November 3, 1862, bound for winter quarters in Texas, Quantrill struck a Union supply train, killing four soldiers and six civilian teamsters before he torched the wagons. Overtaken by cavalry, he fought a skirmish that left six guerrillas dead and 21 wounded, eluding capture once again. On November 5 his men rampaged through downtown Lamar, Missouri, losing six of their number to Yankee marksmen holed up inside the courthouse. Departing Lamar, Quantrill's raiders burned down one-third of the town and escaped into Arkansas.

Border dwellers heard no more of Quantrill until May 1863 when he returned with a vengeance, sacking the small town of Diamond Springs, Kansas. The retreat to Missouri was an orgy of looting and murder, the guerrillas executing soldiers and civilians alike, raiding towns and homesteads, engaged in HIGHWAY ROBBERY of stagecoaches. All but one raider

escaped: 23-year-old Jim Vaughn was captured at Wyandotte, Kansas, and hanged at Fort Leavenworth on May 29.

June 1863 found Quantrill killing in Missouri, slaughtering nine members of a Union patrol near Penick. Shawneetown was the target on June 6, with four civilians murdered and nine homes burned. Ten days later Quantrill struck a Union column outside Kansas City, killing 20 soldiers in a brisk exchange of fire. Apparently sated, he then retired for two months at Blue Springs, enjoying the company of his 15-year-old mistress while the guerrillas rode on without him.

Exasperated Union troops began reprisals in August 1863, arresting and evacuating from Missouri relatives of known guerrillas riding under Quantrill's flag. Those arrested including two cousins of Cole Younger and three sisters of Bloody Bill Anderson. They were confined temporarily in a dilapidated Kansas City jail, which collapsed on August 14, killing five female inmates. One of the dead was Anderson's sister; another was Younger's cousin. Enraged, Quantrill planned a retaliatory raid on the scene of his previous humiliation and incarceration—Lawrence, Kansas. His men struck the town at 5:15 A.M. on August 21, under Quantrill's order to "Kill every man big enough to carry a gun and burn every house." In fact, that bloody day left 185 men and boys dead, while two-thirds of the town's inhabitants were made homeless.

Described by some historians as the worst single atrocity of the Civil War, Quantrill's raid on Lawrence provoked General Thomas Ewing to order the immediate evacuation of all Confederate sympathizers dwelling on a strip of land 50 miles wide and 85 miles long between Osage County, Kansas, and the Missouri River. Uprooted without compensation, some 20,000 families were dispossessed in one stroke, their homes often torched by Jayhawker guerrillas who followed the troops. The victims included Cole Younger's mother, and their loss was not inclined to soften Quantrill's attitude or tactics.

The heat from Lawrence drove Quantrill back to Texas in September, but he returned to southeastern Kansas in early October 1863. On October 6, guerrillas led by Dave Poole struck a wagon train near Baxter Springs, killing two teamsters, and then rode on to a nearby encampment of 150 black troops, killing nine soldiers and wounding 10 more before they were driven off. The same afternoon, Quantrill led the strike on a second army wagon train, capturing and executing 85 Union troops. Many of the corpses were mutilated, a young drummer boy thrown alive into a flaming wagon where he burned to death.

Back in Texas for the winter, Quantrill objected to Bloody Bill Anderson's wedding plans and thereby lost his chief lieutenant, Anderson defecting to lead his own crew of ruthless brigands. Left with some 350 men, Quantrill behaved himself so poorly in Confederate Texas that Brigadier General Ben McCulloch complained to his superiors, saying "We cannot, as a Christian people, sanction a savage, inhuman warfare, in which men are to be shot down like dogs, after throwing down their arms and holding up their hands supplicating for mercy." Furthermore, McCulloch noted, "I have little confidence in men who fight for booty, and whose mode of warfare is little, if any, above the uncivilized Indian." McCulloch formally ordered Quantrill's arrest as an outlaw in March 1864, but through chance or design the bandit leader was never apprehended. Defections multiplied meanwhile, guerrilla William Gregg noting that "This wholesale killing was repugnant to many of the men." Critics note that Gregg's departure from the troop was based on money, specifically a quarrel with George Todd over the division of some $6,000 in loot.

On September 20, 1864, Todd led the first major guerrilla raid since Lawrence, invading Keytesville, Missouri, with 130 riders, disarming the local garrison and torching the courthouse, looting homes and shops at random. Strangely, the only deaths reported were the town sheriff and a prominent Union sympathizer, executed on Todd's order. Five days later, briefly reunited with Bill Anderson, Quantrill and Todd led a chaotic raid on Fayette, Missouri, losing 18 of their number killed and 42 wounded. It was the end of collaboration for Quantrill, permanently separated from both Anderson and Todd.

Two days after the Fayette raid, on September 27, Anderson led 80 men in stolen Yankee uniforms against Centralia, Missouri, looting the down and burning anything they could not steal. The James brothers were among Anderson's raiders, staging their first TRAIN ROBBERY when a hapless engineer pulled into Centralia, Frank James discovering a suitcase with several thousand dollars on board. The train also carried 25 unarmed Union soldiers, wounded or on furlough. Twenty-four of them were executed on the spot, after which the raiders fought a pitched battle with Yankee reinforcements, killing 131 of 150 new arrivals. The dead were stripped of their weapons and uniforms, and some of them were scalped and beheaded.

Time was running out for the Confederacy and its highly irregular warriors. George Todd's band captured a Union officer and several soldiers on October 21, executing all of them, but a Yankee sniper killed Todd the next day outside Independence, Missouri. Four days later, on October 22, Bloody Bill Anderson was killed while leading a charge against bluecoats near Richmond, Missouri. Taking a page from Anderson's own rule book, the victor's cut off his head and mounted it atop a nearby telegraph pole.

William Quantrill had only 33 loyal gunmen left when he fled St. Louis and his teenage mistress in late October 1864, but their number included the James brothers, with Cole and Jim Younger. December found the raiders in Alabama, on unfamiliar ground, kidnapping Union soldiers near Tuscumbia to serve as guides. Bound for Kentucky, they finally reached their destination on January 22, 1865, abducting and murdering three Union soldiers near Hartford. The militia gave chase, capturing Jim Younger and eight other guerrillas outside Danville. (Eight of the nine escaped three months later, with help from local Confederate sympathizers.)

The depleted squad kept raiding, burning a Kentucky railroad depot, capturing a wagon train, and executing seven teamsters. At 2:00 A.M. on February 9, militiamen surprised Quantrill's camp with a volley of fire, killing four guerrillas and scattering the rest. Quantrill fled barefoot from the camp but still managed to elude his pursuers.

The Civil War ended officially on April 9, 1865, but the announced cessation of hostilities meant nothing to Quantrill and his die-hard outlaws. He fought another skirmish with Kentucky militia on April 13, losing two men killed and three wounded. Jesse James and others sacked Holden, Missouri, on May 7, killing eight men and burning five homes, murdering another 15 victims during their retreat. Haunted by premonitions of death, Quantrill remained at large until May 10, when his battered remnant was surrounded on a Kentucky farm and Quantrill was shot in the back while running away. He survived until June 6 and thus passed into legend, remembered for good or ill as the man whose guerrilla disciples would lead a startling crime wave between 1866 and 1882.

R

RAINEY, Donald Dean

Convicted of auto theft in 1948 and armed robbery in 1951, Don Rainey never seemed to learn from his mistakes. On May 25, 1956, he entered the Del Rey branch of the Bank of America in Fresno, California, firing a pistol shot into the wall before he looted the cash drawers of $5,147. Arrested in Mexico and returned to California for trial, he was convicted on federal bank-robbery charges and packed off to Leavenworth, serving nearly eight years before his conditional release in April 1964.

Still on parole eight months later, on December 8 Rainey returned to the same Fresno bank with his 16-year-old son Gerald. Waving a pistol while Gerald brandished a sawed-off shotgun, the father-son team netted $19,995 for their efforts. Unfortunately for the bandits, witnesses secured the license number of their car, which Donald had rented in Fresno using his own name. Federal warrants were issued immediately, charging both Raineys with bank robbery, and Donald was posted to the FBI's "Ten Most Wanted" list on March 26, 1965.

Less than three months later, on June 18, Gerald Rainey was arrested by federal agents in Brownsville, Texas. Faced with the prospect of serious jail time, the boy started to talk. On June 22 G-men were waiting in Nogales, Arizona, when Don Rainey crossed the border from Mexico. Bearded, wearing a cowboy hat pulled down to cover his eyes, Rainey carried $11,000 cash and a loaded .38-caliber pistol, but he had no chance to use either as agents took

Bank robber Donald Rainey recruited his teenage son for a holdup in 1964. (FBI)

him into custody. He was held in lieu of $35,000 bond, pending trial and subsequent conviction on new federal charges.

RANELS, Charles Edward

A native of Conroe, Texas, Ranels logged his first arrest in 1937 at age 15 for an auto theft in Waco. Confined to a state institution for delinquent boys, he escaped but was swiftly recaptured. By 1954 he had served 15 years in various state prisons on convictions for kidnapping, car theft, robbery with firearms, and aiding a prisoner to escape. From all appearances, his latest prison term—resulting from a Fort Worth robbery in 1943—had taught him nothing of the risks inherent in a criminal career . . . but it encouraged him to find new hunting grounds.

On October 8, 1954, Ranels and another gunman robbed a Louisville, Kentucky, supermarket of $3,000. Nineteen days elapsed before the bandits struck again in Louisville, looting a bank of $34,860. Ranels could afford a vacation after that score, but he turned up alone in Lonoke, Kentucky, on May 27, 1955, taking another bank for $9,760 in cash and $15,000 in unsigned traveler's checks. He had the federal government's attention now; his name was added to the FBI's "Ten Most Wanted" list on September 2, 1955.

Celebrity did not slow Ranels down. On January 9, 1956, he robbed a bank in Monticello, Arkansas, of $11,000. He wore no mask, and tellers at the bank were able to identify his mug shots four days later. Some of them had also seen the words "HARD LUCK" tattooed across his fingers.

On December 16, 1956, federal agents traced Ranels to the minuscule community of Dew Drop, Arkansas, near Pine Bluff, 20 miles southeast of Little Rock. A lady friend of Ranels, Opal May, had bought the local grocery store a few months earlier, and neighbors grew suspicious of her male companion, finally putting two and two together from a WANTED flier. Agents armed with Tommy guns and pistols caught the couple sitting down to dinner; They took Ranels by surprise and granted him no opportunity to reach the loaded handgun in his pickup truck outside. In custody, en route to trial and ultimate conviction on a lengthy list of charges, the fugitive was philosophical about his fateful choice of sanctuaries. "I knew you'd get me," he informed arresting officers, "so I decided to hide out."

READ, Mary

An adventurous tomboy who dressed as a man most of her life, Mary Read was successful in duping the British navy and army alike, serving at various times on a man-of-war, in the infantry, and in the cavalry. She found romance on horseback in the latter service, resigning to marry one of her barracks mates, and the newlyweds settled in Holland, opening an inn at Breda called The Three Horseshoes. When her husband died, Read went back into costume and shipped out aboard a Dutch merchant ship bound for the Caribbean.

En route to its destination, the vessel was captured by pirates under the command of "Calico Jack" Rackham and his lover, ANNE BONNY. Surviving members of the Dutch crew were pressed into service aboard Rackham's ship, while Bonny—"not altogether so reserved in point of chastity"—cast a lascivious eye on one of the prisoners. Leading Mary to her cabin, Bonny was removing "his" jacket when she froze, startled at the sight of female breasts.

The two young women became fast friends, Bonny protecting Read's secret from the rest of the crew. They hit stormy weather when Rackham became jealous, threatening to kill Bonny's supposed lover before he was briefed on the scam. In time, Mary found herself drawn to a young pirate on board, whereupon "she suffered the discovery of her sex to be made by carelessly showing her breasts, which were very white." The young sailor liked what he saw and they soon became lovers, but Mary's new man left much to be desired. A hopeless coward, he was so terrified by a shipmate's dueling challenge that Mary had to fight in his place, killing the brawny assailant with one thrust of her sword.

No one questioned Read's status with the crew from that point on, and she became a zealous buccaneer, ready to loot and kill with the rest. In October 1720 Rackham's crew was surprised by a British assault force while celebrating their latest prize. The raiders struck with swords and pistols; most of Rackham's crew retreated to the hold, where they refused to fight. Anne Bonny stood her ground with Mary Read to face the enemy, Read turning on her shipmates with a brace of pistols, shouting, "Come on you bastards, and fight like men!" When they refused to move she shot two pirates, killing one, before she was subdued by the authorities.

At trial a witness said of Read and Bonny that "the two cursed and swore with the best of the males, and never cringed from murder." Both were among the six crew members (including Calico Jack) sentenced to die on various charges. When the judge rhetorically asked for reasons why they should not be hanged, both women rose in unison and said, "We plead our bellies." Startled to discover both were pregnant, the court stayed execution until after their children were born. Fate had other plans for Mary Read, however, and she contracted a fatal illness in prison, dying from natural causes in December 1720.

See also: PIRACY.

RED Army Faction: Terrorist bank robbers

Rooted in left-wing student protests, West Germany's Red Army Faction (RAF) was founded by radical lawyer Horst Mahler, sometime in 1968. Mahler advocated revolutionary violence and defended clients charged with crimes against the state. In April 1968 those clients included 24-year-old Andreas Baader and 27-year-old Gudrun Ensslin, charged with firebombing Frankfurt department stores "to light a torch for Vietnam." Both were convicted and sentenced to three-year prison terms but were released in June 1969 when the verdicts were quashed on appeal. They quickly joined Mahler's growing RAF, as did a sympathetic journalist who covered their trial, 34-year-old Ulrike Marie Meinhof.

After training in guerrilla warfare at a Jordanian camp run by members of the Popular Front for the Liberation of Palestine, the RAF launched a series of daring daylight bank robberies in West Germany, once cracking three banks in a single day. Mahler was arrested in October 1970, ultimately sentenced to 14 years in prison, while Baader assumed de facto leadership of the RAF, collaborating with Ulrike Meinhof to run what became notorious as the "Baader-Meinhof Gang." The gang robbed two banks at Kassell on January 15, 1971, but police pressure grew so intense that the RAF was reduced to recruiting new members from the out-patients list of Heidelberg's Psychiatric Neurological Clinic.

Erratic bloodshed was the inevitable result. A policeman was killed by the RAF in Hamburg on October 22, 1971, and another two months later when the gang robbed a bank at Kaiserslautern on December 22. More raids followed until the RAF had sufficient funds to launch a seemingly indiscriminate "People's War" against the West German government and its international allies. Bombing and assassination were the favored tactics of the RAF in its 1972 heyday, but the group's notorious leaders were already running out of time. Andreas Baader was wounded by Frankfurt police and captured on June 1, 1972, with associates Holger Meins and Jan-Carle Raspe. Six days later, Gudrun Ensslin, packing two pistols, was arrested in Hamburg while she shopped at a stylish boutique.

Ulrike Meinhof was captured the following week in Hanover.

Deprived of anything resembling stable leadership, surviving remnants of the RAF escalated their aimless war on society with a new rash of bombings and shootings. The trial of four Baader-Meinhof leaders (minus Holger Meins, who starved himself to death on a jailhouse hunger strike) began at Stammheim on May 21, 1975. The list of charges filed against Baader, Ensslin, Meinhof, and Raspe ran more than 350 pages, and the trial dragged on for nearly two years. Ulrike Meinhof would not hear the verdict, having hanged herself in jail on May 10, 1976. Eleven months later, on April 28, 1977, the three surviving defendants were convicted on four counts of murder and sentenced to life imprisonment; additional convictions on 34 counts of attempted murder and conspiracy against the state added 15 years to each life sentence.

A series of kidnappings followed, prominent Germans held hostage and murdered when the Bonn government refused to negotiate release of the Baader-Meinhof defendants and other imprisoned TERRORISTS. The last attempt, on October 13, 1977, involved the skyjacking of a Lufthansa flight bearing 87 passengers and crew from Mallorca to Frankfurt. The aircraft was diverted to Mogadishu, Somalia, where members of West Germany's elite GSG-9 antiterrorist unit stormed the plane and killed the four hijackers in the predawn hours of October 18.

German authorities were jubilant over the rescue, while imprisoned Baader-Meinhof leaders watched their last hope for early freedom evaporate in a puff of gunsmoke. On the day of the Mogadishu rescue, Andreas Baader and Jan-Carl Raspe shot themselves to death with smuggled handguns in their isolation cells at Stammheim. Gudrun Ensslin, also confined in solitary, hanged herself with wire the same day. A fourth RAF member, Irmgard Moller, stabbed herself but recovered from the wounds to continue serving time.

REILEY, Edward

A father of four and former operator of an auto-wrecking yard in Bourbonnais, Illinois, Edward Reiley was not the typical family man. He had logged his first arrest at age 10, piling up a record of convictions for burglary, robbery, larceny, auto theft, and possession of burglar tools. By autumn 1958 he was prepared to crack the big time.

On November 4 Ed Reiley robbed a bank in Hamlet, Indiana, making off with $3,390. His next target was a bank in Onarka, Illinois, and he rebounded on January 29, 1959, with a raid against the Farmers and Merchants Bank in Logansport, Indiana, waltzing out with $19,827 in cash. Fleeing the scene, he crashed a state police roadblock, slightly injuring an officer who fired a shotgun blast at his retreating car. The vehicle was traced next day to a garage where it had been dropped off for body work, new paint, and replacement of a shattered rear window. Vehicle registration identified Reiley as the owner, and his link to the series of heists was confirmed on April 25 when witnesses selected Reiley's mug shot as the likeness of a bandit who stole $16,000 from a bank in Des Moines, Iowa.

Reiley's name was added to the FBI's "Ten Most Wanted" list on May 10, 1960. Days later, a used-car dealer in Rockford, Illinois, was visiting the local sheriff's office on unrelated business when he recognized Reiley's poster, remarking that the fugitive had browsed around his lot a short time earlier. The dealer was advised to keep in touch if Reiley showed himself again.

On May 24 Ed Reiley returned to the lot and bought a car. The dealer pocketed his money, made his call to the authorities, and settled back to wait. Six minutes after sheriff's deputies received the all-points bulletin, their suspect's car was sighted at a local drive-in restaurant. Blocked in by a patrol car, Reiley raised his hands without attempting to retrieve a pair of loaded pistols from the trunk. "I'm glad you got me," he remarked. "Now, maybe I can sleep nights." The list of charges filed against him guaranteed that Reiley would be sleeping in a prison cell for several years to come.

RENO Brothers

Unlike the outlaw DALTON, JAMES, and YOUNGER brothers, all of whom came from respectable families, Indiana's Reno brothers learned disdain for law and order at their father's knee. A resident of Seymour in Jackson County—dubbed a "carnival of crime" by one observer from the press—Wilkinson Reno was suspected of arson in nearby Rockford during 1860, burning down a house to drive the tenants out and let him buy their land at a discount. Eldest son Frank Reno was charged with robbing a post office, while next-eldest John was suspected of killing another local hoodlum, but neither ever went to trial. By 1866 the Renos led a brutal gang of thieves in Seymour, prepared to broaden their horizons with a fling at TRAIN ROBBERY.

They were not America's first train robbers, having missed that dubious honor by nine months to the day, but they would be the nation's first *identified* railroad bandits, striking two years before the James-Younger gang allegedly "invented" train robbery in Missouri. On the night of October 6, 1866, the Renos boarded a train outside Seymour and held the express messenger at gunpoint while they shoved two safes out of the baggage car. They cracked one safe, removing $15,000 in currency, but the other—with twice that much inside—resisted their best efforts and was left behind, unopened.

Allan PINKERTON, under contract to protect shipments on the Ohio & Mississippi Railroad, sent three detectives to Seymour, passing themselves off as denizens of the local underworld. Brothers John and Simeon Reno were soon identified as participants in the robbery, with accomplice Frank Sparks. All three were arrested, Sparks and John Reno linked to the holdup by boots that fit prints near the crime scene, but they were released on bail, Pinkerton's case languishing in the hands of inept or corrupt prosecutors.

Undismayed by the arrests, the Reno gang moved on to steal $22,065 from the Daviess County treasury in Gallatin, Missouri. Allan Pinkerton was summoned to work that case, too, deciding that his only hope of nabbing John Reno lay in kidnapping. Arrest warrants were obtained from Missouri and were carried by the Daviess County sheriff to a Cincinnati rendezvous with Pinkerton. Detective Dick Winscott, meanwhile, had wormed his way into the Reno crowd, persuading brother John to accompany him when Winscott went to "meet a friend" at Cincinnati's railway depot. The friend was Allan Pinkerton, backed up by reinforcements on a special train, leaping out to disarm Reno and clap him in irons for a swift getaway, vainly pursued by other members of the gang.

Arraigned the next morning in Gallatin, Reno faced a magistrate who told him, "You're the one who did this work and we're going to hang you from the highest tree in Grand River Bottoms if that money isn't returned!" Confined under round-the-clock guard, Reno later described how "The natives began coming from all directions with their shotguns and coonskin caps and with their hair hanging back down their shoulders. Some of them had not taken the mess from their backs that had grown there during the war." Transferred to Missouri's state prison on January 18, 1868, Reno described his arrival in a subsequent autobiography. "When we arrived at the prison gate I looked up and read in large letters over the entrance: the way of the transgressor is hard; admission twenty-five cents. But I was on the dead-head list and went in free."

Frank Reno led the gang in John's absence, robbing county treasuries and post offices across Indiana, Iowa, and Missouri. In February 1868 they caused "a public calamity" by stealing $14,000 from the Harrison County treasure at Magnolia, Iowa. William Pinkerton, sent to investigate that crime, focused on a Magnolia saloon run by an ex-counterfeiter from Seymour, Indiana. One of its frequent patrons was Michael Rogers, a "pillar of the Methodist church" whose criminal record dated from before the Civil War. Rogers entertained Frank Reno at his home about the same time the Mills County treasury was robbed of $12,000, the burglars escaping on a railroad handcar found discarded at Magnolia. Pinkerton raided Rogers's home on March 31, 1868, arresting Rogers, Frank Reno, and a pair of counterfeiters—Miles Ogle and Albert Perkins—before they could burn $14,000 of their loot. Jailed at Council Bluffs, the four broke out a day later—April 1—and left a taunting message in their cell: APRIL FOOL.

The gang kept raiding. Twelve bandits enlisted to stop another train on May 22, 1868, stealing $96,000 in gold and government bonds earmarked for the U.S. Treasury. Unsatisfied with that haul, the raiders planned another strike against the Ohio & Mississippi line, bribing engineer James Flanders to make an unscheduled stop at Brownstown, Indiana, 10 miles from the gang's base at Seymour. Flanders agreed and then warned his employers. Pinkerton agents were summoned and filled the express car with armed men. The heist went ahead as planned on July 10, 1868, detectives firing as soon as the bandits appeared, but all escaped except for Volney Elliott, cornered in the locomotive. Two more of the raiders—Theodore Clifton and Charlie Roseberry—were caught within 48 hours and jailed with Elliott in Cincinnati for safekeeping.

The rest of the gang had scattered, Frank Reno heading for Canada with Michael Rogers, Miles Ogle, and Albert Perkins. Three others—Henry Jerrell, John Moore, and Frank Sparks—fled to Mattoon, Illinois. A tip led Allan Pinkerton to Mattoon on July 16, accompanied by five armed detectives. Jerrell and Moore were captured in a local saloon; Sparks was cornered and collared in a barn outside

town. The bandits were returned to Indianapolis, ironically confined in the bullet-riddled boxcar from their recent failed holdup, and then shipped out to Seymour by rail. Vigilantes slowed the train by sabotage, and Allan Pinkerton missed his connection in Seymour, hiring a wagon for the last leg of the trip to Brownstown. Two hundred masked men met the wagon en route on July 24, disarming the escort and releasing them on foot, while Jerrell, Moore, and Sparks were lynched on the spot.

William and Simeon Reno were in custody by that time, arrested by Pinkerton detectives at Lexington, Indiana, on July 22. Held for a chaotic preliminary hearing on July 30, the brothers were then packed off to New Albany's stronger jail, where vigilantes promptly surrounded the town. In Windsor, Ontario, Allan Pinkerton led a raiding party against the gang's final hideout, arresting Frank Reno, Al Perkins, Charlie Anderson, and Michael Rogers; gang member Jack Friday escaped from a local saloon, after slugging one of Pinkerton's men with a pool cue. Anderson was found to be a Canadian citizen, thus ruled immune to extradition. Rogers was released on a plea of mistaken identity and fled to Detroit. Two attempts on Pinkerton's life were foiled, and a $6,000 bribe to the presiding judge was rejected, before Reno and Perkins were finally extradited on October 7, 1868. At that, they nearly drowned en route to Detroit when their tugboat foundered and sank midriver.

Reunited at New Albany, brothers Frank, Simeon, and William Reno were awaiting trial with Charlie Anderson on robbery charges when an engineer wounded in their last holdup died on December 7, 1868. Five days later, several hundred lynchers stormed the jail and hanged all four prisoners. None of the mob were ever charged, despite a perfunctory local investigation. Allan Pinkerton raged against lynch law at the time but later changed his tune when his detectives were deployed against the terrorist Molly Maguires in Pennsylvania. On that occasion he declared, "The only way to pursue them as I see it is to treat them as the Renos were treated in Seymour, Indiana. After they were done away the people improved wonderfully and Seymour is a quiet town."

RICHETTI, Adam "Eddie"
One of the Depression era's most notorious bandits, albeit through no real fault of his own, Adam Richetti was born at Strom, Texas, on August 5,

1909. His family moved to Lincolnport, Ohio, three years later, and Richetti had no major problems with the law until 1928. Two days after his 19th birthday, he was arrested for robbery at Hammond, Indiana, later convicted on that charge, and slapped with a sentence of one to 10 years at the Pendleton state reformatory. He served two years and was paroled on October 2, 1930.

Richetti's next recorded escapade occurred on March 9, 1932, when he joined Fred Hamner and the Smalley brothers, L. L. and W. A., to steal $800 from a bank at Mill Creek, Oklahoma. Their take was small, the getaway disastrous. Hamner was killed on the spot, the Smalley brothers wounded and captured at the scene. Richetti, slightly injured, got as far as Sulphur, Oklahoma, before he was arrested two hours after the holdup. Convicted of robbery on April 5, he was packed off to McAlester's state prison, but curiously lax authorities released him on August 25 under a $15,000 bond, pending appeal of his conviction. Richetti promptly skipped and disappeared, leaving his captors to explain their lapse of judgment. He surfaced again on January 12, 1933, teamed with bandits Edgar Dunbar and AUSSIE ELLIOTT to score $3,000 from a bank at Ash Grove, Missouri. Fleeing from the heist, the gang hid out in Bolivar, Missouri, at the home of Adam's brother.

Somewhere between McAlester and Bolivar, perhaps through Aussie Elliott, Richetti met notorious Oklahoma bandit CHARLES "PRETTY BOY" FLOYD. The date of their first meeting is unknown, but Floyd thought enough of Richetti, despite Adam's worsening alcoholism, to take him on as a partner in crime. Together, they stole a car in Castle, Oklahoma, on June 8, 1933. Six days later, they looted a bank at Mexico, Missouri, of $1,638. Two lawmen were killed the same afternoon, near Columbia, with Floyd and Richetti initially blamed for the shootings. (In fact, they were innocent; the case remains unsolved.) On June 16 the duo kidnapped Polk County Sheriff William Killingsworth from Bolivar and fled eastward in the sheriff's vehicle. They dumped his car at Clinton, Missouri, and commandeered another driven by Walter Griffith, releasing both hostages that night at Lee's Summit near Kansas City.

Unknown to Richetti and Floyd, the stage was set for a crime that would make them both notorious from coast to coast, favoring Floyd to the title of "Public Enemy Number One." On June 16, while the two outlaws were driving hell-bent across Mis-

souri, fugitive bank robber FRANK "JELLY" NASH had been captured in Arkansas and placed aboard a train for Kansas City on his way to complete an interrupted term in Leavenworth prison. The following day, Nash and his escorts were confronted by at least three gunmen at Kansas City's Union Station in an apparent rescue attempt. Shooting erupted, leaving Nash and four lawmen dead in what headlines would dub the KANSAS CITY MASSACRE. Eyewitness accounts of the shooting were confused, to say the least, with early suspects including bank robbers HARVEY BAILEY and WILBUR UNDERHILL. Sheriff-turned-gunman VERNON MILLER was soon identified as the leader of the hit team, but speculation on the identity of his cohorts ran rampant. FBI reports—suppressed for more than 60 years—indicated that Nash and several of the dead or wounded officers were, in fact, shot accidentally by a trigger-happy FBI agent.

Thus far, there was nothing to link Richetti or Floyd to the murders. On August 29, 1933, they were named as the gunmen who stole $3,000 from a bank in Galena, Missouri. A month later, on September 21, the outlaws rented a Buffalo, New York, apartment and moved in with their female traveling companions, sisters Rose Ash and Beulah Baird. They were still in Buffalo on October 11, 1934, when FBI spokespersons named Richetti, Floyd, and Vern Miller as the Kansas City Union Station triggermen.

Miller was already dead by that time, shot gangland-style and dumped outside Detroit on November 29, 1933. The case against Floyd amounted to a single .45-caliber cartridge case (allegedly linked to one of Floyd's pistols months after the murders), and some highly dubious testimony extracted from a female associate of Miller's, held incommunicado and without legal counsel by federal agents. As for Richetti, Floyd's known partner, G-men simply assumed that he must be involved in any crime committed by Floyd. Today, in hindsight, almost no one still believes Richetti guilty of the Kansas City massacre. Floyd's involvement is equally problematic, though at least he may have been in shape for the rescue attempt with Frank Nash. Richetti, for his part, was by all reliable accounts sleeping off an all-night drinking binge when the guns went off at Union Station.

It mattered not in October 1934, however, when every pronouncement from J. EDGAR HOOVER's Washington office was accepted by the press as gospel truth. Richetti and Floyd, with their girlfriends, left Buffalo on October 18, 1934, and headed for Oklahoma. Floyd wrecked their car near Wellsville, Ohio, on October 20, sending the sisters to town for a tow truck while he and Richetti hid out in the woods. Suspicious locals saw them lurking and summoned police, who captured Adam while Floyd slipped away. On October 22, G-man MELVIN PURVIS led the flying squad that cornered Floyd near East Liverpool, Ohio, gunning him down in what some witnesses would later call a summary execution.

Adam Richetti, meanwhile, had problems of his own. He was indicted for obstruction of justice on November 6, 1934, but that charge was held in abeyance after Missouri state officials charged him with murder. His trial for the Kansas City massacre opened on June 13, 1935, with a parade of witnesses whose memories had "clarified" and "focused" to the point where those who had named alternate suspects—or who could identify no one—in June 1933 now fingered Richetti and Floyd as the Union Station killers. On June 17, the second anniversary of the massacre, Richetti was convicted of killing police officer Frank Hermanson and sentenced to hang for that crime. Appeals were unavailing, but new technology spared him from the gallows; he was executed in Missouri's new gas chamber on October 7, 1938.

RIDEAU, Wilbert

An African American native of Louisiana, born in 1942, Wilbert Rideau was 19 years old when he robbed a Lake Charles bank of $14,000 in 1961. Fleeing the scene, he took three hostages and later gunned them down while they were pleading for their lives. Bank teller Julia Ferguson died of her wounds; the other two victims survived to testify against Rideau at his murder trial. Although sentenced to death, he was spared in 1972 when the U.S. Supreme Court invalidated death-penalty statutes nationwide, and his sentence was automatically commuted to life imprisonment.

A budding jailhouse journalist, Rideau applied for a position on the staff of Louisiana's state prison newspaper, *The Angolite*, but was rejected. He then started his own publication, *The Lifer*, while writing occasional columns for a syndicate of black newspapers on the outside. In 1976 he was appointed editor of *The Angolite* and swiftly transformed it from a simple mimeographed newsletter into an award-winning magazine. With assistance from inmate coeditor Billy Wayne Sinclair, Rideau's improved *Angolite*

won the Robert F. Kennedy Journalism Award, the American Bar Association's Silver Gavel Award, and the George Polk Award (in 1979, for articles on homosexual rape and a murder in prison). Rideau was also codirector of a documentary prison film, *The Farm*, which was nominated for an Academy Award and won a prize at the 1998 Sundance Film Festival.

By that time, Rideau billed himself as "the most rehabilitated prisoner in America," but parole eluded him, thanks in large part to the embarrassment his reporting caused officials in one of the country's most archaic and brutal prisons. On December 22, 2000, a three-judge panel of the Fifth U.S. Circuit Court of Appeals unanimously overturned Rideau's 1961 conviction, noting that blacks had been systematically and illegally excluded from the grand jury that indicted him. Prosecutors acknowledged that it would be virtually impossible to retry the case 40 years after the fact but vowed to appeal the decision to the U.S. Supreme Court. Wilbert Rideau, meanwhile, was forbidden by his jailers from making any comment to the press.

RINEHART, Ted Jacob

An accomplished burglar and jewel thief, Ted Rinehart was born January 21, 1927, in Poplar Bluff, Missouri. Logging his first arrest at age 17, he went on to compile a record of convictions for breaking and entering, grand larceny, and armed robbery in several states. His modus operandi involved extensive travel and renting inconspicuous houses in middle-class neighborhoods from which he proceeded to raid homes in more affluent areas.

Sentenced to 10 years for a Florida robbery, Rinehart was paroled after serving five and a half years of his term, but his parole was revoked on June 17, 1959. Federal charges of unlawful flight to avoid confinement were filed on July 23, and Rinehart made the FBI's "Ten Most Wanted" list on January 25, 1960. Additional counts charged him with interstate transportation of stolen property, alleged to be the loot from his most recent burglaries.

Fond of high society, Scotch whiskey, and older women, Rinehart once boasted of plans to make 1930s bank robber GEORGE "BABY FACE" NELSON "look like a piker." Unlike Nelson, though, Rinehart did not resist with blazing guns when federal agents traced him to Los Angeles on March 6, 1960, and took him into custody without a fight. In hiding,

Bandit Ted Rinehart boasted of plans to make "Baby Face" Nelson "look like a piker." (FBI)

Rinehart had tried to change his appearance by growing a mustache and gaining 40 pounds, but the disguise proved ineffective, and he was returned to Florida to finish out his time.

ROBBERS' Roost: Utah outlaw sanctuary

Located near the eastern limit of Wayne County in present-day Canyonlands National Park, Robbers' Roost differed from other bandit hideouts of the late 19th century in topography. Neither a valley (like BROWN'S HOLE) nor a sheltered box canyon (like Wyoming's "HOLE-IN-THE-WALL"), the Roost was in fact a plateau on the summit of the San Rafael Swell, largely devoid of trees. Three trails approached Robbers' Roost in the late 1800s, and all were clearly visible to lookouts on the rim, their view extending on a clear day for some 50 or 60 miles in all directions.

The Roost's first white settlers were a quartet of Mormon fugitives—"Destroying Angels" of the Dan-ite clique—sought for the murder of a Gentile physician during the "Mormon War" that preceded America's four-year battle over slavery. Twenty years later, when Utah's dominant church made a show of banning polygamy, more Danites and sundry other hardline dissidents occupied the plateau, but by 1883 they were forced to contend with an influx of horse thieves and gunmen on the run. Righteous farmers soon found themselves outnumbered by felons, and they moved on in search of more peaceful habitation, leaving Robbers' Roost to notorious bandits like the quick-trigger MCCARTY BROTHERS.

Horse theft soon took a backseat to the more profitable trade of cattle rustling, and fledgling outlaw BUTCH CASSIDY rode with the McCarty gang until Wyoming authorities caged him in 1894. Pardoned in January 1896 on condition that he leave the Equality State, Cassidy rode south for a reunion with survivors of the old outfit. His new recruits—soon recognized far and wide as the infamous "WILD BUNCH"—continued to use Robbers' Roost as one of their primary hideouts through the early 1900s until Cassidy fled the United States and his allies were captured or killed.

ROBERTS, Jessie James

A native of Sylvester, Georgia, born on November 13, 1920, Roberts early displayed a fondness for concealed weapons and armed robbery in the mold of his famous namesake. His adult convictions listed counts of larceny, assault with intent to commit armed robbery, attempted escape, interstate transportation of stolen motor vehicles and fraudulent checks, and post-office burglary.

On December 21, 1965, while free on appeal bond after conviction for burglarizing a Tennessee post office, Roberts looted a bank at Quapaw, Oklahoma, of $34,144. Three weeks later, on January 10, 1966, he robbed a bank in Lenox, Georgia, of $38,322, rebounding minutes later with a failed attempt to raid another bank in nearby Alapaha. In that incident Roberts fled under fire from a bank officer, speeding away after one of the clerks tried to grab his pistol. Return fire from the getaway car grazed the banker's head, wounding him slightly.

In flight, Roberts was also charged with burglarizing a Modoc, South Carolina, post office in December 1965, stealing and subsequently cashing numerous postal money orders. His name was added to the FBI's "Ten Most Wanted" list on February 3, 1966, and G-men traced him to Laredo, Texas, five

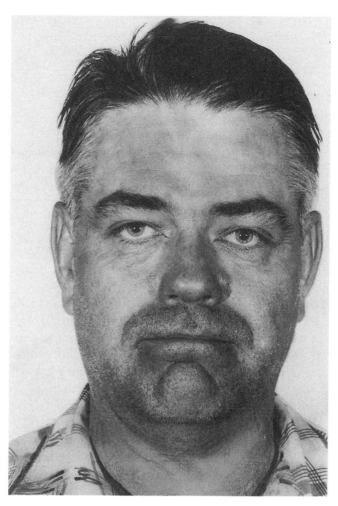

Bank robber Jessie James Roberts, added to the FBI's "Ten Most Wanted" list in 1966. (FBI)

days later, making the arrest without resistance. Roberts was returned to Tennessee to serve his time, with other charges waiting in the wings.

"ROBIN Hood"

Arguably the most famous SOCIAL BANDIT of all time, Britain's legendary HIGHWAYMAN of Sherwood Forest has been regarded for generations as a hero of fable, as fictional as Sherlock Holmes or James Bond. In fact, though, just as Holmes and Bond were crafted by their literary creators from the traits of one or more real-life individuals, so it now appears that the "Robin Hood" of legend may have a sound basis in fact.

Untangling the strands of myth from public records is a Herculean task, compounded by the observation of scholar J. C. Holt that English history includes "a quiverful of possible Robin Hoods" for historians to consider. Holt concludes that the identity of the original Robin "matters less than the persistence of the legend," but true-crime buffs are prone to disagree.

The earliest confirmed entry in what became a long-running series of adventures was *A Gest of Robyn Hode,* an epic poem consisting of 456 four-line stanzas apparently written around 1400. Other poems, tales, and ballads followed, including *Robin Hood and the Monk* (circa 1450), *Robin Hood and the Potter* (circa 1503), and some 30-odd others preserved during the 15th and 16th centuries. In essence they comprised a rambling morality play, recounting the trials and adventures of an outlaw with the proverbial heart of gold who steals from the rich and shares his loot with the poor. Martin Parker's *True Tale of Robin Hood* (1632) claims to be "carefully collected out of the truest writers of our English chronicles," but Parker actually borrowed its "facts" and woodcut illustrations from the wholly fictional *Tale of Adam Bell,* published in 1536.

In fact, the original Robin Hood was almost certainly a mercenary highwayman who extorted money from travelers whom he stopped along Britain's Great North Road sometime in the latter 12th century. His generosity to those less fortunate is unsupported by surviving records of the era—which, in fact, leave amateur detectives with more suspects than solutions in this case.

Among those suspects we find: *Robert Hood,* the servant of a clergyman at Cirencester, who murdered an acquaintance in his master's garden sometime between 1213 and 1216; *Robert Hod,* a Yorkshire outlaw hunted by authorities in 1225; *William Robehod,* a Berkshire fugitive of 1261–62; and the promising *Robin Hood,* jailed in 1354 pending trial for unspecified offenses committed in Rockingham forest. In J. C. Holt's estimation, tales of these and other outlaws whose names are lost to history were merged and garbled over time to create the enduring—and sadly inaccurate—myth of a philanthropic highwayman who never really lived.

Robin Hood's ephemeral record did not prevent a home-grown tourist industry from springing up around his name. Robin Hood's Well on the Great North Road boasted two inns for travelers in the mid-18th century. By 1819, settlers at Loxley were touting a ruined homestead as the famous outlaw's birthplace. The grave of sidekick Little John was likewise "discovered" at Hathersage, while the keepers of St. Anne's Well in Nottingham displayed articles of Robin Hood's "original" clothing and furniture. A church at Edwinstone was touted as the site of Robin's marriage—presumably to the beautiful Maid Marian of legend. Robin Hood's Hills, outside Mansfield, carry the highwayman's name without any apparent link to his real-life career.

Whether he ever lived or not, Robin Hood was a natural for show business and was probably featured in more films and television programs than any other felon. His film credits, with dates and stars who played the mythic role, include: *Robin Hood* (1912, Robert Frazer); *Robin Hood* (1913, William Russell); *Robin Hood* (1922, Douglas Fairbanks); *Robin Hood* (1935, animated); *The Adventures of Robin Hood* (1938, Errol Flynn); *The Bandit of Sherwood Forest* (1948, Cornel Wilde); *The Story of Robin Hood and His Merrie Men* (1952, Richard Todd); *Sword of Sherwood Forest* (1960, Richard Greene); *Wolfshead: The Legend of Robin Hood* (1969, David Warbeck); *Robin Hood* (1973, animated); *Robin Hood* (1973, Brian Bedford); *Robin and Marian* (1976, Sean Connery); *The Zany Adventures of Robin Hood* (1984, George Segal); *Robin Hood: Prince of Thieves* (1991, Kevin Costner); *Robin Hood* (1991, Patrick Bergin); *Robin Hood: Men in Tights* (1993, Cary Elwes); *Robin Hood* (1998, David Wood); and a popular television series called *The New Adventures of Robin Hood* (1997–99, John Bradley).

Above all else, Robin Hood has furnished the English language with a name for altruistic bandits, ranging from California's JOAQUIN MURRIETA to JESSE JAMES and CHARLES "PRETTY BOY" FLOYD. Sadly, when historical records are examined, few of those labeled "Robin Hoods" in the prime of their criminal careers deserve the accolades. Murrieta and James were cold-blooded killers, if not full-blown psychopaths. Floyd may have destroyed bank-mortgage records on one or two occasions as a favor to friends in Oklahoma, but on balance he was a thief who stole for himself and never shied away from violence in pursuit of profit.

Robin Hood may have lived in medieval England, under one name or another, but the altruistic thief his name has come to symbolize is clearly a denizen of fantasy. The closest to an echo of the legend in modern America is found in the case of Byron Shane Chubbuck, a prolific New Mexico bank robber nicknamed "Robin the Hood." Chubbuck pled guilty to 13 bank holdups in 2000, claiming he planned to share his loot with the poor (though no evidence of such largesse could be produced). He later escaped from federal custody but was soon recaptured, charged in early June 2001 with escape and firearms charges, facing life imprisonment under a U.S. "three-strikes" law.

RUSH, Jerry Clarence

A stickup artist with a penchant for escaping from confinement, Jerry Rush was sought by Maryland authorities for breaking out of prison at the time he made the FBI's "Most Wanted" list. His latest crime involved the robbery of a Perth Amboy, New Jersey, bank from which he obtained $100,000 in cash. The money was used to finance a free-wheeling cross-country honeymoon, but bridegroom Rush was already running out of time. Federal warrants listing charges of bank robbery and unlawful flight to avoid confinement were issued in his name, and he made the bureau's Top Ten roster on January 14, 1963. Ten weeks later, on March 25, FBI agents caught him in Miami, closing their net as Rush slid behind the wheel of a brand-new luxury car. Upon conviction on bank-robbery charges, he was sentenced to 29 additional years in a federal penitentiary.

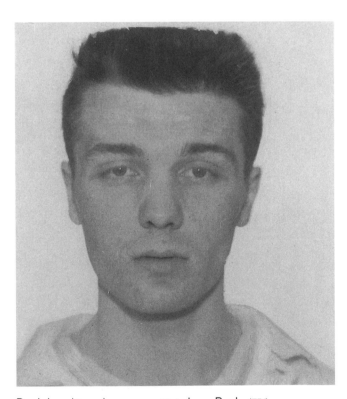

Bank bandit and escape artist Jerry Rush (FBI)

S

SACCO, Nicola, and VANZETTI, Bartolomeo

America's most controversial holdup-murder of the 20th century occurred in South Braintree, Massachusetts, on April 15, 1920. At three o'clock that afternoon, a paymaster and an armed guard for a local shoe factory were shot and killed by two men armed with pistols and robbed of two cash boxes containing $15,776.51. The bandits, seen by several witnesses, tossed their loot into a car occupied by several other men and fled the scene. On April 17 the getaway car was found by police, abandoned in some nearby woods.

Authorities in nearby Bridgewater were already investigating a similar holdup, committed without loss of life. In both cases, the bandits were described as probable Italians. Bridgewater authorities suspected a man named Boda as the getaway driver, noting that he lived with a "radical" named Coacci who faced deportation in the midst of 1920s' widespread FBI "Red Raids." Based on descriptions of the Bridgewater getaway car and tire tracks found near the site where the South Braintree car was abandoned, law enforcers concluded that Boda's automobile—presently garaged for repairs in Cochesett—was the holdup gang's second vehicle. Police were waiting when four Italians arrived to inquire about the car on May 5. Two of them—Nicola Sacco and Bartolomeo Vanzetti—were arrested near the garage; Boda escaped, while a fourth suspect, named Orciani, was jailed on May 6 (and quickly released when employment records placed him at work on the dates of both holdups).

Both Sacco and Vanzetti carried revolvers at the time of their arrest. Five witnesses placed Sacco at the murder scene in South Braintree, while two identified Vanzetti. Both were indicted for double murder on September 14, 1920. Vanzetti, a self-employed fish peddler from Plymouth, was also charged with the Bridgewater holdup, but Sacco was exempted from that case when personnel records from a Stoughton shoe factory proved he had worked on the day in question. On April 15, however, Sacco had taken a day off and thus remained a viable suspect in the South Braintree murders. More damning than the evidence in hand, however, was the fact that both defendants styled themselves as anarchists—a political persuasion calculated to condemn them in the eyes of most prospective jurors when their trial opened at Dedham before Judge Webster Thayer on May 21, 1921.

At trial, prosecutors named Sacco as the gunman responsible for both murders, while Vanzetti was described as a conspirator and occupant of the getaway car. Fifty-nine witnesses testified for the state, including ballistics experts who linked Sacco's pistol to one of four bullets removed from the payroll guard's corpse. "Consciousness of guilt" was attributed to both defendants by their possession of firearms and the various false statements they made to police. The defense called 99 witnesses to counter prosecution evidence, but conviction was a foregone

Nicola Sacco, second from right in foreground, and Bartolomeo Vanzetti, second from left in foreground, were accused of killing two people and stealing $16,000, although it is widely believed that they were convicted because of their anarchistic beliefs. (AP/Wide World Photos)

conclusion in the Red Scare atmosphere of 1921. Both Sacco and Vanzetti were convicted of first-degree murder on July 14, 1921, and condemned to die in the electric chair. After six years of fruitless appeals, both defendants were executed on August 23, 1927, but their deaths did not resolve the controversy that had grown into a global cause célèbre. In fact, with the clear hindsight of eight decades, it appears that Sacco and Vanzetti were almost certainly innocent.

Among the fatal problems of the prosecution's case, we find the following:

(1) Five witnesses identified Sacco in court as a member of the holdup gang. Two of those—Mary Splaine and Frances Devlin—heard gunshots on April 15 while working at the Slater and Morrill shoe factory and ran to a second-floor window in time to see the gang's car speed away, visible for

three seconds or less. Based on that fleeting glimpse, Splaine described Sacco in such detail—including "a good-sized [left] hand . . . that denoted strength"—that a defense psychologist would later term her powers of observation "psychologically impossible." Devlin, for her part, told police in May 1920 that Sacco "look[ed] very much" like one of the bandits but would not "say positively" that he was guilty. At trial, more than a year later, she denied ever doubting his guilt. Shoe-cutter Louis Pelzer failed to identify Sacco in May 1920 but described him as a "dead image" of the holdup gunman in June 1921, this despite testimony from two coworkers that he hid under a workbench when the shots rang out and never approached a window. Witness Lola Andrews, described as "a woman of doubtful reputation," missed the shooting entirely but claimed to identify Sacco as one of two men she saw tinkering with a car outside the shoe factory four hours prior to the holdup. Carlos Goodridge allegedly glimpsed Sacco as the getaway car sped past a South Braintree poolroom; contradicted by four other witnesses (including his employer), Goodridge was discovered after trial to be a fugitive from justice, charged with larceny, who testified under a false name.

(2) Two witnesses, Harry Dolbeare and a railroad worker named LeVangie, were called by the state to identify Vanzetti as a member of the holdup gang. Dolbeare, unfortunately, made his sighting four or five hours prior to the robbery and miles away, claiming he had seen Vanzetti with four other "tough-looking" men in a car that passed him on the street. Witness LeVangie saw the holdup car speed by his railroad crossing with Vanzetti at the wheel; his testimony was contradicted by a coworker who described LeVangie fleeing for cover as the car raced past *and* by the prosecutor whose final summation specifically ruled Vanzetti out as the getaway driver, while still insisting that LeVangie "saw something" on April 15, 1920. Conversely, 31 eyewitnesses to the holdup flatly denied that Vanzetti was a member of the gang, while 13 others corroborated his presence in Plymouth on the afternoon of April 15, 20 miles south of the crime scene.

(3) While five of the Braintree holdup's fatal shots were definitely fired by some weapon other than the pistols owned by Sacco and Vanzetti, two ballistics experts linked one slug to Sacco's .32-caliber Colt automatic. State Police Captain William Proctor found the bullet "consistent with being fired by that pistol," but in later testimony on appeal Proctor denied linking the slug to any particular gun; in fact, he said under oath, he found testimony by the state's second ballistics expert on the same topic to be "entirely unconvincing." That second expert—Charles Van Amburgh—was exposed in 1924 as a friend of Massachusetts prosecutors who perjured himself in other cases, tailoring his testimony to condemn defendants in cases where he thought other evidence proved them guilty. One defendant in an unrelated case was later exonerated despite Van Amburgh's false ballistics testimony, but revelation of his penchant for perjury failed to save Sacco and Vanzetti.

Eyewitnesses and scientific evidence were virtually irrelevant, however, in the circus atmosphere attending the Sacco-Vanzetti trial and America's broader Red Scare. As future U.S. Supreme Court Justice Felix Frankfurter observed in covering the case for

The Atlantic Monthly: "In 1921 the temper of the times made it the special duty of a prosecutor and a court engaged in trying two Italian radicals before a jury of native New Englanders to keep the instruments of justice free from the infection of passion or prejudice. In the case of Sacco and Vanzetti no such restraints were respected. By systematic exploitation of the defendants' alien blood, their imperfect knowledge of English, their unpopular social views, and their opposition to the war, the District Attorney invoked against them a riot of political passion and patriotic sentiment; and the trial judge connived at—one had almost written, cooperated in—the process."

In fact, Judge Thayer's charge to the jury was nothing short of a direct appeal to patriotism. Despite his admonition to consider their verdict in "a purer atmosphere of unyielding impartiality and absolute fairness," Thayer poisoned that atmosphere with his call for military-style discipline. "The Commonwealth of Massachusetts," Thayer proclaimed, "called upon you to render a most important service. Although you knew that such service would be arduous, painful, and tiresome, yet you, like the true soldier, responded to that call in the spirit of supreme American loyalty. There is no better word in the English language than 'loyalty.'" Truth was of little concern to Judge Thayer, as he falsely informed the jury that Captain Proctor had testified "it was [Sacco's] pistol that fired the bullet that caused the death of [victim] Berardelli." In fact, as previously noted, Proctor testified to no such thing. Judge Thayer's prejudice was showcased outside court where he was heard describing the defendants as "dagos" and "sons of bitches." In the wake of their conviction, Thayer asked a friend, "Did you see what I did to those anarchist bastards?"

Attorney William G. Thompson handled the case on appeal, striking at the heart of the prosecution's case. Captain Proctor supplied an affidavit refuting Judge Thayer's interpretation of the ballistics evidence. It read, in part:

I do not intend by that answer [regarding "consistent" features] to imply that I had found any evidence that the so-called mortal bullet had passed through this particular Colt automatic pistol and the District Attorney well knew that I did not so intend and framed his question accordingly. Had I been asked the direct question: Whether I had found any affirmative evidence whatever that this so-called mortal bullet had passed through this particular Sacco's pistol, I should have answered then, as I do now without hesitation, in the negative.

Thompson used Proctor's affidavit as the springboard for his motion to gain a new trial for Sacco and Vanzetti. Judge Thayer rejected that motion in October 1923, oddly acknowledging that "Captain Proctor did not testify that the mortal bullet did pass through Sacco's pistol, but that from his examination of the facts it was simply consistent with it." As for his own lie to the jury on that very point, Thayer had no comment. On May 12, 1926, the Massachusetts Supreme Court found "no error" on Judge Thayer's part, declaring that "as a matter of law" his decisions could not be reversed.

In the meantime, on November 18, 1925, a startling confession to the South Braintree holdup was obtained from Massachusetts prison inmate Celestine Madeiros, a 23-year-old Portuguese career criminal. Madeiros admitted driving the getaway car on April 15, 1920, for an Italian holdup gang that had "done lots of jobs of this kind." He further stated for the record that "Sacco and Vanzetti was not in said crime." His accomplices, rather, were identified as members of the notorious Morelli gang, out on bail from previous indictments and desperate for cash to finance their defense in April 1920. (It didn't help; they were convicted on May 25, 1920, and sentenced to federal prison.) Gang leader Joe Morelli furthermore habitually carried a .32-caliber Colt automatic similar to Sacco's.

The courts and police ignored Madeiros's confession and refused to interrogate members of the Morelli gang in prison, rather maintaining that Madeiros had confessed because he "hoped to get money" from some unidentified source in return for his testimony. Governor Alvan Fuller appointed a special commission to study the case in 1927, its members including a former probate judge plus the sitting presidents of Harvard University and the Massachusetts Institute of Technology. The commission found "no evidence" of justice betrayed, but its report did note Judge Thayer's "grave breach of official decorum" throughout the murder trial.

On August 12, 1927, Governor Fuller granted Sacco and Vanzetti a 12-day stay of execution to permit last-ditch legal maneuvers. Worldwide, protests against their execution turned violent, with riotous demonstrations and multiple injuries reported from London, Geneva, Paris, Casablanca, Berlin, Buenos Aires, Warsaw, Marseilles, Brest, Havana, and other cities. It was all in vain; the defendants were electro-cuted on August 23, 1927. Fifty years later, in 1977, Sacco and Vanzetti were officially exonerated in a special proclamation signed by Massachusetts governor Michael Dukakis.

ST. PAUL, Minnesota: Midwestern gangster refuge

"In St. Paul, gangsters can fuck in the street."

So opens *Saint Mudd*, a crime novel of the Great Depression published in 1992 by best-selling author Steve Thayer. And if the statement is not literally true, it serves to capture the wide-open atmosphere of a city virtually owned by criminals, described by U.S. Attorney General Homer Cummings in 1934 as "a poison spot of crime."

Thayer's lively novel is populated with such real-life desperadoes as JOHN DILLINGER, HOMER VAN METER, GEORGE "BABY FACE" NELSON, and the BARKER GANG. One of those who moves through its pages, retired "public enemy" ALVIN KARPIS, had this to say about St. Paul when he published his memoirs in 1969:

But of all the Midwest cities, the one that I knew best was St. Paul, and it was a crook's haven. Every criminal of any importance in the 1930s made his home at one time or another in St. Paul. If you were looking for a guy you hadn't seen in a few months, you usually thought of two places—prison or St. Paul. If he wasn't locked up in one, he was probably hanging out in the other.

St. Paul's affinity for gangsters was not a new phenomenon in the Depression; rather it dated back to the early 1900s when John J. O'Connor—aka "The Big Fellow"—was sworn in as chief of police. O'Connor's strange view of law and order demanded ruthless punishment for local "disorganized" crime while advertising his city nationwide as a guaranteed sanctuary for gangsters on the run. Hoodlums of every stripe were welcome to spend time and money in St. Paul as long as they obeyed O'Connor's rules.

For starters, new arrivals were required to visit Paddy Griffin's boarding house on Wabasha Street and report their arrival in St. Paul. Griffin informed Chief O'Connor and arranged for suitable lodging. Visiting hoodlums were shadowed by O'Connor's spies—left alone if they minded their manners, or hauled in for a rough dressing down if they got rowdy in public. Local holdups were strictly forbidden, a sacrifice that guaranteed fair warning from police headquarters before any outside authorities could make an arrest.

Chief O'Connor's second-in-command was younger brother Richard O'Connor—aka "The Cardinal." As head of Minnesota's Democratic Party and one of said party's "Big Four" men nationwide, Richard was in an excellent position to warn visiting gangsters of any hostile moves by state police or other agencies that may have wished them ill. Aside from his political concerns, "The Cardinal" also ran a lucrative string of saloons and brothels in St. Paul. The flagship of his operation, Nina Clifford's whorehouse, was conveniently located directly behind his brother's office at police headquarters.

Poor health forced John O'Connor to retire in 1920, while his brother was increasingly distracted by national politics. Replacing them as St. Paul's ruling bosses were "Dapper Danny" Hogan (an Italian, despite the name) and partner Harry Sandlovich, a Russian immigrant better known around St. Paul as Harry Sawyer. They operated from the Green Lantern Café, a speakeasy on Wabasha Street situated within sight of the state capitol. Where the O'Connors had suppressed their enemies, however, Hogan and Sawyer fell short. "Dapper Danny" was killed by a car bomb on December 5, 1928, leaving Harry alone at the helm. Sawyer, in turn, soon proved too soft to control visiting rowdies—or even some of his own men. Police Chief Thomas Dahill, privately opposed to the city's corrupt regime, was likewise unable (or unwilling) to crack down.

By the onset of the Great Depression, sinful St. Paul was ripe for its very own crime wave.

Thomas Holden, of the HOLDEN-KEATING GANG, drove the first wedge on September 2, 1930, when he rented an apartment in St. Paul. A month later he was joined by FRANK "JELLY" NASH, a fugitive from Leavenworth penitentiary. Both had fallen on hard times in their respective criminal careers and were now associated with the Barker Gang, an up-and-coming outfit. Another year would pass before the full gang was assembled in St. Paul, however. On December 31, 1931, the crowd gathered for a New Year's Eve party at Harry Sawyer's Green Lantern included Holden, Nash, Fred Barker, Alvin Karpis, HARVEY BAILEY, and Francis Keating.

The Barker gang launched its first raid from St. Paul five days later, looting the small town of Cambridge, Minnesota, and fleeing straightaway to Harry Sawyer's sanctuary. "Ma" Barker, described years later by J. EDGAR HOOVER as the brains of the gang, rented a St. Paul house with son Fred and Alvin Karpis on February 1, 1932. They enjoyed their home for 12 weeks until the landlady grew suspicious of her tenants and identified the men as wanted murderers from mug shots in a *True Detective* magazine. Police were notified at 1:00 A.M. on April 25, the landlady suggesting that they hurry over and surprise the outlaws while they slept. Instead, the raiders stalled for six long hours while the gang packed up its Tommy guns and slipped away.

That kind of hospitality kept gangsters coming back for more. The Barkers didn't travel far, and St. Paul always lured them back. On December 16, 1932, the gang hit a bank in neighboring Minneapolis, killing two policemen, wounding a third, and gunning down a civilian who showed too much interest in their license plates. Two months later, brothers Fred and Arthur "Dock" Barker rented three apartments in St. Paul, soon joined by cohorts Alvin Karpis and Earl Christman. Again they were recognized, and again police were generous with advance warning, allowing the gang a long head start before their apartments were raided on March 4, 1933.

The raids meant nothing. Ma Barker and Fred were back in St. Paul by early May 1933, Dock Barker and Karpis renting an apartment together on May 28. Frank Nash and his wife spent a night at the flat, passing through, on June 9, 1933. Bright and early next morning, the gang adjourned to a cabin at nearby White Bear Lake to plot a crime that would startle St. Paul. Local brewer William Hamm was kidnapped on June 15 and held for four days before he was released in exchange for $100,000 ransom.

"Respectable" St. Paul was no longer off-limits to the gangs. That point was driven home two months later on August 20 when the Barkers hit a payroll shipment delivered by train to the South St. Paul post office. They escaped with $33,000 in another bloody raid, leaving one patrolman dead at the scene and another gravely wounded.

If Harry Sawyer was unable to control the gangster element, some of his men collaborated in the rampage. One such, Harry Campbell, met with members of the Barker gang at the Dale Apartments in St. Paul on January 1, 1934, to plot the outfit's next kidnapping. Campbell himself proposed the victim—Edward Bremer, scion of a wealthy, well-connected family whose personal friends included Minnesota's governor. Fred Barker and Karpis almost blew the plan on January 13, shooting up a carload of uniformed Northwest Airlines employees whom they mistook for policemen in a dark alley, but the snatch proceeded on schedule over Sawyer's belated objections. Kidnapped on January 17, Bremer was held for three weeks through several bungled ransom drops until his freedom was purchased for $200,000 on February 8.

By then, the Barkers weren't the only Big League game in town. John Dillinger and JOHN "RED" HAMILTON, both wounded in a bank holdup at Mason City, Iowa, on March 13, 1934, arrived in St. Paul that night with Homer Van Meter, seeking medical attention. They huddled with Pat Reilly, a waiter at the Green Lantern Café whose sisters-in-law were married to Alvin Karpis and bank robber TOMMY CARROLL. Reilly drove Dillinger and company to see Dr. N. G. Mortenson, St. Paul's public health officer, waiting with them while their wounds were cleaned and bandaged.

FBI agents came looking for Dillinger in St. Paul on March 31, risking exposure by the town's corrupt police. Red Hamilton was warned in time to flee his apartment before G-men kicked in the door, but Dillinger and Van Meter had another close shave, battling their way clear of an ambush that became a running firefight in the streets. Ironically, the shootout occurred while members of a special grand jury were holding a press conference downtown, announcing results of a three-month investigation into charges of local corruption. Among the panel's findings—

We believe there is no justification for any charges that an excess of crime exists here—we believe further that a comparison with other large cities will prove that St. Paul cannot be shown in an unfavorable light.

Charges of official incompetence and neglect—these charges have not been sustained by evidence.

Charges of collusion between police and underworld— no evidence of centralized graft has been found.

Afternoon headlines of the *Daily News* told a different story: MACHINE GUNS BLAZE AS JURY WHITEWASHES POLICE.

There was more gunfire coming as the tide slowly turned. FBI agents ambushed gangster EDDIE GREEN outside his St. Paul apartment on April 3, 1934, riddling his unarmed body with bullets. Local police

were the triggermen four months later when Homer Van Meter was cornered and killed on August 23.

The last act of St. Paul's gangland drama began in January 1935, after Ma and Fred Barker were killed by FBI agents in Florida. Federal indictments from May 1934 had already charged Dock Barker, Alvin Karpis, and nine others (including "John Doe" and "Richard Roe") for kidnapping Edward Bremer, but a new set of indictments superseded those charges on January 22, 1935, naming 26 conspirators in the abduction. Four of those cited—Ma and Fred Barker, Fred Goetz, and Russell Gibson—were already dead; Harry Sawyer and Harry Campbell joined the new list, along with sundry members and hangers-on of the Barker-Karpis gang.

Dock Barker was among the first to face trial, in April 1935; convicted on May 6, he and several codefendants were sentenced to life imprisonment. Harry Sawyer and wife Gladys were arrested three days before those verdicts were returned in St. Paul, bagged by FBI agents at Pass Christian, Mississippi. Tried with conspirators Bill Weaver and Cassius McDonald in January 1936, Sawyer was convicted and sentenced to life; Weaver received an identical sentence, while McDonald drew a term of 15 years.

St. Paul hoodlum Jack Peifer was arrested by FBI agents on April 18, 1936, charged with participation in the Hamm kidnapping. Four days later he was formally indicted for the crime, along with Alvin Karpis, Dock Barker, and four more defendants. Karpis remained at large until May 1 when he was captured by G-men in New Orleans. Six days later, Harry Campbell and defendant Sam Coker were arraigned on conspiracy charges in both the Hamm and Bremer abductions. At trial in July, Jack Peifer received a 30-year term for the Hamm kidnapping and promptly committed suicide in jail, using a stick of poisoned chewing gum. Three codefendants in that trial drew prison terms ranging from five years to life.

St. Paul, from all appearances, had been dramatically "cleaned up," its reputation as a gangland refuge fading slowly into history. A city ordinance of March 2, 1936, made it official: Henceforth, any resident convicted of a felony within the past 10 years would be required to register with the police— but not for special favors, as in days of old.

SANKEY, Verne

Born in 1890, Sankey worked for the Canadian Pacific railroad and tried his hand at farming in

South Dakota before turning to a life of crime and becoming one of America's most wanted outlaws of the early 1930s. With cohort Gordon Alcorn, Sankey robbed several banks in Canada and the United States before it struck him that kidnapping might be an easier way to earn dishonest dollars. The duo's first target was Haskell Bohn, son of a refrigerator manufacturer in ST. PAUL, MINNESOTA, whom they snatched in June 1932. The take was less than spectacular: Sankey and Alcorn demanded $35,000 but finally settled for $12,000, releasing their captive unharmed. Seven months later they abducted Denver millionaire Charles Boettcher II and drove him to Sankey's South Dakota turkey ranch, where he was ransomed for a more substantial $60,000.

By that time, the partners were wrongly suspected of carrying out the high-ticket Hamm and Bremer kidnappings, in fact committed by the more successful BARKER GANG. Seized by police and FBI agents on January 31, 1934, at a Chicago barbershop, Sankey was returned to South Dakota for trial in the Boettcher case, confined to the state prison at Great Falls for security purposes. He cheated justice there on the night of February 8, using a necktie to hang himself in his cell. Gordon Alcorn had been captured in Chicago six days earlier and later received a life sentence for kidnapping Boettcher.

SAWYER, James Franklin "Frank"

An Oklahoma native, born near Durant on May 1, 1899, Frank Sawyer was the fourth of nine children raised by strict Baptist parents. The religious teaching didn't take in Frank's case, and by age 17 he was robbing banks with accomplices Jim Baldwin and Tom Slaughter. Sawyer's parents cut him loose after loot from one of the holdups was found in their home, so he drifted north to Wichita, working as a dealer in gambling halls. There, he met bank robbers Jeff Davis, Bud Maxwell, and Henry Wells, making it a foursome for a series of holdups during 1917 and early 1918. Drafted by the army in 1918, Sawyer was spared from induction by the unexpected armistice and went back to gambling full time.

One report asserts that in the 1920s Sawyer joined AL SPENCER's notorious bank- and train-robbing gang, but his participation in the outfit's raids has never been confirmed. It is known that Sawyer killed two men in quarrels over cards. The first, bank robber John Moore, accused Frank of cheating and was shot for his trouble. Back in hometown Durant, it was Sawyer's turn to make the accusation, blasting a

dealer named Bleaker. Arrested in Dallas six months later, Sawyer was extradited, convicted of murder, and sentenced to life imprisonment. He entered the state pen at McAlester on April 13, 1920, and escaped two years later, heading back to his old stamping grounds. It is unknown whether he participated with Al Spencer, FRANK NASH, and others in the $20,000 robbery of a mail train near Okesa, Oklahoma, on August 20, 1923, but some reports contend that he was present on September 15 when police and federal agents killed Spencer near Bartlesville, Oklahoma.

Sawyer married in 1923, and while his wife pleaded with him to go straight, Frank saw no percentage in working for wages when it was so much easier to steal. Soon after the birth of his daughter in 1924, Sawyer was arrested and returned to McAlester to finish his life sentence. On February 2, 1930, he was part of a prison work crew assigned to paint the state capitol building in Oklahoma City, but Frank had other plans, eluding careless guards to make good his escape. He hung around Oklahoma City for the next two years, gambling and pulling small robberies to support himself. On May 2, 1932, Sawyer was identified as one of two gunmen who held up a small bank in Union, Missouri. Soon after that heist, he teamed with bandits JIM CLARK and ED DAVIS for a bank job that would change their lives.

The target was a jug in Rich Hill, Missouri, but Sawyer was stricken with a bad case of nerves as he entered the bank and called the raid off before pistols were drawn. The shakes were seemingly a premonition of disaster because the day witnessed another bank robbery, committed by the BARKER GANG at Fort Scott, Kansas. As law enforcers fanned out in pursuit of that gang, missing all concerned with the $47,000 they had stolen, Sawyer and company were caught in the dragnet. No evidence of any kind connected them to the Kansas holdup, but all three were escaped convicts, found riding in a stolen car. Accordingly, they were indicted and convicted for the Fort Scott job and packed off to the state prison at Lansing.

None of them would stay long behind bars. On May 30, 1933, Sawyer, Clark, and Davis were among 11 Lansing inmates who escaped from prison, using pistols smuggled in by Frank Nash. Among the other fugitives were HARVEY BAILEY, BOB BRADY, and WILBUR UNDERHILL. Sawyer split from the others on June 4 after they reached Oklahoma's COOKSON HILLS, supposing that he would do better on his own. Instead, his flight became a comedy of errors. First thumbing rides, Sawyer finally commandeered a car at gunpoint, only to have the motor die. His second acquisition blew a tire, near Middleburg. A third car almost instantly developed problems with the steering rod. Frank's fourth, stolen from a rural farm, carried him a half-dozen miles before it broke down, north of Gracemont. The driver of his fifth stolen car deliberately steered the vehicle into a roadside ditch. The sixth and last car to appear was occupied by Sheriff Horace Crisp and a deputy, investigating the rash of auto theft reports. Confronting Sawyer near Chickasaw, the lawmen quickly disarmed him and pistol-whipped him into unconsciousness.

Sawyer was returned to McAlester for completion of his murder sentence, transferred to the Oklahoma state reformatory in 1946, and finally paroled to Kansas, where a cell awaited him at Lansing. Governor Robert Docking pardoned Sawyer on September 18, 1969, after a belated affidavit from ALVIN KARPIS cleared Frank of involvement in the Fort Scott robbery. Sawyer filed a lawsuit against the state of Kansas, charging false imprisonment, but the case bogged down in legal red tape and was still unresolved at the time of his death.

SAXE, Susan: See POWER, KATHERINE.

SAYADOFF, Jack Daniel

A veteran of crime with convictions for bank robbery in California and Georgia, Jack Sayadoff wasted none of his time in jail on rehabilitation, preferring to think of prison as a kind of vocational school. By learning from his own mistakes and those of others, he surmised, he could become a better, more efficient robber.

Testing out his theory on October 21, 1965, Sayadoff raided a Chicago savings and loan association for $1,549. The take was average at best, and there were countless risks involved in working solo. Determined to better himself, Sayadoff began to shop around for an accomplice.

He found one in the person of Patsy Janakos while traveling in California. Patsy was having custody problems with her three-year-old daughter, and Sayadoff had the solution. Abducting the child's elderly babysitter, Sayadoff and Janakos left her bound and gagged in a Neward, California, home, making off with the child. Their action brought FBI agents

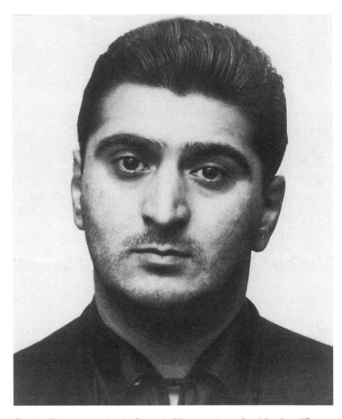

Federal fugitive Jack Sayadoff was identified by his "Born to Love" tattoo. (FBI)

into the case, pursuing charges of kidnapping and interstate transportation of a stolen vehicle.

On December 8, 1965, Jack and Patsy looted a San Francisco bank of $3,131. A month later, on January 6, 1966, they struck a Lakewood savings and loan office, netting another $2,186. On March 14 a bank job in Hampton Township, Pennsylvania, yielded $11,113. Three days later, Sayadoff's name was added to the FBI's "Ten Most Wanted" list.

Sayadoff and his adopted family had settled in Indianapolis on January 18, renting an apartment as "Mr. and Mrs. Jack F. Delano." Tipped to their location in March, FBI agents staked out the dwelling, following Jack and Patsy on their daily rounds until positive identification was confirmed. On March 24, 1966, Sayadoff was arrested at a local shopping center; Patsy Janakos was taken at home a short time later, and her daughter was placed in a Marion County children's shelter. In custody, Sayadoff was identified by a tattoo on his right forearm, reading "Born to Love." Glancing down at the incriminating mark, he offered G-men a rueful smile and said, "So true." Conviction on outstanding federal charges would curtail his love life drastically for years to come.

SCHWARZBERG, Daniel

In a dangerous trade like bank robbery, where flamboyant practitioners have been saddled with nicknames including "Baby Face," "Machine Gun," "Pretty Boy," and "Old Creepy," there is something almost poignant about a thief dubbed "Average Joe." Nicknames can be deceiving, though, and this one's owner was suspected of 17 successful holdups before his luck ran out.

A 43-year-old resident of Boone County, Kentucky, Daniel Schwarzberg took pains to look "average"—sporting a baseball cap and glasses, often carrying a day planner—while he robbed a minimum of 18 banks during a two-year period, striking repeatedly along Interstate Highway 75 in Ohio and Kentucky. He was arrested in July 2000 after looting a bank in Lexington, Kentucky. Grand jury investigation of the holdup series drove Schwarzberg to a plea bargain in federal court, admitting on October 30, 2000 to the robbery of 11 banks. FBI agents consider the remainder of "Average Joe's" holdups solved as well, with Schwarzberg's guilty plea.

SCUTARI, Richard Joseph

A product of the postwar baby boom, born April 30, 1947, at Port Jefferson, New York, Richard Scutari moved with his family to Florida in 1956. He dropped out of high school in his junior year to join the U.S. Navy and was stationed in Spain. Discharged in 1968, Scutari, a qualified scuba diver, worked in Louisiana and on oil rigs in the North Sea, repairing underwater oil pipes. He met his first wife in New Orleans while dating her mother; they married in 1970, and the union produced two daughters before they divorced in 1976. Remarried the same year, Scutari continued his underwater work until 1980 when the mounting death toll among his coworkers convinced him to resign.

By that time Scutari had found new passions in martial arts and extremist right-wing politics. Founding a construction company with his brother Frank, three years his senior, Richard fathered a third child and devoted his free time to the paranoid John Birch Society, absorbing pseudofacts and conspiracy theories that pushed him ever farther to the political

right. In 1979 he attended a Florida seminar hosted by the paramilitary Minutemen, forerunners of the latter-day "militia" movement. Comrades Andrew Barnhill and Ardie McBrearty soon introduced Scutari to Christian Identity—a racist-fringe religion whose disciples believe Jews are the literal offspring of Eve's copulation with Satan in the Garden of Eden, lumping nonwhite races together as soulless "mud people." In 1982 Scutari taught karate to the compound-dwelling racists of James Ellison's Covenant, Sword, and Arm of the Lord in Arkansas, rubbing shoulders with visiting members of the neo-Nazi Aryan Nations. In May 1984 Barnhill and McBrearty invited Scutari to Idaho, there introducing him to colleague Robert Jay Mathews and officially recruiting Scutari for a new paramilitary group called THE ORDER.

Although initially suspicious, Scutari joined The Order after subjecting its leaders to voice-stress analysis and thus convincing himself they were patriots committed to the overthrow of "ZOG"—the "Zionist Occupation Government" in Washington, D.C. Code named "Mr. Black"—based on his dark complexion or his black belt in karate; reports vary—Scutari was in Denver on June 18, 1984, when members of The Order assassinated controversial talk-show host Alan Berg, an outspoken Jew who had publicly insulted the Ku Klux Klan and other racist groups. One month later, on July 16, Scutari was part of the 11-man team that stopped a Brinks armored car outside Ukiah, California, and stole $3.6 million at gunpoint. In the process, Mathews dropped a pistol registered to Andrew Barnhill, and FBI agents were soon in hot pursuit of The Order.

Despite the manhunt, Scutari traveled widely on The Order's behalf in late 1984, distributing stolen cash to the group's leading allies. In November he was one of 11 would-be revolutionaries who signed The Order's declaration of war "for the future of our children, and for our King, Jesus Christ." Mathews was dead by December 8, 1984, killed in a shootout with the FBI on Whidbey Island, Washington, while survivors of the broken movement scattered nationwide. (Frank Scutari, meanwhile, was arrested by G-men in February 1985, convicted as an accessory after the fact to his brother's crimes, and sentenced to three years in prison.)

Richard Scutari was among those named in federal racketeering indictments against The Order on April 12, 1985, but he remained elusive and was added to the FBI's "Ten Most Wanted" list on July 11.

Eight months later, on March 19, 1986, G-men traced their quarry to a brake shop in San Antonio, Texas, where he was employed as "Larry Cupp." Known to his boss and coworkers as a soft-spoken "nice guy," Scutari had no chance to reach the .45-caliber automatic pistol hidden beneath the driver's seat of his car.

By the time of Scutari's arrest, 21 members of The Order had filed guilty pleas or been convicted on various federal charges, facing prison terms that ranged from six months to 100 years. Scutari bypassed trial on those charges with his own guilty plea and received a 60-year prison term—40 years for the Ukiah robbery and 20 more consecutive for racketeering. Tried in Denver for the Alan Berg assassination, Scutari was acquitted in November 1987; two colleagues from The Order were convicted and sentenced to 150 years in prison. Scutari was also among 14 Nazis indicted for sedition in April 1987, but all were acquitted in April 1988. In January 1989 guards at Leavenworth federal prison uncovered a plot by Scutari and two other inmates—Order veterans David Lane and Bruce Pierce—to escape with weapons smuggled in by friends. The plot was foiled and security was tightened, leaving Scutari eligible for parole sometime after 2026—at age 79.

SELLERS, Willie Foster

A member of the loose-knit Dawson gang, renowned for looting banks in northern Georgia through the early 1970s, Willie Sellers was convicted on federal bank-robbery charges in 1975 and sentenced to 45 years in prison. Confined at Marion, Illinois, he was returned to Atlanta in early 1977 to testify in defense of two persons charged with another Georgia robbery. Fulton County deputies intercepted a smuggled shipment of hacksaw blades meant for Sellers on February 25, believing their escape risk had been neutralized.

They were dead wrong.

On March 17, 1977, three armed intruders used bolt cutters to remove the wire screen covering a jail window, passing an acetylene torch through the window to sellers and convicted bank robber Charles Galvin Garrett. Following his escape, Sellers was linked to robberies netting a half-million dollars from banks in Arkansas, Missouri, North Carolina, and Texas. Declared a federal fugitive on charges of bank robbery and unlawful flight to avoid confine-

ment, Sellers was added to the FBI's "Most Wanted" list on June 14, 1977.

Two years later, on June 20, 1979, agents pursuing their investigation of Sellers traced the fugitive to Hartsell Airport in Atlanta where he was surrounded in the freight terminal and arrested without resistance. Declining to reveal the source that led them to Sellers, the G-men merely stated that he was visiting the airport on "legitimate business" when nabbed.

SHANNON, John Wesley, Jr.

An ex-prize fighter and occasional narcotics addict, John Shannon was born on July 9, 1936, in Pleasantville, New Jersey. His pugilistic prowess won him a championship during military service, but in civilian life his violent temper made him an unstable contender. When not squaring off in the ring, he variously found employment as a caddy, a dishwasher, hod carrier, a construction worker, and a hospital orderly. None of the jobs supported his drug habit or his fondness for gambling, and by 1957 he had turned his hand to crime, logging arrests and convictions for larceny, robbery, possession of a weapon, and sodomy.

On May 26, 1967, Shannon joined four accomplices in robbing a Northfield, New Jersey, savings and loan office of $8,881. The take was less than fabulous when split five ways, and three of the bandits were swiftly apprehended and sentenced to prison for their role in the heist. Federal warrants charging Shannon with bank robbery were issued on September 15, and his name was added to the FBI's "Ten Most Wanted" list on May 7, 1968. A month later, on June 5, he was cornered by federal agents in Camden, New Jersey, flushed from his hideout, and taken into custody without resistance. Held for trial on federal charges, Shannon was convicted and imprisoned for his crimes.

SHELTON, Henry Harland

An Indiana native, Henry Shelton was arrested in 1933 for his participation in a Michigan bank robbery that left a cashier dead. Sentenced to a minimum of 60 years, he made his first escape attempt in 1935 without success. His luck was better in the last week of September 1949 when he obtained a pistol, shot it out with guards, and fled the prison grounds accompanied by Samuel Lieb, an inmate serving life for murder.

On September 17 the convicts seized a motorist in northern Michigan. Abducted at knifepoint, their hostage escaped after driving his captors across Wisconsin and Illinois into Indiana. There the trail went cold, but agents of the FBI were joining in the hunt. In flight, the fugitives had racked up federal kidnap charges in addition to their violation of the Dyer Act, forbidding transportation of stolen cars across state lines.

The outlaws surfaced in Kentucky on the evening of October 2 when they tried to rob a Mayfield resident outside his home. The target's wife observed the crime in progress, telephoning the police, and officers arrived to find the fugitives still rifling their victim's pockets. Gunfire was exchanged; Sam Lieb was captured when he tried to jump a fence and cracked his skull instead. Shelton was luckier and managed to escape once more.

He surfaced in Paducah nine days later, holding up a liquor store and fleeing with $1,100. When the FBI created its "Ten Most Wanted" program in March 1950, Shelton's name was posted to the list as number nine. Exactly three months later, he was captured.

A son of Indianapolis, Shelton had never strayed far from home in his travels. Scouring the city, federal agents were told Shelton liked to patronize a certain tavern, turning up with clockwork regularity to slake his thirst. On June 23, 1950, G-men staked out Shelton's favorite bar and settled down to wait.

When Shelton finally appeared with two companions, the agents moved to intercept him, but months of living on the run had honed the convict's paranoia to a razor's edge. He tried to draw the .45 concealed beneath his coat, and agents opened fire before he had a chance to use the weapon, dropping Shelton in his tracks. On recovery, the fugitive faced trial in federal court and was sentenced to a 45-year term in Leavenworth. In the event that he survived to make parole, the term of 60 years to life (with extra time for his escape) would still be waiting for him back in Michigan.

SHERMAN, John William

A member of the radical George Jackson Brigade, linked to numerous West Coast bombings and bank robberies in the 1970s, John Sherman shot it out with police on at least two occasions. Once, during a 1976 Seattle bank robbery, he was wounded by authorities and subsequently captured. Sherman escaped a short time later when an accomplice,

dressed as a medical assistant, shot the guard assigned to escort Sherman from a local hospital. Back on the street, Sherman resumed his career of TERRORISM, ultimately robbing 14 banks and touching off 11 high-explosive charges in the name of "liberation." Cornered at a Tacoma drive-in restaurant in March 1978, Sherman was dressed as a priest when FBI agents surrounded his car and took him into custody. On conviction of bank robbery and escape charges, he was sentenced to 10 years in prison.

On April 24, 1979, Sherman escaped from prison at Lompoc, California, and was declared a federal fugitive on charges of unlawful flight to avoid confinement. His name was added to the bureau's "Ten Most Wanted" list on August 3. Thirty-two months later, after completing extensive investigations in Seattle and Portland, Oregon, federal agents traced Sherman to his hideout in Golden, Colorado. He was taken into custody without incident, surrendering meekly to his captors. Also arrested were Sherman's wife and another female traveling companion, both held on charges of aiding a federal fugitive. Sherman was returned to prison with additional time tacked onto his sentence for the latest escape.

SINGER, Joel

Assisted by his uncle, Jack Frank, Canadian Joel Singer scored a criminal coup on October 24, 1965, using an antitank cannon to blast open the vault in a Brinks office in Syracuse, New York. The bandit escaped with $161,000 in cash and $292,587 in nonnegotiable securities.

By November 1 Frank was in custody, spilling everything he knew about the crime in return for a grant of total immunity from prosecution. According to his statement, he had purchased two 20-mm antitank guns and 200 rounds of armor-piercing ammunition in Alexandria, Virginia. The purchase was Singer's idea, Frank said, and his nephew had fronted the money. Ironically, FBI agents and officers of the Royal Canadian Mounted Police had been aware of the purchase, tracking the weapons on suspicion of a link to TERRORIST activity, but Singer was alerted to the surveillance, and he "stole" the shipment from himself in a warehouse burglary at Plattsburgh, New York, on the night of April 7, 1965. To prove himself, Frank led a team of agents to the bridge near Jones Beach, New York, where the cannon was discarded following the Brinks heist.

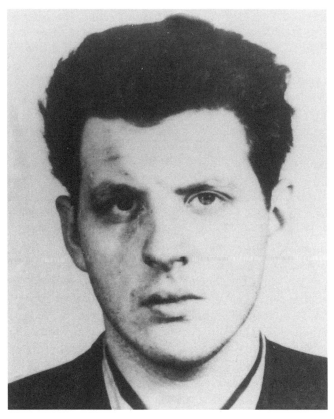

Joel Singer used an antitank gun to crack a Brinks vault in 1965. (FBI)

On November 17, 1965, Joel Singer was indicted on a charge of third-degree burglary. Further charges of first-degree larceny were later filed, and his name was added to the FBI's "Most Wanted" list on November 19. Twelve days later, Singer was arrested by detectives in his native Montreal. A vial of nitroglycerine was found in his car, parked nearby. In his possession the arresting officers found $188.35; no other loot from the Brinks job was ever recovered.

Singer fought extradition, but in vain. Convicted in 1966, he drew a term of five to 10 years in prison. On July 27, 1972, Singer was transferred from the state penitentiary at Clinton, New York, to a mental hospital where he received therapy for an apparent breakdown. On parole in early 1973, he returned to Montreal and was found dead in his apartment there on February 9. An autopsy revealed traces of cyanide in his system, and his death was ruled a suicide.

SKINNER Brothers

Daring practitioners of HIGHWAY ROBBERY in gold-rush-era California, Cyrus Skinner and his younger brother George worked alone for the most part until they were captured together in the early 1850s and packed off to San Quentin state prison. There, they met and were befriended by a clique of veteran bandits that included TOM HODGES (aka Tom Bell) and RICHARD "RATTLESNAKE DICK" BARTER, forming the nucleus of a new gang that would terrorize northern California miners in the last half of the decade.

The outfit's biggest score was accomplished on March 12, 1856, when they robbed a mule train carrying gold dust from the Yreka Mine to Shasta, California, a three-day, 110-mile trip through the Trinity Alps. George Skinner and three others stopped the mule train, stealing $17,000 in dust, while Cyrus, Dick Barter, and BILL GRISTY provided a backup string of 13 stolen mules. Cyrus was arrested days later for stealing horses in Sacramento and was jailed at Auburn, California, pending trial. George hatched a plan to spring his brother, but before the gang could mobilize, members ADOLPH NEWTON and Tom Brown were arrested for their part in the holdup. Brown bargained for his freedom, leading a posse to a cabin on the American River, one mile from Folsom, where George Skinner, Bill Gristy, and Nicanor Rodriguez had their hideout.

The outlaws went for their pistols as raiders burst into the cabin, armed with double-barreled shotguns. Skinner died in the first exchange of fire, but gunsmoke quickly filled the one-room cabin, making accurate shooting impossible. Rodriguez fled out the back but was shot twice and collapsed. Bill Gristy had better luck, shooting his way out the front door and vanishing into the night.

Cyrus Skinner had little time for mourning his kid brother. Convicted of stealing horses, he was sentenced to 14 years at San Quentin but later escaped after serving a fraction of his time. Unfit for any trade but banditry, he relocated to Montana Territory and launched a new crime spree there. He was eventually caught by vigilantes and hanged, one of 22 suspected felons executed without trial between December 1863 and February 1864.

SMITH, Edward: First American bank burglar

While not a bank robber in the traditional sense of daylight raids, drawn guns, and daring getaways, Englishman Edward Smith (aka James Smith, Edward Jones, and James Honeyman) still takes dubious honors as the first-known criminal to penetrate and loot a bank. His tactic of nocturnal burglary would remain the standard for east coast thieves through the 19th century, emulated further west through the 1920s by such operators as the KIMES-TERRILL GANG.

Smith pulled his one and only bank job on March 19, 1831, using duplicate keys to invade the City Bank on New York City's Wall Street, making off with an impressive $245,000. Less clever at evading capture than at stealing cash, Smith spent $60,000 on high living in the space of a few days before he was fingered by informants and taken into custody. Officers recovered $185,000 of the bank loot, while Smith received a relatively lenient sentence for his unfamiliar crime. On May 11, 1931, he was sentenced to five years at hard labor in Sing Sing prison, while his future emulators would serve decades for less successful robberies.

SOCIAL Bandits

As defined by Eric Hobsbawm in his classic work *Bandits* (1969), this term applies to outlaws who arise from downtrodden classes to attack their privileged masters, the resultant depredations reflecting a "universal longing for freedom, heroism and the dream of justice" among the "weak, oppressed and cheated." Reports of social banditry often include—but seldom document conclusively—descriptions of the outlaws sharing loot with their impoverished neighbors, sometimes (rarely) moving on from simple robbery to revolution in the people's name.

The earliest known social bandit may be "ROBIN HOOD," a figure of Medieval British legend whose exploits have been so widely embroidered and fictionalized that his real-life existence is now controversial, most scholars suggesting he was probably a composite figure, cobbled together from scattered reports over several generations. It is impossible to say with any certainty which English felon from the Middle Ages was the source or inspiration for surviving tales of "Robin Hood," and all accounts of his adventures must be taken with a healthy grain of salt.

In the United States, somewhat more recently, America's war with Mexico and the subsequent California gold rush sparked conflict between Anglos and Hispanics, most often settled at gunpoint by vigilantes or militiamen. In the circumstances, it is not surprising that Latinos cheered for bandits like JOAQUIN MURRIETA and Tiburcio Vásquez, who looted homes and ranches up and down the Golden

State. Accounts describing Murrieta as a revolutionary are mistaken, though. His band and others like it robbed and murdered Mexicans, Chinese, and blacks along with Anglos, sometimes stealing no more than a watch or pocket change, and there are no reliable accounts of any raiders sharing loot outside of their respective gangs.

America's next noteworthy social bandits, outlaw brothers FRANK and JESSE JAMES were denizens of the Missouri Ozark region who saw action in the Civil War and never lost their taste for violence. They certainly existed, but what stands in doubt are tales of their generosity to friends, neighbors, even total strangers. A typical story describes Jesse James loaning money to a widow for payment of her mortgage and then riding off to rob the bank that held her deed. No evidence of any such events exists today, but that does not prevent the tale from being handed down as fact. One Hollywood film puts a grim reverse twist on the legend, sending James back to murder the widow and sleep in her house on his way to the gang's last great battle in Northfield, Minnesota.

Australia's social bandits were the "BUSHRANGERS," frequently Irishmen transported from England as convicts for stealing to feed their hungry families. On arrival in the distant penal colony, they found themselves further oppressed by politicians, judges, and policemen in the British mold, driven to banditry when crops and all else failed. Most famous of the lot was EDWARD "NED" KELLY, whose gang robbed banks and trains during the same era when the James brothers were at large in America. His persecution by police is legendary—but again, there is no evidence of Kelly sharing loot with anyone outside his own gang or immediate family.

In Mexico, during the First World War, Francisco "Pancho" Villa led an outlaw band that roughly fit the social-bandit mold, allegedly redistributing wealth through "individual beneficence or indiscriminate largesse," later graduating from cross-border raids to a general's rank in the revolutionary army opposing Mexican dictator Victoriano Huerta. By the time Villa was ambushed and killed in July 1923, Sicily's greatest social bandit was growing up in poverty, learning to hate the politicians and gangsters who squeezed hard-working peasants for their last lira. Salvatore Giuliano was 21 years old in 1943 when he was accused of smuggling grain to his hungry family and was shot and wounded by *carabinieri* who tried in vain to arrest him. By 1944 Giuliano was the leader of a bandit gang that ambushed fascist columns and liberated political prisoners, quickly earning himself a reputation as "the Robin Hood of Sicily." His luck ran out when he tried to bridge the worlds of crime and politics, opposing candidates advanced for office by the ruling party and the Mafia. Giuliano died in a battle with Sicilian police on July 5, 1950, but his legend lives on, memorialized in FICTION AND FILM.

America's last great social bandit was CHARLES "PRETTY BOY" FLOYD, an Oklahoma farm boy gone bad, who hit his stride—and national headlines—in the Great Depression. Floyd was not alone by any means, sharing newsprint with the likes of JOHN DILLINGER and ALVIN KARPIS, but he alone of the Depression-era bank robbers is credited with more than entertainment value to the public. Stories persist of Floyd interrupting bank jobs to collect and burn mortgage papers, thus freeing poor farmers from debt, but in fact no record has survived of such an incident. Regardless, Floyd is still remembered by old-timers in the Sooner State as "the Robin Hood of the COOKSON HILLS."

Whereas the classic social bandits passed into legend for the most part unconsciously, modern pretenders to the mantle work overtime to cultivate the "Robin Hood" image, demanding media attention as they claim to act—and steal—in the name of "The People." South American guerrilla bands such as the MONTONEROS and the TUPAMAROS were notorious in their day for robbing banks and corporate offices, kidnapping wealthy businessmen or politicians, and subjecting them to trials by "people's courts." America's most recent example of such behavior was the SYMBIONESE LIBERATION ARMY, demanding distribution of food to California ghetto residents after the kidnapping of newspaper heiress Patricia Hearst. On the far-right wing of the political spectrum, neo-Nazi bandits such as THE ORDER and affiliated groups have achieved "Aryan hero" status among fringe dwellers of the white supremacist Christian Identity cult by robbing banks and armored cars to finance their guerrilla war against America's "Zionist Occupation Government" in Washington, D.C.

SUTTON, William Francis

Willie Sutton always had a sense of style. To friends and enemies alike he was "The Actor," capable of altering his look and personality to suit his needs in any given situation. Armed with keen intelligence where many of his criminal contemporaries struggled through on nerve alone, he operated in the upper strata of an industry where life expectancies and careers are sometimes measured in hours. Willie played the game for nearly 40 years, and there are some who would suggest he won more often than he lost.

Born in Brooklyn's "Irishtown," young Willie Sutton ran with street gangs in his youth, but he already had his sights on bigger things. While friends were stealing food from pushcarts, playing smash-and-grab with local merchants, Sutton dreamed of going on to law school and defending those whose company he cherished. He could never raise the cash for college, though, and in 1917 romance propelled him into trouble with the law. He burglarized a store belonging to his girlfriend's father, stealing $16,000 that he hoped would finance their elopement. On arrest he was indicted for abduction, burglary, and grand larceny, but the imposing charges were bargained down to mere unlawful entry. Willie spent a year in the reformatory, and the remainder of his sentence was suspended.

Sutton disappeared from official records for a time, returning with a vengeance on July 10, 1921. With an acquaintance, Willie was indicted on a double murder charge after two known enemies were shot outside his favorite pool hall. Running for his life, he joined a team of robbers and safecrackers, picking up an education on the lam before he was arrested and returned for trial. To everyone's surprise, he was acquitted by a jury of his peers.

In April 1926 Sutton was convicted of bank burglary in New York City, sentenced to a term of five to 10 years. Serving time at Sing Sing and Dannemora, he was paroled in August 1929 and worked briefly for Dutch Schultz's bootlegging gang in the Bronx before launching a new career in armed robbery of banks and jewelry stores. Employing makeup and various disguises—often dressing in the uniform of a policeman, a firefighter, or a Western Union messenger—"Willie the Actor" ran up some impressive scores before his next arrest. On October 10, 1930, attired in Western Union garb, he tried to rob the Bay Bridge, Brooklyn, branch of the National City Bank, but a watchman foiled the effort. On October 28 Sutton rebounded, in the same costume, to steal $130,000 worth of gems from the Broadway jewelry store of M. Rosenthal & Son. The jewels were fenced through cronies in the Schultz mob, with a payoff to the Dutchman for his help.

Sutton's luck ran out on June 5, 1931, when he was sentenced to 30 years for bank robbery and returned to Sing Sing. He escaped on December 12,

Bank robber Willie "The Actor" Sutton is booked at the Bergen Street station in Brooklyn, New York, in 1952. (AP/Wide World Photos)

1932, and soon collected new accomplices to help him pick up where he had left off. On July 9, 1933, with cohorts Joe Perlongo and Eddie Wilson, Sutton robbed the Corn Exchange Bank in New York City of $23,838. Six months later, on January 15, 1934, the same trio looted another branch of the Corn Exchange Bank, this time in Philadelphia, of another $10,980. Captured by Philadelphia police on February 5, 1934, Sutton was convicted of his latest capers and sentenced to a prison term of 25 to 50 years.

"The Actor" started to serve his time at Eastern State Prison, but he chafed at confinement, staging four unsuccessful escape attempts during the next 13 years. Transferred to Holmesburg Prison for greater security, he was finally successful, with other inmates, on February 10, 1947. A snowstorm covered the fugitives' tracks, and Willie was soon back

in the business of armed robbery. By this time, there could be no question of "The Actor" going straight. He only knew one trade, and he was still the best in town.

Wrongly suspected in the January 1950 BRINKS ROBBERY, Sutton had his hands full with other capers that year. On March 9, 1950, three armed bandits struck the officers of the Manufacturers Trust Company in Sunnyside, Queens, escaping with $63,933. Bank employees picked Willie's mug shot as a likeness of the gang's leader, and his name was added to the FBI's "Ten Most Wanted" list on March 20, replacing the recently captured WILLIAM NESBIT.

The end came suddenly for Sutton on February 18, 1952, when New York subway rider Arnold Schuster recognized "The Actor" from his WANTED fliers. Summoning police, Schuster watched as Sutton casually surrendered and was taken into custody. By

Willie "The Actor" Sutton was an early addition to the FBI's "Ten Most Wanted" list. (FBI)

then, Willie's accomplices in the Queens robbery had been identified as THOMAS KLING and John De Venuta, both of whom were captured two days later by police in New York City.

(Schuster became an overnight celebrity for fingering Sutton, but his fame would be short lived. Observing Schuster in a television interview, New York Mafia chieftain Albert Anastasia flew into a homicidal rage. "I hate squealers!" he shouted. "Hit that guy!" The contract was fulfilled on March 8, 1952, when Schuster was assassinated near his Brooklyn home. According to the later testimony of defecting mobster Joe Valachi, Schuster's execution was arranged and carried out by Frederick Tenuto, yet another member of the bureau's Top Ten list. Once he had murdered Schuster, Tenuto was himself executed on orders from Anastasia and his body disappeared. His name was removed from the "Most Wanted" list in March 1964 after his fate was publicly revealed.)

On April 1, 1952, Sutton and Kling were convicted of the Queens holdup, each sentenced to a term of 29 years in prison. Sutton received two additional terms of 15 years to life on weapons charges unrelated to the heist, those terms to run consecutively with the remainder of his interrupted 30-year sentence from 1931. (John De Venuta saved himself by turning state's evidence at the trial, and his sentence was suspended.) Sutton was finally paroled on the day before Christmas 1969. He died of natural causes on November 2, 1980, at his sister's home in Spring Hill, Florida.

SYMBIONESE Liberation Army

America's most notorious radical clique of the 1970s sprang from a failed social experiment at California's Vacaville State Prison. Designed to provide education, cultural awareness, and prerelease counseling for inmates approaching parole, the Black Cultural Association (BCA) had enlisted 100 Vacaville inmates by 1971. Collaborating with the BCA were various volunteer tutors from outside the prison, including members of a far-left Oakland collective run by white activists William Wolfe and Russell Little. The BCA's prime mover behind bars was 30-year-old career criminal Donald David DeFreeze, who taught a class on "unisight" aiming to increase awareness of the male role in black families.

Tutors Wolfe and Little staged a quiet coup in 1972, wresting control of the BCA from more moderate hands and shifting the curriculum toward Maoist politics. Star pupil DeFreeze was lost to them in a transfer to Folsom prison, but he escaped from that facility's minimum security wing on March 5, 1973, and soon rejoined his friends on the outside. By that time DeFreeze had dubbed himself "Cinque"—after the leader of a 19th-century slave rebellion—and proclaimed himself "field marshal" of the Symbionese Liberation Army (SLA). DeFreeze apparently took his group's name from a novel by Sam Greenlee, *The Spook Who Sat by the Door* (1959), which portrays armed insurrection in Chicago's ghetto and uses the term *symbiology* in passing to describe collaboration among disparate organisms.

The collaboration DeFreeze had in mind apparently involved himself giving orders to a handful of naive white radicals. Despite its roots in the BCA and proclaimed dedication to oppressed minorities, the SLA apparently had no black members other than DeFreeze. His disciples were unanimously white and thoroughly ashamed of it, to the extent that they shunned their given "slave names" and adopted more exotic names. (Wolfe, for instance, called himself "Cujo," a word of unknown derivation which translated as "unconquerable.") Female recruits—a majority of the SLA's tiny membership—went even further in rejecting their ethnicity, affecting dark makeup and Afro wigs to make themselves "look black."

By autumn 1973 DeFreeze had recruited 11 would-be warriors for his "army," seven of whom were women. Aside from charter members Wolfe and Little there was disaffected Vietnam veteran Joseph Remiro; James Kilgore; Nancy Ling Perry; Patricia M. Soltysik; Camilla C. Hall; Wendy Yoshimura; Angela Atwood; Kathleen Ann Soliah; and a married couple, William and Emily Harris. The SLA made its first move on November 9, 1973, when Little and Remiro ambushed Oakland's black school superintendent, Marcus Foster, and killed him in a barrage of cyanide-tipped bullets. Foster's "crime," according to DeFreeze, was sponsorship of a program to photograph each member of Oakland's mostly black student body. DeFreeze regarded Foster's plan as an attempt to isolate and persecute black militants, thus prompting the elimination of a "peoples' enemy."

Police became lucky two months after Foster's murder, on January 10, 1974, when a van occupied by Little and Remiro was stopped for a traffic violation in Concord, California. The SLA gunmen came out shooting and Little was wounded, captured at the scene. Remiro briefly eluded patrolmen but he was arrested later in the day. Panicked by news of the arrests, other SLA members set fire to a nearby hideout and fled. A search of the smoldering rubble turned up revolutionary pamphlets and a cryptic note in handwriting later identified as "Cinque's." It read: "Patricia Campbell Hearst on the night of the full moon January 7."

Patricia Hearst, who was kidnapped by the Symbionese Liberation Army (SLA) and participated in a bank robbery with her captors, arrives for her trial in 1976. (AP/Wide World Photos)

The SLA had chosen its next target, even though the dates were off.

Patricia Hearst was the 19-year-old granddaughter of William Randolph Hearst, multimillionaire newspaper magnate whose circulation war with rival Joseph Pulitzer helped spark the Spanish-American War in 1898; Patricia's father, Randolph Hearst, owned the *San Francisco Examiner*. On the night of February 4, 1974, a woman knocked on the door of Patty Hearst's Berkeley apartment, asking permission to use the telephone. Two gunmen barged in behind the woman, clubbing 26-year-old Stephen Weed to the floor when he tried to defend his fiancée. The raiders dragged Hearst out to a waiting car and fled in a hail of gunfire unleashed to deter pursuit. SLA involvement in the kidnapping was revealed three days later with arrival of a letter at Berkeley radio station KPFA-FM. Inside the envelope, with a credit card issued to Randolph Hearst, was a letter stating that his daughter had been taken into "protective custody." The SLA's letterhead featured a seven-headed cobra, each head corresponding to one of the group's professed goals: self-determination, cooperative production, creativity, unity, faith, purpose, and collective responsibility.

The SLA made its first ransom demand in a second letter to KPFA on February 12. As a "symbolic gesture of good faith" toward negotiation of Patricia's release, Randolph Hearst was ordered to deliver $70 worth of groceries during the next four weeks to "all people [in California] with welfare cards, Social Security pension cards, food stamp cards, disabled veteran cards, medical cards, parole or probation papers and jail or bail release slips." Enclosed with the letter was a tape recording of Patty Hearst asking her father to comply with the demands. A second tape recording, mailed separately to KPFA, featured "Cinque"-DeFreeze declaring himself "quite willing to carry out the execution of your daughter to save the life of starving men, women and children of every race."

Randolph Hearst declared his willingness to cooperate but warned the kidnappers on February 13 that "we can't meet the cost"—estimated at $400 million—of feeding all California's needy for a month at $70 per head. A third tape from the SLA, received three days later, struck a more reasonable tone. "It was never intended that you feed the whole state," Patty Hearst told her father. "Whatever you come up with is okay." DeFreeze advised Randolph Hearst, "We are quite able to assess the extent of your sincerity, and we will accept sincere efforts on your part." With that in mind, distribution of food worth some $2 million began in San Francisco and the Oakland ghetto on February 22.

By that time, Bay Area law enforcers and reporters had identified DeFreeze as "Cinque." Fingerprints from the burned-out Compton hideaway also identified 26-year-old Nancy Perry as an SLA fugitive at large. A March 9 tape recording mailed to Randolph Hearst demanded television air time for a jailhouse press conference with triggermen Little and Remiro, but Judge Sam Hall rejected the notion. Patty Hearst, on the same tape, warned her father that negotiations for her release would not begin until another $4 million in high-quality food had been distributed to the poor. A third voice—that of a woman who called herself "General Genina"—denounced the groceries passed out so far as "not fit for human consumption."

The next SLA tape, received by authorities on April 5, 1974, included a shocking announcement from Patty Hearst that she had voluntarily "chosen to stay and fight" with "Cinque's" commandos. Ten days later, SLA raiders struck a branch of the Hibernia Bank in San Francisco, stealing $10,960 and wounding two bystanders with wild gunfire as they fled the scene. Security cameras recorded the event, and FBI spokesmen identified one of the armed bandits as Patricia Hearst. Two other bandits appeared to point their carbines at Hearst, but bank guard Edward Shea insisted that Hearst "absolutely was a participant" in the holdup. "She wasn't scared," Shea told reporters. "She had a gun and looked ready to use it. She had plenty of command in her voice. She was full of curse words. She let it be known that she meant business."

From Washington, U.S. Attorney General William Saxbe declared of the SLA, "The entire group we're talking about is common criminals and Miss Hearst is part of it." Randolph Hearst denounced the statement as "irresponsible," but federal warrants were issued on April 15 for Patricia's arrest as a material witness. Also named in the warrants were DeFreeze, Nancy Perry, Patricia Soltysik, and Camilla Hall. San Francisco police announced that the raiding party, with getaway drivers included, had consisted of nine persons. California Attorney General Evelle Younger followed the federal lead on April 17, issuing felony arrest warrants for SLA members William Wolfe, Angela Atwood, and William and Emily Harris on perjury charges for giving false information on applications for their drivers' licenses.

The Hearst family insisted that Patricia had been brainwashed by her captors, a victim of "Stockholm syndrome," in which hostages display sympathy for their kidnappers. Patty Hearst rejected that argument in a tape mailed to San Francisco police on April 24. Calling herself "Tania," Hearst denounced the brainwashing argument as "ridiculous" and confirmed her voluntary participation in the Hibernia holdup. Her father and her fiancée were "pigs," Patricia said; if the bank heist did not prove her loyalty to the SLA, she promised that other actions soon would. A photograph depicted "Tania" wearing a beret and brandishing a carbine, posed before the SLA's seven-headed cobra flag.

Time ran out for Donald DeFreeze and half of his army in May 1974. On May 16 the Harrises were caught shoplifting in a Los Angeles thrift store, scuffling with an employee until Patty Hearst fired an automatic rifle to cover their escape in a stolen van. The next day, a telephone tip led manhunters to an SLA hideout on East 54th Street in Los Angeles. Surrounded by more than 400 police and FBI agents, six SLA members shot it out with police while TV cameras broadcast the battle nationwide. More than 6,000 shots were fired before the house was set afire, either by tear gas rounds or (according to one eyewitness report) FBI agents lobbing hand grenades. Unable or unwilling to approach the burning house, firefighters waited for it to collapse. Inside, with a small arsenal of guns, they found the charred remains of DeFreeze, William Wolfe, Nancy Perry, Patricia Soltysik, Angela Atwood, and Camilla Hall.

"Tania" Hearst remained at large though, voicing grief for her comrades in a tape mailed to Los Angeles radio station KPFK on June 7. After reiterating her revolutionary commitment, she added a more personal note. "Cujo [Wolfe] was the gentlest, most beautiful man I've ever known," she said. "We loved each other so much. *Cujo* means 'unconquerable.' It was the perfect name for him. He conquered life as well as death." Hearst's relatives continued to defend her, but a federal grand jury in San Francisco took her statements seriously, indicting Patricia for armed bank robbery on June 6.

Indicting "Tania" Hearst and catching her were two very different things, however. She was still on the run with her surviving SLA cronies on April 21, 1975, when four armed bandits invaded the Crocker National Bank in Carmichael, California. Before they fled with $15,000 from the tellers' cages, one robber fired an unprovoked shotgun blast and fatally wounded a customer, 42-year-old Myrna Lee Opsahl. The getaway car was found three hours later, abandoned six blocks from the bank; embarrassed police acknowledged placing the vehicle under surveillance a week earlier, based on reports of "suspicious" persons renting a local garage, but the vehicle had somehow disappeared on April 21. Patricia Hearst later identified three members of the holdup team as SLA members Emily Harris, Kathleen Soliah, and James Kilgore.

FBI agents caught a break in the case on September 18, 1975, when a tipster directed them to the SLA's latest hideout in San Francisco's Mission District. William and Emily Harris were surrounded on a street corner and taken into custody without resistance. Moments later G-men raided a nearby apartment where they captured Patty Hearst, Steven Soliah (Kathleen's brother), and 32-year-old Wendy Yoshimura (sought since 1972 for conspiracy to bomb a Naval ROTC building on the University of California campus in Berkeley). Bond was set at $500,000 for each fugitive on September 18, but a federal judge reversed that decision a day later, ordering Patty Hearst held without bail.

Defense arguments focused on Hearst's state of mind, contending that she had been threatened, raped, drugged, and confined to a filthy closet for weeks before the Hibernia holdup. As a result, her mind became "confused and distorted," with fears of impending madness. A defense affidavit maintained: "Her recollections of everything that transpired from shortly after the bank incident up to the time that she was arrested has been as though she lived in a fog in which she was confused, still unable to distinguish between actuality and fantasy, and in a perpetual state of terror." A semblance of sanity had returned, lawyers said, around the time Patty came back to San Francisco with G-men on her trail. Furthermore, the legal team declared, "She is completely convinced of the love and affection of her family and that she will find safety and comfort in its midst."

Perhaps, but a Los Angeles County grand jury remained unconvinced, charging Hearst and the Harrises on October 6 with 11 counts of robbery, kidnapping, and assault related to the May 1974 thrift shop incident. Kathleen and Steven Soliah, meanwhile, were indicted for bank robbery resulting in death, related to the April 1975 Carmichael raid. Federal Judge Oliver Carter found Patricia Hearst mentally competent for trial and ordered the proceedings to begin on January 26, 1976.

Lead defense attorney F. Lee Bailey attacked Hearst's SLA kidnappers as "crazy people" in his opening statement to the jury, contending that the Hibernia holdup had been deliberately staged by DeFreeze and company to complete the brainwashing of "a particularly vulnerable, frightened 19-year-old girl." Furthermore, Bailey asserted, the carbine carried by Hearst in the bank job "was not operable." Testifying on February 9, Hearst told a story of mental and sexual abuse by her captors, recanted professions of love for William Wolfe, and claimed she had fired on the L.A. thrift shop in May 1974 because she was "indoctrinated" to defend SLA members. On cross-examination by the prosecutor, Hearst used her Fifth Amendment privilege 19 times to avoid questions about various other bank holdups.

Patty Hearst was convicted of armed robbery and sentenced to seven years imprisonment, but she served only two years before her sentence was commuted by President Jimmy Carter. (President Bill Clinton officially pardoned Hearst in January 2001.) Los Angeles jurors convicted William and Emily Harris of armed robbery, kidnapping, and auto theft on August 9, 1976; they were indicted for kidnapping Patty Hearst in October 1976 and pled guilty to that charge in 1978, winning parole in the spring of 1983. Russ Little and Joseph Remiro were convicted of Marcus Foster's murder in June 1977 and sentenced to life imprisonment. Kathleen Soliah fled to ST. PAUL, MINNESOTA, where (as "Sarah Jane Olson") she married and bore three children. Arrested on June 16, 1999, after her case was profiled on *America's Most Wanted,* she was returned to California and currently awaits trial. (Soliah's trial was originally scheduled to begin on September 24, 2001, but it was indefinitely postponed by order of a federal appeals court following the prosecution's belated release—in July 2001—of some 23,000 government documents to the defense.) SLA member James Kilgore remains at large, indicted for possession of an unregistered explosive device.

T

TALBOT, Henry J. "Cherokee Bob"

One of five California bandits nicknamed "Cherokee Bob" during the 1850s, Henry Talbot is the subject of some predictable confusion in gold rush–era newspaper reports. Georgia born in 1833, Talbot arrived in California at age 16 and soon developed a brawler's reputation. He logged his first arrest in San Francisco, fined with four others on January 25, 1850, for "riotous and disorderly behavior." A fixture of the Golden State's mining camps over the next three years, Talbot was described by one observer as "a gentleman of great consequence, who had killed six Chilenos in one fight, and although he had been riddled with bullets and sliced with knives, yet he had never failed to get his man when he went for him."

There is no record of that fearsome battle, but Talbot fought his share of duels with knife and pistol, always emerging victorious. By 1854 he was established as a more-or-less professional gambler, partnered with an alleged brother who habitually used the alias "William Ewing" (true name unknown). On February 15, 1854, the Talbot brothers had a fatal altercation with Jamestown hotelkeeper Thomas Brown. "Ewing" fired the killing shot, but "Cherokee Bob" had handed him the pistol and both fled town to escape summary justice.

Talbot settled in Mariposa County, where he found more trouble within two weeks of the Jamestown murder. His new gambling partner, a Mexican named Velásquez, quarreled with a Chilean gambler, and the men agreed to a pistol duel with Talbot serving as Velásquez's second. Velásquez was a miserable shot, missing his opponent six times and suffering two minor wounds before the duelists started to grapple hand-to-hand. Talbot stabbed the Chilean and then slashed the Indian second who came to his aid. Fearing murder charges, Talbot and Velásquez stole horses and rode south, captured by a posse near Millerton. Their wounded opponents survived, but both defendants were convicted of horse theft and sentenced to 10 years' hard labor at San Quentin.

Talbot entered the prison on March 21, 1854, swiftly making friends with a team of hardened outlaws and HIGHWAYMEN that included TOM HODGES and BILL GRISTY. Two days after Christmas 1854, while loading a ship at the prison wharf, Talbot led a mass escape attempt. The convicts overpowered and disarmed their guards, including Captain B. F. Pullen, and commandeered a sloop to make their getaway. Under heavy fire from officers, Talbot used Captain Pullen as a human shield, shouting, "Stand up and be shot like a man, for we all have to die together!"

In fact, although all 22 convicts (and Captain Pullen) were wounded by bullets, only one escapee died in the withering fusillade. Injured as they were, the fugitives still sailed across San Francisco Bay and landed north of Oakland, scattering into the Contra Costa hills. All were soon recaptured, with Talbot not expected to survive. A newspaper account described his wounds: "A rifle ball entered the left side at the arm pit, passed within an inch of the heart, and lodged near the backbone. The bullet has not been taken out, and can be felt with the fingers. . . . Bob has another bullet feelable in his arm. In the calf of his right leg are the marks of the entrance and exit of a bullet."

Still, Talbot surprised his captors and lived on, recovering in time to join another breakout on May 12, 1855. Assigned to a wood-chopping detail with Tom Hodges, Bill Gristy, Jim Smith, and several other inmates that afternoon, he took advantage of a guard's intoxication and fled with the others, this time escaping uninjured. Settling in San Mateo County and earning his keep as a gambler, Talbot made friends with a former California governor, John McDougal, but bad luck continued to dog him. En route to Los Angeles that November, Talbot was wrongly accused of a double murder in Monterey County, jailed in that case on December 21, 1855. He was acquitted, but publicity surrounding the trial brought manhunters to his doorstep, and he was returned to San Quentin as an escapee.

Despite his record, Talbot received a gubernatorial pardon in 1860 and made a beeline for the Comstock Lode in Nevada Territory. On August 6, 1861, he wounded a Carson City constable in a free-wheeling knife fight. Seven weeks later Talbot wounded a second lawman and was finally jailed, jumping bond on both charges and fleeing to the scene of new gold strikes in Washington. America was deep in civil war by then, and the violence seemed inescapable. On April 10, 1862, Talbot killed two soldiers at Walla Walla in a brawl between Union and Confederate partisans. He promptly stole a horse and fled for his life into Montana Territory.

Gambling had played out for "Cherokee Bob"; he was a full-fledged outlaw now. Joining a gang led by rogue sheriff Henry Plummer, Talbot plied his lawless trade with such bandits as the notorious CYRUS SKINNER. Vigilante justice shattered the gang, however, when lynch mobs executed 22 badmen (including Plummer and Skinner) between December 1863 and February 1864. Talbot survived that purge by fleeing to the mining camp of Florence, but his brawler's reputation finally caught up with him on January 2, 1864. After his drunken girlfriend was ejected from a New Year's party, Talbot and sidekick "Poker Bill" Willoughby confronted dance-hall owners Rube Robbins and Jacob Williams in the street outside. All four drew pistols, with Talbot and Willoughby killed in the exchange of gunfire.

TATE, Ray Delano

Launching his criminal career with a long series of juvenile delinquency arrests, Ray Tate went on to collect adult convictions for armed robbery and parole violation. In 1956 he received an indeterminate sentence with 15 years maximum for the robbery of a clothing store in Trenton, New Jersey. At the time of his Trenton arrest, Tate was sought by authorities in Hudson, North Carolina, as a fugitive from the prison work camp there. The compound sentences did not prevent him from being released in time to find more trouble in the new decade.

On June 23, 1960, two gunmen entered the offices of the Yorke Savings and Loan Company in Newark, New Jersey, one brandishing a shotgun and the other wielding a pistol as they raided the cash drawers for $2,704. Retreating to a car outside where an accomplice waited at the wheel, they made their getaway, but two were snared by local officers within the next three days. The missing bandit was identified as Ray Tate from photographs and through interrogation of his partners in the crime. Tate's name was added to the FBI's "Ten Most Wanted" list on November 18, 1960.

One week later, on November 25, Tate telephoned the New York *Daily Mirror* and expressed his wish to end the chase. Later that day he surrendered to a reporter and a photographer in Vancouver, British Columbia. With an exclusive interview in hand, the newsmen turned him over to Canadian authorities for subsequent delivery to the FBI. Conviction on outstanding charges added new time to his pending sentence in North Carolina.

TERRORIST Robberies

Definitions of *terrorism* are as diverse as the scholars and authors who study the subject, some of them so broad as to include most any act of violence, while others flatly contradict each other. Political perspective is crucial; one man's *terrorist* is another's *freedom fighter*, with the difference often determined more by goals than tactics. For the purposes of this discussion, *terrorism* is defined as any use or threat of violence to eliminate, intimidate, or regulate some element within society—be it an ethnic group, a race or gender, a particular religion, collective residents of a specific region, or even a government in power.

Terrorism thus defined may be employed by ruling elements within society—that is, the state or extralegal vigilantes fighting for the status quo—or by insurgents seeking to depose specific rulers. Terroristic acts may be committed in the name of "ethnic cleansing," to suppress dissent, or as a revolutionary instrument. When governments embark on terrorism, they rely on public funds to arm their thugs. Insurgent forces without regular support fall back on other means—and one of those is robbery.

An early example of alleged terrorist robbery in the United States was the case of immigrant anarchists NICOLA SACCO and BARTOLOMEO VANZETTI. Indicted for a Massachusetts payroll robbery that left two persons dead in April 1920, Sacco and Vanzetti were convicted and sentenced to die in a trial that bore more resemblance to a three-ring circus than dispassionate pursuit of justice. Despite clear manipulation (or fabrication) of forensic evidence and subsequent official condemnation of the trial judge's conduct, Sacco and Vanzetti were executed in August 1927. (Fifty years later, the governor of Massachusetts issued a formal proclamation clearing their names.)

In recent years, the United States has witnessed terrorist robberies by factions of both the extreme right and left. On the neofascist right, various paramilitary groups and white supremacist organizations have fattened their coffers by looting banks and armored cars; radicals of the New Left and militant black revolutionaries have done likewise. Both sides, though diametrically opposed in theory, demonstrate equal contempt for law and human life.

First among the right-wing bandits were members of the Minutemen, a Missouri-based precursor of the 1990s "patriot militia" movement founded in 1960 by Robert Bolivar DePugh. On January 19, 1968, self-described Minuteman Henry Floyd Brown detonated a bomb outside the police station in Overland Park, Kansas, using the diversion to rob a nearby bank of $13,000. Traced to an apartment in the area, Brown shot it out with law enforcers, killing Sgt. Eldon Miller of the Kansas State Police. Brown lobbed dynamite at his pursuers, but the fuse burned out prematurely and he was wounded while fleeing the apartment, disarmed, and taken into custody. A search of Brown's flat revealed a small arsenal of weapons and a partially burned list of names—which in turn led FBI agents to three more suspects.

One week after the Kansas holdup, on January 26, 1968, federal officers arrested seven more Minutemen for conspiracy to bomb a police station and rob four banks in the Seattle suburb of Redmond, Washington. Investigation demonstrated that the plot had been hatched by Robert DePugh himself in August 1967. Indicted with cohort Walter Patrick

Peyson, DePugh went underground as a fugitive and remained at large until July 1969 when he was arrested by G-men in Truth or Consequences, New Mexico. Convicted of federal firearms violations and bail jumping, DePugh received an 11-year prison sentence. He was released in May 1973, reporting that prison had taught him "a little humility." DePugh remained active in far-right pamphleteering through the 1980s, his work noteworthy for political paranoia and increasing anti-Semitism.

A decade after DePugh was paroled, in the fall of 1983, members of America's growing neo-Nazi movement organized a hard-core fighting unit called THE ORDER, pledged to racial holy war against "ZOG"—the so-called Zionist Occupation Government in Washington, D.C. Led by Robert Jay Mathews and staffed by recruits from various extremist groups, The Order dabbled ineptly in counterfeiting before its members turned to armed robbery. Between December 1983 and June 1984, raiding parties stole more than $3.9 million in a series of daylight holdups, donating much of their loot to extremist groups including the Aryan Nations, Ku Klux Klan, and the neo-Nazi National Alliance. Bob Mathews died in a shootout with FBI agents on December 8, 1984; 28 more members of The Order were arrested in early 1985, convicted on various charges, and sentenced to prison terms ranging from six months to 250 years.

Another far-right terrorist group involved in armed robberies across America is the so-called Phineas Priesthood, a loosely-knit coalition of white supremacists who feel themselves "called by God" to commit random acts of terrorism. The group is named for Phinehas, a biblical character (see Numbers 25:1–8) who diverted a plague by executing an Israeli man and his Midianite lover—regarded in racist theology as a divine order to punish "race-mixing" with death. The modern group was christened—with its name misspelled—in 1990, by author Richard Kelly Hoskins in his book *Vigilantes of Christendom*. Somewhere between Old Testament times and the 1990s, these neo-Nazi "priests" decided their crusade should be supported by armed robbery.

On August 28, 1991, a Muskogee, Oklahoma, thrift store was robbed for the second time in six weeks, the lone bandit fleeing with $52,000 in cash. Captured after a running battle with police, convicted counterfeiter and self-styled "Phineas Priest" Walter Eliyah Thody told reporters the holdup was meant to finance a series of kidnappings and assassinations targeting "Jewish conspirators" in the United States. Thody was sentenced to life imprisonment in 1992, but three more Phineas Priests were arrested on October 8, 1996, and charged with two bank robberies and several bombings in Spokane, Washington. Defendants Charles Barbee, Robert Berry, and Jay Merrell were convicted and sentenced to life; a fourth defendant in the case, Brian Ratigan, was subsequently convicted and received a 55-year prison term. Their loot—some $108,000—was not recovered, FBI spokespersons suggesting it may have been donated to groups in the far-right racist underground. Suspected Phinean James Cavanaugh Jr. was arrested by federal agents posing as militia members on July 24, 1996, charged with detonating bombs in Spokane and robbing a suburban bank on April 1.

Yet another neo-Nazi gang, the Aryan Republican Army (ARA), was broken up on January 19, 1996, when G-men arrested founder Peter Langan (aka "Commander Pedro") and cohort Richard Guthrie. The defendants were charged with robbing 22 banks in seven Midwestern states and funneling an estimated $250,000 to like-minded terrorist groups across the country. Guthrie committed suicide in jail prior to trial; Langan received a life sentence in one case and 55 years in another. Pennsylvania racist Mark Thomas pled guilty to planning the heists and informed federal agents that the ARA had purchased its illegal weapons from members of a right-wing "survivalist" compound in Oklahoma, dubbed Elohim City. Those guns were supplied primarily by the Kehoe brothers, Chevie and Cheyne, convicted of multiple terrorist murders in 1999. Chevie Kehoe was condemned for those crimes, while his brother and disciple Daniel Lee drew terms of life imprisonment. In exchange for his cooperation, witness Thomas received a minimal eight-year prison term. Another Pennsylvania conspirator, Kevin McCarthy, also pled guilty in federal court and received a five-year sentence. Langan was convicted on five counts of bank robbery on February 10, 1997, by a federal jury in Columbus, Ohio.

On April 22, 1997, three members of the Ku Klux Klan were arrested in Texas for plotting to bomb a natural-gas refinery outside Fort Worth. The three defendants—and a fourth, arrested later —planned to blow up the refinery, endangering hundreds of residents and children at a nearby school, as a diversion for a simultaneous armored-truck heist. All four later pled guilty on conspiracy charges and received prison terms ranging up to 20 years.

One day after the Texas arrests, on April 23, 1997, police in Orlando, Florida, cracked another bank-robbing conspiracy when 28-year-old resident Todd Vanbiber was wounded in the explosion of a homemade pipe bomb. A search of Vanbiber's home revealed weapons and large quantities of neo-Nazi literature, including documents linking Vanbiber to the neo-Nazi National Alliance and a shadowy terrorist group called the League of the Silent Soldier. Investigators jailed three of Vanbiber's National Alliance cohorts on May 9, charging the trio with illegal manufacture of bombs and conspiracy to rob local banks. In September 1997 Vanbiber received a six-year prison term on weapons charges. Thirteen months later, on October 30, 1998, defendant Brian Pickett pled guilty on charges of plotting to detonate bombs in Orlando and loot banks while police were distracted by the blasts.

Left-wing terrorist bandits have robbed fewer American banks than their far-right counterparts, spanning a shorter period, but they claimed a higher toll of human lives. First on the modern scoreboard in September 1970 were college radicals KATHERINE ANN POWER and SUSAN EDITH SAXE. Opposed to the Vietnam war and America's capitalist society in general, Power and Saxe recruited three apolitical ex-convicts to help them rob banks in Philadelphia and Boston. The take was small in both raids, and a Boston policeman was murdered in the second holdup. While their mercenary cohorts were swiftly arrested, Power and Saxe went underground as fugitives and were posted to the FBI's "Ten Most Wanted" list. Saxe was captured in March 1975; Power remained at large until September 1993, when she voluntarily surrendered for trial.

America's most peculiar radical group was the tiny SYMBIONESE LIBERATION ARMY (SLA), organized in October 1973 by escaped convict Donald DeFreeze. A career criminal and belated black militant pledged to violent "liberation" of his people, DeFreeze recruited a handful of white radicals to serve as his shock troops, some of them so guilt-ridden on racial issues that they donned Afro wigs and dark makeup in an effort to look black. The SLA kidnapped newspaper heiress Patricia Hearst in February 1974 and apparently converted her to their cause. Hearst participated in at least two California bank robberies— in April 1974 and April 1975—and SLA bullets claimed the life of a female customer at the second bank. (More bank heists were suspected but never

In this still frame taken from a videotape produced by the Aryan Republican Army, the hooded figure holds money he says was taken in bank robberies to finance the organization that also calls itself the Midwestern Bank Bandits. (AP/Wide World Photos)

proved.) DeFreeze and five of his "soldiers" died in a shootout with Los Angeles police on May 17, 1974; Hearst and several others were later arrested and served prison time on various state and federal charges. Hearst maintains to this day that her participation in SLA crimes was a result of coercive "brainwashing" techniques.

The most prolific left-wing bandits in American history called themselves the MAY 19TH COMMUNIST ORGANIZATION (aka "The Family"). As with their far-right counterparts in The Order, May 19th members were drawn from various radical groups including the Black Panther Party, the Republic of New Afrika, the Black Liberation Army, and the Weatherman faction of Students for a Democratic Society (SDS). Operating on the Eastern Seaboard, mostly in New

York and New Jersey, the group robbed one bank and a half-dozen armored cars between October 1978 and November 1981. May 19th bandits stole more than $2.6 million in those raids, killing two police officers after an October 1981 armored-car holdup at Nyack, New York. Funds were used to support the group's members in hiding and, briefly, to finance social programs for certain poor blacks in New York. Leader Jeral Wayne Williams (aka "Mutulu Shakur") earned a spot on the FBI's "Ten Most Wanted" list before he was captured in February 1986. Other members of the group remained at large until 1987 when they were finally rounded up and convicted on various state and federal charges.

America's most successful leftist robbers, in terms of total loot obtained, were a group of Puerto Rican separatists known as *Macheteros* (literally, "machete wielders"). On September 12, 1983, the group scored the U.S.'s second-largest cash theft on record to that date, stealing $7.1 million from a WELLS FARGO depot in West Hartford, Connecticut. The actual holdup was carried out by Wells Fargo employee Victor Manuel Gerena, who drugged and handcuffed two fellow security guards before looting the vault. Federal warrants were issued on Gerena the following day, but he eluded pursuers, allegedly fleeing to Cuba, where he remains to this day, despite a May 1984 posting on the FBI's "Ten Most Wanted" list. Gerena and two other defendants—Puerto Rican nationalists Juan Enrique Palmer III and Filiberto Inocencio Ojeda Rojas—were formally indicted by a federal grand jury on August 23, 1985. Others added to the list of conspirators over time included Antonio Camacho Negrón, Norman Ramírez Talavera, Robert Maldonado Rivera, and Carlos Ayes Suárez. Ojeda Rojas jumped bail in 1990 and was never seen again, although a court convicted him in absentia on May 6, 1992, and he received a 55-year sentence two months later. The other defendants were present for trial, all but Suárez convicted on charges including robbery, conspiracy, and transportation of stolen funds.

Terrorists in other countries have been more successful with careers in robbery than those in the United States. An early example was witnessed on June 13, 1907, when Bolshevik guerrillas led by Ter-Petrosian (aka "Kamo"), a protégé of Joseph Stalin, ambushed a government cash shipment at Tiflis in Yerevan Square. Armed with guns and explosives, the bandits attacked Cossack guards and killed the horses that had been employed to draw a carriage filled with currency and bonds. Seven bombs were detonated in the crowded square, killing at least a half-dozen persons and wounding 50 more. The raiders escaped with several bags of loot in the resultant confusion and were never apprehended.

French-Canadian terrorists from the Front de Libération du Québec (FLQ) tried their hand at armed robbery on May 28, 1970, stealing $58,775 at gunpoint from the University of Montreal. Three members of the FLQ were captured on June 21 at a hideout in the Laurentians and $28,000 of the holdup loot was recovered from their safe house. Robbery was among the numerous charges filed against 19-year-old Claude Morency, 21-year-old

André Roy, and 21-year-old François Lanctot at their arraignment on July 3, 1970.

The Provisional Irish Republican Army, pledged to driving British occupation troops from Northern Ireland, has also resorted to holdups on occasion, when receipts from voluntary contributions lag. On February 3, 1974, a quartet of PIRA gunmen robbed a branch bank at Stansted Airport, near London, escaping with some $80,000 in cash. Thirteen weeks later, on April 26, PIRA activist Bridget Rose Dugdale and four male accomplices stole 19 paintings valued at $19.2 million from the Irish home of British millionaire Sir Alfred Beit. The guerrillas demanded $1.2 million ransom for safe return of the paintings, but the artwork was recovered undamaged by police on May 3 before the payoff was arranged.

Another European terrorist group prone to robbery was the German RED ARMY FACTION (RAF), nicknamed the Baader-Meinhof Gang after notorious leaders Andreas Baader and Ulrike Meinhof. Linked to a series of bank heists beginning in January 1971, the RAF remained violently active through 1975 when most of its leaders were captured. Meinhof hanged herself in prison on May 10, 1976; Baader and two other high-ranking members of the gang followed suit on October 18, 1977, after an abortive airplane hijacking failed to liberate them from their life prison terms.

Latin America is the hands-down leader in any comparison of terrorist holdups by region. One of the earliest practitioners was Mexican bandit-revolutionary Francisco "Pancho" Villa, whose cross-border raids into the southwestern United States prompted deployment of American troops in Mexico. A decade of guerrilla warfare and sporadic banditry ended in 1923 when Villa was killed in an ambush by Mexican troops.

More recently, in January 1963, four gun-toting members of the leftist Fuerzas Armadas de Liberación Nacional (FALN) staged a daylight robbery at the Museum of Fine Arts in Caracas, Venezuela. Nine hundred visiting students looked on—and one of them was fatally wounded—as the bandits stole priceless paintings by artists including Braque, Cézanne, Gaugin, Picasso, and Van Gogh. The paintings were held for ransom, threatened with destruction if Venezuelan authorities did not comply with the FALN's political demands, but government leaders refused to negotiate, and police later recovered the art work undamaged.

Two years after the FALN's fling at ART THEFT, leftist Uruguayan rebels organized as TUPAMAROS launched a campaign to destabilize their nation's government. Armed robbery was a favorite tactic of the Tupamaros: Between October 1968 and September 1970, the group robbed nine banks, a casino, an oil refinery, and a General Motors plant in Uruguay, stealing more than 564 million pesos (about $3.1 million at the contemporary exchange rate). Such activities prompted harsh government reprisals and the Tupamaros were virtually exterminated by late 1972, with 42 members killed and another 2,600 imprisoned on various charges.

Brazil has been the scene of various armed robberies by terrorist factions since 1968 when a band of guerrillas stole 100,000 cruzeiros (about $24,000) from an armored car of the French and Italian Bank on April 15. Seventeen months later, in September 1969, 15 political prisoners were released from Argentine jails and flown to Mexico City in exchange for the release of kidnapped U.S. Ambassador Charles Burke Elbrick. One of those released, Mario Galgardo Zanconato, held a press conference on September 8 and boasted of robbing eight banks around Minas Gerais to finance revolutionary causes.

Three members of Nicaragua's Frente Sandinista de Liberación Nacional (FSLN) staged three rapid-fire bank robberies on the afternoon of March 17, 1978, stealing an estimated 270,000 cordobas (about $20,455) from bank branches in Managua, Linda Vista, and Altamira. Sandinista rebels toppled the brutal dictatorship of Anastasio Somoza in July 1979, sparking covert (and illegal) American retaliation against the new "communist" regime that later embroiled U.S. presidents Ronald Reagan and George H. W. Bush in the humiliating Iran-Contra scandal, complete with tales of American drug smuggling, White House funding of right-wing terrorism in Nicaragua, and illicit weapons sales to Muslim extremists in the Middle East.

Leftist terrorism in Europe has largely subsided since the collapse of Soviet communism in 1991, and there has been no significant reports of far-left terrorism in the United States since the early 1980s. Widespread guerrilla activity continues in many parts of the so-called Third World, particularly Latin America and Africa, where robbery and ransom kidnapping remain staple activities of cash-poor guerrillas. In the United States, meanwhile, most terrorist activity within the past two decades has been generated by factions of the white supremacist and neo-Nazi fringe, self-described "Patriots" or "Aryans" who regard themselves as living in a state of war against America's elected government. In light of recent history and propaganda outpourings from these groups, it seems probable that armed robbery will persist as a primary means of funding extremist operations.

THOMAS, Joseph Lloyd

Twice imprisoned for auto theft in Indiana, once fined and jailed for possession of an illegal still, Joseph Thomas had apparently gone straight by the late 1950s. Married and the father of two children, he owned a restaurant in Terre Haute, supporting his family through honest labor. Still, the "easy" life of crime had its attractions, which Thomas seemed unable to resist.

According to the federal charges filed against him, Thomas was one of three men who invaded a Shreveport, Louisiana, bank on February 13, 1958,

Joseph Thomas graduated from auto theft and bootlegging to bank robbery in 1958. (FBI)

293

making off with $34,000 in a daring daylight robbery. His accomplices were swiftly captured, but Thomas remained at large, earning a place on the FBI's "Ten Most Wanted" list on October 21, 1959.

By that time he had relocated to the town of Pelzer, South Carolina, traveling as "George Ashley" and using his share of the Shreveport loot to open a used-car agency. His wife also adopted a pseudonym, and their daughters were enrolled at local schools, presenting the perfect image of a normal family. At least one of their neighbors knew better, though, the truth revealed by Joseph's poster hanging in the post office. Tipped to the fugitive's whereabouts, FBI agents surrounded him at a Pelzer gas station on December 10. Thomas surrendered without resistance, but arresting officers discovered he had come prepared: A gun was tucked behind the radio in his car, Thomas had two hacksaw blades strapped to one leg, and his shoes were stuffed with $125 in cash.

Convicted and imprisoned on bank-robbery charges, Thomas was back in Terre Haute as a parolee in 1969. He soon held up another bank and was rewarded with his second posting to the Bureau's Top Ten list on September 2 of that year. Charged with bank robbery and violation of his federal parole, Thomas remained at large until March 8, 1970, when he was arrested in Peoria, Illinois, by FBI special agents Elias Williams, Jerome DiFranco, and John Leuck. (Curiously, the same trio would bag another "Most Wanted" fugitive in Peoria 10 years later.) Thomas was returned to prison as a parole violator, with more time added on conviction for the latest heist.

TOLLETT, Henry Clay

Henry Tollett's criminal career dated from 1923, including convictions for larceny, auto theft, and bank robbery. On his first arrest, for rustling livestock, he was sentenced to a two-year prison term. In 1925 he was given five years for robbery. In 1932 the charge was robbery with firearms and the sentence 30 years. Released on April 16, 1946, after serving 14 years for the robbery of a Konawa, Oklahoma, bank, Tollett seemed incapable of avoiding trouble with the law.

In early 1947 he was arrested in Bakersfield, California, on another robbery charge and was released on bail. He promptly skipped and on May 5 of that year joined an accomplice to rob a bank in Oakland, Oregon, of $31,000 in cash and $1,225 in blank U.S. savings bonds. On July 10 he was arrested in Tulare, California, on charges of child stealing and contributing to the delinquency of a minor; two weeks later, again in Bakersfield, he was charged with carrying a concealed weapon.

The sporadic arrests failed to slow Tollett down. On August 29, 1947, he joined a male accomplice in raiding a Sweet Home, Oregon, bank for $58,000—then the largest haul from a bank heist in Oregon history. By September 10 he was back in Tulare, briefly jailed on a concealed weapons charge. FBI agents arrested him in Bakersfield on September 17, and conviction on federal bank-robbery charges earned him a 25-year prison term. On release, he faced another term of five years to life in California's state prison.

On November 22, 1949, Tollett escaped from the federal lockup on McNeil Island, Washington, by hiding in an outbound shipment of prisonmade furniture. He was seen bailing out of the truck in Tacoma, and the hunt was on. As an escaped convict with a quarter-century of violent felonies behind him, he was added to the FBI's "Ten Most Wanted" list on April 11, 1950.

In the end, Tollett's penchant for returning to his favorite haunts in California was his undoing. FBI investigation turned up evidence that he was traveling the Golden State in spring of 1951, and officers of the California Highway Patrol picked him up near Redding on June 3. Tollett was returned to federal prison for completion of his sentence, with a list of further charges filed against him.

TRAIN Robbery: History

America's first-recorded train robbery was an unplanned act of war. Confederate guerrillas led by William "Bloody Bill" Anderson, disguised in Union blue invaded Centralia, Missouri, on September 27, 1864, and were intent on looting the town when a westbound train from St. Louis pulled into the depot. Anderson's thugs swarmed the train, firing shots into the ceilings of the passenger coaches, relieving civilians of their cash, watches, and jewelry. Several raiders forced their way into the baggage car and forced its clerk to open the safe. Anderson removed $3,000, while guerrilla FRANK JAMES found several thousand more hidden in a suitcase. Twenty-five Union soldiers—some of them wounded, the others on furlough—were removed from the train and executed on Anderson's order before the terrorists left Centralia.

Anderson's crime is generally ignored in the published histories of American train robbery, although some authors credit outlaw brothers Frank and JESSE JAMES with "inventing" the crime nine years later. In fact, while the James boys and their cousins in the YOUNGER clan would indeed become prolific train robbers, they deserve no credit for the first civilian holdup of a train.

That dubious "honor" belongs to an eight-man gang from New York that invaded the Adams Express car on a train bound from New York City to Bridgeport, Connecticut, stealing nearly $700,000 on the night of January 6, 1866. Two safes were battered open and a third left intact with some $50,000 untouched. Allan PINKERTON took the case and soon identified the thieves, whose number included a brakeman on the looted train. Investigators recovered $100,000 of the cash in New York, but the rest was never found.

America's first serial train robbers were the Hoosier RENO BROTHERS, making their first score at Seymour, Indiana, on October 6, 1866. Three members of the gang, jailed a month later, were soon bailed out pending trial. In the meantime, one day after their arrest, a train was derailed near Bristow, Kentucky, by bandits who stole $8,000 from the baggage car. Law enforcers were still tracking those thieves when a gang of 12 derailed another train near Franklin, Kentucky, and stole a U.S. government payroll. Those rapid-fire holdups signaled the beginning of a seven-decade guerrilla war between the railroads and hard-riding bandits who saw the trains as little more than cash boxes on wheels.

Derailment was the method of choice for many would-be train robbers. The Cincinnati Express was wrecked on April 7, 1867, by cross-ties heaped on the line near Wall Station, Pennsylvania. While police soon captured the saboteur, they denied any plot to rob the train. Two months later, on June 12, an attempt to derail another train on the Hudson River line was foiled when watchmen found a switch jammed open with a metal spike. Indiana outlaws MICHAEL COLLEARN and WALKER HAMMONDS emulated the Reno brothers on September 29, 1867, lifting $8,000 from the Adams Express car on a train leaving Seymour, but witnesses helped Pinkerton detectives track the bandits to their lair.

Such imitation brought the Renos out of hiding in early 1868, stealing nearly $100,000 from an Adams Express shipment near Marshfield, Indiana, on May 22. Seven weeks later, on July 10, the gang hit another train at Brownstown, but they came away from the heist empty handed. Six members of the team were rounded up by late July, dispatched by lynch mobs in a vigilante reign of terror that effectively ended train robbery in the Hoosier State.

Holdups continued elsewhere in the country, however. In November 1870, A. C. "GENTLEMAN JACK" DAVIS and his "Seven Knights of the Road" lifted some $41,000 from a WELLS FARGO railroad shipment near Verdi, Nevada. Two months later, another thief took $10,000 in currency from a Central Pacific mail car at Alta, California. In June 1871, bandits caught an express guard sleeping when his train stopped at Meridian, Mississippi, and dragged the safe out of his car without waking him. In October of that year, two more alumni of Quantrill's Raiders, outlaw brothers HILLARY and LEVI FARRINGTON, robbed their first train in Tennessee and shot the express guard.

It was July 1873 before the James-Younger gang robbed its first train, derailing a locomotive near Adair, Iowa, and scalding the engineer to death, stealing an estimated $26,000 from the express car and various passengers. (A commemorative plaque erroneously hails the event as the "world's first robbery of a moving train.") Other train robberies by the James-Younger gang were committed at Gads Hill, Missouri (January 1874); Muncie, Kansas (December 1874); and Rocky Cut, Missouri (July 1876). Pinkerton agents tracked the gang in vain, relieved when the Youngers and other Missouri long riders were killed or captured at Northfield, Minnesota, in September 1876, but they had not heard the last of the James boys.

In the meantime, other gangs were busy looting trains. Two unknown bandits hit the Union Pacific between Bitter Creek and Table Rock, Utah, on August 26, 1875, while others robbed a train at Grand Junction, Iowa, in September 1875. SAM BASS and company stole more than $60,000 in gold coins from a train at Big Springs, Nebraska, in September 1877, rolling on from there to hit more trains at Allen Station, Texas (February 1878); Hutchins, Texas (March 1878); and Eagle Ford and Mesquite, Texas (both in April 1878). Four unknown bandits robbed passengers aboard a train near Perry, Iowa, on May 29, 1878, but they missed $120,000 in the express car. A month later, on June 21, two gunmen robbed a train between Milton Junction and Des Moines, Iowa. Mike Rourke's four-man gang stole $5,000 from a train at Winthrop Junction, Missouri, on August 12, 1878. Two days later, "Big Nose" George Parrot's gang took a cue from new recruit Frank James but botched their first attempted train holdup near Medicine Bow, Wyoming; they killed two posse men but wound up fleeing empty handed.

Beleaguered railroads responded to the rash of holdups by appointing their own private police forces, often staffed by poorly trained "detectives" whose guns were faster than their minds. Various states were pleased to off-load responsibility for pursuing train robbers, passing legislation that granted full police powers to the railroads' private gunmen. Among those jurisdictions were Pennsylvania (in 1865), Ohio (1867), Tennessee (1870), and the District of Columbia (1878). Western states, for the most part, resisted efforts to legitimize railroad police, but they continued to operate as vigilante "regulators," with Wells Fargo detectives apprehending more bandits than most duly authorized lawmen.

The James brothers emerged from retirement in October 1879, stealing $40,000 from a train at Glendale, Missouri. Nine months later, on July 15, 1871, they stopped another train near Winston, Missouri, and executed two unarmed men in what authorities described as settlement of an outstanding grudge. Jesse was murdered at his home by turncoat "friend" Bob Ford in April 1882; brother Frank surrendered for trial six months later and astounded prosecutors when a sympathetic jury set him free.

If railroad barons felt relief at the demise of the James gang, it was short lived. Four days after Jesse's murder, on April 16, 1882, five bandits derailed a train at Rincon, New Mexico, scalding the engineer and the fireman to death and then fleeing empty handed from a mob of outraged passengers. Another bungled robbery was logged in January 1883 when bandits derailed seven cars of a Southern Pacific train near Tehachapi Summit, California; the hapless outlaws killed themselves and 13 passengers, including the wife of former Governor John Downy.

The echoes from that tragic incident had barely faded when bandits struck again, a 12-man gang stopping a train near the Nevada-Utah border. Wells Fargo guard Aaron Ross barred them from the express car and drove them off empty handed, despite three bullet wounds. Another Wells Fargo guard, Samuel Peterson, scattered the outlaws who tried to rob a train at Coolidge, Kansas, in September 1883 but not before they killed the engineer and the fireman. No one saw the bandits who looted a Rock Island railroad express car in March 1886, but the guard was found dead in his blood-spattered car, clutching strands of black hair in one hand and red hair in the other.

Railroad bandits tried their hands at different methods in the closing decades of the 19th century. In lieu of simply wrecking trains and jeopardizing everyone on board, some switched to using "torpedo signals"—small explosive charges placed on the track to warn engineers of trouble on the line ahead and make them stop. Others boarded moving trains and tried to crawl inside express cars without alerting the guards, but few outlaws possessed the requisite athletic skills. Two imaginative "coffin bandits" had themselves boxed as corpses and shipped via railroad express, but both were captured—in Utah (1879) and in Wisconsin (1886)—without obtaining any loot. Fred Wittrock made his $5,000 score in October 1886 with the connivance of Adams Express messenger DAVID FOTHERINGHAM, but Pinkerton detectives saw through the ruse and arrested both thieves in St. Louis. Derailments still occurred from time to time, as with the gang that wrecked a train carrying $1 million near Osage, Kansas, in September 1891. Unfortunately for the bandits, the pile-up buried the loot beyond their reach and they were forced to flee with nothing. Another gang derailed a train crossing Alabama's Cahaba River in December 1897, killing three crewmen and 27 passengers, only to learn that the train had no express car.

RUBE BURROW, with his brother Jim and others, gave southern railroad men fits in the latter 1880s, beginning with his first train robbery at Bellevue, Texas, in December 1886. The take was a disappointing $300, but Burrow improved with practice, twice robbing trains at the same bridge near Ben Brooks, Texas (in June and September 1887), and at Genoa, Arkansas (December 1887). Pinkerton raided the Burrow farm in Lamar County, Alabama, in January 1888, but both brothers escaped. Jim was captured in Montgomery two weeks later, but Rube remained at large, robbing at least two more Alabama trains (in September and December 1888). Finally jailed at Linden, Alabama, in 1890, Rube escaped after two hours in custody but was killed when he hung around town to ambush the merchant who arrested him.

Alabama's problems were a mere sideshow to the action witnessed out west as the century drew to a close. California bandits CHRIS EVANS and JOHN SONTAG seemed to operate as much from hatred of the railroads as from greed, looting their first train at Pixley and killing the brakeman in February 1889. Eleven months later they stole $20,000 from a train at Goshen and murdered a passenger in cold blood.

A second robbery at the same place was foiled in September 1891 when railroad detectives opened fire on the thieves. Evans and Sontag traveled out of state for the November 1891 robbery of a train near Chicago, but they were back in California nine months later, stealing $15,000 from another train near Collis. One manhunter was killed, with two more wounded, when a posse raided Evans's Visalia ranch in August 1892. Evans and Sontag hid out in the mountains until May 1893 when Sontag was killed and Evans was captured near Visalia. Evans escaped again, with his trial in progress, and robbed one more train at Fowler, California, in January 1894 before he was recaptured and sentenced to life imprisonment.

The torch was passed almost immediately to another pair of railroad bandits, JIM BRADY and SAM BROWNING. Together, they robbed at least four California trains between October 1894 and March 1895 at Mikon, Swanson, Castle, and Wheatland. Browning was fatally wounded by express guards in the last holdup, and Brady was soon arrested and was sentenced to life in prison. Further east, authorities hunted the "Black Bart of Wisconsin" for two train robberies in May and August 1889; finally arrested, he was identified—and imprisoned—as Reimund Holzhay. Missouri safecracker Marion Hedgepeth led the gang that robbed a train near Omaha, Nebraska, on November 4, 1890, rebounding to loot others on November 12 (outside Chicago) and November 30 (at Glendale, Missouri). Captured in California on February 10, 1891, Hedgepeth was returned to Missouri for trial and drew a 12-year prison sentence.

A new rash of train robberies in the 1890s led Wade Hampton, U.S. commissioner of railroads, to describe the problem as an "epidemic" in December 1893, but most of the action was seen in the West. While some authorities blamed geography and the region's vast open spaces for encouraging outlaw gangs, William Pinkerton denounced "certain sensational newspapers and yellow covered literature" for "exploiting and extolling the cowardly crimes," thereby "filling the youthful mind with a desire for the same sort of notoriety and adventure." Whatever the cause, western trains were robbed at a rate of one every four days between January and March 1895. Attempted solutions included the doubling or tripling of armed guards aboard express trains, reinforced express cars, occasional decoy trains for some shipments, and concealment of mounted posses in

boxcars. One train surprisingly ignored by bandits was the special that carried $20 million in gold coins (disguised as Asian silk) from San Francisco to the U.S. Treasury in July 1892.

Chief among American train robbers in the early 1890s were the hard-riding DALTON BROTHERS, who graduated from small-time rustlers to raid banks and railroads ranging from Missouri and Oklahoma to as far west as New Mexico and California. Their first train robbery was committed at Alila, California, in February 1891, followed three months later by another in Noble County, Oklahoma. Fledgling outlaw BILL DOOLIN joined the gang for the September 1891 robbery of a train at Leliaetta, Kansas, and another at Red Rock, Oklahoma, in June 1892. One month later, on July 14, the gang looted a train at Adair, Oklahoma, shooting it out with law enforcers in a pitched battle that wounded four officers and killed one civilian bystander. Wells Fargo detective FRED DODGE organized a special "Dalton Posse" to track the gang after Adair, but his effort was too late, frustrated by the gang's annihilation at Coffeyville, Kansas, in October 1892.

Bill Doolin missed the Coffeyville slaughter and rallied stragglers from the Dalton gang into a new band of raiders to plague the railroads. The gang scored its first train near Cimarron, Oklahoma, in June 1893, stealing $1,000 but missing another 10 grand in a safe that was too tough to crack. August 1893 found the gang surprised by law officers at Ingalls, Oklahoma, but they shot their way clear, all but one raider escaping while two deputies were killed. Doolin's gang robbed another train near Dover, Oklahoma, in April 1895, but it would be the last. Four months later, Doolin was ambushed and killed at Lawson, leaving remnants of his gang to carry on alone.

Two of those who sought new leadership in Doolin's absence were DANIEL "DYNAMITE DICK" CLIFTON and "Little Dick" West. Unfortunately, they cast their lot with a pair of hard-luck desperadoes, ex-lawyers Al and Frank Jennings, who had quit the bar after another Oklahoma attorney killed their brother and then won acquittal on murder charges. That was the story, at least, when the Jennings gang was organized, including Clifton, West, brothers Morris and Pat O'Malley, and one Sam Baker—who, unknown to the others, was an active police informant. Sold out by their "friend" from the start, the Jennings bungled three Oklahoma train robberies in August and September 1897. In the first holdup, near

Edmond, they were defeated by a sturdy safe. Two weeks later, outside Muskogee, an engineer drove through their barricade of cross-ties and left them in his dust. At Purcell, alerted by Baker, a posse turned up in place of the expected train and put them to flight. The gang finally scored a reported $30,000 on their fourth attempt, near Berwyn, and the Jennings brothers took off for a vacation in Honduras. Back in Oklahoma on October 1, they stopped a fifth train but used up their dynamite blasting into the express car; they had none left with which to open the safe they found there. Duplicitous Baker had most of the gang in custody by year's end, but Clifton and West bailed out earlier, disgusted with the haphazard raids. Law enforcers killed Clifton in the fall of 1897; Dick West survived a bit longer but was shot by U.S. marshals near Guthrie, Oklahoma, in April 1898.

Far more successful in its efforts was the "WILD BUNCH" led by affable outlaw BUTCH CASSIDY. A career criminal who probably robbed his first train with the MCCARTY BROTHERS near Grand Junction, Colorado, in November 1887, Cassidy dropped out of sight after that until his conviction and imprisonment for rustling livestock in 1894. Back on the range four years later, he organized a band of outlaws dubbed the "Train Robbers' Syndicate" in 1898, and the outfit's first documented holdup of a train was a $50,000 score from the Union Pacific in June 1899 at Wilcox, Wyoming. Cassidy's gang took another $50,000 from the Union Pacific at Tipton, Wyoming, in August 1900 (though railroad spokespeople admitted losing only $54), and $40,000 more was lifted from a train near Wagner, Montana, in early July 1901. Cassidy and cohort HARRY LONGABAUGH (aka "The Sundance Kid") decamped for South America soon after that robbery, allegedly killed by Bolivian soldiers in 1909.

Train robbery, meanwhile, had fallen on hard times in the United States. In 1902 journalist Charles Michelson wrote that "It has not kept pace with the progress of related arts. For this reason, it has become the most hazardous of crimes—not in the commission, that is astonishingly simple, but in getting away. In a country cobwebbed with telegraph lines and honeycombed with detective agencies, with their disheartening outposts of stool pigeons and informers, escape is yearly getting more difficult."

Train robbery was also less rewarding as the western mines played out, shipments of gold and silver dwindling across the continent. Congress raised the ante in 1902 with the Train Robbery Act, making it a federal crime to board any American train with intent to rob or murder. Sixteen holdups were reported in 1901, rising to 22 in 1902, and then dropping to 13 per year in 1903 and 1904, plummeting to seven cases in 1905. In 1907 William Pinkerton felt secure enough to dub train robbers an "almost extinct species," and the only line still logging holdups consistently by 1910 was the Southern Pacific.

Still, noteworthy cases were recorded as America moved toward its Progressive Era and World War I. Bandits JOSEPH BROWN and CHARLES DUNBAR made headlines with their April 1910 holdup of a mail train near Goodyear Station, California, and wound up sentenced to life imprisonment although their grand haul totaled only $17. Two months later, unknown bandits stopped a Southern Pacific train in Cow Creek Canyon, Oregon, but could not open the express car. "Wild Bunch" veteran Ben Kilpatrick stormed his last train near Sanderson, Texas, in March 1912—and was beaten to death by an express messenger armed with an ice mallet. JEAN LABANTA was more successful, robbing three California mail trains between October 1913 and January 1914, confessing all after his arrest for forgery in San Francisco. NOLA ANDERSON and FRANK RYAN looted a train outside Saugus, California, in February 1915, but they were captured soon after while burglarizing a post office. Cocky bandit WES CARLISLE staged a series of one-man railroad heists in early 1915, robbing Union Pacific trains near Green River (February 4) and Laramie, Wyoming (on April 14 and 15). His downfall came from taunting letters to the press, from which an ex-employer recognized his handwriting and tipped authorities.

Train holdups continued sporadically through the 1920s, including two California robberies staged by "King of the Escape Artists" ROY GARDNER in May 1921 at Sacramento and Roseville. By November 1921 1,000 U.S. Marines had been assigned to guard mail shipments, a War Department spokesperson declaring: "When our men go on guard over the mail, that mail must be delivered or there must be a Marine dead at the post of duty." There were no dead marines at Okesa, Oklahoma, though, where AL SPENCER's gang stole $20,000 in Liberty Bonds from a train in August 1923. (FRANK "JELLY" NASH, convicted of participation in that robbery and sent to Leavenworth in May 1924, escaped six years later to

A policeman stands guard by the hijacked mail train at Cheddington station, 40 miles north of London, England, on August 10, 1963. (AP/Wide World Photos)

join the BARKER GANG.) Leathernecks were also missing two months later in Oregon when the lethal DeAUTREMONT BROTHERS robbed another mail train, killing the engineer, the fireman, and the mail clerk. The largest mail robbery of all time was recorded on June 12, 1924, when bandits armed with guns and gas bombs stole $2 million from a train at Round-out, Illinois. Investigation of that crime identified veteran postal inspector William Fahy as the brains behind the holdup, while his front-line troops were the Newton Brothers from Texas.

Holdups continued through the last years of the Roaring Twenties, though with dwindling frequency. Bandits looted a Union Pacific mail car near Rawlings, Wyoming, in August 1926 and escaped with an undisclosed amount of cash. Another 1926 robbery saw the HOLDEN-KEATING GANG lift $130,000 from a mail train at Evergreen Park, Illinois; sentenced to Leavenworth in May 1928, Tom Holden and Francis

Keating escaped together in February 1930 and joined the Barker gang for a series of bank jobs. In September 1928 a loan gunman braced passengers on a train north of Los Angeles, bagging $800. The take was more impressive in November 1928 when robbers stole $50,000 from a mail train near Fort Worth, Texas, but they stashed their bulky loot near a local school, and children tipped police off to the haul. Bandit FRANK ELLIS and company came armed for bear, their equipment including a Thompson submachine gun and a tripod-mounted .30-caliber machine gun, when they robbed a Southern Pacific train near McAvoy, California, in June 1929. Ex-convict Tom Vernon, three months out of Folsom Prison, was alone four months later when he derailed a passenger train near Cheyenne, Wyoming, and robbed the survivors of their pocket change.

The Depression-era 1930s saw train robbery dwindle in America, discouraged in equal parts by a paucity of prospects and the FBI's growing reputation. Frank Ellis staged another robbery in November 1930, stealing close to $50,000 from a train at Nobel Station, California, but it would be his last. Five years later to the day, fugitive bank robber ALVIN KARPIS led the six-man gang that took $34,000 from a mail train at Garrettsville, Ohio, making their escape by airplane. Hard-luck bandits HENRY LOFTUS and HARRY DONALDSON waited another two years to write the last chapter of America's railroad saga in November 1937. Bungling their attempt to rob the Southern Pacific's Apache Flyer near El Paso, they killed one crewman before they were overpowered and disarmed by angry passengers.

Although railroads had girdled the planet by the 1890s, train robbery remained an almost uniquely American pastime. Few foreign bandits chose to emulate the Renos, the James-Younger gang, or the

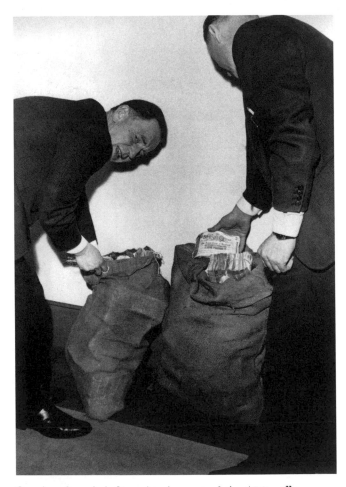

Stacks of cash, believed to be part of the $7.3 million stolen in the Great Train Robbery, were found in a London phone booth. Police were tipped off by an anonymous phone call to Scotland Yard. (AP/Wide World Photos)

Dalton brothers. Two striking exceptions to that rule were recorded from England, however—including the world's first train robbery, in 1855.

That adventure was years in the making, spawned by the venality of one William Pierce, a sticky-fingered clerk for Britain's South-Eastern Railway. Fired in 1850 on suspicion of theft, Pierce brooded on his plight and plotted to achieve revenge. To that end, he recruited veteran forger Edward Agar and solicited two more railroad employees—stationmaster William Tester and express guard James Burgess—to help him steal a shipment of gold bullion valued at some £20,000. The robbers struck on May 15, 1855, admitted by Burgess to the gold car of a train bound from London to Boulogne, France. Copies were made in advance of the keys to the several strongboxes, while the thieves carried bags of lead shot to replace the missing gold. Rifling the strongboxes one at a time, tossing the gold out to confederates along the way and replacing wax seals on the chests as they finished, the robbers bagged £12,000 before they suddenly ran out of shot and had to leave the rest of their intended loot behind.

The robbery was discovered on arrival in Boulogne, by which time Pierce's gang had scattered with the gold. During the next five months they sold it off to underworld fences, but the plot unraveled after Agar was arrested for check forgery in October 1855. Sentenced to life in the Australian penal colony of Botany Bay, Agar was placated by Pierce's promise to support Agar's mistress in England. Pierce broke his word, though, and Agar retaliated by squealing on his accomplices in 1856. Convicted at the Old Bailey in January 1857, Tester and Burgess were sentenced to 14 years each in Australia, while mastermind Pierce received a token two-year sentence. Their crime was hailed in Britain as the "Great Train Robbery" for more than a century until another gang conspired to make a vastly larger haul.

A mail train left Glasgow, Scotland, on the night of August 7, 1963, bearing receipts of a lucrative Boxing Day's shopping—128 bags filled with £5 and £1 notes—to sundry banks in London. At 2:00 A.M. on August 8, engineer Jack Mills stopped the train for a red emergency light at Sears Crossing in Bedfordshire. Before he could identify the problem, his cab was swarmed by hooded bandits armed with blackjacks. Mills and fireman David Whitby were overpowered, beaten senseless, and left handcuffed—with Mills permanently disabled—while the thieves moved on to the mail car. Hacking through the door with an ax, they looted the car, escaping with £2.6 million in used currency.

Four days after the holdup, a tip led police to the farm where the gang had abandoned much of its gear, covered with fingerprints. Robbers Gerald Boale and Roger Cordrey were swiftly arrested, caught with £141,000 of the stolen cash. Panicked, the gang hid another £101,000 near Dorking in Surrey where it was soon discovered by hikers. During the next few weeks, Scotland Yard jailed 10 more participants in the holdup; also arrested, on charges of harboring one fugitive, was attorney John Wheater, who arranged for purchase of the gang's rural hideout. Three more suspects—Bruce Reynolds, Ronald "Buster" Edwards, and James Edward White—were still at large when their associates went to trial. Defendant Ronald Arthur Biggs had his case severed from the rest, leaving 12 bandits to face the bar of justice in January 1964.

One defendant, John Daly, persuaded the court that his fingerprints had found their way into the gang's hideout by innocent means; the charges filed against him were dismissed. Eleven others were convicted on March 26, 1964: Eight defendants found guilty of armed robbery and conspiracy received 30-year prison terms (except for Gerald Boale, who was given 24 years); two convicted of conspiracy alone drew 24-year terms; Roger Cordrey, likewise convicted of conspiracy, received a "lenient" 20-year sentence for cooperating with police; and attorney Wheater was sentenced to three years, with consideration for his service during World War II.

Perhaps surprisingly, the British press was outraged by the sentences handed down, one newspaper declaring them "out of all proportion with everything except the value of the property involved." Four of those convicted saw their prison terms reduced on appeal, but the outcry failed to help Ronald Biggs at his separate trial, resulting in a 30-year prison term. Biggs escaped from prison with cohort Charles Wilson in 1965, and while Wilson was soon recaptured, Biggs fled to Australia and on from there to Brazil where he settled in Rio de Janeiro and was granted immunity from extradition. A successful Rio nightclub operator, Biggs fathered a son in 1976 and later portrayed himself in a motion picture, *The Great Rock 'n' Roll Swindle*. He returned to England in May 2001 at age 71, following a series of debilitating strokes. A tabloid newspaper provided transportation on its private jet, delivering Biggs to a maelstrom of controversy in London. While some papers called for a

Ronald A. Biggs, one of the engineers of the Great Train Robbery, is shown in a photo from 1965. (AP/Wide World Photos)

humanitarian pardon and others demanded strict enforcement of his sentence, a spokesman for Biggs told the public, "This is his swan song. He wants to return to the United Kingdom before he passes away."

TUPAMAROS: terrorist robbers

Formally known as the Movimiento de Liberación Nacional (National Liberation Movement), this Uruguayan guerrilla army took its more common name from Tupac Amaru, an Inca chief who rebelled against Spanish invaders and was burned at the stake. A leftist revolutionary faction organized in 1965, the Tupamaros movement ironically drew most of its members from Uruguay's middle-class and academic ranks rather than from the majority of impoverished peasants. Through the late 1960s, the Tupamaros focused on armed robbery as a means of funding their movement, graduating to concerted revolutionary violence and kidnapping in the 1970s.

Tupamaros bandits were nothing if not flamboyant. On October 7, 1968, they stole 11 million pesos from an Uruguayan branch of the Bank of London and South America. A General Motors plant at Penarol was raided on June 27, 1969, the bandits escaping with 500 million pesos (about $2.6 million dollars). The Bank of London and South America was tapped again, this time for 5 million pesos ($26,000) on September 10, 1969. The entire town of Pando, 20 miles east of Montevideo, was captured by Tupamaros on October 8, 1969, with three banks robbed and 15 persons killed in a battle with authorities. No cash was involved in the June 12, 1970, raid on the Swiss embassy in Montevideo, but Tupamaros gunmen stole documents, typewriters, and a photocopying machine. Five days later, Tupamaros gunmen stole 5,320,000 pesos ($28,000) from a branch of the Union of Uruguay Banks. There were two robberies on June 23: the Banco Palestino del Uruguay losing 18 million pesos ($72,000) and the Banco de Pan de Azucar giving up 8 million pesos ($28,000). One week later, on June 30, the Bank of London and South America was hit a third time for 12 million pesos ($63,000). A disappointing score of 342,000 pesos ($1,800) was gained from a robbery of the Esso Standard Oil Company's Montevideo office on September 11, 1970, but Tupamaros later rebounded to steal 4.75 million pesos ($250,000) from a gambling casino, enhancing their ROBIN HOOD image by distributing the cash to casino employees.

Despite such public gestures supporting their claim that "the Tupamaros are the people and the people are the Tupamaros," the movement had no solid political program and exercised little influence in Uruguay. At the peak of its notoriety, in 1971, the Tupamaros openly supported a dissident party, the Fronte Amplio, but their candidates received only 20 percent of the popular vote. By the close of 1972, the movement was effectively crushed, with 42 Tupamaros dead, another 2,600 imprisoned, and hundreds more dwelling in foreign exile. A tiny remnant of the group claimed credit for an Argentine airplane hijacking in October 1973, but another group was probably responsible. A self-styled Tupamaros leader, Washington Laino Amaral, was arrested for robbery in Mexico City on November 7, 1978. His unsupported claim of recruiting Mexican followers to fight against the Somoza government in Nicaragua spoke volumes about the Tupamaros situation in Uruguay.

UNDERHILL, Wilbur, Jr. "Mad Dog"; "Tri-State Terror"

A native of Joplin, Missouri, born in 1901, Wilber Underhill Jr. changed the spelling of his given name in the belief that substituting *u* for *e* made the name sound more manly. His three elder brothers—Earl, George, and Ernest—all grew up to be criminals, though none would hold a candle to their junior sibling in terms of notoriety. (Underhill's three sisters, by contrast, grew up to lead law-abiding lives, above reproach.) Wilbur was 12 years old when brother George drew a life sentence for killing a Joplin tamale vendor. Wilbur's own wild streak already showed: His mother blamed a childhood accident, telling anyone who would listen, "I don't think it left him quite right."

In fact, Underhill was a volatile psychopath. In his first brush with the law, he was suspected of stealing silverware from a neighbor's home, attempting to convince police that "a stranger" gave it to him. Convicted of burglary in 1918, he spent the next four years in prison. By 1923 he was notorious, albeit anonymously, as Joplin's "Lover's Lane Bandit." Police decoys caught him red handed, and Underhill was sentenced to five years in state prison, paroled in the latter part of 1926. On Christmas Day that year, he teamed with Ike "Skeet" Akins to rob a drugstore in Okmulgee, murdering 19-year-old customer George Fee in the process.

The deadly duo were cornered in Tulsa and arrested on charges of robbery and murder on January 7, 1927. They were still awaiting trial on January 30 when Underhill and Akins used smuggled hacksaw blades to free themselves from the Okmulgee jail, accompanied by inmates Red Gann and Duff Kennedy. Wilbur eluded pursuers, but Akins was captured at Lamar, Missouri, on February 9. Three days later, on his way back to Okmulgee, Akins made another break for freedom and was killed by Sheriff John Russell.

If Underhill was grieving for his late crime partner, he concealed it well. One day after Skeet's death, Wilbur stole $52 from a theater in Picker, Oklahoma. Collared at the scene by Constable George Fuller, he grabbed Fuller's pistol and killed a deputized civilian, Earl O'Neil, before escaping with his meager loot. Captured at Panama, Oklahoma, on March 20, 1927, Underhill was convicted of the Fee murder in Okmulgee and sentenced to life imprisonment on June 3, 1927. After multiple failed attempts to escape from state prison, Wilbur finally succeeded on July 14, 1931.

Twelve days later, in Cherryvale, Kansas, Underhill purchased a car and applied for a driver's license in the name of "Ralph Carraway," winding up his day by robbing a local theater of $300. On August 12, with nephew Frank Underhill, Wilbur robbed a Wichita gas station for the princely amount of $14.68. Speeding from the holdup scene, he crashed into another car and had to have his own towed for repairs at a local garage. Patrolman Merle Colver, assigned to check Wichita's hotels for suspicious new arrivals, came knocking on August 13 and was killed instantly when Wilbur shot him three times in the head. Fleeing on foot, Wilbur engaged in a literal running gunfight with police; a two-year-old boy was killed by police bullets before a lucky shot struck Underhill in the neck, numbing his gun arm. Conviction on his second murder charge earned Wilbur another life sentence, and he entered the Lansing state prison on September 4, 1931. (Nephew Frank, never charged, was apparently "scared straight" and led a blameless life from that day on.)

Despite his homicidal reputation—or, perhaps, because of it—Underhill was included in a mass breakout from Lansing on May 30, 1933. Eleven inmates, using pistols smuggled in by outlaw FRANK NASH, escaped that day and made tracks for the bandit-friendly COOKSON HILLS in Wilbur's native Oklahoma. Other participants in the exodus included HARVEY BAILEY, JIM CLARK, FRANK SAWYER, ED DAVIS, and "BIG BOB" BRADY. On June 16 Bailey and Underhill, with several others, robbed a bank at Black Rock, Arkansas. One day later, both were among the fugitives wrongly accused of killing friend Frank Nash and four lawmen in the headline-grabbing KANSAS CITY MASSACRE. The Bailey-Underhill team took $11,000 from a Clinton, Oklahoma, bank on July 3, 1933, but Wilbur was apparently alone when he stuck up another bank in Canton, Kansas, two days later. He rejoined Bailey's crew in time to help rob another bank at Kingfisher, Oklahoma, on August 9.

Harvey Bailey was out of circulation, wrongly jailed on kidnapping charges three days after the Kingfisher heist, when Underhill surfaced again. On October 6, 1933, he led several unidentified accomplices in looting $3,000 from a bank at Baxter Springs, Kansas. More bank jobs swiftly followed at Galena, Kansas, and Stuttgart, Arkansas. On November 2, Underhill teamed with FORD BRADSHAW and others to lift $13,000 from a bank in Okmulgee.

The heat surrounding Wilbur was intense by then. Newspapers vied for blood-curdling nicknames, one dubbing him "The Southwest Executioner." While a special task force, complete with armored cars, combed the Cookson Hills, Wilbur was cocky enough to present himself at the courthouse in Coalgate, Oklahoma, on November 18 and apply for a marriage license under his own name. His bride, Hazel Jarrett Hudson, was a sister of the outlaw Jarrett brothers. Five days later, Underhill joined other gunmen to take down a bank in Frankfort, Kentucky, as a kind of wedding present for Hazel.

FBI director J. EDGAR HOOVER, infuriated by the seeming negligence of Oklahoma law enforcers, dispatched agent R. H. Colvin to stalk Underhill on a full-time basis. Colvin soon learned that Wilbur had given his wife's Oklahoma City address to the minister who married them to receive their wedding certificate. G-men staked out the house and spotted the honeymooning Underhills a week later, but Wilbur and Hazel were gone by the time reinforcements arrived. Days later, police stormed a farm near Konower, believing that Wilbur was in residence, but he passed them on the highway, going in, and vanished by the time the squad cars could reverse directions.

It was embarrassing for all concerned, the more so after Wilbur, Jack Lloyd, and Ralph Roe tried to burglarize a bank at Harrah, Oklahoma, on December 11. Two days later, the gang was more successful with a bank job at Coalgate. But time was running out for "Mad Dog" Underhill. He simply did not know it, yet.

On the day after Christmas 1933, Wilbur and Hazel rented a house in Shawnee, Oklahoma, sharing the digs with Ralph Roe and his girlfriend, Eva Mae Nichols. Four days later, a strike force of 24 FBI agents, Oklahoma state troopers, and Shawnee patrolmen surrounded the house, led by G-men Colvin and Frank Smith, a Kansas City massacre survivor. Underhill answered calls for his surrender with gunfire, and a pitched battle ensued. Eva Nichols was killed by a rifle shot before Wilbur bolted from the dwelling barefoot in his underwear. Hit five times before he cleared the yard, he still ran for another 16 blocks and broke into a furniture store, where pursuers found him collapsed on one of the beds. Ralph Roe, also wounded, was jailed along with Hazel Underhill. Wilbur hung on for a week, shackled to a bed in the McAlester state prison infirmary, before he died on January 6, 1934. His last words to the jailers at his bedside: "Tell the boys I'm coming home."

"The boys" were not amused by Wilbur's capture. On December 31, Ford Bradshaw led a raiding party into little Vian, Oklahoma, and shot up the town in retaliation for the Shawnee raid. Underhill may have appreciated the gesture, but it did him no good in the end. His tombstone bore the original, hated spelling of his given name as "Wilber."

VAN LEWING, Robert

Born in 1922, Robert Van Lewing chalked up an impressive record of arrests and convictions for robbery before he was named to the FBI's "Ten Most Wanted" list on January 12, 1966, sought on multiple charges of bank robbery. Two months later, he was identified as the lone bandit who entered a St. Louis, Missouri, savings and loan office, flashing a pistol as he handed the teller a note demanding large bills. Van Lewing fled with $2,456 in cash, but his mug shots were identified by three witnesses at the scene. Wise enough to leave St. Louis in the face of mounting heat, he still refused to leave Missouri. Traced to Kansas City on February 6, 1967, Van Lewing was arrested without incident by FBI agents, was subsequently convicted, and was imprisoned for his several holdups.

VAN METER, Homer "Wayne"

A Hoosier native, born at Fort Wayne, Indiana, on December 3, 1906, Homer Van Meter was the son of an alcoholic railroad conductor who ultimately died of "general nervous collapse." Homer ran away from home in sixth grade and made his way to Chicago, working variously as a bellhop and a waiter. His first arrest, at age 17, resulted in a $200 fine for drunk and disorderly conduct in public. A short time later, on June 23, 1923, Van Meter was sentenced to 41 days in jail on a larceny conviction in Aurora, Illinois. By January 11, 1924, when an auto-theft conviction earned him a sentence of one to 10 years at the Illinois state prison in Menard, Homer had syphilis and a tattoo reading "HOPE" on one forearm.

Paroled in December 1924, Van Meter managed to stay out of trouble for barely three months. Teaming up with a former cellmate to rob the passengers aboard a train at Crown Point, Indiana, he took the fall alone, while his sidekick escaped and later died on the lam. On March 12, 1925, Van Meter was convicted of robbery, drawing a 10- to 21-year term at Pendleton Reformatory. There, he met inmates JOHN DILLINGER and HARRY PIERPONT, the former becoming a trusted friend. Pierpont could barely disguise his loathing of Van Meter. Part of the problem was Homer's continual clowning, epitomized by a gag in which he threw his body out of joint and hobbled about like a paralytic for the amusement of fellow convicts. The joking and repeated violations of reformatory rules saw Homer transferred to state prison at Michigan City on July 28, 1925.

In January 1926 Van Meter volunteered for a trip to Chicago to testify in defense of a suspect wrongly identified as his train-robbing companion. Homer escaped from his escort at Union Station, threw his body out of joint, and was begging money on the street outside when the furious guard caught up with him. A week later, with cellmate Charles Stewart, Homer sawed through the bars of his cell and beat a guard unconscious, but he was caught before he reached the prison's outer wall. Confined to solitary for the next two months, Van Meter was beaten by guards on a near-daily basis, emerging with several teeth missing and bruises all over his body. In the wake of his escape attempt, the prison's director of research diagnosed Van Meter's personality as follows:

This fellow is a criminal of the most dangerous type. Moral sense is perverted and he has no intention of following anything but a life of crime. . . . He is a murderer at heart and if society is to be safeguarded, his type must be confined throughout their natural lives.

In the face of that grim prognosis, Van Meter surprised his keepers by cleaning up his act and devoting himself to the study of law—transforming himself, as it were, into a model prisoner. Michigan City's chaplain wrote to the parole board: "I verily believe that Van Meter #11561 is ready to prove that he is no longer the man who got off on such a bad start. He has put off the old man. Judge him by the new man." Van Meter, for his part, told the board: "Through self education, I have become aware of life as a social minded man sees it. The more I read, the more I became convinced that a man has a purpose in life with his duty towards society. That a life dedicated to humanity is far more important than to be a Croesus. I began to age and mellow like a fine old wine."

The parole board bought it and released Van Meter on May 19, 1933. Dillinger was paroled three days later, but they did not immediately reunite, though Dillinger began to rob a series of banks suggested by Homer before they left prison. It was August 18 before Van Meter swung back into action, joining GEORGE "BABY FACE" NELSON, TOMMY CARROLL, and others to steal $30,000 from a bank at Grand Haven, Michigan. On October 23 he was back with Nelson and Carroll, adding JOHN PAUL CHASE and Charles Fisher to the team and looting $32,000 from a bank in Brainerd, Minnesota. When Illinois published its first list of 21 "public enemies" on December 28, 1933, Van Meter ranked 18th, well behind Dillinger but still two slots above an envious "Baby Face Nelson."

It was March 6, 1934, when the bank-robbing team later known as the "second Dillinger gang" cracked its first jug, at Sioux Falls, South Dakota, killing Patrolman Hale Keith in the process and escaping with $49,500 to a hideout in ST. PAUL, MINNESOTA. In addition to Dillinger and Van Meter, participants in that holdup included Nelson, Carroll,

EDDIE GREEN and JOHN "RED" HAMILTON. One week later to the day, the same crew stole $52,000 from a bank in Mason City, Iowa. FBI agents came close to trapping Van Meter and Dillinger in St. Paul on March 31, but the bandits shot their way clear of the trap. Twelve days later, Van Meter and Dillinger invaded a police station in Warsaw, Indiana, making off with various weapons and several bulletproof vests. On April 19 the gang was suspected of stealing $27,000 from a bank at Pana, Illinois.

That kind of action guaranteed intense heat around the gang's usual haunts. On April 20, 1934, five members of the holdup team (excluding Eddie Green) gathered with their women at Little Bohemia Lodge near Rhinelander, Wisconsin. Chicago G-man MELVIN PURVIS was tipped to their presence and staged a poorly planned raid on the night of April 22, killing one innocent bystander and wounding two more, while three of his own men were shot, one fatally. The gangsters all escaped, leaving their molls behind to face arrest and probation on charges of harboring fugitives. Van Meter was riding in a stolen car with Dillinger and Hamilton on April 23 when they blasted their way through a police trap near Hastings, Minnesota. Red Hamilton was wounded in the shootout and died on April 27 at the Illinois home of VOLNEY DAVIS. Van Meter helped bury Hamilton in a gravel pit near Oswego with assistance from members of the BARKER GANG.

On May 4, 1934, three men robbed a bank in Fostoria, Ohio, killing Chief of Police Frank Culp before they fled with $17,000. Witnesses named Dillinger and Van Meter as two of the gunmen, but erroneous identifications were common in those hectic days, and their guilt was never established. Homer and Dillinger spent most of May with Tommy Carroll, hiding in a forest cabin outside East Chicago, Illinois, cruising the back roads by night in a red panel truck. On May 19, a federal grand jury in Madison, Wisconsin, indicted them on charges of harboring each other in their flight from justice. Five days later, while driving their van through East Chicago, Van Meter and Dillinger were stopped by Detectives Martin O'Brien and Lloyd Mulvihill. Some reports call the stop an attempted shakedown, while others describe it as simple bad luck for the lawmen. Either way, Van Meter killed both officers with a burst of submachine-gun fire, the outlaws fleeing to Chicago and the sanctuary only well-connected gangland cronies could provide.

By May 28, when Dillinger submitted to clumsy plastic surgery from Doctor WILHELM LOESER, he and Van Meter were sharing a small Chicago apartment. Home went under the knife on June 3, with results so painfully disappointing that he had to be restrained from killing Loeser on the spot. Six days later, he traveled with Dillinger to Indianapolis, seeking a man they suspected of fingering them for the police stop in East Chicago, but their target managed to elude them and thus saved himself from a one-way ride. By June 21 Homer was out on his own, sharing a rented house with girlfriend Marie Comforti in Calumet City, Illinois.

He was not done with Dillinger, however. On June 30 they were reunited, teamed with "Baby Face" Nelson and a fourth man whose identity remains in dispute, to lift $28,890 from a bank at South Bend, Indiana. It was the gang's last raid and the bloodiest yet. Van Meter killed Patrolman Howard Wagner and was grazed by a bullet in return; four bystanders were also shot and wounded in the getaway. It was July 2 before Homer received medical attention for his scalp wound, but he felt well enough to visit the Chicago World's Fair six days later, with Dillinger and their girlfriends. On July 12, Van Meter and Dillinger huddled with their mob-connected lawyers, discussing plans to rob a train and flee the country.

It was not to be, however. FBI agents led by Melvin Purvis and SAMUEL COWLEY killed Dillinger in Chicago on July 22. That same night, Van Meter and Marie Comforti drove to St. Paul in an effort to escape the heat. Homer did not know it yet, but he had one month and one day to live. A brief visit to Bear Island View Resort at Longville, Minnesota, helped calm his nerves a bit in early August, but he was soon back in St. Paul, looking for action. On August 23 he was ambushed by a four-man police squad and riddled with bullets in a St. Paul alleyway, several of his fingers shot away in what the lawmen called self-defense, but Homer's kinfolk angrily described it as "target practice."

Several theories have been floated to explain the ambush. One version refers to a feud between Homer and "Baby Face" Nelson, with Nelson putting Homer on the spot to save himself the risk of a personal confrontation. Marie Comforti was also suspected, with jealousy the motive after she discovered that Van Meter had been cheating on her in St. Paul. A variation on that theme involved the parents of a young girl he was seeing on the side. Yet another suspect in the setup was a minor local hoodlum, Frank McCarthy, who had scheduled a meeting with Homer on August 23, presumably to pay off a $2,000 debt.

This much is known: When Homer reached the corner of Marion Street and University Avenue that Thursday, four officers were waiting for him in an unmarked car. The party included Chief of Police Frank Cullen, former chief Thomas Brown, and two detectives—all of them armed to the teeth. The officers would later say that Homer ignored their commands to halt, drew a pistol, and ducked into a nearby alley where they were forced to shoot him when he opened fire. If the wounds smacked of overkill—or summary execution—it would not have been the first time that an outlaw was gunned down deliberately in lieu of trial.

The firing squad reported finding $1,323 on Van Meter's body, but Marie Comforti and various gangland associates agreed that he was carrying more than $10,000 on the day he died. By 1939, FBI spokesmen felt confident in proclaiming that St. Paul fixer Harry Sawyer had arranged the shooting and split Homer's loot with the officers who gunned him down. By that time, Sawyer was in prison as an accessory to kidnapping and in no position to defend his dubious reputation. A footnote to the shooting was provided by Volney Davis, after his arrest as a member of the Barker Gang. That outfit, Davis told G-men, was so incensed by Homer's treacherous slaying that ex-chief Tom Brown was penalized by forfeiture of his cut from the gang's latest ransom haul.

It was all academic to Homer Van Meter by that time, however. The wise-cracking clown of the Dillinger gang went home to Fort Wayne for the last time on August 24, 1925, and was buried the following day at Lindenwood Cemetery.

VIKINGS: Early North Atlantic pirates

History's most notorious sea raiders were Scandinavians—mostly from Norway and Denmark—who figured prominently in the history of Western Europe from the eighth to the 11th century. Dubbed "Vikings" in English, after the land of Viken flanking Norway's Oslo Fjord where some originated, the far-ranging PIRATES were known by many other names, as well. The Franks they terrorized generally referred to the raiders as Northmen; Irish victims dubbed the Norwegians *Finngall* and the Danes *Dubgall*, indicating "white" and "black" foreigners; in Finland and Eastern Europe, the looters were called Rus—a term for "rowers" or "oarsmen" that later gave Russia its name.

Wherever they sailed, the Vikings were hardy explorers and ruthless enemies of those whose lands they invaded. They plundered extensively throughout the British Isles and the Frankish Empire, also attacking ports on the Iberian Peninsula and across North Africa. By the ninth century they controlled the Orkney and Shetland islands, with most of the Hebrides; they also conquered a large part of England and established bases on the Irish coast, from which they launched new raids across the Irish Sea and expeditions into the interior of Ireland.

Speculation on the Norse motive for piracy once centered on claims of expanding population in western Norway, but the rest of Scandinavia was relatively uncrowded throughout the Viking era. Modern scholars suggest that a more likely motive was simple greed. As commerce expanded throughout northwestern Europe in the late seventh and early eighth centuries, with major trading centers established at London, Ipswich, York, Dorestad (on the Rhine), and Quentovic (near Boulogne), adventurous pirates were naturally drawn to the feast.

Portland, an island off the Dorset coast, was apparently the first Viking target, raided by the occupants of three long ships during the reign of Beorhtric, king of Wessex (786–802). Initially mistaken for traders by the local reeve, one Beaduheard, the Norsemen slaughtered their host and all his men before looting the port. Lindesfarne, on the east coast of Scotland, was the next port to suffer, in June 793, and raids continued through the remainder of the eighth century: across Northumberland, near Dorchester, in 794; against the Irish towns of Skye, Iona, and Rathlin in 795; and against the monastery of St. Philibert on Noirmoutier—an island off the west coast of France—in 799. King Charlemagne was troubled enough to mount coastal defenses north of the Seine estuary in 800, but his efforts failed to keep the Vikings out of France.

Wherever they touched down, Viking raiders looted towns, plundered monasteries (at least 53 in Ireland alone), and kidnapped victims for ransom or sale into slavery. Sixty-eight residents of Iona were slain in the great raid of 806. Depredations against St. Philibert monastery were so predictable in the years between 819 and 836 that the monks withdrew to mainland France each summer, for their own safety. Franks repelled a fleet of 13 Viking ships from

Flanders and the Seine estuary in 820, but the pirates still managed to loot Aquitaine.

The Emerald Isle remained a favorite hunting ground throughout the Viking era. In 831 the Norsemen raided northern Louth in east-central Ireland and held its king for ransom. A year later, Armagh suffered three raids in a single month, while other Viking crews struck at Derry, Clondalkin, Dromiskin, and the monastery of Lismore. The year 834 witnessed attacks at Glendalough and Slane on Boyne. In 835, Vikings sacked Ferns and Clonmore and then raided Glendalough again in 836. Raids into the Irish interior were also launched in 836, while Viking fleets plied the rivers Boyne and Liffey at will in the following year. A fleet on Lough Neagh plundered the surrounding countryside in 839, and Vikings waged relentless war against the native Picts. Another fleet on Lough Ree staged monastery raids across central Ireland in 844. Norse reinforcements were on the scene by 849, subjugating much of Ireland as a launching pad for raids against new targets, but resistance hung on in Armagh until the settlement was razed by Olaf's invaders in 869. Dublin was sacked by Norse raiders as late as 944.

Britain remained under constant attack while Viking hordes plundered neighboring Ireland. Norse raiders stormed ashore on the Isle of Sheppey in the Thames estuary during 835 and defeated the West Saxons a year later at Carhampton in Somerset. Viking raids along the coast of Wales began in 852 and continued for years thereafter. Vikings based in France attacked Winchester in 860. A "great army" of Norsemen landed in East Anglia in 865 and compelled a surrender with payment of tribute. The same force occupied York in 866 and then returned to East Anglia three years later, defeating and killing Edmund, king of the East Angles, on November 20, 869. Viking raiders based in Dublin captured Dumbarton, the capital of Strathclyde, in 870. One year later, the "great army" from East Anglia failed in its attempt to conquer Wessex but still exacted tribute from the frightened natives there. A second invasion force penetrated Wessex in 875, occupying Wareham and Exeter before treaties were signed; the raiders withdrew from Wessex in 877 to seize control of northeastern Mercia. Rochester was besieged in 885, albeit unsuccessfully. Viking leader Ragnald defeated a combined army of Englishmen and Scots at Cambridge, on the river Tyne, in 914. Four years later he sacked Dunblane, Scotland, and defeated another army on the Tyne. By 919 Ragnald had conquered

York and was recognized as its king. Raids along the Welsh coast occurred with greater frequency after 961, lasting into the mid-11th century.

France also suffered ongoing depredations by Norsemen, meanwhile. The monks of beleaguered St. Philibert's finally abandoned Noirmoutier island entirely in 836. Five years later, in 841, Vikings raided along the Seine valley; they sacked Nantes in 843 and rebounded a year later with strikes at Toulouse, Galice, and al-Andalus. Paris was ransomed for 7,000 pounds of silver in 845. Bordeaux was seized by Norsemen in 848 following a long siege, and Périgueux was looted a year later. The abbey of St.-Martin was attacked at Tours in 852. A Viking base was established at Camarque on the south coast of Frankia in 859, and dragon boats were active along the Somme valley. In 865, Norse plunderers raided the abbey of St.-Benoit at Fleury. Vikings from Loire teamed with Bretons to sack Le Mans in 866. Seven years later, Charles the Bald besieged a Norse army and drove it from Angers. Raiders based in England crossed the Channel in 879 to ravage the Meuse region, but they suffered heavy losses against the East Franks at Thiméon the following year. Paris withstood a Viking siege in 885. Two years of campaigning in western Frankia during 886–88 saw Sens besieged, with raids on other towns including Troyes, Verdun, and Toul. Norsemen launched from the Seine valley were defeated by Breton forces at Saint-Lô in 890. Vikings led by Rollo raided the Seine valley again in 911 and though defeated at Chartres still managed to occupy Rouen.

Elsewhere, the Rhine port of Dorestad suffered at least seven Viking raids between 834 and 865. Hamburg was sacked by Norsemen in 845, and Constantinople was attacked in 860 by the Rus warriors who would later lend their name to vast Russia. A Viking army based at Fulham, England, crossed the Channel to raid along the Lower Rhine in 879. Further raids along the Rhine in 881 included a strike at Cologne, while Vikings in the low countries ravaged Liège, Utrecht, and Aachen.

Viking raids against England resumed in 980 after an interval of quiet. Norsemen attacked East Anglia in 991 and defeated an English army at Maldon, collecting 10,000 pounds of silver as tribute. Annual raids between 997 and 1002 produced another 24,000 pounds of tribute, but payoffs failed to protect the bishop of St. David's, slain by Viking raiders in 999. Sven Forkbeard campaigned in England from 1003 to 1005, and a large Viking fleet arrived in 1006, extorting 36,000 pounds of tribute the following year. Thorkell's army began a new English campaign in 1009, seizing Canterbury in 1012 and executing Archbishop Æltheah before 48,000 pounds of silver ended the rampage. St. David's was attacked repeatedly—in 1073, 1080, and 1091—but Danish king Knut failed to carry out his planned invasion of England in 1085.

Various factors combined to end Viking depredations in the early 12th century. A series of military defeats sapped Norse strength on foreign battlefields, while intermarriage and alliances with former enemies made widespread destruction counterproductive. Perhaps the most significant factor of all was the conversion of many Scandinavians to Christianity, unarmed missionaries from Britain and the Continent succeeding at last where so many militant kings and warlords had failed in the past.

WAH Mee Club Massacre

In the early morning hours of February 19, 1983, three gunmen invaded the Wah Mee Club, a private (and illegal) gambling establishment in Seattle's Chinatown. Three employees were shot as the bandits entered; 11 more—including one woman—were subsequently bound and robbed. When they had collected their loot, the intruders methodically opened fire on their victims with .22-caliber weapons, firing multiple head shots at close range.

One victim of the massacre survived, shot twice in the head, and struggled free of his bonds, staggering outside to call for help. The survivor described his assailants to police, while local newspapers ran their latest series of exposés on rampant gambling in Chinatown. Within 24 hours of the murders, two suspects were arrested, identified as 22-year-old Kwan Fia "Willie" Mak and 20-year-old Benjamin Ng. Loot from the robbery, some $10,000 in all, was recovered in the raid on Ng's home. A third suspect, 26-year-old Hong Kong native Wai-Chiu "Tony" Ng—no relation to Benjamin—remained at large, urgently sought by authorities. A federal warrant was issued on March 31, 1983, charging Ng with unlawful flight to avoid prosecution. On June 14, 1984, he became the first Asian ever posted to the FBI's "Ten Most Wanted" list.

His accomplices faced trial in the meantime. On August 24, 1983, Seattle jurors convicted Benjamin Ng on 13 counts of aggravated murder. He was spared execution and sentenced to life imprisonment on August 26, after the jury failed to return a unanimous recommendation of death. Willie Mak was less fortunate; convicted on October 5, 1983, he was condemned on October 21 and remains on death row today, still appealing his sentence.

Tony Ng was arrested in Calgary, Alberta, on October 4, 1984, by officers of the Royal Canadian Mounted Police. Held on charges of illegal immigration, he was subsequently extradited after American prosecutors promised not to seek the death penalty. Convicted on 13 murder counts in June 1985, Ng received one life sentence for each of the slayings on July 3, 1985. Under Washington law he was required to serve a minimum of 35 years before consideration for parole.

WASHINGTON, Levi

A native of Alligator, Missouri, Levi Washington was on parole from a narcotics conviction when police in New Orleans arrested him, filing charges in three local bank robberies committed between July and November 1967. Before those cases went to trial, the FBI charged Washington with robbing a church in Chicago, and Louisiana surrendered him to Illinois authorities. On August 16, 1968, he escaped from the Cook County jail in Chicago and was declared a federal fugitive on a charge of unlawful flight to avoid prosecution. Washington was added to the bureau's "Ten Most Wanted" list on November 15, 1968.

Three weeks later, on December 5, three gunmen entered a Jackson, Michigan, bank and scooped $37,000 into their satchels, spraying the room with a riot-control chemical as they fled. Witnesses described the bandits and their vehicle, which was discovered by patrolling officers an hour later. Footprints in a snowbank led police to a nearby rooming house, where suspects "Paul Carter" and "Allen Rose" were taken into custody. A search of their room turned up loot from the bank heist, along with a sawed-off .30-caliber carbine and three pistols.

At midnight on December 5 a homemade bomb exploded at Jackson's city hall, wounding two policemen. Officers concluded that the bomb was meant to blow at noon as a diversion for the earlier bank job, but a faulty timer had delayed the blast for 12 hours. Evidence recovered from the scene established that robbery suspects Rose and Carter were responsible for the explosion.

On December 9 a fingerprint comparison revealed "Paul Carter's" true identity as Levi Washington. His cellmate was identified as Louis Carr. Two

Levi Washington robbed four banks prior to his 1968 arrest by federal agents. (FBI)

days later, the elusive third man—Delbert Beard—turned up to visit Carr in jail. Beard gave his name as "August Cerio," but officers were not deceived, and he was taken into custody on the charge of attempting to arrange a jailbreak.

The federal trial of Beard and Carr began in Detroit on July 8, 1969. Levi Washington succeeded in severing his case from the others and was placed on trial separately but in the same courthouse. On the morning of July 23, arriving at court in a prison van, the three defendants made a desperate bid for freedom, fleeing under the guns of federal marshals. Louis Carr was seriously wounded by a gunshot to the chest, and three bystanders suffered minor injuries. Levi Washington, unharmed, was captured in the courthouse basement and was later convicted on all counts, drawing a stiff prison sentence.

WEBSTER, Jim

A notorious gunman and outlaw of the California gold-rush era, Jim Webster's first claim to fame was an 1853 shootout over a mining claim near Timbuctoo in which he killed three armed assailants. A year later, at the mining camp of Washington, California, he was less fortunate, losing two front teeth to an opponent's bullet. A fling at robbery landed Webster in San Quentin prison, where he soon became fast friends with outlaws TOM HODGES, ADOLPH NEWTON, RICHARD "RATTLESNAKE DICK" BARTER, and others. Upon release, he briefly joined the Hodges gang but was arrested at Nevada City in October 1856 and was jailed with Dick Barter and the bandit Farnsworth brothers, Fred and Warren.

Unsuited to captivity, Webster joined Barter in tunneling out of their cell with smuggled tools, broke down the jail's main door, pummeled a guard, and escaped into darkness. Captured three days later at Smartville by lawman/outlaw Henry Plummer, Webster remained behind bars for three weeks but then escaped on November 2 with the Farnsworth brothers. Connivance of a corrupt guard was suspected, as the fugitives apparently had keys to their cell; rumors later circulated that Plummer himself had arranged the escape, hoping to recapture his errant prisoners and claim the outstanding reward.

Webster outsmarted Plummer, though, organizing his own holdup gang and enlisting one of Plummer's erstwhile patrolmen, Wallace Gehr, as a recruit. Arrested at Marysville for robbery in February 1857, Webster was sentenced to 25 years at San Quentin, boasting on arrival at the prison that "I won't be here six months." He was correct, escaping in a mass breakout that August. He remained at large until 1860 when he was shot and killed in a quarrel with another outlaw.

WEEKS, Danny Michael

A native of Roswell, New Mexico, born January 19, 1954, Danny Weeks grew up in company with drug addicts and outlaw bikers, hanging around the fringes of such motorcycle gangs as the Hell's Angels and the Bandidos. Boasting adult convictions for burglary, escape, and possession of marijuana, by 1986 he was confined in Louisiana on convictions for armed robbery and contract murder. On August 23 of that year he joined two other inmates in breaking out of state prison; two days later federal warrants charged him with unlawful flight to avoid confinement.

Fleeing across Texas, Weeks kidnapped female hostages in two separate incidents, releasing his prisoners unharmed in each case. He was also identified as the gunman who held up a savings and loan office in San Antonio, moving on from there to rob a bank in Tucson, Arizona. His name was added to the FBI's "Most Wanted" list on September 29, 1986.

Weeks was still at large 16 months later when the new Fox television network introduced a weekly program called *America's Most Wanted,* profiling fugitives from justice. His case was featured on the program's broadcast of February 28, 1988, and federal agents found him on March 20, pursuing leads provided by a viewer of the show. Apprehended in Washington state, Weeks was returned to prison in Louisiana to face additional time on conviction of the holdups in Arizona and Texas.

WELLS, George Edward

A native of Belmont County, Ohio, Wells was convicted of first-degree murder in the shooting of an Akron tavern owner. Sentenced to die, he won commutation of his sentence to life imprisonment in 1938, 12 hours before he was scheduled for electrocution. In 1961 Wells was paroled after Governor Michael DiSalle commuted his sentence again, this time to second-degree murder.

In October 1967 four gunmen invaded the home of coin collector Norman Kanserski in Middleberg Heights, Ohio, pistol-whipping Kanserski and making off with coins valued at $50,000. A few days later, Wells was linked to the $40,000 robbery of a jewelry store in Breckville, Ohio. Before the year was out, George Westrich, named as a participant in the Kanserski raid, was found shot to death in his car in Independence, Missouri.

Indicted on the relatively minor federal charge of transporting stolen property across state lines, George Wells was added to the FBI's "Ten Most Wanted" list on March 28, 1968. Fourteen months later he was captured by G-men outside a motel in South Point, Ohio. Accompanying Wells at the time of his arrest was Steve Gomori Jr., recently indicted by a federal grand jury in Cleveland for distributing counterfeit $100 bills. Wells was jailed in lieu of $100,000 bond; Gomori's bail was set at $5,000 on new charges of harboring a federal fugitive. Convicted in November 1969 of transporting stolen property, Wells was sentenced to nine years in federal prison.

WELLS Fargo: Security firm and holdup target

On January 24, 1848, a gold nugget the size of a pea was discovered in the millrace at John Sutter's sawmill near Coloma, California. That seemingly minor discovery sparked California's gold rush and simultaneously inaugurated a new era for bandits in America's Wild West. For every prospector who joined the rush, there was a corresponding influx of gamblers, prostitutes, swindlers, and HIGHWAYMEN intent on relieving lucky miners of their gold dust and nuggets. Security was paramount, especially for larger mining firms, and eastern bankers wasted no time in filling the need.

Chief among them were Henry Wells and William Fargo, organizers of the American Express Company in 1850, who pooled their resources to create a new Wells Fargo banking and express company in March 1852. The first Wells Fargo office opened four months later in San Francisco; 55 offices were established through the western states by fall of 1855. Wells Fargo shipped anything and everything—from food and ice to clothing, mail, and farmers' seeds—but the company was best known for its gold and payroll shipments in the West. Hand-crafted Concord stagecoaches were widely used, built for $1,100 each, tipping the scales at 2,200 pounds, and so durable that one pulled from a river after 30 days submerged was still in service a half-century later. Six-horse teams would pull the coaches until they were finally retired for good in 1918. By 1866 Wells Fargo, under company president Louis McLane, monopolized stage lines west of Missouri.

It was big business, and that implied big risk. A band of outlaws led by RICHARD "RATTLESNAKE DICK" BARTER burglarized the safe of a Wells Fargo office at Fiddletown, California, in February 1857. Three years later, Wells Fargo lost $20,000 in a Butte County holdup, but company detective Henry Johnson succeeded in tracking down two of the thieves. Forewarned of a robbery in January 1860, Wells Fargo detectives Daniel Gay and Charles O'Neil replaced the gold in their strongbox with lead shot for the January 15 run from Angel's Camp to Stockton. Hiding in the stage's leather boot, they shot it out with four outlaws who stopped the coach, killing one of California's five known "Cherokee Bobs" and wounding a second gunman before the other two escaped.

Bloody failure has never deterred greedy bandits. Between 1870 and 1884, 347 attempted holdups of Wells Fargo gold coaches were recorded; 226 bandits were convicted during the same period, most tracked down by company detectives under James Hume and John Thacker. One who nearly got away was soft-spoken outlaw Charles Bolton (aka "Black Bart"), who successfully robbed 28 coaches, leaving handwritten poems in place of his stolen loot. Captured on his 29th attempt, fleeing with $4,800 on November 3, 1883, Bolton was sentenced to 10 years in San Quentin and paroled in January 1888, with time off for good behavior. Robert Paul, a shotgun messenger from 1873 to 1878, was promoted to express detective in the latter year and sent to Arizona, where he hired brothers Wyatt and Morgan Earp as stagecoach guards. Paul personally shot it out with bandits on the Tombstone run in 1881, leaving two men dead; intrigue surrounding the abortive holdup led directly to October's blood showdown at the O.K. Corral, pitting the Earps and John "Doc" Holliday against the rival Clanton-McLowery gang.

By 1888 Wells Fargo had expanded nationwide and internationally, with some 300 offices in Mexico and contractual agreements for sale of Wells Fargo travelers checks from banks in Hong Kong. Transport of gold and cash shipments by rail forced the company to deal with a risk of TRAIN ROBBERY, beginning with November 1870's $41,000 holdup of a Central Pacific train in Nevada by "Gentleman Jack" Davis and his "Seven Knights of the Road." Missouri's DALTON GANG raised so much hell with railroads in general and Wells Fargo in particular that company detective FRED DODGE was assigned to track

them full time with a special "Dalton posse." He missed his chance, however, when the outlaw brothers overplayed their hand and were gunned down while trying to rob two banks simultaneously in Coffeyville, Kansas.

Soon after the turn of the 20th century, Edward Harriman gained control of Wells Fargo through his ownership of the Southern Pacific Railroad, moving the company's headquarters to New York City in 1904. By the time America entered World War I, Wells Fargo boasted 10,000 offices and 80,000 miles of railroad track. Expansion into full-service banking preceded the Great Depression in America, and armored trucks replaced the venerable stagecoach for transport of cash, but trouble with bandits continued. With such a far-flung corporate empire and so much cash at stake, it comes as no surprise that Wells Fargo has suffered some of America's most notorious holdups. A sampling of those crimes includes the following.

1969—New York: Three men armed with pistols robbed a Wells Fargo armored truck on November 12 as it returned to Manhattan from Aqueduct Race Track. Their estimated $1.4 million haul set a new U.S. record for theft of cash.

1978—New York: A gang of five or six gunmen broke the standing record on December 19 with the robbery of a Wells Fargo truck on Staten Island. Company spokespersons called it the firm's worst loss ever, with the loot variously estimated between something "in excess of $1 million" and "a shade over $3 million." The bandits surprised two Wells Fargo guards while they were lunching at a delicatessen, then overpowered the driver, and fled with his truck, transferring the cash to a getaway car parked nearby.

1983—Tennessee: Thieves stole $6.5 million from a Wells Fargo office in Memphis. "Final suspect" Nathan Page Gervais surrendered to authorities on July 19, 1984, police announcing that they had recovered $3.2 million of the stolen cash.

1983—Connecticut: Puerto Rican nationalists robbed a Wells Fargo depot at West Hartford in September, escaping with $7.1 million. Company guard Victor Gerena played a key role in the heist, afterward escaping to Cuba; he was posted to the FBI's "Ten Most Wanted" list. Six other suspects, all described as members of the Macheteros terrorist group, were arrested and charged in the holdup. Alleged ringleader Filiberto Ojeda Rios jumped bail in 1990 and disappeared; he was convicted in absentia and received a 55-year prison term in May 1992. Four other defendants were likewise convicted, and the sixth was acquitted of all charges.

1985—New York: Three bandits stole $8 million from a Wells Fargo vault in New York City. Witnesses observed the trio loading their haul into a getaway car and provided information leading to the May 29–30 arrests of defendants Jeffrey Grubczak, Rosario Leanzo, and Thomas Lacarrula.

1994—Florida: Thieves attacked a Wells Fargo truck outside a Miami nightclub on April 11, pistol-whipping the driver and escaping with an estimated $500,000.

1997—Florida: Another U.S. holdup record was established on March 29 when $18.8 million was removed at gunpoint from a Loomis-Fargo vault in Jacksonville. Company employee Philip Noel Johnson, charged with robbery, kidnapping, and money laundering in that case, was arrested on August 30, 1997, when U.S. Customs officers caught him crossing the Mexican border at Brownsville, Texas. On September 18 FBI agents recovered $18.6 million of the loot from a storage facility Johnson had rented in Mountain Home, North Carolina.

1999—California: "Whispering Bandit" Stanley Edward Jamison Jr. was arrested in San Mateo on January 8 following three bank holdups in the San Francisco area. Nicknamed for his habit of passing notes to bank tellers and whispering, "This is a holdup," Jamison pulled his second job at a Wells Fargo bank in Campbell, California, on November 7, 1998. In that peculiar heist, he handed the cashier a note reading "$2,500," while hissing, "Give me twenties, fifties, and hundreds. This is a robbery." Unfortunately, Jamison spoke so softly that the teller could not understand him and asked him to repeat himself. Despite the cryptic note, he fled with $4,201, leaving his image recorded on videotape. At the time of his arrest, Jamison was on parole from a previous bank-robbery conviction, having been released in August 1998 after serving 87 months.

2000—California: FBI spokespersons and officers of the Torrance Police Department sought public assistance in capturing the "Please Hurry Bandit," who was blamed for holdups at 13 Wells Fargo banks in southern California during January. The robber—identified from surveillance photos as a balding, heavy-set African American male in his 40s, earned his nickname from urging bank tellers to "please hurry" after handing them written demands for cash.

2001—Colorado: Gunman Jared Flahiff was arrested in Colorado Springs on March 23 and charged with robbing two Wells Fargo banks in the past week. His arrest climaxed a standoff with police during which Flahiff doused his motel room with gasoline and threatened to set it afire. Authorities obtained warrants for Flahiff's arrest after his 50-year-old father was jailed for a separate bank holdup in Colorado Springs. Arresting officers in that case observed a photo of Flahiff in his father's home and recognized him as the robber captured on surveillance tapes during the two Wells Fargo heists. He was held under $5,000 bond pending trial.

2001—California: San Diego's Bank Robbery Task Force sought public assistance in March to apprehend the elusive "Bilingual Bank Bandit," credited with seven robberies between February 17 and March 12. His first two targets were Wells Fargo banks, robbed on February 17 and 21. Described as a Hispanic male in his late 20s, recognizable by his mustache and long eyelashes, the Bilingual Bandit remains at large today.

WILCOXSON, Bobby Randell, and NUSSBAUM, Albert Frederick

Bobby Wilcoxson and Albert Nussbaum resembled each other closely enough to be mistaken for brothers, but there were also crucial differences between them. One-eyed Bobby was the muscle of the team, quick on the trigger, volatile, and brutal. Albert was the brains, a bookworm with a taste for criminology and chemistry, firearms and explosives. Nussbaum also studied makeup and disguises, poring over the biographies of famous criminals to learn from their achievements and mistakes. He loved to work with guns, but when the chips were down, it would be Wilcoxson who pulled the trigger.

Launching his criminal career in 1952 with a charge of auto theft at age 18, Nussbaum was placed on probation and joined the army. Honorably discharged in 1957, he went into gun-running, picking up arrests over the next two years on charges of burglary and robbery, possession of a dangerous weapon, and interstate transportation of a Thompson submachine gun. The latter charge landed Albert in the federal reformatory at Chillicothe, Ohio, where he met Bobby Wilcoxson, incarcerated for interstate transportation of a vehicle purchased with a fraudulent check. (An African-American inmate, Peter Columbus Curry, also became friendly with

Bobby Wilcoxson and partner Albert Nussbaum favored daylight robberies employing automatic weapons. (FBI)

Nussbaum and Wilcoxson at Chillicothe, returning in later years to play a pivotal role in their downfall.)

Paroled in 1959, Wilcoxson headed south and waited for his friend's release in 1960. They regrouped at Nussbaum's home in Buffalo, New York, in mid-September, raising cash by pulling off a string of local burglaries. The money went for guns and rented cars as they prepared to hit the big time with a string of daring daylight robberies.

On December 5, 1960, the duo struck a savings-and-loan company in Schiller Park, New York, walking out with $5,709 in cash. Their next take, on January 12, was larger, as they made a clean getaway from the M & T Trust Company, carrying $87,288 in their satchel.

The partners split up and invested their loot: Wilcoxson visited Florida, buying into a jewelry store, a lettuce farm, and an automobile dealership; Nussbaum, meanwhile, used an alias to rent a storefront in Buffalo, stockpiling firearms and ammuni-

tion and building an arsenal that grew to include machine guns, grenades, and antitank weapons.

In June 1961 the bandits planned a series of random bombings in Washington, D.C., designed to generate fear of a "mad bomber" at large, distracting police on the day of a planned bank robbery. Trash cans and phone booths were demolished, with Nussbaum placing anonymous calls to the authorities, posing as a fanatic white supremacist, and claiming credit for the blasts. Their final bomb, planted in an office building on June 30, turned out to be a dud, but the partners went ahead with their robbery on schedule, bagging another $19,862.

A short time later, agents from the Bureau of Alcohol, Tobacco and Firearms (BATF) arrested Wilcoxson's father for illegally receiving antitank guns and ammunition. The arrest would ultimately lead them back to Nussbaum's arsenal in Buffalo, but in the meantime there were other targets to be looted.

Staking out a trust company in Rochester, New York, Nussbaum and Wilcoxson raided the office after a Brink's truck had dropped off a shipment of cash. The bandits fled with $57,197, but in their haste they missed another $81,700 lying behind the counter in canvas bags.

Come winter, Pete Curry was fresh out of prison and itching for action. On December 15, 1961, Curry and Wilcoxson entered a bank in Brooklyn, New York, leaving Nussbaum outside at the wheel of their getaway car. When security guard Henry Kraus went for his pistol, Wilcoxson unleashed a burst of submachine gun fire, killing Kraus instantly. Outside, a patrolman responded to the sound of shots and tried to shoot Wilcoxson, but a heavy plate glass door deflected bullets from his revolver. Returning fire, Wilcoxson had a little better luck; the officer was wounded, but a slug that would have pierced his heart was stopped on impact by his badge. The robbers escaped with $32,763, dumping their car and Wilcoxson's weapon nearby. Serial numbers led BATF agents to Nussbaum's gun shop in Buffalo and the separate pieces of a baffling puzzle began to mesh.

On January 30, 1962, federal warrants were issued, charging Wilcoxson with two counts of bank robbery; Nussbaum was named in the warrants as a material witness. Reports of a black bandit in Brooklyn led investigators back to Chillicothe, where officials at the federal lockup remembered Peter Curry's friendship with the wanted fugitives. Arrested on February 13 by FBI agents staking out his mother's home in Brooklyn, Curry soon began to sing.

Enraged by Curry's betrayal, Nussbaum and Wilcoxson plotted to murder their "friend," but they never got the chance. Federal agents uncovered Albert's arsenal near Buffalo, and slugs removed from nearby trees were found to be identical with those employed to murder Henry Kraus. New warrants were prepared, upgrading Nussbaum from a material witness to the status of a full participant in the lethal Brooklyn heist. Wilcoxson's name was added to the FBI's "Ten Most Wanted" list on February 23, 1962, Nussbaum joining him five weeks later, on April 2, 1962.

On June 26, 1962, the bandits raided a savings-and-loan company in Philadelphia, but a teller sent to empty the vault locked himself inside, leaving them with a pitiful $160 in singles. Driving on to Pittsburgh, they struck at a branch bank in a shopping mall, netting $4,373 and overlooking another $10,000.

It seemed apparent that the famous Nussbaum strategy was failing. Quarreling bitterly through summer, Bobby and Albert agreed on one more job together; Nussbaum stubbornly insisted that he would only drive the car, prompting Wilcoxson to offer him a flat $500 fee. On September 19 Wilcoxson looted a Pennsylvania bank of $28,901 and split the take as agreed—$500 for Albert, $28,401 for himself. Furious, Nussbaum stormed out with his handful of cash and the partnership ended; the outlaws would not see each other again until they next met in jail.

On November 3, 1962, Nussbaum's wife returned from a secret meeting with her husband to find FBI agents waiting at her home. With some coaxing from her mother, she was finally persuaded to describe Albert's car, his new disguise, and his probable location. Spotted at 2:00 A.M. the following day, Nussbaum was captured after a brief high-speed chase. Five days later, acting on a "tip" that may have come from Nussbaum, G-men dropped the net on Wilcoxson in Baltimore. Thirty agents ringed the outlaw's home on November 9, armed in expectation of a battle and waiting through the night, until his girlfriend left the house next morning. Bobby followed on her heels, a baby in his arms, and offered no resistance when he found himself surrounded. Convicted of the robbery that led to Henry Kraus's death, Bobby Wilcoxson and Peter Curry were sentenced to life imprisonment. For his participation as the wheelman, Al Nussbaum drew a prison term of 20 years.

WHITE, Alfred James

A master burglar by trade and inclination, Al White was not averse to trying other felonies when times were lean. His record spanned three decades, with arrests on charges that included auto theft, grand larceny, bank robbery, and violation of parole. Ohio locked him up for 14 years on conviction for a bank job. Freed in 1940, he was hauled back three years later after violating terms of his parole.

In summer 1954 policemen in West Hardin, West Virginia, surprised White in the act of burglarizing a lumber yard. He answered their challenge with bullets, ducking return fire and plunging into a nearby river, scrambling to freedom in the darkness of the opposite bank. Identified from fingerprints, he proved more difficult to capture. More than two years passed before his name was added to the FBI's "Most Wanted" list, on January 14, 1957.

White had thus far eluded capture by adherence to a policy of isolation from his fellow humans. Avoiding human contact when he could, White worked odd jobs and passed his leisure time alone. For relaxation he would visit airports, sometimes watching planes take off and land for hours at a time. Addition to the Top Ten list with its attendant fanfare of publicity made it impossible for White to stay anonymous. On January 24 two residents of Memphis saw his published photographs and recognized "Frank Shaw," a tenant of the local George Vincent Hotel. The FBI was notified, and agents bagged White as he emerged from the elevator, headed for his room. Unarmed, he offered no resistance, but a

Albert Nussbaum, captured by FBI agents in 1962 (FBI)

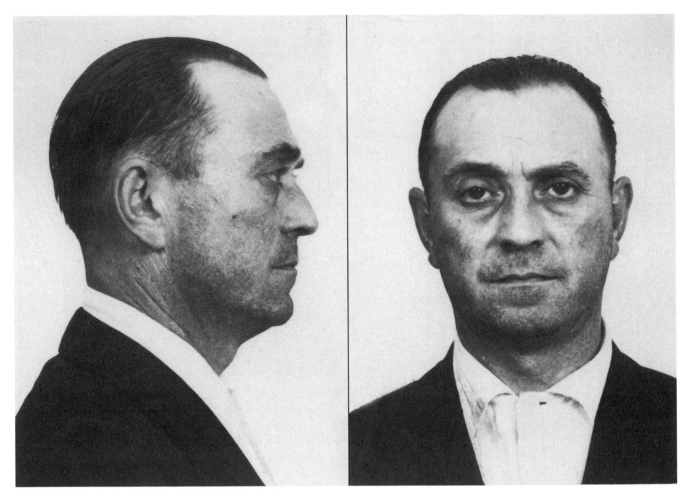

1950s burglar and bank robber Alfred White (FBI)

shakedown of his car and trailer revealed three pistols, an illegal sawed-off shotgun, ammunition, and a quantity of burglar's tools.

In custody, White told his captors he had nearly opted for surrender two months earlier when he was injured in an accident and found that as a fugitive he could not utilize his health insurance. "I shouldn't have been on the FBI list in the first place," he groused. "It must have been the insistence of the West Virginia officers that got me on the list." And it would be those officers' testimony at his trial that sent White off to prison on conviction for assault and burglary.

WHITE, Billy Ray

In September 1967 two gunmen held up a jewelry store in Metairie, Louisiana, escaping with $4,000 worth of diamond rings and other merchandise. In flight they fired three shots at store employees who tried to pursue them, vanishing before police arrived. One of the robbers was quickly arrested by local officers, and he named Billy White as his elusive accomplice.

A month later, in Albuquerque, New Mexico, White invaded the offices of a savings-and-loan association, herding employees into a back room and tying them up before looting the office of $1,650. In November 1967 witnesses identified White as one of two bandits who robbed a trading post at Budsville, 50 miles west of Albuquerque. Netting a mere $300, the thieves went berserk, tying up two hostages and shooting both of them to death. The arrest of White's accomplice brought confirmation of his identity, and murder charges were added to several outstanding counts of armed robbery. On August 13, 1968, White's name was added to the FBI's "Ten Most Wanted" list.

Four days later, acting on a tip, federal agents surrounded a rented home in Wood River, Illinois. The female occupant denied any knowledge of Billy White, granting permission for agents to search the house. White was found in a closet, trying to hold the door shut from inside, and he surrendered without resistance. Three pistols and a quantity of stolen drugs were found inside the house, along with some 200 cartons of stolen cigarettes.

According to the landlord, White had described himself as a traveling insurance agent, required to make long business trips at frequent intervals. Two maps of Illinois recovered in the search showed 70 towns marked with circles; White's girlfriend fingered the locations as the scenes of past or future robberies. In every case, the cash or stolen merchandise was driven back to Wood River where various hot items were unloaded through black market outlets. Held on federal charges, White was extradited to New Mexico for trial and subsequent conviction on two counts of murder.

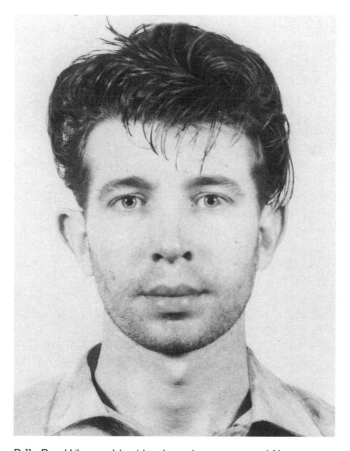

Billy Ray White robbed banks in Louisiana and New Mexico. (FBI)

WHITTEMORE Gang

Career criminal Richard Reese Whittemore was serving time in Maryland for armed robbery when he escaped from the state penitentiary on February 20, 1925, killing prison guard Robert Holtman in the process. Swiftly reunited with his wife Margaret—aka "Tiger Lil"—Whittemore recruited a team of ruthless bandits that included Bernard Mortillaro, Pasquale Chicarelli, Joseph Ross, Morris "Shuffles" Goldberg, Anthony Paladino, and the Kramer brothers, Jake and Leon. Together, this crew would embark on an epic crime spree spanning 12 months and two states.

The Whittemore gang logged its first score only four days after Richard's prison break, ambushing a Baltimore payroll shipment of Western Maryland Dairy, shooting the driver and a guard before escaping with $16,034 in cash. Three weeks later, again in Baltimore, the raiders waylaid bank messenger J. Wahl Holtzman in broad daylight, beating him unconscious and stealing the $8,792 he carried.

It was time to shake the heat of Maryland; Whittemore led his crew to the safer anonymity of New York City. There, on April 5, 1925, they robbed the Metro Sacks jewelry store on West 125th Street, collecting an estimated $16,000 in cash and gems. A month later, on May 9, Whittemore's raiders stopped jeweler Jacques Ross on Grand Street in Manhattan, relieving him of diamonds valued at $25,000.

Another change of scene took the gang to Buffalo, New York, on June 1, 1925, where they held up the Levy Jewelry Company and fled with gems worth $50,000. Back in Manhattan, they raided Stanley's jewelry shop on July 16, bagging another $50,000 haul. The estimated take was identical on September 14, 1925, when the gang struck David Brick's jewelry store on Third Avenue. JEWEL THEFT was becoming a habit for the Whittemore gang. On October 5, 1925, they hit Linherr's shop on Sixth Avenue, Manhattan, for an estimated $30,000 in gems. Barely two weeks later, on October 20, the raiders were waiting for John Sandford, a salesman for Laster and Son, when he parked his car on Broadway. The reported daylight take: $25,000 worth of watches and gems.

Residents of Buffalo, New York, were stunned on October 29, 1925, when a band of six gunmen stopped a federal-reserve-bank vehicle, killing the driver and his armed escort, escaping with some $93,000 cash. Richard Whittemore was instantly suspected, but other big-name outlaws of the period—including GEORGE "DUTCH" ANDERSON—were also named in press reports as likely perpetrators of this crime which ultimately went unsolved.

Whether Whittemore pulled the Buffalo stickup or not, he had other problems on his mind in late October 1925. Bootlegger Edwin "Spike" Kenny was shot and wounded at a Baltimore roadhouse on Halloween, naming Whittemore as his assailant in statements to police. The row had started, Kenny said, when Whittemore took umbrage to the bootlegger's adulterous romance with "Tiger Lil."

Whatever the truth of that story, the battling Whittemores and their crew were back together on December 2, 1925, stealing $75,000 worth of diamonds from M. G. Ernest's jewelry store on Columbus Avenue in New York. Two days before Christmas, they struck again, taking Nassau Street jeweler Folmer Prip for an estimated $10,000. A sour note for the holidays sounded on December 26 when gang member Joe Ross was found shot to death near Elizabeth, New Jersey, victim of a still-unsolved gangland slaying.

After resting up for New Year's, the Whittemore gang went back into action on January 11, 1926, stopping Belgian diamond merchants Albert Goudris and Emanuel Veerman on West 48th Street in Manhattan, robbing them of gems worth $175,000. It was the end, but Whittemore and company did not know their time had run out. They spent the next nine weeks celebrating, spending their ill-gotten loot—and, if we believe later reports from federal watchdog Harry Anslinger, injecting themselves with large quantities of heroin. It may have been the drugs that made them sloppy, allowing New York police to round up the eight surviving gang members on March 19, 1926, without a shot being fired.

Buffalo prosecutors got first crack at Richard Whittemore for the October armored car heist, but their case was weak and jurors deadlocked on April 27, 1926, unable to reach a verdict. A mistrial was declared, and charges in the case were subsequently dropped. If Whittemore was optimistic though, relief was premature. New York authorities surrendered him to Maryland on April 30 for trial in the murder of prison guard Robert Holtman. Convicted on May 21, 1926, Whittemore was condemned on June 10 and hanged on August 11, setting a near record for the greased wheels of justice. The remaining members of his gang were convicted on robbery charges and sentenced to prison in New York.

"WILD Bunch," The

Although some historians maintain the "Wild Bunch" sobriquet was initially coined for the DALTON BROTHERS of Missouri, its most common application is in reference to a later band of Western outlaws led by BUTCH CASSIDY, ranging over a half-dozen states in the years between 1896 and 1903. Most acknowledged members of the gang were dead or in prison by December 1901, but isolated survivors hung on to the only trade they knew, Cassidy and veteran sidekick HARRY LONGABAUGH (aka the "Sundance Kid") escaping to South America where they continued riding and robbing until early 1909.

Affable Butch Cassidy was born Robert LeRoy Parker, a son of honest Mormon parents living in Utah. By the early 1890s he had turned to robbery and rustling under the tutelage of the McCARTY GANG. Arrested with Wyoming accomplice Al Haines for stealing horses in June 1893, Butch was acquitted by sympathetic jurors, but the vote went against him at a second trial on identical charges in 1894. He entered Wyoming's state prison on July 15, 1894, proving himself the proverbial model inmate. Governor William Richards pardoned Cassidy on January 19, 1896, releasing him on the condition that he leave the Cowboy State forever.

True to his word, Cassidy struck off for the notorious outlaw sanctuary of BROWN'S HOLE in northwestern Colorado. There, he soon made friends with bandits Ellsworth "Elza" Lay and Bob Meeks. Lay was a native of Massachusetts (or Ohio, accounts vary) who went bad after moving west to Denver in the mid-1880s. Meeks, born in Utah, had worked the wrong side of the law with Lay for several years before Butch Cassidy arrived to take the pair in hand. On August 13, 1896, they robbed a bank at Montpelier, Idaho, escaping to Brown's Hole with $6,165 in currency and $1,000 in gold and silver. Montana train robber Harry Longabaugh soon joined the team, with others following. Charles Kelly, in his 1938 history of the gang, reports that the Wild Bunch earned its nickname "by practical joking and daredevil stunts" performed at local dances rather than for any flamboyant behavior on the trail.

In any case, the gang's notoriety was sufficient after one successful heist to inspire imitators. A "Junior Wild Bunch" was organized at Brown's Hole in the fall of 1896, without advice or approval from Butch Cassidy. Its members were four would-be badmen, aged 18 to 20: George Bain, George Harris, Joe Rolls, and a youngster known only as Shirley. On October

Members of the Wild Bunch included (from left) Henry Longabaugh, aka "The Sundance Kid," William Carver, Ben Kilpatrick, aka "The Tall Texan," Harvey Logan, aka "Kid Curry," and Robert LeRoy Parker, aka "Butch Cassidy." (AP/Wide World Photos)

13, 1896, Bain, Harris, and Shirley attempted to rob a bank at Meeker, Colorado, while Rolls held their horses nearby. A shootout erupted in the street, leaving all three fledgling bandits dead, while Rolls alone escaped to tell the tale. Cassidy's raiders announced their intent to "smoke up" the town in revenge, but they never made good on the threat.

Around the same time, on October 18, 1896, Cassidy suffered one of his rare failures when he planned to steal a mining payroll from the Union Pacific Railroad at Rock Springs, Wyoming. The Wild Bunch often bribed railroad employees for information on rich shipments, but the technique backfired this time when a Union Pacific agent learned of the impending robbery. Thinking fast, he sent the payroll by train under heavy guard and then drove his empty buckboard along the scheduled route of travel. Bandits were waiting to stop him, but they rode off cursing, empty handed, after searching the agent's carriage.

The gang had better luck on April 21, 1897. Cassidy and Elza Lay stole a payroll from the Denver and Rio Grande Railroad at Castle Gate, Utah, escaping with $8,700 in gold. They celebrated their haul at ROBBERS' ROOST and then settled down to plan their next outing. On June 15, 1897, two masked bandits robbed the post office at Fort Bridger, Colorado, escaping with a meager $123. Bob Meeks was in town at the time, coincidentally or otherwise, and, jailed on suspicion, he soon was identified in custody as one of the Montpelier bank robbers. Convicted in Idaho on September 3,

1897, Meeks drew the maximum 32-year sentence, but he would not remain long in prison. Eating soap to feign illness, he soon escaped from the penitentiary hospital but broke his leg in the attempt. The leg was amputated, and Meeks was later released, an ex-outlaw unable to keep up with the game.

By summer 1897, Wild Bunch members had established a veritable "Outlaw Trail" for themselves, stretching from Robbers' Roost in Utah, northward to Brown's Hole, and central to Wyoming's notorious "HOLE-IN-THE-WALL." Outlaws who joined the team at Hole-in-the-Wall included George "Flat Nose" Curry, David Lant, Patrick "Swede" Johnson, Harry Tracy (dubbed "the JOHN DILLINGER of his time" by one historian), and Bob Lee and his cousins, the three Logan brothers: Harvey, Henry, and Lonny. Canadian native Curry had survived the collapse of Nate Champion's "Red Sash Gang" to lead his own crew of rustlers, operating from a ranch in Johnson County. Tracy and Lant first met in Utah's state prison, escaping together on October 8, 1897, with a hand-carved wooden pistol wrapped in tinfoil. Johnson hailed from Missouri, that "MOTHER OF OUTLAWS" which produced so many famous bandits following the Civil War. Lee and the Logans were Kentucky born and bred. To confuse matters, Harvey and Lonny Logan often used the Curry surname as an alias, though they bore no familial relationship to "Flat Nose" George.

On March 1, 1898, Swede Johnson shot and killed Brown's Hole resident Willie Strang after Strang roused Johnson from sleep with a pan of cold water. News of the murder quickly spread, and a posse set out to nab Johnson that same afternoon. A pitched battle erupted as the posse approached Brown's Hole, leader Valentine Hoy blasted dead from his saddle, but the bandits were outnumbered, with Johnson, Dave Lant, and Harry Tracy captured. All were charged with murder, Lant and Tracy briefly fleeing custody on March 24 and confined to a hastily constructed metal "tank" on recapture. Transferred to Aspen for trial, the duo escaped once more after Tracy whittled another toy pistol. Swede Johnson escaped conviction at his first murder trial and spent two years in jail before a second jury convicted him on reduced charges, as an accomplice. He spent two years in state prison and apparently went straight upon release.

Publicity surrounding the Brown's Hole murders and their aftermath prompted calls for action against what the Denver *News* called "the greatest organized band of thieves and murderers that ever rendezvoused in the west." Wyoming Governor W. A. Richards and Utah Governor Heber Wells issued a joint statement on March 4, calling for "arrest and extermination" of the "Wild Bunch." Colorado's governor joined the chorus 10 days later, but the campaign was aborted in April when the United States declared war on Spain. Unverified reports place several "Wild Bunch" members in the Philippines on active duty during the Spanish-American War, but because they were not named, the stories carry little weight.

On March 5, 1899, a posse seeking rustlers struck at Robbers' Roost. Another pitched battle was fought, but law enforcers came up empty handed when the smoke cleared, their quarry having fled in the confusion. Three months later, on June 2, six bandits robbed a train between LeRoy and Wilcox, Wyoming, 100 miles south of Casper. They demolished the express car with dynamite while cracking the safe, filling their sacks with $30,000 in unsigned bank notes. Identified members of the raiding party included Harvey Logan, Elza Lay, and Sam Ketchum (brother of outlaw Tom ["Black Jack"] Ketchum).

Lay, Logan, and Ketchum were back in action on July 11, 1899, robbing a train near Folsom, New Mexico. A posse from Trinidad, Colorado, surprised the gang in camp at Turkey Creek on the afternoon of July 16. Elza Lay, wounded repeatedly, still managed to kill Hernando County Sheriff Edward Farr. Logan killed posse member H. N. Love and wounded another; Ketchum was mortally wounded. Logan and Lay escaped after 45 minutes, but Ketchum could not mount his horse and was left to the posse. He died of blood poisoning on July 24 at Santa Fe. Enraged, brother Tom tried to rob another train near the same spot on August 16, 1899, but his single-handed effort was disastrous. Wounded and captured the following day, "Black Jack" Ketchum lost an arm before trial on murder charges and was subsequently condemned. At his hanging, on April 26, 1901, he shouted, "Let her go!" and was decapitated by the noose.

Harvey Logan and Elza Lay were running for their lives, meanwhile. On August 22, 1899, an Eddy County rancher summoned law officers with reports of two suspicious strangers lurking on his property. Elza Lay suffered three more wounds in the resultant skirmish and wounded Deputy Rufus Thomas before he was captured; his companion, believed to be Logan, escaped unseen by the posse. Charged as "William McGinnis" with Sheriff Farr's murder, Lay was convicted and sentenced to life imprisonment on October 10, 1899. Lay's sentence was commuted in July 1905 as a reward for helping guards during a 1900 prison riot, and he was released in January 1906. Lay spent the rest of his life as "McGinnis," a respectable saloon owner, and died on November 10, 1934.

While Elza Lay was facing trial in Colorado, Butch Cassidy went to Utah in search of a pardon, selecting prominent judge Orlando Powers as his go-between with Governor Wells. The governor rejected Butch's plea, and Cassidy went back to raiding with a gang of fluid membership that now included outlaws Bill Carver and the Kilpatrick brothers, George and Ben (aka "The Tall Texan"). Before they could make a new score, though, law enforcers whittled down the outfit's old breed. Lonny Logan went home to Missouri in January 1900, and detectives trailed him there, killing him in a 25-minute firefight on February 28. Around the same time, cousin Bob Lee was convicted on various charges and sent to Wyoming's state prison. George Curry, passing his time between heists as a rustler, was killed by a posse near Green River, Utah, on April 17, 1900. A vengeful Harvey Logan led four other gunmen from his Arizona hideout to stalk the leaders of the posse that killed "Flat Nose" George. On May 27, 1900, they ambushed Moab County Sheriff Jesse Tyler and a companion, Sam Jenkins, killing both men in a fusillade of gunfire. Tod Carver was arraigned for the double murder on August 20, 1900, but he broke out of jail prior to trial.

Nine days after Carver's arraignment, on August 29, the Wild Bunch robbed a train at Tipton, Wyoming. Cassidy, Longabaugh, and Harvey Logan were identified, among the five who stopped the train. Controversy prevails over the size of their score. An initial report pegged the haul at $55,000, drastically scaled back a few days later by an "official" report that only $50.40 had been stolen; a third account, published years later, claimed the gang escaped with $40,000.

The gang's next documented raid occurred at noon on September 19, 1900, when Cassidy, Longabaugh, and Bill Carver tapped a bank at Winnemucca, Nevada, for $32,640. They escaped in a flurry of gunshots from neighborhood merchants and shook off a posse, riding to Fort Worth, Texas, for a rendezvous with Ben Kilpatrick and Harvey Logan. The five posed together for a formal photograph, soon noticed by WELLS FARGO detective FRED DODGE as he passed the photographer's shop. By the time a posse gathered, the gang had ridden on to San Antonio and Dodge had missed his chance. The gang lingered in Texas until April 1901, scattering after April 2 when Bill Carver was recognized and killed by Sheriff Ed Bryant at Sonora.

The last major holdup committed by Wild Bunch members as a unit was the robbery of a train near Wagner, Montana, on July 3, 1901. Identified members of the raiding party included Cassidy, Longabaugh, Harvey Logan, and Texas recruit Camilla Hanks, a crony of Bill Carver and the Kilpatrick brothers. Overzealous with their dynamite as usual, the gang destroyed an express car while trying to crack the safe, but they still salvaged $65,000 in currency.

It was the outfit's last hurrah. Camilla Hanks was nearly captured on October 26, 1901, after passing some of the Wagner loot in Nashville, Tennessee. He fled to San Antonio and there spent more of the money, thus attracting law officers who cornered and killed him on April 16, 1902. Ben Kilpatrick was arrested with $7,000 of the Wagner haul on November 8, 1901, in Knoxville, Tennessee. He confessed 10 days later and received a 15-year prison term on December 12. Two days after that sentence was handed down, Harvey Logan shot two policemen in a Knoxville billiards parlor. Captured on June 15, he overpowered two jailers and used the sheriff's horse to escape 12 days later. The absolute lack of pursuit prompted PINKERTON detectives to suggest that local law officers had collaborated with Logan in the jailbreak.

The heat was too much for Butch Cassidy. On February 1, 1902, he rendezvoused in New York City with Harry Longabaugh and Longabaugh's girlfriend, 27-year-old Etta Place. They sailed for Buenos Aires on February 20 and arrived sometime in March, adopting the lifestyle of prosperous ranchers for the next few years. Back home, Harvey Logan was finally captured and convicted of the Wagner train robbery on November 29, 1902, but he soon staged another escape and fled to Colorado where he led the gang that stopped a train near Parachute on July 7, 1903. Disappointed by a near-empty safe, the gang retreated to Glenwood Springs where they were overtaken by a posse. An overnight battle ensued,

Logan finally shooting himself in the head to avoid yet another arrest.

Further west, Wild Bunch fugitive Harry Tracy had made his way to Portland, Oregon, after his 1898 flight from Colorado, teamed up there with outlaw Dave Merrill for a series of holdups and murders. Finally arrested, Tracy and Merrill shot their way out of jail but were soon recaptured, convicted on various charges, and confined to the state penitentiary. There, they staged another bloody break, killing three guards and wounding a fourth before they made good their escape. Tracy married Merrill's sister but later strangled Merrill to death after reading a newspaper's claim that Merrill had informed on him in an effort to win leniency for himself. Traveling along the Washington coast in 1902, Tracy hijacked a fishing boat and sailed to Seattle. Pursued by a local posse, he killed one manhunter and wounded three more before vanishing into the wilderness. Finally cornered near Davenport, Washington, on August 5, 1902, Tracy shot himself to avoid capture.

The straight life paled for Butch Cassidy and Harry Longabaugh after three or four years in Argentina. One account blames them for the February 1905 robbery of a bank in Río Gallegos, Argentina, while others maintain that Butch and Sundance refrained from further banditry until March 1906 when they stole $20,000 from a San Luis bank and killed the banker. They scored another $20,000 at Bahía Blanca a few months later and then robbed a payroll train at Eucalyptus, Bolivia. The bandits stole $10,000 from a Rio Gallegos bank on December 7, 1907, and then rebounded on December 20 to rob a store and kill its manager in Arroyo Pescado. Wild Bunch historian Charles Kelly cites these holdups as "only a few of the many robberies" Butch and Sundance pulled in South America, but because no more are specified, the claim remains impossible to judge. Years after the fact, reports claimed that Cassidy and Longabaugh were trapped and killed by soldiers at San Vincente, Bolivia, in early 1909, but rumors persist that Butch returned to the United States and lived in Washington under an alias until his death from natural causes in 1937.

"Tall Texan" Ben Kilpatrick was the last Wild Bunch member to be killed in action. Riding with sidekick Ole Buck, Kilpatrick tried to rob a train at Sanderson, Texas, on March 13, 1912. The express messenger had no gun, but he was still determined to protect his shipment. Assaulting Kilpatrick with an ice mallet, he bludgeoned the outlaw to death, then seized Kilpatrick's six-gun, and killed Ole Buck before the startled robber could defend himself.

Sixty years after the alleged flame-out in Bolivia, Butch Cassidy and his gang enjoyed a sudden resurgence of popularity in the United States. Two feature films were released in 1969, based wholly or in part on the gang's exploits. *Butch Cassidy and the Sundance Kid,* starring Paul Newman and Robert Redford in the title roles, won an Academy Award for best screenplay by playing down the outfit's violence; Sam Peckinpah's *The Wild Bunch* took a different tack, presenting the screen's first "splatter" Western with a tale of aging badmen on the Mexican border in 1913. Screenwriters clearly had Butch and Sundance in mind a year later when they produced a television pilot titled *Alias Smith and Jones,* starring Peter Duel as Hannibal Heyes (aka "Joshua Smith") and Ben Murphy as Jed "Kid" Curry (aka "Thaddeus Jones"). The pilot was popular enough to spawn a series of the same title, broadcast for three seasons from 1971 to 1973. The 1979 production of *Butch and Sundance: The Early Days* offered a prequel to the 1969 original with Tom Berenger as Butch Cassidy and William Katt as Harry Longabaugh.

WILLIAMS, Donald Keith

A native of Lincoln, Nebraska, Don Williams logged his first arrest in 1952 for larceny. Convicted of burglary in Missouri in 1961, he rolled on from there to collect a prison sentence for armed robbery in Oklahoma. Paroled in 1968 on that conviction, he was subsequently hauled back to prison as a parole violator. Between 1983 and 1986 Williams was named as the bandit in 34 bank robberies, netting more than $100,000 from raids in California, Colorado, Illinois, Minnesota, Oregon, and Washington. Fifteen of those holdups occurred in Los Angeles, where Williams was dubbed the "Veil Bandit" after the cloth veil he wore suspended from a baseball cap to hide his face. (The veil concealed a distinctive muscular condition that caused Donald's right eye to squint.) He also sported body armor on occasion to deflect police bullets, and he sometimes wore radio earphones, as if tuning in to local law enforcement bulletins.

Named as a federal fugitive on bank-robbery charges in May 1984, Williams was elevated to the FBI's "Ten Most Wanted" list on August 8, 1985. Twelve days later, an alert citizen recognized published photographs and directed G-men to the fugitive's Mar Vista apartment in West Los Angeles. Three pistols were seized in the raid, but Williams made no effort to resist arrest. At age 57, facing an accumulated 950 years in prison on various charges, his long run was finally over.

WILLIAMS, George Benjamin

A native of Malheur County, Oregon, George Williams spent most of his adult life in various prisons, confined for robbing banks. It was a specialty of sorts, with criminal convictions dating back to 1931, and Williams could not seem to get the hang of going straight. In December 1965 he set something of a record, looting $19,534 from the same Newcastle, California, bank that he had previously robbed in 1946. On March 18, 1968, his name was added to the FBI's "Ten Most Wanted" list.

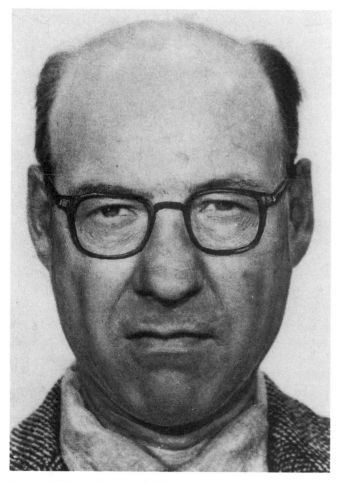

George Williams's bank-robbing career spanned four decades, from the 1930s to 1960s. (FBI)

Exactly two months later, on May 18, a man's skeletal remains were discovered in Pershing County, Nevada, near Lovelock. Unable to identify the bones, Lovelock's sheriff sent them off to Washington for examination by FBI forensic experts. On June 19 comparison of dental charts and other features identified the corpse as that of George Williams, and his file was permanently closed. No cause of death was indicated in published reports of the case.

WOMEN Bandits

Females have traditionally been labeled (by males) as the "weaker" or "gentler" sex, and although many modern women find such terms offensive, the designations are borne out to some extent in American crime statistics. According to the FBI's *Uniform Crime Reports* for 1999 (the latest year with complete statistics available at this writing), male offenders accounted for 78 percent of all American arrests; they committed 90 percent of all murders and robberies, 83 percent of violent crimes overall, and 70 percent of all property crimes reported. Bearing in mind that female felons—always a minority—are more common now than in past generations, notorious women bandits throughout history deserve special mention for their emergence in a field dominated by armed and dangerous men.

The earliest female bandits were probably PIRATES, carving a niche for themselves with cutlass and dagger among men who typically regarded all women as sex objects or potential hostages for ransom. The first woman pirate on record was Alwilda, daughter of a Scandinavian king in the fifth century A.D. who fled an arranged marriage by donning men's clothes and shipping out to sea with a pirate crew, afterward proving herself ruthless enough to replace the ship's captain when he was slain in battle. According to legend, Alwilda led her crew so ably in the Baltic Sea that a special crew was dispatched to hunt her down, ironically commanded by the same Prince Alf of Denmark whom she earlier refused to marry. Captured by Alf after a fierce battle in Gulf of Finland, Alwilda reportedly changed her mind in custody and wed her prince, thus becoming the queen of Denmark.

More substantially documented is the tale of Grace O'Malley, born on the west coast of Ireland around 1530. Twice married and widowed after shipping out with pirates in her teens, O'Malley operated from Rockfleet Castle in County Mayo between 1566 and 1603. At one point she com-

325

manded three galleys and 200 fighting men, offering her services to England's Queen Elizabeth as a mercenary privateer. In the early 1570s O'Malley's raids terrorized Galway merchants to the point that Governor Edward Fitton sent a special expedition to besiege Rockfleet Castle in March 1574. The attackers were repulsed, but O'Malley was captured in 1577 and jailed for 18 months by a judge who called her "a great spoiler, and chief commander and director of thieves and murderers at sea to spoil this province." Negotiations with the British Crown secured her release from prison and ensured a royal title for O'Malley's son upon her death in 1603.

Two of the most notorious women pirates were MARY READ and ANN BONNY, who sailed and fought throughout the Caribbean with Captain John "Calico Jack" Rackham in the early 18th century. Captured with the rest of Rackham's crew in October 1720, Read and Bonny were condemned for murder but escaped the gallows by special dispensation when both were found to be pregnant. A century later, on the South China Sea, widowed Ching Yih Saou took command of her late husband's pirate fleet, ultimately grown to include 800 large junks and 1,000 smaller boats, with an estimated fighting force of 70,000 to 80,000 pirates. After three years of unrestricted raiding, Ching Yih Sao negotiated a treaty with Chinese authorities in April 1810, arranging to keep most of her loot while her lover, pirate Chang Pao, was granted formal military rank and permitted to keep his private fleet of 20 junks. In return for those concessions, Ching Yih Sao surrendered 226 ships and 17,318 pirates (126 of whom were executed and 211 banished). She retired to Canton thereafter and ran a gambling house until her death in 1844 at age 69.

The American West produced a handful of women bandits, with Belle Starr undoubtedly the most notorious. Born Myra Belle Shirley in pre–Civil War Missouri and immortalized by author Burton Rascoe in his book *Belle Starr, "The Bandit Queen"* (1941), she in fact never led a gang or participated in a holdup, restricting her activities to some small-time rustling and conjugal liaisons with various noteworthy badmen. Belle's first lover was Missouri bandit Cole YOUNGER, although he steadfastly denied paternity of the illegitimate daughter whom Belle named Pearl Younger (later a prostitute in Arkansas). Cole was replaced in Myra's bed by Jim Reed, another associate of JESSE JAMES, who was killed by lawmen in August 1874. Bandit Sam Starr "married" Belle

without benefit of clergy in 1880, but she still entertained other lovers. Two of them, John Middleton (a cousin of Jim Reed) and a thief called Blue Duck, were murdered by Sam Starr in May 1885 and July 1886, respectively. Starr lost his last gunfight in December 1886, leaving Belle free to spend time with Choctaw bandit Jack Spaniard (hanged for murder in August 1889), Cherokee outlaw Jim July (killed resisting arrest in January 1890), and Creek Indian Jim French (shot while robbing a store in February 1895). Belle herself was shot and killed from ambush by persons unknown while riding horseback near her home at Younger's Bend, Arkansas, on February 3, 1889. The assassin made sure of his work by firing a second shotgun blast into her face as she lay dying on the ground.

Another "bandit queen," Ann Bassett, was born in 1875 at BROWN'S HOLE, an outlaw refuge on the Wyoming-Colorado border. At age seven she reportedly told playmates, "I don't want to be a lady; I want to be a cowboy." To that end, "Queen Ann" would later share the bed of "WILD BUNCH" outlaw Elza Lay, opening her home to other members of the gang and helping them conceal their loot between holdups. Arrested on a rustling charge in 1911, Bassett postponed her trial for two years with various legal maneuvers and was finally acquitted in 1913. Bassett apparently went straight after that episode and died a more-or-less respectable old maid at Leeds, Utah, in May 1956.

Less is known about the life and criminal career of another Wild Bunch woman, Etta Place. Reports filed by the PINKERTON DETECTIVE AGENCY in 1902 described her as 27 years old, and although some accounts call Place a school teacher, details of her background are virtually nonexistent. As the unmarried lover of bandit HARRY LONGABAUGH, aka "The Sundance Kid," Place accompanied BUTCH CASSIDY when he and Longabaugh fled the United States for South American in February 1902. Described as an active accomplice in several armed robberies between 1906 and 1908, she disappeared from public records before Butch and Sundance fought their reported last battle with Bolivian troops in early 1909. As with her early life, no details of her fate are known today. Actress Katherine Ross twice portrayed Place, in *Butch Cassidy and the Sundance Kid* (1969) and teamed with Pancho Villa in *Wanted: The Sundance Woman* (1976).

The "dry" 1920s witnessed a nationwide crime wave in America, but the decade produced only two noteworthy women bandits, and one of those remains anonymous today. In February 1924 New York police commanders assigned 500 detectives to scour Manhattan and surrounding boroughs a female robber dubbed the "Bob-Haired Bandit," but she managed to avoid arrest. Less fortunate was Margaret "Tiger Lil" Whittemore, married (though not always faithful) to the boss of the infamous WHITTEMORE GANG. The gang robbed numerous jewelers between February 1925 and January 1926, but it was murder that finally sent Richard Whittemore to the gallows, for gunning down one of "Tiger Lil's" extramarital lovers in October 1925. Margaret was captured with the rest of the crew in March 1926 and sentenced to a prison term; husband Richard was hanged on August 11, 1926.

Bank robbery became a form of public entertainment in the Great Depression, with bandits such as JOHN DILLINGER and GEORGE "BABY FACE" NELSON claiming flamboyant headlines from coast to coast. The heist game was still dominated by men, but female bandits were more prominent than usual in the 1930s. Two who rated more publicity than all the rest combined were Texas native BONNIE PARKER and Missouri's Arizona Donnie Clark—better known as "Ma" Barker, alleged brains and leader of the ruthless BARKER GANG.

Bonnie Parker's claim to fame was her association with CLYDE BARROW, a homicidal small-timer who shot his way to notoriety in a series of battles with law enforcers in four states. The Barrow gang rarely scored more than $1,000 from any single job, but with a dozen murders and several jailbreaks to their credit, they ranked as a bona-fide sensation wherever they roamed, from Texas northward to Missouri and beyond. Bonnie herself contributed to the publicity, abandoning various poems in gang hideouts, posing for snapshots—complete with weapons and a cigar clenched in her teeth—that graced the front pages of newspapers across the country.

Ma Barker, by contrast, may have known little or nothing about the criminal activities of her sons and their quick-trigger accomplices. Killed by FBI agents in January 1935 with son Fred, she was posthumously named as the criminal mastermind of the Barker gang, responsible for numerous holdups and murders, along with two high-profile kidnappings that netted the gang $300,000 ransom. J. EDGAR HOOVER took the lead in casting Arizona Barker as a cold-blooded matriarch who schooled her sons in larceny and homicide, but proof of her role as a criminal genius remains nonexistent. Gang member ALVIN KARPIS insisted, years later, that Ma took no part in planning the gang's holdups, suggesting that Hoover and his publicists fabricated the legend in an effort to excuse their killing of an elderly woman. Subsequent efforts by others to portray Ma Barker as a sadistic lesbian serial killer of young women, in addition to her alleged role as America's premier bank robber, are patently absurd.

The Depression's next most notorious woman was probably Kathryn Kelly, alleged kidnapper and full-time publicist for husband GEORGE "MACHINE GUN" KELLY. Another product (some say victim) of the FBI's publicity machine, Kathryn allegedly bought Kelly his first Tommy gun, insisted that he practice with it to become proficient, and coined his fearsome nickname herself while handing out .45-caliber cartridges to friends as souvenirs of those shooting sessions. George Kelly robbed banks with veteran bandits including HARVEY BAILEY and WILBUR UNDERHILL, but FBI spokesmen insist to this day that wife Kathryn planned the 1933 ransom kidnapping of Oklahoma oil man Charles Urschel. When the kidnap gang was rounded up, Kathryn and her mother, Ora Shannon, received life sentences with the rest, but persuasive evidence suggests they may have been framed by overzealous G-men. When their convictions were overturned in 1959, the FBI refused to provide any evidence for retrial, thus permitting both women to go free.

Other women bandits of the Depression era were unequivocally guilty as charged. Eleanor Jarman, aka "The Blond Tigress," was named by Chicago police as the brains behind a gang that pulled 48 holdups in the early 1930s. Described as "a beautiful but vicious animal" who slugged her victims with a blackjack, Jarman was convicted of murder in August 1933 and sentenced to 199 years in prison, but she escaped in 1940 and was never recaptured. Another female escape artist, "Kissing Bandit" EDNA MURRAY was nicknamed "Rabbits" following her third escape from Missouri's women's prison, where she was serving a 25-year term for highway robbery. With lover VOLNEY DAVIS, Murray was sent back to prison in 1935 for participation in one of the Barker gang's kidnappings. VIVIAN CHASE continued the family tradition of larceny after her bank robber husband was killed on the job in 1926; acquitted of a Kansas heist two years later, she was finally convicted of another bank job in 1932 and was murdered by Kansas City mob associates after her escape from prison. STELLA

"SURE SHOT" DICKSON helped husband Bennie rob a South Dakota bank on the eve of her 16th birthday in August 1938. Bennie was killed by FBI agents in April 1939; Stella was sentenced to 10 years in prison.

The 1970s saw a shift to political activism by women bandits, robbing (and sometimes killing) in the name of revolution. Among the first to make headlines were KATHERINE POWER and SUSAN SAXE, added to the FBI's "Ten Most Wanted" list in October 1970 after a lethal bank holdup in Boston. Across the Atlantic, radical women played a leading role in Germany's RED ARMY FACTION (RAF), ranked as one of Europe's most active TERRORIST groups of the tumultuous decade. Better known in media reports as the Baader-Meinhof Gang, the group took its popular name from co-leaders Andreas Baader and Ulrike Meinhof, ably assisted by another female leftist, Gudrun Ensslin. Captured in 1972 and finally convicted after a long trial in 1975, the RAF's leaders committed suicide in October 1977 after an airplane hijacking failed to win their release from confinement. In the United States, women radicals also played an active role in holdups perpetrated by the MAY 19TH COMMUNIST MOVEMENT, but America's strangest radical robbers called themselves the SYMBIONESE LIBERATION ARMY (SLA). Led by a black ex-convict but made up predominantly of young white women, the SLA kidnapped newspaper heiress Patricia Hearst in 1974 and apparently converted her to their cause. Six members died in a 1975 shootout with Los Angeles police, but Hearst and others survived to stand trial and serve prison terms for bank robbery.

A unique case in modern times is that of India's "Bandit Queen" Phoolan Devi, a bona-fide SOCIAL BANDIT whose crimes transcended simple larceny to form the springboard for a successful political career. The daughter of a low-caste family, Devi was forced into marriage by her parents at age 11 later fleeing her abusive husband to join a gang of rural outlaws. Gang-raped by men from the village of Behmai in 1981, she returned with armed cohorts and massacred 22 of Behmai's upper-caste residents in an apparent act of vengeance. Devi remained at large until 1983 when she surrendered to authorities and was sentenced to prison. Paroled in 1994, she joined the Samajwadi Party in Uttar Pradesh and

India's notorious "Bandit Queen" Phoolan Devi, seen here in 1994, earned her name for allegedly murdering 20 upper-caste men to avenge her rape. (AP/Wide World Photos)

collaborated with Oscar-nominated film director Shekhar Kapur on a movie of her life entitled *Bandit Queen*. She was elected to India's parliament in 1995 with broad public support from her district. Devi lost her parliamentary seat in 1998 but rallied for a comeback the following year. On July 25, 2001, she was ambushed and shot to death outside her New Delhi home by gunmen who fled in a motorized rickshaw. Devi's supporters rioted in the wake of her assassination, while suspect Sher Singh Rana confessed to her murder, calling himself a high-caste avenger of the Behmai massacre. Three alleged accomplices to the murder surrendered on July 30. Mourners called Devi's life a "triumph of the human spirit," and headlines proclaimed "A Queen Is Dead."

YOUNG, Jerry Lynn

Alabama-born in October 1942, Jerry Young joined the marines in February 1961, but he found military discipline too rigorous. Convicted of robbing a Richlands, North Carolina, bank of $4,359, he received a dishonorable discharge in March 1962. The rap also carried a six-year federal prison sentence, but Young was paroled in August 1963. He was discharged as a free man on March 1, 1967, upon successful completion of his parole.

The next day, Young raided a bank in Asheville, North Carolina, brandishing a shotgun as he looted the cages of $13,671 in cash. Threatening to kill any pursuers, he fled in a stolen car, firing pistol shots at an employee who briefly gave chase. On April 14 he struck again, robbing a bank in Olive Branch, Mississippi, of $14,919. Identified from photographs, Young was declared a federal fugitive on bank-robbery charges, and his name was added to the FBI's "Ten Most Wanted" list on May 12, 1967.

One month later, on June 15, FBI agents were waiting when Young and accomplice William Webb left their room at an Akron, Ohio, motel. Mindful of Young's boast that he would "never be taken alive," G-men were ready when he reached for a pistol. Confronted with superior firepower, he swiftly reconsidered and surrendered without further incident. Conviction on outstanding charges subsequently sent Young back to federal prison.

Bandit Jerry Young began to rob banks while still a teenage member of the U.S. Marine Corps. (FBI)

YOUNGER Brothers

Natives of Missouri, the outlaw Younger brothers were four of 14 children born to affluent parents before the American Civil War; the entire brood included eight sons and six daughters. Clan patriarch Henry Washington Younger was a county magistrate, the holder of several U.S. mail contracts, and one of Missouri's richest planters, with several farms held in his name. He was also a pro-Southern slave owner, but he opposed secession from the Union until violence from "Bleeding Kansas" spilled over onto his own home turf. The sons who later turned to banditry included Thomas Coleman "Cole" Younger, born in 1844; Jim Younger, born in 1848; John Younger, born in 1851; and Bob Younger, the baby of the family, born in 1853.

Trouble began for the Younger family in autumn 1860 when Kansas "Jayhawker" guerrillas raided their homestead, stealing 40 horses and four wagons valued at $4,000. That crime was still unavenged on April 13, 1861, the night after Fort Sumter was shelled by Confederate artillery, when Cole Younger quarreled with a leader of the Kansas irregulars—one Irwin Walley—at a local dance. Bystanders separated the men, but Cole's opponent later led a lynching party to the Younger farm in search of him. The mob was disappointed because Cole had already left home to join WILLIAM CLARKE QUANTRILL's guerrillas, raiding into Kansas with first cousins FRANK and JESSE JAMES. Before year's end, 10-year-old John Younger reportedly helped brother Jim kill four Union soldiers in Clay County. Union forces were suspected on July 20, 1862, when Henry Younger was ambushed and murdered near Harrisonville, $500 stolen from his corpse. (The killers missed another $2,200 hidden in a money belt.) Cole blamed his old enemy Irwin Walley for the murder but later explained his failure to retaliate in a letter written from prison:

In relation to Walley I will say: if I were what the world paints me, there could be no excuse except cowardice for my neglect to kill him. During the war I did everything in my power to get hold of him, but failed. . . . When I returned home from the war . . . I could have killed Walley nearly any time, but only by assassination—slipping up to his house and shooting him through a window. Some people might have perpetrated such a deed, but I could not pollute my soul with such a crime. . . . I could not shoot him like a dog, especially when I knew he had a wife and children.

Cole Younger was among the earliest recruits for Quantrill's raiders and one of the band's fiercest warriors, though he later resigned in disgust at Quantrill's increasingly brutal methods. Years later, in his autobiography, Cole described the change that made him reconsider his allegiance to Quantrill:

Where at first there was only killing in ordinary battle, there became to be no quarter shown. The wounded of the enemy next felt the might of this individual vengeance, acting through a community of bitter memories, and from every stricken field there began, by and by, to come up the substance of this awful bulletin: Dead, such and such a number—wounded, none.

While it lasted, though, Cole Younger threw himself into the guerrilla war effort with total commitment. Once, it was claimed, he disguised himself as an old woman to spy on Union troops at Independence, Missouri—riding sidesaddle with a basket of fresh produce—but his six-feet height and 170 pounds soon betrayed him, sparking a gunfight in which he killed one Yankee before escaping under fire. Cole was present on August 21, 1863, when Quantrill's band sacked Lawrence, Kansas, leaving 185 men and boys dead in the ruins, but reports that place 10-year-old brother Bob at his side are certainly erroneous. The Younger home in Clay County was among those evacuated and burned by Union forces in retaliation for the Lawrence massacre, Bersheba Younger departing with four children and two black servants for the relative safety of Texas.

The Confederate surrender at Appomattox left Dixie in turmoil. Missouri had never left the Union, but tempers ran high on both sides of the slavery question, and wartime damage in the "burned-over district" adjoining the Kansas state line was as bad as anyplace below the Mason-Dixon Line. Many of Quantrill's guerrillas had entered the war to settle private scores, and their blood debts did not disappear with the cease-fire. Others had learned a habit of casual violence that proved impossible to break. John Younger, barely 15 years old, shot and killed a man who slapped him with a fish in 1866; jurors agreed with him that gunning down an unarmed man was "self-defense" and set him free. Brothers Cole and Jim, meanwhile, were reunited with their wartime cronies in a veritable band of brothers—Frank and Jesse James, Ed and Clell Miller, Wood and Clarence Hite, George and Oliver Shepherd, with others—to pick up where their wartime raiding had left off.

The goal this time was profit, though they sometimes dressed it up in politics or seized an opportunity to kill old foes encountered by chance. The gang robbed its first bank at Liberty, Missouri, on February 14, 1866, escaping with $15,000 in gold coins, some currency and silver, plus $45,000 in bonds that proved worthless. Riding out of town, one of the gunmen casually murdered an unarmed college student, 19-year-old George Wymore (or Wynmore). Cole and Jim Younger were identified as members of the 10-man raiding party.

Spring found Cole Younger in Texas, visiting his mother near Sycene. One of Bersheba Younger's neighbors was another transplanted Missourian, saloonkeeper John Shirley, whose teenage daughter Myra caught Cole's eye. The fact of their romance is indisputable, but its outcome remains controversial. Myra Belle Shirley later named her first illegitimate child Pearl Younger, insisting the girl was Cole's daughter, going so far as to name her later homestead in Arkansas Younger's Bend. Cole, for his part, denied paternity for the rest of his life and apparently shunned further contact with the woman who entered Western history as "Queen of the Bandits" Belle Starr.

The James-Younger gang was back in action on October 30, 1866, stealing $2,000 from a bank at Lexington, Missouri. Seven months later, on May 23, 1867, they hit a Richmond, Missouri, bank for $4,000 in gold. Townspeople opened fire as they fled, but guerrilla training served the bandits well, enabling them to kill Richmond's mayor, jailer B. G. Griffin, and Griffin's 15-year-old son as they rode out of town. Warrants were issued for seven suspects in that case, with several arrested and later convicted, but indictments overlooked the James and Younger brothers.

A year after the Richmond holdup, on May 20, 1868, Jesse James and Cole Younger entered a bank at Russellville, Kentucky, seeking change for a $50 bill. Informed the bill was counterfeit, they cheerfully agreed and drew their pistols, demanding real cash in exchange. James and Younger were bagging their loot—$14,000 in gold, silver, and currency—when a cashier ran for daylight, raising the alarm despite a parting bullet wound. Outside, as vigilantes gathered, one of the outlaws wounded a second man to discourage the rest and they fled without pursuit. It was a good score but a costly one as PINKERTON detectives were employed for the first time to track down the gang.

Known for long lulls between holdups, the James-Younger gang pulled its next verified job on December 7, 1869, when Jesse, Frank, and Cole Younger robbed a bank at Gallatin, Missouri. The take was a disappointing $700, and Jesse executed cashier John Sheets, a former Union officer, before the bandits fled in a hail of vigilante gunfire. On June 3, 1871, the gang did better, lifting $45,000 from a bank at Corydon, Iowa. Ten months later, on April 29, 1872, they scored a pitiful $200 from a bank at Columbia, Kentucky, killing cashier R. A. C. Martin in the process. Bob Younger entered the scene that year, joining the James brothers on September 26 to steal $10,000 from the Kansas City fairgrounds. A bank at Sainte Genevieve, Missouri, was the target on May 23, 1873. Two months later, on July 21, the gang pulled its first TRAIN ROBBERY, derailing a passenger train east of Council Bluffs, Iowa, and stealing $7,000 from the passengers. Fleeing, they left engineer John Rafferty scalded to death in the ruins of his locomotive and the fireman clinging to life with painful burns.

No target was too large or small for the James-Younger gang. On January 15, 1874, they stopped a stagecoach near Malvern, Arkansas, and robbed the passengers of pocket change. Two weeks later they invaded Gads Hill, Missouri, and commandeered the railroad depot, robbing the inbound train of some $2,000, leaving behind a handwritten press release that described their latest exploit as "The Most Daring Train Robbery on Record!"

It was too much for the Pinkerton Detective Agency. Spies were dispatched to Missouri in the guise of livestock buyers, infiltrating bandit territory in the Ozark Mountains. One of the agents, John Whicher, was ambushed and killed by persons unknown on March 15, 1874, while en route from Kearney, Missouri, to the homestead occupied by Jesse James's mother. One day later, detectives Louis Lull and James Wright, led by ex-lawman E. B. Daniels, met Jim and John Younger on a backwoods road in St. Clair County. When the gunsmoke cleared, Daniels and John Younger were dead and Lull mortally wounded. James Wright and Jim Younger escaped from the battle unscathed.

Twenty months passed before the gang's next verified outing, stealing $60,000 worth of cash and valuables from passengers aboard a train at Muncie, Kansas, on December 13, 1875. Another stagecoach fell prey to the gang on May 12, 1876, between San Antonio and Austin, Texas; the gang bagged $3,000 without firing a shot. Two months later, on July 7, they netted $15,000 from a train holdup at Otterville, Missouri.

The gang's last hurrah involved a foray to the north, far removed from the Missouri farms and wilderness where they could count on friends and relatives for shelter. Jesse James was counting on surprise to help them loot a bank at Northfield, Minnesota, without difficulty. Cole Younger opposed the plan but went along when brothers Jim and Bob outvoted him. Frank James, Clell Miller, Charlie Pitts, and Bill Chadwell filled out the ranks as the gang started north, riding 300 miles to their target.

The Northfield raid of September 7, 1876, was a bloody fiasco. Cashier J. L. Heywood was killed for refusing to open the safe; teller A. E. Bunker was wounded in the shoulder by Bob Younger as he fled crying for help. Outside, one of the raiders shot and killed Norwegian immigrant Nicholas Gustavson as armed vigilantes appeared on the street, blazing away with rifles and shotguns. Clell Miller was the next to fall, blasted dead from his saddle. Bill Chadwell was blinded by birdshot and then drilled through the heart by a rifle bullet. Jim Younger was shot in the face, his jaw shattered. Brother Bob's horse was killed and his own right elbow smashed by a bullet as he ran for cover. Cole Younger, already hit in the shoulder, rode back for his brother and hauled Bob up behind him to ride double. Every surviving member of the gang was wounded by bullets or shot as they rode out of Northfield through a withering crossfire.

Nor was the bad news over yet. With nothing but fresh wounds to show for the holdup, the gang was surprised by a posse near Shieldsville on September 11, another of their horses killed before they escaped with four men riding double. They had traveled only 15 miles from Northfield in four days with vigilante patrols manning every major road and bridge in the district. Jesse James went too far on September 13,

asking Cole to put brother Jim out of his misery, and the cousins split up, Charlie Pitts remaining with the Younger team. At 2:00 A.M. the next day, Pitts and the Youngers fought their way past guards on the Blue Earth River bridge and shook off a posse that rode in pursuit.

Skulking near Mankato, the fugitives were reduced to stealing chickens for their dinner, a circumstance that made them feel "real mean," in Jim Younger's recollection. On September 21 one of the gang approached a farm 150 miles northwest of Northfield, trying to buy bread and eggs, but his stiff walk and barely hidden guns prompted a report to Sheriff James Glispin at Madelia. A posse surrounded the bandits in a nearby patch of timber, killing Charlie Pitts in the first barrage of fire and inflicting further wounds on all three Youngers before they surrendered. Cole was hit 11 times, while Jim had stopped a total of 10 slugs; Bob, the sole brother still able to stand, was better off with only a half-dozen wounds.

The brothers all defied physicians' expectations by surviving to stand trial. All were convicted and sentenced to 25-year prison terms. Bob died of tuberculosis in prison on September 16, 1889, but his brothers survived to make parole. Jim Younger stayed in Minnesota and later committed suicide in a ST. PAUL hotel room. Cole Younger published his memoirs in 1903 and joined Frank James as star attractions with a Wild West show, but the old wounds from Northfield were still painful, and the cousins were soon estranged once more. Cole tried religion next, preaching sermons with "his own misspent life as a text" until he died at Lee's Summit, Missouri, on March 21, 1916. Legends still circulate about the Younger gang, some claiming that a portion of their loot—$500,000 in some sensational accounts—lies hidden, waiting to be claimed on some Missouri homestead or among the limestone caves once used as bandit hideouts.

Z

ZAVADA, George

Jailed for the first time in March 1933 at age 17, George Zavada spent nearly four years in the Ohio state reformatory before his release in January 1937. Fourteen months later, on March 21, 1938, he was sentenced to 25 years on conviction for three armed robberies in Cleveland. Between 1938 and 1961 Zavada logged time in the Tennessee state prison, plus federal lockups at Alcatraz, Atlanta, and Leavenworth. Released from the latter prison on October 24, 1961, he drove west to renew his acquaintance with hoodlum Howard Jensen, a crony from his days at Alcatraz in the 1950s.

In the early spring of 1963, Zavada and Jensen teamed up to rob a supermarket in Whittier, California, making off with $2,633. In May they were joined by ex-convict Clarence Kostich in robbing a motel and another supermarket. Zavada was emerging as the brains of the gang, plotting their raids, and his partners soon dubbed him "The King." Zavada grew so fond of the nickname that he had it embroidered on his underwear.

On June 4, 1963, "King" George led his subjects into a Culver City savings-and-loan office, bagging $3,034 at gunpoint. A month later, on July 9, they relieved a Los Angeles bank of $10,049, making a clean getaway. Raiding the United California Bank in Canoga Park on July 26, Zavada vaulted over the teller's cage to retrieve $33,771 in cash.

Throughout the crime spree, Zavada lived in San Francisco, traveling south when a holdup was sched-

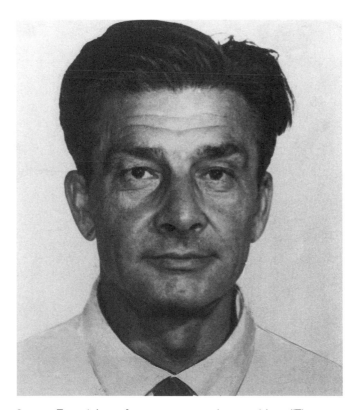

George Zavada's outlaw partners nicknamed him "The King," a name he wore embroidered on his underwear. (FBI)

uled. Jensen and Kostich were less security-conscious, and their negligence backfired on August 8, 1963, when they were caught with guns and stolen money at a Hollywood motel. The outlaws tried to bluff their way through questioning, but a telephone number found in Jensen's room led police to Zavada. Arrested in San Francisco, Zavada was returned to Los Angeles and there confessed his role in the holdups.

On December 23, 1963, Zavada failed to appear in court for his trial. "The King" was otherwise engaged with an abortive bank heist in Reno, Nevada. Working with ex-convicts Joseph Anderson and Thomas Lombardi, Zavada was frustrated by a bank manager who refused to open the vault. Fleeing with small change, the outlaws sideswiped an oil truck in their haste to get away.

Zavada and Lombardi fared a little better in their next outing on January 20, 1964, lifting $7,696 from a savings-and-loan office in Los Angeles. On March 13 they tapped an L.A. bank for $4,478, rebounding a week later with another bank job, net-

ting $13,000 for their effort. By that time, the FBI was hot on Zavada's trail, and agents nearly bagged him on April 17, settling for Tom Lombardi when they missed their prey by minutes. Lombardi and Zavada were charged with three counts of bank robbery on May 6, 1964, and Zavada made the FBI's "Ten Most Wanted" list the same day.

On June 12, 1964, following a Sacramento bank heist that netted $73,000, Zavada's car was spotted outside a house in San Jose, California. Federal agents surrounded the house, closing in as Zavada emerged, but "The King" chose to fight for his freedom. Drawing a pistol, Zavada had no time to fire before a well-placed shot laid him out on the lawn. Pleading guilty to all counts in federal court on October 26, 1964, Zavada received another 25-year term at Leavenworth. He died in prison of natural causes in June 1965.

Bibliography

Hundreds of sources were utilized for this work. What follows is a bibliography of selected sources. Many works consulted in reference to individual entries are mentioned in the text.

Aalders, Gerard, and Cees Wiebes. *The Art of Cloaking Ownership: The Case of Sweden*. Amsterdam: Amsterdam University Press, 1996.

Adams, Ramon. *Sixguns and Saddle Leather: A Bibliography of Books and Pamphlets on Western Outlaws and Gunmen*. Norman, Okla.: University of Oklahoma Press, 1969.

Alcorn, Robert. *The Count of Gramercy Park*. London: Hurst & Blackett, 1955.

Appler, Augustus. *The Guerrillas of the West or the Life, Character and Daring Exploits of the Younger Brothers*. St. Louis: Eureka Publishing Co., 1876.

Aswell, Thomas. *The Story of Bonnie and Clyde*. Ruston, La.: H.M.G. Inc., 1968.

Audett, James. *Rap Sheet*. New York: Sloane, 1954.

Barndollar, Lue. *What Really Happened on October 5, 1892*. Coffeyville, Kan.: Coffeyville Historical Society, 1992.

Barnes, Bruce. *Machine Gun Kelly: To Right a Wrong*. Perris, Calif.: Tipper, 1991.

Bartholomew, Ed. *Biographical Album of Western Gunfighters*. Houston: Frontier Press, 1958.

Barton, O. S. *Three Years with Quantrell [sic]: A True Story Told by His Scout John McCorkle*. 1914. Reprint. Norman, Okla.: University of Oklahoma Press, 1992.

Beamis, Joan M., and William E. Pullen. *Background of a Bandit: The Ancestry of Jesse James*. s.n., 1971.

Beebe, Lucius, and Charles Clegg. *U.S. West: The Saga of Wells Fargo*. New York: E. P. Dutton, 1948.

Berkow, Ira. *The Man Who Robbed the Pierre*. New York: Atheneum, 1987.

Betenson, Lula. *Butch Cassidy, My Brother*. Provo, Utah: Brigham Young University Press, 1975.

Block, Eugene. *Great Train Robberies of the West*. New York: Coward-McCann, 1959.

Boessenecker, John. *Gold Dust & Gunsmoke*. New York: John Wiley & Sons, 1999.

Boley, Edwin. *The Masked Halters*. Seymour, Ind.: Graessle-Mercer, 1977.

Bower, Tom. *Nazi Gold*. New York: HarperPerennial, 1998.

Brant, Marley. *Jesse James: The Man and the Myth*. New York: Berkley, 1998.

———. *The Outlaw Youngers: A Confederate Brotherhood*. Lanham, Md.: Madison Books, 1992.

Breihan, Carl. *The Escapades of Frank and Jesse James*. New York: Frederick Fell, 1974.

———. *Saga of Jesse James*. Caldwell, Idaho: Caxton Printers, 1991.

Bronaugh, Richard. *The Youngers Fight for Freedom*. Columbia, Mo.: E. W. Stevens, 1906.

Brownlee, Richard. *Gray Ghosts of the Confederacy: Guerrilla Warfare in the West, 1861–1865*. Baton Rouge: Louisiana State University Press, 1958.

Bruns, Roger. *The Bandit Kings: From Jesse James to Pretty Boy Floyd*. New York: Crown, 1995.

Buel, James. *The Border Outlaws*. St. Louis: Daniel Linahan, 1881.

Butler, Daniel, and Alan Ray. *America's Dumbest Criminals*. Nashville, Tenn.: Rutledge Hill Press, 1995.

———. *Crimes and MisDumbMeanors*. Nashville, Tenn.: Rutledge Hill Press, 1998.

———. *These Aren't My Pants!* Nashville, Tenn.: Rutledge Hill Press, 1999.

———. *Wanted! Dumb or Alive*. Nashville, Tenn.: Rutledge Hill Press, 1996.

———. *The World's Dumbest Criminals*. Nashville, Tenn.: Rutledge Hill Press, 1997.

Callahan, Clyde, and Byron Jones. *Heritage of an Outlaw— The Story of Frank Nash*. Hobart, Okla.: Schoonmaker, 1979.

Cantor, George. *Bad Guys in American History*. Dallas, Tex.: Taylor Publishing, 1999.

Cantrell, Dallas. *Youngers' Final Blunder*. Kansas City, Mo.: Naylor Publishing, 1973.

Castel, Albert. *William Clarke Quantrill: His Life and Times*. Ithaca, N.Y.: Cornell University Press, 1958.

Cheshes, Jay, and Jason Kersten. "America's Most Wanted Sweethearts." *Maxim* (April 2000): 91–102.

Chesnoff, Richard. *Pack of Thieves: How Hitler and Europe Plundered the Jews and Committed the Greatest Theft in History.* New York: Doubleday, 1999.

Clayton, Merle. *Union Station Massacre.* New York: Bobbs-Merrill, 1975.

Clemens, Nancy. *American Bandits.* Girard, Kan.: Haldeman-Julius Publications, 1938.

Clemente, George. *The Cops Are Robbers.* Boston: Quinlan Press, 1987.

Connelly, William. *Quantrill and the Border Wars.* 1909. Reprint. New York: Pageant, 1956.

Conquest, Robert. *Stalin: Breaker of Nations.* New York: Penguin, 1991.

Cook, D.J. *Hands Up: or, Twenty Years of Detective Life in the Mountains and on the Plains.* Norman, Okla.: University of Oklahoma Press, 1958.

Cook, Philip. *Robbery in the United States: An Analysis of Recent Trends and Patterns.* Washington, D.C.: U.S. Department of Justice, 1983.

Cooper, Courtney. *Ten Thousand Public Enemies.* Boston: Little, Brown, 1935.

Cordingly, David. *Under the Black Flag.* San Diego: Harvest Books, 1995.

Cordry, H. D., Jr. *Oklahoma Outlaw and Lawman Map, 1865–1935.* Oklahoma City: Oklahoma Heritage Association, 1990.

Corey, Herbert. *Farewell, Mr. Gangster!* New York: D. Appleton-Century, 1936.

Costello, Peter. *The Real World of Sherlock Holmes.* New York: Carroll & Graf, 1991.

Cromie, Robert, and Joseph Pinkston. *Dillinger: A Short and Violent Life.* New York: McGraw-Hill, 1962.

Croy, Homer. *He Hanged Them High.* New York: Duell, Sloan and Pierce, 1952.

———. *Jesse James Was My Neighbor.* New York: Duell, Sloan and Pierce, 1949.

———. *Last of the Great Outlaws: The Story of Cole Younger.* New York: Duell, Sloan and Pierce, 1956.

———. *Trigger Marshal.* New York: Duell, Sloan and Pierce, 1958.

Cummins, Jim. *Jim Cummins the Guerrilla.* Denver: Reed Publishing, 1903.

Dacus, Joseph. *The Illustrated Lives and Adventures of Frank and Jesse James and the Younger Brothers.* St. Louis, N. Dak.: Thompson and Co., 1882.

Dalton, Emmett. *Beyond the Law.* Coffeyville, Kan.: Coffeyville Historical Society, n.d.

———. *When the Daltons Rode.* Garden City, N.Y.: Doubleday, Doran, 1931.

Dawidowicz, Lucy. *The War Against the Jews 1933–1945.* New York: Holt, Rinehart & Winston, 1975.

DeNevi, Don. *Western Train Robberies.* Milbrae, Calif.: Celestial Arts, 1976.

DeSimone, Donald. *"I Rob Banks: That's Where the Money Is!": The Story of Bank Robber Willie Sutton and the Killing of Arnold Schuster.* New York: Shapolsky, 1991.

Dewhurst, H. S. *The Railroad Police.* Springfield, Ill.: Charles C. Thomas, 1955.

Dibble, R. F. *Strenuous Americans.* New York: Boni and Liveright, 1923.

Dillon, Richard. *Wells Fargo Detective: The Biography of James B. Hume.* New York: Coward-McCann, 1969.

Dodge, Fred. *Under Cover for Wells Fargo.* Boston: Houghton Mifflin, 1969.

Drago, Harry. *Outlaws on Horseback.* New York: Dodd, Mead & Co., 1964.

———. *Road Agents and Train Robbers.* New York: Dodd, Mead & Co., 1973.

———. *Wild, Wooly and Wicked.* New York: Potter, 1960.

Dugan, Mark, and John Boessenecker. *The Gray Fox: The True Story of Bill Miner, Last of the Old Time Outlaws.* Norman, Okla.: University of Oklahoma Press, 1992.

East, William. *The Monon Express Robbery.* Indianapolis: Carlon & Hollenbeck, 1891.

Edelheit, Abraham, and Hershel Edelheit. *History of the Holocaust: A Handbook and Dictionary.* Boulder, Colo.: Westview Press, 1994.

Edge, L. L. *Run the Cat Roads.* New York: Dembner Books, 1981.

Edwards, John. *Noted Guerrillas.* St. Louis: Bryan, Brand and Co., 1877.

Elliott, David. *Last Raid of the Daltons.* New York: Books for Libraries Press, 1971.

Elliott, David, and Ed Bartholomew. *The Dalton Gang and the Coffeyville Raid.* Fort Davis, Tex.: Frontier Book Co., 1968.

Elman, Robert. *Fired in Anger: The Personal Handguns of America's Heroes and Villains.* Garden City, N.Y.: Doubleday, 1968.

Facts On File Yearbooks, 60 vol. New York: Facts On File, 1941–2000.

Fass, Paula. *Kidnapped: Child Abduction in America.* Cambridge, Mass.: Harvard University Press, 1997.

Fernandez, Ronald. *Los Macheteros.* New York: Prentice Hall, 1987.

deFord, Miriam. *The Real Bonnie and Clyde.* New York: Ace, 1968.

———. *The Real Ma Barker.* New York: Ace, 1970.

Ford, Paul. *The Great K & A Train Robbery.* New York: International Assn. of Newspapers and Authors, 1901.

Fordham, Peta. *The Robbers' Tale: The Real Story of the Great Train Robbery.* London: Houghter and Stoughton, 1965.

Friedlander, Saul. *Nazi Germany and the Jews, Vol. I: The Years of Persecution.* New York: HarperCollins, 1997.

Furneaux, Rupert. *Robert Hoodhouse.* London: Stevens, 1960.

Gard, Wayne. *Frontier Justice.* Norman, Okla.: University of Oklahoma Press, 1949.

Gaute, J. H. H., and Robin Odell. *The Murderers' Who's Who.* London: Harrap, 1979.

Gentry, Curt. *J. Edgar Hoover: The Man and the Secrets.* New York: W. W. Norton, 1991.

Gibson, Walter, ed. *The Fine Art of Robbery.* New York: Grosset & Dunlap, 1966.

Girardin, G. Russell, and William Helmer. *Dillinger: The Untold Story.* Bloomington, Ind.: Indiana University Press, 1994.

Glasscock, C. B. *Bandits and the Southern Pacific.* New York: Frederick A. Stokes, 1929.

Goodrich, Thomas. *Black Flag: Guerrilla Warfare on the Western Border, 1861–1865.* Bloomington, Ind.: Indiana University Press, 1995.

Gosling, John. *The Great Train Robbery.* London: W. H. Allen, 1964.

Gottesman, Ronald, ed. *Violence in America.* 3 vol. New York: Charles Scribner's Sons, 1999.

Goulart, Ron. *Lineup, Tough Guys.* Los Angeles: Sherbourne, 1966.

Graves, Richard. *Oklahoma Outlaws.* Oklahoma City: State Printing and Publishing Co., 1915.

Greene, A. C. *The Santa Claus Bank Robbery.* New York: Knopf, 1972.

Gutman, Israel, ed. *Encyclopedia of the Holocaust.* 2 vol. New York: Macmillan, 1990.

Hale, Donald. *We Rode with Quantrill.* Lee's Summit, Mo.: Donald R. Hale, 1975.

Haley, J. Evetts. *Robbing Banks Was My Business.* Canyon, Tex.: Palo Duro Press, 1973.

Hall, Angus, ed. *The Gangsters.* New York: Paradise, 1975.

Hamilton, Floyd. *Public Enemy No. 1.* Dallas, Tex.: Acclaimed Books, 1978.

Hanes, Bailey. *Bill Doolin, Outlaw.* Norman, Okla.: University of Oklahoma Press, 1968.

Harkey, Dee. *Mean as Hell.* Albuquerque: University of New Mexico Press, 1948.

Harmon, S. W. *Hell on the Border.* Fort Smith, Ark.: Hell on the Border Publishing Co., 1953.

Hatch, Alden. *American Express: A Century of Service.* Garden City, N.Y.: Doubleday, 1950.

Hauge, Elmer. *Bank Robbery in California: A 35-Year Comparison of California with the Rest of the United States, and an Intensive Study of 1965 Offenses.* Sacramento, Calif.: Bureau of Criminal Statistics, 1967.

———. *Bank Robberies: California Compared with Other States, 1931–1968.* Sacramento, Calif.: Bureau of Criminal Statistics, 1969.

Haven, Charles, and Frank Belden. *A History of the Colt Revolver.* New York: Bonanza Books, 1940.

Hawkes, Harry. *The Capture of the Black Panther: Casebook of a Killer.* London: Harrap, 1978.

Heilbron, W. C. *Convict Life at the Minnesota State Prison.* St. Paul: W. C. Heilbron, 1909.

Helmer, William. *The Gun That Made the Twenties Roar.* New York: Macmillan, 1969.

Helmer, William, and Rick Mattix. *Public Enemies: America's Criminal Past, 1919–1940.* New York: Checkmark Books, 1998.

Higham, Charles. *Trading with the Enemy: The Nazi-American Money Plot.* New York: Barnes & Noble, 1995.

Hinton, Ted, and Larry Grove. *Ambush: The Real Story of Bonnie and Clyde.* Bryan, Tex.: Shoal Creek, 1979.

Hogg, Wilgus. *The First Train Robbery.* Louisville, Ky.: Data Courier Inc., 1977.

Holbrook, Stewart. *Robbing the Steamcars.* Fort Wayne, Ind.: Public Library of Fort Wayne and Allen County, 1958.

Hollon, W. Eugene. *Frontier Violence: Another Look.* New York: Oxford University Press, 1974.

Holt, J. C. *Robin Hood.* London: Thames and Hudson, 1989.

Hoover, J. Edgar. *Persons in Hiding.* Boston: Little, Brown, 1938.

Horan, James. *Desperate Men: Revelations from the Sealed Pinkerton Files.* New York: G. P. Putnam's Sons, 1951.

———. *The Pinkertons.* New York: Crown Publishers, 1967.

Huntington, George. *Robber and Hero.* Northfield, Minn.: Christian Way Co., 1895.

Jacobs, Timothy. *The Gangsters.* New York: Mallard, 1990.

James, Jesse. *Jesse James, My Father.* Independence, Mo.: Sentinel Publishing, 1899.

James, Stella. *In the Shadow of Jesse James.* Thousand Oaks, Calif.: Revolver Press, 1989.

Jeffers, H. Paul. *Bloody Business: Scotland Yard's Most Famous and Shocking Cases.* New York: Pharos Books, 1992.

Jenkins, John, and H. Gordon Frost. *I'm Frank Hamer: The Life of a Texas Peace Officer.* Austin, Tex.: Pemberton, 1968.

Jennings, Al, and Will Irvin. *Beating Back.* New York: D. Appleton, 1914.

Johnson, Lester. *The Devil's Front Porch.* Lawrence, Kan.: University of Kansas Press, 1970.

Jones, J. Harry. *The Minutemen.* Garden City, N.Y.: Doubleday, 1968.

Karpis, Alvin, and Bill Trent. *The Alvin Karpis Story.* New York: Coward-McCann & Geoghegan, 1971.

Karpis, Alvin, and Robert Livesey. *On the Rock.* Don Mills, Ontario: Musson/General, 1980.

Keating, H. R. F. *Great Crimes.* London: Weidenfeld & Nicholson, 1982.

Kelly, Charles. *The Outlaw Trail: A History of Butch Cassidy and His Wild Bunch.* New York: Bonanza Books, 1959.

Kelly, George [pseud.], Jim Dobkins, and Ben Jordan. *Machine Gun Man: The True Story of My Incredible Survival into the 1970s.* Phoenix, Ariz.: UCS, 1988.

Kerby, Phil. *With Honor and Purpose.* New York: St. Martin's, 1998.

Kimani, John. *Life and Times of a Bank Robber.* Nairobi: Spear Books, 1988.

King, Jeffrey. *The Life and Death of Pretty Boy Floyd.* Kent, Ohio: Kent State University Press, 1998.

Kirchner, L. R. *Triple Cross Fire: J. Edgar Hoover & the Kansas City Union Station Massacre.* Kansas City, Mo.: Janlar, 1993.

Kirkpatrick, E. E. *Voices from Alcatraz*. San Antonio, Tex: Naylor, 1947.

Kooistra, Paul. *Criminals as Heroes: Structure, Power and Identity*. Bowling Green, Ohio: Bowling Green State University Press, 1989.

Lake, Carolyn, ed. *Under Cover for Wells Fargo: The Unvarnished Recollections of Fred Dodge*. Boston: Houghton Mifflin, 1969.

Lane, Brian, and Wilfred Gregg. *The Encyclopedia of Mass Murder*. London: Headline, 1994.

———. *The Encyclopedia of Serial Killers*. London: Headline, 1992.

Latta, Frank. *Dalton Gang Days*. Santa Cruz, Calif.: Bear State Books, 1976.

Levine, Itamar. *The Fate of Stolen Jewish Properties*. Jerusalem: Institute of the Jewish World Congress, 1997.

Lindberg, Richard. *To Serve and Collect*. New York: Praeger Press, 1991.

Louderback, Lew. *The Bad Ones*. New York: Fawcett, 1968.

Love, Robertus. *The Rise and Fall of Jesse James*. New York: G. P. Putnam's Sons, 1926.

Maccabee, Paul. *John Dillinger Slept Here: A Crook's Tour of Crime and Corruption in St. Paul, 1920–1936*. St. Paul: Minnesota Historical Press, 1995.

MacDonald, John. *Armed Robbery: Offenders and Their Victims*. Springfield, Ill.: Thomas, 1975.

Macintyre, Ben. *The Napoleon of Crime*. New York: Farrar, Straus and Giroux, 1997.

Mackay, James. *Allen Pinkerton: The First Private Eye*. New York: John Wiley & Sons, 1996.

Maddox, Web. *The Black Sheep*. Quannah, Tex.: Nortex, 1975.

Maurice, Rene, and Ken Follett. *Under the Streets of Nice*. Toronto: PaperJacks, 1989.

Maxwell, Hu. *Evans and Sontag: The Famous Bandits of California*. Fresno, Calif.: Fresno City and County Historical Society, 1981.

McCall, Andrew. *The Medieval Underworld*. New York: Barnes & Noble, 1979.

McCorkle, John. *Three Years with Quantrill*. Armstrong, Mo.: n.p., 1914.

McCormick, Harry, and Mary Carey. *Bank Robbers Wrote My Diary*. Austin, Tex.: Eakin, 1985.

McPhee, Michele. "The Models, the Mob and the Murder." *Maxim* (May 2000): 127–136.

Messick, Hank. *Gangs and Gangsters: The Illustrated History of Gangs from Jesse James to Murph the Surf*. New York: Ballantine, 1974.

Metz, Leon. *The Shooters*. El Paso, Tex.: Mangan Books, 1976.

Miller, George. *The Trial of Frank James for Murder*. Columbia, Mo.: E.W. Stephens, 1898.

Miller, Rick. *Bounty Hunter*. College Station, Tex.: Creative Publishing, 1988.

Mills, George. *Rogues and Heroes from Iowa's Amazing Past*. Ames, Iowa: Iowa State University Press, 1972.

Milner, E. R. *The Lives and Times of Bonnie and Clyde*. Carbondale, Ill.: Southern Illinois University Press, 1996.

Moore, Lucy. *The Thieves' Opera*. San Diego: Harvest Books, 1997.

Myers, John. *Doc Holiday*. Lincoln, Neb.: University of Nebraska Press, 1995.

Newton, Michael. *Cop Killers*. Port Townsend, Wash.: Loompanics Unlimited, 1998.

———. *Killer Cops*. Port Townsend, Wash.: Loompanics Unlimited, 1997.

Newton, Willis, Joe Newton, Claude Stanush, and David Middleton. *The Newton Boys: Portrait of an Outlaw Gang*. Austin, Tex.: State House Press, 1994.

Nichols, Lynn. *The Rape of Europa: The Fate of Europe's Treasures in the Third Reich and the Second World War*. New York: Vintage Books, 1995.

Odell, Robin. *Landmarks in 20th Century Murder*. London: Headline, 1995.

O'Neal, Bill. *Encyclopedia of Western Gun-Fighters*. Norman, Okla.: University of Oklahoma Press, 1979.

Palmer, Henry. "The black-flag character of the war on the border." *Kansas Historical Collections* 9 (1905–1906): 455–466.

Parker, Emma, and Nell Cowan. *Fugitives: The Story of Clyde Barrow and Bonnie Parker*. Dallas: Ranger Press, 1934.

Patterson, Richard. *Train Robbery: The Birth, Flowering, and Decline of a Notorious Western Enterprise*. Boulder, Colo.: Johnson Books, 1981.

———. *The Train Robbery Era: An Encyclopedic History*. Boulder, Colo.: Pruett Publishing, 1991.

Phillips, Charles, and Alan Axelrod. *Cops, Crooks, and Criminologists*. New York: Checkmark Books, 2000.

Pileggi, Nicholas. *Wise Guy: Life in a Mafia Family*. New York: Pocket Books, 1985.

Pinkerton, William. *Train Robberies and Train Robbers*. Fort Davis, Tex.: Frontier Book Co., 1968.

Pointer, Larry. *In Search of Butch Cassidy*. Norman, Okla.: University of Oklahoma Press, 1977.

Pool, James. *Hitler and His Secret Partners*. New York: Pocket Books, 1997.

Porter, Adam. "Pirates of Panang." *Bizarre* 31 (May 2000): 64–68.

Powers, Richard. *G-Men: Hoover's FBI in American Popular Culture*. Carbondale, Ill.: Southern Illinois University Press, 1983.

Prassel, Frank. *The Great American Outlaw: A Legacy of Fact and Fiction*. Norman, Okla.: University of Oklahoma Press, 1993.

———. *The Western Peace Officer: A Legacy of Law and Order*. Norman, Okla.: University of Oklahoma Press, 1972.

Preece, Harold. *The Dalton Gang: End of an Outlaw Era*. New York: Hastings House, 1963.

Purvis, Melvin. *American Agent*. Garden City, N.Y.: Doubleday, Duran, 1936.

Quimby, Myron. *The Devil's Emissaries*. New York: Curtis Books, 1969.

Read, Piers. *The Train Robbers*. London: W. H. Allen, 1978.

Reed, Lear. *Human Wolves: Seventeen Years of War on Crime.* Kansas City, Mo.: Brown-White-Lowell, 1941.

Robinson, Charles, III. *The Men Who Wear the Star: The Story of the Texas Rangers.* New York: Random House, 2000.

Rosen, Victor. *A Gun in His Hand.* New York: Gold Medal, 1951.

Rosie, George. *The Directory of International Terrorism.* Edinburgh: Mainstream Publishing, 1986.

Ross, James. *I, Jesse James.* Thousand Oaks, Calif.: Dragon Publishing, 1988.

Rothert, Otto. *The Outlaws of Cave-in-Rock.* Cleveland: A. H. Clark, 1924.

Runyon, Tom. *In the Life.* New York: W. W. Norton, 1953.

Sabljak, Mark, and Martin Greenberg. *Most Wanted: A History of the FBI's Ten Most Wanted List.* New York: Bonanza, 1990.

Samuelson, Nancy. *The Dalton Gang Family.* Mead, Kans.: Back Room Printing, 1989.

———. *The Dalton Gang Story.* Eastford, Conn.: Shooting Star Press, 1992.

Sanborn, Debra. *The Barrow Gang's Visit to Dexter.* Dexter, Iowa: Bob Weesner, 1976.

Sawyer, Peter, ed. *The Oxford Illustrated History of the Vikings.* Oxford: Oxford University Press, 1997.

Schultz, Duane. *Quantrill's War.* New York: St. Martin's, 1996.

Settle, William. *Jesse James Was His Name.* Columbia, Mo.: University of Missouri Press, 1966.

Shalloo, J. P. *Private Police.* Philadelphia: American Academy of Political and Social Science, 1933.

Shirley, Glenn. *Belle Starr and Her Times.* Norman, Okla.: University of Oklahoma Press, 1990.

———. *Gunfight at Ingalls.* Stillwater, Okla.: Barbed Wire Press, 1990.

———. *Heck Thomas, Frontier Marshal.* Norman, Okla.: University of Oklahoma Press, 1981.

———. *Law West of Fort Smith.* Lincoln: University of Nebraska Press. 1968.

———. *Six Gun and Silver Star.* Albuquerque: University of New Mexico Press, 1955.

———. *Toughest of Them All.* Albuquerque: University of New Mexico Press, 1953.

———. *West of Hell's Fringe: Crime, Criminals and the Federal Peace Officer in Oklahoma Territory, 1889–1907.* Norman, Okla.: University of Oklahoma Press, 1978.

Sifakis, Carl. *The Encyclopedia of American Crime.* New York: Facts On File, 1984.

———. *The Mafia Encyclopedia.* New York: Facts On File, 1999.

Smith, Brent. *Terrorism in America: Pipe Bombs and Pipe Dreams.* Albany, N.Y.: State University of New York Press, 1994.

Smith, Robert. *Daltons! The Raid on Coffeyville, Kansas.* Norman, Okla.: University of Oklahoma Press, 1996.

Spooner, Mary. *Soldiers in a Narrow Land: The Pinochet Regime in Chile.* Berkeley, Calif.: University of California Press, 1994.

Steel, Phillip. *In Search of the Daltons.* Springdale, Ark.: Frontier Press, 1985.

———. *Jesse and Frank James: The Family History.* Gretna, La.: Pelican Publishing, 1987.

Steele, Phillip, and Marie Scoma. *The Family Story of Bonnie and Clyde.* Gretna, La.: Pelican Publishing, 2000.

Steele, Sean. *Heists: Swindles, Stickups, and Robberies That Shocked the World.* New York: MetroBooks, 1995.

Sterling, William. *Trails and Trials of a Texas Ranger.* Norman, Okla.: University of Oklahoma Press, 1968.

Stuart, Hix. *The Notorious Ashley Gang: A Saga of the King and Queen of the Everglades.* Stuart, Fla.: St. Lucie Publishing, 1928.

Sutton, Willie, and Edward Linn. *Where the Money Was.* New York: Viking Press, 1976.

Theoharis, Athan, ed. *The FBI: A Comprehensive Reference Guide.* New York: Checkmark Books, 2000.

Thurman, Steve. *"Baby Face" Nelson.* Derby, Conn.: Monarch, 1961.

Toland, John. *The Dillinger Days.* New York: Random House, 1963.

Treherne, John. *The Strange History of Bonnie and Clyde.* New York: Stein & Day, 1984.

Triplett, Frank. *The Life, Times, and Treacherous Death of Jesse James.* St. Louis: J. H. Chambers, 1882.

Triplett, William. *The Flowering of the Bamboo.* Kensington, Md.: Woodbine House, 1985.

Underwood, Sid. *Depression Desperado: The Chronicle of Raymond Hamilton.* Austin, Tex.: Eakin, 1995.

Unger, Robert. *The Union Station Massacre: The Original Sin of Hoover's FBI.* Kansas City, Mo.: Andrews, McNeel, 1997.

Vincent, Isabel. *Hitler's Silent Partners: Swiss Banks, Nazi Gold, and the Pursuit of Justice.* New York: William Morrow, 1997.

Volkman, Ernest. *The Heist: How a Gang Stole $8,000,000 At Kennedy Airport and Lived to Regret It.* New York: F. Watts, 1986.

Wallis, Michael. *Pretty Boy: The Life and Times of Charles Arthur Floyd.* New York: St. Martin's, 1992.

Ward, Bernie. *Families Who Kill.* New York: Pinnacle, 1993.

Waters, William. *A Gallery of Western Badmen.* Covington, Ky.: Americana, 1954.

Webb, Walter. *The Texas Rangers: A Century of Frontier Defense.* Boston: Houghton Mifflin, 1935.

Webber, Bert. *Oregon's Great Train Holdup.* Fairfield, Wash.: Ye Galleon Press, 1973.

Weber, Louis, ed. *The Holocaust Chronicle.* Lincolnwood, Ill.: Publications International, 2000.

Webster, Paul. *Pétain's Crime: The Full Story of French Collaboration in the Holocaust.* London: Macmillan London Ltd., 1990.

Wellman, Paul. *A Dynasty of Western Outlaws.* Garden City, N.Y.: Doubleday, 1961.

Westlie, Bjørn. *Coming to Terms with the Past—The Process of Restitution of Jewish Property in Norway.* Jerusalem: Institute of the World Jewish Congress, 1996.

West, C. W. *Outlaws and Peace Officers of Indian Territory.* Muskogee, Okla.: Muskogee Publishing, 1987.

Whitehead, Don. *The FBI Story.* New York: Random House, 1956.

Wilson, Colin. *The Mammoth Book of True Crime.* New York: Carroll & Graf, 1998.

————. *The Mammoth Book of Unsolved Crimes.* New York: Carroll & Graf, 1999.

Wilson, Colin, Damon Wilson, and Rowan Wilson. *World Famous Robberies.* Bristol, England: Parragon, 1994.

Wilson, Neill, and Frank Taylor. *Southern Pacific: The Roaring Story of a Fighting Railroad.* New York: McGraw-Hill, 1952.

Woodside, John, et al. *The Young Brothers Massacre.* Springfield, Mo.: Springfield Publishing, 1932.

Wright, Richard. *Armed Robbers in Action: Stickups and Street Culture.* Boston: Northeastern University Press, 1997.

Yonover, Neal. *Crime Scene USA.* New York: Hyperion, 2000.

Younger, Coleman. *The Story of Cole Younger by Himself.* Chicago: Henneberry, 1903.

Zabludoff, Sidney. *And It All Disappeared.* Jerusalem: Institute of the World Jewish Congress, 1998.

————. *Movements of Nazi Gold.* Jerusalem: Institute of the World Jewish Congress, 1998.

Index

Page numbers in **boldface** indicate major treatment of a subject. *Italic* page numbers indicate photographs.

Herrado, Rafael 177
Heywood, J. L. 149, 334
Higgins, Jack 105–106
hijacking **132–135**
Hildebrand, Fred 109
Hill, David 104
Hill, Henry 134, 182, 232
Hill, J. R. 76
Himmelsbach, Ralph 65
Himmler, Heinrich 217
Hinton, Ted 24, 26, 27, 126
Hirsch, Frederick 67, 68
Hite, Clarence 332
Hite, Wood 150, 332
Hitler, Adolf 5, 211, 212, 213,, 214, 215, 217, 219
Hlavaty, Joe 109
Ho Chi Minh 188
Hobsbawm, Eric 279
Hodges, Tom 28, 122, 123, 133, **135–137**, 225, 278, 287, 288, 312
Hoeh, Gustav 151
Hofer, Walter 217
Hoffman, Charles 2
Hoffmann, Heinrich 213, 218
Hogan, Danny 271
Holden, Thomas 11, 12, 19, 36, 81, 103, 137–138, *138*, 162, 163, 167, 197, 205, 209, 270, 299
Holden-Keating Gang **137–138**, 299
Hole-in-the-Wall (Wyo.) 45, 52, **138–139**, 180, 264, 322
Holland, William 150
Holliday, John 314
Hollis, Herman 56, 66, 223–224
Holloway, W. M. 179
Holt, J. C. 265
Holtan, Richard **139**, *140*
Holtman, Robert 319, 320
Holtzman, J. Wahl 319
Holzhay, Reimund 297
Homer, Leslie 236
Hood, Elizabeth 135, 136
Hood, Robin *See* Robin Hood
Hoover, J. Edgar 13, 20, 45, 55, 56, 66, 86, 87, 91, 92, 101, 103, 106, 112, **139–141**, 161, 165, 175, 210, 224, 248, *249*, 250, 251, 252, 271, 304, 327
Hope, Bob 105
Hornigold, Benjamin 3
Hoskins, Richard 289

Hothan, Lois 246
Houston, Tom 89
Howard, Clarence 56
Howard, Joe 17–18, 162
Hoy, Perry 255
Hoy, Valentine 322
Hubbard, Millard **141**
Huddleston, Ned 44
Huerta, Victoriano 279
Hume, James 314
Humphrey, H. D. 24, 157
Hungary 212, 217
Hunsicker, Horace 164
Hunt, Alva-Dewey 141
Hunter, Freddie 164–165
Hunter, W. H. 174
Hunt-Gant Gang **141**
Huston, Patrick **141–142**, *141*

I

Idaho 32, 52, 178, 180, 227, 228, 229, 230, 231, 275, 320, 321–322
Illinois 13, 54, 57, 58, 77, 85, 86, 96, 102, 107, 129, 130, 137, 141, 151, 153, 174, 175, 178, 196, 201, 203, 221, 223–224, 23, 259, 260, 261, 276, 294, 306, 307, 319, 324; Chicago 6, 7, 11, 12, 13, 14, 19, 20, 32, 33, 36, 40, 45, 46, 50, 54, 55, 56, 60, 64, 66, 84, 85, 86, 87, 90, 91–92, 97, 103, 112, 114, 115, 119, 128, 129, 133, 134, 137, 138, 148, 151, 152, 153, 162, 163, 164, 169, 176–177, 178–179, 196, 199, 200, 203, 204, 205, 210, 220, 221, 222, 223, 231, 237, 238, 248, 249–252, 273, 274, 282, 297, 299, 305, 306, 307, 311, 327; Springfield 33, 115
India 5, 242, 243, 244, 328329; Thugee cult 132–133
Indiana 11, 29, 33, 40, 46, 50, 51, 55, 58, 60, 63, 82–85, 86, 128, 133, 151, 157, 174, 183, 209, 222, 235–237, 238, 260, 261, 262, 276, 277, 293, 294, 295, 306, 307; Fort Wayne 59, 23, 305, 307; South Bend 36, 56, 87, 90, 113–114, 167, 223; State Police 82, 175–176, 236–237
Indonesia 244
Inman, Elmer **143–144**, 170

Inman, Lavona 143
International Maritime Organization 243, 244
Iowa 11, 24, 26, 27, 50, 51, 81, 91, 106, 114, 122, 137, 147, 148, 157, 167, 196, 197, 295, 333; Davenport 37, 118, 150; Des Moines 7, 39, 260, 295; Mason City 50, 55, 86, 122, 128, 222, 272, 306; Sioux City 90, 224; State Bureau of Investigation 114; Training School for Boys 90
Iran 243
Iran-Contra scandal 293
Ireland 133, 144, 152, 308, 325–326; Dublin 6, 308
Irish National Liberation Army 144
Irish Republican Army **144**
Irish Republican Socialist Party 144
Italy 5, 6, 215–216, 217, 218, 279–280

J

Jackson, Albert 18
Jackson, Frank 29
Jacubanis, David **145**, *145*
Jamaica 240
James, Frank 14, 71, 105, 133, 138, **145–150**, 203, 238, 254, 256, 260, 279, 294, 295, 296, 300, 323–334
James, Henry 6
James, Jerry **150–151**
James, Jesse 3, 8, 14, 54, 71, 82, 87, 102, 105, 114, 133, 138, **145–150**, 179, 203, 204, 238, 254, 256, 260, 266, 279, 295, 296, 300, 326, 332–334
James, R. H. 222
James, Robert 146
Jamison, Stanley, Jr. 315
Jarman, Eleanor **151**, 327
Jefferson, Thomas 8
Jenkins, James 60, 84, **151–152**, *152*
Jenkins, Joe 236
Jenkins, Sam 323
Jenkinson, C. 206
Jennings, Al 61, 297–298
Jennings, Frank 61, 297–298
Jennings, Henry 36
Jensen, Howard 335